UNDERSTANDING PRODUCTS LIABILITY LAW

TERRENCE F. KIELY

Professor of Law

DePaul University College of Law

BRUCE L. OTTLEY

Professor of Law

DePaul University College of Law

LexisNexis™

Library of Congress Cataloging-in-Publication Data

Kiely, Terrence F.
  Understanding products liability law / Terrence F. Kiely, Bruce L. Ottley.
    p. cm.
  Includes index.
  ISBN 0-8205-6108-8 (perfect bound)
  1. Products liability — United States. I. Ottley, Bruce L. II. Title.
  KF1296.K54 2006 346.7303'8 — dc22   2005032589

Editorial Offices
744 Broad Street, Newark, NJ 07102 (973) 820-2000
201 Mission St., San Francisco, CA 94105-1831 (415) 908-3200
701 East Water Street, Charlottesville, VA 22902-7587 (434) 972-7600
www.lexis.com

(Pu

DEDICATION

To Sidni and Younghee

PART II

**Chapter 11: RESEARCH AND PRACTICE IMPLICATIONS
               OF CHOICE OF THEORY** ...

Chapter 1

THE DEVELOPMENT OF PRODUCTS LIABILITY LAW

SYNOPSIS

§ 1.01 INTRODUCTION

More than most areas of the law, an understanding of the theory and practice of products liability law requires an understanding of its history and development. In part, this is because the laws governing the liability of those who manufacture and sell products that cause injury or death have undergone fundamental changes since the middle of the nineteenth century. While the recovery of damages resulting from defective products originally was governed (and limited) by principles of contract law, the theories of liability gradually expanded to include negligence, beginning in the second decade of the twentieth century, and strict liability, starting in the mid-1960s. As a result of those developments, no single theory of liability now governs lawsuits against product manufacturers and sellers. Instead, a claim for damages may be based upon one or more of a number of complex theories: express warranty; implied warranty; misrepresentation; negligence; strict liability. In recent years a number of individuals and govern-

ment entities also have filed suits against manufacturers and sellers of products such as lead paint, pesticides found in contaminated groundwater, and alcohol using nuisance theory or including a nuisance count along with the traditional products liability theories.[1] The adoption by the American Law Institute (ALI) in 1997 of the Restatement (Third) of Torts: Products Liability promises further change in the approaches to recovery for products that cause harm. Because the different causes of action in products liability actions, along with their elements, defenses, and damages, are the result of a constantly evolving process, it is necessary to begin by putting them into perspective and explaining how and why products liability law has developed.

§ 1.02 THE INFLUENCE OF CONTRACT LAW

Products liability law has its origins in early nineteenth century cases where a defect in a product meant that it did not meet the buyer's expectations. However, during the second quarter of the nineteenth century, buyers who suffered bodily injuries as a result of product defects began to bring claims alleging negligence in the manufacturing of the goods.[2] Because negligence was a developing area of the law at that time, courts looked to contract law to define the scope of the duty owed by manufacturers and sellers. As a result, persons seeking compensation for bodily injuries caused by defective products faced the two principal limitations of contract law: *caveat emptor* and privity. Although these doctrines have been rejected or severely limited over the years, they have exerted an extremely important influence on the development of products liability law.

[A] *Caveat Emptor*

Until the early nineteenth century, people bought most of the goods they needed for their personal and commercial use directly from the makers of those goods. The complexity of products and the layers of distribution that arose during the industrial revolution did not yet exist. As a result, buyers usually knew the manufacturers and had an opportunity to inspect their products before they purchased them. Because buyers and sellers bargained with each other for the goods they bought and sold, the right to recover for any defects in the products was governed by the contract of sale. However, with the coming of the industrial revolution, manufacturers became insulated from the buyers of their products due to the increase of middlemen,

---

[1] *See* State of Rhode Island v. Lead Industries Association, 2005 R.I. Super. LEXIS 95 (R.I. Super. Ct. 2005); Sabater v. Lead Industries Association, Inc., 704 N.Y.S. 2d 800 (N.Y. Sup. Ct. 2000); Goodwin v. Anheuser-Busch Co., Inc., No. BC310305, 2005 WL 280330 (Cal. Super. Ct. Jan. 28, 2005); Donald G. Gifford, *Public Nuisance as a Mass Products Liability Tort*, 71 U. CIN. L. REV. 741 (2003).

[2] Dixon v. Bell, 5 Maule & Selwyn 198 (1816).

such as wholesalers and retailers. This also meant that buyers no longer were able to bargain with the manufacturers of the items they purchased. In addition, the rise of large factories and the complexity of many of the new mass-produced goods meant that buyers were unable to inspect them before purchase or to understand how they operated. Because the lawsuits seeking compensation for the bodily injuries caused by defects in these new products threatened their industries, manufacturers sought protection from liability in the traditional requirements of contract law. As a result, courts continued to apply the earlier common law rule of *caveat emptor* (let the buyer beware).[3] A defense of this rule was offered by the Supreme Court in its 1871 decision in *Barnard v. Kellogg*:[4]

> No principle of the common law has been better established, or more often affirmed, both in this country and in England than that in sales of personal property, in the absence of express warranty, where the buyer has an opportunity to inspect the commodity, and the seller is guilty of no fraud . . . the maxim of caveat emptor applies. . . . And there is no hardship in it, because if the purchaser distrusts his judgment he can require of the seller a warranty that the quality or condition of the goods he desires to buy corresponds with the sample exhibited. If he is satisfied without a warranty, and can inspect and declines to do it, he takes upon himself the risk that the article is merchantable. And he cannot relieve himself and charge the seller on the ground that the examination will occupy time, and is attended with labor and inconvenience. . . . Of such universal acceptance is the doctrine of caveat emptor in this country, that the courts of all the States in the Union where the common law prevails, with one exception (South Carolina), sanction it.[5]

Demands by businesses during the late nineteenth century that government leave the regulation of commerce to the laws of the marketplace led to a philosophy of *laissez-faire*.[6] Ideas of the freedom and sanctity of contract resulted, among other things, in the rejection of any idea that a general implied warranty accompanied the sale of goods. At the same time, however, courts recognized the need to create exceptions to the rule of *caveat emptor* to protect buyers from harm in specific situations. This led courts to hold that, even in the absence of fraud or an express warranty, an "implied warranty of merchantability" or an "implied warranty of fitness for a particular purpose" accompanied the sale of some products. These implied warranties began the movement (that culminated with the adoption of

---

[3] National Oil Co. v. Rankin 75 P. 1013 (Kan. 1904). For a detailed study of the doctrine, see Walton H. Hamilton, *The Ancient Maxim Caveat Emptor*, 40 YALE L.J. 1133 (1931).

[4] 77 U.S. (10 Wall.) 383 (1871).

[5] *Id.* at 388-389. *See also* Slaughter's Administrator v. Gerson, 80 U.S. 379 (1871).

[6] *See* John W. Metzger, *The Social Revolution in Products Liability*, 49 ILL. B.J. 710 (1961).

strict liability in the 1960s) toward focusing on the dangerous condition of products themselves rather than on any fault in the process of manufacturing or selling them. Thus, as early as 1815, a New York court held that there was an implied warranty of fitness in the sale of food.[7] According to the Illinois Supreme Court, the imposition of such a warranty was based upon public policy:

> Where . . . articles of food are purchased from a retail dealer for immediate consumption, the consequences resulting from the purchase of an unsound article may be so serious and may prove so disastrous to the heath and life of the consumer that public safety demands that there should be an implied warranty on the part of the vendor that the article sold is sound and fit for the use for which it was purchased.[8]

Similarly, where a person sold drugs, medicines or other chemicals, the rule of *caveat emptor* did not apply if the buyer was not an expert and relied on the knowledge and skill of the seller. In such a case, there was an implied warranty of fitness for the use to which the product usually was put or was recommended by the seller.[9] According to Kentucky's highest court: "As applicable to the owners of drugs stores, or persons engaged in vending drugs and medicines by retail, the legal maxim should be reversed. Instead of caveat emptor, it should be caveat vendor."[10] Finally, courts came to hold that the rule of *caveat emptor* did not apply if the seller undertook to furnish goods for a particular purpose specified by the buyer.[11]

Despite the exceptions to the rule of *caveat emptor*, the concept of general implied warranties of merchantability and fitness did not begin to gain acceptance until the early twentieth century. Changing views about how the marketplace actually operated made the idea that consumers were able to bargain with sellers from a position of equal knowledge and strength a fiction. In addition, the injuries and deaths that resulted from a general lack of any government regulation of contracts led to pressure for the protection of workers and consumers. Among the many reforms of the progressive era were the implied warranty provisions adopted by the Uniform Sales Act (USA) in 1906[12] that created the basis for the current implied warranty provisions in Article 2 of the Uniform Commercial Code (UCC).[13]

---

[7] Van Bracklin v. Fonda, 7 Am. Dec. 339 (N.Y. 1815). *See also* Ward v. Morehead City Sea Food Co., 87 S.E. 958 (N.C. 1916).

[8] Wiedeman v. Keller, 49 N.E. 210, 211 (Ill. 1897).

[9] Thomas v. Winchester, 6 N.Y. 397 (N.Y. 1852); Salmon v. Libby, McNeil & Libby, 114 Ill. App. 258 (Ill. App. Ct. 1904).

[10] Fleet and Semple v. Hollenkemp, 52 Ky. (1 B. Mon.) 219 (1852).

[11] Shoenberger v. Mcewen, 15 Ill. App. 496 (Ill. App. Ct. 1884).

[12] *See* Uniform Sales Act § 15(2) (implied warranty of merchantability) and §§ 15(1), 15(4) and 15(5) (implied warranty of fitness for a particular purpose).

[13] *See* UCC § 2-314 (implied warranty of merchantability) and § 2–315 (implied warranty of fitness for a particular purpose).

[B] *The Privity Rule*

Although exceptions to the rule of *caveat emptor* developed during the nineteenth century, they extended the right to recover no further than the immediate buyer of the defective product. That was in keeping with the general requirement that, ordinarily, a contract created no duties except to the parties to it and to their privies.[14] Although originally a requirement of contract law, privity of contract between the plaintiff and defendant became an essential element in negligence actions as well. Thus, at common law, a person injured by a product had no cause of action against the manufacturer of the product unless that person was in privity of contract with the manufacturer. However, as with the rule of *caveat emptor*, the privity rule became subject to a number of judicially-created exceptions.

The origin of the privity rule in products liability cases was the 1842 English decision in *Winterbottom v. Wright*[15] in which Winterbottom, a coachman, suffered permanent injuries when the mail-coach he was driving collapsed. The coach had been built by Wright, who had contracted with the Postmaster General to supply coaches for the delivery of mail and to keep those coaches in good repair. The Postmaster-General then contracted with Atkinson to supply horses and drivers for the coaches to deliver the mail. Winterbottom was, in turn, one of the coachmen hired by Atkinson under that contract. Although not a party to the contract between Wright and the Postmaster-General, Winterbottom's declaration stated that, "by virtue of the said contract," Wright undertook a duty "to keep the carriage in a safe condition."[16] Winterbottom alleged that his right to recover was based upon his knowledge of, and reliance upon, the contract and that Wright's "omission" resulted in his injuries.

In what one of the judges, Lord Abinger, termed "an action of first impression,"[17] the Court of Exchequer dismissed Winterbottom's suit against Wright because there was no privity of contract between the parties. Although Wright breached the duty that he undertook to keep the coaches in a state of good repair, another of the judges, Baron Rolff, explained that the duty arose solely out of the contract between Wright and the Postmaster-General. Since Winterbottom was not a party to that contract, Wright owed him no duty of care.[18] The emphasis by the judges on the privity rule was prompted by their fear that, if Winterbottom was permitted to recover, "every passenger, or even any person passing along the road, who was

---

[14] 2 Edwin A. Jaggard, Handbook of the Law of Torts § 260 (1895).

[15] 152 Eng. Rep. 402 (Ex. 1842).

[16] *Id.* at 405.

[17] *Id.* at 404.

[18] *Id.* at 405. Although Baron Rolff did not use the word "negligence" or "tort" in his opinion, Lord Abinger referred to the case as an "action of tort" at the end of his opinion. *Id.* at 405.

injured by the upsetting of the coach, might bring a similar action."[19] Since Lord Abinger felt that, unless liability was limited to those who had entered into the contract, "the most absurd and outrageous consequences, to which I see no limit, would ensue,"[20] the third judge in the case, Baron Alderson, concluded:

> The only safe rule is to confine the right to recover to those who enter into the contract; if we go one step beyond that, there is no reason why we should not go fifty. The only real argument in favour of the action is that this is a case of hardship; but that might have been obviated, if the plaintiff had made himself a party to the contract.[21]

Although Winterbotton based his action on Wright's "omission" in the performance of his contract with the Postmaster-General and not on tort, the *dicta* of Lord Abinger and Baron Alderson was interpreted by courts in England and in the United States to mean that a manufacturer or seller of a defective product was not liable, either in contract or in negligence, to a buyer in the absence of a contractual relationship between them.[22] As a result, the duty in negligence actions against manufacturers and sellers for defective products was defined as arising solely out of the contract of sale. Since the contract of sale applied only to the parties who entered into that contract, the privity rule prevented a consumer or user from recovering damages from the manufacturers or seller of the product for their injuries unless the purchase had been made directly from the manufacturer.[23]

American courts expressed similar fears as those stated in *Winterbottom* about the "far-reaching consequences" to the "general prosecution of mercantile business" of extending liability in negligence actions to persons who were not in privity of contract with the manufacturer or seller of a product.[24] One reason for this fear was that manufacturers and sellers did not know who would use their products or where or how they would be used. This was the concern expressed by the Pennsylvania Supreme Court in *Curtin v. Somerset*,[25] in which a hotel guest was injured when a porch col-

---

[19] *Id.*

[20] *Id.*

[21] *Id.*

[22] Goodlander Mill Co. v. Standard Oil Co., 63 F. 400 (7th Cir. 1894); Bragdon v. Perkins-Campbell Co., 87 F.109 (3d Cir. 1898); Davidson v. Montgomery Ward, 171 Ill. App. 355 (Ill. App. Ct. 1912). For a discussion of Winterbottom v. Wright in the United States, see Francis H. Bohlen, *The Basis of Affirmative Obligations in the Law of Tort,* 44 AM. L. REG. (N.S.) 209 (1905).

[23] Huset v. J. I. Case Threshing Machine Co., 120 F. 865 (8th Cir. 1903); Losee v. Clute, 10 Am. Rep. 638 (N.Y. 1873); Loop v. Litchfield, 42 N.Y. 351 (N.Y. 1870).

[24] Lebourdais v. Vitrified Wheel Co., 80 N.E. 482, 483 (Mass. 1907).

[25] 21 A. 244 (Pa. 1891).

lapsed. The court denied recovery for negligence in an action based upon the construction of the porch, declaring:

> The consequences of holding the opposite doctrine would be far reaching. If . . . a manufacturer who constructs a boiler, piece of machinery, or a steamship, owes a duty to the whole world, that his work or his machine or his steamship shall contain no hidden defect, it is difficult to measure the extent of his responsibility, and no prudent man would engage in such occupations upon such conditions. It is safer and wiser to confine such liabilities to the parties immediately concerned.[26]

Courts restricted the scope of a manufacturer's liability by using one of the essential elements of negligence: causation. They took the position that injuries to persons other than the immediate buyer of the product were not "the natural or probable effect of negligence" in the manufacture of products. That was because such injuries were not foreseeable and the act of the purchaser "insulated" the negligence of the manufacturer from the buyer.[27]

[C] *Exceptions to the Privity Rule*

Although it became a general rule of common law that a manufacturer or seller of a product was not liable, regardless of its negligence, to third persons with whom it had no contractual relations, courts developed a number of exceptions to the privity requirement.[28] These exceptions, which led to the development of the modern rules of negligence, strict liability, and misrepresentation, fell into four broad categories. First, privity did not protect a manufacturer or seller's negligence where the product was "imminently" or "inherently" dangerous to human life or health.[29] As with implied warranties (and later strict liability), this exception was based on the condition of the product itself rather than any conduct by the manufacturer or seller. The classic example of this is *Thomas v. Winchester*,[30] a case decided in 1852, just ten years after *Winterbottom v. Wright*. In *Thomas*, a chemist negligently labeled a bottle of poison as harmless medicine and sold it to a retail druggist who, in turn, sold it to a man who purchased it for his wife. As in *Winterbottom*, there was no privity of contract between the chemist and the woman who took the poison. However, despite the absence of privity of contract, the New York Court of Appeals distinguished *Winterbot-*

---

[26] *Id.* at 245.

[27] Huset, 120 F. at 865.

[28] *See* FRANCIS H. BOHLEN, STUDIES IN THE LAW OF TORTS 109-155 (1926); THOMAS M COOLEY & ARCHIBALD H. THROCKMORTON, A TREATISE ON THE LAW OF TORTS § 345 (1930).

[29] For a list of cases dealing with this exception, see *Huset*, 120 F. at 870. *See also* Edward Levi, *An Introduction to Legal Reasoning*, 15 U. CHIC. L. REV. 501, 506-519 (1948).

[30] 6 N.Y. 397 (N.Y. 1852).

tom, saying that negligent mislabeling "put human life in imminent danger" and was much more likely to affect a remote purchaser than the druggist to whom the chemist sold it.[31] Because the extent of the danger posed by the mislabeled poison could be foreseen, the "duty" owed by the chemist did not arise out of the contract of sale but in selling a dangerous product which the chemist knew would be put into the stream of commerce. Thus, the chemist owed a duty of care to anyone who foreseeably could take the poison, not just to the immediate purchaser.[32] The "inherently dangerous" exception to the privity requirement later was extended from drugs to the manufacturer of a household item, a coffee urn.[33]

The second exception to the privity rule arose when a property owner's negligence injured a person who was invited by the property owner to use his defective product on his property.[34] The application of this exception was far more limited than the first one. The leading example is *Devlin v. Smith*,[35] in which a painter hired a scaffold-builder to construct a scaffold for the specific purpose of enabling his workers to stand on it to paint the 90 foot dome of a courthouse. The scaffold was constructed negligently and, while one of the workers was using it, it gave way, resulting in the death of the worker. Since the builder undertook to construct a scaffold for workers to use while painting, any negligence in the construction of the scaffold would result in the workers falling from a significant height. As in *Thomas v. Winchester*, injury to persons who were not party to the contract "would be a natural and necessary consequence of the builder's negligence."[36] Since the builder's duty of care extended to the workers who used his scaffold, the New York Court of Appeals held that a jury should decide whether the death of the worker was caused by the builder's breach of that duty in the construction of the scaffold.[37]

The third exception to the privity rule involved persons who sold products which they knew were imminently dangerous to life or health but concealed the dangers from the buyers.[38] Under this exception, both the condition of the product and the manufacturer's knowledge and concealment of the danger posed by it were essential. In *Huset v. J. I. Case Threshing Machine*

---

[31] *Id.* at 409.

[32] *Id.* at 409-410.

[33] Statler v. George A. Ray Manufacturing Co., 88 N.E. 1063 (N.Y. 1909).

[34] For a list of cases dealing with this exception, see *Huset*, 20 F. at 870-71. *See also* Coughtry v. Globe Woolen Co., 1874 N.Y. LEXIS 92 (N.Y. 1874).

[35] 89 N.Y. 470 (N.Y. 1882).

[36] *Id.* at 478.

[37] *Id.* at 479.

[38] The earliest example of this exception is an English decision, Lanridge v. Levy, 150 Eng. Rep. 863 (Ex. 1837). For a list of American cases dealing with this exception, see *Huset v. J. I. Case Threshing Machine Co.*, 120 F. 865, 871 (8th Cir. 1903).

Co.,[39] the defendant manufactured a thrashing machine that it sold to the employer of the plaintiff. The machine had an iron covering over the top of the cylinder which employees walked on while operating the machine. However, due to a defect in the construction, the covering was unable to hold the weight that was placed upon it. As a result, it collapsed and the plaintiff's leg was crushed. Although the manufacturer knew that the machine was dangerous when it shipped it to the plaintiff's employer, it concealed the defective and dangerous condition so that it could not be discovered by persons using the machine. The Court of Appeals held the manufacturer liable since it negligently produced a product "imminently dangerous to the lives and limbs of those who should use the machine" and knowingly concealed the dangerous condition of the product when it shipped it to the retailer.[40] Similarly in *Kuelling v. Roderick Lean Manufacturing Co.*,[41] a farmer injured by a road roller alleged that the manufacturer "intentionally, willfully, maliciously, negligently, and fraudulently" constructed a machine that was unfit for its use and concealed the dangers so they could not be seen on inspection.[42] The New York Court of Appeals found not only "fraudulent deceit and concealment" of the dangers in the product but also what amounted to "an affirmative representation" that the product was fit for its intended use.[43] In such a situation, the manufacturer was liable to any person, including those not in privity of contract, who was injured because of the fraudulent deceit and concealment.[44]

The final exception to the requirement of privity arose in cases where the seller was guilty of fraud. In an English case, *Langridge v. Levy*,[45] the son of the buyer of a gun was severely injured when the gun exploded while he was using it. The seller had told the buyer's father that the gun had been manufactured by a well-known gun-maker and was a "good, safe and secure gun."[46] In fact, the seller knew that the gun had been made by a different gun-maker and was "a very bad, unsafe, ill-manufactured, and dangerous gun, wholly unsound and of very inferior materials."[47] Since the son had not been a party to the contract for the sale of the gun and since the gun was not inherently dangerous, the Court of Exchequer rejected liability based on the warranty as a contract. The court feared, as had the court in *Winter-bottom v. Wright*, that permitting anyone to recover whenever a duty was

---

[39] 120 F. 865 (8th Cir. 1903).

[40] *Id.* at 872-73.

[41] 75 N.E. 1098 (N.Y. 1905).

[42] *Id.* at 1099.

[43] *Id.* at 1101.

[44] *Id.* at 1102.

[45] 150 Eng. Rpt. 863 (Ex. 1837).

[46] *Id.*

[47] *Id.*

imposed by contract would lead to an "indefinite extent of liability."[48] Instead, the court based its finding of the seller's liability for the son's injuries on fraud: the seller knowingly made a false statement that a product was safe in order to induce a sale; the person to whom the false statement was made relied upon it in purchasing and using the product; and the person injured was the person to whom the false statement was made or a person within the seller's contemplation at the time of the sale.[49] These elements later became the basis for the independent theory of fraudulent misrepresentation.

§ 1.03 THE RISE OF NEGLIGENCE

Just as changing views about the nature of the marketplace led to the decline of the doctrine of *caveat emptor*, social and economic changes in the United States during the first half of the twentieth century resulted in the rejection of the privity limitations in negligence cases and led, ultimately, to the creation of a new theory of strict liability in products liability cases. Scholars have posited a number of forces that were responsible for these changes: increasing governmental control and responsibility for the welfare of the individual; increasing mechanization and the growing complexity of product design; the rise of the welfare state; increasing urbanization; a policy of "internalizing" costs to achieve an efficient level of manufacturing operations; the gradual evolution of the fault system; and the rise of the the- ory of enterprise liability.[50] The first tangible effect these changing views had on products liability law came in 1916 when Judge Benjamin Cardozo, writing for the New York Court of Appeals in *MacPherson v. Buick Motor Co.*,[51] rejected the privity rule in negligence cases.

[A] *The Fall of Privity*

In *MacPherson*, the defendant, an automobile manufacturer, sold an automobile to a retail dealer who resold it to the plaintiff. One of the wheels on the automobile was made of defective wood and, when its spokes sud-

---

[48] *Id.* at 530.

[49] *Id.* at 531-532.

[50] For a discussion of these factors, see George L. Priest, *The Invention of Enterprise Liability: A Critical History of the Intellectual Foundations of Modern Tort Law*, 14 J. LEGAL STUDIES 461 (1985). Priest takes the position that modern product liability law is the result of the enterprise theory which provides that "business enterprises ought to be responsible for losses resulting from products they introduce into commerce." *Id.* at 463.

[51] 111 N.E. 1050 (N.Y. 1916). For a discussion of the case, see James Henderson, *MacPherson v. Buick Motor Co.: Simplifying the Facts While Reshaping the Law*, in Robert L. Rabin & Stephen D. Sugarman (eds.), TORT STORIES 41 (2003).

denly collapsed while the plaintiff was driving the automobile, he was injured. The wheel had been manufactured by another company and purchased by the defendant for incorporation into the automobile. In a negligence action brought by the plaintiff, the question for the court was whether the automobile manufacturer owed a duty of care to anyone except the immediate purchaser (the retail dealer) of the automobile. Since the manufacturer did not know of the defect in the wheel and conceal it, and since there was no evidence that the defect could have been discovered by ordinary inspection, the case did not fall into the exceptions to the privity rule of *Huset v. J. I. Case Threshing Machine Co.* and *Kuelling v. Roderick Lean Manufacturing Co.*

The manufacturer in *MacPherson* argued that, since an automobile is not an "inherently" dangerous product, it was not liable to a third-party in "simple negligence."[52] In deciding whether the manufacturer owed a duty of care to anyone except the immediate purchaser, Judge Cardozo began by analyzing the exceptions to the privity rule set forth in *Thomas v. Winchester*. However, rather than simply add automobiles to the growing list of exceptions to the privity rule based on "inherently" dangerous products, Judge Cardozo "buried the general rule under the exception."[53] Judge Cardozo concluded:

> We hold . . . that the principle of *Thomas v. Winchester* is not limited to poisons, explosives, and things of like nature, to things which in their normal operation are implements of destruction. If the nature of a thing is such that it is reasonably certain to place life and limb in period when negligently made, it is then a thing of danger. Its nature gives warning of the consequences to be expected. If to the element of danger there is added knowledge that the thing will be used by persons other than the purchaser, and used without new tests, then, irrespective of contract, the manufacturer of this thing of danger is under a duty to make it carefully.[54]

In his opinion, Judge Cardozo emphasized that the case dealt with the liability of a manufacturer of a finished product who puts it on the market knowing that it will be used without inspection by its customers. For Judge Cardozo, a manufacturer's duty to third parties in such a situation required a showing of the foreseeability of harm. That meant that the manufacturer had to have knowledge of a danger posed by the product and had to know that the danger was probable, not merely possible. Foreseeabilty also required that the manufacturer must know that, in the usual course of things, the danger would not be limited to the immediate buyer of the product. In keeping with proximate cause as a limit on liability in negligence

---

[52] 111 N.E. at 1050.

[53] William L. Prosser, *The Assault Upon the Citadel (Strict Liability to the Consumer)*, 69 YALE L.J. 1099, 1100 (1960).

[54] MacPherson v. Buick Motor Co., 111 N.E. 1050, 1053 (N.Y. 1916).

cases, Judge Cardozo held that the proximity or remoteness of the relationship between the manufacturer and the person injured by the product was a factor for the jury's consideration.[55]

The discussion of forseeability and proximate cause was not simply part of a redefinition of what constituted "a thing of danger" for purposes of broadening *Thomas v. Winchester*. Judge Cardozo concluded his opinion by stating that he had severed the tie of negligence to contract law in products liability cases. "We have put aside the notion that the duty to safeguard life and limb, whenever consequences of negligence may be foreseen, grows out of contract and nothing else. We have put the source of obligation where it ought to be. We have put its source in the law."[56]

Applying his negligence analysis to the facts in *MacPherson*, Judge Cardozo held that the nature of automobiles is such that probable danger is foreseeable if they are constructed defectively. Since the automobile in the case "was designed to go fifty miles an hour," injury was almost certain to happen if the wheels were defective. The manufacturer knew of that danger and also knew that the automobile would be used by persons other than the immediate buyer, an automobile dealer who bought it for resale. Proximate cause did not limit the manufacturer's liability since, according to Judge Cardozo, the dealer was the person least likely to use the automobile.[57] Finally, Judge Cardozo refused to hold that the automobile manufacturer was not liable because it had purchased the wheels from a reputable component-part manufacturer. Since the defendant was a manufacturer of automobiles, it was responsible for the finished product and had a duty to subject the component parts to ordinary testing.[58]

[B] *The Adoption of Negligence*

MacPherson did not mean the immediate end to the privity requirement in negligence cases. Although in 1946 the Massachusetts Supreme Judicial Court stated that "[t]he doctrine of the *MacPherson* case is now generally accepted,"[59] some state courts did not eliminate entirely the privity requirement in negligence actions until later.[60] However, *MacPherson* began the development of what now is the modern law of negligence in products lia-

---

[55] *Id.*

[56] *Id.*

[57] *Id.*

[58] *Id.* at 1055.

[59] Carter v. Yardley & Co., 64 N.E.2d 693, 700 (Mass. 1946).

[60] The Illinois Supreme Court, for example, waited until 1965 to abolish privity entirely in negligence suits. *See* Suvada v. White Motor Co., 210 N.E.2d 182 (Ill. 1965). Maine did not abolish privity in products liability cases until 1982. *See* Adams v. Buffalo Forge Co., 443 A.2d 932 (Me. 1982).

bility cases.[61] Beginning in the 1920s, the theory of negligence expanded to apply to manufacturers of component parts[62] to include property damage,[63] and to give a right of action to bystanders[64] and other non-purchasers.[65]

The influence of *MacPherson* also can be seen in the Restatement of the Law of Torts, adopted by the American Law Institute in 1934. Chapter 14 of the Restatement was devoted to the "Liability of Persons Supplying Chattels for the Use of Others." Section 388, which was entitled "Chattel Known to be Dangerous for Intended Use," drew upon the language of *MacPherson* and applied negligence to "one who supplies directly or through a third person a chattel for another to use." Such suppliers were liable for bodily harm if they knew or should have known that the chattel was likely to be "dangerous for the use for which it was supplied"; did not have any reason to believe that the user of the product would realize the dangerous condition; and failed to use "reasonable care" to inform the user of the dangerous condition. Other sections dealt specifically with manufacturers and held them liable for a "Chattel Known to be Dangerous"[66] and for the "Negligent Manufacture of Chattel; Dangerous Unless Carefully Made."[67] Although liability was limited to products that posed "an unreasonable risk of causing substantial bodily harm," in those situations liability was not limited by privity and extended liability to "those who lawfully use [the product] for a purpose for which it is manufactured and to those whom the supplier should expect to be in the vicinity of its probable use."[68] Retailers also had a duty to take reasonable steps to prevent injury from a known danger in the products they sold when they should know that the danger was likely to pass unnoticed to the buyer or others likely to use the product.[69] By the late 1950s, the influence of the Restatement sections was such that the "Liability of Suppliers of Chattels" based on negligence had become an all but universal part of tort law.[70] The acceptance of negligence as a theory of recovery in products liability and the influence of the sections of Chapter 14 is reflected in the fact that they were retained in the Restatement (Second) of Torts, adopted by the American Law Institute in 1965.

---

[61] *See* FOWLER V. HARPER, A TREATISE ON THE LAW OF TORTS § 106 (1933).

[62] Smith v. Peerless Glass Co., 181 N.E. 576 (N.Y. 1932).

[63] Marsh Wood Products Co. v. Babcock & Wilcox Co., 240 N.W. 392 (Wis. 1932).

[64] McLeod v. Linde Air Products Co., 1 S.W.2d 122 (Mo. 1927).

[65] Reed & Barton Corp. v. Maas, 73 F.2d 359 (1st Cir. 1934) (applying Wisconsin law).

[66] RESTATEMENT OF THE LAW OF TORTS § 394 (1934).

[67] *Id.* § 395.

[68] *Id.*

[69] *Id.* at § 399.

[70] *See* 2 FOWLER V. HARPER & FLEMING JAMES, JR., THE LAW OF TORTS §§ 28.1-28.14 (1956) *and* WILLIAM L. PROSSER, HANDBOOK OF THE LAW OF TORTS § 84 (2d ed. 1955).

[C] *Res Ipsa Loquitur*

With the elimination of the privity requirement in products liability actions based upon negligence, a plaintiff had to show that the manufacturer or seller owed a duty of reasonable care in connection with the manufacture or sale of the product, that the manufacturer or seller breached that duty, and that the injuries that resulted were caused by the breach of the duty. The principal difficulty with a negligence action, however, is that the plaintiff has the burden of pleading and proving how the manufacturer or seller breached the duty. The plaintiff must show both that the product was defective and that the manufacturer or seller failed to exercise reasonable care in its manufacture or sale. In some cases, the defect may not be the result of any negligence. In other cases, the plaintiff may not know the specific circumstances that led to the injury or who was responsible for the defect.

In order to overcome the hurdle of establishing a *prima facie* case in such situations, some courts turned to the evidentiary rule of *res ipsa loquitur*. In *Escola v. Coca Cola Bottling Co.*[71] a waitress suffered severe injuries when a soft drink bottle broke in her hand while she was restocking the restaurant's refrigerator. In her suit against the company that bottled and delivered the defective bottle to her employer, she claimed that the company had been negligent in selling "bottles containing said beverage which on account of excessive pressure of gas or by reason of some defect in the bottle was dangerous . . . and likely to explode."[72] However, since the waitress could not prove any specific acts of negligence on the part of the bottling company, she relied on the rule of *res ipsa loquitur*. The company alleged that the rule did not apply, since exclusive control of the item causing the injury is an essential element of *res ipsa loquitur* and, in this case, the bottle had been out of its control for some time.[73] The California Supreme Court, however, held that it was not necessary for the plaintiff to eliminate every remote possibility of injury after the bottle left the defendant's control. It was sufficient if there was evidence "permitting a reasonable inference that it was not accessible to extraneous forces and that it was carefully handled by plaintiff or any third person who may have touched it."[74] In *Escola*, the court held that the record supported an inference that the bottle had not been damaged by any extraneous force after the defendant had delivered it to the restaurant. Thus, the bottle had to have been defective at the time it left the defendant's control.

---

[71] 150 P.2d 436 (Cal. 1944). For a discussion of the case, see Mark Geistfeld, *Escola v. Coca Bottling Co.: Strict Products Liability Unbound*, in Robert and Stephen D. Sugarman (eds.), Torts Stories 229 (2003).

[72] 150 P.2d at 437.

[73] *Id.* at 438.

[74] *Id.* at 439.

§ 1.04 FROM NEGLIGENCE TO STRICT LIABILITY

With the growing acceptance of negligence as a basis of products liability actions, the first arguments were made during the 1940s and 1950s for a new theory of liability that would go beyond negligence and base liability not on the conduct of the manufacturer but on the condition of the product.[75] While warranties already provided such a basis of liability in contract law, warranties still were limited by the privity requirement.[76] In the twenty years preceding the American Law Institute's adoption in 1965 of section 402A of the Restatement (Second) of Torts, a series of decisions and law review articles laid the ground work for strict liability by proposing new bases for liability and modifying existing ones.[77]

[A] *The Theory Behind Strict Liability*

The first articulation of a rational for a tort theory of strict liability in products liability cases came in 1944 in *Escola v. Coca Cola Bottling Co.*[78] The real significance of that decision is not its extension of *res ipsa loquitur* to situations in which the plaintiff was able to negate the possibility that the injury might have been caused by the negligence of some intervening party. Instead, its importance lies in Justice Roger Traynor's concurring opinion. He took a position that was not argued by any of the parties: liability should be grounded in absolute liability. According to Justice Traynor: "In my opinion it should now be recognized that a manufacturer incurs an absolute liability when an article that he has placed on the market, knowing that it is to be used without inspection, proves to have a defect that causes injury to human beings."[79] Justice Traynor based his support for absolute liability not on "inherent dangers" or the consumer expectations that had marked the decline of *caveat emptor* and privity but on enterprise liability, the idea that business should be liable for the inevitable injuries that resulted from its activities. More specifically, Justice Traynor's offered three rationales for absolute liability. First, he stated that it would provide an incentive for manufacturers to produce safer products and minimize the losses to society from those products.

> Even if there is no negligence, . . . public policy demands that responsibility be fixed wherever it will most effectively reduce the

---

[75] For articles by Fleming James, Leon Green, Marcus Plant, and Noel Dix dealing, from differing points of view, with the question whether manufacturers should be held strictly liable, see 24 TENN. L. REV. 923-1018 (1957).

[76] *See* Fleming James, *Products Liability*, 34 TEX. L. REV. 192 (1955).

[77] For a discussion of the evolution of strict liability theory from the 1930s to the 1960s, see George L. Priest, *The Invention of Enterprise Liability: A Critical History of the Intellectual Foundations of Modern Tort Law*, 14 J. LEGAL STUDIES 461 (1985).

[78] 150 P.2d 436 (Cal. 1944).

[79] *Id.* at 440.

hazards to life and health inherent in defective products that reach the market. It is evident that the manufacturer can anticipate some hazards and guard against the recurrence of others, as the public cannot.[80]

Secondly, Justice Traynor felt that the manufacturer was better able than the consumer to absorb or pass on the costs from the inevitable losses that result from defective products.

Those who suffer injury from defective products are unprepared to meet its consequences. The cost of an injury or loss of time or health may be an overwhelming misfortune to the person injured, and a needless one, for the risk of injury can be insured by the manufacturer and distributed among the public as a cost of doing business. It is to the public interest to discourage the marketing of products having defects that are a menace to the public.[81]

Finally, Justice Traynor saw absolute liability as a means to eliminate the problems of proof that confronted plaintiffs in negligence actions. "An injured person . . . is not ordinarily in a position to refuse [a showing of proper care] or identify the cause of the defect, for he can hardly be familiar with the manufacturing process as the manufacturer himself is."[82]

Although Justice Traynor's concurring opinion later would provide a major rationale for the adoption of strict liability in products liability cases, it received little attention at the time and 20 years would go by before his position would be accepted. However, the 1950s and early 1960s saw an increased interest in strict liability in general and products liability in particular. The two most prolific advocates of strict liability during those decades were Professors Fleming James and William Prosser. However, they took different views as to what the basis of strict liability should be. Professor James advocated a system of "strict enterprise liability" that would help reduce the number of accidents resulting from defective products and administer the losses from such accidents in a way that would minimize their individual and social costs.[83] While Professor James felt that traditional negligence and warranty were not equipped to meet the modern challenges presented by accidents from defective products and should be abandoned, he took the position that courts could develop a new warranty theory for products liability cases "which is tailored to meet modern needs in that field."[84] In contrast, Professor Prosser, in his two influential articles,

---

[80] *Id.* at 440-441.

[81] *Id.* at 441.

[82] *Id.*

[83] Fleming James, *General Products — Should Manufacturers Be Liable Without Negligence?* 24 TENN. L. REV. 923 (1957).

[84] Fleming James, *Products Liability*, 34 TEX. L. REV. 192, 228 (1955).

The Assault Upon the Citadel[85] in 1960 and *The Fall of the Citadel*[86] in 1966, analyzed the entire area of products liability law and urged: "If there is going to be strict liability in tort, let there be strict liability in tort, declared outright, without an illusory contract mask."[87] Although Professor James' warranty theory, "tailored to meet modern needs," initially was the victor in the competition for a new approach to products liability, the ultimate winner was the tort strict liability theory of Professor Prosser.

[B] *"The Fall of the Citadel of Privity"*

Despite the abolition of the privity requirement for products liability actions brought in negligence, courts continued to hold that actions for breach of warranty were contract actions and thus could be brought only by the party to the contract.[88] As with the earlier privity requirement in negligence, there was an exception in food cases. Parties who were not in privity to the manufacturer could bring an action against the manufacturer on the ground that the implied warranty ran with the sale of the food.[89] According to the Texas Supreme Court, the reason for that was that "the liability of the manufacturer and vendor [of food] is imposed by operation of law as a matter of public policy for the protection of the public, and is not dependent on any provision of the contract, either expressed or implied."[90]

Just as *MacPherson v. Buick Motor Co.* eliminated privity in negligence cases, "[t]he fall of the citadel of privity"[91] in warranty actions came in 1960 when the New Jersey Supreme Court decided *Henningsen v. Bloomfield Motors.*[92] Based upon an implied warranty of fitness, the court extended protection of that warranty to the "ultimate purchaser" and to other foreseeable users of the product. In *Henningsen*, a husband purchased a new automobile manufactured by Chrysler and sold by Bloomfield Motors, an automobile dealership. The husband gave the automobile to his wife as

---

[85] William Prosser, *The Assault Upon the Citadel (Strict Liability to the Consumer)*, 69 YALE L.J. 1099 (1960).

[86] William Prosser, *The Fall of the Citadel (Strict Liability to the Consumer)*, 50 MINN L. REV. 791 (1966).

[87] Prosser, *supra*, note 85, at 1134.

[88] Paul Harris Furniture Co. v. Morse, 139 N.E.2d 275 (Ill. 1956). *See* HARPER & JAMES, *supra*, note 70, § 28.16.

[89] In *Ward v. Morehead City Sea Food Co.*, 87 S.E. 958 (N.C. 1916), the North Carolina Supreme Court held that a packer was liable in negligence in packing fish it knew were unfit for human consumption. The court based its finding of negligence on a violation of state statutes making it a crime to sell adulterated food. *See* Mazetti v. Armour & Co., 135 P. 633 (Wash. 1913) *and* William Prosser, *The Assault Upon the Citadel*, 69 YALE L.J. 1099 (1960).

[90] Decker & Sons v. Capps, 164 S.W.2d 828, 831-832 (Tex. 1942).

[91] William Prosser, *The Fall of the Citadel (Strict Liability to the Consumer)*, 50 MINN L. REV. 791 (1966).

[92] 161 A.2d 69 (1960).

a gift and, while driving it, she was injured when a defect in the steering mechanism caused the automobile to crash into a wall. The husband and wife brought suit against the manufacturer and dealer of the automobile. Their complaint was based upon breach of express and implied warranties and upon negligence. At the trial, the judge dismissed the negligence counts and the case was submitted to the jury solely on the issue of breach of implied warranty of merchantability. The jury returned a verdict for the plaintiffs against both defendants.

The problem for the plaintiffs was the sales contract for the automobile signed by the husband. It contained, in 8½ inches of fine print on the back of the contract, a "warranty" provision that limited the manufacturer's liability to replacing defective parts within 90 days of the sale or until the car had been driven 4000 miles, whichever came first, if the part was shipped, at the buyer's expense, to the manufacturer's factory and an examination revealed that the part was defective. The provision also stated that the repair warranty was "expressly in lieu of all other warranties expressed or implied, and all other obligations or liabilities" on the part of the manufacturer. That language not only disclaimed all implied warranties, it barred all claims for consequential damages for personal injury resulting from a defect in the automobile.[93]

Writing for a unanimous New Jersey Supreme Court, Justice Francis reviewed the history and rationale for warranties and the privity doctrine and the limited exceptions to the privity requirement, beginning with food.[94] However, he then stated that there was "no rational doctrinal basis" for distinguishing between a defective bottle of a beverage and a defective automobile.[95] While a defective beverage could make a person sick, a defective automobile had an even greater potential to cause harm. Under modern methods of manufacturing and marketing, the ordinary purchaser has no opportunity or ability to inspect an automobile to determine its fitness. Thus, the court felt that the remedies in such a situation should not depend "upon the intricacies of the law of sales" or be based solely on privity of contract. Instead, they should rest on "the demands of social justice."[96] The court then held that, "under modern marketing conditions, when a manufacturer puts a new automobile in the stream of trade and promotes its purchase by the public, an implied warranty that it is reasonably suitable for use as such accompanies it into the hands of the ultimate purchaser."[97] The court concluded by taking one more giant step when it stated the implied

---

[93] *Id.* at 74.

[94] *Id.* at 80-81.

[95] *Id.* at 83.

[96] *Id.*

[97] *Id.* at 84.

warranty of merchantability extended not only to the "ultimate purchaser" of the automobile but also to

> members of his family, and to other persons occupying or using it with his consent. It would be wholly opposed to reality to say that use by such persons is not within the anticipation of the parties to such a warranty of reasonable suitability of an automobile for ordinary highway operation. Those persons must be considered within the distributive chain.[98]

Although *Henningsen* involved a defective automobile, personal injuries, and what the New Jersey Supreme Court considered an extremely unfair standard-form sales contract, the effect of the decision was not limited to its facts. By invalidating the disclaimer of liability for injuries in the standard form sales contract provided by the manufacturer, the court eliminated the ability of manufacturers to use the most important limitations of contract law — disclaimers and privity — to restrict their liability for personal injuries. In addition, since recovery did not depend upon proof of negligence or knowledge of any defect, courts were well on their way toward strict liability. Although *Henningsen* did not use the term "absolute liability" or "strict liability," it articulated the rationale upon which the transition from warranty to strict liability ultimately would be made.

[C] *The Triumph of Strict Liability in Tort*

The final steps toward the development of a tort theory of strict liability in products liability cases began in 1963 with the California Supreme Court decision in *Greenman v. Yuba Power Products*.[99] In *Greenman*, a woman purchased a combination power tool that could be used as a saw, drill and lathe and gave it to her husband for Christmas as a present for his home workshop. Two years later, he bought an attachment to use the machine as a lathe. While using it as a lathe, a piece of wood flew out of it and struck the husband on the forehead, causing serious injury. About ten and a half months later, he gave the retailer and manufacturer written notice of a claim for breach of warranty and filed a suit for breach of warranty and negligence.

The plaintiff introduced evidence that the saw had been defectively designed and manufactured by the defendant. The jury returned a verdict for the plaintiff after it concluded that the manufacturer was negligent and that the statements in the manufacturer's brochure constituted an express warranty. On appeal, the manufacturer argued that the plaintiff did not give notice of the breach of warranty within a reasonable time and

---

[98] *Id.* at 100.

[99] 377 P.2d 897 (Cal. 1963). For an analysis of Justice Roger Traynor's opinion, see RICHARD A. EPSTEIN, MODERN PRODUCTS LIABILITY LAW 36-48 (1980).

that the claim was barred by the Civil Code. However, Justice Roger Traynor, writing for a unanimous court, rejected the "timely notice" argument, stating that the notice provision was not "an appropriate one for the court to adopt in actions by injured consumers against manufacturers with whom they have not dealt."[100]

As in his concurring opinion in *Escola* 19 years earlier, Justice Traynor did not limit his analysis to the theories put forth by the plaintiff. Instead, he used the case as the opportunity to impose liability based on strict liability. According to Justice Traynor: "A manufacturer is strictly liable in tort when an article he places on the market, knowing that it is to be used without inspection for defects, proves to have a defect that causes injury to a human being."[101] After listing a variety of situations, beginning with food, in which strict liability long had been applied by the courts because of the hazard posed by the product if it was defective, Justice Traynor stated:

> Although in these cases strict liability usually has been based on the theory of an express or implied warranty running from the manufacturer to the plaintiff, the abandonment of the requirement of a contract between them, the recognition that the liability is not assumed by agreement but imposed by law . . . , and the refusal to permit the manufacturer to define the scope of its own responsibility for defective products . . . makes clear that the liability is not one governed by the law of contract warranties but by the law of strict liability in tort. Accordingly, the rules defining and governing warranties that were developed to meet the needs of commercial transactions cannot properly be invoked to govern the manufacturer's liability to those injured by its defective products unless those rules also serve the purposes for which such liability is imposed.[102]

Although Justice Traynor referred to Harper and James' treatise on torts, Prosser's law review articles, and to his own concurring opinion in *Escola* to provide support for his reasons for imposing strict liability, his opinion was a triumph of the enterprise liability theory. According to Justice Traynor, the purpose of strict liability is "to insure that the costs of injuries resulting from defective products are borne by the manufacturers that put such products on the market rather than by the injured persons who are powerless to protect themselves."[103] Since strict liability based upon "the intricacies of the law of sales" did not fully achieve that goal, it was necessary to develop a new theory based upon strict liability in tort. Under that new theory it was sufficient for the plaintiff to prove that "he was injured while using the

---

[100] *Id.* at 900.

[101] *Id.*

[102] *Id.* at 901.

[103] *Id.*

[power tool] in a way it was intended to be used as a result of a defect in design and manufacture of which plaintiff was not aware that made the [power tool] unsafe for its intended use."[104]

The year after it held manufacturers strictly liable in *Greenman*, the California Supreme Court applied strict liability to retailers in *Vandemark v. Ford Motor Co.*,[105] The court justified its extension of strict liability to include retailers on a number of business, safety, and economic grounds:

> Retailers like manufacturers are engaged in the business of distributing goods to the public. They are an integral part of the overall producing and marketing enterprise that should bear the cost of injuries resulting from defective products. . . .In some cases the retailer may be the only member of the enterprise reasonably available to the injured plaintiff. In other cases the retailer himself may play a substantial part in insuring that the product is safe or may be in a position to exert pressure on the manufacturer to that end; the retailer's strict liability thus serves as an added incentive to safety. Strict liability on the manufacturer and retailer alike affords maximum protection to the injured plaintiff and works no injustice to the defendants, for they can adjust the costs of such protection between them in the course of their continuing relationship.[106]

§ 1.05 THE RESTATEMENTS

The decision in *Greenman* was followed two years later (1965) by the ALI's statement of a general principle of strict liability in § 402A of the Restatement (Second) of Torts. That section, which was the work of Professor William Prosser who served as the Reporter for the entire Restatement (Second) of Torts, provides:

(1) One who sells any product in a defective condition unreasonably dangerous to the user or consumer or to his property is subject to liability for physical harm thereby caused to the ultimate user or consumer, or to his property, if

    (a) the seller is engaged in the business of selling such a product, and

    (b) it is expected to and does reach the user or consumer without substantial change in the condition in which it is sold.

(2) The rule stated in subsection (1) applies although

    (a) the seller has exercised all possible care in the preparation and sale of his product, and

---

[104] *Id.*

[105] 391 P.2d 168 (Cal. 1964).

[106] *Id.* at 262-263.

(b) the seller or consumer has not bought the product from or entered into any contractual relation with the seller.

Caveat:

The Institute expresses no opinion as to whether the rules stated in this Section may not apply

(1) to harm to persons other than users or consumers

(2) to the seller of a product expected to be processed or otherwise substantially changed before it reaches the user or consumer or

(3) to the seller of a component part of a product to be assembled.

Although § 402A is part of the Restatement (Second) of Torts, only California had adopted strict tort liability for defective products at the time the section was approved by the ALI. Thus, rather than a restatement of existing law, the section was a statement of what Professor Prosser felt the law should be in the hope that courts would move in that direction. Strict liability under § 402A differs from negligence or warranty in that it does not require any fault by the manufacture of the product (*see* § 402A(2)(a)), any representation about the product by the seller, or any reliance by the buyer on the skill or judgment of the seller (§ 402A(2)(b)). Since § 402A does not depend upon a contract, it is not affected by the specific requirements of a warranty, such as notice or disclaimers of privity. However, section 402A does not make the seller an insurer of the consumer's safety. Instead of absolute liability, it adopts a system of liability that does not require negligence or a warranty.

Within two decades, almost every state either had adopted § 402A or some variation of it.[107] At the present time (2005), only five states — Delaware, Massachusetts, Michigan, North Carolina and Virginia — do not have some form of strict tort liability in products liability cases. However, section 402A is a product of the 1960s. Like many other innovations during that decade, its effects continue to be felt in American society after more than a generation. As the late 1990s pointed toward a new century, the ALI attempted to move products liability law in a new direction by replacing § 402A with the Restatement (Third) of Torts: Products Liability ("Restatement (Third)"). However, unlike § 402A, which covers strict liability in a single section, the Restatement (Third) consists of 21 sections, which critics see both as a traditional "restatement" of what the courts have done and as advocating changes in a number of areas of the law, particularly design defects.[108] The sections of the Restatement (Third) address almost every aspect of products liability law:

---

[107] Seven states – Alabama, Colorado, Georgia, Maine, Mississippi, Ohio, and Tennessee – have statutory or judicially-created standards for strict liability that are based on § 402A but differ from it in some respects.

[108] *See* Larry S. Stewart, *Courts Overrule ALI 'Consensus' on Products*, TRIAL, November 2003, at 18.

- the liability of a commercial seller or distributor for harm caused by defective products;

- the categories of product defects;

- circumstantial evidence supporting an inference of a product defect;

- noncompliance and compliance with product safety statutes and regulations;

- the liability of a commercial seller or distributor of product components for harm caused by products into which the components are integrated;

- the liability of a commercial seller or distributor for harm caused by defective prescription drugs and medical devices;

- the liability of a commercial seller or distributor for harm caused by defective food products;

- the liability of a commercial seller or distributor for defective used products;

- the liability of a commercial product seller or distributor for harm caused by misrepresentation;

- the liability of a commercial product seller or distributor for harm caused by a post-sale failure to warn;

- the liability of a commercial product seller or distributor for harm caused by a post-sale failure to recall a product;

- the liability of successor for harm caused by defective products sold commercially by a predecessor;

- the liability of a successor for harm caused by the successor's own post-sale failure to warn;

- selling or distributing as one's own a product manufactured by another;

- general rule governing the causal connection between a product defect and harm;

- increased harm due to a product defect;

- apportionment of responsibility between or among the plaintiff, sellers, and distributors of defective products, and others;

- disclaimers, limitations, waivers, and other contractual exculpations as defenses to products liability claims for harm to persons;

- the definition of a "product";

- the definition of "one who sells or otherwise distributes";

- the definition of "harm to persons or property": recovery for economic loss.

Since its adoption by the ALI in 1997, the Restatement (Third) has generated widespread discussion in the literature and by the courts.[109] Whether the sections of the Restatement (Third) ultimately will supplant § 402A will be decided by state court judges. An indication of the initial reaction of the courts can be seen in a study published by J. Denny Shupe and Todd Steggerda in 2003.[110] Their study found that the Restatement (Third) had been cited by twenty-six state supreme courts as well as federal courts and the United States Supreme Court.[111] However, because the sections of the Restatement (Third) are much more complex than § 402A, no court has adopted or rejected the Restatement (Third) in its entirety. Instead, Shupe and Steggerda found that some state supreme courts had adopted one or more sections of the Restatement while some of those same states and other states had rejected other sections of the Restatement. Shupe and Steggerda also found that nineteen state supreme courts had discussed provisions of the Restatement (Third) without adopting or rejecting them.

§ 1.06 CHOICE OF THEORIES IN A PRODUCTS LIABILITY CASE

In most states, plaintiffs can choose from a number of different theories in framing their products liability claims: express and implied warranty; intentional, negligent, or innocent misrepresentation; negligence, and strict liability. Which theory or theories they choose depends upon the facts of each case, including any statements made by the seller, the difficulty and expense of proof, the relationship between the injured party and the manufacturer or seller, the type of damages sought, anticipated defenses, and the statute of limitations and repose. Their choice also is determined by the differences among the states in the requirements for the particular theories, by who bears the burden of proof on particular issues, and by the tests for determining whether the product was defective.

---

[109] For discussion of whether states should adopt the Restatement (Third), see Matthew R. Sorenson, *A Reasonable Alternative? Should Wyoming Adopt the Restatement (Third) of Torts: Products Liability?* 3 Wyo. L. Rev. 257 (2002); Robert D. Klein, *A Comparison of the Restatement (Third) of Torts: Products Liability and the Maryland Law of Products Liability*, 30 U. Balt. L. Rev. 273 (2001); Thomas V. Van Flein, *Prospective Application of the Restatement (Third) of Torts: Products Liability in Alaska*, 17 Alaska L. Rev. 1 (2000).

[110] J. Denny Shupe and Todd Steggerda, *Survey of the Reactions of the Highest Courts of the States to the Restatement (Third) of Torts: Products Liability*. The study is adapted from J. Denny Shupe and Todd Steggerda, *Toward a More Uniform and 'Reasonable' Approach to Products Liability Litigation: Current Trends in the Adoption of the Restatement (Third) and Its Potential Impact on Aviation Litigation*, 66 J. Air L. & Com. 129 (2000). A copy of the 2003 study was provided to the authors of this book and has not yet been published.

[111] Geier v. American Honda Motor Co., 529 U.S. 861 (2000).

Mention also must be made of the approach taken in six states — Connecticut,[112] Indiana,[113] Kansas,[114] Louisiana,[115] New Jersey,[116] and Washington[117] — that have enacted products liability statutes that, while not making substantial changes in the traditional standards of warranty, negligence and strict liability, create the exclusive remedy for all products liability actions brought in their states and preclude common law claims for harm caused by a defective product.[118] An example of these statutes is the Kansas Product Liability Act ("KPLA"),[119] which is based on the Model Uniform Product Liability Act ("Model Act").[120] The purpose both of the Model Act and the KPLA is "to consolidate all products liability actions, regardless of theory into one theory of legal liability."[121] In order to achieve this goal, the KPLA defines a "product liability claim" as "any claim or action brought for harm caused by the manufacture, production, making, construction, fabrication, design, formula, preparation, assembly, installation, testing, warnings, instructions, marketing, packaging, storage or labeling of the relevant product."[122] The KPLA applies to every "product liability claim" regardless of the substantive theory of recovery. This includes, but is not limited to "any action based on strict liability in tort, negligence, breach of express or implied warranty, breach of, or failure to, discharge a duty to warn or instruct, whether negligent or innocent, misrepresentation, concealment or nondisclosure, whether negligent or innocent, or under any other substantive legal theory."[123] The comprehensiveness of the KPLA is illustrated further by the fact that it applies to every "product seller," a term that is defined as "any person or entity that is engaged in the business of selling products, whether the sale is for resale, or for use or consumption.

---

[112] Connecticut Products Liability Act, CONN. GEN. STAT. § 52-572m (1991). For an analysis of the Act, see JAMES H. ROTONDO & PAUL D. WILLIAMS, CONNECTICUT PRODUCT LIABILITY LAW (1998).

[113] Indiana Product Liability Act, IND. CODE ANN. § 34-20-1-1 (2001).

[114] Kansas Product Liability Act, KAN. STAT. ANN. § 60-3301 (1994).

[115] Louisiana Products Liability Act, LA. REV. STAT. ANN. § 9:2800.51 (1997). See Thomas C. Galligan, Jr., The Louisiana Products Liability Act: Making Sense Of It All, 49 LA. L. REV. 629 (1989).

[116] The Products Liability Act, N.J. STAT. ANN. § 2A:58C-1 (2000).

[117] Washington Product Liability Act, WASH. REV. CODE § 7.72.010 (1992).

[118] Gerrity v. R.J. Reynolds Tobacco Co., 818 A.2d 769 (Conn. 2003); Savina v. Sterling Drug, Inc., 795 P.2d 915 (Kan. 1990).

[119] KAN. STAT. ANN. §§ 60-3301 et. seq. (1994).

[120] 44 Fed. Reg. 62,714 et seq. (1979). In 1967 Department of Commerce promulgated a Model Uniform Products Liability Act for adoption by the states. Although no state has adopted the model act, it has influence some state products liability statutes such as the one in Kansas. In addition, sections of the act have been adopted by some states.

[121] Patton v. Hutchinson Wil-Rich Manufacturing Co., 861 P.2d 1299, 1311 (Kan. 1993).

[122] KAN. STAT. ANN. § 60-3302(c) (1994).

[123] Id. See Savina v. Sterling Drug, Inc., 795 P.2d 915 (Kan. 1990).

The term includes a manufacturer, wholesaler, distributor or retailer of the relevant product."[124] Finally, the KPLA defines "harm" to include "(1) damage to property; (2) personal physical injuries, illness and death; (3) mental anguish or emotional harm attendant to such personal physical injuries or death." However, "harm" does not include direct or consequential economic loss.[125] Although the KPLA does not define "direct or consequential economic loss," case law indicates that such loss includes damages for inadequate value, costs or repair, replacement costs and loss of use of the defective product.[126]

The elements of a "product liability claim" are not set out in the KPLA. However, Kansas courts have stated that, to establish a *prima facie* case based either on neglience or strict liability under the KPLA, the plaintiff must prove three elements: (1) the "harm" resulted from a condition in the product; (2) the condition of the product was an unreasonably dangerous one; and (3) the unreasonably dangerous condition of the product existed at the time it left the manufacturer's control.[127] Thus, regardless of the theory of recovery in Kansas, proof that a product defect caused the plaintiff's injury is a prerequisite to recovery under the KPLA and the condition that caused the injury — whether it is a design defect, a manufacturing defect, or a failure to warn — must have existed at the time the product left the defendant's control.[128]

---

[124] *Id.* § 60-3302(a).

[125] *Id.* § 60-3302(d).

[126] Koss Construction v. Caterpillar, 960 P.2d 255 (Kan. Ct. App. 1998).

[127] Stadtherr v. Elite Logistics, Inc., 2002 U.S. Dist. LEXIS 9701 (D. Kan. 2002) (applying Kansas law).

[128] Messer v. Amway Corp., 210 F. Supp. 2d 1217 (D. Kan. 2002) (applying Kansas law).

Chapter 2

WARRANTY

SYNOPSIS

§ 2.01 THE ROLE OF WARRANTY IN PRODUCTS LIABILITY LITIGATION

Most of the attention in products liability law focuses on tort law and its theories of negligence and strict liability. However, warranty law also plays a very important role in products liability litigation. Actions for breach of warranty are governed by Article 2 of the Uniform Commercial Code (UCC) which has been adopted in every state except Louisiana.[1] In 2003 the American Law Institute (ALI) and the National Conference of Commissioners on Uniform State Laws (NCCUSL) published for adoption by the states a Revised Article 2 that includes a revision of the sections dealing with warranties. At the time of writing this book (2005), no state yet has enacted Revised Article 2. If and when states do adopt Revised Article 2, judicial decisions interpreting and applying it will be some years in the future. Because of the uncertainty about the acceptance and interpretation of the sections of Revised Article 2, this chapter focuses exclusively on actions for breach of express and implied warranties under Article 2 of the UCC as applied by the courts in 2005. This chapter also examines actions under the Magnuson-Moss Warranty Act,[2] the federal statute that provides warranty protection for the sale of consumer products to the public.

As with negligence and strict liability in tort, there are advantages and disadvantages of bringing a products liability action based on breach of warranty. One reason why "buyers"[3] often allege breach of warranty is that the proof may be simpler than with a tort. The focus of a warranty claim is on the condition of the goods — whether they complied with the express representations made by the seller or the "merchantability" implied by law — rather than on any "fault" on the part of the seller in the failure of the goods to possess the required quality.[4] In addition, although persons who suffer personal injury or damage to property other than the product frequently include breach of warranty counts in their complaints along with counts for negligence and strict liability,[5] persons who claim only loss of the product

---

[1] Louisiana's sales law is similar to, but is not based on, the UCC.

[2] 15 U.S.C. § 2301. The act is discussed *infra* at § 2.09.

[3] The UCC uses the word "buyer" in its sections dealing with warranties. However, UCC § 2-318 has expanded horizontal privity to include persons who are not the actual "buyer" of the goods. *See infra* § 2.05.

[4] Vlases v. Montgomery Ward & Co, Inc., 377 F.2d 846 (3d Cir. 1967) (applying Pennsylvania law).

[5] *See* Denny v. Ford Motor Co., 6662 N.E.2d 730, 739 (N.Y. 1995) ("the causes of action for strict products liability and breach of implied warranty of merchantability are not identical in New York and. . .the latter is not necessarily subsumed by the former. It follows that, under the circumstances presented, a verdict such as the one occurring here — in which the manufacturer was found liable under an implied warranty cause of action and not liable under a strict products cause of action — is theoretically reconcilable under New York law."). *See also* Stones v. Sears, Roebuck & Co., 558 N.W.2d 540 (Neb. 1997); McLaughlin v. Michelin Tire Corp., 778 P.2d 59 (Wyo. 1989); Realmuto v. Straub Motors, Inc., 322 A.2d 440 (N.J. 1974).

or economic damages are limited to actions for breach of warranty. This is because the economic loss doctrine bars recovery for such damages in actions based on negligence or strict liability.[6] A third advantage of breach of warranty theories is that the statute of limitations usually is longer than for negligence or strict liability.[7] As a result, plaintiffs who otherwise would bring claims for personal injury or property damage in negligence or strict liability use breach of warranty if the statute of limitations under those theories has run. Finally, alleging breach of warranty in the complaint may enable the buyer, during the discovery process, to obtain information about the seller's operations that would not be relevant in a negligence or strict liability action.

At the same time, however, there are important limitations that buyers must consider before using breach of warranty theories in products liability actions. Although the requirement of horizontal privity has been liberalized by the UCC,[8] the contract basis of warranty means that vertical privity still is more restrictive than in negligence and strict liability. Another hurdle for buyers in breach of warranty actions is that they are required, as a prelude to filing their suits, to notify the seller of the breach within a "reasonable time" after discovering it.[9] Failure to do so may bar their warranty action. Finally, and most importantly, the UCC permits a seller, in some situations, to disclaim express and implied warranties entirely or to limit the buyer's remedy to "repair or replacement."[10]

§ 2.02 EXPRESS WARRANTIES

[A] *Introduction*

> *All of the new Ford cars have a Triplex shatter-proof glass windshield — so made that it will not fly or shatter under the hardest impact. This is an important safety factor because it eliminates the dangers of flying glass — the cause of most of the injuries in automobile accidents. In these days of crowded, heavy traffic, the use of this Triplex glass is an absolute necessity.*[11]

---

[6] Purina Mills, Inc. v. Odell, 948 S.W.2d 927 (Tex. App. 1997). Economic loss includes the loss of the benefit of the bargain resulting from the diminished value from defective goods as well as consequential damages such as the cost of repair or replacement of the defective goods and lost profits resulting from a loss of use of the goods. The economic loss doctrine is discussed in detail in Chapter 10.

[7] UCC § 2-725. *See* Cleveland v. Square-D Co., 613 S.W.2d 790 (Tex. App. 1981). The statute begins to run on the date of sale of the goods (Pitts v. Northern Telecom, Inc., 24 F. Supp. 2d 437 (E.D. Pa. 1998) (applying Pennsylvania law)). For a discussion of the statute of limitations in warranty actions, see Chapter 9.

[8] *See* UCC § 2-318.

[9] UCC § 2-607(3). The notice requirement is discussed *infra* at § 2.06.

[10] *See* UCC § 2-719. These limitations are discussed *infra* at § 2.07.

[11] Baxter v. Ford Motor Co., 12 P.2d 409, 410 (Wash. 1932).

The above statement, included in printed materials furnished by an automobile manufacturer to potential purchasers of its cars in the 1932 case *Baxter v. Ford Motor Company*[12] is a classic example of an express warranty.[13] It is a representation of fact made by the seller of a product to a potential buyer that the product has a particular quality and will perform in a specific manner (i.e., the windshield "will not fly or shatter under the hardest impact"). In *Baxter*, a pebble from a passing vehicle struck the windshield of one of the manufacturer's cars, causing small pieces of glass to fly into the eyes of the purchaser of that car, resulting in injuries. The Washington Supreme Court held that the purchaser could proceed with an action for breach of express warranty against the manufacturer.[14]

With the adoption of § 2-313(1) of the Uniform Commercial Code (UCC), an express warranty now is created in one of three ways:

(a) Any affirmation of fact or promise made by the seller to the buyer which relates to the goods and becomes part of the basis of the bargain creates an express warranty that the goods shall conform to the affirmation or promise.

(b) Any description of the goods which is made part of the basis of the bargain creates an express warranty that the goods shall conform to the description.

(c) Any sample or model which is made part of the basis of the bargain creates an express warranty that the whole of the goods shall conform to the sample or model.

Why the windshield shattered was not an issue in *Baxter*. That was in keeping with the view, still followed in most states after adoption of the UCC, that an action based on breach of express warranty does not require the buyer to prove that there was an identifiable defect in the goods.[15] Instead, it is sufficient for the buyer to show that the product did not perform as expressly warranted. However, an action based on UCC § 2-313 does require the buyer to establish a number of elements.[16] First, an express

---

[12] 12 P.2d 409 (Wash. 1932).

[13] For a brief review of the historical development of express warranties, see *Southwest Bell Telephone Co. v. FDP Corp.*, 811 S.W.2d 572, 574-575 (Tex. 1991).

[14] *Id.* at 413. At the second trial, the jury found for the plaintiff, and the Washington Supreme Court affirmed. *See* Baxter v. Ford Motor Co., 35 P.2d 1090 (1934).

[15] Collins v. Uniroyal, Inc., 315 A.2d 16 (N.J. 1974) ("A cause of action for breach of express warranty. . .does not depend upon a defect in the goods. Indeed, the affirmative establishment by the defendant of freedom from defect would be irrelevant to such an action.") *Id.* at 17. *See also* Harte v. Stuttgart Autohaus, Inc., 706 P.2d 394 (Ariz. Ct. App. 1985). However, in a few states, proof of a defect in the goods is essential to establish a breach of an express warranty. *See* McLaughlin v. Michelin Tire Corp., 778 P.2d 59 (Wyo. 1989).

[16] In about 10 states, breach of express warranty claims are not governed exclusively by the UCC. For a discussion of state products liability statutes and express warranty, see Louis R. Frumer & MELVIN I. FRIEDMAN, PRODUCTS LIABILITY § 9.02[1][b] (2004).

warranty must guarantee that "goods" are of a specific quality. A promise to repair defects in goods is not a warranty about their quality.[17] Second, the defendant must have been a "seller" of the goods. UCC § 2-103(1)(d) defines a "seller" as "a person who sells or contracts to sell goods." The term includes both manufacturers and retailers of goods.[18] Third, the "seller" must have made an "affirmation of fact or promise," given a "description," or provided a "sample or model" of its goods. Fourth, the affirmation, description, sample or model must have formed "part of the basis of the bargain" between the seller and the buyer. Fifth, the buyer must establish that the express warranty was breached because the goods did not conform to the seller's statements about their quality or performance. Finally, the breach of the warranty must have been the cause of the injury to the buyer.[19] However, despite these elements, most products liability cases involving express warranties center on only two questions: (1) Did the seller make an "affirmation of fact or promise" or give a "description" of the goods? and (2) Was that statement or description "part of the basis of the bargain" between the seller and the buyer?

[B] *Statement of Fact v. Opinion*

In any action for breach of express warranty, the buyer must prove that, in the contract of sale, the seller made an "affirmation of fact or promise" or provided a "description of the goods." An affirmation of fact or description of goods can take a number of different forms. Among these are written statements or pictures in advertising brochures,[20] instructions manuals,[21] or product literature;[22] oral statements by salespersons;[23] and samples or

---

[17] In *Cosman v. Ford Motor Co.*, 674 N.E.2d 61 (Ill. App. Ct. 1996), the Illinois Appellate Court stated that a promise to repair goods was not a warranty about the quality of the goods. According to the court, "a promise to repair can more honestly be read as an admission that the thing sold might break, rather than a legally enforceable prediction that it will never need tending to." *Id*. at 68.

[18] In *Hughes v. The Tobacco Institute, Inc.*, 278 F.3d 417 (5th Cir. 2001) (applying Texas law), one of the few cases in which the meaning of a "seller" under § 2-313 was an issue, the court held that a trade association was not a "seller" and was not liable for breach of express warranties made by its members.

[19] Rodarte v. Philip Morris, Inc., 2003 U.S. Dist. LEXIS 25067 (C.D.Calif. 2003) (applying California law).

[20] Neville Construction Co. v. Cook Paint & Varnish Co., 671 F.2d 1107 (8th Cir. 1982) (applying Nebraska law); Touchet Valley Grain Growers, Inc., v. Opp & Seibold General Construction, Inc., 831 P.2d 724 (Wash. 1992).

[21] Kinlaw v. Long Manufacturing N.C., Inc., 259 S.E.2d 552 (N.C. 1979). *But see* Corral v. Rollins Protective Services Co., 732 P.2d 1260 (Kan. 1987) (holding that the statements in a manual for a fire alarm were instructional and not an express warranty).

[22] Beyette v. Ortho Pharmaceuticals Corp., 823 F.2d 990 (6th Cir. 1987) (applying Michigan law).

[23] Crothers v. Cohen, 384 N.W.2d 562 (Minn. Ct. App. 1986).

models of the goods.[24] Past deliveries of the goods also may set the description of quality warranted.[25] However, in all of these situations, the buyer must plead and prove the exact representation or the specific advertisement used by the seller.[26] Although comment 5 to UCC § 2-313 states that "all descriptions by merchants must be read against the applicable trade usages with the general rules as to merchantability resolving any doubts," many states treat the issue of whether a particular affirmation or description amounts to a warranty as a question for the trier of fact to decide.[27]

The most difficult issue in express warranty cases is determining whether the seller's representation of the goods was a statement of fact or simply an expression of opinion. According to UCC § 2-313(2), it is not necessary for the creation of an express warranty that the seller use formal words such as "warrant" or "guarantee" or even have the specific intention to make a warranty.[28] However, both the UCC and the cases make it clear that "representations which merely express the seller's opinion, belief, judgment, or estimate do not constitute a warranty."[29] Although courts state that they use a reasonable person standard to determine whether language is an affirmation of fact or a statement of opinion,[30] it often is difficult to draw a distinction between the two. For example, an Illinois court interpreted assurances by the seller of a 10 year-old used car that the car was "mechanically sound," "in good condition," and had "no problems" to be "affirmations of fact and descriptions of the car that created an express warranty."[31] In contrast, an Alabama court held that statements that a vehicle was "a good car" and "in good shape" were not representations of material fact but statements of opinion, "sales talk," and "puffery."[32] Similarly, a statement by a company that its copying machines and their component parts were of "high quality" was held to be a statement of the seller's opinion, "the kind of puffing to be expected in any sales transaction, rather than a positive aver-

---

[24] UCC § 2-313(1)(c). *See* Jones v. Davenport, 2001 Ohio App. LEXIS 226 (Ohio Ct. App. 2001).

[25] UCC § 2-313 cmt. 5. *See* The Shutter Shop, Inc v. Amersham Corp., 114 F. Supp. 2d 1218 (M.D. Ala. 2000) (applying Alabama law).

[26] Rodarte v. Philip Morris, Inc., 2003 U.S. Dist. LEXIS 25067 (C.D. Calif. 2003) (applying California law).

[27] Moore v. Mack Trucks, Inc., 40 S.W.3d 888 (Ky. Ct. App. 2001).

[28] James River Equipment Co. v. Beadle County Equipment, Inc., 646 N.W.2d 265 (S.D. 2002).

[29] UCC § 2-313(2). *See* Beyette v. Ortho Pharmaceutical Corp., 823 F. 2d 990 (6th Cir. 1987) (applying Michigan law); McLaughlin v. Michelin Tire Corp., 778 P.2d 59 (Wyo. 1989).

[30] Rawson v. Conover, 20 P.3d 876 (Utah 2001).

[31] Weng v. Allison, 678 N.E.2d 1254, 1256 (Ill. App. Ct. 1997).

[32] Scoggin v. Listerhill Employees Credit Union, 658 So.2d 376 (Ala. 1995). *See also* Oak Point Associates v. Southern States Screening, Inc., 1994 U.S. Dist. LEXIS 6912 (S.D.N.Y. 1994 (applying New York law); Web Press Service Corp. v. New London Motors, Inc., 525 A.2d 57 (Conn. 1987); Klages v. General Ordinance Equipment Co., 367 A.2d 304 (Pa. Super. Ct. 1976).

ment of the fact describing a product's capabilities to which an express warranty could attach."[33]

Because of the wide variety of statements made about goods by sellers, there is no clear test for distinguishing between a statement of fact and an expression of opinion. The determination depends upon the circumstances surrounding each particular case. Among the factors courts consider is the specificity of the representation. The more specific the statement about the characteristics of goods, the more likely a court will hold that it constitutes a warranty.[34] Thus, the Oklahoma Supreme Court held that a jury was entitled to find that a statement that a new automobile engine "would be guaranteed for six thousand miles or six months" was an express warranty.[35] According to the court, the statement was not an expression of opinion but a "definite and unqualified statement that the engine was 'guaranteed' for the specific time or distance."[36] However, a statement in a sales brochure that a particular model fishing boat "delivers the kind of performance you need to get to the prime offshore fishing grounds" was held to be merely a commendation of the boat's performance and not a description of a specific characteristic of the boat.[37]

Closely related to the specificity of the statement is whether the representation was objective in nature, i.e., whether it was capable of being proven true or false. Thus, statements that a pressing machine was "one year old" (when it was at least five years old) and was "in perfect condition" were specific and objective enough to create an express warranty.[38] However, advertising language that bungee cords were "Premium Quality" was held to be puffery as "generalized statements of salesmanship" and not "descriptions of particular characteristics of the goods."[39] Similarly, assertions in a brochure that a yacht offered the "best performance" and "superb handling" were held to be "characteristic of an opinion" since they relied on "inherently subjective words."[40]

---

[33] Royal Business Machines, Inc. v. Litton Business Systems, Inc., 633 F.2d 34, 42 (7th Cir. 1980) (applying Indiana law).

[34] Downie v. Abex Corp., 741 F.2d 1235 (10th Cir. 1984) (applying Utah law).

[35] Scovil v. Chilcoat, 424 P.2d 87, 92 (Okla. 1967).

[36] *Id.*

[37] Bayliner Marine Corp. v. Crow, 509 S.E.2d 499 (Va. 1999). *See also* Royal Business Machines, Inc. v. Litton Business Systems, Inc., 633 F.2d 34 (7th Cir. 1980) (a statement by company representatives that experience and testing had shown that the frequency of repair of their copying machines was "very low" and would remain so, lacked the specificity of an affirmation of fact).

[38] Kates Millinery, Ltd. v. Benay-Albee Corp., 450 N.Y.S.2d 975 (N.Y. Civ. Ct. 1982).

[39] Anderson v. Bungee International Manufacturing Corp., 44 F. Supp. 2d 534, 541 (S.D.N.Y. 1999) (applying New York law).

[40] Boud v. SDNCO, Inc., 54 P.3d 1131 (Ut. 2002).

Courts also compare the knowledge and sophistication of the buyer and the seller about the goods. They ask whether the seller made a representation of fact about the goods that the buyer would not be expected to know or expressed an opinion about an aspect on which they each would have an opinion.[41] Thus, courts often hold that statements made by cigarette companies about their products are not express warranties because it long has been common knowledge that smoking is addictive and a health risk.[42] Finally, courts look to see whether the representation concerned the present condition of goods or was a specific reference to the future. A representation about the present quality or performance of goods without a specific reference to the future is not an express warranty of their future performance, even if the representation implies that the goods will perform a certain way in the future.[43]

[C] *Basis of the Bargain*

Under UCC § 2-313(1) a buyer must show that the "affirmation of fact," "description," or "sample or model" was "made part of the basis of the bargain." Since the term "basis of the bargain" is not defined by the UCC,[44] courts are divided as to whether the phrase means that the buyer must have relied specifically upon the language of the express warranty in deciding whether to purchase the goods.[45] This is important because, in many cases, buyers do not become aware of the sellers' specific representations about the goods until after they purchase them, take them home, and read the literature contained in the boxes.

Under the old Uniform Sales Act (USA), reliance was a key element of an action for breach of an express warranty.[46] With the adoption of the UCC, several states interpret "part of the basis of the bargain" to be a continuation of the USA requirement that the buyer must show some type of reliance upon the affirmation of fact or description in deciding to purchase the goods.[47] Under this view, the "basis of the bargain" is part of the deter-

---

[41] Liberty Lincoln-Mercury, Inc. v. Ford Motor Co., 171 F.3d 818 (3d Cir. 1999) (applying New Jersey law); Peterson v. North American Plan, 354 N.W.2d 625 (Neb. 1984); Valley Datsun v. Martinez, 578 S.W.2d 485 (Tex. App. 1979).

[42] White v. R. J. Reynolds Tobacco Co., 2000 U.S. Dist. LEXIS 16172 (S.D. Tex. 2000) (applying Texas law).

[43] Employers Mutual Casualty Co. v. Collins & Aikman Floor Coverings, Inc., 2004 U.S. Dist. LEXIS 7172 (S.D. Iowa 2004) (applying Iowa law).

[44] According to one court, the term describes "the commercial relationship between the parties as to the product." *See* Autzen v. John C. Taylor Lumber Sales, Inc., 572 P.2d 1322, 1325 (Or. 1977).

[45] Compaq Computer Corp. v. Lapray, 2004 Tex. LEXIS 435 (Tex. 2004).

[46] Uniform Sales Act § 12.

[47] McManus v. Fleetwood Enterprises, Inc., 320 F.3d 545 (5th Cir. 2003) (applying Texas law); Freeman v. Hoffman-La Roche, Inc., 618 N.W.2d 827 (Neb. 2000); Smith v. Anheuser-Busch, Inc., 599 A.2d 320 (R.I. 1991).

mination of whether the language of the representation constituted an express warranty since statements of fact and descriptions tend to become part of the basis of the bargain.[48] However, in states that take this view, a buyer who establishes that the seller's representation was a statement of fact often fails to show the necessary reliance on the statement. This has been a particular problem for smokers in their suits against tobacco companies. Courts have held that reliance on the manufacturers' representations about their products is not established simply from the fact that buyers purchased particular brands of cigarettes. Buyers must show that they saw the companies' advertisements making claims about their cigarettes or disputing the link between smoking and health problems and that they relied on those advertisements in their decisions to begin smoking or to switch from one brand to another.[49]

The majority of states take the view that the phrase "basis of the bargain" in UCC § 2-313 means that it is no longer necessary for buyers to show reliance on an affirmation or promise before statements by sellers can be an express warranty.[50] This view is based upon comment 3 to the section which states that "no particular reliance on [the affirmations of fact made by the seller] need be shown to weave them into the fabric of the agreement." An example of a case where reliance was inferred is *Bernick v. Jurden*,[51] in which the plaintiff brought an action against the manufacturer of a mouth guard for injuries he suffered while playing ice hockey. Although neither the plaintiff nor his mother (who purchased the mouth guard) actually read the advertising label, the North Carolina Supreme Court held that the reliance of the plaintiff could be inferred from allegations of the purchaser or user of the product, if the natural tendency of the seller's representations is to induce purchase or use. Since the manufacturer promoted the product in hockey catalogue advertisements and in parent guides, the court concluded that the natural tendency of a representation that the mouth guard provided "maximum protection to the lips and teeth" was to induce the purchase of the product.

Although most representations about products are made before their sale, comment 7 to UCC § 2-313 states that "[t]he precise time when words of description or affirmation are made or samples are shown is not material." Instead:

> The sole question is whether the language or samples or models are fairly to be regarded as part of the contract. If language is used after the closing of the deal (as when the buyer taking delivery asks and

---

[48] Stang v. Hertz Corp., 490 P.2d 475 (N.M. Ct. App. 1971).

[49] *See* Hughes v. The Tobacco Institute, Inc., 278 F.3d 417 (5th Cir. 2001) (applying Texas law); American Tobacco Company, Inc. v. Grinnell, 951 S.W.2d 420 (Tex. 1997).

[50] Lutz Farms v. Asgrow Seed Co., 948 F.2d 638, 645 (10th Cir. 1991) (applying Colorado law).

[51] 293 S.E.2d 405 (N.C. 1982).

receives an additional assurance), the warranty becomes a modification, and need not be supported by consideration if it is otherwise reasonable and in order.

An example of a post-sale statement that became "part of the basis of the bargain" is *Bigelow v. Agway, Inc.*,[52] in which a farmer sued the manufacturer and distributor of a chemical used to treat hay before baling. The farmer was told that the chemical would permit him to bale hay at a higher moisture level than normal. Two months after the sale and use of the chemical, the defendant's salesman guaranteed that hay treated with the chemical was safe to bale even though the hay contained a moisture level well above normal. The farmer baled the hay and the level of moisture resulted in a fire that destroyed his entire crop. The Court of Appeals held that the salesman's representation was a basis of the bargain, even though it was made two months after the sale. According to the court, "it is undisputed that the [salesman's] visit [after the delivery of the chemical] . . . was to promote the sale of the product. Thus, [his representations] might constitute an actionable modification of the warranty."[53]

§ 2.03 IMPLIED WARRANTY OF MERCHANTABILITY

[A] *Introduction*

In addition to express warranties, the Uniform Commercial Code creates two types of implied warranties: an implied warranty of merchantability[54] and an implied warranty of fitness for a particular purpose.[55] Often, buyers include counts alleging a breach of each type of these warranties in their complaints.[56]

The oldest and most common implied warranty is the implied warranty of merchantability.[57] Unlike an express warranty and an implied warranty of fitness for a particular purpose that are created by representations made by the seller, an implied warranty of merchantability arises by law from a contract for the sale of most goods if "the seller is a merchant with respect to goods of that kind."[58] The seller does not have to make any statement

---

[52] 506 F.2d 551 (2d Cir. 1974) (applying Vermont law).

[53] *Id.* at 555 n. 6.

[54] UCC § 2-314.

[55] UCC § 2-315.

[56] *See, e.g.,* Dickerson v. Mountain View Equipment, 710 P.2d 621 (Idaho Ct. App. 1985).

[57] As early as 1815, courts recognized an implied warranty in the sale of food. *See* Van Bracklin v. Fonda, 12 Johns. 468 (N.Y. 1815). For a proposed modern use of this warranty, see Franklin E. Crawford, *Fit for Its Ordinary Purpose? Tobacco, Fast Food and The Implied Warranty of Merchantability*, 63 OHIO ST. L.J. 1165 (2002/2003).

[58] UCC § 2-314(1). *See* Mocek v. Alfa Leisure, Inc., 7 Cal. Rptr. 3d 546 (Cal. Ct. App. 2003).

about the goods in order to create an implied warranty of merchantability. The warranty is a representation about the quality (i.e., "merchantability") of goods that the law implies in the sales contract based upon the facts and circumstances of the transaction, the nature of the goods, trade usages, and the knowledge common to the community about the goods.[59] An example of this is the implied warranty of merchantability that accompanies the sale of a new automobile by an automobile dealer. The warranty is a promise that the automobile is in the proper condition for the ordinary functions for which an automobile is intended. However, it is not a guarantee that nothing ever will go wrong with the automobile. There is a breach of this warranty only if a defect existed in the automobile at the time of sale. However, it is not necessary that a defect become evident immediately after the sale of the automobile. Instead:

> [E]vidence of reasonable and proper handling of a product between the time it left the possession and control of the defendant manufacturer or seller and the time of the occurrence of the injury is an indication that the defect alleged to have existed at the time of the injury did not come into being in the interim, but existed prior thereto.[60]

As with an express warranty, there are a number of elements that a buyer must establish in order to recover damages for a breach of an implied warranty of merchantability under UCC § 2-314: (1) the "seller" must have been a "merchant with respect to goods" of the kind in question; (2) the goods must not have been "merchantable" at the time of the sale; (3) the buyer must have suffered injury or damage to his or her property; (4) the injury or damage must have been caused, in fact, by the defective nature of the goods; and (5) the buyer must have given the required notice of the injury to the seller.[61] An implied warranty of merchantability can be excluded or modified only in a manner that complies with UCC § 2-316.

[B] *The Seller as Merchant of the Goods*

Unlike an express warranty and an implied warranty of fitness for a particular purpose that apply to any "seller," an implied warranty of mer-

---

[59] Because of the general health risks associate with cigarettes are commonly known by the community, courts have held that no expectation of safety for their consumption arises when they are purchased. American Tobacco Co., Inc. v. Grinnell, 951 S.W.2d 420 (Tex. 1997).

[60] Alvarez v. American Isuzu Motors, 749 N.E.2d 16, 24 (Ill. App. Ct. 2001) (*quoting* Fullreide v. Midstates Beverage Co., 388 N.E.2d 1070, 1073 (Ill. App. Ct. 1979).

[61] JAMES J. WHITE & ROBERT S. SUMMERS, UNIFORM COMMERCIAL CODE, 360-369 (5th ed. 2000). One court has reduced a claim for breach of implied warranty to two elements: (1) the product was defective, and (2) the defect caused the plaintiff's injuries. Hollister v. Dayton-Hudson Corp., 201 F.3d 731 (6th Cir. 2000) (*citing* Piercefield v. Remington Arms, 133 N.W.2d 129 (Mich. 1965).

chantability requires that the "seller" be a "merchant with respect to goods of that kind."[62] The UCC defines a "merchant" as

> [A] person who deals in goods of the kind or otherwise by his occupation holds himself out as having knowledge or skill peculiar to the practices or goods involved in the transaction or to whom such knowledge or skill may be attributed by his employment of an agent or broker or other intermediary who by his occupation holds himself out as having such knowledge or skill.[63]

Using this definition, courts have held that an implied warranty applies to merchants who sell both new goods and used goods.[64] However, an implied warranty of merchantability does not extend to the casual sale by an individual of personal goods[65] or to a single isolated transaction by a merchant of goods with which it otherwise does not deal.[66] Such a warranty also does not extend to a claim by an ultimate purchaser for economic loss against a manufacturer of a component part.[67] In addition, while the definition of a "merchant" includes a commercial restaurateur, a court held that it did not apply to a voluntary association of mothers of high school band students who sold food to raise money.[68] Finally, since UCC Article 2 applies to "transactions in goods," if the defective goods were provided as part of a transaction that was primarily one for services rather than for goods, no implied warranty of merchantability applies.[69]

The UCC defines "goods" to include "all things (including specifically manufactured goods) which are moveable at the time of identification to the contract of sale."[70] However, goods need not be "manufactured" to be covered by an implied warranty of merchantability. For example, granite blocks

---

[62] Lish v. Compton, 547 P.2d 223 (Utah 1976).

[63] UCC § 2-104(1). *See* Siemen v. Alden. 341 N.E.2d 713 (Ill. App. Ct. 1975).

[64] Whittle v. Timesavers, Inc:, 614 F. Supp. 115 (W.D. Va. 1985) (applying Virginia law); Dickerson v. Mountain View Equipment Co., 710 P.2d 621 (Idaho Ct. App. 1985). For the quality expected of used goods, see UCC § 2-314 cmt. 3 and *International Petroleum Services, Inc. v. S & N Well Service, Inc.*, 639 P.2d 29 (Kan. 1982).

[65] UCC § 2-314 cmt. 3. *See* Smith v. Stewart, 667 P.2d 358 (Kan. 1983); Ballou v. Trahan, 334 A.2d 409 (Vt. 1975).

[66] Mozee v. Kuplen, 1990 U.D. Dist. LEXIS 11974 (D. Kan. 1990) (applying Kansas law); Donald v. City National Bank, 329 So.2d 92 (Ala. 1976); Foley v. Dayton Bank & Trust, 696 S.W.2d 356 (Tenn. Ct. App. 1985).

[67] In *Hininger v. Case Corp.*, 23 F.3d 124 (5th Cir. 1994), the Fifth Circuit felt that the Texas Supreme Court would distinguish between the manufacturer of a finished product and a component part manufacturer because of the component supplier's inability to disclaim effectively its warranty liability. That distinction, along with the purchasers' lack of any expectation that the component part manufacturer would respond to defects in the finished product, led the court to hold that the purchaser had no implied warranty action.

[68] Samson v. Riesing, 215 N.W.2d 662 (Wis. 1974).

[69] Brandt v. Boston Scientific Corp., 792 N.E.2d 296 (Ill. 2003).

[70] UCC § 2-105(1).

sold to a headstone manufacturer were held to be "goods" covered by an implied warranty when monuments made from the stone discolored.[71] Also included within the definition of "goods" under the UCC are "the unborn young of animals and growing crops and other identified things attached to realty." Thus, cattle have been held to be "goods" under the section even though they are not manufactured.[72]

[C] *Merchantability*

Key to recovery for a breach of an implied warranty of merchantability is a showing that the goods were not "merchantable" at the time of the sale. Although the UCC does not define that term, some basis for determining the merchantability of goods is provided by UCC § 2-314(2) which requires that the goods meet "at least" six standards:

(a) pass without objection in trade under the contract description; and

(b) in the case of fungible goods, are of fair average quality within the description; and

(c) are fit for the ordinary purposes for which such goods are used; and

(d) run, within the variations permitted by the agreement, of even kind, quality and quantity within each unit and among all units involved; and;

(e) are adequately contained, packaged and labeled as the agreement may require; and

(f) conform to the promises or affirmations made on the container or label if any.

Unless excluded or modified according to UCC § 2-316, other implied warranties may arise from the course of dealings between the parties or from the usage of trade.[73] In all situations, whether the goods were "merchantable" is a question for the trier of fact.[74]

An action for breach of an implied warranty of merchantability is similar to one in express warranty or strict liability in that it is not necessary for the buyer to prove any fault by the seller.[75] In addition, the inquiry in such

---

[71] Willis Mining, Inc. v. Noggle, 509 S.E.2d 731 (Ga. Ct. App. 1998).

[72] Vince v. Broome, 443 So.2d 23 (Miss. 1983).

[73] *See* UCC § 2-314(3) and cmt. 11.

[74] Criscuolo v. Mauro Motors, Inc., 754 A.2d 810 (Conn. App. Ct. 2000).

[75] Delta Marine, Inc. v. Whaley, 813 F. Supp. 414 (E.D.N.C. 1993) (applying North Carolina law).

an action is not whether the goods were the best or whether they met the buyer's every expectation. Instead, courts focus on UCC § 2-314(2)(c) and ask whether the goods were "fit for the ordinary purposes for which such goods are used"[76] i.e., whether the goods were of an average quality when compared to that generally acceptable in the trade for goods of the kind.[77] How courts make this determination is illustrated by *Coffer v. Standard Brands, Inc.*,[78] in which the plaintiff was eating nuts from a bottle of mixed nuts manufactured by the defendant when he bit down on a nut that had not been shelled, damaging his teeth. In affirming a directed verdict against the plaintiff's claim for breach of implied warranty, the North Carolina appellate court held that the goods impliedly were warranted to be nuts and that a natural incident of nuts is their shells. According to the court, the nuts were "fit for the ordinary purposes" under UCC § 2-314(2)(c). In determining whether the nuts met the other merchantability standards set out in UCC § 2-314(2), the court looked to state and federal regulations governing the sale of mixed nuts. Those regulations permitted a small percentage of naturally occurring unshelled nuts in a container of shelled nuts. Thus, the presence of a small quantity of unshelled nuts did not make the shelled nuts objectionable in the trade within the meaning of UCC § 2-314(2)(a). Finally, the court looked at whether the clear glass jar containing the nuts, that revealed only shelled nuts, was a "promise or affirmation of fact" of what was inside within the meaning of UCC § 2-314(2)(f). The court did not feel that such a designation was consistent with the nature of the goods inside the container.[79]

A few courts hold that a cause of action for breach of an implied warranty requires only a showing that the goods did not meet the standards of UCC § 2-314(2), regardless of whether they were defective.[80] However, most courts speak of an implied warranty as a guarantee that the goods will perform in the ordinary way that goods of that kind should perform.[81] For these courts, a showing that the product was defective is an essential element under all theories of recovery in products liability: negligence, strict liability and breach of an implied warranty.[82] However, states differ over whether the requirements for a defect are the same for implied warranty of

---

[76] *See* Brazier v. Hasbro, Inc., 2004 U.S. Dist. LEXIS 4064 (S.D.N.Y. 2004) (applying New York law).

[77] Castro v. QVC Network, 139 F.3d 114 (2d Cir. 1998) (applying New York law); Norcold, Inc. v. Gateway Supply Co., 798 N.E.2d 618 (Ohio Ct. App. 2003).

[78] 226 S.E.2d 534 (N.C. Ct. App. 1976).

[79] *Id.* at 537-539.

[80] Hyundai Motor Co. v. Rodriguez, 995 S.W.2d 665 (Tex. 1999); Maldonado v. Creative Woodworking Concepts, Inc., 796 N.E.2d 662, 666 (Ill. App. Ct. 2003).

[81] Employers Mutual Casualty Co. v. Collins & Aikman Floor Coverings, Inc., 2004 U.S. Dist. LEXIS 7192 (S.D. 2004).

[82] McLaughlin v. Michelin Tire Corp., 778 P.2d 59 (Wyo. 1989); Lariviere v. Dayton Safety Ladder Co., 525 A.2d 892 (R.I. 1987).

merchantability as for strict liability. In *Larsen v. Pacesetter Systems, Inc.*,[83] for example, the Hawaii Supreme Court held that, in order to bring an action in implied warranty for personal injury, a buyer must show product unmerchantability sufficient to avoid summary judgment on the issue of defectiveness in a tort strict liability action. This requires applying the balancing factors in the risk/benefit analysis or the consumer expectation test to implied warranty as well as strict liability actions.[84]

For some other states, the implied warranty of merchantability is breached when the goods are defective to a normal buyer who makes ordinary use of them.[85] This requires the buyer to prove only that something went wrong with the goods consistent with the existence of a defect.[86] While most buyers attempt to establish the specific condition in the goods that made them not of an acceptable quality, in some cases that may not be possible. In those cases, the buyer will attempt to draw an inference of a defect from circumstantial evidence that he or she used the goods in an ordinary manner and that they did not function as they should have.[87] This does not require use of the risk/benefit analysis. How circumstantial evidence can provide a sufficient basis for a finding of a defect is illustrated by *Dewitt v. Eveready Batteries, Inc.*,[88] in which a buyer was injured when batteries he purchased for a lantern leaked. In a suit against the manufacturer of the batteries, for breach of the implied warranty of merchantability, the North Carolina Supreme Court held that the buyer did not have to prove a specific defect in order to meet his burden of proof. The court held that the buyer raised a genuine issue of material fact by producing circumstantial evidence of a defect in the batteries by showing: (1) the malfunction of the batteries; (2) expert testimony as to a variety of possible causes that were due to defects in the batteries; (3) use of the batteries in their ordinary manner when the buyer was injured; (4) the possibility of similar accidents to that involving the buyer; (5) the elimination of possible causes of the accident unrelated to the manufacturer; and (6) proof that such an accident ordinarily does not occur in the absence of a manufacturing defect.[89]

---

[83] 837 P.2d 1273 (Haw. 1992).

[84] Cigna Insurance Co. v. OY Saunatec, Ltd., 241 F.3d 1 (1st Cir. 2001) (applying Massachusetts law). See also *Hollister v. Dayton-Hudson Corp.*, 201 F.3d 731 (6th Cir. 2000), in which the Sixth Circuit, applying Michigan law, stated that a claim for a breach of an implied warranty required a showing that the product sold was in a defective condition. In *Hollister*, the plaintiff claimed that the product was defective because of a design defect and the failure to warn of the dangers.

[85] *See* Landree v. University Medical Products, USA, Inc., 2004 U.S. Dist. LEXIS 3165 (D. Minn. 2004) (applying Minnesota law).

[86] Fleck v. Titan Tire Corp., 177 F. Supp. 2d 605 (E.D. Mich. 2001) (applying Michigan law).

[87] Alvarez v. American Isuzu Motors, 749 N.E.2d 16 (Ill. App. Ct. 2001).

[88] 565 S.E.2d 69 (N.C. 2002).

[89] *Id.* at 151-154.

[D] *Unforeseeable Use of the Goods*

An implied warranty of merchantability is based on the idea that the goods are fit for the ordinary purposes for which they are used. As in negligence cases, "ordinary purposes" include all of the foreseeable uses of the goods, even if they are not intended specifically by the seller. According to one court: "[A] manufacturer must anticipate the environment in which its product will be used, and it must design against the reasonably foreseeable risks attending the product's use in that setting."[90] Thus, the basis of the analysis is the foreseeability of the use of a product. The manufacturer must anticipate the intended as well as the reasonably foreseeable misuses of its products.[91] However, buyers in such actions must prove that, at the time of the injury or damage, they were using the goods in a reasonable manner, i.e., a manner that the seller reasonably could have foreseen.[92]

§ 2.04 IMPLIED WARRANTY OF FITNESS FOR A PARTICULAR PURPOSE

[A] *Introduction*

UCC § 2-315 sets out the requirements for an implied warranty of fitness for a particular purpose:

> Where the seller at the time of contracting has reason to know any particular purpose for which the goods are required and that the buyer is relying on the seller's skill or judgment to select or furnish suitable goods, there is unless excluded or modified under the next section an implied warranty that the goods shall be fit for such purpose.

Based upon this section, courts have stated that a plaintiff must establish four elements to prove a breach of an implied warranty of fitness for a particular purpose: (1) a sale of goods; (2) the seller had reason to know any particular purpose for which the goods were required; (3) the plaintiff, as the buyer of the goods, relied upon the seller's skill or judgment to select suitable goods; and (4) the goods were not fit for the particular purpose for which they were used.[93]

---

[90] Venturelli v. Cincinnati, Inc., 850 F.2d 825, 827 (1st Cir. 1988) (applying Massachusetts law).

[91] Cigna Insurance Co. v. OY Saunatec, Ltd., 241 F.3d 1 (1st Cir. 2001) (applying Massachusetts law).

[92] *Venturelli*, 850 F.2d 825.

[93] *See* Malawy v. Richards Manufacturing Co., 501 N.E.2d 376, 382 (Ill App. Ct. 1986).

An example of an implied warranty of fitness is *Klein v. Sears Roebuck and Co.,*[94] in which plaintiff's parents decided to purchase a riding lawn mower as a gift for him. They visited a local Sears store where they consulted a salesman about the intended purchase. They told the salesman that they had no experience with lawnmowers and that the property on which the mower would be used contained numerous hills. The salesman recommended a particular brand and model of mower but conditioned the sale on his inspection of the property. When the mower was delivered a few days later, the salesman inspected the property and stated that it was suitable for the property but that it should be driven vertically up and down the hills. The plaintiff used the mower without incident for a year but then, while mowing vertically up a 19 degree hill, the mower tipped over, severely injuring his hand. In an action against Sears for breach of an implied warranty of fitness for a particular purpose, the jury awarded the plaintiff damages and the Fourth Circuit affirmed.

In *Klein*, all three elements necessary for the creation of an implied warranty of fitness for a particular purpose under UCC § 2-315 were present. First, at the time of the sale, the salesman knew the "particular purpose" for which the lawnmower was required (mowing a large lot with numerous hills). Second, the salesman also knew that the buyers were relying on his skill and judgment to select a suitable mower, since they told him they had no experience with lawnmowers. Finally, the buyers in fact relied upon the salesman's skill to select the particular brand and model of lawnmower.[95]

Unlike an implied warranty of merchantability, the implied warranty of fitness in *Klein* did not arise from the sale itself. Instead, like an express warranty, it arose from the recommendation of a particular brand and model and representation that the lawnmower was suitable for the plaintiff's property made by the salesman and relied upon by the buyers. *Klein* also illustrates the concept of a defect in an implied warranty of fitness case. The lawnmower tipped over while it was being used in the manner intended by the buyers (to mow a property with hills) and that intended use was known to the salesman. The failure of the lawnmower to function in the way represented by the salesman, coupled with the other requirements of UCC § 2-315, resulted in the product being sufficiently defective for the plaintiff to recover. The defect was not in the lawnmower itself but in the conduct of the salesman in furnishing one that was not fit for the buyers' particular purpose.[96]

Four other general comments must be made about implied warranties of fitness. First, although the implied warranty of merchantability was not an

---

[94] 773 F.2d 1421 (4th Cir. 1985) (applying Maryland law).

[95] *See also* Daniell v. Ford Motor Co., 581 F. Supp. 728 (D. N.M. 1984) (applying New Mexico law); Stones v. Sears, Roebuck & Co., 558 N.W.2d 540 (Neb. 1997).

[96] *McLaughlin v. Michelin Tire Corp.*, 778 P.2d 59 (Wyo. 1989).

issue in *Klein*, implied warranties of merchantability and fitness for a particular purpose are not mutually exclusive. Both warranties can exist for a single product and a buyer may bring an action alleging breaches of both implied warranties.[97] Similarly, an implied warranty of fitness also may overlap with express warranties. In *Filler v. Rayex Corp.*,[98] the seller sold sunglasses that were advertised as "baseball sunglasses." Based on this advertising, the buyer purchased the sunglasses and wore them while playing baseball. The sunglasses splintered when hit by a baseball and injured the buyer. The court found that seller breached both an express warranty and an implied warranty of fitness because the sunglasses were advertised as being fit for the particular purpose of being able to be worn while playing baseball. Second, although the seller in *Klein* was a "merchant," implied warranties of fitness are not limited to merchants as are implied warranties of merchantability.[99] It is sufficient that the defendant is a "seller" within the meaning of the UCC. Third, while *Klein* involved simply the sale of a product, an implied warranty of fitness for a particular purpose also may arise where goods are provided as part of a service. Thus, when a beauty parlor operator used a waving solution on a customer in connection with administering a permanent wave, the service carried with it the implied warranty that the product used on the customer was reasonably fit for the purpose for which it was to be used.[100] Finally, although *Klein* involved the sale of a new lawnmower, implied warranties of fitness for a particular purpose apply to the sale both of new and used goods.[101]

[B] *The "Particular Purpose"*

While an implied warranty of merchantability is meant to guarantee that the goods are fit for the ordinary purposes for which such goods are used, an implied warranty of fitness provides that goods are fit for the "particular purpose" for which the buyer made known to the seller. UCC § 2-315, comment 2, states:

> A "particular purpose" differs from the ordinary purpose for which the goods are used in that it envisages a specific use by the buyer which is peculiar to the nature of his business whereas the ordinary purposes for which goods are used are those envisaged in the con-

---

[97] Lariviere v. Dayton Safety Ladder Co., 525 A.2d 892 (R.I. 1987).

[98] 435 F.2d 336 (7th Cir. 1970) (applying Indiana law).

[99] International Petroleum Services, Inc. v. S & N Well Service, Inc., 639 P.2d 29 (Kan. 1982).

[100] Newmark v. Gimbel's Inc., 246 A.2d 11 (N.J. Super. Ct. App. Div. 1968). *See also* Levondosky v. Marina Assoc., 731 F. Supp. 1210 (D.N.J. 1990) (applying New Jersey law); Skelton v. Druid City Hosp. Bd., 459 So.2d 818 (Ala. 1984).

[101] International Petroleum Services, Inc. v. S & N Well Service, Inc., 639 P.2d 29 (Kan. 1982).

cept of merchantability and go to uses which are customarily made of the goods in question. For example, shoes are generally used for the purpose of walking upon ordinary ground, but a seller may know that a particular pair was selected to be used for climbing mountains.

The "particular purpose" of goods is narrower than the "ordinary purpose" covered by an implied warranty of merchantability. The "particular purpose" envisages a specific use by the buyer that is peculiar to the nature of his or her business while the "ordinary purpose" goes to uses that customarily are made of the goods.[102] The purchase of a boat as a personal pleasure craft on an lake is within the "ordinary purpose" of a boat. If the buyer did not intend to use the boat for any purpose other than its ordinary purpose, there is no implied warranty of fitness.[103] Thus, in *Klein*, the buyers sought to purchase a lawnmower that would be suitable for a specific use: a large lot with numerous hills. Most courts now take the position that UCC § 2-315 applies only when "goods do not fulfill the specific need for which they were purchased."[104] If the seller was not aware of the "particular purpose" for which the goods were to be used, there is no implied warranty of fitness.[105] An example of this is *Bayliner Marine Corp. v. Crow*,[106] in which the buyer purchased a fishing boat from the seller. The particular purpose for which the boat was intended was use as an offshore fishing boat capable of traveling 30 miles per hour. Although the buyer informed the seller that he intended to use the boat for offshore fishing and discussed the speed with him, the evidence did not show that the buyer informed the seller that a boat incapable of traveling 30 miles an hour was unacceptable to him. As a result, the Virginia Supreme Court found that no implied warranty of fitness for a particular purpose attached to the sale of the boat. In some situations, circumstances alone, without any specific statement from the buyer to the seller, may give rise to an implied warranty "if the circumstances are such that the seller has reason to realize that the purpose intended or that the reliance exists."[107]

[C] *Reliance*

In determining whether or not goods are covered by an implied warranty of fitness, the trier of fact must decide whether the buyer relied on "the seller's skill or judgment to select or furnish suitable goods." In *Klein*, the buyers specifically told the salesman that they had no experience with

---

[102] *See* UCC § 2-315 cmt. 2.

[103] Smith v. Stewart, 667 P.2d 358 (Kan. 1983).

[104] Stones v. Sears, Roebuck & Co., 558 N.W.2d 540, 547 (Neb. 1997).

[105] Ambassador Steel Co. v. Ewald Steel Co., 190 N.W.2d 275 (Mich. Ct. App. 1971).

[106] 509 S.E.2d 499 (Va. 1999).

[107] *See* UCC § 2-315 cmt. 1.

lawnmowers and told him they wanted him to recommend a mower that would be suitable to their son's property. However, in most cases such direct statements are absent. While it is not necessary that the buyer have told the seller of the particular purpose in purchasing the goods, it is necessary that the seller had reason to know of the buyer's particular purpose and that the buyer was relying on the seller's skill or judgment to furnish the appropriate goods.[108]

Whether the statements of the parties or the circumstances surrounding the transaction support a finding that the buyer relied on the seller's skill or judgment is an issue for the trier of fact.[109] Among the factors that influence a court's determination of this issue is the relative expertise of the parties with the goods sought for purchase.[110] In *Barb v. Wallace*,[111] the buyer purchased a gasoline-powered engine for use in a go-cart. When he attempted to start the engine, it exploded, severely injuring him. The buyer alleged that he told the seller that he intended to use the engine in a go-cart and that the seller told him that the engine "ran real good" and that it could be used in a go-cart "cause the shaft was out the side of the engine."[112] The seller, however, argued that the buyer's judgment and skill was just as good as his since, at the time of the purchase, the buyer was taking a course in auto mechanics and had worked on small engines. The Maryland appellate court felt that this presented a factual dispute for the jury. However, the court said that the fact that the buyer may have had some experience with the goods did not necessarily preclude the possibility that he relied on the seller's knowledge of the capabilities of the particular engine.[113]

Another factor that courts consider when determining the existence of an implied warranty of fitness is whether or not the buyer participated in the selection of the goods. Where a buyer inspected the goods before purchase, there is less likelihood of reliance on the seller's skill and judgment. This extends to cases where a buyer had an agent examine the goods before purchase. In *Sessa v. Riegle*,[114] a buyer sent his agent to examine a horse before purchasing it. He purchased the horse after the agent examined it and without any reliance on the seller's judgment. As a result, the Pennsylvania federal court held there was no implied warranty of fitness because the buyer relied on statements from his own agent rather than from the seller. This position is supported by UCC § 2-316(3)(b) which states:

---

[108] Bergquist v. MacKay Engines, Inc., 538 N.W.2d 655 (Iowa Ct. App. 1995).

[109] Norcold, Inc. v. Gateway Supply Co., 798 N.E.2d 618 (Ohio Ct. App. 2003).

[110] Conservation Load Switch, Inc. v. Ohio Univ., 2004 Ohio Misc. LEXIS 93 (Ohio Ct. Claims 2004); Catania v. Brown, 231 A.2d 668 (Conn. Cir. Ct. 1967).

[111] 412 A.2d 1314 (Md. Ct. Spec. App.1980).

[112] *Id.* at 1315-1316.

[113] *Id.* at 1319.

[114] 427 F. Supp. 760 (E.D. Pa. 1977) (applying Pennsylvania law).

when the buyer before entering into the contract has examined the goods or the sample or model as fully as he desired or has refused to examine the goods there is no implied warranty with regard to defects which an examination ought in the circumstances to have revealed to him.

A third factor that may influence a court in deciding whether or not there was reliance is whether the goods were manufactured according to specifications provided by the buyer. If they were, an argument for an implied warranty of fitness is weakened since the buyer did not rely on the seller's skill or judgment.[115] The position is supported by UCC § 2-316, comment 9, which states:

> The situation in which the buyer gives precise and complete specifications to the seller is not explicitly covered in this section, but this is a frequent circumstance by which the implied warranties may be excluded. The warranty of fitness for a particular purpose would not normally arise since in such a situation there is usually no reliance on the seller by the buyer.

Finally, although purchase of a particular brand of goods does not necessarily mean that the buyer did not rely on the seller's judgment, a buyer's claim of reliance will be weakened if he or she insisted upon purchasing a particular brand. In *Siemen v. Alden*,[116] the buyer heard that a particular brand of "gang-rip saw" was of good quality and decided to purchase one. When he went to the dealer, there was a six month delay for the brand he wanted. The buyer purchased a used saw of the same brand thinking that it would be of the same high quality. The Illinois appellate court held that the buyer acted on his own opinion of the brand rather than on any judgment by the seller. As a result, no implied warranty of fitness attached to the sale of the used saw. The position is supported by UCC § 2-315, comment 5 which states, in part, that "[i]f the buyer himself is insisting on a particular brand he is not relying on the seller's skill and judgment and so no warranty results."

§ 2.05 SCOPE OF WARRANTIES

[A] *Introduction*

The common law required privity of contract between the seller and the buyer of goods in all actions based upon a breach of an express or implied warranty.[117] A buyer or user of goods was barred from recovering against

---

[115] Controltek, Inc. v. Kwikee Enterprises, Inc., 585 P.2d 670 (Or. 1978); Layne Atlantic Co. v. Koppers Co., Inc., 201 S.E.2d 609 (Va. 1974).

[116] 341 N.E.2d 713 (Ill. App. Ct. 1975).

[117] Wood v. Advanced Rumely Thresher Co., 234 N.W. 517 (N.D. 1931).

those in the chain of distribution with whom he or she did not have a direct contractual relationship. The effect of this was to prevent consumers from bringing suits for breach of warranty against manufacturers, manufacturers of component parts, and wholesalers, and to limit their suits to their immediate retail seller. Although "the citadel of privity" began to decline in the early part of the twentieth century, first in cases involving the sale of food[118] and then in negligence cases,[119] the New Jersey Supreme Court was the first court to abolish privity as a defense in actions based on breach of implied warranties.[120] Although a number of states have followed New Jersey's lead, privity has not disappeared in warranty actions.

Fundamental to the role of privity in breach of warranty actions is the classification of *vertical* and *horizontal* privity. *Vertical privity* deals with whom the buyer can sue. Cases in which vertical privity is an issue involve buyers who did not purchase the goods directly from the named defendant.[121] An example of this is the buyer who purchases defective goods from a retail store and then brings an action against the manufacturer of those goods. Although the buyer is in the chain of distribution from the manufacturer, the buyer's contractual relationship (i.e., privity) extends no further than to the retailer. In contrast, *horizontal privity* deals with who can sue. Cases in which horizontal privity is an issue involve users of defective goods who were not the purchasers of the goods and thus are outside the direct chain of distribution. An example of the problem of horizontal privity is *Henningsen v. Bloomfield Motors, Inc.*,[122] in which a woman was injured while driving an automobile that had been purchased and given to her as a present by her husband. Since she was not the purchaser of the automobile, Mrs. Henningsen was not in the chain of distribution. She was able to recover only because the New Jersey court struck down the privity requirement.

The role that privity plays in breach of warranty actions has become more complicated in recent years. Although the UCC governs horizontal privity cases, vertical privity has been left to the individual states. As a result, who can be sued for breach of warranty often depends upon whether the buyer is seeking damages for personal injury, property damage, economic loss, or consequential damages. In addition some states take different approaches to privity in cases of express and implied warranties. They permit recovery for breach of implied warranty in situations where it is restricted for breach of express warranty.[123] One reason for this is that

---

[118] Mazetti v. Armour & Co., 135 P. 633 (Wash. 1913).

[119] MacPherson v. Buick Motor Co., 111 N.E. 1050 (N.Y. 1916).

[120] Henningsen v. Bloomfield Motors, Inc., 161 A.2d 69 (N.J. 1960).

[121] Rheem Manufacturing Co. v. Phelps Heating & Air, 714 N.E.2d 1218 (Ind. Ct. App.1999).

[122] 161 A.2d 69 (N.J. 1960).

[123] Nobility Homes of Texas, Inc. v. Shivers, 557 S.W.2d 77 (Tex. 1977); Reichhold Chemical, Inc. v. Haas, 1989 Ohio App. LEXIS 4129 (Ohio Ct. App. 1989).

implied warranties arise by operation of law without specific adoption by the seller.[124]

[B] *Horizontal Privity*

UCC § 2-318 offers the states three alternative versions of the scope of a seller's liability for an express or implied warranty:[125]

Alternative A

A seller's warranty whether express of implied extends to any natural person who is in the family or household of his buyer or who is a guest in his home if it is reasonable to expect that such person may use, consume, or be affected by the goods and who is injured in person by breach of the warranty. A seller may not exclude or limit the operation of this section.

Alternative B

A seller's warranty whether express of implied extends to any natural person who may reasonably be expected to use, consume or be affected by the goods and who is injured in person by breach of the warranty. A seller may not exclude or limit the operation of this section.

Alternative C

A seller's warranty whether express of implied extends to any person who may reasonably be expected to use, consume or be affected by the goods and who is injured by breach of the warranty. A seller may not exclude or limit the operation of this section with respect to injury to the person of an individual to whom the warranty extends.

Alternative A, which has been adopted by the largest number of states, is, by its wording, the most restrictive of the three approaches to privity. It extends the protection of an express or implied warranty to "any natural person who is in the family or household of his buyer or a guest in his home if it is reasonable to expect that such person may use, consume or be affected by the goods."[126] However, there is no "third-party exception" and if the plaintiff is not within the group set out in Alternative A, the warranty

---

[124] *See* Tex Enterprises, Inc. v. Brockway Standard, Inc., 66 P.3d 625 (Wash. 2003).

[125] The three alternatives offered by UCC § 2-318 are not exhaustive. A number of states have adopted variations on the alternatives. In addition, California has not adopted UCC § 2-318.

[126] Smith v. Mitlof, 198 F. Supp. 2d 492 (S.D.N.Y. 2002) (applying New York law). Some states have abolished the distinction between "natural" and "legal" persons." JKT Co., Inc. v. Hardwick, 265 S.E.2d 510 (S.C. 1980).

extends only to the first buyer or user of the product.[127] In addition, it limits recovery to injuries "in person" from the breach of the warranty. This excludes property damage and economic loss.

Although the extent of the protection of a warranty under Alternative A appears to be limited, some states have held that its list of potential plaintiffs is not necessarily exhaustive. For example, Illinois courts have expanded the class to include employees of the ultimate purchaser who suffer personal injury.[128] In *Reed v. City of Chicago*,[129] an Illinois federal district court further expanded the category of plaintiffs who can recover for personal injury by holding that the estate of a man who hanged himself while in jail could bring a suit for breach of express and implied warranties against the manufacturer of the paper gown that the man used to kill himself. According to the court, the beneficiary of any warranty made by the manufacturer of the gown included potentially suicidal detainees. In designing and manufacturing the gown, the manufacturer knew that its users would be jail detainees. Since the safety of those detainees was explicitly or implicitly part of the bargain between the manufacturer and the city (which bought the gowns), a person detained by the city should be able to enforce the protections of any warranties.[130]

Alternative B to UCC § 2-318 is broader. Although it also applies to a "natural person," it omits the requirement that the third party be in the family, household or guest of the buyer. Instead, it extends protection of the warranty to anyone who "may reasonably be expected to use, consume or be affected by the goods." However, it still limits recovery to personal injuries. Thus, a buyer who claimed injury to his boat was unable to recover under a warranty claim because he suffered property damage.[131]

The most expansive (but least adopted) alternative is Alternative C. It permits "any person who may reasonably be expected to use, consume or be affected by the goods" to bring an action for breach of warranty. Since this alternative is not limited to "natural" persons, it also includes corporations. In addition, it does not limit recovery to personal injury. Instead, anyone who is "injured by breach of the warranty" may bring an action.[132]

[C] *Vertical Privity*

The more difficult question in breach of warranty cases has been vertical privity. This is because whether privity is required to recover against a

---

[127] Barnett v. Royal Cup, Inc., 968 F. Supp. 690 (N.D. Ga. 1997) (applying Georgia law).

[128] Thomas v. Bombardier-Rotax Motorenfabrik, 869 F. Supp. 551 (N.D. Ill. 1994) (applying Illinois law).

[129] 263 F. Supp. 2d 1123 (N.D. Ill. 2003) (applying Illinois law).

[130] *Id.* at 1126.

[131] Hedges v. United States, 2003 U.S. Dist. LEXIS 23383 (D.V.I. 2003) (applying Virgin Islands law).

[132] Stoney v. Franklin, 2001 Va. Cir. LEXIS (Va. Cir. Ct. 2001).

remote seller (i.e., the manufacturer of goods sold by a retailer) is not covered explicitly by UCC. Comment 3 to UCC § 2-318 states that the section "is not intended to enlarge or restrict the developing case law on whether the seller's warranties, given to his buyer who resells, extends to other persons in the distributive chain." Thus, the drafters of the UCC left it to the courts to determine whether vertical privity is required in a warranty actions between a buyer and a remote seller. As a result, there are a number of different approaches to vertical privity.

The majority of states have abandoned the vertical privity requirement, in all or certain situations, either by statute or by judicial decision.[133] The New Jersey Supreme Court, for example, held that, in a case involving economic and consequential damages, the absence of privity between the ultimate purchaser of a truck and a remote supplier did not prevent the extension to the purchaser of the warranties the supplier gave to the manufacturer.[134] Other states have abolished the requirement of vertical privity only in cases where the buyer seeks personal injury or property damages.[135] According to one court, the reason for the privity requirement is to prevent "a manufacturer from being held liable for damages of unknown and unlimited scope."[136] Although a number of states still require privity in order to recover economic and consequential damages,[137] a growing number permit non-privity plaintiffs to recover such losses.[138] Finally, even states that take a strict approach to vertical privity recognize two exceptions to the rule: where the immediate seller of the product was an agent of the manufacturer and where the manufacturer participated significantly in the sale of the product.[139]

Some states still require vertical privity between the buyer and the defendant regardless of the type of damage.[140] In *Keaton v. A.B.C. Drug Co.*,[141] a woman taking a bottle of bleach from a shelf in a store was injured when bleach splashed on her face due to a unseen loose cap on the bottle. In her suit against the store for breach of an implied warranty of merchantability

---

[133] Michels v. Monaco Coach Corp., Inc., 298 F. Supp. 2d 642 (E.D. Mich. 2003) (applying Michigan law); Hyundai Motor America, Inc. v. Goodin, 822 N.E.2d 947 (Ind. 2005).

[134] Spring Motors Distributors, Inc. v. Ford Motor Co., 489 A.2d 660 (N.J. 1985).

[135] Szajna v. General Motors Corp., 503 N.E.2d 760 (Ill. 1986). Although the purchasers of automobiles in *Szajna* could not bring an action based on implied warranty against the manufacturers because of the lack of privity, the court stated that the UCC creates implied warranties "running from the dealer to the purchaser." *Id.* at 767.

[136] *Id.* at 767.

[137] Tex Enterprises, Inc. v. Brockway Standard, Inc., 66 P.3d 625 (Wash. 2003); Mekertichian v. Mercedes-Benz U.S.A., 807 N.E.2d 1165 (Ill. App. Ct. 2004); Hyundai Motor America, Inc. v. Goodin, 804 N.E.2d 775 (Ind. Ct. App. 2004).

[138] AgGrow Oils LLC v. National Union Fire Ins. Co. Of Pittsburgh, 276 F. Supp. 2d 999 (D. N.D. 2003) (applying North Dakota law).

[139] Hyndai Motors America, Inc, 804 N.E.2d at 787.

[140] *See* Friedlein v. E.I. du Pont de Nemours & Co., 68 F. Supp. 2d 1061 (N.D. Iowa 1999).

[141] 467 S.E.2d 558 (Ga. 1996).

because it displayed the bleach at a dangerous height with a loose cap, the Georgia Supreme Court stated that, in order to recover, she had to have privity with the store. However, the court held that, by taking possession of bottle with intent to purchase it, the woman established the required privity.

§ 2.06 NOTICE

[A] *Introduction*

One aspect of an action for breach of warranty that sets it apart from negligence and strict liability is the requirement that the buyer give the seller notice of the breach of warranty before filing suit.[142] Under UCC § 2-607(3), "[w]here tender has been accepted, the buyer must within a reasonable time after he discovers or should have discovered any breach notify the seller of the breach or be barred from any remedy."[143] Courts have given a number of reasons for making notice a prerequisite for recovering damages. Notice provides the seller with an opportunity to correct any defect in the goods. Notice also makes it possible for the parties to resolve any problems with the goods through negotiations. Finally, and perhaps most important, notice minimizes the possibility of prejudice to the seller by giving it the opportunity to investigate the claim and take whatever steps may be required to defend itself or to minimize its damages while the facts still are fresh in the minds of the parties.[144] Because of the importance of the notice requirement, it is excused only in two situations: where the seller already had actual knowledge of the defect of the particular product, or where the buyer or consumer suffers personal injury. In the second situation, the notice requirement is satisfied by filing a lawsuit against the seller.[145]

[B] *"Buyer"* and *"Seller"*

Since UCC § 2-607 requires the "buyer" to notify the "seller" of any breach of warranty, the first question is who qualifies as a "buyer" and a "seller." The issue of who is a "buyer" has arisen when the potential plaintiff either did not purchase the goods (i.e., was a third-party beneficiary) or purchased the goods from a retailer rather than the manufacturer whom

---

[142] For a detailed examination of the notice requirement in one state, see Lisa Macrito, *A Buyer's Obligation to Give Notice of a Defective Product in Illinois*, 89 ILL. B.J. 34 (2001).

[143] Hubbard v. General Motors Corp., 1996 U.S. LEXIS 6974 (S.D.N.Y. 1996) (applying New York law).

[144] Palmer v. A. H. Robins Co., 684 P.2d 187 (Colo. 1984); Maybank v. S.S. Kresge Co., 273 S.E.2d 681 (N.C. 1981); Wal-Mart Stores, Inc. v. Wheeler, 586 S.E.2d 83 (Ga. Ct. App. 2003).

[145] Allstate Insurance Co. v. Daimler Chrysler, 2004 U.S. Dist LEXIS 3811 (N.D. Ill. 2004) (applying Illinois law).

they are suing (i.e., was a subpurchaser). Although comment 5 to UCC § 2-607(3)(a) states that the section extends to requiring the third-party beneficiary to notify the seller that an injury has occurred, most courts have looked, instead, to the language of the UCC. UCC § 2-103(1)(d) defines a "buyer" as "a person who buys or contracts to buy goods." Using this definition and interpreting UCC § 2-607(3)(a) literally, courts have held that notice of a breach of warranty is required only from actual buyers[146] and subpurchasers[147] of the goods. Nonbuyer beneficiaries of goods have no obligation to provide notice.[148] Thus, in *Tomczuk v. Town of Cheshire*,[149] a young girl was visiting the home of her friend and while there was injured due to a defect in a bicycle owned by her friend. The Connecticut court held that, since the young girl was a third-party beneficiary and not the "buyer" of the bicycle, she was not required to give notice to the manufacturer.

Closely related to the issue of who is a "buyer" is that of who the buyer must notify (i.e., who is a "seller"). For example, if a buyer wishes to bring a breach of warranty action against an automobile manufacturer, must the buyer notify the manufacturer or is it sufficient for the buyer to notify the dealer who sold the automobile? The majority of courts that have considered the question have held that buyers need only notify the immediate seller of the goods, not remote sellers such as the manufacturer.[150] The reason for this is that, for purposes of UCC § 2-607, courts view each transaction in the marketing chain as separate.[151] However, courts in a few states have required the buyer to notify the remote manufacturer directly.[152]

[C] *Adequate Notice*

Another problem with the notice requirement of § 2-607 is determining what constitutes adequate notice. Comment 4 to the section states that "[t]he content of the notification need merely be sufficient to let the seller know that the transaction is still troublesome and must be watched." Noti-

---

[146] Phipps v. General Motors Corp., 363 A.2d 955 (Md. Ct. App. 1976).

[147] Snell v. G. D. Searle & Co., 595 F. Supp. 654 (N.D. Ala. 1984) (applying Alabama law); Goldstein v. G. D. Searle & Co., 378 N.E.2d 1083 (Ill. App. Ct. 1978).

[148] Ayala v. Joy Manufacturing Co., 1983 U.S. Dist. LEXIS 18967 (D. Colo.1983) (applying Colorado law); Mattos, Inc. v. Hash, 368 A.2d 993 (Md. Ct. App. 1976). See, however, *Ratkovich v. SmithKline and French Lab.*, 711 F. Supp. 436 (N.D. Ill. 1989) (applying Illinois law) in which the court held that the UCC intended the notice provision to extend to third-party beneficiaries.

[149] 217 A.2d 71 (Conn. Super. Ct. 1965).

[150] Hubbard v. General Motors Corp., 1996 U.S. LEXIS 6974 (S.D.N.Y. 1996) (applying New York law); Sullivan v. Young Brothers & Co., Inc., 893 F. Supp. 1148 (D. Me. 1995) (applying Maine law).

[151] Firestone Tire and Rubber Co. v. Cannon, 452 A.2d 192 (Md. Ct. Spec. App. 1982).

[152] Compaq Computer Corp. v. Lapray, 135 S.W.3d 657 (Tex. 2004); Berry v. G.D. Searle & Co., 309 N.E.2d 550 (Ill. 1974).

fication does not have to include a statement of all of the objections that the buyer has with the goods or be a claim for damages. In interpreting UCC § 2-607, courts have been liberal in interpreting what constitutes sufficient notice. Oral notice to the seller is acceptable as is returning the goods to the seller for repair.[153] A letter from a buyer's attorney to the manufacturer of a ladder stating that the attorney had been retained by the buyer to represent him in his claim for personal injuries resulting from the seller's faulty equipment also was held to be sufficient notice even though it did not identify the equipment or indicate that the buyer was injured when he fell from a ladder.[154] Finally a buyer's calling his dissatisfaction with the goods to the attention of the manufacturer's repairman was held to be adequate notice.[155]

[D] *"Reasonable Time"*

A third issue in interpreting UCC § 2-607 is what constitutes "a reasonable time" within which to give the seller notice. This depends upon the nature, the purpose, and the circumstances of the particular case. Comment 4 to UCC § 2-607 states that what constitutes a reasonable time where the buyer is a retail consumer is judged differently from a reasonable time when the buyer is a merchant. The comment goes on to state that "the rule of requiring notification is designed to defeat commercial bad faith, not to deprive a good faith consumer of his remedy." Thus, in cases involving retail consumers, many courts hold that delay alone is not sufficient to prevent recovery.[156] Instead, the seller must show that the delay in giving notice prejudiced it by increasing the claim for damages, hindering the discovery of evidence, or resulting in the loss of evidence that might have helped the seller defend against the claim.[157] The burden is on the seller to show that the delay resulted in prejudice. However, other courts hold that a showing of prejudice is not required.[158] Notification within a reasonable period of time is a condition precedent to recovery and that without proof of notification, a warranty action must fail. These courts look simply to the length of time after the buyer discovered the defect and whether there was

---

[153] Tufano Motorcar, Inc. v. Equipment and Resources International, Ltd., 1992 Conn. Super. LEXIS 2777 (Conn. Super. Ct. 1992).

[154] Lariviere v. Dayton Safety Ladder Company, 525 A.2d 892 (R.I. 1987).

[155] Vintage Homes, Inc. v. Coldiron, 585 S.W.2d 886 (Tex. App. 1979).

[156] Maybank v. S.S. Kresge Co., 273 S.E.2d 681 (N.C. 1981) (a delay of three years was not unreasonable as a matter of law under the facts of the case); Wal-Mart Stores, Inc. v. Wheeler, 586 S.E.2d 83, 85 (Ga. Ct. App. 2003).

[157] Smith v. Robertshaw Controls Co., 2003 U.S. Dist. LEXIS 23639 (D. Mass. 2003) (applying Massachusetts law) (a water heater accidently was destroyed after a year of being stored in case an insurance adjuster wanted to inspect it; the failure of the owner to notify the manufacturer of the accident during that year deprived it of the opportunity to inspect it.).

[158] San Antonio v. Warwick Club Ginger Ale Co., 248 A.2d 778 (R.I. 1968).

an explanation for the delay in providing notice. Thus, an unexplained delay of giving notice for almost four years after an accident was held to be unreasonable.[159]

§ 2.07 DISCLAIMERS AND LIMITATIONS OF WARRANTIES

Although selling goods without a warranty, or with limitations on the buyer's remedy if the goods are defective, may send a message to potential buyers that the seller does not stand behind its product, UCC § 2-316 permits a seller to exclude or modify warranties. In addition, UCC § 2-719 allows a seller to limit the remedies or damages available to a buyer. If a seller follows the procedures set out in these sections, a buyer may be prevented from recovering all or part of the damages caused by the failure of the goods.[160] However, disclaimers and limitations of warranties are not favored by the courts and are construed strictly against a seller.[161]

[A] *Exclusion or Modification of Warranties*

[1] Express Warranties

UCC § 2-316(1) permits a seller to exclude or limit an express warranty but only when it is "reasonable." Since a seller is not required to provide a buyer with an express warranty, a seller may include a provision in the contract stating that none is given. However, if the seller makes a representation that amounts to an express warranty, the UCC makes it difficult to disclaim or modify that warranty if it formed "part of the basis of the bargain." Thus, a seller cannot make an affirmation of fact about goods and then insert a provision in the sales contract excluding "all warranties, express or implied."[162] In order for a disclaimer or modification of an express warranty to be valid, its language must be consistent with the language of the express warranty.[163] In addition, although the UCC does not require that the language of a disclaimer of an express warranty to be "conspicuous," as it does for an implied warranty of merchantability, the New Jersey Supreme Court has stated that "it is inconceivable that such a disclaimer or

---

[159] Salmon Rivers Sportsman Camps. Inc. v. Cessna Aircraft Co., 544 P.2d 306 (Idaho 1975).

[160] *See* Moore v. Mack Trucks, 40 S.W.3d 888 (Ky. Ct. App. 2001).

[161] James River Equipment Co. v. Beadle County Equipment, Inc., 646 N.W.2d 265 (S.D. 2002).

[162] UCC § 2-316 cmt. 1.

[163] Boud v. SDNCO, Inc., 54 P.3d 1131 (Utah 2002); Mercedes-Benz of North America, Inc. v. Dickenson, 720 S.W.2d 844 (Tex. App. 1986).

limitation of an express warranty which is other than clear and conspicuous could be regarded as valid and enforceable."[164]

An example of what one court called "the remote case in which a seller has effectively limited an express warranty" is *Jones v. Davenport*,[165] in which the buyer was building a new home and contracted with the seller for the brick work on the outside of the house and interior fireplaces. The buyer selected the brick on his own and verified the color and style on a sample board belonging to the seller. However, the majority of the brick delivered to the site was not the color the buyer ordered and the few that were correct contrasted and diminished the appearance of the house. The Ohio appellate court held that, although the sample board created an express warranty, the board also contained a disclaimer that read: "Samples prepared to show general color and texture. Usual color variations from these samples may be expected."[166] Since the buyer admitted that he read the disclaimer when he viewed the sample board, the court held that anyone would have seen that any warranty was limited by the disclaimer language.

[2] Implied Warranties of Merchantability

UCC § 2-316(2) recognizes a seller's right to exclude or modify an implied warranty of merchantability. However, the section imposes two important requirements on the right and the omission of either of the requirements makes an attempted disclaimer ineffective.[167] First, the language of the disclaimer specifically must mention "merchantability."[168] Second, if the disclaimer is in writing, it must be "conspicuous."[169] UCC § 2-201(10) defines "conspicuous" as a term,

> so written, displayed, or presented that a reasonable person against which it is to operate ought to have noticed it. Whether a term is 'conspicuous' or not is a decision for the court. Conspicuous terms include the following:
>
> (A) a heading in capitals equal to or greater in size than the surrounding text, or in contrasting type, font, or color to the surrounding text of the same or lesser size; and
>
> (B) language in the body of a record or display in larger type than the surrounding text, or in contrasting type, font, or color to the

---

[164] Gladden v. Cadillac Motor Car Division, 416 A.2d 394, 399 (N.J. 1980).

[165] 2001 Ohio App. LEXIS 226 (Ohio Ct. App. 2001).

[166] *Id.* at *18.

[167] Providence & Worcester Railroad Co. v. Sargent & Greenlead, Inc., 802 F. Supp. 680, 687 (D. R.I. 1992) (applying Rhode Island law).

[168] Jordan v. Carlisle Construction Co., 2001 U.S. Dist. LEXIS 24287 (D.Neb. 2001) (applying Nebraska law); McCormick Machinery, Inc. v. Julian E. Johnson & Sons, Inc., 523 So.2d 651 (Fla. Dist. Ct. App. 1988).

[169] Tennessee Carolina Transportation, Inc. v. Strick Corp., 196 S.E.2d 711 (N.C. 1973); Leland Industries, Inc. v. Suntek Industries, Inc., 362 S.E.2d 441 (Ga. Ct. App. 1987).

surrounding text of the same size, or set off from surrounding text of the same size by symbols or other marks that call attention to the language.

Cases dealing with whether a disclaimer of an implied warranty of merchantability was "conspicuous" turn on whether the size of the type and color of the printed disclaimer distinguished it from other provisions in the contract.[170] A textbook example of what constitutes a conspicuous disclaimer is *Mitsch v. General Motors Corp.*, [171] in which the plaintiffs purchased a used automobile from a General Motors dealership in 2002. Over the next 18 months, the plaintiffs experienced various problems with the vehicle and took it to two General Motors dealerships for repairs. When the repairs proved unsuccessful, the plaintiffs sought to revoke the acceptance of the vehicle, alleging among other things, breach of implied warranty of merchantability against General Motors and the dealership.[172] The defendants asserted that there was no warranty since the purchase agreement stated that the vehicle was sold "as is — no warranty."[173] The Illinois Appellate Court affirmed the grant of summary judgment to the defendants even though the disclaimer did not use the word "merchantability." According to the court the conspicuousness of the disclaimer outweighed any other concerns:

> [T]he term "as is" appeared prominently at the top of the disclaimer along with notice that plaintiffs would bear the entire expense of repairing or correcting any defects that currently existed in the vehicle or may develop in the future. The disclaimer was in all capital letters, the terms "entire expense" and "without" were underlined, and plaintiff . . . signed his name below that provision. . . .[W]e conclude that the "as is" was sufficient to disclaim the implied warranty of merchantability and that the prominent placement and size of the disclaimer in the purchase agreement are fatal to the plaintiff's argument.[174]

[3] Implied Warranties of Fitness for a Particular Purpose

UCC § 2-316(2) also provides for the exclusion or modification of an implied warranty of fitness for a particular purpose. Although the disclaimer of such a warranty may be in general language, it must be "by a writing and conspicuous." According to the section, language to exclude all

---

[170] Koellmer v. Chrysler Motors, Inc., 276 A.2d 807 (Conn. Super. Ct. 1970).

[171] 2005 Ill. App. LEXIS 699 (Ill. App. Ct. 2005).

[172] *Id.* at 2-3.

[173] *Id.* at 3.

[174] *Id.* at 10-11.

implied warranties of fitness is sufficient if it states: "There are no warranties which extend beyond the description of the face hereof." However, the restrictive attitude of some courts towards the disclaimer of implied warranties is expressed in their view that, even if a disclaimer strictly complies with the language of UCC § 2-316(2), a court still may find it unconscionable as a matter of law and thus unenforceable.[175]

[4] "As Is" Disclaimers

An alternative method of disclaiming implied warranties is provided by UCC § 2-316(3). This section provides that, "unless the circumstances indicate otherwise, all implied warranties are excluded by expressions like 'as is,' 'with all faults' or other language which in common understanding calls the buyer's attention to the exclusion of warranties and makes plain that there is no implied warranty."[176] According to comment 7 to UCC § 2-316, these are terms of ordinary commercial usage that are understood to mean that the buyer takes the entire risk as to the quality of the particular goods. Since the subsection does not specifically state that the seller must mention the term "merchantability" or require that the language of the disclaimer be "conspicuous," courts are split whether to read those requirements into UCC § 2-316(3).[177] Despite the UCC provision, approximately a dozen states and the District of Columbia do not permit the "as is" sale of consumer products.

Since UCC § 2-316(3) applies only to implied warranties, an "as is" clause cannot exclude an express warranty. An example of this is *Gable v. Boles*,[178] in which a salesman sold a used boat to a buyer, claiming that it was "winterized." The buyer signed a sales contract that stated that the boat was sold "as is." In reality, the boat had not been "winterized" and, as a result, it did not operate properly. The Alabama appellate court held that the salesman's claim that the boat was "winterized" created an express warranty that was not defeated by the subsequent "as is" clause in the contract for sale.

[B] *Limitations on Warranties*

In many sales situations, sellers will warrant in the sales contract that its goods are free from defects for a limited period of time (i.e., one year) or, in the case of automobiles, for a certain number of miles they are driven. The seller then will limit the extent of its liability if the goods are defective dur-

---

[175] Schmaltz v. Nissen, 431 N.W.2d 657, 661-662 (S.D. 1988).

[176] Rawson v. Conover, 20 P.3d 876 (Utah 2001).

[177] *See* Gaylord v. Lawler Mobile Homes, Inc., 477 So.2d 382 (Ala. 1985) (holding that the requirements are not required); Gindy Manufacturing Corp. v. Cardinale Trucking Corp., 268 A.2d 345 (N.J. Super. Ct. 1970) (the requirements applied to § 2-316(3)).

[178] 718 So.2d 68 (Ala. Civ. App. 1998).

ing that time by inserting a limitation of remedy provision in the sales contract. An example of such a provision is one that stated:

> UNDER NO CIRCUMSTANCES WILL SELLER BE LIABLE
> FOR ANY INCIDENTAL OR CONSEQUENTIAL DAMAGES, OR
> FOR ANY OTHER LOSS, DAMAGES OR EXPENSE OF ANY
> KIND, INCLUDING LOSS OF PROFITS ARISING IN CONNEC-
> TION WITH THIS CONTRACT OR WITH THE USE OR INABIL-
> ITY TO USE SELLER'S PRODUCTS FURNISHED UNDER THIS
> CONTRACT. . . .BUYER'S REMEDY IS LIMITED TO EITHER (i)
> REPAIR OR REPLACEMENT OF THE DEFECTIVE PART OR
> PRODUCT, OR AT SELLER'S OPTION, (ii) RETURN OF THE
> PRODUCT AND REFUND OF THE PURCHASE PRICE, AND
> SUCH REMEDY SHALL BE BUYER'S ENTIRE AND EXCLU-
> SIVE REMEDY.[179]

Limitation of remedy clauses in contracts are a means of allocating the
risks between the seller and the buyer. UCC § 2-719(1) provides that a
sales contract may limit the damages that a buyer may recover or limit
the remedy to "return of the goods and repayment of the price or to repair
and replacement" of the defective goods.[180] UCC § 2-791(3) also permits a
seller to limit or exclude consequential damages unless the "limitation or
exclusion is unconscionable."[181] This section provides that, while consequential damages for breach of warranty may be excluded unless "unconscionable," such a limitation with respect to damages for personal injuries
is "prima facie unconscionable." In cases involving consumer goods, the
limitation of consequential damages for personal injury is considered prima
facie unconscionable.[182] However, where the buyer's loss is commercial,
such a limitation is not prima facie unconscionable.[183] In addition, a limitation that is presented as part of a warranty may be so deceptive, confusing or misleading as to be invalid.[184]

A seller's ability to created an exclusive or limited remedy also becomes
ineffective if the remedy fails of its "essential purpose."[185] Thus, if the
seller limits the buyer's remedy to repair of the defective goods and the
seller is unable to correct the defect within a reasonable period of time, the

---

[179] Kearney & Trecker Corp. v. Master Engraving Co., 527 A.2d 429, 431 (N.J. 1987).

[180] For an example of a seller limiting its liability for consequential damages for any
breach of warranty, see *Moore v. Mack Trucks, Inc.*, 40 S.W.3d 888 (Ky. Ct. App. 2001).

[181] Schmaltz v. Nissen, 431 N.W.2d 657 (S.D. 1988).

[182] Figueroa v Boston Scientific Corp., 254 F. Supp. 2d 361 (S.D.N.Y. 2003) (applying New
York law); Collins v. Uniroyal, Inc., 315 A.2d 16 (N.J. 1974); Moore v. Coachman Industries, Inc.,
499 S.E.2d 772 (N.C. Ct. App. 1998).

[183] Gladden v. Cadillac Motor Car Division, 416 A.2d 394 (N.J. 1980).

[184] *Id.*

[185] UCC § 2-719(2).

exclusive remedy fails.[186] However, courts are split on the effect of the failure of the exclusive remedy to achieve its essential purpose. A number of courts have adopted the view that the failure of the limited remedy also invalidates the exclusion of consequential damages. Others hold that the exclusion of consequential damages is independent of the limited warranty so that if the repair or replacement remedy fails, the validity of the exclusion of consequential damages depends on the intention of the parties.[187]

§ 2.08 DAMAGES FOR BREACH OF WARRANTY

If goods to not comply with an express or implied warranty, the buyer may suffer one or more of five different types of damages: loss of value of the product; damage to (or loss of) the product; economic loss from the inability to use the product; personal injury; or damage to property other than the product. Courts have stated that the purpose of the UCC is to shift those losses from the individual victims to those responsible for manufacturing or selling the product.[188] Since the UCC does not make any distinction between damages recoverable for the breach of an express warranty and the breach an implied warranty, damages for both are governed by UCC § 2-714 and § 2-715.

UCC § 2-714 provides that a buyer who accepts goods that turn out not to conform to the express or implied warranty may recover for the decreased value of the goods. This is defined as the difference between the value of the goods accepted and the value they would have had if they had been as warranted, unless special circumstances show proximate damages of a different amount.[189] In order to give the buyer the benefit of the bargain, this may require compensation for: (1) the cost to replace the goods, or (2) the cost to repair the goods.[190] Plaintiffs also may suffer personal injury, property damage, or economic loss as the result of a breach of a warranty. UCC § 2-714(3) provides for recovery of incidental and consequential damages under § 2-715 in proper cases.

Incidental damages are those costs that a buyer incurs in dealing with the breach of a warranty. Although the UCC does not define incidental expenses, UCC § 2-715(1) states that they include "the expenses reasonably incurred in inspection, receipt, transportation and care and custody of goods

---

[186] Ford Motor Co. v. Mayes, 575 S.W.2d 480 (Ky. Ct. App. 1978).

[187] Kearney & Trecker Corp. v. Master Engraving Co., 527 A.2d 429 (N.J. 1987).

[188] See McDonald v. Mazda Motors of America, 603 S.E.2d 456, 460 (Ga. Ct. App. 2004).

[189] See Gill v. Bluebird Body Co., 2005 U.S. Dist. LEXIS 4611 (M.D. Ga. 2005) (applying Georgia law); Mayberry v. Volkswagen of Am., Inc., 692 N.W.2d 226 (Wis. 2005); Chapman v. Upstate RV & Marine, 610 S.E.2d 852 (S.C. Ct. App. 2005).

[190] See Schroeder v. Barth, Inc., 969 F.2d 421, 423-424 (7th Cir. 1992) (applying Indiana law); Davis Industries Sales, Inc. v. Workman Construction Co., 856 S. W.2d 355 (Mo. Ct. App. 1993).

rightfully rejected, any commercially reasonable charges, expenses, or commissions in connection with effecting cover and any other reasonable expenses incident to the delay or other breach." An example of an award of incidental damages is *Keller v. Inland Metals All Weather Conditioning, Inc.*,[191] in which an Idaho trial court found that the defendants breached express and implied warranties that a dehumidifier sold to the plaintiffs for use in their athletic club was fit for its intended purpose. The trial court held that the plaintiffs were entitled to recover for the decreased value of the dehumidifier as well as incidental or consequential damages. The Idaho Supreme Court affirmed the award for incidental damages, saying that the plaintiffs were entitled to recover expenses reasonably incurred in the inspection, receipt, transportation and care and custody of the dehumidifier and any reasonable expense incident to the delay or breach. Those incidental expenses were: (1) $1,092 for the time one of the plaintiff's employees spent gathering temperature and humidity data during the period between the installation of the dehumidifier and the filing of this lawsuit; (2) $1,001.00 for the time another employee spent transporting water samples for testing during the same time period; (3) $700 the plaintiffs spent to have additional testing of the water and air in their athletic club. The court found that those expenses reasonably were incurred in inspecting the dehumidifier to determine whether it conformed to the express warranty and that they were caused by defendant's breach.

The UCC also permits recovery of consequential damages that result from a seller's breach of warranty. Consequential damages resulting from seller's breach include injury to person or property proximately resulting from any breach of warranty. UCC § 2-715(2) defines consequential damages as:

(a) any loss resulting from general or particular requirements and needs of which the seller at the time of contracting had reason to know and which could not reasonably be prevented by cover or otherwise; or

(b) injury to person or property proximately resulting from any breach of warranty.[192]

Consequential damages for lost profits are permitted if they meet the requirements of foreseeability and certainty.[193] This requires the buyer to show (1) the seller to have known, or have had reason to know, at the time of contracting, that if it breached the warranty the buyer would suffer lost

---

[191] 76 P.3d 977 (Idaho 2003).

[192] *See* Federal Insurance Company v. The Village of Westmont, 649 N.E.2d 986 (Ill. App. Ct. 1995) (property damage); Garavalia v. Heat Controller, Inc., 570 N.E.2d 1277 (Ill. App. Ct. 1991) (personal injury).

[193] The foreseeability and certainty requirements for consequential damages arise out of the English case, *Hadley v. Baxendale*, 156 Eng. Rep. 145 (Ex. 1854).

profits, (2) the lost profits were readily ascertainable, and (3) the lost profits could not have been reasonably prevented.[194]

A few states permit the award of punitive damages when the breach of warranty is willful or the result of a tort such as fraud.[195] However, punitive damages are not favored and generally are not available in breach of warranty cases.[196]

§ 2.09 THE MAGNUSON-MOSS ACT

In response to the misuse of express warranties and disclaimers by manufacturers and sellers, Congress enacted the Magnuson-Moss Warranty-Federal Trade Commission Improvement Act (the "Act")[197] in 1975. The Act does not create new warranties or preempt the UCC unless a section is inconsistent with the Act.[198] Instead, the Act regulates the terms of a written warranty and any implied warranty in order to "improve the adequacy of information available to consumers, prevent deception, and improve competition in the marketing of consumer products."[199] In order to accomplish these goals, the Act permits a "consumer"[200] to bring an action against a "supplier"[201] or "warrantor"[202] of a "consumer product"[203] for the failure to

---

[194] Lewis v. Mobil Oil Corp., 438 F.2d 500 (8th Cir. 1971) (applying Arkansas law); Parker Tractor & Implement Co. v. Johnson, 819 So. 2d 1234 (Miss. 2002).

[195] RESTATEMENT (SECOND) OF CONTRACTS § 355 (1981) ("Punitive damages are not recoverable for a breach of contract unless the conduct constituting the breach is also a tort for which punitive damages are recoverable.") See West v. Jayne, 484 N.W.2d 186 (Iowa 1992); Romero v. Mervyn's, 784 P.2d 992 (N.M. 1989); Gasque v. Mooers Motor Car, Inc., 313 S.E.2d 384 (Va. 1984).

[196] See MacKenzie v. Chrysler Corporation, 607 F.2d 1162 (5th Cir.1979) (applying Mississippi law); Rhodes v. McDonald, 548 S.E.2d 220 (S.C. Ct. App. 2001).

[197] 15. U.S.C. §§ 2301-2312.

[198] Murphy v. Mallard Coach Co., 582 N.Y.S.2d 528 (N.Y. App. Div. 1992).

[199] 15 U.S.C § 2302(a). See Sorce v. Naperville Jeep Eagle, Inc., 309 Ill.App.3d 313 (1999).

[200] A "consumer" is any individual or business who buys a "consumer product" and any person "to whom such product is transferred during the duration of an implied or written warranty. . .applicable to the product." Id. § 2301(3). The effect of this section is to eliminate the defense of horizontal privity that exists under some versions of UCC § 2-318. Under the Act, a "consumer" does not include buyers who purchase products "for purposes of resale" or for commercial purposes.

[201] A "supplier" is "any person engaged in the business of making a consumer product directly or indirectly available to consumers." In keeping with the goals of the Act, it applied to the creation of a "written warranty." Id. § 2301(4).

[202] A "warrantor" is any supplier or other person who gives or offers to give a written warranty or who is or may be obligated under an implied warranty. Id. § 2301(5).

[203] A "consumer product" includes tangible personal property distributed in commerce that normally is used for personal, family, or household purposes and may include property attached to or installed on real property. This excludes products purchased for resale and commercial products. Id. § 2301(1).

honor a "written warranty"[204] or an "implied warranty."[205] The Act prohibits tie-in sales provisions as a condition for a written or implied warranty.[206]

Although the Act does not require a supplier to provide a written warranty to a consumer, if it does, the warranty must comply with the disclosure requirements of the Act.[207] The terms of the Act go beyond the UCC and specify that the warranty "fully and conspicuously disclose in simple and readily understood language the terms and conditions of such warranty."[208] The Act contains a list of the information that may be required in the warranty.[209] All written warranties must be designated either as a "full warranty" or a "limited warranty."[210] In order to be a full warranty, a number of conditions must be met. The "warrantor" (1) must provide a remedy within a reasonable time and without charge to the consumer for any defect or failure to conform with the warranty; (2) must not impose any limitation on the duration of any implied warranty; (3) must not exclude or limit consequential damages for the breach of any written or implied warranty unless the limitation or exclusion appears conspicuously on the face of the warranty; and (4) must permit the consumer to elect a refund or replacement of the product without charge if, after a reasonable number of attempts, the defect cannot be remedied.[211] A warranty that does not meet all of the standards for a full warranty is a "limited warranty."[212]

In order to protect consumers, the Act prohibits a full warranty from disclaiming or modifying an implied warranty.[213] However, a limited warranty may limit an implied warranty to the duration of the limited written warranty "if such limitation is conscionable and is set forth in clear and unmistakable language and prominently displayed on the face of the warranty."[214]

Remedies available under the Act for failure to honor a warranty include damages and injunctions.[215] The type and amount of damages under the Act

---

[204] A "written warranty" is defined as a written promise that the product is free of defects or will meet a specific level of performance over a specified time period.

[205] The Act defines an "implied warranty" as an "an implied warranty arising under state law. . .in connection with the sale by a supplier of a consumer product." *Id.* § 2301(7). Thus, an "implied warranty" under the Act is an implied warranty of merchantability under the UCC. *See* Alvarez v. American Isuzu Motors, 749 N.E.2d 16 (Ill. App. Ct. 2001).

[206] 15 U.S.C. § 2302(c).

[207] Boelens v. Redman Homes, Inc., 748 F.2d 1058, 1061 (5th Cir. 1984).

[208] 15 U.S.C. § 2302(a).

[209] *Id.*

[210] *Id.* § 2303.

[211] *Id.* § 2304(a).

[212] *Id.* § 2303(a)(2).

[213] *Id.* § 2308(a).

[214] *Id.* § 2308(b).

[215] *Id.* § 2310.

depend upon state law.[216] Damages may include recovery of the purchase price, market price of a replacement, or loss in value of the product. State law determines whether punitive damages are available under the Act.[217] In addition to damages, a consumer also may recover court costs and expenses as well as reasonable attorney fees.[218]

Enforcement of the Act lies with the Attorney General or the Federal Trade Commission (FTC).[219] The Act also provides for a class action[220] or a individual right of action to a consumer who is "damaged by the failure of a supplier, warrantor, or service contractor to comply with any obligation under this chapter, or under a written warranty, implied warranty, or service contract."[221] The consumer may bring the action in federal or state court. Because of the jurisdictional requirements for bringing a claim under the Act in federal court,[222] most suits are brought in state court. However, before bringing a suit, the class or an individual consumer must give the supplier a reasonable opportunity to "cure" the failure to comply with the Act.[223] In addition, the Act allows warrantors to establish informal dispute resolution procedures if they meet stated requirements.[224] If a warrantor establishes a dispute resolution procedure that meets the Act's requirements, a consumer may not file a civil action until he or she has attempted to resolve the dispute through those procedures.[225]

---

[216] Mitsch v. General Motors Corp., 2005 Ill. App. LEXIS 699 (Ill. App. Ct. 2005).

[217] Kelly v. Fleetwood Enterprises, Inc., 377 F.3d 1034, 1039 (9th Cir. 2004); Boelens v. Redman Homes, Inc., 748 F.2d 1058, 1069 (5th Cir. 1984).

[218] *Id.* § 2310(d)(2).

[219] *Id.* § 2310.

[220] Id. § 2310(a).

[221] *Id.* § 2310(d)(1).

[222] Individual claims under the Act may only be brought in federal court if the amount in controversy is at least $50,000.00. In addition, for class actions, there must be at least 100 named plaintiffs whose individual claims exceed $25 each. *Id.* § 2310(d).

[223] 15 U.S.C. § 2310(e).

[224] *Id.* § 2310(a).

[225] *Id.*

Chapter 3

MISREPRESENTATION

SYNOPSIS

§ 3.01 INTRODUCTION

Closely related to breach of express warranty and breach of implied warranty of fitness for a particular purpose are products liability actions based upon claims of fraudulent, negligent, or innocent misrepresentations.[1] Although both breach of warranty and misrepresentation claims require a

---

[1] "Breach of these warranties provides an independent basis of liability under the Uniform Commercial Code and may be combined in the same case with a claim for misrepresentation" RESTATEMENT (THIRD) OF TORTS: PRODUCTS LIABILITY § 9 cmt. *e* (1998).

showing that the manufacturer or seller made a false or misleading statement about the qualities of its product, there are significant differences
between the two causes of action. First, unlike breach of warranty, which
is a contract action, misrepresentation is a tort and does not require any contractual relationship between the parties, even though a misrepresentation
usually arises in a contractual setting.[2] Secondly, breach of warranty focuses
on the condition of the product and whether it had the qualities attributed
to it by the manufacturer or seller. Fault on the part of the person providing the express warranty or implied warranty of fitness is not an element
of proof in that determination. While the condition of the product also is
important in misrepresentation actions, the focus in such cases is on the
state of mind of the person who made the statement about the product
and whether the person who acted upon it was justified in doing so. Fraud,
recklessness, or negligence may be crucial to this analysis. Thirdly, despite
the expansion of potential plaintiffs in breach of warranty actions, the
scope of persons who can recover for a misrepresentation is broader. Finally,
there are important differences between the damages that can be awarded
for breach of warranty and misrepresentation.

In addition to the differences between breach of warranty and misrepresentation, there are significant differences between the three categories
of misrepresentation as well. Although the Restatement (Third) deals with
all three categories of misrepresentation in § 9, they are distinct causes of
action with their own requirements. This makes it necessary to examine
each form of misrepresentation separately.

§ 3.02 FRAUDULENT MISREPRESENTATION

[A] *Introduction*

The oldest of the theories of misrepresentation is based upon fraud and
deceit in a statement made by the manufacturer or seller of a product.[3] In
recent years, advertising and mass marketing have given rise to claims of
fraudulent and deceptive representations concerning a variety of products
including automobiles,[4] IUDs,[5] prescription medicine,[6] silicon breast
implants,[7] and tobacco.[8]

---

[2] Keller v. A.O. Smith Harvestone Products, Inc., 819 P.2d 69 (Colo. 1991).

[3] *See* Langridge v. Levy, 150 Eng.Rep. 863 (1837), *aff'd*, 150 Eng.Rep. 1458 (1838).

[4] Clark v. McDaniel, 546 N.W.2d 590 (Iowa 1996).

[5] Adams v. G.D. Seale & Co., 576 So.2d 728 (Fla. Ct. App. 1991).

[6] In re Rezulin Products Liability Litigation, 133 F. Supp. 2d 272 (S.D.N.Y. 2001) (applying
Mississippi law); Freeman v. Hoffman-La Roche, Inc., 618 N.W.2d 827 (Neb. 2000).

[7] Barrow v. Bristol-Myers Squibb Co., 1998 U.S. Dist. LEXIS 23187 (M.D. Fla. 1998) (applying Florida law).

[8] Cipollone v. Liggett Group, Inc., 505 U.S. 504 (1992).

Courts require plaintiffs to prove a number of elements in order to establish a *prima facie* case of fraudulent misrepresentation.[9] Despite differences in language among the states as to the exact formulation of the requirements, six elements are at the heart of recovery for fraud: (1) a misrepresentation; (2) concerning an existing material fact; (3) knowledge of the falsity of the representation, or recklessness based on insufficient information, by the person who made it; (4) an intention to induce the person to whom the misrepresentation was made to rely on it; (5) justifiable reliance on the misrepresentation by the person to whom it was made; and (6) resulting damage. These elements also are reflected in § 310 of the Restatement (Second) of Torts, which states:

> An actor who makes a misrepresentation is subject to liability to another for physical harm which results from an act done by the other or a third person in reliance upon the ruth of the representation, if the actor
>
> (a) intends his statement to induce or should realize that it is likely to induce action by the other, or a third person, which involves an unreasonable risk of physical harm, and
>
> (b) knows
>
>> (i)   that the statement is false, or
>>
>> (ii) that he has not the knowledge which he professes.

Unlike claims based on beach of express warranty, the Federal Rules of Civil Procedure, as well as many state codes of civil procedure, require a plaintiff to plead the circumstances constituting a fraudulent misrepresentation "with particularity."[10] Many states also place a heightened burden of proof on a plaintiff in a case of fraudulent misrepresentation, i.e., "clear and convincing evidence," as opposed to a "preponderance of the evidence," the usual standard for recovery in civil cases.[11]

[B] *A False Statement of a Material Fact*

The first requirement for fraudulent misrepresentation is that the defendant made a false statement about a material fact concerning the product. A statement of "fact" has been defined as one that "(1) admits of being

---

[9] For examples of the different formulations of the required elements, see *Montgomery Rubber and Gasket Co., Inc. v. Belmont Machinery Co., Inc.*, 308 F. Supp. 2d 1293 (M.D. Ala. 2004) (applying Alabama law); *Valente v. Sofamor*, 48 F. Supp. 2d 862 (E.D. Wis. 1999) (applying Wisconsin law); *Small v. Lorillard Tobacco Co., Inc.*, 679 N.Y.S.2d 593 (N.Y. 1998); *Allen v. Mac Tools Inc.*, 671 So. 2d 636 (Miss. 1996); *Dobbin v. Pacific Coast Coal Co.*, 170 P.2d 642 (Wash. 1946).

[10] Federal Rules of Civil Procedure, Rule 9(b). *See* Hearn v. R. J. Reynolds Tobacco Co., 279 F. Supp. 2d 1096 (D. Ariz. 2003) (applying Arizona law).

[11] Marvin Lumber and Cedar Co. v. PPG Industries, Inc., 223 F.3d 873 (8th Cir. 2000) (applying Minnesota law).

adjudged true or false in a way that (2) admits of empirical verification."[12] A "material fact" is one that influences a person's decision whether or not to purchase a product.[13] The requirement that a statement be one of material fact is meant to distinguish it from a nonactionable expression of opinion or sales "puffery" that often is associated with the advertising of products.[14] The distinction between "fact" and "opinion" is illustrated by the statements the manufacturer of a roof made to a customer about its product in *Cummings v. HPG International, Inc.*[15] In that case, the manufacturer's statement that the roof would last for 20 years was held to be a statement of "fact," while its statement that the roof "would perform better and last the same or longer than other commercial roof systems on the market" fell into the "opinion category, as normal commercial puffing."[16] The difficulty in distinguishing between the two types of statements is illustrated by the manufacturer's additional statement that the roof was suitable for the variable climate of the particular state. Although that statement was close to the line between the two categories, the Court of Appeals concluded that it was, arguably, more like a statement of "fact" than "opinion."[17]

A misrepresentation usually is contained in advertising, product literature, or an oral statement made by the seller. In addition, it can result from the concealment of a material fact about a product.[18] While silence does not amount to a misrepresentation where the parties are experienced business people, a manufacturer or seller has a duty to disclose information about a product in a number of situations, including where it has superior knowledge about the product and the purchaser lacks expertise with it.[19] A fraudulent misrepresentation also can be created by a statement that is a "half-truth" about a product. An example of this is *St. Joseph Hospital v. Corbetta Construction Co.*,[20] in which the Illinois Appellate Court upheld a verdict against the manufacturer-supplier of wall paneling installed in a hospital. The manufacturer failed to disclose to the architect and the builder that testing by an independent company had revealed that the paneling had

---

[12] Presidio Enterprises, Inc. v. Warner Bros. Distributing Corp., 784 F.2d 674, 679 (5th Cir. 1986).

[13] The Shutter Shop, Inc. v. Amersham Corp., 114 F. Supp. 2d 1218 (M.D. Ala. 2000) (applying Alabama law); Trenholm v. Ratcliff, 646 S.W.2d 927 (Tex. 1983).

[14] Hubbard v. General Motors Corp., 1996 U.S. Dist. LEXIS 6974 (S.D.N.Y. 1996) (applying New York law); In re All Terrain Vehicle Litigation, 771 F. Supp. 1057 (C.D. Cal. 1991).

[15] 244 F.3d 16 (1st Cir. 2001) (applying Massachusetts law).

[16] *Id.* at 21.

[17] *Id.*

[18] Finch v. Hughes Aircraft Co., 469 A.2d 867 (Md. 1984); Kuelling v. Roderick Lean Manufacturing Co., 75 N.E. 1098 (N.Y. 1905).

[19] Wright v. Brooke Group Ltd., 114 F. Supp. 2d 797 (N.D. Iowa 2000). *See* RESTATEMENT (SECOND) OF TORTS § 551.

[20] 316 N.E.2d 51 (Ill. App. Ct. 1974).

a flame spread 17 times the maximum allowed under the city building code. When the testing company refused to rate the wall-paneling because the flame spread was so high, the manufacturer told the contractor that the paneling "does not carry a flame spread rating of any kind."[21] Although that statement technically was true, the Illinois court held that it was fraudulent since the failure to disclose the dangerously high flame spread was misleading. "In other words, a half-truth is sometimes more misleading than an outright lie."[22]

[C] *Scienter*

The second element of a fraudulent misrepresentation is that the person who made the statement had the requisite degree of knowledge of its falsity (*scienter*). According to the Restatement (Second) of Torts, § 526, a misrepresentation is fraudulent if the person who makes it "(a) knows or believes that the matter is not as he represents it to be, (b) does not have the confidence in the accuracy of his representation that he states or implies, or (c) knows that he does not have the basis for his representation that he states or implies."[23] This element of *scienter* often is the most difficult for a plaintiff to prove. It requires proof of what the manufacturer or seller knew about its product at the time they made the statement. In *Gillham v. Admiral Corp.*,[24] for example, the Sixth Circuit upheld a judgment against a manufacturer for compensatory and punitive damages resulting from a fire ignited by one of its televisions. The evidence showed that the manufacturer used unsafe high voltage transformers in its television sets. The evidence also supported the jury's finding that the manufacturer knew that its transformers were causing fires because of their design and knew that the safety device designed to contain fires was ineffective. However, despite that knowledge, the manufacturer not only failed to inform prospective purchasers of the danger, it told them that the television sets were safe.

Although the evidence in *Gillham* showed that the manufacturer knew of the dangers posed by the product, it is not necessary for the plaintiff to prove that the person making the allegedly fraudulent representation had actual knowledge of its falsity. If a person makes a false statement with reckless disregard of the lack of information as to the truth of the statement, a court will infer the person's knowledge of its falsity.[25]

---

[21] *Id.* at 69.

[22] *Id.* at 71.

[23] *See* Neri v. R. J. Reynolds Tobacco Co. Inc., 2000 U.S. Dist. LEXIS 22223 (N.D. N.Y. 2000) (applying New York law) (a smoker failed to show that a tobacco company knew that its statement included false statements at the time it was published).

[24] 523 F.2d 102 (6th Cir. 1975) (applying Ohio law).

[25] Aaron v. Hampton Motors, Inc., 124 S.E.2d 585 (S.C. 1962); Hurley v. Frontier Ford Motors, Inc., 299 N.E.2d 387 (Ill. App. Ct. 1973).

[D] *Intent to Induce Reliance on the Misrepresentation*

The third element of fraudulent misrepresentation is that the manufacturer or seller who made the false statement did so with the intent to induce the user to act or rely on the statement in a way that created a risk of harm.[26] In order to establish this element, the user of the product must show that the manufacturer or seller not only knew that the statement was false but also knew that the user would rely upon it.[27] While the misrepresentation usually will create a risk of harm to the person to whom the statement was made or who read the advertising or product literature, a person who makes a fraudulent misrepresentation may be liable to third persons who are within the class of persons whom they should expect to act based upon their misrepresentation.[28] Thus, privity is not required for fraudulent misrepresentation.

[E] *Justifiable Reliance*

The requirement of an intent to induce action or reliance is tied to the fourth element of fraudulent misrepresentation: a plaintiff must show not only that he or she relied upon the truth of the representation but also that the reliance was justified.[29] The California Supreme Court has stated that "[r]eliance exists when the misrepresentation or nondisclosure was an immediate cause of the plaintiff's conduct which altered his or her legal relations, and when without such misrepresentation or nondisclosure he or she would not, in all reasonable probability, have entered into the contract or other transaction."[30] Thus, in *Valente v. Sofamor*,[31] the plaintiffs failed to show that they or their doctors relied on the allegedly fraudulent misrepresentations made by the manufacturers of orthopedic bone screws when they decided to undergo spinal fusion surgery. As a result, the plaintiffs could not show the necessary causal connection between their continued back pains and the alleged misrepresentations. The requirement of showing justifiable reliance has been a particular issue in lawsuits against tobacco companies in which smokers allege that they began smoking or

---

[26] Roginsky v. Richardson-Merrell, Inc., 378 F.2d 832 (2d Cir. 1967) (applying New York law).

[27] Reservoir Manor Corp. v. Lumbermens Mutual Casualty Co., 137 N.E.2d 912 (Mass. 1956).

[28] Learjet Corp. v. Spenlinhauer, 901 F.2d 198 (1st Cir. 1990) (purchaser of an airplane relied upon a statement made by the airplane manufacturer for certification to the FAA); Tetuan v. A.H. Robbins Co., 738 P.2d 1210 (Kan. 1987) (patient brought suit against the manufacturer of the Dalkon Shield relying on her physician).

[29] Miller v. Pfizer Inc., 196 F. Supp. 2d 1095 (D. Kan. 2002 (applying Kansas law); White v. R. J. Reynolds Tobacco Co., 109 F. Supp. 2d 424 (D. Md. 2000) (applying Maryland law).

[30] Alliance Mortgage Co. v. Rothwell, 900 P.2d 601, 608 (Cal. 1995).

[31] 48 F. Supp. 2d 862 (E. D. Wis. 1999) (applying Wisconsin law).

continued smoking because of representations in the company advertisements.[32] Such suits have been dismissed where the plaintiffs could not show that they actually relied upon the advertisements made by the companies in their decisions to smoke.[33] Simply having read newspapers and magazines during the time when the alleged statements were made was not sufficient to establish reliance.[34]

[F] *Damages*

Reliance upon the misrepresentation leads to the final element the plaintiff must establish for fraudulent misrepresentation: harm resulting from reliance on the statement. Most cases involve claims for "physical harm"[35] resulting from the misrepresentation either to the person to whom the false statement was made or to a third person who acted in reliance on the representation. In addition, one of the advantages of suing for fraudulent misrepresentation is that a plaintiff also may recover punitive damages.[36] While some states hold that the economic loss doctrine bars claims of fraudulent misrepresentation when the only damage is to the product itself, other states hold that the doctrine does not apply to fraudulent misrepresentation.[37]

§ 3.03 NEGLIGENT MISREPRESENTATION

[A] *Elements of an Action*

In addition to fraudulent misrepresentation, a manufacturer or seller also may be liable for negligent misrepresentation. As they do with fraudulent misrepresentation, courts define the elements of this tort in a num-

---

[32] Neri v. R. J. Reynolds Tobacco Co., 2000 U.S. Dist. LEXIS 22223 (N.D.N.Y. 2000) (applying New York law).

[33] Tompkins v. R. J. Reynolds Tobacco Co., 92 F. Supp. 2d 70 (N.D.N.Y. 2000) (applying New York law).

[34] Allgood v. R. J. Reynolds Tobacco Co., 80 F.3d 168 (5th Cir. 1996) (applying Texas law); Small v. Lorillard Tobacco Co. Inc., 679 N.Y.S. 2d 593 (N.Y. 1998).

[35] RESTATEMENT (SECOND) OF TORTS § 310 (1965). THE RESTATEMENT (THIRD) § 9 (1998) speaks of "harm to persons or property."

[36] In *Robinson Helicopter Co., Inc. v. Dana Construction*, 102 P.3d 268 (Cal. 2004), the jury found the defendant liable for fraudulent misrepresentation and awarded compensatory damages of $1.5 million and punitive damages of $6 million. *See also* Gillham v. Admiral Corp., 523 F.2d 102 (6th Cir. 1975) (applying Ohio law); First National Bank of Louisville v. Brooks Farms, 821 S.W.2d 925 (Tenn. 1991).

[37] Robinson Helicopter Co., Inc. v. Dana Construction, 102 P.3d 268 (Cal. 2004); Tietsworth v. Harley-Davidson, 677 N.W.2d 233 (Wis. 2004). *See* R. Joseph Barton, *Note: Drowning in a Sea of Contract: Application of the Economic Loss Rule to Fraud and Negligent Misrepresentation Claims*, 41 WM. AND MARY L. REV. 1789 (2000).

ber of ways.[38] One of the most detailed statements of the elements of negligent misrepresentation was provided by a California court which stated
that a plaintiff must establish that: (1) the defendant made a representation as to a past or existing material fact; (2) the representation was untrue;
(3) regardless of his actual belief, the defendant made the representation
without any reasonable ground for believing it was true; (4) the representation was made with the intent to induce the plaintiff to rely upon it; (5)
the plaintiff was unaware of the falsity of the representation, acted in
reliance upon the truth of the representation and was justified in relying
upon the representation; and (6) as a result of the reliance upon the truth
of the representation, the plaintiff suffered damage.[39] As with fraudulent
misrepresentation, the elements of negligent misrepresentation also are
contained in the Restatement (Second) of Torts. Section 311 of the Restatement provides:

> (1) One who negligently gives false information to another is sub-
>   ject to liability for physical harm caused by action taken by the
>   other in reasonable reliance upon such information, where such
>   harm results
>
>   (a) to the other, or
>
>   (b) to such third persons as the actor should expect to be put in
>   peril by the action taken.
>
> (2) Such negligence may consist of failure to exercise reasonable
>   care
>
>   (a) in ascertaining the accuracy of the information, or
>
>   (b) in the manner in which it is communicated.

An action for negligent misrepresentation requires the plaintiff to prove
that the defendant made a false statement of a material fact (as opposed to
an opinion) about the product and that the plaintiff justifiably relied on the
statement to his or her detriment.[40] However, the scope of those who can
recover for a negligent misrepresentation is not as broad as for other types
of negligence. According to one California court, the "class of persons entitled to rely upon the representations is restricted to those to whom or for
whom the misrepresentations were made. Even though the defendant

---

[38] *See* Jimenez v. Daimler Chrysler Corp., 269 F. 3d 439 (4th Cir. 2001) (applying South Carolina law); Cummings v. HPG International, Inc., 244 F.3d 16 (1st Cir. 2001) (applying Massachusetts law); Wilson v. Dryvit Systems, Inc., 206 F. Supp. 2d 749 (E.D.N.C. 2002) (applying
North Carolina law). *See also* RESTATEMENT (SECOND) OF TORTS § 311 (1965).

[39] Friedman v. Merck & Co., Inc., 131 Cal. Rptr. 2d 885, 900 (Cal. Ct. App. 2003). For a
shorter statement of the elements, see *Pabon v. Hackensack Auto Sales, Inc.*, 164 A.2d 773 (N.J.
Super. Ct. 1960).

[40] *Jimenez*, 269 F. 3d 439.

should have anticipated that the misinformation might reach others, he is not liable to them."[41]

As with fraudulent misrepresentation, the failure to disclose information also may be the basis for a negligent misrepresentation claim.[42] However, the crucial difference between the two forms of misrepresentation is the defendant's mental state. Unlike fraudulent misrepresentation, in which the plaintiff must prove that the defendant actually knew that the statement was false, the degree of culpability required to establish negligent misrepresentation is less stringent. In a negligent misrepresentation action, it is sufficient for the plaintiff to prove that the defendant was negligent in making the statement to the plaintiff. This places the focus on the degree of care taken by the person making the statement in discovering the truth or falsity of the statement and requires the plaintiff to prove that an ordinary person who engaged in the particular business would not have made the false statement to a customer.[43]

Negligent misrepresentations usually result from oral statements, advertising, or product literature provided by the manufacturer or seller of the product. However, most cases of negligent misrepresentation involve sellers rather than manufacturers. These sellers also can include third parties, such as those who endorse products manufactured by someone else.[44] In the classic case of *Hanberry v. Hearst Corp.*,[45] the California Court of Appeal recognized a cause of action for negligent misrepresentation against a publishing company that advertised, in one of its magazines, that a certain brand of shoes met the "Good Housekeeping's Consumers' Guaranty Seal," that the shoes were a good product and that "the advertising claims made for them in our magazine are truthful."[46] The plaintiff read the advertisement, purchased a pair of the shoes, and was injured when she slipped on a vinyl floor, allegedly because the shoes were defective. In allowing the complaint, the court stated that the plaintiff alleged that the magazine permitted its seal to be used in connection with shoes it had not tested or inspected or, if it had inspected and examined the shoes, had done so negligently. According to the court, if either of those allegations was true, the defendant's conduct would amount to negligent misrepresentation.

All of the elements required for negligent misrepresentation are illustrated by another frequently cited case, *Pabon v. Hackensack Auto Sales,*

---

[41] *Friedman*, 131 Cal. Rptr. 2d at 901.

[42] *Id.*

[43] Cummings v. HPG International, Inc., 244 F.3d 16 (1st Cir. 2001) (applying Massachusetts law); Cunningham v. C. R. Pease House Furnishing Co., 69 A. 120 (N.H. 1908).

[44] *See* Walters v. Seventeen Magazine, 244 Cal. Rptr. 101 (Cal. Ct. App. 1987) (defendant did not sponsor or endorse the product by advertising it in its magazine).

[45] 81 Cal. Rptr. 519 (Cal. Ct. App. 1969).

[46] *Id.* at 521.

Inc.,[47] in which the service manager of an automobile dealership told the plaintiff that the "clicking" and "chopping" sensation in the steering of his automobile was because it was "a new car. Don't worry about it. It'll wear out."[48] However, the service manager never checked the steering system and the plaintiff was injured in a crash when the steering locked. The New Jersey appellate court held that a jury could find the dealership liable for negligent misrepresentation. According to the court: "Negligence may be inferred not only from Hackensack's failure or refusal to repair or even to examine the reported defect, but also from its representation to [the plaintiff] that the steering deficiency was normal and should cause him no concern."[49]

[B] *Damages*

Damages for negligent misrepresentation are more limited than those for fraudulent misrepresentation. Because the action is based upon negligence, punitive damages are not available to plaintiffs.[50] Courts also have refused to recognize a cause of action for negligent misrepresentation resulting in emotional distress. A plaintiff may recover for a negligent misrepresentation that involves a risk of harm only if actual physical harm results.[51]

Damages for negligent misrepresentation usually are limited to situations where the defective product caused personal injury or damage to property other than the product itself. This is because most states follow the economic loss doctrine which bars a person from recovering purely economic losses (i.e., loss of the product itself) in tort actions based upon strict liability and negligence (including negligent and innocent misrepresentations). In such cases, a cause of action lies only in contract for breach of warranty.[52] However, many states recognize an exception to the economic loss doctrine for a negligent misrepresentation where the plaintiff's damages were caused by a negligent misrepresentation by a person in the business of supplying information for the guidance of others in their business transactions. Most of the litigation involving this exception has turned on the question of whether the defendant was in the business of supplying information and whether the information was ancillary to the sale or in connection with the sale of other merchandise.[53]

---

[47] 164 A.2d 773 (N.J. Super. Ct. 1960).

[48] *Id.* at 784.

[49] *Id.*

[50] Klein v. Sears Roebuck and Co., 773 F.2d 1421 (4th Cir. 1985) (applying Maryland law).

[51] Friedman v. Merck & Co., Inc., 131 Cal. Rptr. 2d 885 (Cal. Ct. App. 2003).

[52] *See* Moorman v. National Tank Co., 435 N.E.2d 443 (Ill. 1992); Advanced Drainage Systems, Inc. v. Lowman, 437 S.E.2d 604 (Ga. Ct. App. 1993).

[53] Haimberg v. R & M Aviation, Inc., 2001 U.S. App. LEXIS 4429 (7th Cir. 2001) (applying Illinois law); Trans Helicoptere Service v. Jet Support Services, Inc., 2004 U.S. Dist. 5287 (N.D. Ill. 2004) (applying Illinois law). *See* R. Joseph Barton, *Note: Drowning in a Sea of Contract: Application of the Economic Loss Rule to Fraud and Negligent Misrepresentation Claims*, 41 WM. AND MARY L. REV. 1789 (2000).

If a negligent misstatement results in personal injury or property damage, the defendant is liable both to the person to whom it was made and "to such third persons as the actor should expect" to rely on the statement.[54] In *Cunningham v. C. R. Pease House Furnishing Co.*,[55] the defendant retailer sold a stove blackening chemical to a woman. Two days later her daughter was injured while using the product. Although the defendant dealt with the mother and probably did not think about whether she had a daughter who might use the product as well, the New Hampshire Supreme Court permitted the case to go to the jury, stating that the defendant "knew the mother bought it to use on her stove and that other members of the family were likely to use it; consequently the plaintiff can recover, if her mother could have recovered had she been injured instead of the plaintiff."[56]

§ 3.04 INNOCENT (STRICT LIABILITY) MISREPRESENTATION

[A] *Restatement (Second) of Torts, Section 402B*

The third category of misrepresentation does not require any showing of fault on the part of the person making the statement. According to § 402B of the Restatement (Second) of Torts, which has been adopted by approximately half of the states:

> One engaged in the business of selling chattels who, by advertising, labels, or otherwise, makes to the public a misrepresentation of a material fact concerning the character or quality of a chattel sold by him is subject to liability for physical harm to a consumer of the chattel caused by justifiable reliance upon the misrepresentation, even though
>
> (a) it is not made fraudulently or negligently, and
>
> (b) the consumer has not bought the chattel from or entered into any contractual relation with the seller.[57]

Section 402B has its origins in a series of cases, beginning in the 1930s, holding manufacturers liable to consumers who relied on their express representations concerning the safety or quality of products.[58] Although those cases were brought in contract under a theory of breach of an express warranty, the decisions of the courts, rejecting contractual privity, were part of

---

[54] RESTATEMENT (SECOND) OF TORTS § 311 (1965).

[55] 69 A. 120 (N.H. 1908).

[56] *Id.* at 121.

[57] RESTATEMENT (SECOND) OF TORTS § 402B cmt. c (1965).

[58] For a discussion of the evolution of the theory of misrepresentation in § 402B, see *American Safety Equipment Corp. v. Winkler*, 640 P.2d 216, 219-220 (Colo. 1982).

the gradual move toward strict liability in tort. In *Baxter v. Ford Motor Co.*,[59] a man was injured when a pebble struck the windshield of a new automobile he was driving, shattering the glass and injuring his eyes. In the sales literature that the automobile manufacturer furnished to dealers for distribution to potential customers were statements such as: "All of the new Ford cars have a Triplex shatter-proof glass windshield — so made that it will not fly or shatter under the hardest impact."[60] Since ordinary consumers were unable to discover the truth of such a statement, the Washington Supreme Court held the manufacturer liable, even though the plaintiff had purchased the automobile from a third party, a dealership, and was not in privity of contract with the manufacturer. The reason for this, according to the court, was that its decision did not rest on express warranty

> "but rather on the principle that the original act of delivering an article is wrong, when, because of the lack of those qualities which the manufacturer represented it as having, the absence of which could not be readily detected by the consumer, the article is not safe for the purposes for which the consumer would ordinarily use it."[61]

The second influence on § 402B were a series of decisions in the 1950s and early 1960s holding manufacturers strictly liable for representations they made to consumers using what the courts termed "modern merchandising practices." In *Rogers v. Toni Home Permanent Co.*,[62] for example, a woman suffered injury to her hair and scalp after using a home permanent advertised by the manufacturer to be "Very Gentle." The Ohio Supreme Court focused on the extensive use of advertising by manufacturers to promote their products directly to consumers in newspapers, magazines, signboards, and on radio and television. The advertising extolled the qualities and benefits of the products in "glowing terms" and consumers relied heavily on those advertisements in making their purchasing decisions. In such situations:

> "The warranties made by the manufacturer in his advertisements and by the labels on his products are inducements to the ultimate consumers and the manufacturer ought to be held to strict accountability to any consumer who buys the product in reliance on such representations and later suffers injury because the product proves to be defective or deleterious."[63]

---

[59] 12 P.2d 409 (Wash. 1932).

[60] *Id.* at 411.

[61] *Id.* at 412.

[62] 147 N.E.2d 612 (Ohio 1958).

[63] *Id.* at 615-616. *See also* Randy Knitwear, Inc. v. American Cyanamid Co., 181 N.E.2d 399 (N.Y. 1962); Hamon v. Digliani, 174 A.2d 294 (Conn. 1961).

[B] *"Engaged in the Business of Selling Chattels"*

Following the approach taken by the courts in cases such as *Baxter* and *Rogers*, liability under § 402B is not based upon whether the product is defective but upon whether the product conforms to the manufacturer's express statements about the product. Although fraud or negligence in making the statements is not required, section 402B does not create absolute liability. Instead, the section has its own distinct requirements that a plaintiff must prove in order to establish a *prima facie* case. The first requirement of these is that the defendant was "engaged in the business of selling chattels." In deciding who is a "seller" for purposes of § 402B, court have adopted the definition of the term used in the context of strict liability under § 402A: "anyone in the business of selling any type of chattel."[64] Those "in the business" of selling include not only manufacturers but also wholesalers, retailers, and distributors.[65] Neither § 402B nor the comments to it define what constitutes a "chattel." As a result, courts have looked both to the ordinary dictionary meaning of the term and to the way it is used in cases involving § 402A: tangible property.[66] Applying this definition of "chattels" to a claim of misrepresentation under § 402B, one federal court held that it did not to apply to ideas and expressions in a book.[67]

[C] *"Material Fact" Concerning "the Character or Quality of the Chattel"*

The second element in an action under § 402B is that the misrepresentation was a statement of a "material fact" concerning "the character or quality of the chattel." As with the other forms of misrepresentation, liability under § 402B arises only from an affirmative, express, and specific misrepresentation of material fact concerning the product.[68] An implied representation of the product's character or quality is not sufficient.[69] In *Crocker v. Winthrop Laboratories*,[70] the plaintiff's husband died as the result of a weakened condition brought on by addiction to a drug. The drug

---

[64] RESTATEMENT (SECOND) OF TORTS § 402B cmt. *e* (1965). *See* Kirby v. B. I. Incorporated, 2003 U.S. Dist. LEXIS 16964 (N.D. Tex. 2003) (applying Texas law).

[65] RESTATEMENT (SECOND) OF TORTS § 402B cmt. *e* (1965).

[66] Winter v. G. P. Putnam's Sons, 938 F.2d 1033 (9th Cir. 1991); Pitler v. Michael Reese Hosp., 415 N.E.2d 1255 (Ill. App. Ct. 1980).

[67] Winter, 938 F.2d 1033.

[68] English v. Suzuki Motor Co., Ltd., 1997 U.S. App. LEXIS 19865 (10th Cir. 1997) (applying Colorado law); Kirby v. B. I. Incorporated, 2003 U.S. Dist. LEXIS 16964 (N.D. Tex. 2003) (applying Texas law); Klages v. General Ordinance Equipment Co., 367 A.2d 304 (Pa. Super. Ct. 1976).

[69] Hilbrenner v. Kawasaki Motors Corp., 1988 U.S. Dist. LEXIS 8373 (W.D. Mo. 1988) (applying Missouri law).

[70] 514 S.W.2d 429 (Tex. 1974).

company argued that, because of the state of medical knowledge and the rare susceptibility of the user, the addiction could not have been foreseen. In affirming the judgment of the trial court for the plaintiff, the Texas Supreme Court held that, regardless of those facts, when a drug company "positively and specifically represents its product to be free and safe from all dangers of addiction," the company will be liable for misrepresentation if the treating physician relies on the representation and it proves to be false and results in harm.[71]

In contrast to a statement of a "material fact" concerning the quality of the product, are statements of general assurances of good quality, opinion, and sales talk characterized as "puffing."[72] As with the other forms of misrepresentation, section 402B does not apply to these statements. In *Hauter v. Zogarts*,[73] the defendant manufactured a training device designed to help unskilled golfers improve their game. The labels on the shipping carton and the cover of the instruction booklet urged players to "drive the ball with full power" and stated: "COMPLETELY SAFE BALL WILL NOT HIT PLAYER." The plaintiff was seriously inured by a golf ball while using the product. The California Supreme Court held that the statement fell within the ambit of § 402B, leading the plaintiff to believe that he could use the product with safety. According to the court: "The assertion that the [product] is completely safe, that the ball will not hit the player, does not indicate the seller's subjective opinion about the merits of the product but rather factually describes an important characteristic of the product."[74]

[D] *Advertising*

Section 402B contains two caveats, in the first of which the drafters took no position on whether the section should apply "where the representation is not made to the public, but to an individual."[75] However, according to comment h, section 402B is limited to "misrepresentations which are made by the seller to the public at large, in order to induce purchase of the chattels sold, or are intended by the seller to, and do, reach the public." These misrepresentations may be made to the public "in newspapers or television, by literature distributed to the public through dealers, by labels on the product sold, or leaflets accompanying it, or in any other manner, whether it be oral or written."[76] In keeping with trends in modern advertising, the post-

---

[71] *Id.* at 433.

[72] RESTATEMENT (SECOND) OF TORTS § 402B cmt. *g* (1965). *See* Adkins v. Ford Motor Co., 446 F.2d 1105 (6th Cir. 1971) (applying Tennessee law); Hittle v. Scripto-Tokai Corp., 166 F. Supp. 2d 142 (M.D. Pa. 2001) (applying Pennsylvania law); Chandler v. Gene Messer Ford, Inc., 81 S.W.3d 493 (Tex. App. 2002).

[73] 534 P.2d 377 (Cal. 1975).

[74] *Id.* at 381.

[75] Lewis & Lambert Metal Contractors, Inc. v. Jackson, 914 S.W.2d 584 (Tex. App. 1994).

[76] RESTATEMENT (SECOND) OF TORTS § 402B cmt. *h* (1965).

ing by a manufacturer or seller of an advertisement on its internet website also has been held to be a "public representation."[77] However, statements made by an automobile salesman to prospective buyers have been held not to be made to the "public at large."[78]

Another issue related to representations made to the public is whether an advertisement must be for the specific model or brand of the product at issue or whether it can include similar types of goods. Although three cases in the 1970s and 1980s were divided on the question,[79] the most recent decision is *Ladd v. Honda Motor Co.*[80] in which the plaintiff alleged that the defendant misrepresented the handling characteristics of all-terrain vehicles by advertising that they were safe enough to be operated by children. The defendant argued that the plaintiff could not recover unless he could prove that it had misrepresented the handling characteristics of the particular model of all-terrain vehicle involved in the case. The plaintiff replied that his claim could rest on proof that the defendant misrepresented the handling characteristics of all-terrain vehicles in general. The Tennessee court felt that manufacturers should not be able to insulate themselves from liability under § 402B by using general advertisements of an entire product line. It held that manufacturers would be liable if their general advertisements of a product line contain representations of the "character or quality" of particular models in the product line.

[E] *"Justifiable Reliance"*

As with fraudulent and negligent misrepresentation, it is essential to a claim under § 402B that there was "justifiable reliance" on the misrepresentation concerning the product and that physical harm resulted from the reliance.[81] However, comment j to § 402B states that "[t]he reliance need not necessarily be that of the consumer who is injured. It may be that of the ultimate purchaser of the chattel, who because of such reliance passes it on to the consumer who is in fact injured, but is ignorant of the misrepresentation." Thus, a person who purchases a product in justifiable reliance upon statements about it, and then permits another person to use the product, has provided the element of reliance even though the person using the product never knew of the statements.[82]

---

[77] Kirby v. B. I. Incorporated, 2003 U.S. Dist. LEXIS 16964 (N.D. Tex. 2003) (applying Texas law).

[78] Chandler v. Gene Messer Ford, Inc., 81 S.W.3d 493 (Tex. App. 2002).

[79] *See* Haynes v. American Motors Corp., 691 F.2d 1268 (8th Cir. 1982) (applying Arkansas law); Collins v. Wayne Corp., 621 F.2d 777 (5th Cir. 1980) (applying New Mexico law); Jacobson v. Benson Motors, Inc., 216 N.W.2d 396 (Iowa 1974).

[80] 939 S.W.2d 83 (Tenn. Ct. App. 1996).

[81] RESTATEMENT (SECOND) OF TORTS § 402B cmt. j (1965). *See* Burton v. Danel Medical, Inc., 1999 U.S. Dist. LEXIS 2619 (Pa. 1999) (applying Pennsylvania law).

[82] Westlye v. Look Sports, Inc., 22 Cal. Rptr. 2d 781 (Cal. Ct. App. 1993).

It is a factual question in each case whether the representation influenced the purchase or use of the product.[83] According to comment j to § 402B, the rule "does not apply where the misrepresentation is not known, or there is indifference to it, and it does not influence the purchase or subsequent conduct." However, since § 402B applies to "consumers," the person injured need not have been the purchaser of the product and need not have been the one who relied on the advertising before using it.[84] An example of this is *Ladd v. Honda Motor Co.*,[85] in which a man who purchased an all-terrain vehicle admitted that he did not rely on the defendant's advertising in deciding whether to buy it. Instead, he bought it because his brother had the same vehicle. However, he did rely on the company's advertising showing children riding all-terrain vehicles in deciding to let the plaintiff (the 12-year-old son of friends) ride it. According to the Tennessee appellate court, "the reliance required by § 402B need not be that of the injured consumer but may be that of the purchaser who passes the product along to the ultimate consumer."[86]

[F] *Damages*

Finally, a plaintiff in an action under § 402B must have suffered "physical harm" caused by the misrepresentation. However, the second caveat to § 402B leaves open the question of whether the section applies "where physical harm is caused to one who is not a consumer of the chattel."[87] Liability under this section is limited to physical harm to a person or property and does not include economic loss unaccompanied by physical damage.[88]

§ 3.05 RESTATEMENT (THIRD) OF TORTS: PRODUCTS LIABILITY

Section 9 of the Restatement (Third) of Torts: Products Liability deals with the liability of a manufacturer or seller for harm caused by misrepresentation. The section states: "One engaged in the business of selling or otherwise distributing products who, in connection with the sale of a product, makes a fraudulent, negligent or innocent misrepresentation of material fact concerning the product is subject to liability for harm to persons or property caused by the misrepresentation."

---

[83] Baughn v. Honda Motor Co., 727 P.2d 655 (Wash. 1986); American Safety Equipment Corp. v. Winkler, 640 P.2d 216 (Colo. 1982).

[84] RESTATEMENT (SECOND) OF TORTS § 402B cmt. *i* (1965).

[85] 939 S.W.2d 83 (Tenn. Ct. App. 1996).

[86] *Id.* at 101.

[87] There are no cases discussing this caveat. *See* RESTATEMENT (THIRD) OF TORTS § 9 Reporters Note 2 (1998).

[88] Ritter v. Custom Chemicides, Inc., 912 S.W.2d 128 (Tenn. 1995).

This section, which is based on §§ 310, 311, and 402B of the Restatement (Second) of Torts, imposes strict liability on a seller and applies to fraudulent, negligent, and innocent misrepresentations. The section does not require the plaintiff to show that the product was defective at the time of sale or distribution.[89]

§ 3.06 DECEPTIVE TRADE PRACTICES STATUTES

[A] *Introduction*

In addition to common law misrepresentation, the federal government, all 50 states, and the District of Columbia have enacted "consumer protection," "consumer fraud," "unfair trade practices" or "deceptive trade practices" statutes that provide an additional basis for products liability actions. These statutes date from the early 1960s when the national consumer protection movement expanded governmental regulation and oversight of consumer goods. The purpose of these statutes is to protect the public from false, deceptive, or misleading representations or statements in the advertising, marketing, and sale of products and services.[90] Most of the statutes provide for a private cause of action. As with common law misrepresentation, the language and details of the statutes differ from state to state. However, there are three elements that are similar in all of the statutes: (1) a deceptive act or practice must be part of a business transaction; (2) an intent that the consumer rely on the deception; and (3) damages to the consumer as a result of that reliance. Many of the statutes permit successful plaintiffs to recover not only compensatory damages (and, in some instances, treble damages), but also attorneys fees and costs.[91] Some statutes also permit the recovery of punitive damages.[92]

---

[89] For a discussion of this section by a court that did not adopt it, see *Miller v. Pfizer Inc.*, 196 F. Supp. 2d 1095 (D. Kan. 2002).

[90] An example of this are the lawsuits brought against alcohol manufacturers alleging unfair and deceptive marketing practices by targeting underage consumers through advertisements. *See* Goodwin v. Anheuser-Busch Cos., Inc., 2005 WL 280330, at *4 (Cal. Super. Ct. Jan. 28, 2005).

[91] For examples of the consumer protection statutes, see Illinois Consumer Fraud and Deceptive Business Practices Act (815 ILL. COMP. STAT. 505/1 (2002)); New Jersey Consumer Fraud Act (N.J. STAT. ANN. § 56:8-1 (2001)); Texas Deceptive Trade Practices-Consumer Protection Act (TEX. BUS. & COM. § 17.41 (Vernon 2002)); Wisconsin Deceptive Trade Practices Act (WIS. STAT. § 100.18 (2004)).

[92] *See* Florida Deceptive and Unfair Trade Practices Act (FLA. STAT. § 501.201 (2002)); (HAW. REV. STAT. § 480-13 (2002)); New Mexico Unfair Trade Practices Act (N.M. STAT. ANN. § 57-12-10 (Michie 1978)).

[B] *The Food Industry and Deceptive Trade Practice Statutes*

An example of the consumer protection statutes are the New York laws that prohibit "deceptive acts or practices in the conduct of any business, trade or commerce"[93] as well as all "false advertising in the conduct of any business, trade or commerce."[94] The most highly publicized and controversial case involving the New York statutes is *Pelman v. McDonald's Corporation*,[95] in which the parents of two teenagers filed a lawsuit against McDonald's restaurants on behalf of their children. The lawsuit was based on three counts that alleged that: (1) McDonald's promotional representations created the false impression that its food products were nutritional and part of a healthy lifestyle if consumed daily; (2) McDonald's failed to disclose adequately that the use of certain food additives and processing techniques made its food less healthy than represented; and (3) McDonald's deceptively represented that nutritional information was readily available to its customers when, in fact, the information was not available at a significant number of its restaurants in New York.[96] The complaint also asserted that as a result of the children eating at McDonald's three to five times a week between 1987 and 2002, they developed "obesity, diabetes, coronary heart disease, high blood pressure, elevated cholesterol intake, related cancer, and/or other detrimental and adverse health effects."[97]

As in other states, the New York consumer protection statutes require a plaintiff to show that the statements were consumer-oriented, that they were misleading in a material respect, and that the plaintiff was injured as a result of them. In cases of false adverting under § 350 of the New York statute, a plaintiff also must show that he or she relied upon the allegedly false advertisement.[98] In *Pelman*, the district court judge granted McDonald's motion to dismiss the complaint. The judge held that the customers failed to allege that the plaintiffs specifically relied to their detriment upon any particular representation made in any McDonald's advertisement or promotional material. The judge also dismissed the same claims under § 349 on the ground that the plaintiffs failed to make a sufficient causal connection between their consumption of McDonald's food and their alleged injuries.

On appeal of the dismissal of the action under § 349, the Second Circuit reversed and reinstated the plaintiffs' claims. According to the court, no showing of reliance is required in an action based on § 349 since it goes

---

[93] N.Y. GEN. BUS. LAW § 349 (McKinney 2004).

[94] *Id.* § 350.

[95] 396 F.3d 508 (2d Cir. 2005).

[96] *Id.* at 510.

[97] *Id.*

[98] *Id.* at 511.

beyond common law fraud and covers other deceptive practices. In particular, the Second Circuit focused on the district court judge's statement that he dismissed the complaint for failure to answer a series of questions about other factors that may have played a role in their weight gain and health problems.

> What else did the plaintiffs eat? How much did they exercise? Is there a family history of the diseases which are alleged to have been caused by McDonald's products? Without this additional information, McDonald's does not have sufficient information to determine if the foods are the cause of the plaintiffs' obesity or if instead McDonald's foods are only a contributing factor.[99]

The Second Circuit held that these questions were more appropriate to the discovery stage than to the pleading stage and that the complaint should not have been dismissed for the failure to answer them.

Pelman illustrates some of the similarities and differences between the consumer protection statutes and common law misrepresentation. Like misrepresentation, an action under the consumer protection statutes requires a plaintiff to allege and prove that the statements were deceptive or that the advertising was false in a material respect, that the plaintiff relied on it in deciding whether to buy or use the product, and was injured as a result of the deceptive practice or false advertising. A key difference, however, is that, under the consumer protection statutes, a plaintiff does not have to prove an intent to deceive; innocent misrepresentations are actionable if they are "deceptive" or part of "false advertising."

In response to *Pelman* and other lawsuits filed by consumers against the food industry for obesity, Congress and a number of state legislatures introduced "commonsense consumption acts" to protect producers and retailers of foods. The legislation provides that a "manufacturer, packer, distributor, carrier, holder, seller, marketer or advertiser of food" is exempt from civil liability arising out of "weight gain, obesity, a health condition associated with weight gain or obesity, or other generally known condition allegedly caused by or allegedly likely to result from long-term consumption of food."[100] Although the House of Representatives passed the "Personal Responsibility in Food Consumption Act" in October 2005,[101] the Senate has not adopted similar legislation.[102] However, approximately twenty states have enacted laws to protect the food industry in their states from weight and health-related lawsuits.[103] None of these laws, however, prohibits suits based on false or deceptive advertising or on negligence resulting from tainted food.

---

[99] *Id.* at 511-512.

[100] MODEL COMMONSENSE CONSUMPTION ACT § 2.

[101] H. R. 554, 109th Cong. (1st Sess. 2005).

[102] S. 908 was introduced in the Senate on April 26, 2005.

[103] For an example, see the Illinois Commonsense Consumption Act, 745 ILL. COMP. STAT. 43/1 (2005).

Chapter 4
NEGLIGENCE AND STRICT LIABILITY: POLICIES, PARTIES, AND PRODUCTS

SYNOPSIS

§ 4.01 INTRODUCTION

The theories of liability used most frequently by plaintiffs in products liability cases are those based on tort: negligence and strict liability. Because of the historic evolution of products liability law, these two theories have come to share many common elements and plaintiffs frequently include

counts alleging both in their complaints.[1] Despite their similarities, however, there are a number of important differences between negligence and strict liability. This chapter begins an examination of the use of negligence and strict liability in products liability cases by focusing on the elements of proof required for each theory, the underlying policies that support them, the scope of persons who may be plaintiffs and defendants, and the range of items that courts have held to be a "product." The following six chapters examine the application of negligence and strict liability theory to the three different types of product defects (design, manufacturing, and failure to warn), the methods of proving that a product was defective, the requirement that a product defect have been both the factual and proximate cause of the plaintiff's injuries, the various defenses available to a manufacturer or seller, and the types of damages that an injured person may recover.

§ 4.02 AN OVERVIEW OF NEGLIGENCE AND STRICT LIABILITY

[A] *Negligence*

When Judge Benjamin Cardozo wrote in 1916, in *MacPherson v. Buick Motor Co.*,[2] that the liability of a manufacturer was not limited to the immediate buyer of its product if that product was "reasonably certain to place life and limb in peril when negligently made,"[3] he did more than reject the traditional privity requirement that had limited recovery in negligence actions. His opinion began a revolution that, first, made it possible to judge the liability of a manufacturer or seller of a defective product according to the principles of negligence law[4] and, later, led to strict liability.[5]

As used by lawyers and judges, the term "negligence" applies both to conduct and to a complex cause of action. The most common definition of negligent conduct is "the failure to do something which a reasonably careful person would do, or the doing of something which a reasonably careful person would not do"[6] under the particular circumstances of the case. Thus,

---

[1] For an example, see *Cooper v. Zimmer Holdings, Inc.*, 320 F. Supp. 2d 1154 (D. Kan. 2004), in which the plaintiff asserted claims based not only on negligence and strict liability but also on breach of express and implied warranties and a violation of the Kansas Consumer Protection Act. However, for an argument that a plaintiff's choice between negligence and strict liability in design defect and failure to warn cases largely is a rhetorical preference, see Richard L. Cupp, Jr. & Danielle Polage, *The Rhetoric of Strict Liability Versus Negligence: An Empirical Analysis*, 77 N.Y.U. L. REV. 874 (2002).

[2] 111 N.E. 1050 (N.Y. 1916).

[3] *Id.* at 1053.

[4] *See* RESTATEMENT (SECOND) OF TORTS § 395 (1965).

[5] *Id.* § 402A.

[6] Mangrum v. Pigue, 2004 Ark. LEXIS 686 at *11 (Ark. 2004).

in a negligence action, the plaintiff must focus on the conduct of the manufacturer or seller and prove that the defect in the product, that was the cause of the injuries, was the result of their failure to use reasonable skill or care, i.e., their fault.[7] The evidentiary difficulties that a plaintiff faces in establishing that the conduct of the manufacturer or seller fell below the requisite standard of care for a reasonable person have been mitigated in some situations by the development of the concepts of negligence *per se*[8] and *res ipsa loquitur*.[9] However, the fact that the situations in which those doctrines are available to a plaintiff are limited was an important argument used by supporters of strict liability beginning in the 1960s.

Another widely cited definition of negligent conduct was articulated by Judge Learned Hand in *United States v. Carroll Towing Co.*[10] Under what has come to be known as the "Hand formula," liability depends upon whether the burden ("B") of taking adequate precautions to prevent the harm is less than the probability ("P") that the injury-causing act will occur discounted by the gravity of the injury ("L") if it does occur. According to Judge Richard Posner, "[t]he [Hand] formula translates into economic terms the conventional test for negligence. . . .Unreasonable conduct is merely the failure to take precautions that would generate greater benefits in avoiding accidents than the precautions would cost."[11] Although the Hand formula has not been adopted explicitly by courts, its cost-benefit analysis underlies the way most lawyers and judges approach the question of whether conduct was negligent. In products liability cases, it is used to determine whether the design of a product was negligent and whether the manufacturer or seller should have warned of dangers in using the product.

In addition to conduct, the term "negligence" also is used by lawyers and judges to describe a cause of action that requires a plaintiff to establish four interrelated elements. In a products liability action, a plaintiff first must establish that the manufacturer or seller owed her a duty to use reasonable care in the design, manufacture, or sale of its product. Second, a plaintiff must prove that the manufacturer or seller breached that duty of care. A breach of a duty of care is defined as the failure to exercise the standard of care of a "reasonable person" under the circumstances of the case.[12] In a

---

[7] Oanes v. Westgo, Inc., 476 N.W.2d 248 (N.D. 1991); Cronin v. J.B.E. Olson Corp., 501 P.2d 1153 (Cal. 1972).

[8] *See* Reed v. Landstar Ligon, Inc., 314 F.3d 447 (10th Cir. 2002) (applying Oklahoma law); Kemp v. Medtronic, Inc., 2001 U.S. App. LEXIS 1344 (6th Cir. 2001) (applying Ohio law).

[9] *See* Escola v. Coca Cola Bottling Co., 150 P.2d 436 (Cal. 1944); State Farm Mutual Automobile Insurance Co v. Wrap-On Co., 626 So.2d 874 (La. Ct. App. 1993).

[10] 159 F.2d 169 (2d Cir. 1947). For a discussion of the case, see Stephen G. Gilles, *United States v. Carroll Towing Co.: The Hand Formula's Home Port*, in Robert L. Rabin & Stephen D. Sugarman (eds.), TORT STORIES 11 (2003).

[11] McCarty v. Pheasant Run, Inc., 826 F.2d 1554, 1557 (7th Cir. 1987).

[12] Trull v. Volkswagen of America, Inc., 320 F.3d 1 (1st Cir. 2002) ("reasonably prudent automobile manufacturer").

products liability case, this requires a determination of whether the conduct of the manufacturer or seller fell below the acceptable standard of care in the design, manufacture, or distribution of the product or in providing warnings regarding the use of the product. Third, a plaintiff must establish that she suffered personal injury or property damage. If the only harm was to the product itself, a plaintiff is unable to recover in negligence and must rely on warranty theory. Finally, a plaintiff must prove that the breach of the duty was the factual and proximate cause of her injuries or damages.[13]

Despite the development of strict liability beginning in the 1960s, negligence still is an important theory for plaintiffs to consider in products liability cases. There are a number of reasons for this. First, five states (Delaware, Massachusetts, Michigan, North Carolina and Virginia) have not adopted strict liability in tort. For a plaintiff in these states, negligence is the only tort theory available in a products liability case. Second, proving that a manufacturers or seller was "at fault" in designing, manufacturing, or failing to warn of the dangers associated with the use of a product may make a jury more sympathetic to a plaintiff's claims and increase the damages it awards. Third, in some situations the expiration of the statute of limitations or statute of repose may prevent a plaintiff from bringing an action in strict liability, leaving only a negligence count. Fourth, negligence provides an additional net for a plaintiff during the discovery process and may result in more information about a defendant's product than would be available solely under a strict liability theory. Finally, many plaintiffs' attorneys feel that there is no disadvantage to including a negligence count in their complaints since they can dismiss the claim voluntarily at a later date if they do not have enough evidence to support their negligence count. On the other side, the principal reasons why a plaintiff may not plead negligence in a products liability action include the additional proof required to establish "fault" and the ability of a defendant, in many states, to raise contributory negligence as a defense.

[B] *Strict Liability*

Justice Roger Traynor articulated a number of reasons for holding a manufacturer "absolutely liable" in tort in his concurring opinion in the 1944 case of *Escola v. Coca Cola Bottling Co.*[14] However, his rationale was not adopted by a court until almost twenty years later in *Greenman v. Yuba Power Products, Inc.*,[15] an opinion also written by Justice Traynor. The framework for the system of strict liability in a products liability case was established three years later when the ALI adopted § 402A of the Restate-

---

[13] Stahlecker v. Ford Motor Co., 667 N.E.2d 244 (Neb. 2003); Merrill v. Navegar, Inc., 28 P.3d 116 (Cal. 2001); Sims v. General Motors Corp., 751 P.2d 357 (Wyo. 1988).

[14] 150 P.2d 436 (Cal. 1944).

[15] 377 P.2d 897 (Cal. 1962).

ment (Second) of Torts. That system was revised in 1997 with the adoption of the Restatement (Third) of Torts: Products Liability.

Although in some aspects strict liability is similar to warranty theory, an action based on § 402A does not require any representation about the product by the seller or reliance by the buyer on the skill or judgment of the seller. In addition, strict liability does not depend upon a contract, nor is it affected by the specific requirements of a warranty action such as privity, notice or by disclaimers.[16] Strict liability, however, is not intended to be what one court has called "an enveloping net of absolute liability"[17] that entitles an injured person to recover from any member of the production or distribution chain.[18] Instead, the purpose of the system of strict liability created by § 402A is to permit the injured party to recover without the requirement of proving negligence.[19] Liability depends upon three conditions.[20] First, the product must have been in a "defective condition unreasonably dangerous to the user or consumer or to his property." Second, the seller of the product must have been "engaged in the business of selling such a product." Third, the product must have been expected to and did reach the user or consumer "without substantial change in the condition in which it is sold."

According to one court, requiring the plaintiff to prove that the product was in a "defective condition unreasonably dangerous" "serves the useful function of placing some limits on the liability of a manufacturer or seller."[21] Other states construe the language of § 402A as creating a single standard and interpret the term "unreasonably dangerous" as the definition of a "defective condition."[22] Still other states have rephrased the requirements of § 402A and state that a plaintiff must prove that the injury resulted from a "condition of the product" and that condition was "an unreasonably dangerous one."[23] A few states, however, have rejected the "unreasonably dangerous" language in § 402A.[24] In *Cronin v. J.B.E. Olson Corp.*,[25] the

---

[16] *See* RESTATEMENT (SECOND) OF TORTS § 402A cmt. *m* (1965).

[17] Nesselrode v. Executive Beechcraft, Inc., 707 S.W.2d 371, 375 (Mo. 1986). See also *Potter v. Chicago Pneumatic Tool Co.*, 694 A.2d 1319, 1328-1329 (Conn. 1997) in which the Connecticut Supreme Court stated that "strict liability does not transform manufacturers into insurers, nor does it impose absolute liability. . . . Strict tort liability merely relieves the plaintiff from proving that the manufacturer was negligent and allows the plaintiff to establish instead the defective condition of the product as the principal basis of liability."

[18] Coney v. J.L.G. Industries, Inc., 454 N.E.2d 197 (Ill. 1983).

[19] Trujillo v. Berry, 738 P.2d 1331 (N.M. Ct. App. 1987).

[20] *See* Fuchsgruber v. Custom Accessories, Inc., 628 N.W.2d 833, 838 (Wis. 2001).

[21] The Union Supply Co. v. Pust, 583 P.2d 276, 282 (Colo. 1978).

[22] McAlpine v. Rhone-Poulenc Ag Co., 16 P.3d 1054 (Mont. 2000); Seattle-First National Bank v. Tabert, 542 P.2d 774 (Wash. 1975).

[23] Sollami v. Eaton, 772 N.E.2d 215 (Ill. 2002).

[24] Caterpillar Tractor Co. v. Beck 593 P.2d 871 (Alaska 1979); Berkebile v. Brandtly Helicopter Corp., 337 A.2d 893 (Pa. 1975).

[25] 501 P.2d 1153 (Cal. 1972).

California Supreme Court chose to adopt, instead, only the "defective" language of *Greenman v. Yuba Power Products, Inc.*[26] The court criticized the "unreasonably dangerous" phrase of the Restatement (Second) as introducing the negligence concept of foreseeability into strict liability analysis. The court then went on to state:

> A bifurcated standard is of necessity more difficult to prove than a unitary one. But merelyproclaiming that the phrase "defective condition unreasonably dangerous" requires only a single finding would not purge that phrase of its negligence complexion. We think that a requirement that a plaintiff also prove that the defect made the product "unreasonably dangerous" places upon him a significantly increased burden and represents a step backward in the area pioneered by this court.[27]

Although *Cronin* is widely cited in opinions and in the literature, the vast majority of courts have declined to follow its elimination of the "unreasonably dangerous" portion of § 402A's definition of strict liability. However, the Restatement (Third), §§ 1-2, supports the position taken in *Cronin* by stating that anyone who sells a "defective product" is liable for the harm it causes.

The elements required to establish strict liability highlight the important similarities and differences between that theory and negligence. Common to strict liability and negligence is the requirement that the user or consumer show that the product was defective and unreasonably dangerous when it left the control of the manufacturer or seller. As will be discussed in detail in the next three chapters, a product may be defective because of its design, the way in which it was manufactured, or because of the failure to warn of dangers associate with the use of the product. In a negligence action, fault on the part of the manufacturer or seller in creating or passing on the defect is an essential element that an injured person must establish in order to recover.[28] In an action under § 402A, however, the focus is on the condition of the product itself.[29] A manufacturer or seller is liable for the injury or loss resulting from a defective product that it puts into the stream of commerce even in the absence of any fault. Thus, while users and consumers often include separate counts of negligence and strict liability in the same complaint, they rely on strict liability in those cases in which it is difficult or impossible to prove fault.

---

[26] 377 P.2d 897 (Cal. 1962).

[27] Cronin v. J. B. E. Olson Corp., 501 P.2d 1153, 1162 (Cal. 1972).

[28] East River S.S. Corp. v. Transamerica Delaval, Inc., 476 U.S. 858 (1986); Phillips v. Kimwood Mach. Co., 525 P.2d 1033 (Or. 1974); Greenman v. Yuba Power Prods., 377 P.2d 897 (Cal. 1963).

[29] Gonzales v. Caterpillar Tractor Co., 571 S.W.2d 867 (Tex. 1978).

[C] *Policy Reasons Underlying Strict Liability*

Although Judge Cardozo's opinion in *MacPherson* abolished the privity requirement in negligence cases, it did not create a new theory of recovery. Instead, it brought products liability cases within the orbit of the existing negligence theory. However, Justice Traynor's opinions in *Escola* and *Greenman* and the adoption of § 402A created a new, and what has become highly controversial, tort theory of recovery for products liability cases. Since almost every word in § 402A has been the subject of debate and litigation, it is necessary to examine briefly the policy considerations underlying strict liability.

Comment *c* to § 402A sets out four policy justifications to support the adoption of the doctrine of strict liability:

> the seller, by marketing his product for use and consumption, has undertaken and assumed a special responsibility toward any member of the consuming public who may be injured by it; the public has the right to and does expect, in the case of products which it needs and for which it is forced to rely upon the seller, that reputable sellers will stand behind their goods; that public policy demands that the burden of accidental injuries caused by products intended for consumption be placed upon those who market them, and be treated as a cost of production against which liability insurance can be obtained; and that the consumer of such products is entitled to the maximum protection and the proper persons to afford it are those who market the products.[30]

These justifications for strict liability — the assumption of a duty to the public that uses the product, consumer expectations, loss shifting, and the need to protect consumers — are not new to comment *c*. Two of them — the need to protect consumers and the idea that losses caused by defective products should be shifted to manufacturers and sellers who are better able to bear the losses — echo the reasons given by Justice Traynor in his concurring opinion in *Escola*. The first of the reasons offered by Justice Traynor in that case was loss minimization. "Even if there is no negligence, . . . public policy demands that responsibility be fixed wherever it will most effectively reduce the hazards to life and health inherent in defective products that reach the market."[31] Unlike the old maxim of *caveat emptor* that held it was the buyer's responsibility to determine the quality of a product before purchasing it, Justice Traynor took the view that the manufacturer

---

[30] Comment *c* has been cited by courts in support of their adoption of § 402A. *See* O.S. Stapley Co. v. Miller, 447 P.2d 248, 251-52 (Ariz. 1968). For two other discussions of the policy reasons supporting strict liability, see *Harber v. Altec Industries, Inc.*, 812 F. Supp. 954, 957-958 (W.D. Mo., 1993) (applying Missouri law); FRANK J. VANDALL, STRICT LIABILITY: LEGAL AND ECONOMIC ANALYSIS 20-22 (1989).

[31] Escola v. Coca Cola Bottling Co., 150 P.2d 436, 440 (Cal. 1944).

is in the best position to reduce injuries and losses caused by its defective products. Strict liability would provide the required incentive for manufacturers to produce safer products.

A second justification for strict liability found both in comment *c* to § 402A and in Justice Traynor's concurring opinion is that it places the losses that result from defects in manufactured products on those best able to bear those losses. "The cost of an injury and the loss of time or health may be an overwhelming misfortune to the person injured and a needless one, for the risk of injury can be insured by the manufacturer and distributed among the public as a cost of doing business."[32] According to this rationale, a manufacturer is in the best position to distribute the costs of the risks created by its defective products. It can self-insure or purchase insurance from a third party and then either spread the cost of that insurance among all consumers by charging a proportionately higher price for its product or absorb the cost of that insurance and reduce the profit it would otherwise make from the sale of its product. Under such a system, consumers will be less likely to have to bear the full burden of the losses they suffer from defective products.

More recently, the Pennsylvania Supreme Court spoke forcefully about the policy that led it to adopt strict liability and of the need to recognize that "strict liability is not a type of mongrel derivative of negligence."[33] According to the court:

> Strict liability was intended to be a cause of action separate and distinct from negligence, designed to fill a perceived gap in our tort law. . . .This court recognized that in a modern industrial society, liability should not necessarily be predicated only on a finding that the defendant failed to exercise due care. Rather, we adopted the strict liability cause of action, finding "that the risk of loss must be placed upon the supplier of the defective product without regard to fault. . . ."[34]

These risk reduction, loss spreading and consumer expectations rationales have been cited by numerous courts in support of their adoption of strict liability.[35] In addition to these justifications, another policy reason has been cited by courts in support of strict liability. In *Escola*, Justice Traynor stated that a system of strict liability would eliminate the problems of proof that result from negligence. "An injured person . . . is not ordinarily in a position to refute [evidence of negligence] or identify the cause of the defect, for he

---

[32] *Id*. at 441.

[33] Phillips v. Cricket Lighters, 841 A.2d 1000, 1007 (Pa. 2003).

[34] *Id*. (*quoting* Azzarello v. Black Bros. Co., Inc., 391 A.2d 1020, 1024 (Pa. 1978)).

[35] *See* Fuchsgruber v. Custom Accessories, Inc., 628 N.W.2d 833 (Wis. 2001); Leong v. Sears Roebuck and Co., 970 P.2d 972 (Haw. 1998); Queen City Terminals, Inc. v. General American Transportation Corp., 653 N.E.2d 661 (Ohio 1995).

can hardly be familiar with the manufacturing process as the manufacturer himself is."[36] This rationale has found support as the complexity of modern products and the methods of manufacturing has come to mean that, frequently, only the manufacturer is in a position to know whether a product is properly designed and safe for its intended use.[37] Because of the costs involved in proving whether a product was negligently designed, manufactured, or marketed, strict liability has been put forward as a means of reducing the litigation costs incurred by a plaintiff and ensuring that a manufacturer or seller that places a defective product on the market does not escape liability because the plaintiff is unable to prove negligence.[38] This view is reflected in comment *a* to § 2 of the Restatement (Third) which states:

> By eliminating the issue of manufacturer fault from plaintiff's case, strict liability reduces the transaction costs involved in litigating that issue. . . .In many cases manufacturing defects are in fact caused by manufacturer negligence but plaintiffs have difficulty proving it. Strict liability therefore performs a function similar to the concept of res ipsa loquitur, allowing deserving plaintiffs to succeed notwithstanding what would otherwise be difficult or insuperable problems of proof.

In response to the cost-savings rationale, a counter-argument can be made that strict liability does not make recovery any easier for a plaintiff or reduce economic and resource costs. Instead, strict liability simply substitutes a different set of elements of proof from those required in a negligence action. While the negligence concept of fault is not among those elements, proving and defending against the numerous elements required for strict liability can be as complex and expensive for plaintiffs and defendants as those required for negligence.

§ 4.03 POTENTIAL PLAINTIFFS

In deciding whether to bring a products liability action in negligence or strict liability, the first question a potential plaintiff must ask is whether he or she meets the test for who can be a plaintiff. In a negligence action, this means that a plaintiff must establish that the manufacturer or seller owed him or her a duty of care. In a case based on strict liability, a plaintiff must show that he or she was a "user or consumer" of the product within the meaning of § 402A. Although these tests usually result in the same group of persons being able to bring actions under both theories, the different approaches taken by the two theories require separate examination.

---

[36] *Escola*, 150 P.2d at 441.

[37] *See* Sprung v. MTR Ravensburg, Inc., 788 N.E.2d 620 (N.Y. 2003).

[38] Harber v. Altec Industries, Inc., 812 F. Supp. 954 (W.D. Mo. 1993) (applying Missouri law).

[A] *The Duty Issue in Negligence*

The duty to act with "reasonable care" imposed by negligence law does not extend to the world at large. In cases where the existence of a duty of care is an issue, it is a question of law that must be decided by the judge.[39] This requires the judge to determine, usually in the context of a motion for summary judgment, whether the plaintiff and defendant stood in such a relationship to one another that the law imposes an obligation on the defendant to act reasonably for the protection of the particular plaintiff.[40] The question of duty is the threshold issue that precedes consideration of breach and causation. A trial judge can dismiss, as a matter of law, a complaint based on negligence if he or she determines that the defendant did not owe a duty to the plaintiff under the facts of the case.

With the fall of privity as a requirement in negligence cases, the scope of the duty owed by manufacturers and sellers is very broad. By marketing their products to the public, they owe a duty of care not only to the purchasers of those products but also to all foreseeable consumers, users, and persons in possession of the products.[41] However, a new fact situation may create a question of the existence of a duty to a particular person (i.e., bystander, unintended user of a product). In such cases, courts consider a number of often vague factors. The most frequently cited of these factors is the foreseeability of an injury to the plaintiff.[42] Although courts do not require plaintiffs to prove that the particular injury they suffered was foreseeable, some injury to persons in their class must have been likely to result from the negligent design, manufacture, or marketing of the product. However, more than a mere possibility of injury is required since, with hindsight, everything is foreseeable. According to the California Supreme Court, "[f]oreseeability is not to be measured by what is more probable than not, but includes whatever is likely enough in the setting of modern life that a reasonably thoughtful [person] would take account of it in guiding practical conduct."[43] In addition to foreseeability, other factors that guide courts in their duty analysis include the likelihood of injury; the closeness of the connection between the injury and the conduct; the moral blame attached to the conduct; the magnitude of the burden on the defendant in guarding against the injury; the consequences of placing the burden on the defendant;

---

[39] Gamradt v. Federal Laboratories, Inc., 380 F.3d 416 (8th Cir. 2004) (applying Minnesota law); Carter Lincoln-Mercury, Inc. v. Emar Group, Inc., 638 A.2d 1288 (N.J. 1994).

[40] National Bank of Bloomington v. Westinghouse Electric Corp., 600 N.E.2d 1275 (Ill. App. Ct. 1992).

[41] Hopkins v. Chip-In-Saw, Inc. 630 F.2d 616 (8th Cir. 1980) (applying Arkansas law); Rossell v. Volkswagen of America, 709 P.2d 517 (Ariz. 1985).

[42] Kirk v. Hanes Corp., 771 F. Supp. 856 (E.D. Mich. 1991) (applying Michigan law); Haase v. Badger Mining Corp., 682 N.W.2d 389 (Wis. 2004).

[43] Bigbee v. Pacific Tel. & Tel., 665 P.2d 947, 952 (Cal. 1983) (*quoting* 2 HARPER & JAMES, LAW OF TORTS, § 18.2 at p. 1020).

and public policy and social requirements.[44] However, these factors rarely are independently determinative of a duty and courts give them different weight depending upon the facts of the particular case.

An example of a court analyzing all of these factors to determine whether manufacturers and sellers owed a duty to a plaintiff in a products liability case is *Halbrook v. Honda Motor Co., Ltd.*,[45] in which two children were killed when a motorcycle struck the automobile in which they were riding as passengers. The parents of the children brought a wrongful death action against the companies that manufactured and sold the motorcycle. Because Michigan is one of the five states that has not adopted strict liability in tort, the parents alleged negligence in the design, manufacture, marketing and distribution of the product. The basis of their claim was that the companies manufactured and marketed a motorcycle that was dangerous and unsuitable for highways since it could travel too fast and neither an inexperienced rider nor other drivers could appreciate its capabilities. The trial court granted summary judgment to the companies based on a finding that they did not owe the children a duty.

In affirming the grant of summary judgment, the Michigan Court of Appeals reviewed five factors that it considered relevant to the determination of a duty of care. First, the court felt that it was foreseeable to the manufacturer both that motorists speed and that excessive speed can cause accidents. That was true particularly in this case where the manufacturer and sellers advertised the speed and acceleration abilities of the motorcycle as part of their marketing campaign. However, even though the foreseeability of injury factor weighed in favor of the plaintiffs, the court stated that a duty of care does not depend solely on foreseeability.[46]

The court looked to a second factor — the degree of certainty of the injury — and found that, unlike foreseeability, it weighed against the plaintiffs. That was because the court concluded that it was not certain that a motorcycle designed to travel at high speeds would cause injury to persons other than those riding on it. The risk of harm also depended upon the way in which the driver handled the motorcycle. Even if the motorcycle had been designed to travel no faster than the maximum speed limit, the court felt that it was not certain that the accident and injuries would have been prevented.[47]

The third factor considered by the court — the closeness of the connection between the defendants' conduct and the deaths of the children — also weighed in favor of the defendants. The deaths of the children were not

---

[44] Lamkin v. Towner, 563 N.E.2d 449 (Ill. 1990); J.S. v. R.T.H., 714 A.2d 924 (N.J. 1998).

[45] 569 N.W.2d 836 (Mich. Ct. App. 1997).

[46] *Id*. at 839.

[47] *Id*.

closely connected to the fact that the motorcycle could be driven in excess of the speed limit. Instead, the Michigan court found that the accident was more closely connected to the failure of driver of the automobile to yield the right of way and the motorcycle driver's reckless driving.[48]

The fourth factor — the moral blame attached to the conduct — required the Michigan court to look at the participants in the accident and determine who was the most blameworthy. The court found that the manufacturer and sellers were the least blameworthy since they did not cause the motorcycle driver to speed or the driver of the automobile to ignore the oncoming motorcycle. The court felt that the policy of preventing future harm could be promoted by imposing a duty on motorcycle manufacturers to design and market vehicles with limited speed and acceleration capabilities. However, the danger of a motorcycle depends heavily on its driver. In addition, the court felt that the legislature, not the courts, should determine what speed limitations should be set for motorcycles.[49]

Finally, the Michigan court considered the burdens and consequences of imposing a duty on the defendants. It held that motorcycle manufacturers should not be liable to persons in this type of case. The court felt that if it imposed a duty on manufacturers to protect persons who could be injured by the misuse of their products, the result would be a significant increase in litigation. Although, in some situations, a manufacturer is in a better position to bear the costs of litigation and redistribute them to the general public, the court found that, in this case, the burden would be too great.[50]

[B] *The "User or Consumer" in Strict Liability*

In order for a plaintiff to recover in an action based upon strict liability under § 402A, the person must have been the "ultimate user or consumer of the defective product." According to comment *l* to § 402A, this term is not limited to the purchaser of the product but also may be a member of the family of the purchaser, his or her employee, a guest, or a donee from the purchaser. In addition, the comment states that "it is not necessary that the ultimate user or consumer have acquired the product directly from the seller . . . [or even] have purchased the product at all." The comment goes on to define "consumers" to include not only those who consume the product but also a person who prepares it for consumption, which it defines as "all ultimate uses for which the product is intended." A "user" includes those who passively enjoy the benefits of the product, such as passengers in automobiles and in airplanes, as well as those who use the product by work-

---

[48] *Id.* at 839–840.

[49] *Id.* at 840.

[50] *Id.*

ing on it.[51] Comment *l*'s definitions have been adopted by state products liability statutes[52] and by court decisions.[53]

[C] *Bystanders*

In addition to persons who are "uses or consumers" of products, nonusers and nonconsumers of products, such as bystanders, passers-by, rescuers, and pedestrians, also may be injured by defective products.[54] The issue of whether a bystander can recover has arisen both in negligence and strict liability cases. Every court that has considered the question in a negligence case has held that the duty of care owed by manufacturers extends to bystanders injured by their products.[55]

Section 402A states that it expresses no opinion on whether the section should apply to "persons other than users or consumers." However, comment *o* to that section takes the position that there may be "no essential reason why such plaintiffs should not be brought within the scope of the protection afforded, other than that they do not have the same reasons for expecting such protection as the consumer who buys a marketed product." One of the first cases holding that § 402A was available to bystanders was *Elmore v. American Motors Corp.,*[56] in which a defective automobile manufactured by the defendant went out of control and struck the plaintiff's on-coming vehicle. The California Supreme Court based its decision on what it viewed as the principal policy reason for strict liability: "to *insure* that the costs of injuries resulting from defective products are borne by the manufacturers that put such products on the market rather than by the injured persons who are powerless to protect themselves."[57] The court concluded by saying:

---

[51] Bray v. Marathon Corp., 588 S.E.2d 93 (S.C. 2003).

[52] For an example, INDIANA CODE § 34-6-2-29 (1998), defines a "user" for purposes of the state's products liability act as:

    (1) a purchaser;

    (2) any individual who uses or consumes the product;

    (3) any person who, while acting for or on behalf of the injured party, was in possession and control of the product in question; or

    (4) any bystander injured by the product who would reasonably be expected to be in the vicinity of the product during its reasonably foreseeable use.

[53] *See* Anderson v. Smith, 514 N.W.2d 54 (Wis. Ct. App. 1993).

[54] For cases involving the liability of manufacturers to rescuers, see McCoy v. American Suzuki Motor Corp., 961 P.2d 952 (Wash. 1998); Govich v. North American Systems, Inc., 814 P.2d 94 (N.M. 1991); Guarino v. Mine Safety Appliance Co., 255 N.E.2d 173 (N.Y. 1969).

[55] For examples, see *Moning v. Alfono,* 254 N.W.2d 759 (Mich. 1977); *Ragin v. Porter Hayden Co.,* 754 A.2d 503 (Md. Ct. Spec. App. 2000). *See also* RESTATEMENT (SECOND) OF TORTS § 395 cmt *i* (1965).

[56] 451 P.2d 84 (Cal. 1969).

[57] *Id.* at 88.

If anything, bystanders should be entitled to greater protection than the consumer or user where injury to bystanders from the defect is reasonably foreseeable. Consumers and users, at least have the opportunity to inspect for defects and to limit their purchases to articles manufactured by reputable manufacturers and sold by reputable dealers, whereas the bystander ordinarily has no such opportunities.[58]

Other state courts also have extended strict liability to include bystanders.[59] In addition, some state statutes specifically include bystanders within the definition of "consumers" who are entitled to recover.[60]

The term "bystander" usually applies to persons in the immediate vicinity of the product during its use. However, a few courts have expanded its scope to include "domestic bystanders"[61] such as a wife who contracted cancer from inhaling asbestos fibers brought home over many years on the clothes of her husband who worked with the product.[62] By including the cleaning of the clothes, which took place away from the site where the asbestos was used, for purposes of determining who is a bystander, the courts recognizing "domestic bystanders" have expanded recovery to include activities not related to the actual use of the product.

Like § 402, the Restatement (Third) does not state explicitly whether bystanders are entitled to recover. However, the language of § 1 of the Restatement (Third), which states that sellers are liable "for harm to persons or property caused by the defect," does not limit liability to consumers or users and arguably is broad enough to include bystanders.

[D] *Unintended Users and Uses of Products*

Although courts agree that a broad group of persons may recover under negligence and strict liability theories in products liability cases, they are divided over whether the duty owed by manufacturers and sellers in negligence and the definition of "user and consumer" in § 402A extends to unforeseeable or unintended users of a product. Most products liability cases involve injuries to persons who were both the foreseeable and the intended

---

[58] *Id.* at 89.

[59] For examples, see *Moss v. Polyco, Inc.*, 522 P.2d 622 (Okla. 1974); *Howes v. Hansen*, 201 N.W.2d 825 (Wis. 1972); *Darryl v. Ford Motor Co.*, 440 S.W.2d 630 (Tex. 1969); *Threats v. General Motors Corp.*, 890 S.W.2d 327 (Mo. Ct. App. 1994).

[60] *See* INDIANA CODE § 34-6-2-29(4) (1998).

[61] Dube v. Pittsburgh Corning, 870 F.2d 790 (1st Cir. 1989).

[62] Stegemoller v. ACandS, Inc., 767 N.E.2d 974 (Ind. 2002). For a review of the cases, see *Lunsford v. Saberhagen Holdings, Inc.*, 106 P.3d 808 (Wash. Ct. App. 2005) (plaintiff alleged that his cancer was caused by his childhood exposure to asbestos dust brought home by his father, who worked as an insulation installer).

users of the products. However, in some cases, a product may have been used by someone who was foreseeable but was not an intended user. An example of this are products such as disposable cigarette lighters that are marketed to adults and intended for their use that fall into the hands of small children, resulting in injuries to them or to other persons.[63] While some courts permit recovery if the plaintiff was a foreseeable user of the product, others require the plaintiff to have been the intended user.

One the first cases to consider the question of an unintended user of a product was *Winnett v. Winnett*,[64] in which the Illinois Supreme Court used the foreseeability of harm test to determine who is entitled to recover in an action based on § 402A:

> In our judgment the liability of a manufacturer properly encompasses only those individuals to whom injury from a defective product may reasonably be foreseen and only those situations where the product is being used for the purpose for which it was intended or for which it is reasonably foreseeable that it may be used.[65]

According to the court, foreseeability means not only what might occur but also what is objectively reasonable to expect.[66] In *Winnett* a four-year-old was injured when her fingers were caught in the conveyor belt of a forage wagon. The Illinois Supreme Court held the scope of the forage wagon's "intended use" did not include use by a four-year-old child. Because the child was not a "user or consumer" of the product, the court applied a foreseeability test and concluded that it was not "objectively reasonable to expect" the child to place her fingers in the moving screen or belt of the forage wagon.[67] Thus, the court affirmed the dismissal of the plaintiff's complaint.

The same foreseeability test resulted in a plaintiff being able to recover in another Illinois case, *Palmer v. Avco Distributing Corp.*,[68] in which an eleven-year-old child was injured when his leg was caught in the agitator mechanism of a fertilizer spreader designed and manufactured by the defendant. In that case, the Illinois Supreme Court found evidence that farmers customarily allowed people to ride on their farm equipment and that children often accompany their parents by riding on vehicles for pleasure and for work. The court concluded that it was "objectively foreseeable that children of plaintiff's age might ride inside fertilizer spreaders."[69] The

---

[63] *See* Palmer v. Avco Distributing Corp., 841 A.2d 1000 (Pa. 2003).

[64] 310 N.E.2d 1 (Ill. 1974).

[65] *Id*. at 4.

[66] *Id*. at 5.

[67] *Id*.

[68] 412 N.E.2d 959 (Ill. 1980).

[69] *Id*. at 962.

court distinguished *Winnett,* which it said contained no allegation that it was customary for young children to roam unattended near operating farm machinery.[70]

Although many courts use the foreseeability of harm test to determine the scope of the liability of a manufacturer or seller, the Pennsylvania Supreme Court has held that, for purposes of strict liability, a product need only be reasonably safe for its intended user, not for all foreseeable users. *Phillips v. Cricket Lighters*[71] involved a fact situation that has come before a number of courts: persons were killed when a child started a fire while playing with a cigarette lighter that did not have child-proof features. The manufacturers and sellers of the lighters in those cases argued that they owed no duty to those injured since the child was an unintended user of their products. In keeping with its view that negligence and strict liability are distinct legal theories and should not be mixed, the Pennsylvania Supreme Court in *Phillips* stated that the concept of foreseeability had overtones of negligence and should not be imported into strict liability.[72] Because the five-year-old child in *Phillips* was not an intended user of the cigarette lighter, the court held that the manufacturer was not liable under a strict liability theory.

Because the court in *Phillips* viewed negligence and strict liability as separate causes of action, it was able to reject the plaintiff's claim in strict liability while still holding the manufacturer owed those killed in the fire a duty of care in negligence. The court based its finding of a duty on five factors: the relationship between the purchaser of the lighter and the manufacturers; the social utility of the manufacture of the lighter without child safety features; the nature of the risk imposed and the foreseeability of harm resulting from children playing with lighters lacking safety features; the consequences (increased cost) of imposing a duty on the manufacturer of lighters; the overall public interest in imposing a duty on lighter manufacturers to produce a lighter with child proof features.[73] In the Pennsylvania court's view, all five factors weighed in favor of imposing a duty of care on the manufacturer.

§ 4.04 POTENTIAL DEFENDANTS

[A] *Persons "Engaged in the Business of Selling"*

The question of who is a proper defendant in a products liability action arises more often in strict liability actions than it does in negligence cases. This is because the language of § 402A imposes liability only on a person

---

[70] *Id.*

[71] 841 A.2d 1000 (Pa. 2003).

[72] *Id.* at 1006.

[73] *Id.* at 1008-1010.

who "sells" a product in a "defective condition unreasonably dangerous to the user or consumer." However, section 402A does not define a "seller"; it requires only that such a person must be "engaged in the business of selling" the product that injured the plaintiff. According to one federal court, the broader rationale for strict liability explains the specific requirement that the defendant must be a "seller" of the product:

> If the defendant is not engaged in the business of selling the product, then it cannot be said to have "undertaken and assumed [the] special responsibility toward . . . the consuming public." Furthermore, such a defendant has not been afforded the opportunity to treat the risk of producing the product "as a cost of production against which liability insurance [could have been] obtained." Finally, a defendant . . . that did not place the product in commerce has no ability to control the quality of the product or the conformance of the product with its design. The public should not expect to rely upon someone who has not placed the product in the stream of commerce.[74]

Comment *f* to § 402A states that, since the section "applies to any person engaged in the business of selling products for use or consumption," it therefore applies to any manufacturer of such a product, to any wholesale or retail dealer or distributor, and to the operator of a restaurant. Although a few states have statutes[75] or decisions[76] that limit strict liability to the manufacturer and exclude the wholesaler and retailer, most courts and products liability statutes have adopted the views expressed in comment *f* and apply strict liability to everyone in the chain of production and distribution.[77] These persons include: manufacturers,[78] apparent manufactur-

---

[74] Goldsmith v. Olon Andrews, Inc., 941 F.2d 423, 426 (6th Cir. 1991).

[75] The Indiana Products Liability Act (IND. CODE § 34-20-1 (1998)), for example, provides that a strict liability action can be brought only against the manufacturer of a product or the manufacturer of the part of the product alleged to be defective unless the court is unable to exercise jurisdiction over the manufacturer. In such a case, the distributor or seller of the product is considered the manufacturer of the product. *See* Kennedy v. Guess, Inc., 806 N.E.2d 776 (Ind. 2004).

[76] *See* Sam Shainberg Co. of Jackson v. Barlow, 258 So.2d 242 (Miss. 1972).

[77] *See* the Kansas Product Liability Act (KAN. STAT. ANN. § 60-3302(a) (1994)) which defines "product seller" to mean "any person or entity that is engaged in the business of selling products, whether the sale is for resale, or for use or consumption."

[78] Greenman v. Yuba Power Products, Inc., 377 P.2d 897 (Cal. 1962).

ers,[79] wholesalers and distributors,[80] assemblers,[81] retailers,[82] dealers,[83] persons who sell or distribute as their own products manufactured by another;[84] trademark licensors,[85] and lessors and bailors.[86] These same groups of defendants are found in negligence actions as well. Interpreting § 402A to include a broad group of nonmanufacturering sellers who are not responsible for creating the defect has been justified on a number of grounds. Among the reasons that courts have given are: the integral role nonmanufacturing parties play in the production and marketing of defective products; the fact that nonmanufacturing parties often can shift the loss, through indemnification, to the party who, in fact, created the defect; a feeling that nonmanufacturers are in a position to exert pressure on manufacturers for safer products; and the public policy rationale that those in the chain of distribution are involved in, and derive a profit from, placing the defective product in the stream of commerce.[87]

The Restatement (Third) reflects the expansive view of who should be liable for defective products. Section 1 imposes liability on "[o]ne engaged in the business of selling or otherwise distributing products who sells or distributes a defective product." Comment e states that "all commercial sellers and distributors of products, including nonmanufacturing sellers and distributors such as wholesalers and retailers, are subject to liability for selling products that are defective." Section 20(b) defines the term "otherwise distributes":

---

[79] Long v. United States Brass Corp., 333 F. Supp. 2d 999 (D. Colo. 2004) (applying Colorado law).

[80] Fuchsgruber v. Custom Accessories, Inc., 628 N.W.2d 833 (Wis. 2001); Giuffrida v. Panasonic Industrial Co., 607 N.Y.S.2d 72 (N.Y. App. Div. 1994).

[81] Weyerhaeuser Co. v. Thermogas Co., 620 N.W.2d 819 (Iowa 2000).

[82] Moss v. Polyco, 522 P.2d 622 (Okla. 1974); Vandermark v. Ford Motor Co., 391 P.2d 168 (Cal. 1964).

[83] Sabloff v. Yamaha Motor Co., Ltd., 273 A.2d 606 (N.J. App. Div. 1971), aff'd, 283 A.2d 321 (N.J. 1971).

[84] RESTATEMENT (THIRD) OF TORTS § 14 (1998) states:

One engaged in the business of selling or otherwise distributing products who sells ordistributes as its own a product manufactured by another is subject to the same liabilityas though the seller or distributor were the product's manufacturer.

[85] Torres v. Goodyear Tire & Rubber Co., 786 P.2d 939 (Ariz. 1990); Connelly v. Uniroyal, Inc., 389 N.E.2d 155 (Ill. 1979).

[86] For a review of the cases, see Samuel Friedland Family Enterprises v. Amoroso, 630 So.2d 1067 (Fla. 1994) and Kemp v. Miller, 453 N.W.2d 872 (1990). Section 20(b) of the Restatement (Third) applies strict liability to lessors and bailors who "in a commercial transaction . . . [provide a] product to another either for use or consumption or as a preliminary step leading to ultimate use or consumption." Comments c and f to § 20 state that it applies to commercial product leases and product bailments.

[87] Zamora v. Mobil Corp., 704 P.2d 584 (Wash. 1985); Dunham v. Vaughan & Bushnell Manufacturing Co., 247 N.E.2d 401 (Ill. 1969).

One otherwise distributes a product when in a commercial transaction other than a sale, one provides the product to another either for use of consumption or as a preliminary step leading to ultimate sale or consumption. Commercial nonsale product distributors include, but are not limited to, lessors, bailors, and those who provide products to others as a means of promoting either the use or consumption of such products or some other commercial activity.

Although retailers are strictly liable for defects in the products they sell, an actual sale is not required before strict liability attaches. Thus, an automobile dealer that supplied vehicles to its sales staff as a means of promoting the vehicles was held strictly liable for an injury to a third party caused by one of those vehicles.[88] Similarly, sellers who distribute free samples of their products in the hope of making future sales have been held strictly liable for defects in those products.[89] In addition, a seller that provides a product to a customer for a trial period before the actual sale may be strictly liable for an injury caused by the product during that time.[90] In *Mulhern v. Outboard Marine Corp*,[91] the Wisconsin Supreme Court held that the terms "sell" and "seller" in § 402A were merely descriptive and that a product need not actually be sold if it is injected into the "stream of commerce" by other means.[92] The court reasoned that the stream of commerce requirement was consistent with the application of § 402A. The court concluded that the actual sale of the product was not important as long as the defendant was in the business of selling such a product and placed the product in the stream of commerce.[93] The Restatement (Third) continues this approach. Comment *b* to § 1 states that the section applies "not only to sale transactions but also to other forms of commercial product distribution that are the functional equivalent of product sales."

[B] *Special Categories of Sellers*

Courts have given a broad interpretation to § 402A's requirement that the defendant be "engaged in the business of selling." However, there are some areas where courts either are divided as to whether a particular group that participates in placing a product in the stream of commerce should be

---

[88] Beattie v. Beattie, 786 A.2d 549 (Del. Super. Ct. 2001).

[89] McKisson v. Sales Affiliates, Inc., 416 S.W.2d 787 (Tex. 1987). *See also* RESTATEMENT (THIRD) OF TORTS: PRODUCTS LIABILITY § 20 cmt. *b* (1998).

[90] Robert F. Bullock, Inc. v. Thorpe, 353 S.E.2d 340 (Ga. 1987).

[91] 432 N.W.2d 130 (Wis. 1988).

[92] *Id.* at 134.

[93] *Id.*

strictly liable[94] or impose special requirements for liability. The following subsections examine three of those groups.

[1] Component Part Manufacturers

Most products today are composed of a number of component parts produced by different manufacturers and then assembled by the final product manufacturer. Because they no longer are limited by privity, plaintiffs frequently include component part manufacturers as defendants in their products liability suits. Section 402A and comment *q* take no position on the extent of the liability of a component part manufacturer for a defect in the finished product. In response to this silence, courts have held that a component part manufacturer is liable for an injury caused by a finished product if the injury was caused by a component part that was defective at the time it left the control of the part manufacturer. A component part manufacturer also may be liable if it participated in the design of the final product or in the integration of its part into the final product and that part caused the finished product to be defective.[95] However, a component part manufacturer is not liable for supplying a non-defective part or a non-defective part that becomes defective because of substantial change by the assembler of the finished product. These positions are reflected in § 5 of the Restatement (Third) which states:

> One engaged in the business of selling or otherwise distributing components who sells or distributes a component is subject to liability for harm to persons or property caused by a product into which the component is integrated if:
>
> (a) the component is defective in itself . . . and the defect causes the harm; or
>
> (b) (1) the seller or distributor of the component substantially participates in the integration of the component into the design of the product; and
>
>   (2) the integration of the component causes the product to be defective . . . and

---

[94] An example of an area where courts are divided is the liability of trade associations that voluntarily create and set safety standards. See *Meneely v. S.R. Smith, Inc.*, 5 P.3d 49 (Wash. Ct. App. 2000), holding that they can be liable in negligence. However, for a review of cases holding that trade associations are not liable, see *Bailey v. Edward Hines Lumber Co.*, 719 N.E.2d 178 (Ill. App. Ct. 1999).

[95] For a review of the cases dealing with component part manufacturers, see *Thorndike v. DaimlerChrysler Corp.*, 2003 U.S. Dist. LEXIS 8626 (D. Me. 2003); *Bostrom Seating, Inc. v. Crane Carrier Co.*, 140 S.W.3d 681 (Tex. 2004); *Mesa Vista South Townhome Assoc. v. California Portland Cement Co.*, 12 Cal. Rptr. 3d 863 (Cal. Ct. App. 2004).

(3) the defect in the product causes the harm.[96]

The rationale for the Restatement (Third)'s position is stated in comment *a* to § 5: "If the component is not itself defective, it would be unjust and inefficient to impose liability solely on the ground that the manufacturer of the integrated product utilizes the component in a manner that renders the integrated product defective." Thus, a plaintiff must show that the component part was defective when if left the control of the component part manufacturer, that the defect in the component part was the cause of her injury, and that the final product manufacturer did not change the component part substantially.

An example of the liability of a component part manufacturer is *Jimenez v. Superior Court*,[97] in which the California Supreme Court held that a window manufacturer could be held strictly liable for damages that its defective windows caused to other parts of the homes in which they were installed. The court rejected the window manufacturer's argument that it merely supplied component parts of the mass-produced homes, which were the finished products sold to consumers. According to the court:

> The policies underlying strict products liability in tort . . . are equally applicable to component manufacturers and suppliers. . . . For purposes of strict products liability, there are 'no meaningful distinctions' between, on the one hand, component manufacturers and suppliers and, on the other hand, manufacturers and distributors of complete products; forboth groups, the 'overriding policy considerations are the same.'[98]

According to the court, the "overriding policy considerations" that justified strict liability were: first, component part manufacturers are "an integral part of the overall producing and marketing enterprise"; second, they may be "the only member of that enterprise reasonably available to the injured plaintiff"; and, finally, they may be in the best position to ensure product safety, and can adjust the costs of liability in the course of their continuing business relationship with other participants in the manufacturing and marketing process.[99]

In order to overcome the policy arguments in favor of strict liability, the window manufacturer in *Jimenez* raised two arguments. First, it contended that, since the windows were shipped in parts and assembled and installed

---

[96] For a discussion of the Restatement's position, see *Davis v. Komatsu America Industries, Corp.*, 42 S.W.3d 34 (Tenn. 2001), and David A. Fischer, *Product Liability: A Commentary on the Liability of Suppliers of Component Parts and Raw Materials*, 53 S.C. L. REV. 1137 (2002); Hildy Bowbeer, *Liability for Component Parts and Raw Materials*, 10 KAN. J.L. & PUB. POL'Y 110 (2000).

[97] 58 P.3d 450 (Cal. 2002).

[98] *Id.* at 454.

[99] *Id.*

by the home builder, they underwent "substantial change" from the time they left the control of the manufacturer. The court answered that argument by stating that "[t]he mere assembly of a product that is sold in parts is not a 'substantial change' in the product."[100] Second, the window manufacturer claimed that it did not have physical control over the windows when they were installed in the homes. In response, the court stated: "Rarely, if ever, are defective products still in the control of a manufacturer, distributor, or retailer at the time of injury to the consumer. What matters is whether the windows were defective when they left the factory, and whether these alleged defects caused the injuries."[101]

[2] Sellers of Used Products

Courts are divided on the question of whether a commercial seller of used goods can be strictly liable if the product is defective. The majority of states hold that § 402A is not applicable to commercial sellers of used products in the absence of an allegation that the seller created the defect in the product.[102] One of the first cases to deal with the question of liability for the sale of used products was *Peterson v. Lou Backrodt Chevrolet Co.*[103] In that case, the Illinois Supreme Court refused to extend strict liability to a used car dealer and restricted the "creation of the risk" to the actual creation of a defect. The court justified the exemption of sellers of used products from strict liability on four grounds: first, unlike sellers and distributors of new products, sellers of used products are outside the original chain of production and marketing that placed the product in the stream of commerce; second, sellers of used products lack the ability to exert pressure upon manufacturers to produce safe products; third, sellers of used products are not entitled to indemnification from the party who actually created the defect; and finally, if strict liability were imposed upon sellers of used products, they would become, in effect, insurers against defects that came into existence after the chain of distribution was completed and while the product was under the control of one or more consumers.[104]

Almost twenty years after *Peterson*, a federal district court in Missouri, in *Harber v. Altec Industries, Inc.,*[105] reviewed the cases and policy consid-

---

[100] *Id.*

[101] *Id.*

[102] For a review of the cases and arguments for and against extending strict liability to sellers of used products, see *Allenberg v. Bentley Hedges Travel Service, Inc.*, 22 P.3d 223 (Okla. 2001).

[103] 329 N.E.2d 785 (Ill. 1975).

[104] *Id.* at 787. *See also* Pacific National Insurance Co. v. Gormsen Appliance Co., 284 Cal. Rptr. 78 (Cal. Ct. App. 1991).

[105] 812 F. Supp. 954 (W.D. Mo. 1993), *aff'd*, 5 F.3d 339 (8th Cir. 1993).

erations both for and against imposing strict liability on commercial sellers of used goods. The court concluded that extending strict liability to sellers of used goods would not further the rationales behind strict liability: risk spreading, risk reduction through increased inspection, risk reduction through market pressure, and meeting consumer expectations.[106] The only factor that it found weighed in favor of strict liability of sellers of used goods was victim compensation.[107] Although that is an important goal, the court felt that it did not outweigh all of the factors that weighed heavily against strict liability in such cases.[108]

Courts that have held dealers in used goods liable under § 402A also have appealed to the policy justifications behind the adoption of strict liability.[109] They have pointed out that the term "seller" does not require that the person be the first in the chain of sellers. They also have reasoned that strict liability would encourage risk reduction because dealers would increase their inspection and maintenance before resale.[110] Thus, courts have imposed strict liability on sellers of used goods that rebuild or recondition the used goods.[111] Section 8 of the Restatement (Third) also imposes liability for personal injury or property damage on commercial sellers or distributors of used products but only if the defect:

(a) arises from the seller's failure to exercise reasonable care; or

(b) is a manufacturing defect . . . and the seller's marketing of the product would cause a reasonable person in the position of the buyer to expect the used product to present no greater risk of defect than if the product were new; or

(c) is a defect . . . in a used product remanufactured by the seller or a predecessor in the commercial chain of distribution of the used product; or

(d) arises from a used product's noncompliance . . . with a product safety statute or regulation applicable to the used product.

---

[106] *Id*. at 961-965.

[107] *Id*. at 965.

[108] *Id*. at 965-966.

[109] *See* Galindo v. Precision American Corp., 754 F.2d 1212 (5th Cir. 1985) (applying Texas law); Harber v. Altec Industries, Inc., 812 F. Supp. 954 (W.D. Mo. 1993) (applying Missouri law); Nelson v. Nelson Hardware, Inc., 467 N.W.2d 518 (Wis. 1991).

[110] *See* Stanton v. Carlson Sales, Inc., 728 A.2d 534 (Conn. Super. Ct. 1998); Jordan v. Sunnyslope Appliance Propane & Plumbing Supplies Co., 660 P.2d 1236 (Ariz. Ct. App. 1983).

[111] Crandell v. Larkin and Jones Appliance Co., 334 N.W.2d 31 (S.D. 1983).

[3] Successor Corporations

One of the most litigated, and controversial, issues in products liability law is the liability of a successor corporation for injuries caused by a product manufactured and marketed by its predecessor company, the total assets of which have been acquired by merger or purchase by the successor corporation.[112] Courts deal with this problem by holding that a corporation that merges with another corporation assumes the latter corporation's liabilities;[113] however, a corporation that purchases all of the assets of another corporation is not liable for the liabilities of the transferor.[114] Courts recognize four exceptions to this general rule of nonliability of a successor corporation: (1) the transaction amounts to a consolidation or merger of the purchaser and seller corporation; (2) the purchaser corporation is merely a continuation of the seller corporation; (3) there is an express or implied agreement to assume the selling corporation's liabilities; or (4) the transaction is for the fraudulent purpose of escaping liability for the seller's obligations.[115] In those four situations, a corporation that purchases the assets of the other corporation assumes the latter's debts and liabilities.[116] Section 12 of the Restatement (Third) adopts this approach to the liability of a successor corporation.[117]

The first two of the above exceptions to the general rule of nonliability of a successor corporation, which involve the most commonly litigated situations, are based on the concept that a successor corporation that effectively takes over a company in its entirety should carry the predecessor's liabilities as a concomitant to the benefits it derives from the goodwill purchased. Courts reason that allowing recovery in tort against a successor corporation is merely an extension of the concept of products liability, which calls for the burden of consumer injuries to be borne by the manufacturer, who can transfer the costs to the general public as a component of the selling price. Strict liability assures that a responsible source is available to compensate the injured party.[118]

---

[112] For a discussion of successor liability, see Marie T. Reilly, *Making Sense of Successor Liability*, 31 HOFSTRA L. REV. 745 (2003); Note, *Successor Liability, Mass Tort, and Mandatory-Litigation Class Action*, 118 HARV. L. REV. 2357 (2005).

[113] Myers v. Pulameister Inc., 596 N.E.2d 754 (Ill. App. Ct. 1992).

[114] City Management Corp. v. U.S. Chemical Co., Inc., 43 F.3d 244 (6th Cir. 1994).

[115] Dayton v. Peck, Stow, & Wilcox Co., 739 F.2d 690 (1st Cir. 1984) (applying Massachusetts law); Savage Arms, Inc. v. Western Auto Supply Co., 19 P.3d 49 (Alaska 2001).

[116] *See* Arnold Graphics Indus. v. Independent Agent Center, 775 F.2d 38, 42 (2d Cir. 1985) (applying New York law); Dayton v. Peck, Stow & Wilcox Co., 739 F.2d 690, 692 (1st Cir. 1984) (applying Massachusetts law); Tucker v. Paxson Mach. Co., 645 F.2d 620, 622 (8th Cir. 1981) (citing Missouri law).

[117] For a discussion of the history and rational for these exceptions, see RESTATEMENT (THIRD) OF TORTS: PRODUCTS LIABILITY § 12 cmts. *a* and *b* (1998).

[118] *See Dayton*, 739 F.2d 690; *Tucker*, 645 F.2d 620.

When a *de facto* merger or consolidation is alleged, a court must determine the substance of the agreement, regardless of the title put on it by the parties.[119] If the parties have not complied with the statutory requirements for a *de jure* merger, but still have achieved virtually all the results of a merger, a court may hold the surviving corporation liable for the conduct of the transferor corporation as if the merger were *de jure*. Courts generally impose four requirements for the recognition of the purported sale of assets as a *de facto* merger: (1) continuity of the business enterprise between the seller and buyer, including continuity of management, personnel, physical location, assets, and general business operations; (2) continuity of shareholders which results from the purchasing corporation paying for the acquired assets with shares of its own stock, this stock ultimately coming to be held by the shareholders of the seller corporation so that they become a constituent part of the purchasing corporation; (3) the seller corporation ceases its ordinary business operations, liquidates, and dissolves as soon as legally and practically possible; and (4) the purchasing corporation assumes those obligations of the seller ordinarily necessary for the uninterrupted continuation of normal business operations of the seller corporation.[120]

Since a successor corporation often continues to manufacture and market the products of its predecessor, courts have considered whether to adopt an additional "product line" exception for successor corporations.[121] Under this exception, a successor corporation that continues to manufacture a product of the business it acquires, regardless of the method of acquisition or any possible attribution of fault, assumes strict liability for products manufactured and sold before the change of corporate ownership. Although some courts recognize the "product line" exception in products liability cases, a majority of states, and the Restatement (Third), reject the exception as incompatible with the doctrine of strict liability in tort.[122] These courts base their rejection of a product line exception on one or more of three arguments: (1) the exception is inconsistent with elementary products liability principles, and strict liability principles in particular, in that it results in an imposition of liability without a corresponding duty; (2) the exception threatens small successor businesses with economic annihilation because of

---

[119] Philadelphia Electric Co. v. Hercules, Inc., 762 F.2d 303 (3d Cir. 1985) (applying Pennsylvania law).

[120] *See* Arnold Graphics Industries v. Independent Agent Center, 775 F.2d 38 (2d Cir. 1985) (applying New York law); Keller v. Clark Equipment Co., 715 F.2d 1280 (8th Cir. 1983) (applying North Dakota law).

[121] Ray v. Alad Corp., 560 P.2d 3 (Cal. 1977).

[122] For a discussion of the states that have adopted and rejected the product line theory, see *Pearson v. National Feeding Systems, Inc.*, 90 S.W.3d 46 (Ky. 2002); *Guzman v. MRM/Elgin*, 567 N.E.2d 929 (Mass. 1991); *Guerrero v. Allison Engine Co.*, 725 N.E.2d 479 (Ind. Ct. App. 2000). Under the RESTATEMENT (THIRD) OF TORTS: PRODUCTS LIABILITY § 12 (1998), the liability of a successor corporation does not include the product line exception.

the difficulty involved in obtaining insurance for defects in a predecessor's product; and (3) the exception is essentially a radical change in the principles of corporation law, and, as such, should be left to legislative action.[123]

[C] *Persons Not Covered by Strict Liability*

Despite the broad scope of potential defendants in a products liability action, courts have not imposed strict liability on everyone involved with the manufacture or distribution of a defective product. Parties that have been held not to be strictly liable for a defective product include:

Employers: A large number of products liability cases involve workers who were injured by machinery during their course of their employment. Because state workers' compensation laws are the exclusive remedy for employees who suffer personal injuries in the course of their employment, these workers are not able to bring negligence or strict liability actions against their employers, even where their employers designed and manufactured the product for the use of their employees.[124] However, injured employees may bring products liability suits against the manufacturers and sellers of the machines that caused their injuries.

Government Contractors: The government contractor defense protects suppliers and contractors from liability for design defects where the United States approved reasonably precise specifications, the equipment conformed to those specifications, and the supplier warned the United States about the dangers in the use of the equipment.[125]

Installers and Repairers: A person who simply installs a product manufactured by someone else is not strictly liable under § 402A.[126] Similarly, a person who repairs a product after it has been manufactured and sold is not strictly liable.[127] The reason for this is that the policy behind strict liability does not apply to a person who is not involved in the sale of the product, receives no profit from placing it in the stream of commerce and thus has no influence over the manufacturer.[128] However, an installer or repairer who also manufacturers or supplies the defective product may be strictly

---

[123] *See* Conn v. Fales Division of Mathewson Corp., 835 F.2d 145 (6th Cir. 1987) (applying Kentucky law); Niccum v. Hydra Tool Corp., 438 N.W.2d 96 (Minn. 1989); Ray v. Alad, 560 P.3d 3 (Cal. 1977).

[124] However, an employer's immunity does not apply to intentional torts. Vermett v. Fred Christen & Sons Co., 741 N.E.2d 954 (Ohio 2000). For a discussion of workers' compensation statutes, see Chapter 9.

[125] Boyle v. United Technologies Corp., 487 U.S. 500 (1988). The government contractor defense is discussed in detail in Chapter 9.

[126] Counts v. MK-Ferguson Co., 862 F.2d 1338 (8th Cir. 1988) (applying Missouri law).

[127] Caine v. Tech Air of CT, Inc., 2003 Conn. Super. LEXIS 2645 (Conn. Super. Ct. 2003).

[128] Hinojasa v. Automatic Elevator Co., 416 N.E.2d 45, 47 (Ill. App. Ct. 1980).

liable.[129] Similarly, an installer or repairer may be liable in negligence for their work.[130]

Occasional Sellers: An occasional seller that is not engaged in selling the product as part of its business is not strictly liable unless it actually created the defect.[131] This includes both the individual who makes an isolated sale of an item and a company that sells equipment if its primary business is not selling such equipment.[132] According to comment *f* to § 402A, the reason for excluding occasional sellers from strict liability is

> the ancient one of the special responsibility for the safety of the public undertaken by one who enters into the business of supplying human beings with products which may endanger the safety of their persons and property, and the forced reliance upon that undertaking on the part of those who purchase such goods. This basis is lacking in the case of the ordinary individual who makes the isolated sale, and he is not liable to a third person, or even to his buyer, in the absence of his negligence.[133]

The Restatement (Third) also applies only to manufacturers and other commercial sellers and distributors who are engaged in the business of selling or distributing the type of product that harmed the plaintiff. Since it does not apply to a noncommercial seller or distributor, "it does not apply to one who sells foodstuffs to a neighbor, nor does it apply to the private owner of an automobile who sells it to another."[134]

Premises Owners: Courts have refused to hold that someone who simply owns the premises on which a defective product was located is strictly liable.[135]

Service Providers: Strict liability does not apply to transactions that involve both a "service," such as those provided by physicians, dentists and hospitals, and a "sale" of a product if the service is the primary purpose of the transaction and the transfer of the product is secondary.[136] The Restate-

---

[129] Lukowski v. Vecta Educational Corp., 401 N.E.2d 781 (Ind. Ct. App. 1980).

[130] Ayala v. V. & O. Press Co., 512 N.Y.S.2d 704 (N.Y. App. Div. 1987).

[131] Sprung v. MTR Ravensburg, Inc., 788 N.E.2d 620 (N.Y. 2003); Engel v. Corrigan Company-Mechanical Contractors, Inc., 148 S.W.3d 28 (Mo. Ct. App. 2004).

[132] Geboy v. TRL, Inc., 159 F.2d 993 (7th Cir. 1998) (applying Wisconsin law); Gebo v. Black Clawson Co., 703 N.E.2d 1234 (N.Y. 1998) (casual seller may have a limited duty to warn the buyer of known, non-obvious defects).

[133] For a discussion of the policy reasons involved in deciding whether an occasional seller is strictly liable, see *Carollo v. Al Warren Oil Co.*, 820 N.E.2d 994 (Ill. App. Ct. 2004).

[134] RESTATEMENT (THIRD) OF TORTS: PRODUCTS LIABILITY § 1 cmt. *c* (1998).

[135] Peterson v. Superior Court, 899 P.2d 905 (Cal. 1995); Armstrong v. Cione, 738 P.2d 79 (Hi. 1987); Siciliano v. Capitol City Shows, Inc., 475 A.2d 19 (N.H. 1984).

[136] *See* Budding v. SSM Healthcare System, 19 S.W.3d 678 (Mo. 2000); Royer v. Catholic Medical Center, 741 A.2d 74 (N.H. 1999); Cafazzo v. Central Medical Health Services, Inc., 668 A.2d 521 (Pa. 1995). However, if there is a clear "sale" of a product, courts have been willing

ment (Third) adopts this position as well, stating that "[s]ervices, even when provided commercially, are not products."[137] Thus, courts have held that the sale/service exempts pharmacist from strict liability for dispensing prescription drugs.[138] However, as with installers and repairers, suppliers of product-related services may be liable in negligence.

[D] *Distributor Statutes*

In order to help nonmanufacturing sellers avoid the expenses of defending products liability suits, some states have enacted statutes permitting their dismissal under certain conditions. While some of these statutes apply only to suits based on strict liability,[139] others apply to negligence actions as well.[140] Although each statute is different, one example is the North Dakota Product Liability Act.[141] The statute provides that, in any products liability action against a defendant who did not manufacture the product, the nonmanufacturing defendant must, when answering or otherwise pleading, "file an affidavit certifying the correct identity of the manufacturer of the product allegedly causing the personal injury, death, or damage to property."[142] Defendants who file an uncontroverted affidavit certifying the identity of the manufacturer then are dismissed from the action unless the plaintiff can show:

(a) That the certifying seller exercised some significant control over the design or manufacture of the product, or provided instructions or warnings to the manufacturer relative to the alleged defect in the product which caused the personal injury, death, or damage to property.

(b) That the certifying seller had actual knowledge of the defect in the product which caused the personal injury, death, or damage to property.

(c) That the certifying seller created the defect in the product which caused the personal injury, death, or damage to property.[143]

---

to impose strict liability, at least on non-medical workers who also provide a "service" to their customers. *See* Newmark v. Gimbel's, Inc., 258 A.2d 697 (N.J. 1969).

[137] RESTATEMENT (THIRD) OF TORTS: PRODUCTS LIABILITY § 19(b) (1998).

[138] *See* Madison v. American Home Products Corp., 595 S.E.2d 493 (S.C. 2004); Makripodis by Makripodis v. Merrell-Dow Pharmaceuticals, 523 A.2d 374 (Pa. Super. Ct. 1987); Docken v. Ciba-Geigy, 739 P.2d 591 (Or. Ct. App. 1987).

[139] *See* the Illinois Distributor Statute, 735 ILL. COMP. STAT. 5/2-621 (2002).

[140] *See* N.J. STAT. ANN. § 2A:58C-9 (2000); TEX. CIV. PRAC. & REM. CODE § 82.003 (Vernon 2003).

[141] N.D. CENT. CODE, § 28-01.2-01 (2003).

[142] *Id.* § 28-01.3-04 (1).

[143] *Id.* § 28-01.3-04(2). *See* Paracelsus Healthcare Corp. v. Phillis Electronics North America, 2000 U.S. Dist. LEXIS 20607 (D. N.D. 2000) (applying North Dakota law).

At any time before the trial begins, however, the plaintiff may move to vacate the dismissal order and reinstate the certifying seller if the plaintiff can show either that the applicable statute of limitation bars a products liability action against the manufacturer of the product or that the identity of the manufacturer given to the plaintiff by the certifying defendant was incorrect.[144]

The North Dakota statute also provides for indemnification of the seller for damages and costs in certain situations where a suit is filed against it. Thus, if an action is filed against a seller, and the plaintiff alleges that

- a product was defectively designed, contained defectively manufactured parts, had insufficient safety guards, or had inaccurate or insufficient warnings; that the condition existed when the product left the manufacturer's control;

- the seller has not substantially altered the product; and

- the defective condition or lack of safety guards or adequate warnings caused theplaintiff's injury or damage,

then, the manufacturer of the product must assume the cost of defense of the action, and any liability that may be imposed on the seller. The obligation to assume the seller's cost of defense also extends to actions in which the manufacturer and seller ultimately are found not liable.[145] This is in keeping with the purpose of the statute which is to relieve retailers when they are sued only because they sold the product.[146]

§ 4.05 WHAT IS A PRODUCT?

[A] *Introduction*

Essential to the application of § 402A is a finding that the plaintiff was injured by a "product" that was in a "defective condition unreasonably dangerous" to the user or consumer when it left the control of the manufacturer or seller.[147] A determination that the item that injured the plaintiff was a "product" is not an issue in negligence cases since the focus is on whether the manufacturer or seller owed a duty to the plaintiff and the causal connection between the conduct of the manufacturer or seller and the harm.

---

[144] *Id.* § 28-01.3-04(3).

[145] *Id.* § 28-01.3-05.

[146] Kaylor v. Iseman Mobile Homes, 369 N.W.2d 101 (N.D. 1985).

[147] Courts have stated that strict liability applies only to a "product" that is in a finished condition when it left the manufacturer's control. Ettinger v. Triangle-Pacific Corp., 799 A.2d 95 (Pa. Super. Ct. 2002).

Section 402A and its comments do not define a "product." However, comment *d* provides a list of some examples of products where strict liability applies. According to the comment:

> The rule stated in this section is not limited to the sale of food for human consumption or other products for intimate body use, although it will obviously include them. It extends to any product sold in the condition, or substantially the same condition, in which it is expected to reach the ultimate user or consumer. Thus the rule stated applied to an automobile, a tire, an airplane, a grinding wheel, a water heater, a gas stove, a power tool, a riveting machine, a chair and an insecticide.

States that have enacted products liability statutes have included very broad definitions of a "product" in those statutes. For example, Arkansas defines a "product" as "any tangible object or goods produced."[148] However, since only a few states have products liability statutes, it is up to the courts to determine whether specific items are a "product" within the meaning of § 402A. In making their decisions, courts have stated that "the policy reasons underlying the strict products liability concept should be considered in determining whether something is a product . . . rather than . . . focus[ing] on the dictionary definition of the word."[149]

The definition of a "product" in the Restatement (Third) reflects the comments to § 402A, state statutes such as the one in Arkansas, and the decisions of state courts. According to § 19 of the Restatement (Third), "[a] product is tangible personal property distributed commercially for use or consumption." Because of the breadth of this definition, the specific question of what constitutes a "product" is not an issue in most situations. However, there have been a number of cases in which courts have been required to decide whether the particular item that was the source of the plaintiff's injuries or damages was a "product" within the meaning of § 402A. The following subsections briefly examine six of those areas.

[B] *Animals*

In the debate over whether animals, such as household pets and commercial livestock, are "products" for purposes of § 402A, courts are divided between those that follow the New York approach or the Illinois approach. In *Beyer v. Aquarium Supply Co.*,[150] a store employee became ill after com-

---

[148] Ark. Code Ann. § 16-116-102(2) (Michie 2003). In *Engelhardt v. Rogers Group, Inc.*, 132 F. Supp. 2d 757 (E.D. Ark. 2001), a federal district court applied the Arkansas statute and concluded that a resurfaced highway was not a "product."

[149] Lowrie v. City of Evanston, 365 N.E.2d 923, 928 (Ill. App. Ct. 1977). *See also* Kaneko v. Hilo Coast Processing, 654 P.2d 343 (Haw. 1982); Perez v. Fidelity Container Corp., 682 N.E.2d 1150 (Ill. App. Ct. 1997).

[150] 404 N.Y.S.2d 778 (N.Y. Sup. Ct. 1977)

ing in contact with allegedly diseased hamsters that had been distributed by the defendant. In a suit based on strict liability, a New York court rejected the defendant's argument that the doctrine of strict liability should be limited to cases involving manufactured products. Since the court viewed the purposes of strict liability as distributing the inevitable losses of commercial activity and promoting the marketing of safe products, it stated that "[t]here is no reason why a breeder, distributor or vendor who places a diseased animal in the stream of commerce should be less accountable for his actions than one who markets a defective manufactured product."[151] Connecticut[152] and Oregon[153] courts also have taken the position that animals are "products."

The opposite position is taken by those states that follow the Illinois approach that animals are not "products" within the meaning of § 402A.[154] In *Whitmer v. Schneblk,*[155] the owners of a dog that bit a young child sought indemnification under strict liability from the seller of the animal. The Illinois Appellate Court refused to apply strict liability, saying that the nature of the item must be fixed when it leaves the manufacturer's control and that it must reach the consumer without substantial change.[156] The court concluded that a dog's character is shaped by the purchaser who creates the risk and should bear the liability.[157] Similarly, in *Anderson v. Farmer Hybria Co.*[158] the Illinois Appellate Court held that pigs were not products under § 402A. In *Anderson*, pigs purchased from the defendant arrived in a diseased condition that spread to the plaintiff's other pigs. The court denied the plaintiff's claim for damage in strict liability, saying:

> While a "product" may be unchanged from its natural state, viable and not the result of manufacturing processes, it must also be of a fixed nature at the time it leaves the seller's control. . . . .Living creatures . . . are by their nature in a constant process of internal development and growth and they are also participants in a constant interaction with the environment around them as part of the development. . . . .[N]owhere in the commentary to section 402A are living things brought within the definition of a "product," nor have the plaintiffs been able to cite us to any case from any jurisdiction which has held a living creature to be a "product."[159]

---

[151] *Id.* at 779.

[152] Worrell v. Sachs, 563 A.2d 1387 (Conn. Super. Ct. 1989) (puppy).

[153] Sease v. Taylor's Pets, Inc., 700 P.2d 1054 (Or. Ct. App. 1985) (rabid pet skunk).

[154] *See* Kaplan v. C Lazy U Ranch, 615 F. Supp. 234 (D. Col. 1985) (applying Colorado law) (horse ride); Blaha v. Stuard, 640 N.W.2d 85 (S.D. 2002) (dog); Latham v. Wal-Mart Stores, Inc., 818 S.W.2d 673 (Mo. Ct. App. 1991) (parrot).

[155] 331 N.E.2d 115 (Ill. App. Ct. 1975).

[156] *Id.* at 119.

[157] *Id.*

[158] 408 N.E.2d 1194 (Ill. App. Ct. 1980).

[159] *Id.* at 1199.

Although an animal may not be a "product" for purposes of strict liability, a retailer still may be liable for the under a theory of negligence for the failure to warn of diseases in the animal.[160]

[C] *Blood and Human Tissue*

Each year thousands of persons suffer injury or death as the result of blood borne pathogens resulting from transfusions. These pathogens include malaria, syphilis, brucellosis, hepatitis and the human immunodeficiency virus (HIV). Some courts initially held that the hospitals that performed blood transfusions were strictly liable on the grounds that blood was a "product" for purposes of § 402A.[161] However, state legislatures quickly overruled those decisions by enacting blood shield statutes which provide that hospitals and distributors of blood products are not strictly liable for injuries caused by blood transfusions.[162] Some of these statutes, and the cases interpreting them, hold that blood is not a "product" for purposes of strict liability,[163] while others classify the transfusion of blood as a medical "service" rather than a "sale,"[164] or hold that blood is an unavoidably unsafe product.[165] Courts have used the same rationales to hold that tissue banks are not strictly liable for providing human tissue for use in medical procedures.[166] The Restatement (Third) reflects these views by stating that "[h]uman bloods and human tissue, even when provided commercially, are not subject to the rules of this Restatement."[167]

---

[160] Malicki v. Koci, 700 N.E.2d 913 (Ohio Ct. App. 1997) (parakeet).

[161] DeBattista v. Argonaut-Southwest Ins. Co., 403 So.2d 26 (La. 1981); Rostocki v. Southwest Florida Blood Bank, Inc., 276 So.2d 475 (Fla. 1973); Cunningham v. MacNeal Memorial Hosp., 266 N.E.2d 897 (Ill. 1970).

[162] For examples of these statutes, see ALA. CODE § 7-2-314(4) (2002); 745 ILL. COMP. STAT. 40/1 (2002); KY. REV. STAT. ANN. § 139.125 (Michie 2001); S.C. CODE ANN. § 44-43-10 (Law. Coop. 2002).

[163] Samson v. The Greenville Hospital System, 377 S.E.2d 311 (S.C. 1989).

[164] For examples, see ALA. CODE § 7-2-314(4) (2002); CAL. HEALTH AND SAFETY CODE § 1606 (West 1990) KY. REV. STAT. ANN. § 139.125 (Michie 2001). *See* McKee v. Cutter Laboratories, Inc., 866 F.2d 219 (6th Cir. 1989) (applying Kentucky law); Brandt v. Boston Scientific, 792 N.E.2d 296 (Ill. 2003); McCombs v Southern Regional Medical Center, 504 S.E.2d 747 (Ga. Ct. App. 1998).

[165] Doe v. Miles Laboratories, Inc., 927 F.2d 187 (4th Cir. 1991) (applying Maryland law); Chauvin v. Sisters of Mercy Health System, 818 So.2d 833 (La Ct. App. 2002).

[166] Condos v. Musculoskeletal Transplant Foundation, 208 F. Supp. 2d 1226 (D. Utah 2002) (applying Utah law); Cryolife, Inc. v. Superior Court of Santa Cruz County, 2 Cal Rptr. 3d 396 (Cal. Ct. App. 2003).

[167] RESTATEMENT (THIRD) OF TORTS: PRODUCTS LIABILITY § 19(c) (1998). *See also* the discussion of "human bloods and human tissue" in § 19 cmt. *c.*

[D] *Electricity*

Another subject that has given rise to a number of cases is electricity. Many of these cases have arisen as the result of accidental contact with allegedly defective high voltage transmission lines. These cases raise two questions for the courts: first, is electricity a "product" for purposes of § 402A and, second, if it is a "product," have the elements of strict liability been met when the injury results from contact with transmission lines?

As to the first issue, most courts have held that electricity can be a "product" for purposes of § 402A.[168] The rational for this position was stated in *Elgin Airport Inn v. Commonwealth Edison Co.*,[169] in which the plaintiff sought recovery for damages sustained by its air-conditioning system when the defendant delivered dangerous low-voltage electricity. According to the Illinois Appellate Court: "[E]lectrical energy is artificially manufactured, can be measured, bought and sold, exchanged in quantity and quality, delivered wherever desired and has been held by our Supreme Court to be personal property whose unlawful transportation is larceny."[170] Although the Illinois Supreme Court later reversed on the grounds that the level of current was not unreasonably dangerous, the court accepted the Appellate Court's finding that electricity is a "product" within the meaning of section 402A.[171] However, the opposite position is taken by courts that hold that electricity is a "service," not a "product" and that strict liability does not apply to services. According to the Ohio Supreme Court: "Consumers . . . are not paying for individual products but for the privilege of using [the electric company's] service."[172]

Although courts are not in complete agreement as to whether electricity is a "product" or a "service," they do agree that personal injury or property damage caused by contact with a high voltage transmission line does not fall within § 402A.[173] Courts have given a number of reasons for their position that electricity is not a "product" prior to delivery to the consumer: (1) the electricity flowing through the power line was not in a "marketable" condition at the time of the injury;[174] (2) defects in the transmission lines car-

---

[168] *See* Houston Lighting & Power Co. v. Reynolds, 765 S.W.2d 784 (Tex. 1988); Smith v. Home Light & Power Co., 734 P.2d 1051 (Colo. 1987); Ransome v. Wisconsin Electric Power Co., 275 N.W.2d 641, 643 (Wis. 1979).

[169] 410 N.E.2d 620 (Ill. App. Ct. 1980).

[170] *Id.* at 624.

[171] Elgin Airport Inn, Inc. v. Commonwealth Edison Co., 432 N.E.2d 259 (Ill. 1982).

[172] Otte v. Dayton Power & Light Co., 523 N.E.2d 835, 839 (Ohio 1988). *See also* Bowen v. Niagara Mohawk Power Corp., 590 N.Y.S.2d 628 (N.Y. App. Div. 1992).

[173] *See* Smith v. Home Light and Power Co., 734 P.2d 1051 (Colo. 1987); Wirth v. Mayrath Industries, Inc. 278 N.W.2d 789 (N.D. 1979); Wood v. Public Service Company of New Hampshire 317 A.2d 576 (N.H. 1974).

[174] Genaust v. Illinois Power Co. 343 N.E.2d 465 (Ill. 1976).

rying the electrical current are not sufficient to create liability since the lines are not "packaging" for the current, are not sold to the consumer, and remain owned by and under the exclusive control of the electric company at the time of the injury;[175] and (3) until the electricity has passed through the customer's electric meter, it has not been placed in the "stream of commerce."[176] The Restatement (Third) retains the distinction between pre- and post-delivery. According to § 19, electricity is a product when "the context of [its] distribution and use is sufficiently analogous to the distribution and use of tangible personal property that it is appropriate to apply the rules stated in this Restatement."

[E] *Information*

Another question that has confronted courts is whether "information" contained in books, maps, charts and the electronic media is a "product" for purposes of § 402A. Courts have been unwilling to extend strict liability to publishers for ideas contained in books or magazines.[177] The leading case in this area is *Winter v. G. P. Putnam's Sons*,[178] in which the plaintiff became ill from eating mushrooms after relying on information in *The Encyclopedia of Mushrooms* published by the defendant. Although the physical book was a "product," the Ninth Circuit refused to apply § 402A to the information contained in the book on the ground that the language of strict liability reflects its focus on tangible items. The court also felt that the "cost" of applying strict liability to words and idea in books would be too high. According to the court:

> We place a high priority on the unfettered exchange of ideas. We accept the risk that words and ideas have winds we cannot clip and which carry them we know not where. The threat of liability without fault (financial responsibility for our words and ideas in the absence of fault or a special undertaking or responsibility) could serious inhibit those who wish to share thoughts and theories.[179]

Although the plaintiff in *Winter* argued that strict liability be applied only to books that give instruction on how to accomplish a physical activity and that are intended to be used as part of an activity that is inherently dan-

---

[175] Monroe v. Savannah Elec. & Power Co., 471 S.E.2d 854 (Ga. 1996).

[176] For a discussion of the tests used by courts to determine whether electricity has been "sold," see *Darling v. Central Vermont Public Service Corp.*, 762 A.2d 826 (Vt. 2000). *See also* Bryant v. Tri-County Electric Membership Corp., 844 F. Supp. 347 (W.D. Ky. 1994) (applying Kentucky law); Bowen v. Niagara Mohawk Power Corp., 590 N.Y.S.2d 628 (N.Y. App. Div. 1992).

[177] Jones v. J. B. Lippincott, 694 F. Supp. 1216 (D. Md. 1988); Herceg v. Hustler Magazine, 565 F. Supp. 802 (S.D. Tex. 1983); Appleby v. Miller, 554 N.E.2d 773 (Ill. App. Ct. 1990).

[178] 938 F.2d 1033 (9th Cir. 1991) (applying California law).

[179] *Id.* at 1035.

gerous, the Ninth Circuit felt that the such a limitation was "illusory."[180] However, one area where courts have been willing to impose strict liability is to nautical and airline maps and charts. Courts have justified this on the grounds that maps and charts are analogous to other navigational instruments such as a compass or radar which, when defective, will be dangerous[181] and that maps and charts are used for their physical characteristics rather than for ideas.[182]

In recent years, the rise of new forms of communication has confronted courts with the question whether video games, movies, and internet sites are "products."[183] In *James v. Meow Media, Inc.*,[184] a high school student shot several of his fellow students, killing three and wounding a number of others. The parents of the victims brought suit in negligence and strict liability, alleging that the shooter regularly watched video games, movies and internet sites produced by the defendant firms that "desensitized" him to violence and caused him to kill his fellow students. The federal district court in Kentucky held that the firms owed no duty in negligence to protect third parties from how viewers or players processed the ideas and images in their games, movies and internet sites. This is consistent with the approach of courts which uniformly have refused to expand the scope of negligence to media broadcasters and publishers for allegedly defective information.[185] The court also held that, while the video game cartridges and movie cassettes were tangible "products," the "words and pictures" they contained were not "products" for purposes of § 402A.[186] Other courts have followed this approach and have held that intangible thoughts, ideas, and expressive content are not "products" within the meaning of strict liability.[187]

[F] *Raw Materials*

Section 402A contains a "caveat" that "[t]he Institute expresses no opinion as to whether the rules stated in this Section may not apply . . . (2) to the seller of a product expected to be processed or otherwise substantially

---

[180] *Id.*

[181] Way v. Boy Scouts of America, 856 S.W.2d 230 (Tex. App. 1993).

[182] Fluor Corp. v. Jeppesen & Co., 216 Cal. Rptr. 68 (Cal. Ct. App. 1985).

[183] Wilson v. Midway Games, Inc., 198 F. Supp.2d 167 (D. Conn. 2002) (apply Connecticut law). For a discussion of the applicability of § 402A to information sold and distributed on the internet, see Nathan D. Leadstrom, *Note: Internet Web Sites as Products Under Strict Products Liability: A Call for an Expanded Definition of Product*, 40 WASHBURN L.J. 532 (2001).

[184] 300 F.3d 683 (6th Cir. 2002) (applying Kentucky law).

[185] Brandt v. The Weather Channel, 42 F. Supp. 2d 1344 (S.D. Fla. 1999) (applying Florida law); Birmingham v. Fodor's Travel Publications, Inc., 833 P.2d 70 (Haw. 1992).

[186] *See* Richard C. Ausness, *The Application of Product Liability Principles to Publishers of Violent or Sexually Explicit Material*, 3 FLA. L. REV. 603 (2000).

[187] Wilson v. Midway Games, Inc., 198 F. Supp. 2d 167 (D. Conn. 2002) (applying Connecticut law).

changed before it reaches the user or consumer." While comment *e* states that § 402A normally will apply to articles that have undergone processing before sale, courts have not limited strict liability to such items. Their position is supported by comment p which provides that "the mere fact that the product is to undergo processing, or other substantial change, will not in all cases relieve the seller of liability." In a number of cases, courts have held that items that have not been manufactured or processed before sale can be products. These include such materials as aluminum,[188] asbestos,[189] and lumber.[190] However, in *Apperson v. E. I. DuPont de Nemours & Co.*,[191] the Seventh Circuit held that raw material, Teflon, manufactured by one company and incorporated into a dental implant by another company was not a "product" within the meaning of § 402A. The court distinguished inherently dangerous raw materials, such as asbestos, from raw materials with safe uses, such as Teflon, which only become dangerous when incorporated into specialized devices.[192]

Although the Restatement (Third) does not explicitly mention raw materials, comment *c* to § 5 states that "[p]roduct components include raw materials. . . .Thus, when raw materials are contaminated or otherwise defective within the meaning of § 2(a), the seller of the raw materials is subject to liability for harm caused by such defects." However, the comment also states that a "basic raw material such as sand, gravel, or kerosene cannot be defectively designed." Liability for the use of such materials lies not with the supplier but with the person who incorporates them into the finished product.

[G] *Real Estate*

Although most products liability cases involve items of personal property, courts also have considered whether strict liability applies to real property. In an early case from California,[193] the state's appellate court held that "in terms of today's society, there are no meaningful distinctions between . . . mass production and the sale of homes and the mass production and sale of automobiles and that the pertinent overriding policy considerations are the same."[194] In keeping with that view, the California Court of Appeal, in *Del*

---

[188] Davis v. Wells Aluminum Southeast, Inc., 323 S.E.2d 215 (Ga. Ct. App. 1984).

[189] Jenkins v. T & N PLC, 52 Cal. Rptr. 2d 642 (Cal. Ct. App. 1996).

[190] Wilkinson v. Bayshore Lumber Co., 227 Cal. Rptr. 327 (Cal. Ct. App. 1986); Housman v. C. A. Dawson & Co., 245 N.E.2d 886 (Ill. App. Ct. 1969).

[191] 41 F.3d 1103 (7th Cir. 1994) (applying Illinois law).

[192] *Id.* at 1107.

[193] Kriegler v. Eichler Homes, Inc., 74 Cal. Rptr. 749 (Cal. Ct. App. 1969).

[194] *Id.* at 752. *See also* Kaneko v. Hilo Coast Processing, 654 P.2d 343 (Haw. 1982) (a manufacturer could be strictly liable for a defective component part in a prefabricated building that had to be assembled); Avner v. Longridge Estates, 77 Cal. Rptr. 633 (Cal. Ct. App. 1969) (devel-

Mar Beach Club Owners v. Imperial Contracting,[195] held that a developer could be held strictly liable for the defective design and construction of a multi-unit residential project. Since the homeowners did not have the opportunity to participate in the design or construction of the project, the court felt that their individual units appeared to "fit the classic mold of buyers of mass-produced housing."[196]

Despite the view of the California courts, courts in other states have looked to the specific requirements of strict liability and held that buildings and similar structures are not "products" within the meaning of § 402A. In *Papp v. Rocky Mountain Oil*,[197] the Montana Supreme Court found that an oil "treater" or "separator" facility was not a product. In *Papp*, the widow of an oil and gas worker brought a strict liability action against the lessee of a "separator" facility when her husband was killed after inhaling sulphide gas while completing work on an auxiliary flow line in the facility. In affirming summary judgment for the defendants, who were in the business of extracting oil and gas for refinement, the court held that the facility was not a "product" for purposes of strict liability: (1) the defendants were not in the business of selling separator facilities; (2) the separator facility did not reach the stream of commerce but, instead, passed "from one lessee to another";[198] and (3) the decedent was not a consumer using the facility after it reached the stream of commerce.[199] In addition to Montana, Illinois courts have held that a condominium unit,[200] a multilevel open-air parking garage,[201] and a sheltered-care facility[202] were not products for purposes of strict liability. The courts offered three justifications for their decisions: (1) the drafters of the § 402A did not contemplate a structure such as a building to be a proper subject for a strict liability action;[203] (2) other remedies are available against those responsible for faulty construction on the theories of negligence and implied warranty;[204] and (3) there is no difficulty of access to a remote manufacturer or supplier and no mass production over which to distribute the risk of injury.[205]

---

opers of homes on hillside property could be strictly liable for damages caused by inadequate drainage and improper compaction of the fill on the development); Schipper v. Levitt & Sons, Inc., 207 A.2d 314 (N.J. 1965).

[195] 176 Cal. Rptr, 886 (Cal. Ct. App. 1981).

[196] *Id.* at 893.

[197] 769 P.2d 1249 (Mont. 1989).

[198] *Id.* at 1256.

[199] *Id.* at 1255.

[200] Heller v. Cadral Corp., 406 N.E.2d 88 (Ill. App. Ct. 1980).

[201] Lowrie v. City of Evanston, 365 N.E.2d 923 (Ill. App. Ct. 1977).

[202] Immergluck v. Ridgeview House, Inc., 368 N.E.2d 803 (Ill. App. Ct. 1977).

[203] *Lowrie*, 365 N.E.2d at 928.

[204] *Id.* at 929.

[205] *Immergluck*, 368 N.E.2d at 805.

Just as courts are divided over whether buildings are products, there is no single view as to whether their component parts are products. The Illinois Appellate Court in *Boddie v. Litton Unit Handling Systems,*[206] for example, cited with approval cases from a number of states that applied strict liability "to products which would be clearly classifiable as real estate fixtures or have specifically held such items to be products for strict liability purposes."[207] The court held these cases were in accord with comment *d* to § 402A, which lists such fixtures as a water heater and a gas stove as examples of products.[208] However, subsequent decisions from the Illinois Appellate Court and the Seventh Circuit have held that specific parts of structures become an integral part of those structures and thus were no longer products for purposes for strict liability.[209]

The Restatement (Third) takes the same approach to real property that it does to electricity. According to § 19, real property may be a product when "the context of [its] distribution and use is sufficiently analogous to the distribution and use of tangible personal property that it is appropriate to apply the rules stated in this Restatement."

---

[206] 455 N.E.2d 142 (Ill. App. Ct. 1983).

[207] *Id.*

[208] *Id.*

[209] *See* Hilliard v. Lummus Co., Inc., 834 F.2d 1352, 1354 (7th Cir. 1987) (applying Illinois law); St. Louis v. Rockwell Graphic Systems, 581 N.E.2d 93 (Ill. App. Ct. 1991); Billman v. Crown-Trygg Corp., 563 N.E.2d 903 (Ill. App. Ct. 1990); Cross v. Ainsworth Seed Co., 557 N.E.2d 906 (Ill. App. Ct. 1990); Duncavage v. Allen, 497 N.E.2d 433 (Ill. App. Ct. 1986); Calumet Country Club v. Roberts Environmental Control Corp., 483 N.E.2d 613 (Ill. App. Ct. 1985); Hubbard v. Chicago Housing Authority, 487 N.E.2d 20 (Ill. App. Ct. 1985).

Chapter 5

DESIGN DEFECTS

SYNOPSIS

---

§ 5.01 PRODUCT DEFECTS

Almost every product is capable of causing injuries when used in certain ways. However, the fact that a product "caused" the plaintiff's injuries is not enough, in itself, to hold a manufacturer or seller liable for those injuries.[1] Instead, before an injured person can recover in an action based upon either negligence or strict liability, every state also requires the person to prove

---

[1] Seattle-First National Bank v. Tabert, 542 P.2d 774 (Wash. 1975); Kutzler v. AMF Harley-Davidson, 550 N.E.2d 1236 (Ill. App. Ct. 1990).

that there was a "defect" in the product at the time it left the control of the manufacturer or seller. In addition, most states require a showing that the particular "defect" made the product "unreasonably dangerous."[2] Whether or not a product was in a defective condition that made it unreasonably dangerous when it left the defendant's control is at the heart of products liability law and is the subject of almost all litigation. This litigation not only involves issues about what makes a product "defective" and "unreasonably dangerous" and the proof required to establish that, it also raises questions about the economic and societal consequences of a finding that a product was defective.[3]

Courts and statutes define a product "defect" in very broad language: an "imperfection";[4] an "injury-producing hazard accompanying normal use of a product";[5] and "a condition of a product that renders it unsafe for normal or anticipated handling and consumption."[6] Because a defect is not limited to the mechanics or the function of a product but includes anything that makes it "unreasonably dangerous,"[7] it is impossible to list all of the types of imperfections or hazards that can constitute a defect.[8] Although strict liability under § 402A requires a product to be in a "defective condition," neither that section nor the comments to it define a defect. Instead, comment h to § 402A states simply that a "product is not in a defective condition when it is safe for normal handling and consumption." The comments to § 402A, however, list a number of sources that can give rise to a defective condition in a product. These include harmful ingredients that are not characteristic of the product, either as to their presence or quantity; foreign objects in a product; decay or deterioration of a product before sale; the way in which a product is prepared or packaged; or the failure to provide adequate directions or warnings about a product.[9] A product also may be defective because

---

[2] Kinser v. Gehl Co., 184 F.3d 1259 (10th Cir. 1999) (applying Kansas law); Farnham v. Bombardier, Inc., 640 A.2d 47 (Vt. 1994); RESTATEMENT (SECOND) OF TORTS § 402A (1965) (a product must be in a "defective condition unreasonably dangerous").

[3] For one expression of "uneasiness" over the economic and societal "impact" of products liability law, see the "Conclusion" to Judge Arlin Adams' opinion for the court in Dawson v. Chrysler Corp., 630 F.2d 950, 962-963 (3d Cir. 1980).

[4] Singleton v. Manitowoc Co., Inc., 727 F. Supp. 217, 221 (D. Md. 1989) (applying Maryland law).

[5] Boudreau v. Baughman, 368 S.E.2d 849, 860 (N.C. 1988).

[6] TENN. CODE ANN. § 29-28-102(2) (2000).

[7] Anderson v. M. W. Kellogg Co., 766 P.2d 637, 643 (Colo. 1988).

[8] See W. Page Keeton, *The Meaning of Defect in Products Liability Law*, 45 MO. L. REV. 579 (1980).

[9] RESTATEMENT (SECOND) OF TORTS § 402A cmts. h and j (1965). See also the discussion of the various ways a product may be defective in *Barker v. Lull Engineering Co.*, 573 P.2d 443, 453 (Cal. 1978).

of the absence of a safety device[10] or because it was not "crashworthy."[11] Whether a product was defective for purposes of negligence and strict liability also depends upon whether it was unavoidably unsafe, whether the risk of the harm was "open and obvious" to the consumer or user, whether the product had been altered, and whether the product was being used for its intended or foreseeable purpose. In recent years, determining whether a product is defective has been complicated further by the issues involved in the lawsuits filed against the manufacturers and sellers of such products as asbestos,[12] cell phones,[13] drugs and medical devices,[14] fast foods,[15] fire arms,[16] medical implants,[17] and tobacco.[18]

Although the comments to § 402A list some of the sources of product defects, they do not categorize the types of defects. Despite the silence of that section as to the forms that a defect can take, courts, as well as the Restatement (Third), classify product defects under three broad headings:[19] (1) design defects; (2) manufacturing defects; and (3) inadequate instructions or warnings concerning the use or risks of a product. These three categories also are used in analyzing defects in negligence cases. Each of the categories not only has its own characteristics and tests for determining whether the product was defective but also presents its own unique problems of proof. The remainder of this chapter focuses on design defects. The following two chapters examine manufacturing defects and the failure to warn about dangers associated with a product or to provide adequate instructions about the use of a product.

---

[10] *See* Shreve v. Sears, Roebuck & Co., 166 F. Supp. 2d 378 (D. Md. 2001) (applying Maryland law); Ogletree v. Navistar International Transportation Corp., 522 S.E.2d 467 (Ga. 1999); Prentis v. Yale Manufacturing Co., 365 N.W.2d 176 (Mich. 1984).

[11] Huff v. White Motor Corp., 565 F.2d 104 (7th Cir. 1977) (applying Indiana law); Larsen v. General Motors Corp., 391 F.2d 495 (8th Cir. 1968) (applying Minnesota law); Sumnicht v. Toyota Motor Sales, U.S.A., Inc., 360 N.W.2d 2 (Wis. 1984).

[12] Halphen v. Johns-Manville Sales Corp., 484 So.2d 110 (La. 1986); Arena v. Owens Corning Corp., 74 Cal. Rptr. 2d 580 (Cal. Ct. App.1998).

[13] *See, e.g.,* Pinney v. Nokia, Inc., 402 F.3d 430 (4th Cir. 2005); Newman v. Motorola, Inc., 2003 U.S. App. LEXIS 21367 (4th Cir. 2003).

[14] Grundberg v. Upjohn Co., 813 P.2d 89 (Utah 1991); Johnson v. American Cyanamid Co., 718 P.2d 1318 (Kan. 1986); Feldman v. Lederle Laboratories, 479 A.2d 374 (N.J. 1984).

[15] *See* Alyse Meislik, *Weighing in on the Scales of Justice: The Obesity Epidemic and Litigation Against the Food Industry*, 46 Ariz. L. Rev. 781 (2004).

[16] Gower v. Savage Arms, Inc., 166 F. Supp. 2d 240 (E.D. Pa. 2001) (applying Pennsylvania law).

[17] Metronic, Inc. v. Lohr, 518 U.S. 470 (1996).

[18] Cipollone v. Liggett Group, 505 U.S. 504 (1992).

[19] *See, e.g.,* Momen v. United States, 946 F. Supp. 196 (N.D.N.Y. 1996) (applying New York law); Gorton v. American Cyanamid Co., 533 N.W.2d 746 (Wis. 1995); Banks v. ICI Americas, Inc., 450 S.E.2d 671 (Ga. 1994); Restatement (Third) of Torts: Products Liability § 2 (1998).

§ 5.02 DESIGN DEFECT

[A] *Characteristics of a Design Defect*

The largest number of products liability cases that reach trial involve an allegation that the plaintiff's injuries were caused by a design defect in the product in question. The design of a product includes the manufacturer's specifications, choice of materials, as well as the structure of the product.[20] Despite the volume of litigation, design defects remain the most difficult for a plaintiff to identify and to prove. In part this is because, unlike a manufacturing defect, which is unintended and often can be identified by comparing the particular product alleged to have caused the plaintiff's injuries with the manufacturer's own design for the product or with other units of the same product line produced by the manufacturer, there are no objective standards by which to judge a design defect.[21] The aspect of a design that makes a product defective is not the result of a mistake on the part of the manufacturer. Instead, it is the consequence of the manufacturer's intentional choice of the specifications or materials used for the product and is inherent in every unit of the particular model produced by the manufacturer.[22] The design choice makes all of those products unsafe when put to their intended or foreseeable use. Because of the economic and societal consequences of finding that a manufacturer's entire product line is defective,[23] courts and commentators continually seek to devise appropriate standards for judging whether a product's design made it unreasonably dangerous. As will be discussed in detail in § 5.03, the most frequently used of the standards that courts have developed to determine whether a defect in a product makes it unreasonably dangerous are the "consumer expectations test" and the "risk-utility analysis."

---

[20] Boudreau v. Baughman, 368 S.E.2d 849 (N.C. 1988); Husky Industries v. Black, 434 So.2d 988 (Fla. Dist. Ct. App. 1983); Jones v. White Motor Corp., 401 N.E.2d 223 (Ohio Ct. App. 1978). In most cases, the manufacturer of a product also designed it. However, in some situations, the purchaser provided the design specifications to the manufacturer. In such a situation, the court in *Sepulveda-Esquivel v. Central Machine Works*, 84 P.3d 895 (Wash. Ct. App. 2004), held that the manufacturer was not liable.

[21] Prentis v. Yale Manufacturing Co., 365 N.W.2d 176 (Mich. 1984); O'Brien v. Muskin Corp., 463 A.2d 298 (N.J. 1983); Caterpillar Tractor Co. v. Beck, 593 P.2d 871 (Alaska 1979).

[22] *Boudreau*, 368 S.E.2d at 860; Leichtamer v. American Motors Co., 424 N.E.2d 568 (Ohio 1981); Caterpillar Tractor Co., 593 P.2d 871.

[23] In *Thibault v. Sears, Roebuck & Co.*, 395 A.2d 843, 846 (N.H. 1978), the New Hampshire Supreme Court expressed this concern when it stated: "The utility of the product must be evaluated from the point of view of the public as a whole, because a finding of liability for defective design could result in the removal of an entire product line from the market." *See also* Lewis v. Coffing Hoist Division, Duff-Norton Co., Inc., 528 A.2d 590, 596 (Pa. 1987) (Hutchinson, J., dissenting).

[B] *Negligence, Strict Liability, and Product Designs*

[1] Introduction

Plaintiffs frequently include separate counts of negligence and strict liability in their design defect complaints against manufacturers.[24] In recent years, some courts have fused negligence theory with strict liability theory to determine whether a product was defective.[25] As a result, one court has said of a design defect case that "there is almost no difference between a prima facie case in negligence and one in strict liability."[26] Reflecting the approach developed by many state courts, section 2 of the Restatement (Third) applies a negligence (i.e., risk-utility) analysis as the standard for judging design defect and failure to warn cases[27] while retaining strict liability (i.e., consumer expectations) as the test for manufacturing defects. However, despite the shift from strict liability to negligence in design defect cases,[28] there is a fundamental distinction between the two theories: "Negligence theory concerns itself with determining whether the conduct of the defendant was reasonable in view of the foreseeable risk of injury; strict liability is concerned with whether the product itself was unreasonably dangerous."[29]

[2] Negligent Design

The elements that a plaintiff must establish in an action alleging negligence in the design of a product are the same as those in other negligence cases. According to one court, a negligent design claim has three basic requirements: "(1) a duty to anticipate and design against reasonably foreseeable hazards; (2) breach of that duty; and (3) injury proximately caused

---

[24] *See* Trull v. Volkswagen of America, Inc., 320 F.3d 1 (1st Cir. 2002) (applying New Hampshire law); Stahlecker v. Ford Motor Co., 667 N.W.2d 244 (Neb. 2003); Bishop v. GenTec Inc., 48 P.3d 218 (Utah 2002).

[25] *See, e.g.*, Solo v. Trus Joist MacMillan, 2004 U.S. Dist. LEXIS 4107 (D. Minn. 2004) (applying Minnesota law); Jones v. Amazing Products, Inc., 231 F. Supp. 2d 1228 (N.D. Ga. 2002) (applying Georgia law).

[26] Colon v. BIC USA, Inc., 199 F. Supp. 2d 53, 83 (S.D.N.Y. 2001) (quoting Denny v. Ford Motor Co., 662 N.E.2d 730 (N.Y. 1995)). *See* Sheila Birnbaum, *Unmasking the Test for Design Defect: from Negligence [to Warranty] to Strict Liability to Negligence*, 33 VAND. L. REV. 539 (1980).

[27] RESTATEMENT (THIRD) OF TORTS: PRODUCTS LIABILITY § 2 (1998). This section was adopted by the Iowa supreme court in Wright v. Brooke Group, 652 N.W.2d 159 (Iowa 2002).

[28] *See* Burt v. Makita USA, Inc., 212 F. Supp. 2d 893, 899 (N.D. Ind. 2002) ("a negligence standard is applied to claims involving design defects" under the Indiana Products Liability Law).

[29] Dart v. Wiebe Manufacturing, Inc., 709 P.2d 876, 880 (Ariz. 1985). *See also* Syrie v. Knoll International, 748 F.2d 304 (5th Cir. 1984) (applying Texas law); Slisze v. Stanley-Bostitch, 979 P.2d 317 (Utah 1999); Bilotta v. Kelley Co., 346 N.W.2d 616 (Minn. 1984).

by the breach."[30] The standard of care imposed by the duty in a negligence action does not require the manufacturer to design a product that is accident-proof, is incapable of causing injury, or that incorporates every available safety device.[31] Instead, a manufacturer has a duty to use ordinary care so that the design will make the product reasonably safe for its intended use[32] or for a use that was reasonably foreseeable.[33] In deciding whether the design of a product is reasonably safe, some courts have adopted the definition used by the consumer expectations test discussed in the next section: a product is "unreasonably dangerous" if it is "dangerous to an extent beyond which would be expected by the ordinary consumer who purchases it."[34]

In a negligence case, the focus is on the manufacturer's conduct and whether the manufacturer acted reasonably in choosing the specifications, materials or structure for the product in light of the risks it knew about or should have known about.[35] In determining whether a manufacturer acted reasonably in designing a product, courts hold a manufacturer to the standard of "an expert in the field." As such, the manufacturer is required it to "keep reasonably abreast of scientific knowledge and discoveries touching his product and of techniques and devices used by practical men in his field."[36] Deciding what such an expert would do in choosing a design for a product has led many plaintiffs, manufacturers, and courts to abandon reliance on consumer expectations and to analyze the purpose, costs, and risks and benefits of the manufacturer's design, as well as reasonable alternative designs, by examining a series of factors. These include: the likelihood and gravity of the potential harm and the burden of precautions that effectively would avoid the harm; the style, type, and particular purpose of

---

[30] Wagatsuma v. Patch, 879 P.2d 572, 583 (Haw. 1994). *See also* Kirk v. Hanes Corporation of North Carolina, 771 F. Supp. 856 (E.D. Mich. 1991) (applying Michigan law); Oanes v. Westgo, Inc., 476 N.W.2d 248 (N.D. 1991).

[31] Westinghouse Electric Corp. v. Nutt, 407 A.2d 606 (D.C. 1979); Morrell v. Precise Engineering, Inc., 630 N.E.2d 291 (Mass. App. Ct. 1994).

[32] Messer v. Amway Corp., 210 F. Supp. 2d 1217 (D. Kan. 2002) (citing Garst v. General Motors Corp., 484 P.2d 47 (Kan. 1971)).

[33] Burt v. Makita USA, Inc., 212 F. Supp. 2d 893 (N.D. Ind. 2002) (applying the Indiana Products Liability Act); Hillrichs v. Avco Corp., 514 N.W.2d 94 (Iowa 1994); Micallef v. Miehle Co., 348 N.E.2d 571 (N.Y. 1976). This standard has been adopted by § 395 of the Restatement (Second) of Torts which states:

> A manufacturer of a chattel made under a plan or design which makes it dangerous for the uses for which it is manufactured is subject to liability to others whom he should expect to use the chattel or to be endangered by its probable use for physical harm caused by his failure to exercise reasonable care in the adoption of a safe plan or design.

[34] *Messer*, 210 F. Supp. 2d 1217 at 1233 (applying Kansas law).

[35] Trull v. Volkswagen of America, Inc., 320 F.3d 1 (1st Cir. 2002) (applying New Hampshire law); Enrich v. Windmere Corp., 616 N.E.2d 1081 (Mass. 1993); McLaughlin v. Michelin Tire Corp., 778 P.2d 59 (Wyo. 1989).

[36] Feldman v. Lederle Laboratories, 479 A.2d 374, 386-387 (N.J. 1984), quoting 2 FOWLER HARPER & FLEMING JAMES, THE LAW OF TORTS § 28.4 (1956).

the product; the cost of an alternative design, since the product's marketability may be adversely affected by a cost factor that greatly outweighs the added safety of the product; and the price of the product itself.[37]

[3] Strict Liability

In contrast to a negligence case, which focuses on whether the manufacturer took reasonable care in selecting the design of the product, the emphasis in a strict liability case is on the design of the product itself and whether the design made it unreasonably dangerous at the time it left the control of the manufacturer.[38] The effect that the different approaches taken by negligence and strict liability to design defects can have on the outcome of a case is illustrated by *Phillips v. Cricket Lighters,*[39] in which a two-year-old boy accidently started a fire with a disposable butane cigarette lighter he found in his mother's purse. The fire resulted in the deaths of three persons. In a suit against the manufacturers and distributors of the lighters, the Pennsylvania Supreme Court held that the manufacturer was not strictly liable for failing to design the lighters with child-resistant features. According to the court, the design of the lighters was not unreasonably dangerous for their intended users, who did not include young children. At the same time, however, the court held that the manufacturer owed the plaintiffs a duty of care and that it was a question for the jury whether it breached that duty in failing to foresee that the lighters could be used by children and in not designing the product with child safety devices.[40]

Section 402A does not mention design defects specifically. Thus, in order to establish a *prima facie* case in a design defect case, a plaintiff must establish the general elements for liability under the section. In most states, these elements require proof that (1) the design of the product resulted in a "defective condition unreasonably dangerous" to the ultimate user or consumer of the product; (2) the product was expected to and did reach the user or consumer "without substantial change in the condition in which it was sold"; (3) the defective design must have been the cause of the plaintiff's injuries; (4) the defendant that sold the product was engaged in the business of selling such products; and (5) the plaintiff suffered injuries as a result.[41]

---

[37] Wagatsuma v. Patch, 879 P.2d 572, 584 (Haw. 1994). *See also* Peck v. Bridgeport Machines, 237 F.3d 614 (6th Cir. 2001) (applying Michigan law); Metzgar v. Playskool Inc., 30 F.3d 459 (3d Cir. 1994) (applying Pennsylvania law); Ogletree v. Navistart International Transportation Corp., 522 S.E.2d 467 (Ga. 1999).

[38] Freeman v. Hoffman-La Roche, Inc., 618 N.W.2d 827 (Neb. 2000); Denny v. Ford Motor Co., 662 N.E.2d 730 (N.Y. 1995); Caterpillar Tractor Co. v. Beck, 593 P.2d 871 (Alaska, 1979).

[39] 841 A.2d 1000 (Pa. 2003).

[40] *Id.* at 1108-09.

[41] The Union Supply Company v. Pust, 583 P. 2d 276, 282-283 (Colo. 1978).

In *Phillips*, the Pennsylvania court held that the lighters were not in a "defective condition unreasonably dangerous" to the ultimate user or consumer of the product which it defined as the intended user, thus excluding young children.

Some courts also have held that a product is not in a "defective condition unreasonably dangerous" if it performed as intended by its design. This position has been very controversial in cases involving firearms. In *McCarthy v. Olin*,[42] for example, a gunman killed six people and wounded nineteen when he entered a commuter train and opened fire, using a gun loaded with Winchester "Black Talon" hollow point bullets that are designed to "bend upon impact into six ninety-degree angle razor-sharp petals . . . that increase the wounding power of the bullet by stretching, cutting and tearing tissue and bone as it travels through the victim."[43] The plaintiffs brought suit against the manufacturer of the bullets in strict liability, alleging that the bullets were "unreasonably designed and ultrahazardous."[44] The Second Circuit, however, affirmed the lower court's dismissal of the design defect claim, stating that "[t]he bullets were not in defective condition nor were they unreasonably dangerous for their intended use because the Black Talons were purposely designed to expand on impact and cause severe wounding."[45]

[C] *Enhanced Injury Doctrine*

In most design defect cases, the plaintiff alleges that the defective design was the cause both of the accident and of his or her injuries. However, in many cases involving motor vehicles,[46] the defective design was not the cause of the initial accident. Instead, the design defect was the cause of a "second collision" in which the plaintiff suffered separate injuries or injuries more severe than they would have been had the design of the product not been defective.[47] The defect that causes or enhances the injuries in an automobile may be in the design of the airbags, dashboard, door locks, fuel system, restraint system, roof, or side impact protection. In *Richardson v. Volkswagenwerk, A.G.*,[48] for example, the plaintiff was the driver of a Volkswagen involved in a head-on collision with a Ford Mustang. Although the

---

[42] 119 F.3d 148 (2d Cir. 1997) (applying New York law).

[43] *Id.* at 152. *See also* Holliday v. Sturm, Ruger & Co., 770 A.2d 1072 (Md. Ct. Spec. App. 2001).

[44] *McCarthy*, 119 F.3d at 151.

[45] *Id.* at 155.

[46] In addition to automobiles, enhanced injury issues have arisen in cases involving aircraft, boats, lawn mowers, and motorcycles, snowmobiles, snowplows, and tractors. For a list of cases, see RESTATEMENT (THIRD) OF TORTS: PRODUCTS LIABILITY § 16, Reporter's Note (1998).

[47] Whitted v. General Motors Corp., 58 F.3d 1200 (8th Cir. 1995).

[48] 552 F. Supp. 73 (W.D. Mo. 1982).

design of the Volkswagen was not responsible for the initial collision, that accident resulted in a "second collision" in which the plaintiff's body struck the Volkswagen's allegedly defective dashboard and assist grip. In his suit against the automobile manufacturer, the plaintiff was able to seek damages only for those injuries that resulted from him striking the dashboard or for his enhanced injuries resulting from the collision.[49] Thus, evidence about the cause of the initial accident is not relevant.[50]

The enhanced injury doctrine[51] has its origins in a 1968 decision, *Larsen v. General Motors Corp.*,[52] in which the Eighth Circuit held that, where the plaintiff's injuries or enhanced injuries are due to the manufacturer's failure to use reasonable care to avoid subjecting the user of its products to an unreasonable risk of injury, negligence principles are applicable.[53] In *Larsen*, the plaintiff alleged that the automobile manufacturer's negligent design of a steering assembly caused his injuries in an automobile accident. In reply, General Motors argued that it had "no duty whatsoever to design and manufacture a vehicle which is otherwise 'safe' or 'safer' to occupy during a collision."[54] According to the court, however, although "automobiles are not made for the purpose of colliding with each other, a frequent and inevitable contingency of normal automobile use will result in collisions and injury-producing impacts."[55] Given the reality of automobile accidents, the court concluded:

> No rational basis exists for limiting recovery to situations where the defect in design or manufacture was the causative factor of the accident, as the accident and the resulting injury, usually caused by the so-called "second collision" of the passenger with the interior part of the automobile, all are foreseeable. Where the injuries or enhanced injuries are due to the manufacturer's failure to use rea-

---

[49] *See* Mickle v. Blackmon, 166 S.E.2d 173 (S.C. 1969).

[50] *See* Thomas Harris, *Enhanced Injury Theory: An Analytic Framework*, 62 N.C. L. Rev. 643 (1984) ("In enhanced injury [crashworthiness] cases, . . . a claimant's fault in causing the accident is not a basis for reducing his recovery. . . . [A] manufacturer's duty is that of minimizing the injurious effects of contact however caused"). *See also* Reed v. Chrysler Corp., 494 N.W.2d 224 (Iowa 1992).

[51] In *Caiazzo v. Volkswagenwerk A. G.*, 647 F.2d 241, 243 n. 2 (2d Cir. 1981), the court distinguished between "crashworthiness," which it defined as "the protection that a passenger motor vehicle affords its passengers against personal injury or death as a result of a motor vehicle accident" and "second collision," which it said "usually refers to the collision between a passenger and an interior part of the vehicle following an impact or collision. The term has also been applied to ejection cases…in which the second collision is between an occupant of the car and the ground." However, because the difference between the two is minimal and courts use the terms interchangeably, "enhanced injury doctrine" will be used to describe both.

[52] 391 F.2d 495 (8th Cir. 1968).

[53] *Id.* at 502.

[54] *Id.* at 497.

[55] *Id.* at 502.

sonable care to avoid subjecting the user of its products to an unreasonable risk of injury, general negligence principles should be applicable. The sole function of an automobile is not just to provide a
means of transportation, it is to provide a means of safe transportation or as safe as is reasonably possible under the present
state of the art.[56]

Under the enhanced injury doctrine as formulated by *Larsen* and applied
by courts, a "manufacturer is under a duty to use reasonable care in the
design of its vehicle to minimize the unreasonable risk of injuries in the
event of collisions."[57] This duty means that a manufacturer is liable not only
for a design defect that causes an initial accident, it also is liable for the
damage or injury that would not have occurred as a result of the initial accident if the design had not been defective. The enhanced injury doctrine
now has been adopted in every state and is applicable both in negligence and
in strict liability cases.[58]

In some enhanced injury cases, the plaintiff or the weather, rather than
a third party, was responsible for the initial accident. In such a case, the
manufacturer is liable only for the injuries or enhanced injuries caused by
the defect in the product. In other cases, however, a third party was responsible for the initial accident while the defective design caused the enhanced
injuries. If it is possible to separate the plaintiff's injuries between those
caused by the initial collision and those that resulted from the second collision, the jury will apportion liability between the manufacturer and all others whose fault combined to cause the plaintiff's injuries. However, if the
plaintiff's injuries cannot be divided between the first collision and the second collision, the manufacturer and third parties are jointly and severally
liable for all of the plaintiff's injuries, unless the jurisdiction has eliminated joint and several liability.[59]

More difficult for the courts is the question of who bears the burden of
proof for purposes of apportioning the damages. The majority of states follow the Restatement (Second) of Torts[60] and hold that the plaintiff must
prove only that the design defect was a "substantial factor in producing
damages over and above those which were probably caused as a result of the
original impact or collision."[61] Under this approach, once the plaintiff meets
the burden of proving that the defective design was a substantial factor in

---

[56] *Id.*

[57] *Id.*

[58] *See, e.g.,* Polk v. Ford Motor Company, 529 F.2d 259 (8th Cir. 1976) (applying Missouri
law); Miller v. Todd, 551 N.E.2d 1139 (Ind. 1990); Leichtamer v. American Motors Co., 424
N.E.2d 568 (Ohio 1981).

[59] For a discussion of joint and several liability, see Chapter 10.

[60] *See* RESTATEMENT (SECOND) OF TORTS §§ 433, 433A & 433B (1965).

[61] Mitchell v. Volkswagenwerk, A. .G., 669 F.2d 1199, 1206 (8th Cir. 1982).

causing or enhancing his or her injuries, the burden of proof shifts to the manufacturer to show which injuries were the result of the initial collision and those attributable to the defective design.[62] A minority of states, however, follow the approach set out in *Huddell v. Levin*[63] and require the plaintiff to prove precisely and exactly the injuries attributable to the initial collision and those caused by the alleged design defect.[64]

Unlike § 402A, the Restatement (Third) states that "a manufacturer has a duty to design and manufacture its product so as reasonably to deduce the foreseeable harm that may occur in an accident brought about by causes other than a product itself."[65] According to § 16 of the Restatement (Third):

(a) When a product is defective at the time of commercial sale or other distribution and the defect is a substantial factor in increasing the plaintiff's harm beyond that which would have resulted from other causes, the product seller is subject to liability for the increased harm.

(b) If proof supports a determination of the harm that would have resulted from other causes in the absence of the product defect, the product seller's liability is limited to the increased harm attributable solely to the product defect.

(c) If proof does not support a determination under Subsection (b) of the harm that would have resulted in the absence of the product defect, the product seller is liable for all of theplaintiff's harm attributable to the defect and other causes.

(d) A seller of a defective product who is held liable for part of the harm suffered by the plaintiff under Subsection (b), or all of the harm suffered by the plaintiff under Subsection (c), is jointly and severally liable with other parties who bear legal responsibilities for causing the harm, determined by applicable rules of joint and several liability.

§ 5.03 TESTS FOR DETERMINING A DESIGN DEFECT

[A] *Introduction*

Negligence and strict liability set out, in broad terms, what a plaintiff must prove in a design defect case. In negligence actions, juries and judges use the multifactored risk-utility analysis mentioned above to determine

---

[62] Trull v. Volkswagen of America, Inc., 187 F.3d 88, 101-102 (1st Cir. 1999).

[63] 537 F.2d 726, 737-738 (3d Cir. 1976).

[64] *See also* Caiazzo v. Volkswagenwerk, A.G., 647 F.2d 241 (2d Cir. 1981); Stonehocker v. General Motors Corp., 587 F.2d 151, 158 (4th Cir. 1978); Yetter v. Rajeski, 364 F. Supp. 105, 109 (D. N.J. 1973).

[65] RESTATEMENT (THIRD) OF TORTS: PRODUCTS LIABILITY § 16 cmt. *a* (1998).

whether the manufacturer acted reasonably in selecting the design of the product. Although there are differences in the details, most states permit a plaintiff in a strict liability action to show that the design resulted in a product that was unreasonably dangerous by using some form of two different tests: the consumer expectation test and/or the risk-utility analysis. Ordinarily, the determination of whether the plaintiff has met its requirement of showing that a product was defective and unreasonably dangerous is at the heart of a design defect case and thus is a question of fact for the jury.[66] However, in Pennsylvania, it is for the trial judge, not the jury, to make a social policy determination whether a product was unreasonably dangerous.[67]

In deciding whether a product is unreasonably dangerous, a large number of states initially used the "consumer expectations test," which examines the operation and safety of a product from the perspective of the expectations of an ordinary consumer.[68] However, that test has been criticized by those who point out that it asks only whether an ordinary consumer expected the harm. These critics suggest that the test protects poor manufacturing standards since, if a dangerous design is widespread, it comes to be expected by consumers and cannot be unreasonably dangerous.[69] This has led the majority of states to adopt a "risk-utility" analysis. As its name indicates, this analysis examines whether the benefits of having the product with the particular design outweigh its risks of harm and the costs of a safer product.[70] The shift from the consumer expectations test to the risk-utility analysis has been more than a simple change in the applicable test. Since the risk-utility analysis is a negligence-based test with its origins in the Learned Hand formula,[71] the move to such an analysis has resulted in a pull-back from strict liability in design defect cases. Although the majority of states, as well as the Restatement (Third), now have adopted some form of a risk-utility analysis for design defect cases, about 25 states still use the consumer expectations test either as an alternative to risk-utility analy-

---

[66] *See* Korando v. Uniroyal Goodrich Tire Co., 637 N.E.2d 1020 (Ill. 1994); Cole v. Lantis Corp., 714 N.E.2d 194 (Ind. Ct. App. 1999).

[67] Azzarello v. Black Brothers Co., Inc., 391 A.2d 1020 (Pa. 1978). This pretrial inquiry requires the court to balance the risks and benefits of manufacturer design choices. No other state has adopted the *Azzarello* approach.

[68] For an analysis of the consumer expectations test, see Douglas A. Kysar, *The Expectations of Consumers*, 103 COLUM. L. REV. 1700 (2003), and Jerry J. Phillips, *Consumer Expectations*, 53 S.C. L. REV. 1047 (2002).

[69] *See, e.g.*, J. BEASLEY, PRODUCTS LIABILITY AND THE UNREASONABLY DANGEROUS REQUIREMENT, 399 (1981). The test was criticized by the Colorado Supreme Court in Camacho v. Honda Motor Co., 741 P.2d 1240, 1246 (Colo. 1987).

[70] For a summary of the variations in the two tests, see John F. Vargo, *The Emperor's New Clothes: The American Law Institute Adorns a "New Cloth" for Section 402A Products Liability Design Defects – A Survey of the States Reveals a Different Weave*, 26 U. MEM. L. REV. 493, 951-955 (1996).

[71] United States v. Carroll Towing Co., 159 F.2d 169 (2nd Cir. 1947).

sis or, in a few cases, as the sole test. One result of this is that a product may be found to be defectively designed under the consumer expectations test but not under the risk-utility analysis.[72] Finally, a few states have done explicitly what many others have done implicitly: incorporated the risk-utility factors into the consumer expectation analysis of the design of the product.[73]

[B] *Consumer Expectations Test*

[1] Introduction

Under the consumer expectations test (sometimes referred to as the "consumer contemplation" test,[74] the "reasonable expectations" test,[75] or the "user-contemplation" test[76]), the question of whether the defect in the design makes the product "unreasonably dangerous" depends upon whether the danger posed by the design is greater than an ordinary consumer would expect when using the product in an intended or reasonably foreseeable manner.[77] The focus of the test is on the reasonable safety expectations of an "ordinary consumer" concerning the product rather than on the product itself or any negligence in the design decision of the manufacturer. The consumer expectation test has its genesis not only in the UCC's principles of implied warranty of merchantability and implied warranty of fitness for a particular purpose, but also in comment *g* to § 402A which states that a product is in a "defective condition" if it is, "at the time it leaves the seller's hands, in a condition not contemplated by the ultimate consumer, which will be unreasonably dangerous to him."

An example of the use of the consumer expectations test is *Hansen v. Baxter Healthcare Corp.,*[78] in which a friction-fit IV catheter that had been inserted into a patient's jugular vein became detached, resulting in her death. In a suit against the manufacturer of the catheter, the estate of the patient alleged, among other things, that the tubing on the catheter was unreasonably dangerous because it was designed without a Luer-lock con-

---

[72] Cunningham v. Mitsubishi Motors Corp., 1993 U.S. Dist. LEXIS 21299 (S.D. Ohio 1993).

[73] *See* Potter v. Chicago Pneumatic Tool Co., 694 A.2d 1319 (Conn. 1997); Seattle-First National Bank v. Tabert, 542 P.2d 774 (Wash. 1975).

[74] *See, e.g.*, Haddix v. Playtex Family Products Corp., 138 F.3d 681 (7th Cir. 1998); Gray v. Manitowoc Co., Inc., 771 F.2d 866 (5th Cir. 1985).

[75] Vincer v. Esther Williams All-Aluminum Swimming Pool Co., 230 N.W.2d 794, 798 (Wis. 1975).

[76] *See, e.g.*, Scoby v. Vulcan-Hart Corp., 569 N.E.2d 1147 (Ill. App. Ct. 1991).

[77] Nesselrode v. Executive Beechcraft, Inc., 707 S.W.2d 371 (Mo. 1986); Barker v. Lull Engineering Co., 573 P.2d 443, 454 (Cal. 1978); Force v. Ford Motor Co., 879 So.2d 103 (Fla. Dist. Ct. App. 2004).

[78] 764 N.E.2d 35 (Ill. 2002).

nection and that the friction-fit connection failed when the catheter was used in a reasonably foreseeable manner.[79] In response, the manufacturer contended that, consistent with the learned intermediary doctrine,[80] the healthcare professionals who inserted the catheter, rather than the patient herself, should be considered the "consumer" of the product for purposes of the consumer expectations test. In addition, the manufacturer argued that, as in the case of a prescriptive medical device, the patient was not familiar enough with the catheter to have any "expectations" about how it would work or about its safety. The Illinois Supreme Court, however, rejected both of the manufacturer's arguments. According to the court, the evidence showed that the decision to purchase the catheter was made solely by the nursing products committee at the hospital, that the chair of the committee relied upon the manufacturer to advise him about the proper uses for the catheter, and that the person who purchased the device from the manufacturer's sales representative was not a physician. Thus, the court concluded that the catheter was more like atypical prescription products such as contraceptives where courts have held that the ordinary consumer expectation test is applicable. In addition, the court found that a patient, who was conscious after surgery, reasonably could have expected that her IV catheter connection, if properly designed and manufactured, would be safe for its intended purpose. Since the patient was the person who used the catheter and would be harmed by the product if it failed, the court held that her expectations of the product performance and safety should be the test.[81]

The consumer expectations test has been called a "simple test"[82] that is "reliable and easy to administer."[83] However, while all states apply the test exclusively in manufacturing defect cases, only about a dozen do so in design defect cases.[84] Instead, most of the states that have retained the consumer expectations test use it as an alternative to the risk-utility analysis in design defect cases.[85] In states that use the consumer expectations test,

---

[79] Id. at 38.

[80] The learned intermediary doctrine is discussed in detail in Chapter 7.

[81] Id. at 43-45.

[82] Todd v. Societe BIC, S.A., 21 F.3d 1402, 1406 (7th Cir. 1994).

[83] Rebecca Tustin Rutherford, Comment, Changes in the Landscape of Products Liability Law: An Analysis of the Restatement (Third) of Torts, 63 J. AIR L. & COM. 209, 224 (1997).

[84] One state that continues to be committed to the consumer expectations test exclusively is Wisconsin. See Green v. Smith & Nephew AHP, Inc., 629 N.W.2d 727 (Wis. 2001). For a list of "roughly a dozen jurisdictions that adhere to the consumer expectation test," see McCathern v. Toyota Motor Corp., 985 P.2d 804, 809 n. 5 (Or. Ct. App. 1999).

[85] Since surveys of states differ, no attempt will be made to list which states use the consumer expectations test either as the exclusive test in design defect cases or as an alternative along with the risk-utility test. One list can be found in John F. Vargo, The Emperor's New Clothes: The American Law Institute Adorns a "New Cloth" for Section 402A Products Liability Design Defects — A Survey of the States Reveals a Different Weave, 26 U. MEM. L. REV. 493, 951-955 (1996).

either alone or as an alternative to the risk-utility analysis, there are four related questions that can arise when the test is used.

[2] Who is an Ordinary Consumer?

As in the *Hanson* case, one question that may arise in a design defect case is whether the person using the product at the time of the injury was an "ordinary consumer." Most juries and judges determine a consumer's expectations of a product not by those of the particular consumer of the product but by the objective test set out in comment *i* to § 402A: "The article sold must be dangerous to an extent beyond that which would be contemplated by the ordinary consumer who purchases it, with the ordinary knowledge common to the community as to its characteristics."[86] This definition of the ordinary consumer is also the test of what makes a defective condition in a product "unreasonably dangerous" under the consumer expectations test.[87]

In the vast majority of cases, whether the plaintiff was, in fact, an ordinary consumer of the product is not an issue. However, in some cases, the person who used the product was not an intended user. An example of this are small children who, without permission, use products that were designed for use by adults. Most courts analyze these cases by focusing on the "intended use" and the "intended users" of the product.[88] A few courts, however, have approached the question of liability from the perspective of whether the characteristics of the product should be judged according to the expectations of adults rather than the young children who used the product.[89] An example of this is *Todd v. Societe Bic S.A.*,[90] in which a four-year-old child found a disposable cigarette lighter that was in the living room of the home in which she lived. She took it upstairs where she set fire to some papers on the floor, resulting in the death of a twenty-two-month-old child who was sleeping in the home. In their suit based upon negligence and strict

---

[86] In *Heaton v. Ford Motor Co.*, 435 P.2d 806, 808 (Or. 1967), the Oregon Supreme Court stated:

> In deciding what a reasonable consumer expects, the jury is not permitted to decide how strong products should be, nor even what consumers should expect. . . .The jury is supposed to determine the basically factual question of what reasonable consumers do expect.

See also Brown v. Sears, Roebuck & Co. 328 F.3d 1274 (10th Cir. 2003) (applying Utah law); Lamkin v. Towner, 563 N.E.2d 449 (Ill. 1990); Dart v. Wiebe Manufacturing Co., 709 P.2d 876 (Ariz. 1985); Vincer v. Esther Williams All-Aluminum Swimming Pool Co., 230 N.W.2d 794 (Wis. 1975).

[87] *See* IND. CODE § 34-6-2-146 (1998).

[88] *See* Phillips v. Crickett Lighters, 841 A.2d 1000 (Pa. 2003). For a discussion of the "intended user" defense, see Chapter 9.

[89] *See* Bellotte v. Zayre Corp., 352, A.2d 723 (N.H. 1976); Vincer, 230 N.W.2d 794.

[90] 21 F.3d 1402 (7th Cir. 1994) (applying Illinois law).

liability against the manufacturer, the parents alleged that the design of the lighter was unreasonably dangerous because it did not include a child-resistant feature.[91] They argued that, instead of looking to the expectations of the ordinary consumer, the court should look to those of a foreseeable user of the lighter — a child — in applying the consumer expectations test.[92]

The Seventh Circuit rejected the parents' arguments, holding that § 402A and Illinois law confined the consumer expectations test to "ordinary consumers." According to the court, it would work an "absurdity" to expand the test to foreseeable users where children are involved. Since children "lack knowledge common to the community regarding consumer products" and do not perceive the dangers present in almost any product, they are not "ordinary consumers."[93] Children frequently engage in dangerous activities because they do not understand the risk of injury. According to the court, if children were the standard to measure consumer expectations,

> manufacturers would face absolute liability every time a child was injured by a product. The child's attorney would march into court and claim the product failed to perform in the manner the child expected. The attorney would be right, but the failure would not be due to a deficiency in the product, but to the natural deficiency children have in their knowledge of consumer products.[94]

Since the cigarette lighters were intended for use by adults — not a four-year-old child — and since an adult is expected to know that lighters cause fires, the court in *Todd* held that the design of the lighters did not make them unreasonably dangerous in the contemplation of the ordinary consumer who purchases them.

[3] What Does an Ordinary Consumer Expect of a Product?

Hansen and *Todd* point to a second question that can arise when consumer expectations test is used: does an ordinary consumer have sufficient knowledge or familiarity with the design of the product to have reasonable expectations about its safety or performance in the given situation? Two examples of the "ordinary knowledge" and expectations that consumers have about products were given by the court in *Todd v. Societe BIC, S.A.*:[95]

---

[91] *Id.* at 1404.

[92] *Id.* at 1407.

[93] *Id.* at 1408.

[94] *Id.* The expectations of an adult rather than a beginning teenage smoker were used to determine the expectations of the average consumer about the risks of smoking. *See* Insolia v. Philip Morris, Inc., 216 F.3d 596 (7th Cir. 2000) (applying Wisconsin law).

[95] 21 F.3d 1402, 1407 (7th Cir. 1994).

[A] pair of rubber soled shoes are not unreasonably dangerous simply because the person wearing them slips on a wet floor, because "it is a matter or common knowledge that shoes are more likely to slip when wet than dry. . . .." But if a hammer breaks when striking a steel peg, sending a metal fragment into the user's eye, the hammer is unreasonably dangerous because ordinary consumers do not expect hammers to chip on impact.

Similarly, in *Anderson v. Weslo, Inc.*,[96] the Washington appellate court stated:

The ordinary consumer buys a trampoline in order to jump on it. Anytime a person jumps on a trampoline, he or she could fall and be injured. The dangers of jumping are therefore obvious enough to be contemplated by the ordinary consumer.

However, the dangers of many products are not as obvious to consumers as rubber shoes, hammers and trampolines. An example of an increasingly complex product that frequently tests the limits of consumers' expectations is the automobile. In *Soule v. General Motors Corp.*,[97] the California Supreme Court gave some simple examples of what it felt an ordinary consumer could expect of automobiles: "[T]he ordinary consumers of modern automobiles may and do expect that such vehicles will be designed so as not to explode while idling at stoplights, experience sudden steering or brake failure as they leave the dealership, or roll over and catch fire in two-mile-per-hour collisions."[98] More difficult, however, was the situation in *Heaton v. Ford Motor Co.*,[99] in which the Oregon Supreme Court stated that a truck traveling 35 miles an hour and hitting a five- or six-inch rock was not so common an occurrence that the average person would know from personal experience what to expect of a truck under the circumstances. This led the court to affirm the involuntary nonsuit in the case, saying that to allow the jury to decide on its own intuition how strong a truck wheel should be would convert the concept of strict liability into absolute liability.

When dealing with consumer expectations about the safety of specific internal systems of an automobile such as airbags and seatbelts, courts increasingly look to "the expectation of performance, not the technical considerations of the product."[100] That was the attitude of the Sixth Circuit in *Hisrich v. Volvo Cars of North America, Inc.*,[101] in which an air bag deployed

---

[96] 906 P.2d 336 (Wash. Ct. App. 1995).

[97] 882 P.2d 298 (Cal. 1994).

[98] *Id.* at 308 n. 3.

[99] 435 P.2d 806 (Or. 1967).

[100] Hisrich v. Volvo Cars of North America, Inc., 226 F.3d 445, 455 (6th Cir. 2000) (applying Ohio law).

[101] 226 F.3d 445 (6th Cir. 2000) (applying Ohio law).

and killed a six-year-old girl after a low-speed collision. In reversing the jury verdict for the manufacturer, the Sixth Circuit held that it was not necessary that an ordinary consumer know "the technical considerations that influence the design of the airbag system in [the plaintiff's] Volvo."[102] Instead, a consumer needs to have only an expectation of the normal operation and safety of the product to satisfy the test. Similarly, in *Force v. Ford Motor Co.*,[103] the Florida appellate court held that, while ordinary consumers may not know the technical aspects of how seatbelts work, they are familiar enough with the item to have developed expectations about the function they perform and their safety.[104] That was sufficient for application of the consumer expectations test.

Since the consumer's expectations are a question of fact, courts favor leaving the question to the general experience of the jury.[105] According to the Connecticut Supreme Court: " 'The jury can draw their own reasonable conclusions as to the expectations of the ordinary consumer and the knowledge common in the community at large.' "[106] An example of leaving this question to the jury, even in a case involving a complicated medical device, is *Mele v. Howmedica, Inc.*,[107] in which the plaintiff alleged injury resulting from a device that was implanted during hip replacement surgery. The device used a cable that passed through the bone and created a risk of chafing off bone particles. As in *Hansen*, the manufacturer claimed that the plaintiff did not know of the particular device when he had the hip replacement and thus did not have any expectations about the safety of the system. However, the Illinois Appellate Court held that, even if implantees did not have expectations specific to the particular part of the artificial hip, they may have had relevant expectations about the safety of the artificial hip as a whole. Although jurors are entitled to use their own experiences to determine what an ordinary consumer would expect in such a situation, plaintiffs and manufacturers often attempt to influence that decision by presenting evidence going to the ordinary purpose of the product, the characteristics of the product, and any representations the manufacturer made about the product in advertisements.[108]

---

[102] *Id.* at 455.

[103] 879 So.2d 103 (Fla. Dist. Ct. App. 2004).

[104] *Id.* at 109.

[105] In *Buehler v. Whalen*, 70 Ill. 2d 51 (Ill. 1977), for example, the Illinois Supreme Court held that a jury did not need testimony from consumers to reach its conclusion that car buyers do not expect their cars to burst into flames in collisions.

[106] Giglio v. Connecticut Light & Power Co., 429 A.2d 486, 489 (Conn. 1980) (*quoting* Slepski v. Williams Ford, Inc., 364 A.2d 175, 178 (Conn. 1975)).

[107] 808 N.E.2d 1026 (Ill. App. Ct. 2004).

[108] Charles E. Cantú, *Distinguishing the Concept of Strict Liability for Ultra-Hazardous Activities from Strict Products Liability Under Section 402A of the Restatement (Second) of Torts: Two Parallel Lines of Reasoning That Never Should Meet*, 35 AKRON L. REV. 31, 45-47 (2001).

[4] When Does the Consumer Expectations Test Apply?

Closely related to the issue of whether an ordinary consumer has suffi-cient knowledge of a product to have expectations about its safety is the question whether the facts of a case are appropriate for the test. The ques-tion arises because the consumer expectations test and risk-utility analysis are used as alternative tests. Some states limit the consumer expectations test to what two leading commentators have called "res-ipsa-like cases that do not require the application of a general standard to determine defective design. For all the rest . . . risk-utility balancing is mandated."[109] In those states, the consumer expectations test is used in cases involving "a simple product which poses an obvious danger,"[110] a design that is "self-evident[ly] . . . not reasonably suitable and safe,"[111] cases where the failure of the product was simple,[112] or cases where the everyday experience of the users permits a conclusion about the product's safety without the need for expert opinion.[113] Other courts, however, take the position that the consumer expectations test is not negated automatically by a product's complexity.[114] In *Cunningham v. Mitsubishi Motors Corp.*,[115] for example, the issue arose in the context of consumers' expectations about automobile seatbelts. The Ohio federal court concluded that consumer expectations test was appro-priate because consumers had been "bombarded with information regarding the importance of wearing seat belts because of the protection which they provide."[116] The court stated that it was not willing to preclude the use of the consumer expectation test

> in a situation involving a familiar consumer product which is tech-nically complex or uses a new process to accomplish a familiar func-

---

[109] James A. Henderson & Aaron D. Twerski, *Achieving Consensus on Defective Product Design*, 83 CORNELL L. REV. 867, 899-900 (1998).

[110] Haddix v. Playtex Family Products Corp., 138 F.3d 681, 684 (7th Cir. 1998) (since tam-pons are a simple product and pose an obvious danger, the consumer expectations test, not the risk-utility analysis, was the proper test to use in a motion for summary judgment). Similarly, in *Miles v. S. C. Johnson & Son, Inc.*, 2002 U.S. Dist. LEXIS 10511 (N.D. Ill. 2002), the district court found that Crystal Draino drain cleaner was a simple, obviously dangerous product and that only the consumer expectations test applied.

[111] Suter v. San Angelo Foundry & Machine Co., 406 A.2d 140, 150 (N.J. 1979).

[112] Morson v. Superior Court, 109 Cal. Rptr. 2d 343 (Cal. Ct. App. 2001).

[113] Soule v. General Motors Corp., 882 P.2d 298, 308 (Cal. 1994) ("the consumer expectations test is reserved for cases in which the everyday experience of the product's users permits a con-clusion that the product's design violated minimum safety assumptions, and is thus defective regardless of expert opinion about the merits of the design.").

[114] *See* Hansen v. Baxter Healthcare Corp., 764 N.E.2d 35 (Ill. 2002) (medical device); Jackson v. General Motors Corp., 60 S.W.3d 800 (Tenn. 2001) (seatbelt).

[115] 1993 U.S. Dist. LEXIS 21299 (S.D. Ohio 1993). *See also* Force v. Ford Motor Co., 879 So.2d 103 (Fla. Dist. Ct. App. 2004).

[116] 1993 U.S. Dist. LEXIS 21299, at *14.

tion. Many familiar consumer products involve complex technology. In addition, manufacturers are constantly altering the methods in which products perform familiar functions. Thus, to conclude that the consumer expectation test cannot be used because a product is technologically complex or because a new process is used to achieve a familiar result would be to significantly reduce the use of that test. . . . Because of their long usage and consumer familiarity with the measure of safety which seat belts provide, consumer expectations do provide useful guidance.[117]

[C] *Risk-Utility Analysis*

[1] Introduction

The consumer expectations test is the standard used by § 402A to determine whether a product is unreasonably dangerous. However, manufacturers frequently make choices in the design of their products that involve weighing a number of factors and alternatives. This has led many courts and commentators to criticize the consumer expectations test as unsatisfactory for determining whether the design of a product created a defective condition that made it unreasonably dangerous.[118] In *Soule v. General Motors Corp.*,[119] for example, the defendant argued that the consumer expectations test was an "unworkable, amorphic, fleeting standard" that was "deficient and unfair in several respects." The defendant set out five reasons to support its contention.

> First, it defies definition. Second, it focuses not on the objective condition of products, but on the subjective, unstable, and often unreasonable opinions of consumers. Third, it ignores the reality that ordinary consumers know little about how safe the complex products they use can or should be made. Fourth, it invites the jury to isolate the particular consumer, component, accident and injury before it instead of considering whether the whole product fairly accommodates the competing expectations of all consumers in all situations. Fifth, it eliminates the careful balancing of risks and benefits which is essential to any design issue.[120]

---

[117] *Id.* at *14-15.

[118] *See* Birnbaum, *supra* note 26, at 593. For judicial expressions of the limitations of the consumer expectations test, see *Turner v. General Motors, Camacho v. Honda Motor Co.*, 741 P.2d 1240 (Colo. 1987).

[119] 882 P.2d 298 (Cal. 1994).

[120] *Id.* at 309-10. Professor John Wade also criticized the consumer expectations test as the exclusive test for determining a design defect on the ground that in "many situations. . .the consumer would not know what to expect, because he would have no idea how safe the product could be made." John Wade, *On the Nature of Strict Liability for Products*, 44 Miss. L.J. 825, 829 (1973).

In response to earlier criticisms of the consumer expectations test, the California Supreme Court, in *Barker v. Lull Engineering Co., Inc.*,[121] developed a "risk-utility analysis" for design defect cases. In *Barker*, a construction worker was injured seriously when the lift truck he was operating became unbalanced on a steep grade and dropped the lumber it was carrying. Although the worker jumped out of the cab of the truck when it started to tip, he jumped directly into the path of the falling lumber. The worker sued the truck manufacturer, claiming that the truck should have been equipped with "outriggers," large mechanical arms extending from the sides of the machine, to provide stability on steep grades. The trial court judge instructed the jury under the consumer expectation test and the jury returned a verdict for the manufacturer on the grounds that an ordinary consumer would expect the lift truck to tip on steep terrain. On appeal, however, the California Supreme Court reversed, holding that the consumer expectations test was an "undue restriction on the application of strict liability principles."[122] The court stated that, previously, it had "flatly rejected the suggestion that recovery in a products liability action should be permitted only if a product is more dangerous than contemplated by the average consumer, refusing to permit the low esteem in which the public might hold a dangerous product to diminish the manufacturer's liability for injuries caused by the product."[123] To deal with the inadequacy of the consumer expectations test, the court did not reject it but, instead, adopted a new approach that permitted a plaintiff to show that a design was defective by using either of two alternative tests: consumer expectations and risk-utility analysis.

> First, a product may be found defective in design if the plaintiff establishes that the product failed to perform as safely as an ordinary consumer would expect when used in an intended or reasonably foreseeable manner. Second, a product may alternatively be found defective in design if the plaintiff demonstrates that the product's design proximately cause his injury and the defendant fails to establish, in light of the relevant, factors, that, on balance, the benefits of the challenged design outweigh the risks of danger inherent in such design.[124]

In response to the second alternative of the *Barker* test, the majority of courts have adopted some form of a risk-utility analysis (sometimes referred

---

[121] 573 P.2d 443 (Cal. 1978). *See also* Soule v. General Motors Corp., 882 P.2d 298 (Cal. 1994).

[122] *Barker*, 573 P.2d at 451.

[123] *Id.*

[124] *Id.* at 456. The California Supreme Court reconsidered the first consumer expectations portion of the *Barker* test in *Soule v. General Motors Corp.*, 882 P.2d 298 (Cal. 1994).

to as the "risk-benefit" analysis,[125] the "danger-utility" analysis,[126] or the "cost-benefit" analysis[127]) to determine whether a product was unreasonably dangerous.[128] While a few states have made the risk-utility analysis their exclusive test for determining whether a product was unreasonably dangerous, most states have followed the approach in *Barker* and made it an alternative to the consumer expectations test.

The risk-utility analysis recognizes that there are benefits as well as risks in almost every product. In order to determine whether the risks make the product unreasonably dangerous, it is necessary to weigh those risks against the benefits.[129] In design defect cases, a product is unreasonably dangerous when the evidence establishes that the risk of the challenged design outweighs the benefits from the design.[130] This involves "balancing the likelihood and gravity of harm . . . against the burden of the precaution which would be effective to avoid the harm,"[131] a process that is similar to the formula articulated by Judge Learned Hand in *United States v. Carroll Towing Co.*[132] The effect of this process, according to the New York Court of Appeals, has been to bring

---

[125] Hisrich v. Volvo Cars of North America, Inc., 226 F.3d 445 (6th Cir. 2000) (applying Ohio law); Jennings v. BIC Corp., 181 F.3d 1250 (11th Cir. 1999) (applying Florida law).

[126] Espeaignnette v. Gene Tierney Co., 43 F.3d 1 (1st Cir. 1994) (applying Maine law); Camacho v. Honda Motor Co., 741 P.2d 1240 (Colo. 1987); Scoby v. Vulcan-Hart Corp., 569 N.E.2d 1147 (Ill. App. Ct. 1991).

[127] Tokio Marine & Fire Ins. Co., Ltd. v. Grove Manufacturing Co., 958 F.2d 1169 (1st Cir. 1992) (applying Puerto Rican law).

[128] According to Professors Henderson and Twerski, "[a] strong majority of American jurisdictions adopt the risk-utility test for design defect." *See* James A. Henderson & Aaron D. Twerski, *Product Design Liability in Oregon and the New Restatement*, 78 OR. L. REV. 1, 10 (1999). The authors set out a long list of cases adopting risk-utility analysis. *See id.* at n. 31.

[129] Lamkin v. Towner, 563 N.E.2d 449 (Ill. 1990).

[130] Metzgar v. Playskool Inc., 30 F.3d 459 (3d Cir. 1994); Sperry-New Holland v. Prestage, 617 So.2d 248 (Miss. 1993); Voss v. Black & Decker Manufacturing Co., 450 N.E.2d 204 (N.Y. 1983).

[131] Burke v. Illinois Power Co., 373 N.E.2d 1354, 1367 (Ill. App. Ct. 1978).

[132] 159 F.2d 169 (2d Cir. 1947). Under the Hand formula, liability depends upon whether the burden of adequate precautions (B) is less than the probability of injury (P) x the gravity of the injury if it does occur (L). According to one commentator:

> When a jury decides that the risk of harm outweighs the utility of a particular design that the product is not as safe as it could be, it is saying that in choosing the particular design and cost trade-offs, the manufacturers exposed the consumer to greater risk of danger than he should have. Conceptually and analytically, this approach bespeaks negligence.

Birnbaum, *Unmasking the Test for Design Defect: Negligence [to Warranty] to Strict Liability to Negligence*, 33 VAND. L. REV. 593, 610 (1980). For examples of judicial decisions taking this view, see *Nunnally v. R.J. Reynolds Tobacco Co.*, 869 So.2d 373 (Miss. 2004), and *Banks v. ICI Americas, Inc.*, 450 S.E.2d 671 (Ga. 1994).

the inquiry in design defect cases closer to that used in traditional negligence cases, where the reasonableness of an actor's conduct is considered in light of a number of situational and policy-driven factors. While efforts have been made to steer away from the fault-oriented negligence principles by characterizing the design defect cause of action in terms of a product-based rather than a conduct based analysis . . . the reality is that the risk/utility balancing test is a 'negligence-inspired' approach, since it invites the parties to adduce proof about the manufacturer's choices and ultimately requires the fact finder to make ' judgment about the [manufacturer's] judgment.'[133]

[2] Factors Used in Risk-Utility Analysis

In balancing the risks inherent in a product's design against the utility or benefit derived from the challenged design, the fact-finder weighs a number of factors. The most frequently cited of these is the list of seven factors first set out by Dean John W. Wade in a 1973 law review article.[134] These factors are:

(1) The usefulness and desirability of the product, i.e., its utility to the user and to the public as a whole.

(2) The safety aspect of the product, i.e., the likelihood that it will cause injury and the probable seriousness of the injury.

(3) The availability of a substitute product which will meet the same need and not be as unsafe.

(4) The manufacturer's ability to eliminate the unsafe character of the product without impairing its usefulness or making it too expensive to maintain its utility.

(5) The user's ability to avoid danger by the exercise of care in the use of the product.

(6) The user's anticipated awareness of the dangers inherent in the product and their avoidability because of public general knowledge of the obvious condition of the product, or the exercise of suitable warnings or instructions.

---

[133] Denny v. Ford Motor Co., 662 N.E.2d 730, 735 (N.Y. 1995). *See also* Banks v. ICI Americas, Inc., 450 S.E.2d 671, 674 (Ga. 1994) ("The balancing test that forms the risk-utility analysis is thus consistent with Georgia law, which has long applied negligence principles in making the determination whether a product was defectively designed.").

[134] John Wade, *On the Nature of Strict Tort Liability for Products*, 44 MISS. L.J. 825, 837-38 (1973). Among the numerous cases that have cited the Wade factors are *Binakonsky v. Ford Motor Co.*, 133 F.3d 281 (4th Cir. 1998) (applying Maryland law); *Surace v. Caterpillar, Inc.*, 111 F.3d 1039 (3d Cir. 1997 (applying Pennsylvania law); *Sperry-New Holland v. Prestage*, 617 So.2d 248 (Miss. 1993); *Camacho v. Honda Motor Co.*, 741 P.2d 1240 (Colo. 1987); *Byrns v. Riddell*, 550 P.2d 1065 (Ariz. 1976).

(7) The feasibility, on the part of the manufacturer, of spreading the loss by setting the price of the product or carrying liability insurance.

Courts rarely analyze in detail all seven of the Wade factors in a single decision. However, one case that did is *Riley v. Becton Dickinson Vascular Access, Inc.*,[135] in which the plaintiff, a nurse, contracted the HIV virus when she was stuck with an I.V. catheter needle after starting an IV in a patient in a hospital where she worked. The plaintiff argued that the design of IV catheter made it unsafe for its intended use because the needle, contaminated by the patient's blood, remained exposed after it was withdrawn from the catheter, permitting a needle-stick accident to occur.[136] In analyzing the claims of the plaintiff and the defenses of the manufacturer of the IV catheter, the federal district court applied Pennsylvania law which had adopted the risk-utility test.

The court began by considering the usefulness and desirability of the I.V. catheter, i.e., its utility to the user and to the public as a whole. The court stated that sharp needles are essential for many medical procedures such as taking blood samples and delivering medications and intravenous fluids and thus are highly useful both to the medical professional and the public as a whole.[137] That led the court to the second factor: the safety aspect of the I.V. catheter, i.e., the likelihood that it would cause injury and the probable seriousness of the injury. In *Riley*, this required the court to consider not only the likelihood of a needle stick from the use of the I.V. catheter but also the likelihood of a stick with a needle that was HIV contaminated and the likelihood of contracting HIV from the stick. Based upon calculations from evidence submitted by the parties, the court concluded that the risks of HIV exposure and HIV infection from an I.V. catheter were very low.[138] The manufacturer had only three reports of HIV infection from its catheter during the 16-year period when it sold an estimated 1.5 billion of the devices.[139]

The third factor analyzed by the court was the availability of a substitute product that would meet the same need and not be as unsafe. The plaintiff argued that there was an available substitute for the defendant's I.V. catheter; one manufactured by another company permitted the needle to be retracted into a plastic sheath as it was withdrawn from the tube attached to the patient's vein.[140] While such an alternative design would reduce the incidence of needle sticks, the court pointed to evidence that the alternative

---

[135] 913 F. Supp. 879 (E.D. Pa. 1995) (applying Pennsylvania law).

[136] *Id.* at 880.

[137] *Id.* at 884.

[138] *Id.* at 884-886.

[139] *Id.* at 886.

[140] *Id.*

catheter had a number of drawbacks and that studies showed that complaints about the protected catheter indicated that it required improvements.[141] Thus, while an alternative design was available and could reduce the number of needle sticks, it was not certain that the alternative was safer overall when compared with other aspects of the alternative design.

The fourth factor was the manufacturer's ability to eliminate the unsafe character of I.V. catheter without impairing its usefulness or making it too expensive to maintain its utility. In *Riley*, the court found that there was only one alternative for the defendant's I.V. catheter and that alternative had its own risks. In addition, the cost of the alternative catheter was almost twice that of the defendant's device. The court concluded that it was not possible to eliminate the unsafe feature of the defendant's I.V. catheter without impairing its utility since the costs of the only available product were much higher, the risks associated with the unsafe design could not be eliminated completely, and there were problems (other than the risk of a needle stick) associated with the use of the alternative design that required extensive training to lessen and which could not be eliminated entirely.[142]

The fifth factor in court's risk-utility analysis was the user's ability to avoid danger by the exercise of care in the use of I.V. catheter. Since the design of the alternative catheter in *Riley* could not prevent completely needle sticks from the use of I.V. catheters, the court concluded that it was unlikely that even extreme caution and adherence to recommended procedures could enable healthcare workers to avoid the dangers completely.[143] The court felt that healthcare workers had some ability to reduce risks inherent in the use of I.V. catheters by taking appropriate precautions.[144]

The sixth factor was the user's anticipated awareness of the dangers inherent in I.V. catheter and their avoidability because of public general knowledge of the obvious condition of the product, or the exercise of suitable warnings or instructions. The court opined that the record indicated the widespread awareness among healthcare workers of the potential dangers of a needle stick. Even the plaintiff did not argue that she was unaware of the danger.[145]

The final factor in the court's risk-utility analysis was the feasibility, on the part of the manufacturer, of spreading the loss by setting the price of the product or carrying liability insurance. The plaintiff in *Riley* suggested that, if the manufacturer of the I.V. catheter was liable for her injury, it could lead to the withdrawal of the device from the market or to an increase

---

[141] *Id.* at 886-888.

[142] *Id.* at 888-889.

[143] *Id.* at 889-890.

[144] *Id.* at 890.

[145] *Id.*

in its cost.[146] The court, however, concluded that a potential manipulation of the market for I.V. catheters should not be undertaken as the result of one of only three accidents over a 16-year period, especially when the alternative design had its own dangers and drawbacks.[147] In addition, the court felt there would be no adverse consequences to the plaintiff from not shifting the loss to the manufacturer since the loss would be borne by the plaintiff's employer and its workers' compensation system.[148] Thus, balancing all of the factors in the risk-utility analysis led the court to conclude that, although the defendant's I.V. catheter was dangerous because it was capable of causing serious injury, it was not unreasonably dangerous for purposes of § 402A.[149]

[3] Reasonable Alternative Design

Of the factors used in risk-utility analysis, the one that has received the most attention is whether a "substitute product" was available at the time of manufacture that would meet the same need as the challenged product and not be as unsafe. In *Hansen v. Baxter Healthcare Corp.*,[150] discussed above in connection with the consumer expectations test, the Illinois Supreme Court also affirmed the jury's finding for the plaintiff based on a risk-utility analysis. According to the court, there was sufficient evidence that, first, a connector existed that would have prevented an unintentional disconnection of the catheter and that, second, the cost would have been only between three and five cents per unit.[151] However, for many products there is no alternative design that will reduce the risk of injury without drastically altering the nature of the product. In *Anderson v. Weslo, Inc.*,[152] for example, the Washington appellate court held that the risk-utility analysis was not applicable in a case involving a teenager injured while using a trampoline because, "[g]iven the nature and purpose of a trampoline, it is impossible to imagine an alternative design that would have prevented [the plaintiff's] harm."[153]

Some states, including Washington in the *Anderson* decision, require proof that an alternative design was of greater overall safety than the

---

[146] *Id.* at 891.

[147] *Id.*

[148] *Id.*

[149] *Id.* at 892.

[150] 764 N.E.2d 35 (Ill. 2002).

[151] *Id.* at 45. *See also* Honda of America Manufacturing, Inc. v. Norman, 104 S.W.3d 600 (Tex. App. 2003). In *Colon v. BIC USA, Inc.*, 199 F. Supp. 2d 53 (S.D.N.Y. 2001), the court held that there was insufficient evidence that the design of a disposable cigarette lighter was unreasonably dangerous since there was no evidence of a feasible alternative design.

[152] 906 P.2d 336 (Wash. Ct. App. 1995).

[153] *Id.* at 340.

design the manufacturer actually used.[154] An example of the failure to meet this requirement is *Allen v. Minnstar*,[155] in which the Tenth Circuit affirmed summary judgment in favor of the manufacturer of a boat engine that was alleged to be defective because of the absence of a propeller guard on the boat. According to the court, the plaintiff failed to show "an alternative, safer design, practicable under the circumstances and available at the time of the defendants' placing the boat and engine in the stream of commerce."[156] However, a number of states have refused to require the plaintiff to prove that a reasonable alternative design was available at the time the product was manufactured. In *Banks v. ICI Americas, Inc.*,[157] the Georgia Supreme Court held that a jury may consider evidence that "an alternative design would have made the product safer than the original design and was a marketable reality and technologically feasible" but refused to make such proof mandatory in every case.[158]

In a lengthy footnote in *Potter v. Chicago Pneumatic Tool Co.*,[159] the Connecticut Supreme Court surveyed the states that had considered the role of feasible alternative designs in design defect cases and found four different approaches.[160] First, the court found that six states did not require a plaintiff to show a feasible alternative design in order to establish a manufacturer's liability for design defect.[161] Second, sixteen states held that a feasible alternative design was only one of several factors that the trier of fact could consider in determining whether a product design was defective.[162] Third, three states required the defendant, not the plaintiff, to

---

[154] *See, e.g.*, Tex. Civ. Prac. & Rem. Code Ann. § 82.005 (Vernon 2005) (in a design defect case, "the burden is on the claimant to prove by a preponderance of the evidence that there was a safer alternative design."); Wankier v. Crown Equipment Corp., 353 F.3d 862 (10th Cir. 2003) (applying Utah law); Richards v. Michelin Tire Corp., 21 F.3d 1048 (11th Cir. 1994) (applying Alabama law); Burt v. Makita Corp., 212 F. Supp. 2d 893 (N.D. Ind. 2002) (applying Indiana law); Rossell v. Volkswagen of America, 709 P.2d 517 (Ariz. 1985); Maxted v. Pacific Car & Foundry Co., 527 P.2d 832 (Wyo. 1974).

[155] 8 F.3d 1470 (10th Cir. 1993) (applying Utah law).

[156] *Id.* at 1479.

[157] 450 S.E.2d 671 (Ga. 1994).

[158] *Id.* at 674-675.

[159] 694 A.2d 1319 (Conn. 1997).

[160] *Id.* at 1331 n. 11.

[161] *Id. See* Karns v. Emerson Electric Co., 817 F.2d 1452 (10th Cir. 1987) (applying Oklahoma law); French v. Grove Manufacturing Co., 656 F.2d 295 (8th Cir. 1981) (applying Arkansas law); Kallio v. Ford Motor Co., 407 N.W.2d 92 (Minn. 1987); Rahmig v. Mosley Machinery Co., 412 N.W.2d 56 (Neb. 1987); Couch v. Mine Safety Appliances Co., 728 P.2d 585 (Wash. 1986); Sumnicht v. Toyota Motor Sales, U.S.A., Inc., 360 N.W.2d 2 (Wis. 1984).

[162] *Id. See* Warner Fruehauf Trailer Co. v. Boston, 654 A.2d 1272, 1277 (D.C. App. 1995); Brooks v. Beech Aircraft Corp., 902 P.2d 54, 61 (N.M. 1995); Banks v. ICI Americas, Inc., 450 S.E.2d 671 (Ga. 1994); Jenkins v. Amchem Products, Inc., 886 P.2d 869 (Kan. 1994); Camacho v. Honda Motor Co., Ltd., 741 P.2d 1240 (Colo. 1987); McCourt v. J. C. Penney Co., 734 P.2d 696 (Nev. 1987); Peterson v. Safway Steel Scaffolds Co., 400 N.W.2d 909, 913 (S.D. 1987); Dart v. Wiebe Manufacturing, Inc., 709 P.2d 876 (Ariz. 1985); Montgomery Elevator Co. v. McCullough, 676 S.W.2d 776 (Ky. 1984); Radiation Technology, Inc. v. Ware Construction Co., 445 So. 2d 329

prove that the product was not defective.[163] Finally, eight states required that the plaintiff prove a feasible alternative design in order to establish a prima facie case of design defect.[164]

In *Potter*, the Connecticut Supreme Court rejected a requirement that the plaintiff establish a reasonable alternative design. In that case, the plaintiffs were shipyard workers who alleged that defects in the pneumatic hand tools they used created excessive vibrations that caused their injuries. The jury returned a verdict for the plaintiffs and the defendant argued that it was time for the court to abandon the consumer expectation test and to adopt the requirement that the plaintiff must prove the existence of a reasonable alternative design in order to prevail on a design defect claim.[165] The Connecticut Supreme Court rejected the defendant's argument for two reasons: First, the court felt that requiring proof of a feasible alternative design imposed an undue burden on plaintiffs that could preclude otherwise valid claims from jury consideration. The reason for that was that such proof would require plaintiffs to retain an expert witness even in cases in which jurors could infer a design defect from circumstantial evidence.[166] Second, the court felt that, in some situations, a product may be in a "defective condition unreasonably dangerous" even though there is no feasible alternative design. In such cases, the manufacturer is strictly liable despite the fact that there is no reasonable alternative design.[167]

One of the most important sections of the Restatement (Third) is § 2(b) which requires a plaintiff to show a reasonable alternative design in a design defect case. According to the section, a product

> is defective in design when the foreseeable risks of harm posed by the product could have been reduced or avoided by the adoption of a reasonable alternative design by the seller or by other distributor, or a predecessor in the commercial chain of distribution, and the

---

(Fla. 1983); Claytor v. General Motors Corp., 286 S.E.2d 129 (S.C. 1982); Chown v. USM Corp., 297 N.W.2d 218 (Iowa 1980); Morningstar v. Black & Decker Manufacturing Co., 253 S.E.2d 666 (W. Va. 1979); Cepeda v. Cumberland Engineering Co., 386 A.2d 816 (N.J. 1978); Wilson v. Piper Aircraft Corp., 577 P.2d 1322 (Or. 1978); Vantour v. BodyMastersSportsIndustries, Inc., 784 A.2d 1178 (N.H. 2001).

[163] *Id. See* Ontai v. Straub Clinic & Hospital, Inc., 659 P.2d (Haw. 1983); Caterpillar Tractor Co. v. Beck, 593 P.2d 871 (Alaska 1979); Barker v. Lull Engineering Co., 573 P.2d 443 (Cal. 1978).

[164] *Id. See* General Motors Corp. v. Edwards, 482 So. 2d 1176 (Ala. 1985); Voss v. Black & Decker Mfg. Co., 450 N.E.2d 204 (N.Y. 1983); Owens v. Allis-Chalmers Corp., 326 N.W.2d 372 (Mich. 1982). *See also* 735 Ill. Comp. Stat. 5/2-2104 (2004); La. Rev. Stat. Ann. § 9:2800.56 (West 1997); Miss. Code Ann. § 11-1-63 (f) (ii) (2002); Ohio Rev. Code Ann. § 2307.75(F) (Anderson 2005); Tex. Civ. Prac. & Rem. Code Ann. § 82.005 (Vernon 2005).

[165] *Potter*, 694 A.2d at 1331.

[166] *Id.* at 1332.

[167] *Id.*

omission of the alternative design renders the product not reasonably safe.[168]

According to comment *d* to § 2:

> Subsection (b) adopts a reasonableness ("risk-utility balancing")
> test as the standard for judging the defectiveness of product designs.
> More specifically, the test is whether a reasonable alternative design
> would, at reasonable cost, have reduced the foreseeable risk of harm
> posed by the product and, if so, whether the omission of the alter-
> native design by the seller . . . rendered the product not reasonably
> safe. . . .Under prevailing rules concerning allocation of burden of
> proof, the plaintiff must prove that such a reasonable alternative
> was, or reasonably could have been, available at the time of sale or
> distribution.[169]

[4] Burden of Proof

As with many areas of products liability law, there is a disagreement
among the courts as to who bears the burden of proving that the risks of the
design of a product outweigh its benefits. In *Barker v. Lull Engineering
Co.*,[170] the California Supreme Court did more than establish two alternative tests for determining design defect liability. The court concluded that,
in a strict liability action using risk-utility analysis, a plaintiff may recover
if he "demonstrates that the product's design proximately caused his injury
and the defendant fails to establish, in light of the relevant factors, that, on
balance, the benefits of the challenged design do not outweigh the risk of
danger inherent in such design."[171] Under the *Barker* court's assignment of
the burden of proof, once a plaintiff makes a *prima facie* showing that the
product's design proximately caused the injuries, the burden shifts to the
defendant to prove that the benefits outweigh the risks.

Although the majority of states have adopted *Barker's* two-pronged
approach to proving whether the design of a product made it unreasonably dangerous, only three other states have followed its lead in shifting the
burden of proof to the defendant.[172] The majority of states have chosen,

---

168 RESTATEMENT (THIRD) OF TORTS: PRODUCTS LIABILITY § 2(b) (1998). For a discussion of the
attitude of states towards § 2(b), see Cami Perkins, *The Increasing Acceptance of Restatement (Third) Risk Utility Analysis in Design Defect Claims*, 4 NEV. L.J. 609 (2004), and Frank
J. Vandall & Joshua F. Vandall, *A Call for an Accurate Restatement (Third) of Torts: Design
Defect*, 33 U. MEM. L. REV. 909 (2003).

169 *Id.* at cmt. *d*.

170 573 P.2d 443 (Cal. 1978).

171 *Id.* at 456.

172 Lamkin v. Towner, 563 N.E.2d 449 (Ill. 1990); Ontai v. Traub Clinic & Hospital, Inc., 659
P.2d 734 (Haw. 1983); Caterpillar Tractor Co. v. Beck, 593 P.2d 884 (Alaska 1979).

instead, to follow the traditional approach to burden of proof in design
defect cases. Under the risk-benefit analysis, the plaintiff must produce
evidence that the danger posed by the product's design, the likelihood that
harm will occur, the gravity of the harm if it occurs, and the feasibility of
a safer alternative design outweigh the cost of that alternative design and
the negative consequences for the product from an alternative design.[173]

[D] *Alternative Tests*

States use a variety of approaches to determine whether the design of a
product is defective. While some states define a design defect solely in terms
of the consumer expectations theory[174] or solely in terms of risk utility
analysis,[175] most states follow the lead of the California Supreme Court in
Barker v. Lull Engineering Co.[176] and use the two tests as alternatives.[177]
The two tests are not mutually exclusive and either or both can be used in
a case. Other states have developed variations on these two approaches. In
Potter v. Chicago Pneumatic Tool Co.,[178] the Connecticut Supreme Court
restated its support for the consumer expectations test, while recognizing
that there are situations in which the complex design of a product makes it
difficult or impossible for the ordinary consumer to have any expectations
of safety about it.[179] To deal with these cases, the court adopted a modified
consumer expectations test, under which

> a consumer's expectations may be viewed in light of various factors
> that balance the utility of the product's design with the magnitude
> of its risks. We find persuasive the reasoning of those jurisdictions
> that have modified their formulation of the consumer expectation
> test by incorporation of the risk-utility factors into the ordinary
> consumer expectation analysis. . . .Thus, the modified consumer

---

[173] Austin v. Mitsubishi Electronics America, Inc., 966 F. Supp. 506 (E.D. Mich. 1997)
(applying Michigan law): Armentrout v. FMC Corp., 842 P.2d 175 (Colo. 1992); Dart v. Wiebe
Manufacturing Inc., 709 P.2d 876 (Ariz. 1985); Knitz v. Minster Machine Co., 432 N.E.2d 814
(Ohio 1982); Wilson v. Piper Aircraft Corp., 579 P.2d 1287 (Or. 1978).

[174] *See* Green v. Smith & Nephew AHP, Inc., 629 N.W.2d 727 (Wis. 2001); Rojas v. Lindsay
Mfg. Co ., 701 P.2d 210, 212 (Idaho 1985); Ritter v. Narragansett Elec. Co., 283 A.2d 255, 263
(R.I. 1971).

[175] *See* Banks v. ICI Americas, Inc., 450 S.E.2d 671 (Ga. 1994); Armentrout v. FMC Corp.,
842 P.2d 175, 183 (Colo. 1992); Radiation Tech., Inc. v. Ware Construction Co., 445 So.2d 329,
331 (Fla. 1983); Thibault v. Sears, Roebuck & Co., 395 A.2d 843, 846 (N.H. 1978).

[176] 573 P.2d 443 (1978).

[177] For examples, see *Peck v. Bridgeport Machines, Inc.*, 237 F. 3d 614 (6th Cir. 2001)
(applying Michigan law); *Halliday v. Strum, Ruger & Co.*, 792 A.2d 1145 (Md. 2002); *Lamkin
v. Towner*, 563 N.E.2d 449 (Ill. 1990); *Dart v. Wiebe Manufacturing Co.*, 709 P.2d 876 (Ariz.
1985); *Ontai v. Straub Clinic and Hospital*, 659 P.2d 734 (Haw. 1983).

[178] 694 A.2d 1319 (Conn. 1997).

[179] *Id.* at 1333.

expectation test provides the jury with the product's risks and utility and then inquires whether a reasonable consumer would consider the product unreasonably dangerous.[180]

Under the *Potter* approach, the consumer expectation test establishes the product's risks and utility. The inquiry then is whether a reasonable consumer, with that information, would consider the product's design unreasonably dangerous. The Connecticut court listed a number of factors — basically those set out earlier by Professor John Wade — the jury could consider in weighing the risk and utility.[181]

Although the Connecticut court in *Potter* adopted a modified consumer expectation test, it did not require the plaintiff to present evidence of the product's risks and benefits in every case. Instead, it said that the ordinary consumer expectations test should be used in situations where "the everyday experience of the particular product's users permits the inference that the product did not meet minimum safety expectations."[182] In contrast, the court stated that risk-utility balancing of the modified test should be reserved for cases where "the particular facts do not reasonably permit the inference that the product did not meet the safety expectations of the ordinary consumer."[183] Under this approach, it is the function of the court to determine when a jury instruction on the ordinary consumer expectation test or the modified test is appropriate.[184]

In 1996, one year before the *Potter* decision, a study by John Vargo found that six states applied a modified consumer expectation test that incorporated certain risk-utility factors into the consumer expectation test and substituted the "reasonable consumer" for the "ordinary consumer."[185] Although *Potter* has attracted considerable attention from commentators, no state explicitly has adopted the modified consumer expectation test since 1997.

The Tennessee Products Liability Act[186] also recognizes two tests for determining whether a product was unreasonably dangerous: the consumer expectations test and the "reasonably prudent manufacturer" test.[187] The

---

[180] *Id.*

[181] *Id.* at 1333–34.

[182] *Id.* at 1334.

[183] *Id.*

[184] *Id.*

[185] John F. Vargo, *The Emperor's New Clothes, The American Law Institute Adorns a "New Cloth" for Section 402A Products Liability Design Defects — A Survey of the States Reveals a Different Weave*, 26 U. MEM. L. REV. 493, 540-41, 952 (Index 4) (1996).

[186] TENN. CODE ANN. § 29-28-101 (2000).

[187] *Id.* § 29-28-102(8). *See* Clinton H. Scott, *Defective Condition or Unreasonably Dangerous Under the Tennessee Products Liability Act: Just What Does It Mean?* 33 U. MEM. L. REV. 945 (2003).

consumer expectations test looks at whether a product was unreasonably dangerous from the perspective of the expectations of an ordinary consumer who uses it. The prudent manufacturer test requires the determination of whether a prudent manufacturer would have marketed the product knowing its dangerous condition. Unlike the modified consumer expectation test developed in *Potter* that asks whether a reasonable consumer, knowing the product's risks and utility, would consider the product unreasonably dangerous, the Tennessee test assumes that a prudent manufacture would engage in the risk-utility analysis and consider such factors as the product's usefulness, the costs involved with an alternative design, and the seriousness and likelihood of potential harm in making its decision whether to market the product.

§ 5.04 OPEN AND OBVIOUS DANGERS

One question that arises both in negligence cases and under strict liability is whether a plaintiff should be barred from recovery if the risk created by the design of the product, such as the absence of a safety device, was "open and obvious."[188] An "open and obvious,"or "patent," danger is defined as "an unsafe aspect of the product that is an inherent characteristic of the product and that would be recognized by the ordinary person who uses or consumes the product with the ordinary knowledge common to the class of persons for whom the product is intended."[189] In negligence cases, using a product that contains an open and obvious danger is treated as factor in considering whether the plaintiff was contributorily negligent.[190] In strict liability cases, the consumer expectations test and risk-utility analysis take different approaches to their treatment of such a danger. In most states that apply the consumer expectations test, an open and obvious danger created by the design bars recovery because the consumer did not expect the product to be safe.[191] An example of this is *Kutzler v. AMF Harley-Davidson*[192] in which the plaintiff suffered multiple fractures and severe injuries to his leg when the motorcycle he was riding was sideswiped by an automobile that crossed the center line of the highway. The plaintiff brought suit against the

---

[188] For a justification of the open and obvious rule, see *Campo v. Schofield*, 95 N.E.2d 802 (N.Y. 1950). *Campo* was overruled by *Micallef v. Miehle Co.*, 348 N.E.2d 571 (N.Y. 1976).

[189] N.J. STAT. ANN. § 2A:58C-3(a)(2) (2000).

[190] RESTATEMENT (SECOND) OF TORTS § 398 cmt *b* (1965) states: "If the dangerous character of the plan or design is known to the user of the chattel, he may be in contributory fault if the risk involved in using it is unreasonably great or if he fails to take those special precautions which the known dangerous character of the chattel requires."

[191] Sandage v. Bankhead Enterprises, Inc., 177 F.3d 670 (8th Cir. 1999) (applying Missouri law); Brewer v. Harley-Davidson, Inc., 1999 U.S. App. LEXIS 2962 (10th Cir. 1999) (applying Oklahoma law); Kirk v. Hanes Corporation of North Carolina, 771 F. Supp. 856 (E.D. Mich. 1991) (applying Michigan law).

[192] 550 N.E.2d 1236 (Ill. App. Ct. 1990). *See also* Shaffer v. AMF Inc., 842 F.2d 893 (6th Cir. 1988).

manufacturer of the motorcycle alleging it was unreasonably dangerous because it was designed with extra-wide gas tanks and not equipped with crash bars. The Illinois Appellate Court, however, dismissed the case on the ground that the extra-wide gas tank and absence of crash bars were obvious both to someone who looked at the motorcycle as well as to a rider who sat down on it. Since the motorcycle could not be expected to protect the rider from sideswipes, the design was not unreasonably dangerous and the motorcycle did not fail to perform in a manner reasonably to be expected in light of its design.

With the adoption of the risk-utility analysis, the open and obvious danger is not, in itself, a bar to recovery. Instead, the obviousness of the risk is only one of the factors that the jury considers in determining the product's risk. An open and obvious risk will bar recovery only when it outweighs the other factors that are considered in weighing the risks against the benefits of the product as designed.[193] The Restatement (Third) takes this position based on the drafters view that, in the strong majority of states, the open and obvious nature of a product is not necessarily an absolute bar to recovery.[194]

Although recognized by the majority of states, the open and obvious doctrine is not accepted by all states. In New Mexico, for example, the doctrine has been abolished in negligence cases. In *Smith ex. rel. Smith v. Bryco Arms*,[195] a 15-year-old accidently shot his 14-year-old friend with a .22 caliber handgun. The plaintiffs argued that the gun was defective because its design did not incorporate safety devices and warnings designed to prevent foreseeable unintentional shooting accidents. In reversing the trial court's grant of summary judgment for the manufacturer, the New Mexico Supreme Court noted that, although the dangers of a gun may be open and obvious, the state had abolished the doctrine. As a result, "a risk is not reasonable simply because it is open and obvious to persons using ordinary care."[196]

§ 5.05 STATE OF THE ART

In many products liability cases, the manufacturer will attempt to show that the design of its product was not defective because it was the "state-of-the-art" at the time of manufacture. In *Potter v. Chicago Pneumatic Tool Co.*,[197] the plaintiffs alleged that defects in the design of the pneumatic

---

[193] *See* Swix v. Daisy Manufacturing Co., 373 F.3d 678 (6th Cir. 2004) (applying Michigan law); Ogeltree v. Navistar International Transportation Corp., 500 S.E.2d 570 (Ga. 1998); Sperry-Holland v. Prestage, 617 So.2d 248 (Miss. 1993).

[194] RESTATEMENT (THIRD) OF TORTS: PRODUCTS LIABILITY § 2 cmt. *d* (1998). See *Blue v. Environmental Engineering, Inc.*, 828 N.E.2d 1128 (Ill. 2005), adopting the RESTATEMENT (THIRD) position.

[195] 33 P.3d 638 (N.M. 2001).

[196] *Id.* at 650.

[197] 694 A.2d 1319 (Conn. 1997).

hand tools they used in their work created excessive vibrations that caused their injuries. The manufacture presented testimony that they "produced the safest and highest quality tools that they were able to design." A representative of one of the defendant's customers also testified that the defendants tools were the best for his company's purposes and that his company would be in a "tough situation" if it had to replace the defendant's tools.[198] The plaintiff, however, presented evidence that one of the manufacturer's competitors had produced a tool since 1976 that reduced vibration and that the manufacturer has been aware of the tool.[199] Thus, in order to make their case, both the plaintiff and the manufacturer presented evidence of the "state-of-the-art" at the time the manufacturer produced its hand tools. The concept of the state-of-the-art has two separate but related meanings in products liability cases. In one sense, the state-of-the-art is more than just the industry custom. It is the level of relevant "technical, mechanical and scientific knowledge of manufacturing, designing, testing, or labeling the same or similar products which was in existence and reasonably feasible for use at the time of manufacture."[200] In this sense, it is an elusive standard. It can be determined only by balancing a wide-ranging pool of data from academic, professional, and industry sources. These, in turn, must be analyzed in light, not only of basic consumer expectations but also technological and financial realities. In this sense, the totality of such materials has a direct bearing on the jury's decision on the adequacy of the challenged design.

Although manufacturers in some cases have argued that state-of-the-art is available only in failure to warn cases, courts hold that it is available in design defect cases as well. However, it is not available in manufacturing defect cases.[201] Plaintiffs, on the other hand, often argue that while state-of-the-art is relevant in negligence cases, it should not be used in strict liability cases. Since negligence cases focus on the conduct of the manufacturer in selecting the particular design of the product, state of the art evidence is relevant to whether the manufacturer acted reasonably in selecting the design. If a safer design was available and feasible, a manufacturer is negligent in not adopting that design. However, plaintiffs argue that state-of-the-art should not be admissible in strict liability cases since the evidence focuses the jury's attention on the manufacturer's conduct in choosing the design. Although some courts take the position that state-of-the-art is not a defense to strict liability, the majority of courts have rejected that argument and hold that state of the art evidence is relevant to helping the jury determine whether he product was defective and unreasonably danger-

---

[198] *Id.* at 1344.

[199] *Id.*

[200] *See* ARIZ. REV. STAT. § 12-681(8) (2003); *Potter*, 694 A.2d at 1346.

[201] *Id.* at 1346–47.

ous.[202] This applies both in cases using the consumer expectations test and risk-utility analysis.[203]

The most difficult question for courts has been how to treat evidence of the state-of-the- art. In some states, proof that the product conformed with the state-of-the-art when it first was sold is an affirmative defense to a defective design claim.[204] New Jersey has codified the state-of-the-art defense in a provision that states:

> In any products liability action against a manufacturer or seller for harm allegedly caused by a product that was designed in a defective manner, the manufacturer or seller shall not be liable if:
>
> (1) At the time the product left the control of the manufacturer, there was not a practical and technically feasible alternative design that would have prevented the harm without substantially impairing the reasonably anticipated or intended function of the product.[205]

At the same time, however, New Jersey holds that the state-of-the-art defense is not applicable, if the court finds, by clear and convincing evidence, that:

(1) The product is egregiously unsafe or ultra-hazardous;

(2) The ordinary user or consumer of the product cannot reasonably be expected to have knowledge of the product's risks, or the product poses a risk of serious injury to persons other than the user or consumer; and

(3) The product has little or no usefulness.[206]

Other states take the position that compliance with the state of the art does not entitle the manufacturer to a judgment in its favor. In Indiana, for example, there is a rebuttable presumption that a product was not defective if, before the sale by the manufacturer, the product:

(1) was in conformity with the generally recognized state-of-the-art applicable to the safety of the product at the time the product was designed manufactured, packaged or labeled; or

---

[202] *Id.* at 1347.

[203] *Id.* at 1348.

[204] *See, e.g.*, Ariz. Rev. Stat. § 12-683(1) (2003); Iowa Code § 668.12 (1998). *See also* Falada v. Trinity Industries, Inc., 642 N.W.2d 247 (Iowa 2002).

[205] N.J. Stat. Ann. § 2A:58C-3(a) (2000). *See also* Neb. Rev. Stat. § 25-21 (1995).

[206] N.J. Stat. Ann. § 2A:58C-3b (2000).

   (2) complied with applicable codes, standards, regulations, or spec-
      ifications established, adopted, promulgated, or approved by
      the United States or Indiana.[207]

This presumption arose in response to complaints by manufacturers that courts were giving insufficient weight to their compliance with government safety standards. As a result, the presumption is mandatory and, unless rebutted, allows the conclusion that the manufacturer was not negligent. In order to overcome the presumption, the plaintiff must show that the reasonably prudent manufacturer would have taken additional precautions even though the product complied with government regulations.[208]

---

[207] IND. CODE § 34-20-5-1 (1998). *See also* KY. REV. STAT. § 411.310(2) (1997).

[208] Schultz v. Ford Motor Co., 822 N.E.2d 645 (Ind. Ct. App. 2005).

Chapter 6

MANUFACTURING DEFECTS

SYNOPSIS

§ 6.01 MANUFACTURING DEFECTS

[A] *Deviation from the Design*

Even if a product is designed properly, it still may be unreasonably dangerous due to a defect that arose during the manufacturing process. The archetypal example of such a defect is *MacPherson v, Buick Motor Co.*,[1] the first case in which a court permitted a plaintiff to recover for a manufacturing defect using ordinary negligence principles. In that case, the plaintiff did not allege that his injury was due to a design that made all Buick automobiles defective. Instead, he claimed that the particular Buick automobile that he purchased was defective because one of its wheels was man-

---

[1] 111 N.E. 1050 (N.Y. 1916).

ufactured with defective wood that caused the spokes to crumble. Similarly, the basis of the plaintiff's suit in *Escola v. Coca-Cola Bottling Co.*[2] was not that the design of Coca-Cola bottles was defective. Instead, the plaintiff alleged that her injuries were caused either by excessive gas in the particular bottle that exploded and injured her or by the manufacturer's negligence in failing to detect a weakness in that bottle before it refilled it.

In contrast to the complexity of a design defect, courts have referred to a manufacturing defect as "a fairly straightforward concept"[3] and stated that defining the standard and meaning of such a defect is "relatively easy."[4] The reason for this is that, unlike a design defect, which results from a condition in the product that was intended by the manufacturer and is present in every unit of the product model, a manufacturing defect is "a physical departure from a product's intended design"[5] that usually is random and affects only one or a small percentage of the products of a specific design.[6] Unless the product has been destroyed,[7] a manufacturing defect usually can be shown by an objective standard: comparing the particular product that caused the plaintiff's injuries with the manufacturer's own design specifications for that product or with a product from the same manufacturer produced according to the design.[8] This "deviation from the design" test has been adopted as the definition of a manufacturing defect by courts and by products liability statutes:

> A product is defective in manufacture or construction if, when it left the control of its manufacturer, it deviated in a material way from the design specifications, formula, or performance standards of the manufacturer, or from otherwise identical units manufactured to the same design specifications, formula, or performance standards. A product may be defective in manufacture or construction as

---

[2] 150 P.2d 436 (Cal. 1944). For a more recent version of *Escola*, see *Lee v. Crookston Coca-Cola Bottling Co.*, 188 N.W. 2d 426 (Minn. 1971).

[3] Jones v. Amazing Products, Inc., 231 F. Supp. 2d 1228, 1236 (N.D. Ga. 2002) (applying Georgia law).

[4] O'Brien v. Muskin Corp., 463 A.2d 298, 304 (N.J. 1983).

[5] RESTATEMENT (THIRD) OF TORTS: PRODUCTS LIABILITY § 1 cmt. *a* (1998).

[6] Wood v. Old Trapper Taxi, 952 P.2d 1375 (Mont. 1997).

[7] The difficulty of proving a manufacturing defect when the product is not available for inspection by either party is illustrated by *Ford Motor Co. v. Gonzales*, 9 S.W.3d 195 (Tex. App. 1999).

[8] In *Myrlak v. Port Authority of N.Y. and N.J.*, 723 A.2d 45, 51 (N.J. 1999), the New Jersey Supreme Court defined a manufacturing defect as a deviation "from the design specifications, formulae, or performance standards of the manufacturer or from otherwise identical units manufactured to the same manufacturing specifications or formula." (*quoting* the New Jersey Products Liability Act, N.J. STAT. ANN. § 2A:58C-2a). For similar definitions of a manufacturing defect, see *Wheeler v. Ho Sports, Inc.*, 232 F.3d 754 (10th Cir. 2000) (applying Oklahoma law); *Guilbeault v. R. J. Reynolds Tobacco Co.*, 1999 U.S. Dist. LEXIS 8365 (D.R.I. 1999) (applying Rhode Island law); *Dierks v. Mitsubishi Motors Corp.*, 256 Cal. Rptr. 230 (Cal. 1989).

described in this section even though its manufacturer exercised all possible care in its manufacture or construction.[9]

An example of the use of this deviation test is *In re Coordinated Latex Glove Litigation*,[10] in which the plaintiff alleged that the latex gloves she used at work contained natural or artificial substances that caused her to suffer latex allergies. Although the jury found a manufacturing defect and awarded the plaintiff compensatory damages, the trial court judge granted the manufacturer's post-trial motion for judgment notwithstanding the verdict (JNOV). The California appellate court held that the trial judge properly granted the motion since the gloves "did not differ from the manufacturer's intended result, nor did they have materially significant differences among identical units from the same product line."[11] The Restatement (Third) also adopts this deviation test by stating that a product has a manufacturing defect "when the product departs from its intended design even though all possible care was exercised in the preparation and marketing of the product."[12] An example of this is *Wright v. Brooke Group Ltd.*,[13] in which the Iowa Supreme Court adopted § 2 and then held that a "plaintiff may not recover from a cigarette manufacturer under a manufacturing defect theory when the cigarettes smoked by the plaintiff were in the condition intended by the manufacturer."[14]

[B] *Manufacturing Defects and Design Defects*

Most of the early products liability cases involved only claims of manufacturing defects. Although manufacturing defects remain a source of litigation, in recent years the number of appellate court decisions involving only a manufacturing defect has been eclipsed by design and failure to warn cases.[15] In part this is because, unless the product was destroyed, it

---

[9] OHIO REV. CODE ANN. § 2307.74 (2005). In *Barker v. Lull Engineering Co.*, 573 P.2d 443, 454 (Cal. 1978), the California Supreme Court stated:

> In general, a manufacturing or production defect is readily identifiable because a defective product is one that differs from the manufacturer's intended result or from other ostensibly identical units of the same product line. For example, when a product comes off the assembly line in a substandard condition it has incurred a manufacturing defect.

See also Freeman v. Hoffman-La Roche, Inc., 618 N.W.2d 827 (Neb. 2000); Corcoran v. Sears, Roebuck and Co., 711 A.2d 371 (N.J. Super. Ct. App. Div. 1998).

[10] 121 Cal. Rptr. 2d 301 (Cal. Ct. App. 2002).

[11] *Id.* at 316.

[12] RESTATEMENT (THIRD) OF TORTS: PRODUCTS LIABILITY § 2(a) (1998). Comment *c* to § 2 goes on to state that "a manufacturing defect is a departure from a product's unit design specifications."

[13] 652 N.W.2d 159 (Iowa 2002).

[14] *Id.* at 178.

[15] For a case in which the plaintiff alleged only a manufacturing defect, see *Montez v. Ford Motor Co.*, 161 Cal. Rptr. 578 (Cal. Ct. App. 1980).

often is fairly easy to determine whether the product deviated from the manufacturer's intent. The elaborate debates over the risks and benefits of the product and alternative products that characterize design defect and failure to warn cases, and which have moved those cases away from strict liability and toward a negligence analysis, are not present in manufacturing defect cases. In manufacturing defect cases, the design and identical products can be used to show that the particular product was defective. As a result, if a product did not conform to its intended design, the manufacturer usually will settle the case or will contest only the issue of damages, unless it believes that the defect was not, in fact, a cause of the injury.

Another reason for the decline of cases alleging only a manufacturing defect is the sophistication of modern products. In many cases, it is difficult to determine whether the defective condition that caused the plaintiff's injury was due only to a manufacturing defect or whether it was due to the design, manufacture, or failure to warn of the dangers. As a result, plaintiffs usually allege some combination of all three theories in separate counts in their complaints.[16]

The difficulty of determining whether an injury was due to a manufacturing defect or to a design defect was discussed by the court in *In re Coordinated Latex Glove Litigation*.[17] After holding that the trial judge properly granted a JNOV to the plaintiff's claim that the latex gloves she used at work contained a manufacturing defect, the California appellate court discussed the close relationship between manufacturing and design defects and the difficulty of distinguishing between the two. For example, a defect that results from the failure of a quality control technique intended to determine the rate of flaws in a particular product may be characterized as a manufacturing defect. However, the manufacturer's choice as to the particular type of quality control technique to use frequently is made on the basis of cost considerations and thus is analogous to the choice of one design over another. This makes it difficult to distinguish the particular source of the defect.[18] As in other latex glove litigation, the plaintiffs' theories had "aspects common to both the design defect and manufacturing defect theories" in that "the materials from which the latex gloves were made contained excessive amounts of latex rubber proteins close to the surface of the gloves, causing the plaintiffs to become sensitized to them and to develop or to exacerbate an existing allergy."[19] Because determining the source of the

---

[16] An early example of a plaintiff alleging both a design and a manufacturing defect is *Greenman v. Yuba Power Products, Inc.*, 377 P.2d 897 (Cal. 1963). For other examples, see *Medtronic v. Lohr*, 518 U.S. 470 (1996); *Transue v. Aesthetech Corp.*, 341 F.3d 911 (9th Cir. 2003) (applying California law); *Shreve v. Sears, Roebuck & Co.*, 166 F. Supp. 2d 378 (D. Md. 2001) (applying Maryland law).

[17] 121 Cal. Rptr. 2d 301 (Cal. Ct. App. 2002).

[18] *Id.* at 311(*citing* 1 MARSHALL SHAPO, THE LAW OF PRODUCTS LIABILITY ¶ 9.01(2), at 9-5 to 9-6 (3d ed. 1994)).

[19] *Id.* (quoting *Morson v. Superior Court*, 109 Cal. Rptr. 2d 343, 354 (Cal. Ct. App. 2001)).

allergic reactions involved the science of the manufacturing and preparation procedures, as well as the medical aspects of an individual's allergic reactions to various substances, the court concluded that it was useless to focus on a distinction between the raw materials from which the product was made and the actual construction of the product itself for purposes of determining whether the defect was the result of design or manufacture.[20]

§ 6.02 THE DIVERSITY OF MANUFACTURING DEFECTS

[A] *Types of Manufacturing Defects*

As the cases in the last section illustrate, manufacturing defects can arise in products as diverse as automobiles, soft drink bottles, work gloves, and cigarettes. Because the production process often involves the integration of a large number of component parts and equipment with human labor and skill, there are countless opportunities for mistakes to occur, even if the manufacturer adopts the most rigorous quality-control system.[21] Defects in finished products can result from

- the raw materials or the component parts used in the product;[22]

- human or mechanical error in assembling the components of the product;[23]

- human or mechanical error in manufacturing the product;[24]

- missing parts in the product;[25]

- foreign objects in the product;[26]

- impure ingredients in the product.[27]

---

[20] *Id.*

[21] *See* John W. Wade, *On the Nature of Strict Tort Liability for Products*, 44 MISS. L.J. 825, 825 (1973) ("The prototype [products liability] case was that in which something went wrong in the manufacturing process, so that the product had a loose screw or a defective or missing part or a deleterious element, and was not the safe product it was intended to be.").

[22] Bell v. T.R. Miller Mill Co., Inc., 768 So.2d 953 (Ala. 2000); Magnuson v. Kelsey-Hayes Co., 844 S.W.2d 448 (Mo. 1992).

[23] Jenkins v. General Motors Corp., 446 F.2d 377 (5th Cir. 1971) (applying Georgia law); USX Corp. v. Salinas, 818 S.W.2d 473 (Tex. App. 1991).

[24] Keeler v. Richards Manufacturing Co., Inc., 817 F.2d 1197 (5th Cir. 1987) (applying Texas law); Doupnik v. General Motors Corp., 275 Cal. Rptr., 715 (Cal. Ct. App. 1990).

[25] Yamaha Motor Co., Ltd. v. Thornton, 579 So.2d 619 (Ala. 1991); Morris v. Chrysler Corp., 303 N.W.2d 500 (Neb. 1981).

[26] See the discussion of these defects in the context of food and drink cases at § 6.05, *infra*. *See also* Glover v. BIC Corp., 6 F.3d 1318 (9th Cir. 1993) (applying Oregon law).

[27] See the discussion of these defects in the context of food and drink cases at § 6.05, *infra*. *See also* Van Wyk v. Norden Laboratories, 345 N.W.2d 81 (Iowa 1984).

Although most manufacturing defects originate at the factory during the manufacturing process itself, they also can arise after shipment. In such a situation, the Restatement (Third) states that the commercial distributor or seller of the product is liable as if the product had been manufactured defectively.[28] This is because the test for strict liability under the Restatement (Third) is whether "the product was defective when it left the hands of the given seller in the distributive chain."[29]

[B] *Testing and Inspection*

Two important aspects of the manufacturing process that can result in defects in a product are the testing and inspection of a product before it is distributed and the labeling and packaging of a product. The failure to test arises in two types of situations: first, where adequate tests for defects were not conducted either during or after the production process and a product containing a defect was placed on the market and, second, where the particular product was not defective but the properties of the product in general were not tested adequately before it was placed on the market.[30] The extent of testing and inspecting that a manufacturer must perform is an issue where the necessary equipment and processes require considerable time and expense. In negligence cases, courts have held that manufacturers have a duty to conduct those tests and inspections that are reasonably necessary to ensure that the product is safe.[31] In order to establish what tests or inspections are reasonably necessary, the plaintiff must establish a standard of care and show the manufacturer's deviation from it.[32] The standard of care may be based on the industry-wide custom of testing or inspections, the past practices of the manufacturer, or expert testimony.[33] However, in order to succeed, the plaintiff must establish not only what tests

---

[28] RESTATEMENT (THIRD) OF TORTS: PRODUCTS LIABILITY § 2 (1998).

[29] *Id.* at cmt. *c.*

[30] Borel v. Fiberboard Paper Products Corp., 493 F.2d 1076 (5th cir. 1973 (applying Texas law); Ford Motor Co. v. Zahn, 265 F.2d 729 (8th Cir. 1959) (applying Minnesota law); Mercer v. Pittway Corp., 616 N.W.2d 602 (Iowa 2000). Oregon defines a "product liability civil action" as "a civil action brought against a manufacturer, distributor, seller or lessor of a product for damages for personal injury, death or property damage arising out of: (1) Any design, inspection, testing, manufacturing or other defect in a product . . ." OR. REV. STAT. § 30.900 (1997).

[31] Nicklaus v. Hughes Tool Co., 417 F.2d 983 (8th Cir. 1969) (according to the court, it was not necessary to determine whether the law of California, the place of manufacturing and testing, or Arkansas, the place of the accident, applied in the case, since there was no significant difference in the law of the two states that was applicable to the case); Lindquist v. Ayerst Laboratories, Inc., 607 P.2d 1339 (Kan. 1980).

[32] Scittarelli v. The Providence Gas Co., 415 A.2d 1040 (R.I. 1980).

[33] *See* Bogosian v. Mercedes-Benz of North America, Inc., 104 F.3d 472 (1st Cir. 1996) (applying Rhode Island law); 1836 Callowhill St. v. Johnson Controls, Inc., 819 F. Supp. 460 (E.D. Pa. 1993) (applying Pennsylvania law); West v. Broderick & Bascom Rope Co., 197 N.W.2d 202 (Iowa 1972).

or inspections should have been performed but that those tests or inspections would have detected the defect.[34] Although most testing and inspection cases involve manufacturers, a seller also may be liable if it is customary to inspect the particular product, such as an automobile, prior to delivering it to the buyer.[35]

[C] *Labeling and Packaging*

A product also may be defective because of the labeling and packaging used for its distribution. Examples of this are a number of cases in which glass soft drink or beer bottles exploded in the hands of those who had purchased them or who were stacking them in restaurants.[36] Comment *h* to § 402A sets out the reasons for imposing liability for defective packaging:

> No reason is apparent for distinguishing between the product itself and the container in which it is supplied; and the two are purchased by the user or consumer as an integrated whole. Where the container is itself dangerous, the product is sold in a defective condition. Thus a carbonated beverage in a bottle which is so weak or cracked, or jagged at the edges, or bottled under such excessive pressure that it may explode or otherwise cause harm to the person who handles it, is in a defective and dangerous condition. The container cannot logically be separated from the contents where the two are sold as a unit, and the liability stated in this section arises not only when the consumer drinks the beverage and is poisoned by it, but also when he is injured by the bottle while he is handling it in preparatory to consumption.

Packaging cases are as diverse as the products they contain.[37] Many of the labeling and packaging cases involve the containers in which chemicals are sold.[38] Although manufacturers owe a duty of care to those who purchase or work near chemicals to exercise reasonable care in packaging them,[39] the issue in many of these cases has not been whether the chemi-

---

[34] Messer v. Amway Corp., 2004 U.S. App. LEXIS 16445 (10th Cir. 2004) (applying Kansas law); Weiss v. Chrysler Motors Corp., 515 F.2d 449 (5th Cir. 1975).

[35] Langford v. Chrysler Motors Corp., 513 F.2d 1121 (2d Cir. 1975) (applying New York law); Bass v. General Motors Corp., 447 S.W.2d 443 (Tex. App. 1968).

[36] *See* Bredberg v. Pepsico, 551 N.W.2d 321 (Iowa 1996); Van Duzer v. Shoshone Coca Cola Bottling Co., 741 P.2d 811 (Nev. 1987); Falstaff Brewing Corp. v. Williams, 234 So.2d 620 (Miss. 1970); Escola v. Coca-Cola Bottling Co., 150 P.2d 436 (Cal. 1944).

[37] Welge v. Planters Lifesavers Co., 17 F.3d 209 (7th Cir. 1994) (glass jar containing peanuts); Levondosky v. Marina Assoc., 731 F. Supp. 1210 (D.N.J. 1990) (glass containing a drink); Tenaglia v. Procter & Gamble, Inc., 737 A.2d 306 (Pa. Super. Ct. 1999) (cardboard box of diapers); Martin v. Burger King, 1998 Mass. Super. LEXIS 607 (Mass. Supp. 1998) (packages in which french fries were sold); Corbin v. Camden Coca-Cola Bottling Co., 290 A.2d 441 (N.J. 1972) (carton containing soft-drink bottles).

[38] Chandler v. Moreland Chemical Co., 154 S.E.2d 502 (N.C. 1967).

[39] Waering v. BASF Corp., 146 F. Supp. 2d 675 (M.D. Pa. 2001) (applying Pennsylvania law).

cals were packaged in a reasonable manner but whether the claim of negligent packaging was preempted by federal statutes.[40]

§ 6.03 NEGLIGENT AND STRICT LIABILITY THEORIES

As in design defect cases, a plaintiff can bring a manufacturing defect case based upon an allegation of negligence and/or strict liability. In order to establish a *prima facie* case under either theory, a plaintiff must establish:[41] (1) a defect in the manufacture of the product that made it unreasonably dangerous;[42] (2) the defect existed at the time the product left the control of the manufacturer or seller;[43] (3) the defect was the cause in fact and proximate cause of the plaintiff's injuries.[44] In addition, in a negligence action, the plaintiff must prove not only that there was a manufacturing defect but also that the defect was the result of the failure of the defendant to exercise reasonable skill and care in the manufacturing process.[45] One advantage of alleging both negligence and strict liability in a manufacturing defect case is that, if the manufacturer is found to be not liable under one of the theories, it still may be liable under the other.

[A] *Negligence*

There is little distinction between a negligent manufacturing claim and other types of common law negligence.[46] A plaintiff must establish first that the manufacturer owed him or her a duty of care. A duty arises if the nature of the product is such that it is reasonably certain to endanger human life if it is not manufactured properly and the plaintiff was the purchaser or a foreseeable user of the product. The plaintiff also must prove the manufacturer's fault, i.e., it failed to use reasonable skill and care in the construction, testing, or inspection of the product, and that the

---

[40] See the Federal Insecticide, Fungicide and Rodenticide Act (FIFRA), 7 U.S.C. §§ 136-136y, and the Hazardous Materials Transportation Act, 49 U.S.C. § 5125. *See also* Hawkins v. Leslie's Pool Mart, Inc., 184 F.3d 244 (3rd Cir. 1999); Jeffers v. Wal-Mart Stores, Inc., 171 F. Supp. 2d 617 (S.D. W.Va. 2001); Lucas v. Bio-Lab, Inc., 108 F. Supp. 2d 518 (E.D. Va. 2000); Lyall v. Leslie's Poolmart, 984 F. Supp. 587 (E.D. Mich. 1997).

[41] Johnson v. Michelin Tire Corp., 812 F.2d 200 (5th Cir. 1987) (applying Texas law); Myrlak v. Port Authority of N.Y. and N.J., 723 A.2d 45 (N.J. 1999); State Farm Fire & Casualty Co. v. Chrysler Corp., 523 N.E.2d 489 (Ohio 1988).

[42] Mixon v. Chrysler Corp., 663 S.W.2d 713 (Ark. 1984).

[43] Welge v. Planters Lifeavers Co., 17 F.3d 209 (7th Cir. 1994) (applying Illinois law); Kerr v. Corning Glass Works, 169 N.W.2d 587 (Minn. 1969).

[44] *Johnson*, 812 F. 2d 200; Lee v. Crookston Coca-Cola Bottling Co., 188 N.W.2d 426 (Minn. 1971).

[45] Larsen v. General Motors Corp., 391 F.2d 495 (8th Cir. 1968) (applying Minnesota law).

[46] Doe v. Solvay Pharmacies, Inc., 350 F. Supp. 2d 257 (D. Me. 2004) (applying Maine law).

defect in the product that resulted from the lack of due care was the cause-in-fact as well as the proximate cause of his or her injuries.[47] The standard of care by which the manufacturer's conduct is measured in a negligence case is that of a reasonably prudent manufacturer.[48] In *MacPherson v. Buick Motor Co.*,[49] Judge Cardozo stated that the manufacturer owed the user of the automobile a duty since the very nature of an automobile is a warning that, unless its wheels are constructed properly, injury is almost certain to occur. The standard of reasonable care in the manufacture of products was reflected in § 395 of the Restatement of Torts, adopted in 1934, which has been carried over into the Restatement (Second) of Torts, adopted in 1965. That section provides in part:

> A manufacturer who fails to exercise reasonable care in the manu-facture of a chattel which, unless carefully made, he should recog-nize as involving an unreasonable risk of causing physical harm to those who use it . . . is subject to liability for physical harm caused to them by its lawful use in a manner and for a purpose for which it is supplied.[50]

Because of the difficulties of proving that a manufacturing defect in a product was the result of a breach of a duty on the part of the manufacturer, even with the help of the doctrine of *res ipsa loquitur*, most plaintiffs bring their manufacturing defect claims in strict liability as well as negligence.

[B] *Strict Liability*

Section 402A provides for strict liability when a product is in a "defective condition unreasonably dangerous to the user or consumer" and applies it even though the manufacturer or seller "has exercised all possible care in the preparation" of the product. The Restatement (Third) goes beyond § 402A and asks only whether the manufacturing defect departed from the product's "intended design."[51] Comment *a* to § 2 states that imposing strict liability for a manufacturing defect that departs from the "intended design" furthers several broad objectives. Although the Restatement does not use the terms, these objectives can be categorized as promoting safety, overcoming the difficulties of proving fault, and fulfilling consumer expectations.

> On the premise that tort law serves the instrumental function of creating safety incentives, imposing strict liability on manufactur-ers for harm caused by manufacturing defects encourages greater investment in product safety than does a regime of fault-based lia-

---

[47] Pouncey v. Ford Motor Co., 464 F.2d 957 (5th Cir. 1972) (applying Alabama law); Willis v. Floyd Brace Co., 309 S.E.2d 295 (S.C. Ct. App. 1983).

[48] Holder v. Keller Industries, Inc., 2000 Tex. App. LEXIS 910 (Tex. App. 2000).

[49] 111 N.E. 1050 (N.Y. 1916).

[50] RESTATEMENT (SECOND) OF TORTS § 395 (1965).

[51] RESTATEMENT (THIRD) OF TORTS: PRODUCTS LIABILITY § 2(a) (1998).

bility under which, as a practical matter, sellers may escape their appropriate share of responsibility. Some courts and commentators also have said that strict liability discourages the consumption of defective products by causing the purchase price of products to reflect, more than would a rule of negligence, the costs of defects. . . .

In many cases manufacturing defects are in fact caused by manufacturer negligence but plaintiffs have difficulty proving it. Strict liability therefore performs a function similar to the concept of res ipsa loquitur, allowing deserving plaintiffs to succeed notwithstanding what would otherwise be difficult or insuperable problems of proof. Products that malfunction due to manufacturing defects disappoint reasonable expectations of product performance. Because manufacturers invest in quality control at consciously chosen levels, their knowledge that a predictable number of flawed products will enter the marketplace entails an element of deliberation about the amount of injury that will result from their activity. Finally, many believe that consumers who benefit from products without suffering harm should share, through increases in the prices charged for those products, the burden of unavoidable injury costs that result from manufacturing defects.[52]

§ 6.04 TESTS FOR DETERMINING A MANUFACTURING DEFECT

[A] *Consumer Expectations Test*

Definitions of a manufacturing defect are based on the idea that such a defect is a deviation from the intended design of the product. However, these definitions do not state how to determine whether the deviation from the design is so serious as to make the product unreasonably dangerous for purposes of liability. Although manufacturers sometimes attempt to convince courts to adopt a risk-benefit analysis to determine whether the manufacturing defect is actionable, state courts, in keeping with § 402A, comment *g*, use the consumer expectations test in manufacturing defect cases. According to one court, the reason for using this test is that

> [m]anufacturing defect cases involve products which are flawed, i.e., which do not conform to the manufacturer's own specifications, and are not identical to their mass-produced siblings. The flaw theory is based upon a fundamental consumer expectancy: that a mass-produced product will not differ from its siblings in a manner that makes it more dangerous than the others.[53]

---

[52] RESTATEMENT (THIRD) OF TORTS: PRODUCTS LIABILITY § 2 cmt. *a* (1998).

[53] Ford Motor Co. v. Pool, 688 S.W. 2d 879, 881 (Tex. App. 1985), *aff'd in part and rev'd in part*, 715 S.W.2d 629 (Tex. 1986).

The consumer expectations test requires the consumer to show that, at the time the product left the seller's hands, it was "in a condition not contemplated by the ultimate consumer, which will be unreasonably dangerous to him." Even those states that have adopted the risk-utility analysis for design defect and failure to warn cases retain the consumer expectations test in manufacturing defect cases. An example of the consumer expectations test is *Ridgway v. Ford Motor Co.*,[54] in which the plaintiff suffered severe burns when his truck burst into flames while he was driving it. In his action against the manufacturer of the truck, the plaintiff alleged both negligence and strict liability due to a manufacturing defect in the fuel system and/or the electrical system. In reversing the grant of summary judgment on the plaintiff's strict liability claim, the Texas appellate court stated: "The manufacturing defect theory is based upon a consumer expectancy that a mass-produced product will not differ from its counterparts in a manner which makes it more dangerous than the others."[55]

Crucial to the consumer expectations test is that the product was being used as intended at the time of the injury. In *Fitzgerald Marine Sales v. LeUnes*,[56] the plaintiff alleged that a defect in the manufacture of the steering wheel of his motorboat was the cause of his injury. The plaintiff and another man were riding in the boat when it took a sharp turn to the right. The plaintiff attempted to use the steering wheel as a restraint but it broke in his hand and he was thrown into the water. In his suit against the boat manufacturer, the plaintiff alleged that the steering wheel was unreasonably dangerous because it was not strong enough to prevent him from being thrown into the water. The jury was instructed that a product is "unreasonably dangerous" when it is "dangerous to an extent beyond that which would be contemplated by the ordinary user of the product, with the ordinary knowledge common to the community of such users as to the product's characteristics."[57] The Texas court looked to the "purpose of a steering wheel on a motorboat" and said that it was to steer the boat, not to serve as a restraining device. Since there was no evidence that the steering wheel was unreasonably dangerous for its intended purpose of steering the boat, the court held that the steering wheel was not defective as a matter of law.[58]

Although the consumer expectations test has been criticized widely in design defect and failure to warn cases, and has been replaced by the risk-utility analysis by states and by the Restatement (Third), the test has been retained for manufacturing defects. The reason for this, according to one critic, is that

---

[54] 82 S.W.3d 26 (Tex. App. 2002).

[55] *Id.* at 30.

[56] 659 S.W.2d 917 (Tex. App. 1983).

[57] *Id.* at 918.

[58] *Id.*

[t]he consumer expectations test for strict liability operates effectively when the product defect is a construction or manufacturing defect. . . . An internal standard exists against which to measure the product's condition — the manufacturer's own design standard. In essence, a product flawed in manufacture frustrates the manufacturer's own design objectives. Liability is imposed on manufacturers in these cases even if the manufacturer shows it acted reasonably in making the product.[59]

[B] *Rejection of the Risk-Utility Analysis*

Although courts have not adopted the risk-utility analysis in manufacturing defect cases, this has not stopped some manufacturers from using it in negligence cases in an attempt to show that the risk of injury was low enough that their manufacturing process was reasonable. An example of this is *Ford Motor Co. v. Zahn*,[60] in which the plaintiff was a passenger in an automobile. When the driver applied the brakes suddenly to avoid a collision, the plaintiff was thrown forward, causing his head to hit the dashboard ash-tray. The plaintiff alleged that the ash-tray was defective because its upper right-hand corner was sharp and it had a jagged protrusion, caused by a dull cutting die. The manufacturer argued that the sampling process used to inspect the ash-trays was not negligent because of the nature, position, and size of the defect and because the foreseeability of the occurrence and the injury were low. According to the manufacturer, the only harm that could be anticipated from the defect was a cut finger or torn clothes and that since, the foreseeable risk was low, its inspection was reasonable. The Eighth Circuit, however, rejected the manufacturer's argument and affirmed the jury's verdict for the plaintiff. According to the court, while the risk of danger from the defective ash tray was not as great as other risks, the plaintiff did suffer a serious injury. The jury was entitled to consider that automobiles are fast moving and that emergencies frequently arise which require the sudden application of the brakes that thrown passengers against the dashboard.[61] Passengers expect that they will not be injured by sharp objects on the dashboard.

§ 6.05 FOOD AND DRINK CASES

A frequent source of claims against food processors and restaurants are harmful substances in food and drink products that make them defective.[62]

---

[59] Keith Miller, *Design Defect Litigation in Iowa: The Myths of Strict Liability*, 40 DRAKE L. REV. 465, 473 (1991).

[60] 265 F.2d 729 (8th Cir. 1959) (applying Minnesota law).

[61] *Id.* at 731-732.

[62] In this section, the word "food" is used to include both food and drink products.

The basis of these claims, which can be based on breach of warranty, negligence, or strict liability,[63] is that the presence of the harmful ingredient was due to a defect in the manufacture or preparation of the food products.[64] In analyzing these claims, courts use two different tests: the "foreign-natural" test and the "consumer expectations" test.

[A] *Foreign-Natural Test*

The first test used by courts in cases involving harmful substances in food is the foreign-natural test. Using this test, courts distinguish between an injury caused by a harmful object or substance that is "foreign" to the food product and an injury caused by an item that is "natural" to the product. If the injury was caused by a "foreign" substance in the food, courts have no difficulty holding the manufacturer or restaurant liable for breach of warranty, negligence, or strict liability. Among the items that courts have held to be a "foreign" substance in food are: a condom in a soft drink;[65] a decomposed housefly in a soft drink;[66] a dead mouse in a soft drink bottle;[67] a decomposed human toe in chewing tobacco;[68] rocks in breakfast cereal;[69] metal in a soup can;[70] glass in ice cream;[71] and a small metal screw in chewing gum.[72] A consumer is barred, however, from recovery if the injury was caused by an object that occurs "naturally" in any ingredient in the food. Among the items that courts have held are found "naturally" in food prod-

---

[63] Doyle v. The Pillsbury Co., 476 So.2d 1271 (Fla. 1985).

[64] In addition to foreign substances in food and drink products are cases involving bottles that exploded during handling. The classic example of this is *Escola v. Coca-Cola Bottling Co.*, 150 P.2d 436 (Cal. 1944) in which the California Supreme Court expanded the doctrine of *res ipsa loquitur* to a situation where the bottle had been out of the control of the defendant for a considerable period of time. Cases now are brought using strict liability. See Bredberg v. PepsiCo, 551 N.W.2d 321 (Iowa 1996); Tyler v. Natchitoches Coca-Cola Bottling Co., 491 So. 2d 358 (La. 1986).

[65] Hagan v. Coca-Cola Bottling Co., 804 So.2d 1234 (Fla. 2001).

[66] LeBlanc v. Louisiana Coca-Cola Bottling Co., 60 So.2d 873 (La. 1952).

[67] Anderson v. Tyler, 274 N.W. 48 (Iowa 1937); Paul v. Rogers Bottling Co., 6 Cal. Rptr. 867 (Cal Ct. App. 1960).

[68] Pillars v. R. J. Reynolds Tobacco Co., 78 So. 365 (Miss. 1918).

[69] Elliott v. Kraft Foods North America, Inc., 118 S.W.3d 50 (Tex. App. 2003).

[70] Campbell Soup Co. v. Dusek, 135 So.2d 414 (Miss. 1961).

[71] Amdal v. F. W. Woolworth Co., 84 F. Supp 657 (N.D. Iowa 1949) (applying Iowa law).

[72] Hickman v. William Wrigley, Jr. Co., 768 So.2d 812 (La. Ct. App. 2000).

ucts are a fish bone in fish chowder;[73] and a turkey bone in a creamed turkey dish.[74]

The first case to articulate the "foreign-natural" test was *Mix v. Ingersoll Candy Co.*,[75] in which a restaurant customer who ordered a chicken pot pie was injured when he swallowed a fragment of a chicken bone contained in the pie. In affirming the dismissal of the customer's complaint against the restaurant for negligence and breach of implied warranty, the California Supreme Court distinguished earlier cases where plaintiffs had been permitted to recover:

> All of the cases are instances in which the food was found not to be reasonably fit for human consumption, either by reason of the presence of a foreign substance, or an impure and noxious condition of the food itself, such as for example, glass, stones, wires or nails in food served, or tainted, decayed, diseased, or infected meats or vegetables. . . .

> [D]espite the fact that a chicken bone may occasionally be encountered in a chicken pie, such chicken pie, in the absence of some further defect, is reasonably fit for human consumption. Bones which are natural to the type of meat served cannot legitimately be called a foreign substance, and a consumer who eats meat dishes ought to anticipate and be on his guard against the presence of such bones. At least he cannot hold the restaurant keeper whose representation implied by law is that the meat dish is reasonably fit for human consumption, liable for any injury occurring as a result of the presence of a chicken bone in such chicken pie.[76]

Although the "foreign-natural" test has been used by many courts,[77] it has been criticized by courts and commentators on a number of grounds. First,

---

[73] Webster v. Blue Ship Tea Room, 198 N.E.2d 309 (Mass. 1964). In defending the tradition of fish chowder and the occasional presence of fish bones in it, the judge in the case stated:

> It is not too much to say that a person, sitting down in New England to consume a good New England fish chowder, embarks on the gustatory adventure which may entail the removal of some fish bones from his bowl as he proceeds. . . . We should be prepared to cope with the hazards of fish bones, the occasional presence of which in chowders is, it seems to us, to be anticipated, and which, in light of a hallowed tradition, do not impair their fitness or merchantability. *Id.* at 312.

[74] Goodwin v. Country Club of Peoria, 54 N.E.2d 612 (Ill. App. Ct 1944).

[75] 59 P.2d 144 (Cal. 1936). In *Mexicali Rose v. Superior Court*, 822 P.2d 1292, 1304 (Cal. 1992), the California Supreme Court overruled *Mix* "to the extent" that it "precludes a cause of action in negligence when injuries are caused by substances natural to the preparation of the food served."

[76] *Mix*, 50 P.2d at 148. *See also* Brown v. Nebiker, 296 N.W. 366 (Iowa 1941) (a pork chop contained a bone sliver).

[77] Webster v. Blue Ship Tea Room, 198 N.E.2d 309 (Mass. 1964); Adams v. Great Atlantic and Pacific Tea Co., 112 S.E.2d 92 (N.C. 1960); Lewis v. Handel's Homemade Ice Cream & Yogurt, 2003 Ohio App. LEXIS 3196 (Ohio Ct. App. 2003); Note, *The Demise of the Foreign-Natural Test in North Carolina — Goodman v. Wenco Foods*, 16 CAMPBELL L. REV. 275, 289 (1994).

it sometimes can be difficult to make a bright line distinction between ingredients that are "foreign" or "natural" to a product. For example, is a bone "foreign" to a meat dish or soup or is it a "natural" part of the food? This difficulty has led commentators and courts to a second criticism that there is no logical basis for treating the two types of substances differently if they cause injury.[78] According to one court, a "nutshell natural to nut meat can cause as much harm as a foreign substance, such as a pebble, piece of wire or glass."[79] Courts also have criticized the "foreign-natural" test for not meeting the expectations of consumers who purchase and consume food and drink products. According to the Illinois Supreme Court:

> In an era of consumerism, the foreign-natural standard is an anachronism. It flatly and unjustifiably protects food processors and sellers from liability even when the technology may be readily available to remove injurious natural objects from foods. The consumer expectation test, on the other hand, imposes no greater burden upon processors or sellers than to guarantee that their food products meet the standards of safety that consumers customarily and reasonably have come to expect from the food industry.[80]

[B] *Consumer Expectations Test*

In response to the criticisms of the foreign-natural test, most states have turned to the consumer expectations test.[81] Under this test, whether the injurious substance is "foreign" or "natural" is irrelevant. Instead, liability is based on whether the consumer had a reasonable expectation that the

---

[78] According to one commentator:

> The distinction makes bad sense. It makes even worse law. If the *Mix* court were taken seriously, one is confronted by the ludicrous spectacle of the chef in the local hashhouse carefully culling the chicken chow mein to remove any ground glass, tacks or other debris he might encounter while disdainfully ignoring the serrated chicken bones therein on the assumption that the *Mix* decision immunizes him from liability.

Mitchel J. Ezer, *The Impact of the Uniform Commercial Code on the California Law of Sales Warranties*, 8 UCLA L. REV. 281, 304 (1961). *See also* O'Dell v. Dijon's Packing Co., 585 P.2d 402 (Okla. Ct. App. 1978). However, for a defense of the "foreign-natural" test, see the dissent of Justice James Heiple in *Jackson v. Nestle-Beich, Inc.*, 589 N.W.2d 547, 552-53 (Ill. 1992) (Heiple, J., dissenting).

[79] Zabner v. Howard Johnson's, Inc. 201 So. 2d 824, 826 (Fla. Dist. Ct. App. 1967).

[80] *Jackson, Inc.*, 589 N.E.2d at 551 (*quoting* Note, *Products Liability — The Test of Consumer Expectation for "Natural" Defects in Food Products*, 37 OHIO ST. L.J. 634, 651-652 (1976)). In *Jackson*, the plaintiff broke his tooth on a pecan shell embedded in candy.

[81] In *Yong v. Marriott Corp.*, 656 F. Supp. 445, 448 (D. Md. 1987), the district court stated that the "'reasonable expectation' test has largely displaced the natural/foreign test. . . ." *See also* Schafer v. JLC Food Systems, Inc., 2005 Minn. LEXIS 216 (Minn. 2005); Harris-Teeter, Inc. v. Burroughs, 399 S.E.2d 801 (Va. 1991); Phillips v. Town of West Springfield, 540 N.E.2d 1331 (Mass. 1989). For a discussion of the evolution from the foreign/natural test to the consumer expectations test, see *Porteous v. St. Ann's Cafe & Deli*, 713 So. 2d 454 (La. 1998).

harmful substance would not be found in the food product.[82] However, if the manufacturer or restaurant can show that the customer reasonably should have expected the substance in his food, the customer is barred from recovery.[83] A frequently cited example of the consumer expectation test is *Jackson v. Nestle-Beich, Inc.*,[84] in which the plaintiff broke a tooth on a pecan shell when she bit into a piece of chocolate-covered candy. In rejecting the foreign-natural test, the Illinois Supreme Court stated:

> [W]e do not find that manufacturers of products such as Nestle describes serve so important a public service that they merit treatment substantially different from that of manufacturers of other products. In this regard, we believe the consumer's reasonable expectations as to the contents of food products, as the gauge of strict liability, adequately balances consumers' interest in the defect-free products and such manufactures' interest in reasonable cost of doing business.
>
> With an awareness of that test, consumers and their attorneys need ask themselves only one question before deciding to bring an action of this type: Would a reasonable consumer expect that a given product might contain the substance or matter causing a particular injury? . . . The test thus provides a reasonable and concrete standard to govern actions of this sort.[85]

The position adopted by the Illinois court in *Jackson* echoed the position taken thirty years earlier by the Wisconsin Supreme Court in *Betehia v. Cape Cod Corp.*,[86] in which the plaintiff encountered a chicken bone in a sandwich.

> There is a distinction between what a consumer expects to find in a fish stick and in a baked or fried fish, or in a chicken sandwich made from sliced white meat and in roast chicken. The test should be what is reasonably expected by the consumer in the good as served, not what might be natural to the ingredients of that food prior to preparation. What is to be reasonably expected by the consumer is a jury question in most cases; at least we cannot say as a matter of law that a patron in a restaurant must expect a bone in

---

[82] Mitchell v. Fridays, 748 N.E.2d 89 (Ohio Ct. App. 2000) (clam shell in a clam strip); Goodman v. Wenco Foods, Inc., 423 S.E.2d 444 (N.C. 1992) (bone in a hamburger); Hochberg v. O'Donnell's Restaurant, Inc., 272 A.2d 846 (D.C. 1971) (unpitted olive in a martini); Zabner v. Howard Johnson's, Inc., 201 So.2d 824 (Fla. Dist. Ct. App. 1967) (walnut shell in maple walnut ice cream).

[83] Vitiello v. Captain Bill's Restaurant, 594 N.Y.S.2d 295 (N.Y. App. Div. 1993) (customer should expect small bones in fish).

[84] 589 N.E.2d 547 (Ill. 1992).

[85] *Id.* at 550.

[86] 103 N.W.2d 64 (Wis. 1960).

a chicken sandwich whether because chicken bones are occasionally found there or are natural to chicken.[87]

The Restatement (Third) also rejects the "foreign-natural" test and adopts the consumer expectations test for food cases. According to § 7 of the Restatement, "[o]ne engaged in the business of selling or otherwise distributing food products who sells or distributes a food product that is defective . . . is subject to liability for harm to persons or property caused by the defect." The section goes on to state that "a harm-causing ingredient of the food product constitutes a defect if a reasonable consumer would not expect the food product to contain that ingredient."[88]

[C] *Hybrid Test*

Although most states use either the foreign/natural test or the consumer expectations test in food cases, California has adopted an approach that combines the two tests. In *Mexicali Rose v. Superior Court*,[89] a restaurant patron suffered throat injury after he swallowed a one-inch bone contained in an enchilada. Although the California Supreme Court rejected the "foreign-natural" test of *Mix* as the exclusive test for determining liability when a substance causes injuries, it was unwilling to adopt the pure consumer expectations test. Instead, the court said that liability should be based on the consumer's expectations within the context of the foreign-natural test. In dismissing the patron's warranty and strict liability claim, the court stated its new approach:

> If the injury-producing substance is natural to the preparation of the food served, it can be said that it was reasonably expected by its very nature and the food cannot be determined unfit or defective. A plaintiff in such a case has no cause of action in strict liability or implied warranty. If, however, the presence of the natural substance is due to a restauranteur's failure to exercise due care in food preparation, the injured patron may sue under a negligence theory.
>
> If the injury-causing substance is foreign to the food served, then the injured patron may also state a cause of action in implied warranty and strict liability, and the trier of fact will determine whether the substance (i) could be reasonably expected by the average consumer and (ii) rendered the food unfit or defective.[90]

---

[87] *Id.* at 68-69.

[88] The rationale for the consumer expectations test in food cases is discussed in the RESTATEMENT (THIRD) § 7 cmt. *b* (1998). *See* Schafer v. JLC Food Systems, 2005 Minn LEXIS 216 (Minn. 2005).

[89] 822 P.2d 1292 (Cal. 1992).

[90] *Id.* at 1303-04.

[D] *Proof of a Food Defect*

As with all products liability cases, a consumer in a food case must prove that the food or drink was in fact defective, that the harmful ingredient or condition existed when the product left the control of the manufacturer or seller, and that the harmful ingredient or condition was the cause of the injuries. The difficulties that a plaintiff can face in proving that food was defective and the cause of the injuries are illustrated by *Anderson v. Piccadilly Cafeteria, Inc.,*[91] in which a restaurant customer became very ill shortly after eating a fruit salad that she said was discolored and "didn't look good."[92] However, no one else who ate salads in the restaurant that day became ill and one of the customer's doctor testified that she did not have any symptom usually associated with food borne diseases. Since there was no proof that the salad was contaminated, the Louisiana court held that the customer's illness may have been due to the fact that different people reacted differently to the appearance, taste, or smell of foods, whether wholesome or contaminated. Since courts hold that an emotional response is not a basis for liability without proof that the food was harmful, the court held that the restaurant was not liable. Although the customer in *Anderson* was unable to recover for the reasons stated above, she had eaten some of the salad that was the subject of the litigation. If she had not, her recovery would have been barred by the "impact rule." In order to recover for physical and psychological injuries caused by food products, a plaintiff must have consumed at least a portion of the food or drink.[93] Merely seeing unwholesome food is not sufficient.[94]

Proving that the harmful condition existed at the time it left the control of the manufacturer also can be a problem for the plaintiff. In *Shoshone Coca-Cola Bottling Co. v. Dolinski,*[95] the plaintiff suffered physical and mental distress when he partially consumed the contents of a bottle of soft drink that contained a decomposed mouse. The bottler argued that the plaintiff failed to present sufficient proof to establish that the mouse was in the bottle when it left the bottler's possession. However, the plaintiff offered the expert testimony of a toxicologist who examined the bottle and contents on the day the plaintiff drank from it. It was his opinion that the mouse "had been dead for a long time" and that the dark stains (mouse feces) that he found on the bottom of the bottle must have been there before the soft drink was added to the bottle. The jury accepted that evidence and the Nevada Supreme Court affirmed the verdict and judgment.

---

[91] 804 So. 2d 75 (La. Ct. App. 2001).

[92] *Id.* at 76.

[93] Coca-Cola Bottling Co. of Plainview v. White, 545 S.W. 2d 279 (Tex. App. 1977).

[94] Doyle v. The Pillsbury Co., 476 So.2d 1271 (Fla. 1985).

[95] 420 P.2d 855 (Nev. 1966).

The requirement of proof can be a particular problem if the plaintiff is unable to identify the object in the food product that caused the injury.[96] That was the issue in *Schafer v. JLC Food Systems, Inc.*,[97] in which the plaintiff experienced a sharp pain to her throat immediately after swallowing a bite of a muffin. Although the specific cause of the pain never was determined because the muffin was not saved, the Minnesota Supreme Court held that circumstantial evidence, within limits, could be used to establish a *prima facie* showing that the muffin was defective. The limits on the use of circumstantial evidence are:

    (1) the injury-causing event was of a kind that would ordinarily only occur as a result of a defective condition in the food product;

    (2) the defendant was responsible for a condition that was the cause of the injury; and

    (3) the injury-causing event was not caused by anything other than a food product defect existing at the time of the food product's sale.[98]

In *Schafer*, the fact that a cut was found on the plaintiff's throat immediately after the event made it more probable than not that the muffin was defective and permitted the case to be submitted to the jury.

---

[96] Wieland v. C. A. Swanson & Sons, 223 F.2d 27 (2d Cir. 1955); Kneibel v. RRM Enterprises, 506 N.W.2d 664 (Minn. Ct. App. 1993).

[97] 2005 Minn. LEXIS 216 (Minn. 2005).

[98] *Id.* at *17.

Chapter 7

WARNING DEFECTS

SYNOPSIS

§ 7.01 CHARACTERISTICS OF A WARNING DEFECT

[A] *Warnings and Instructions*

A manufacturer has a duty to design and to manufacture products that are reasonably safe for their intended purposes and foreseeable uses. However, even if a product meets all of the design and manufacturing requirements, it still may be unreasonably dangerous if the manufacturer fails to warn or to provide adequate warnings about a product's dangers or fails to provide instructions or to provide adequate instructions about how to use a product safely.[1] An over-the-counter medicine, for example, may be designed and manufactured in a manner that makes it safe and beneficial for use by a large number of people. At the same time, however, the medicine may cause serious side-effects if taken by certain groups of persons, such as pregnant women or those with high blood pressure, or if taken too frequently, for too long a period of time, in too large a dose, or in connection with certain other medicines. Courts have held that a manufacturer has an obligation to warn users and consumers of over-the-counter medicines directly of the foreseeable risks associated with such products and to give them adequate instructions about how to use the medicines in a safe manner.[2]

Courts often use the term "failure to warn" to include both the failure to provide adequate warnings about the dangers of a product and the failure to supply adequate instructions about a product's use.[3] The reason for this is that the purpose of both warnings and instructions is the same: to prevent a product from being unreasonably dangerous by giving consumers information about the product of which they are not aware.[4] In the case of an over-the-counter medicine, for example, a warning must inform users of any ingredients in the product that might pose an unreasonable risk of harm to certain types of persons (i.e., children) or to persons with certain conditions (i.e., high blood pressure). By making consumers aware of the risks, an effective warning permits them to decide whether or not the potential benefits of the medicine outweigh its risks.[5] Requiring the manufacturer to provide instructions or directions with a medicine enables consumers

---

[1] Donohue v. Phillips Petroleum Co., 866 F.2d 1008 (8th Cir. 1989) (applying Missouri law); Lewis v. Sea Ray Boats, Inc., 65 P.3d 245 (Nev. 2003); Feldman v. Lederle Laboratories, 479 A.2d 374 (N.J. 1984); DaimlerChrysler Corp. v. Hillhouse, 2004 Tex. App. LEXIS 11471 (Tex. App. 2004).

[2] The "learned intermediary doctrine" does not apply to over-the-counter medicines. For a discussion of the doctrine, see § 7.06.

[3] Delaney v. Deere and Co., 999 P.2d 930 (Kan. 2000).

[4] RESTATEMENT (SECOND) OF TORTS § 402A cmt. *j* (1965). *See also* Seibel v. Symons Corp. 221 N.W.2d 50 (N.D. 1974).

[5] Ontai v. Staub Clinic and Hospital, Inc., 659 P.2d 734 (Haw. 1983).

who use the product to do so safely and effectively by knowing the recommended dosage, how often to take the medicine, and what activities or other medicines to avoid while taking it.[6]

Although warnings and instructions involve different types of information about a product, there is a close relationship between the two. This is because, in some situations, a manufacturer or seller that provides a warning about the risks of the use of a product also must provide adequate instructions about how to use the product safely.[7] Similarly, a manufacturer or seller that provides instructions for the use of a product must include a warning of the risks of the failure to follow those instructions.[8] An example of this is *Midgley v. S.S. Kresge Co.*,[9] in which a store sold, under its own label, a telescope for viewing the sun. The accompanying instruction book contained a warning that stated: "Caution: Please refrain from looking up the sun [*sic*] without attaching the sun glass. Also the sun should not be seen through the finderscope."[10] However, the accompanying manual did not provide adequate instructions for the use of the telescope since it contained no diagrams or illustrations for the proper installation of the sun filter. As a result, a 13-year-old user who purchased a telescope suffered irreparable solar burn to the retina of his eye as a result of improper assembly of the sun filter on the telescope. In holding that the jury should have considered the manufacturer's liability for failure to warn under a theory of strict liability as well as negligence, the court discussed the interrelationship between instructions and a warning:

> [A] product requiring assembly and use in conformity with the supplier's directions is defective if the supplier fails to warn adequately of conditions and circumstances created by such assembly or use which would render the product dangerous to the user. Therefore, the supplier is strictly liable for injury proximately resulting from composing and furnishing a set of instructions for assembly and use which does not adequately avoid the danger of injury.[11]

---

[6] Veil v. Vitek, Inc., 803 F. Supp. 229 (D. N.D. 1992) (applying North Dakota law); Finn v. G.D. Searle & Co., 677 P.2d 1147 (Cal. 1984); Palmer v. Hobart Corp., 849 S.W.2d 135 (Mo. Ct. App. 1993).

[7] Texsun Feed Yards, Inc. v. Ralston Purina Co., 447 F.2d 660 (5th Cir. 1971) (applying Texas law).

[8] Hiigel v. General Motors Corp., 544 P.2d 983 (Colo. 1975); Oberg v. Advanced Transformer Company, Inc., 569 N.E.2d 50 (Ill. App. Ct. 1991).

[9] 127 Cal. Rptr. 217 (Cal. Ct. App. 1976).

[10] *Id.* at 219.

[11] *Id.* at 221.

[B] *Persons Who Have a Duty to Warn*

In most cases, the duty to warn is imposed on the manufacturer of a product,[12] as well as on the manufacturer of specific component parts. In *Walton v. AVCO Corp.*,[13] for example, the manufacturer of a helicopter had an independent duty to warn service centers and owners of the defective engine, even though the engine was manufactured by another company that had issued a "Service Instruction" to service centers when it learned of the defect. The liability of the helicopter manufacturer was based on three factors: it had incorporated a defective part into the helicopter; it had subsequent knowledge of the engine's defect; and the manufacturer of a product is considered to be an expert concerning its products and to know of the risks connected with their use. Component part manufacturers, such as the one that produced the engine in *Walton*, also may have a duty to warn of known dangers in the use of the products they sell.[14] In addition to manufacturers, those in the chain of distribution of a product also may have a duty to warn. This is the position taken by the Restatement (Third) which states that "sellers down the chain of distribution must warn when doing so is feasible and reasonable."[15] One example of "sellers down the chain of distribution" who have a duty to warn are automobile dealers. Since they have an opportunity to inspect their vehicles before the sale, they have a duty to warn potential buyers of the dangers posed by such features as airbags.[16]

[C] *Negligence and Strict Liability*

A claim alleging a failure to warn may be brought in implied warranty of merchantability, negligence, and/or strict liability.[17] However, a reading of § 388 of the Restatement (Second) of Torts, the comments to § 402A, and

---

[12] Germann v. F.L. Smithe Machine Co., 395 N.W.2d 922 (Minn. 1986). Under § 12 of the RESTATEMENT (THIRD), a corporation that acquires assets from another corporation is liable for harm caused by defective products sold by the predecessor only in limited situations. However, under § 13, a successor corporation is liable for its own failure to warn after acquiring the assets of another corporation when certain conditions are met and when a reasonable person in the successor corporation's position would warn.

[13] 610 A.2d 454 (Pa. 1992).

[14] However, there is no duty to anticipate and to warn of how components parts, not in themselves defective, might become dangerous when integrated into a product designed and manufactured by someone else. *See* Brennaman v. R.M.I. Co., 639 N.E.2d 425 (Ohio 1994).

[15] RESTATEMENT (THIRD) OF TORTS: PRODUCTS LIABILITY § 2 cmt. *i* (1998). *See* Santoro v. Donnelly, 2004 U.S. Dist. LEXIS 22849 (S.D.N.Y. 2004) (applying New York law); Tellez-Cordova v. Campbell Hausfeld/Scott Fetzger Co., 28 Cal. Rptr. 744 (Cal. Ct. App. 2004); Grady v. American Optical Corp., 702 S.W.2d 911 (Mo. Ct. App. 1985).

[16] *See* Juliano v. Toyota Motor Sales, U.S.A., Inc., 20 F. Supp. 2d 573 (S.D.N.Y. 1998).

[17] In *Richter v. Limax International, Inc.*, 45 F.3d 1464 (10th Cir. 1995) (applying Kansas law), the jury found a manufacturer liable both in negligence and in strict liability for its failure to warn of the dangers of a trampoline. *See also* Russell v. G. A. F. Corp., 422 A.2d 989 (D.C. 1980); Spuhl v. Shiley, Inc., 795 S.W.2d 573 (Mo. Ct. App. 1990).

§ 2 of the Restatement (Third) shows that, in practice, there is no real difference between negligence and strict liability in failure to warn cases.[18] As a result, most states use a negligence analysis in failure to warn cases, whether the claim is brought in negligence or strict liability.[19] The basis of negligence analysis is § 388 of the Restatement (Second) of Torts. This section, which focuses on the manufacturer's conduct, sets out the criteria for determining when there is a duty to warn and the standard of reasonable care required for a warning. Section 388, which has been cited widely by courts,[20] provides:

> One who supplies directly or through a third person a chattel for another to use is subject to liability to those whom the supplier should expect to use the chattel with the consent of the other or to be endangered by its probable use, for physical harm caused by the use of the chattel in the manner for which and by which a person for whose use it is supplied, if the supplier
>
> (a) knows or has reasons to know that the chattel is or is likely to be dangerous for the use for which it is supplied, and
>
> (b) has no reason to believe that those for whose use the chattel is supplied will realize its dangerous condition, and
>
> (c) fails to exercise reasonable care to inform them of its dangerous condition or the facts which make it likely to be dangerous.

Section 402A does not mention warning defects explicitly. However, as in negligence cases, the comments to the section state that liability is based on the failure to exercise reasonable care in discovering and warning of a risk of harm. Comment *h* to § 402A provides that, where a seller "has reason to anticipate that danger may result from a particular use, as where a drug is sold which is safe only in limited doses, he may be required to give adequate warning of the danger (see comment *j*) and a product sold without such warning is in a defective condition." Comment *j* then states that, because many products cannot be made entirely safe for all of their uses, "[i]n order to prevent the product from being unreasonably dangerous, the seller may be required to give directions or warning . . . as to its use."[21] Unlike § 402A,

---

[18] *See* Taylor v. Monsanto Co., 150 F.3d 806 (7th Cir. 1998) (applying Indiana law); Perlmutter v. United States Gypsum Co., 54 F.3d 659 (10th Cir. 1995) (applying Colorado law); Forest v. E.I. DuPont de Nemours & Co., 791 F. Supp. 1460 (D. Nev. 1992) (applying Nevada law).

[19] *See Richter*, 45 F.3d at 1468 ("Kansas applies the same test to whether a manufacturer met his duty to warn under negligence as it does under strict liability."). *See also* Johnson v. Zimmer, Inc., 2004 U.S. Dist. LEXIS 6007 (D. Minn. 2004) (applying Minnesota law); Roberts v. Performance Site Management, Inc., 2004 Ohio App. LEXIS 2470 (Ohio Ct. App. 2004); Olson v. Prosoco, Inc., 522 N.W.2d 284 (Iowa 1994).

[20] Among the cases that have endorsed this section are *Tipton v. Michelin Tire Co.*, 101 F.3d 1145 (6th Cir. 1996) (applying Kentucky law); *Allen v. IBM*, 1997 U.S. Dist. LEXIS 8016 (D. Del. 1997) (applying Delaware law); *Gray v. Badger Mining Corp.*, 676 N.W.2d 268 (Minn. 2004).

[21] *See* Anderson v. Owens-Corning Fiberglas Corp., 810 P.2d 549 (Cal. 1991).

section 2(c) of the Restatement (Third) lists "inadequate instructions or warnings" as one of three categories of a product defect. It then states that a product

> is defective because of inadequate instructions or warnings when the foreseeable risks of harm posed by the product could have been reduced or avoided by the provision of reasonable instructions or warnings by the seller or other distributor . . . and the omission of the instructions or warnings renders the product not reasonably safe.[22]

[D] *Design Defects and the Failure to Warn*

In many cases, a plaintiff alleges that a product was defective both in its design and because the manufacturer or seller failed to provide adequate warnings.[23] In jurisdictions that use a risk-utility analysis for design defect cases, courts often consider whether a warning was given as one of the factors that weighs in the balance of risk against utility.[24] However, the Restatement (Third) takes the position that, where a safer alternative design is available and reasonable for a product, the manufacturer must adopt that safer design rather than simply warn consumers of the dangers that exist in the design. Only in situations where there is no reasonable alternative design may warnings or instructions be sufficient to make the product reasonably safe.[25] An example of a case alleging that the design of a product was unreasonably dangerous because it did not contain an adequate warning of the dangers or provide an instruction on how to use it is *Strum, Ruger & Company, Inc. v. Bloyd*,[26] in which the plaintiff was struck in the ankle by a bullet that was fired from a revolver that accidentally was dropped on a concrete floor. The revolver had been hidden under the floor mat of the car by its owner and fell out when the plaintiff removed the mat to clean the inside of the car. The Kentucky Supreme Court held that a gun was not designed defectively because, when it was sold new, the gun was accompanied by a pamphlet warning of its unsafe mechanism and advising a user how the gun should be carried.[27] The manufacturer was under a duty only to design a gun that was safe for its anticipated reasonable use and that use was covered by the warning that accompanied the sale. Since

---

[22] For a discussion of § 2(c), see Restatement (Third) of Torts: Products Liability § 2 cmts. *i-o* (1998). *See also* Krummel v. Bombardier Corp., 206 F.3d 548 (5th Cir. 2000) (applying Louisiana law); Blue v. Environmental Engineering, Inc., 828 N.E.2d 1128 (Ill. 2005).

[23] *See* Rivera v. Philip Morris, Inc., 395 F.3d 1142 (9th Cir. 2005); Unrein v. Timesavers, Inc., 394 F.3d 1008 (8th Cir. 2005).

[24] Rogers v. Ingersoll-Rand Co., 144 F.3d 841 (D.C. Cir. 1998) (applying D.C. law).

[25] Restatement (Third) of Torts: Products Liability § 2 cmt. *l* (1998).

[26] 586 S.W.2d 19 (Ky. 1979).

[27] *Id.* at 20-21.

the manufacturer could not have anticipated the way in which the accident occurred, there was no defect in the design or in the warning.

Although some cases analyze a warning as part of the design of a product, the two defects are different conceptually. As was discussed in Chapter 5, a product contains a design defect if it fails to meet consumer expectations or if the risks of the design outweigh its benefits. In a failure to warn case, the design and the manufacture of the product meet all of the design requirements yet still contains a danger that is known to the manufacturer but is not obvious to the ordinary user or consumer.[28] Although § 2(c) of the Restatement (Third) recognizes the failure to warn as a category of product defects, it does not set out explicitly the elements of a failure to warn case. However, within the section are many of the questions that must be analyzed in a failure to warn case. First, when does a manufacturer or seller have a duty to provide a warning or instructions to consumers? Although § 2(c) of the Restatement (Third) defines a product as defective when "foreseeable risks of harm" could be reduced or avoided by instructions or warnings, it does not define when "foreseeable risks of harm" trigger a duty to warn. Is there a duty to warn if the "foreseeable risks of harm" are "open and obvious"? Second, if there is a duty to provide warnings or instructions, to whom must they be given? Third, what constitutes "reasonable instructions or warnings"? What is the effect of "reasonable instructions or warnings?" Finally, does the duty to provide warnings end with the sale of the product or must a warning be given to consumers if the risk of harm was not known until after the sale of the product? When, if ever, does the duty extend to recalling and retrofitting a product? The remainder of this chapter examines these questions and others related to warning defects.

§ 7.02 WHEN A WARNING MUST BE GIVEN

[A] *Introduction*

Even if a product is designed and manufactured properly, it is impossible to eliminate all of the dangers or risks that can result from every possible use.[29] In order that the risks not make a product unreasonably dangerous, it may be necessary for the manufacturer to provide a warning or to include instructions for the proper use of the product. Thus, the first question that must be asked in every case alleging inadequate warnings or instructions about the dangers of a product is: Did the manufacturer or seller have a duty to warn of the particular dangers connected with the use of the product? This is a question of law for the court to decide.[30]

---

[28] For a discussion of the differences between design defect claims and failure to warn claims, see *Hollister v. Dayton Hudson Corp.*, 201 F.3d 731 (6th Cir. 2000) (applying Michigan law).

[29] Wolfe v. Ford Motor Co., 376 N.E.2d 143 (Mass. App. Ct. 1977).

[30] American Tobacco Co. v. Grinnell, 951 S.W.2d 420 (Tex. 1997).

The easiest cases to decide are those involving products such as alcohol, cigarettes, medicines, and some food items where the question of when a warning must be provided has been answered by government regulations mandating that the products carry health warnings about their contents or specific dangers in their use.[31] Since there is no issue of a duty to warn in those cases, the question becomes whether the plaintiff's injuries were within the scope of the dangers covered by the warning.[32] More difficult, however, are the vast majority of cases involving products where a warning is not required by government regulations. Not only is it impossible to warn of every possible danger in every product, warnings are not cost free. There is a monetary cost in labeling, package inserts, and instruction manuals as well as a psychological cost. If a manufacturer includes too many warnings along with a product, the value of the warnings to users and consumers may be depreciated. In *Scott v. Black and Decker, Inc.,*.[33] the plaintiff alleged that the manufacturer was liable for failing to warn that its electric portable band saw was dangerous if used in a flammable atmosphere. Although the Fifth Circuit upheld the warnings as adequate, the extensive list may have resulted in "warning overload" that made the product less safe by causing the buyer to ignore the warnings.

> The owner's manual, which Black & Decker issues with each saw, lists twenty safety warnings on the first inside page, including instructions to ground the tool adequately, to wear proper apparel, to keep guards in place, to maintain properly, etc., in addition to an explicit warning about use of the saw in explosive atmospheres. The saw itself had a label instructing the user to read the owner's manual before using the tool.[34]

Because most states use a negligence analysis in failure to warn cases, whether they are brought in negligence or strict liability,[35] the focus is on what the manufacturer knew or should have known about the risk of harm at the time the product was sold or distributed.[36] A duty to warn is imposed

---

[31] In August 2005 the Attorney General of California filed suit against nine fast-food restaurants and food companies seeking to force them to put labels on all containers of french fries and potato chips sold in the state warning that the products contain chemicals known to cause cancer. California requires warnings on a broad range of products and supermarkets post signs warning of mercury in certain types of fish.

[32] Thongchoom v. Graco Children's Products, Inc., 71 P.3d 214 (Wash. Ct. App. 2003).

[33] 717 F.2d 251 (5th Cir. 1983) (applying Louisiana law).

[34] *Id.* at 254. After setting out the extent of the warnings, the court stated of the manufacturer: "More it cannot do; to require it to place a specific warning encompassing these facts on the saw is beyond the 'reasonable steps'" demanded by earlier cases. *Id.*

[35] Varano v. Jabar, 197 F.3d 1 (1st Cir. 1999) (applying Maine law); O'Flynn v. Owens-Corning Fiberglas, 759 So.2d 526 (Miss. Ct. App. 2000).

[36] *See* Strasser v. Transtech Mobile Fleet Service, Inc., 613 N.W.2d 142 (Wis. 2000); Moore v. Vanderloo, 386 N.W.2d 108, 116 (Iowa 1986); Woodill v. Parke Davis & Co., 402 N.E.2d 194 (Ill. 1980). A few states hold that it is irrelevant whether the manufacturer knew of the danger or should have known of the risk of danger. *See* Halpern v. Johns-Manville Sales Corp., 484

when a manufacturer: (1) knew or should have known that the product posed a sufficiently serious risk of harm when used for its intended or reasonably foreseeable purposes, and (2) had no reason to believe that the users or consumers of the product would be aware of and understand the risk of harm.[37] Foreseeability means a serious risk of harm that is objectively reasonable to expect, not just what conceivably might occur.[38] What is objectively "reasonable" to expect means that the manufacturer is required to warn not only of dangers from the intended use of its product but also of the dangers from the foreseeable unintended use of the product.[39] In deciding what risks were foreseeable, courts hold manufacturers to the standard of an expert regarding its products.[40]

Since the duty to warn is based on the foreseeability of the risk of harm, a manufacturer is liable only for risks that were known or knowable at the time of manufacture of the product. It is not liable for failing to warn of unknowable risks. The California Supreme Court's decision in *Anderson v. Owens Corning Fiberglass Corp.*[41] is illustrative of this principle. In *Anderson*, the court held that a defendant in a products liability action based on an alleged failure to warn of a risk of harm could present evidence of the "state of the art," that is, evidence that the particular risk was neither known nor knowable by application of scientific knowledge available at the time of the manufacture or distribution of the product. The court stated, "exclusion of state of the art evidence, when the basis of liability is a failure to warn, would make a manufacturer the virtual insurer of its product's safe use, a result that is not consonant with established principals of strict liability."[42] The overwhelming majority of jurisdictions accept this premise, which is consistent with comment *j* to the Restatement § 402A, which confines a duty to warn to a situation in which a seller "has knowledge or by the application of reasonable, developed human skill and foresight should have knowledge of…the danger."[43]

So. 2d 110 (La. 1986); Elmore v. Owens-Illinois, Inc., 673 S.W.2d 434 (Mo. 1984); Phillips v. Kimwood Machine Co., 525 P.2d 1033 (Or. 1974).

[37] Daniel v. Ben E. Keith Co., 97 F.3d 1329 (10th Cir. 1996) (applying Oklahoma law); Sheckells v. AGV-USA Corp., 987 F.2d 1532 (11th Cir. 1993) (applying Georgia law); Sollami v. Eaton, 772 N.E.2d 215 (Ill. 2002); Glittenberg v. Doughboy Recreational Industries, 491 N.W.2d 208 (Mich. 1992); Crocker v. Winthrop Laboratories, 514 S.W.2d 429 (Tex. 1974).

[38] Sollami v. Eaton, 772 N.E.2d 215 (Ill. 2002).

[39] RESTATEMENT (SECOND) OF TORTS § 402A cmt. *h* (1965); RESTATEMENT (THIRD) OF TORTS: PRODUCTS LIABILITY § 2 cmt. *p* (1998); Lugo v. LJN Toys, 552 N.E.2d 162 (N.Y. 1990).

[40] Borel v. Fiberboard Paper Products Corp., 493 F.2d 1076 (5th Cir. 1973) (applying Texas law); Feldman v. Lederle Laboratories, 479 A.2d 374 (N.J. 1984); Garlock, Inc. v. Gallagher, 814 A.2d 1007 (Md. Ct. Spec. App. 2003).

[41] 810 P.2d 549 (1991).

[42] *Id.* at 550. *See also* Woodill v. Parke Davis & Co., 402 N.E.2d 194 (Ill. 1980).

[43] *See* RESTATEMENT (SECOND) OF TORTS § 402A cmt. *j* (1965).

[B] *Unavoidably Unsafe Products*

Even if a product is manufactured according to the "state of the art," it may be "unavoidably unsafe" because of the present limits of knowledge about the design or manufacture of the product. In many situation, the inability to produce a reasonably safe product is a sufficient reason not to manufacture and sell it. However, some products, particularly drugs and medical devices, are a great benefit to a large number of people despite being "unavoidably unsafe." If the product is useful and it is beneficial to have it on the market, comment *k* to § 402A provides that it will not be considered "defective" or "unreasonably dangerous" and the manufacturer will not be strictly liable for the unfortunate consequences of its use provided the product is "properly prepared, and accompanied by proper directions and warning."[44]

Although comment *k* has been adopted in the overwhelming majority of states that have considered the matter,[45] states interpret comment *k* in a number of different ways and there is considerable disagreement concerning its application. A few states interpret comment *k* to make all prescription drugs exempt from strict liability. Under this view, a prescription drug that is properly manufactured and accompanied by an adequate warning of the risks known to the manufacturer at the time of sale is not defectively designed as a matter of law.[46] The majority of states, however, apply it on a case-by-case basis, holding that the interests in developing and marketing prescription drugs can be met without giving manufacturers blanket immunity.[47] Thus, in *Castrignano v. E.R. Squibb & Sons*,[48] the Rhode Island Supreme Court held that a case-by-case method of determining the applicability of comment *k* in drug products cases was the most appropriate method.[49] The court also held that comment *k* is not applicable to allegations that a prescription drug manufacturer failed adequately to warn of risks associated with its drug. In such cases, the court held, where the basis of the plaintiff's complaint is the failure to warn adequately, strict liability theory is a properly pled cause of action. The court observed that, although comment *k* cites examples, its language does not establish definitely the boundaries of its exemption.[50] The comment suggests that a

---

[44] RESTATEMENT (SECOND) OF TORTS § 402A cmt. *k* (1965).

[45] *See* Schwartz, *Unavoidably Unsafe Products: Clarifying the Meaning and Policy Behind Comment k*, 42 WASH. & LEE L. REV. 1139 (1985).

[46] Young v. Key Pharmaceuticals, 922 P.2d 59 (Wyo. 1996); Grundberg v. Upjohn Co., 813 P.2d 89 (Utah 1991); Brown v. Superior Court (Abbott Laboratories), 751 P.2d 470 (Cal. 1988).

[47] *See, e.g.*, Tobin v. Astra Pharmaceutical Products, Inc., 993 F.2d 528 (6th Cir. 1993); Hill v. Searle Laboratories, 884 F.2d 1064 (8th Cir. 1989); Castrignano v. E.R. Squibb & Sons, Inc., 546 A.2d 775 (R.I. 1988).

[48] Castrignano v. E.R. Squibb, 546 A.2d 775 (R.I. 1988).

[49] *Id.* at 781.

[50] *Id.* at 780.

drug properly prepared and marketed, and accompanied by proper warnings when the situation calls for it, could not be subject to strict liability when it satisfies the risk-benefit analysis. Satisfying this standard qualifies a drug as unavoidably unsafe. Although the comment speaks of proper warnings, its language does not address exempting drugs from strict liability for failure to warn of the dangers created by their use. Thus, the *Castrignano* court concluded that the exemption applies only to allegations of a defective design. In order to avoid liability for failure to warn, the manufacturer must pass the test set out in comment *j* of the Restatement.

[C] *Open and Obvious Dangers*

An essential element for a duty to warn is unequal knowledge between the manufacturer and the user about the dangers posed by the product.[51] The Restatements make it clear that a manufacturer has no duty to warn if, from an objective point of view, the knowledge of the risk posed by a product is open, obvious, and generally appreciated by users of the product. Section 388(b) of the Restatement (Second) of Torts states that, in negligence cases, there is a duty to warn only if the manufacturer "has no reason to believe that those for whose use the chattel is supplied will realize its dangerous condition."[52] Similarly, comment *j* to § 402A states that, in cases based on strict liability, the seller is not required to warn when the danger or potential danger in a product "is generally known and recognized."[53] Finally, comment *j* to § 2 of the Restatement (Third) states:

> In general, a product seller is not subject to liability for failing to warn or instruct regarding risks and risk-avoidance measures that should be obvious to, or generally known by, foreseeable product users. When a risk is obvious or generally known, the prospective addressee of a warning will or should already know of its existence. Warning of an obvious or generally known risk in most instances will not provide an effective additional measure of safety.[54]

In keeping with the position taken by the Restatements, the vast majority of courts also have adopted an "open and obvious" exception to the duty to warn.[55] According to one court, "nothing of value is gained by a warning regarding a dangerous condition that already is obvious to the average con-

---

[51] Seegers Grain Co. v. United States Steel Corp., 577 N.E.2d 1364 (Ill. App. Ct. 1991).

[52] *See also* RESTATEMENT (SECOND) OF TORTS § 388 cmt *k* (1965).

[53] RESTATEMENT (SECOND) OF TORTS § 388 cmt *j* (1965).

[54] RESTATEMENT (THIRD) OF TORTS: PRODUCTS LIABILITY § 2 cmt. *j* (1998).

[55] *See* Ahrens v. Ford Motor Co., 340 F.3d 1142 (10th Cir. 2003) (applying Oklahoma law); Burke v. Spartanics, Ltd., 252 F.3d 131 (2d Cir. 2001) (applying New York law); Kuras v. International Harvester Co., 820 F.2d 15 (1st Cir. 1987) (applying R.I. law).

sumer and is generally appreciated."[56] A few states, however, either reject the open and obvious doctrine[57] or have rejected an all-or-nothing approach and, instead, treat the obviousness of the risk as a factor for the trier of fact to consider in determining liability.[58]

The problem for courts is determining what risks are open and obvious. The test is an objective one based upon whether a "reasonable person"[59] could recognize and appreciate the risk. Although this requirement is easy to state, its application depends upon the facts of each case. Because of the great variety of products, the ways in which they are used, and the risks they may present, it is impossible to give an exact definition of when a risk is open and obvious to a reasonable person. Whether a particular danger is open and obvious depends on a number of factors: (1) the complexity of the product; (2) the knowledge, age, background, experience, intelligence, and training of the injured person; (3) the extent to which the required contact of the injured person with the device is routine and repetitive; and (4) whether the injured person was distracted.[60] The complexity of these factors makes it a question of fact for the jury to decide. Among the various dangers that have been held to be open and obvious to a reasonable person are:

- a disposable butane lighter,[61]

- consuming alcohol,[62]

- diving into a shallow swimming pool,[63]

- driving with a foot sticking out of a golf cart,[64]

- a handgun,[65]

---

[56] Blue v. Environmental Engineering, Inc., 803 N.E.2d 187, 194 (Ill. App. Ct. 2002). *See also* Jamieson v. Woodward & Lothrop, 247 F.2d 23 (D.C. Cir. 1957); Caterpillar, Inc. v. Shears, 911 S.W.2d 379 (Tex. 1995).

[57] *See* Harris v. Karri-On Campers, Inc., 640 F.2d 65 (7th Cir. 1981) (applying West Virginia law); Tacke v. Vermeer Manufacturing Co., 713 P.2d 527 (Mont. 1986).

[58] *See* Horton v. American Tobacco Co., 667 So.2d 1289 (Miss. 1995); Armentrout v. FMC Corp., 842 P.2d 175 (Colo. 1992); House v. Armour of America, Inc., 886 P.2d 542 (Utah Ct. App. 1994).

[59] Sollami v. Eaton, 772 N.E.2d 215 (Ill. 2002); Sauder Custom Fabrication, Inc. v. Boyd, 967 S.W.2d 349 (Tex. 1998).

[60] Figgie International, Inc., Snorke-Economy Div. v. Tognocchi, 624 A.2d 1285 (Md. Ct. Spec. App. 1993).

[61] Adams v. Perry Furniture Co., 497 N.W.2d 514 (Mich. Ct. App. 1993).

[62] Brown Forman Corp. v. Brune, 893 S.W.2d 640 (Tex. App. 1994).

[63] Spaulding v. Lesco International Corp., 451 N.W.2d 603 (Mich. Ct. App. 1990).

[64] Vela v. Yamaha Motor Corp., 2002 Tex. App. LEXIS 3185 (Tex. App. 2002).

[65] *See* Perkins v. F.I.E. Corp., 762 F.2d 1250 (5th Cir. 1980); Mavilia v. Stoeger Industries, 574 F. Supp. 107 (D. Mass. 1983); Resteiner v. Sturm, Ruger & Co., 566 N.W.2d 53 (Mich. Ct. App. 1997); Richardson v. Holland, 741 S.W.2d 751 (Mo. Ct. App. 1988); Riordan v. Int'l Armament Corp., 477 N.E.2d 1293 (Ill. App. Ct. 1985).

- a meat grinder,[66]

- operating a front-end loader without a roll bar,[67]

- riding on a motorcycle,[68]

- riding unrestrained in an open cargo bed of a pickup truck,[69]

- smoking,[70]

- jumping on a a trampoline.[71]

However, courts have held that it was not open and obvious to a reasonable person that:

- a fire-causing electrical problem also could knock out a smoke alarm,[72]

- a body-care product could be fatal if ingested by a child,[73]

- a small child could choke on a marshmallow[74] or a toy block.[75]

In deciding whether a risk was open and obvious, courts also have drawn a distinction between an reasonable adult's ability to recognize and appreciate certain risks and a child's ability. In *Bunch v. Hoffinger Industries, Inc.*,[76] an 11-year-old became a quadriplegic after diving into a four-foot-deep above-ground swimming pool. In her suit against the manufacturer of the pool liner, the plaintiff alleged a failure to warn of the dangers of diving into a shallow pool. At trial, the plaintiff stated that she vaguely remembered stickers on the pool liner that said: "No diving in shallow water" and showed a man making a "pike," or vertical, dive with the word "caution." The plaintiff said she believed the label warned her "[n]ot to dive like that."[77] After an extensive review of diving cases involving adults and children, the California appellate court concluded it was not evident that, "as a matter of law, the dangers of 'shallow' or surface diving into a shallow pool are open and

---

[66] Liroano v. Hobart Corp., 170 F.3d 264 (2d Cir. 1999) (applying New York law).

[67] Bates v. Richland Sales Corp., 803 N.E.2d 977 (Ill. App. Ct. 2004).

[68] Shaffer v. AMF Inc., 842 F.2d 893 (6th Cir. 1988) (applying Ohio law).

[69] Josue v. Isuzu Motors America, Inc., 958 P.2d 535 (Haw. 1998).

[70] Gibbs v. Republic Tobacco, L.P., 119 F. Supp. 2d 1288 (M.D. Fla. 2000) (applying Florida law).

[71] Sollami v. Eaton, 772 N.E.2d 215 (Ill. 2002).

[72] Laaperi v. Sears, Roebuck & Co., 787 F.2d 726 (1st Cir. 1986) (applying Massachusetts law).

[73] Green v. A.P. Products, Ltd., 691 N.W.2d 38 (Mich. Ct. App. 2004).

[74] Emery v. Federated Foods, Inc., 863 P.2d 426 (Mont. 1993).

[75] Metzgar v. Playskool, Inc., 30 F.3d 459 (3d Cir. 1994) (applying Pennsylvania law).

[76] 20 Cal. Rptr. 3d 780 (Cal. App. Ct. 2004).

[77] *Id.* at 785.

obvious to minors."[78] Since other courts had considered prior swimming and diving experience, familiarity with the pool in question, and the public's general awareness of diving dangers in determining whether the danger is open and obvious to adults, the court felt that it was "absurd and somewhat illogical to consider these factors in determining an awareness of danger but to ignore or exclude the age of the diver."[79]

Although it was foreseeable that the swimming pool in *Bunch* would be used by an 11-year-old, the product was not marketed specifically to children. In cases where a product's primary marketing target is children, courts have required that whether a risk is open and obvious be determined by a "reasonable child" standard rather than an adult "reasonable person" test. In *Swix v. Daisy Manufacturing Co., Inc.*,[80] a child who used an air rifle and his parents brought an action against the rifle's manufacturer alleging defective design and failure to warn of known danger. The Sixth Circuit stated that in determining whether a danger was open and obvious, "the focus is the typical user's perception and knowledge of whether the relevant condition or feature that creates the danger associated with use is fully apparent, widely known, commonly recognized, and anticipated by the ordinary user or consumer."[81] The court reasoned that, since the median age of the purchasers of the gun was 12 years old, the objective "reasonable child standard" applied with respect to the manufacturer's duty to warn, even though the air rifle was to be used under the direct supervision of any adult.[82]

Some courts permit manufacturers in strict liability failure to warn cases to present evidence of the plaintiff's knowledge of the risk based on common knowledge in the particular industry. In *Campos v. Firestone Tire & Rubber Co.*,[83] a tire mechanic brought a products liability action against the manufacturer of the rim assembly, alleging product defect and failure to warn. The New Jersey Supreme Court held the manufacturer had a duty to warn the tire mechanic of the danger of inserting his hand into the protective cage while the tire was being inflated.[84] However, the court also held that the tire mechanic's knowledge of the danger as a result of a prior accident which occurred when he inserted his hand into cage while the tire was being

---

[78] *Id.* at 796 (*quoting* Klen v. Doughboy Recreational, Inc., 643 N.E.2d, 1360, 1369-1370 (Ill. App. Ct. 1994)).

[79] *Id.*

[80] 373 F.3d 678 (6th Cir. 2004).

[81] *Id.* at 686.

[82] *Id.* at 686-688. *See also* Klen v. Asahi Pool, Inc., 643 N.E.2d 1360, 1366 (Ill. App. Ct. 1993) (when a 14-year-old was injured after diving into an swimming pool, the Illinois Appellate Court held that the question of whether the risk was open and obvious must be judged by the "reasonable or objective class of 14-year olds.").

[83] 485 A.2d 305 (N.J. 1984).

[84] *Id.* at 310.

inflated was relevant to the question of causation, i.e., whether manufacturer's failure to warn of danger was the cause of mechanic's injury.[85] Similarly, in *ExParte Chevron Chemical Co.*,[86] employees of a gas company sued the manufacturer of a plastic pipe after the pipeline exploded during an installation, alleging negligent failure to warn of danger of static electricity and alleging liability under the Alabama Extended Manufacturer's Liability Doctrine (AEMLD). However, the Alabama Supreme Court held the manufacturer did not have duty to warn the gas company or its employees of a danger that was common knowledge in the industry, and published in a manual given to the very employees who were injured.[87]

§ 7.03 PERSONS WHO MUST BE WARNED

[A] *Users, Consumers, and Bystanders*

Once it is determined that a manufacturer or seller has a duty to provide a warning or instructions about the use of a product, the next question that must be asked is: to whom must the warning be provided? The Restatements and cases take the position that, a manufacturer has a duty "to warn those persons it should reasonably foresee would be likely to use its product or who are likely to come into contact with a latent danger inherent in the product's use."[88] In negligence cases, section 388 of the Restatement (Second) of Torts requires that a warning be given to those who should be expected to use the product or to be endangered by its probable use. The comments to § 402A state that, in strict liability cases, the warning must be given to the "ultimate user or consumer."[89] In the case of consumer goods that are sold to the general public, these sections mean the same thing: the manufacturer must provide the warning directly to the users along with the product.[90] Depending upon the product, these warnings can be printed directly on the product package or they may be placed on package inserts or in instruction manuals.

The purpose of such warnings is to enable the users or consumers of a product to make an informed decision about whether and how to use it. However, if a warning would not facilitate a user's decision process, the manufacturer has no duty to provide one to the user. In *Stevens v. Cessna Aircraft Co.*,[91] a California court held that the manufacturer of an small air-

---

[85] *Id.* at 311.

[86] 720 So.2d 922 (Ala. 1998).

[87] *Id.* at 926.

[88] Taylor v. Monsanto Co., 150 F.3d 806, 808 (7th Cir. 1998) (applying Indiana law).

[89] RESTATEMENT (SECOND) OF TORTS § 402A cmt. *j* (1965).

[90] Johnson v. Harley-Davidson Motor Company Group, Inc., 2004 Iowa App. LEXIS 344 (Iowa Ct. App. 2004); RESTATEMENT (SECOND) OF TORTS § 388 (1965).

[91] 170 Cal. Rptr. 925 (Cal. Ct. App. 1981).

plane had no duty to warn the passengers of the plane's load capacity. According to the court, whether the plane could fly safely with a particular total weight of passengers depended on too many factors for the passengers to make an informed decision based on a warning. In such a situation, passengers depend on the pilot to determine the safe load capacity.[92]

The duty to warn also may extend to persons other than user or consumers. According to the Restatement (Third), it may be necessary to provide instructions and warnings "to others who a reasonable seller should know will be in a position to reduce or avoid the risk of harm."[93] An example of persons who are "in a position to reduce or avoid the risk of harm" from a product are physicians who act as learned intermediaries between drug manufacturers and patients. In some situations, a manufacturer also may have a duty to warn bystanders. However, before a court will impose a duty to warn a bystander, it must determine who was the primary recipient of the warning, whether a warning would have been seen by the bystander, and whether the lack of the warning was the cause of the bystander's injury.[94]

[B] *Persons with Allergic Reactions*

In a number of cases, the question has arisen whether manufacturers must provide warnings to persons who have allergic reactions to nonprescription drugs, chemicals used in consumer goods, or ingredients in food products.[95] The comments to § 402A,[96] the Restatement (Third),[97] and the cases[98] all agree that whether manufacturers have a duty to warn these persons depends on three factors. First, the product must contain an ingredient to which a "substantial number of persons" in the general population are allergic. Although courts have not quantified what constitutes a "substantial number," the plaintiff must show that the reaction was not unique. However, if the risk posed by the allergic reaction is a severe harm, the "substantial number" required for a warning is less than if the potential harm

---

[92] *Id.* at 926.

[93] RESTATEMENT (THIRD) OF TORTS: PRODUCTS LIABILITY § 2 cmt. *i* (1998).

[94] Scordino v. Hopeman Brothers, Inc., 662 So.2d 640 (Miss. 1995); Daniels v. Bucyrus-Erie Corp., 516 S.E.2d 848 (Ga. Ct. App. 1999). For a discussion of the learned intermediary doctrine, see § 7.06.

[95] Livingston v. Marie Callenders, Inc., 85 Cal. Rptr. 2d 528 (Cal. Ct. App. 1999) (MSG in soup); Kaempfe v. Lehn & Fink Products. Corp., 249 N.Y.S.2d 840 (N.Y. App. Div. 1964) (aluminum sulphate in spray-on deodorant).

[96] RESTATEMENT (SECOND) OF TORTS § 402A cmt. *j* (1965).

[97] RESTATEMENT (THIRD) OF TORTS: PRODUCTS LIABILITY § 2 cmt. *k* (1998).

[98] *See, e.g.*, Guilbeau v. W. W. Henry Co., 85 F.3d 1149 (5th Cir. 1997) (applying Louisiana law); Guevara v. Dorsey Laboratories, 845 F.2d 364 (1st Cir. 1988) (applying Puerto Rican law); Griggs v. Combe, Inc., 456 So.2d 790 (Ala. 1984).

is not serious. Second, the ingredient must be one whose danger is not generally known to consumers or one that consumers would not expect to find in the product. If it generally is known that the particular product contains an ingredient to which a substantial number of persons are allergic, there is no duty to warn. Finally, the manufacturer must have known, or should have known, at the time of sale, that the product contained an ingredient to which a "substantial number" of persons were allergic.

[C] *Bulk Supplier/Sophisticated User/Sophisticated Supplier Doctrine*

Despite the broad duty imposed on manufacturers to provide warnings and instructions about their products, there are some situations where they may not be required to provide the warnings directly to the ultimate users and consumers of products. One of these, products covered by the "learned intermediary doctrine," is discussed in detail in § 7.06. Three others — the "bulk supplier" doctrine, the "sophisticated intermediary" doctrine and the "sophisticated user" doctrine — are closely related affirmative defenses.[99]

The "bulk supplier" doctrine holds that the manufacturer of products that are sold in bulk, such as asbestos or industrial chemicals, may fulfill its duty to warn the employees who use the products by relying on an intermediary distributor that has knowledge of the risks to warn the ultimate users.[100] There are two rationales behind this doctrine. First, where a manufacturer delivers a product in a bulk container to an intermediary, the intermediary repackages the product and then resells it. This makes it impossible for the manufacturer to warn the ultimate users directly of the risks since the product is not provided to those users in the manufacturer's own packaging.[101] Second, products provided in bulk often have a number of uses and are reformulated by the intermediary for those uses. This results in the manufacturer not knowing of the particular risks since it may not know exactly how its product will be used.[102]

Although the intermediary to whom the bulk goods are sold has its own obligation to warn, one court has pointed out that there is no "bright line rule" to determine whether the manufacturer's reliance on the intermediary to provide the necessary warning was reasonable.[103] Instead, it depends upon

---

[99] For a detailed discussion of these three doctrines, see *Gray v. Badger Mining Corp.*, 676 N.W.2d 268 (Minn. 2004).

[100] Hoffman v. Houghton Chemical Corp., 751 N.E.2d 848 (Mass. 2001); Ex parte Chevron Chemical Company, 720 So.2d 922 (Ala. 1998). The doctrine has its origins in the RESTATEMENT (SECOND) OF TORTS § 388 cmt. *n* (1965).

[101] Wood v. Phillips Petroleum, 119 S.W.3d 874 (Tex. App. 2003).

[102] *Hoffman*, 751 N.E.2d at 856-857.

[103] *Id.* at 856.

(1) the dangerous condition of the product;

(2) the purpose for which the product is used;

(3) the form of any warnings given;

(4) the reliability of the third party as a conduit of necessary infor-
     mation about the product;

(5) the magnitude of the risk involved; and

(6) the burdens imposed on the supplier by requiring that he
     directly warn all users.[104]

Even when the bulk supplier is entitled to rely on the intermediary to provide the necessary warnings about a product, the manufacturer still must
provide adequate information to the intermediary so that it is informed of
the potential dangers and is in a position to pass on the warnings to the ultimate users.[105]

The "sophisticated user" doctrine provides that a manufacturer has no
duty to warn the ultimate user of a product if it has reason to believe that
the user knows or should know of the particular dangers involved with the
product.[106] The rationale for this doctrine is that, if the risks of the product already are known by the user, an additional warning will have little
deterrent effect.[107] In *House v. Armour of America, Inc.*,[108] the plaintiff's
husband, a corrections officer who was a member of a SWAT team, was
killed while carrying out an arrest. The plaintiff alleged that the manufacturer of the fabric used in the body armor vest her husband had been wearing at the time was strictly liable for failing to warn him of the limitations
and capabilities of the vest. In reply, the manufacturer argued that the
husband was a sophisticated user since he had been "a highly and specially
trained prison officer" who was "clearly knowledgeable regarding the characteristics of soft body armor vests."[109] However, after reviewing the record,
the Utah Supreme Court concluded that there was insufficient evidence
that any training given to the husband and SWAT team involved the use and
capabilities of body armor. Since the SWAT team had purchased body armor
only a few years before the incident, the court stated that, when the husband

---

[104] *Id. (quoting* Goodbar v. Whitehead Brothers, 591 F. Supp. 552, 557 (D. W.Va. 1984)).

[105] Donahue v. Phillips Petroleum Co., 866 F.2d 1008, 1012 (8th Cir. 1989) (applying Missouri law).

[106] *Id. See also* Jones v. Flowserve FCD Corp., 2003 U.S. App. LEXIS 17523 (5th Cir. 2003)
(applying Louisiana law); East Penn Manufacturing Co. v. Pineda, 578 A.2d 1113 (D.C. Ct. App.
1990).

[107] Hall v. Ashland Oil, 625 F. Supp. 1515 (D. Conn. 1986) (applying Connecticut law);
Hill v. Wilmington Chemical Corp., 156 N.W.2d 898 (Minn. 1968).

[108] 929 P.2d 340 (Utah 1996).

[109] *Id.* at 345.

was killed, his SWAT team "not only lacked knowledge about the capabilities of body armor, but also lacked experience in using the product."[110]

Closely related to the "sophisticated user" doctrine is the "sophisticated intermediary" doctrine. Under this doctrine the duty to warn is satisfied when the manufacturer provides a product directly to an intermediary such as an employer who then passes on the information about the dangers to the employee/users.[111] In such a situation, the manufacturer of the product does not have a duty to warn the ultimate user directly of the risks from use of the product if: (1) the product is sold to an intermediary that has knowledge or sophistication equal to the manufacturer's; (2) the manufacturer adequately warned the intermediary; and (3) the manufacturer reasonably can rely on the intermediary to warn the ultimate user.[112] Unlike the "bulk supplier" doctrine, the "sophisticated user" doctrine and the "sophisticated intermediary" doctrine do not require the product to be supplied to the ultimate user through an intermediary or that the product be supplied in bulk.

In some situations, courts have refused to apply the bulk supplier/sophisticated user doctrines. An example of this is *Oman v. Johns-Mansville Corp.*,[113] in which the Fourth Circuit found that the product (asbestos) was very dangerous, that the burden on the manufacturer in placing a warning on the product was not great, that the employer was unaware of the danger for a long time, and that, when the employer became aware of the danger, it failed to warn its employees.[114]

§ 7.04 ADEQUACY OF THE WARNING

[A] *Criteria for Determining the Scope and Adequacy of a Warning*

Once it is determined that a manufacturer has a duty to warn of the dangers of a product and to whom the warning must be given, the next question is whether the warning was "one calculated to bring home to a reasonably prudent user of the product the nature and extent of the danger

---

[110] *Id.*

[111] Conley v. Lift-All Company, Inc., 2005 U.S. Dist. LEXIS 15468 (S.D. Ind. 2005) (applying Indiana law); Cotton v. Buckeye Gas Products Co., 840 F.2d 935 (D.C. Cir. 1988) (applying Virginia law).

[112] *See* First National Bank & Trust Co. v. American Eurocopter Corp., 378 F.3d 682 (7th Cir. 2004) (applying Indiana law); Beale v. Whitehead Brothers Co., 769 F.2d 213 (4th Cir. 1985) (applying Virginia law); Gray v. Badger Mining Corp., 676 N.W.2d 268 (Minn. 2004).

[113] 764 F.2d 224 (4th Cir. 1985) (applying Virginia law).

[114] *Id.* at 233. *See also* Hunnings v. Texaco, Inc., 29 F.3d 1480 (11th Cir. 1994) (applying Florida law); Fisher v. Professional Compounding Centers of America, Inc., 311 F. Supp. 2d 1008 (D. Nev. 2004) (applying Nevada law); Union Carbide Corp. v. Kavanaugh, 2004 Fla. App. LEXIS 8725 (Fla. Ct. App. 2004) (applying Florida law).

involved in using the product."[115] Whether a warning was adequate to inform "a reasonably prudent user of the product" of the risks of the product is an issue for the trier of fact.[116] However, a manufacturer does not have to warn of every possible danger involving the use of the product. In *Anderson v. Weslo, Inc.*,[117] the plaintiff, a sixteen-year-old who was a "very experienced, although self-taught, trampoline user" was injured while attempting to do a double flip on a trampoline manufactured by the defendant. He brought an action in negligence and strict liability action against the manufacturer, alleging, among other things, that the user's manual failed to warn him of the kinds of injuries that could result from doing somersaults on the trampoline. The Washington appellate court affirmed the grant of summary judgment for the manufacturer. Although the warnings on the trampoline did not inform the plaintiff of every possible injury that could occur while using the product, they did warn of the general risk of injury and of the serious risk of injury when doing somersaults. The court also felt that it was obvious to an ordinary person that they could land on any part of their body, including their head, neck, or back, and suffer serious injury. Thus, the court held that the manufacturer's warnings adequately informed users of the risk, and that proximate cause had not been established as a matter of law.

In order to help juries and courts decide whether a warning was adequate, the New Mexico appellate court set out five general criteria.[118] According to the court: (1) a warning must indicate adequately the scope of the danger; (2) a warning must communicate reasonably the extent or seriousness of the harm that could result from the danger; (3) the physical aspects of the warning — conspicuousness, prominence, relative size of print, — must be adequate to alert a reasonably prudent person to the danger; (4) a simple directive warning (i.e., "Do not use") may be inadequate, without some indication of consequences from failure to follow the directive; and (5) the means to convey the warning must be adequate.[119] In applying these factors, courts require that the form of the warning was such that it was able to catch the attention of reasonable users or consumers in the circumstances of their use of the product.[120] However, even if the form of the warning was

---

[115] Evridge v. American Honda Motor Co., 685 S.W.2d 632, 636 (Tenn. 1985). *See also* Spruill v. Boyle-Midway, Inc., 308 F.2d 79 (4th Cir. 1962) (applying Virginia law).

[116] Huff v. Elmhurst-Chicago Stone Co., 419 N.E.2d 561 (Ill. App. Ct. 1981). However, the adequacy of a warning is a matter of law for the court to decide if reasonable minds cannot differ as to its sufficiency. Jacobs v. E.I. du Pont de Nemours & Co., 67 F.3d 1219 (6th Cir. 1995) (applying Tennessee law).

[117] 906 P.2d 336 (Wash. Ct. App. 1995).

[118] First National Bank in Albuquerque v. Nor-Am Agricultural Products, Inc., 537 P.2d 682 (N.M. Ct. App. 1975).

[119] *Id.* at 691-692. For similar statements of the criteria for an adequate warning, see Oman v. Johns-Manville Corp., 764 F.2d 224 (4th Cir. 1985) (applying Virginia law); Lewis v. Sea Ray Boats, Inc., 65 P.3d 245 (Nev. 2003).

[120] White v. ABCO Engineering Corp., 221 F.3d 293 (2d Cir. 2000) (applying New Jersey law).

sufficient, the content also must be understandable to ordinary users of the product and give them a reasonable indication of the nature and extent of the danger posed by the product.[121]

[B] *Form of the Warning*

In most cases a warning about the dangers associated with the use of a product will be placed on the product itself and/or in a package insert along with any instructions for the user to read before using the product. An example of the use of warnings on the label, product inserts, and direct mailings is *Barnes v. The Kerr Corp.*[122] In *Barnes*, warnings that mixing dental amalgam presented a health risk were printed on the jars in which the capsules were sent. The labels stated in capital letters that the product CONTAINED METALLIC MERCURY and featured an image of a skull and crossbones next to the word POISON. On a chart of different hazards, including flammability, reactivity, and health hazards, the labels also warned that metallic mercury presented a "serious health hazard." The labels recommended using protective gear such as glasses, gloves, and a face mask when handling the amalgams, and warned that ingesting the mercury could cause "Neurotoxic/Nephrotoxic effects," that the inhalation of mercury could cause "Bronchiolitis, Pneumonitis and Pulmonary Edema," and that even skin contact could have harmful effects, including "redness and irritation to the eyes and skin."[123] In addition to the warnings on the label, each jar contained an insert with directions and an additional detailed warnings. After the instructions about how to use the product, the word WARNING appeared in bold, capital letters, followed by a paragraph setting out the dangers of, and precautions against, mercury poisoning.[124] A third warning was provided to users of the product in the Material Safety Data Sheet (MSDS), a regularly updated document that was mailed to dentists who purchased the defendant's products. The MSDS described mercury as a "hazardous ingredient" and stated that chronic mercury poisoning could cause a number of medical problems.[125] The Sixth Circuit concluded that the warnings provided to users by the manufacturer were sufficient as a matter of law. Specifically, the court stated that the warnings (1) adequately indicated the scope of the danger; (2) gave detailed advice on how to use the dental amalgam capsules in order to avoid mercury poisoning; and (3) openly displayed and presented the warning in three separate media.[126]

---

[121] Cottam v. CVS Pharmacy, 764 N.E.2d 814 (Mass. 2000); DaimlerChrysler Corp. v. Hillhouse, 161 S.W.3d 541 (Tex. App. 2004).

[122] 418 F.3d 583 (6th Cir. 2005) (applying Tennessee law).

[123] *Id.* at 586.

[124] *Id.*

[125] *Id.*

[126] *Id.* at 591.

Not only must the warning be on the product or in package inserts, it must be in a form designed to catch the attention of a reasonable user of the product.[127] In deciding whether the form of a warning was adequate, a jury often will consider the position of warning, its color, the size of print, and the symbols used to call the user's attention to the warning or cause the user to be more likely to read the label and warning than not.[128] In *Barnes*, for example, the court was influenced in its holding that the warnings were adequate as a matter of law by the fact that they were in capital letters on the labels and were accompanied by a skull and crossbones.[129] In most cases, however, the form of the warning does not rise to the level of "a matter of law" and is, instead, a question for the jury. An example of a court leaving to the jury the question of whether the size of a warning and its location on a product were sufficient to communicate the risks is *Casey v. Pactiv*,[130] in which the manufacturer of a turkey roasting pan placed a notice on the side of the pan that it could hold a turkey weighing up to 20 pounds. The plaintiff cooked an 18-pound turkey in the pan. However, when the plaintiff lifted the sides of the pan to remove the finished turkey from the oven, the pan collapsed, spilling hot juices onto his legs and feet. The plaintiff suffered severe second and third-degree burns, requiring several surgeries and skin grafts. In his suit against the manufacturer, the plaintiff alleged negligent design and failure to give an adequate warning. The manufacturer filed a motion for summary judgment, arguing that the warnings on the pan were adequate to avoid the type of accident that the plaintiff suffered.

The Massachusetts court noted that the roasting pan contained two warnings. First, in "very small print," the pan's label said:

> Perfect for roasts up to 20 lbs when bottom of pan is properly supported. Caution: do not lift by sides only. To avoid spilling *always* support bottom of pan with a cookie sheet.[131]

Second, embossed on the bottom of the pan, the manufacturer directed the user to "SUPPORT THE BOTTOM." The court noted, however, that the label for the product also stated that the pan was "reusable" and "sturdy."[132] These words appeared in large print, immediately above the fine print indi-

---

[127] Henry v. General Motors Corp., 60 F.3d 1545 (11th Cir. 1995) (applying Georgia law) (yellow sticker on a truck jack was adequate since the plaintiff, who was illiterate, knew that it signified a warning and did not ask anyone to read it to him).

[128] Pavlik v. Lane Ltd./Tobacco Exporters International, 135 F.3d 876 (3d Cir. 1998) (applying Pennsylvania law); Jones v. Amazing Products, 231 F. Supp. 2d 1228, 1247 (N.D. Ga. 2002) (applying Georgia law).

[129] For another example of the form of warnings that was held to be adequate as a matter of law, see *Bartholic v. Scripto-Tokai Corp.*, 140 F. Supp. 2d 1098 (D. Colo. 2000) (applying Colorado law).

[130] 2004 Mass. Super. LEXIS 200 (Mass. Super. Ct. 2004).

[131] *Id.* at *3 (emphasis in original).

[132] *Id.* at *3-4 (capitalization in original).

cating that the pan should be supported with a cookie sheet. The court concluded that it could not hold that the statement "caution: do not lift by sides" was adequate as a matter of law, particularly since the label was not permanent. The label was placed on a wrapper that had to be removed and thrown away before the pan could be used.[133] Thus, the court denied the manufacturer's motion for summary judgment, holding that "the inconspicuous nature of the caution on the label, the size of the print, its contradictory words, its failure to be complete and accurate regarding the inherent dangers in the use of this pan, and its failure to mention the possibility of the pan 'collapsing' may all be considered by the jury."[134]

[C] *Content of the Warning*

In addition to providing a warning in a form that reaches the attention of the user of the product, a manufacturer also must ensure that the content of the warning "convey[s] a fair indication of the nature and extent of the danger to the mind of a reasonably prudent person."[135] The extent of the content of the warning depends on the foreseeability of the use of the product and the type of danger involved.[136] An example of a warning for an otherwise safe product is *Kelso v. Bayer Corp.*,[137] in which the plaintiff used a 12-hour extra moisturizing nasal spray continuously for three years. At the end of that time, he learned that his continued use of the product had caused permanent nasal tissue damage that would require multiple sinus surgeries. The plaintiff sued the manufacturer of the spray in strict liability, alleging that it failed to warn him adequately of the dangers associated with the product. The warning on the spray package read:

Do not exceed recommended dosage.

> Stop use and ask a doctor if symptoms persist. Do not use this product for more than 3 days. Use only as directed. Frequent or prolonged use may cause nasal congestion to recur or worsen.[138]

---

[133] *Id.* at *9.

[134] *Id.* at *11.

[135] Spruill v. Boyle-Midway, Inc., 308 F.2d 79, 85 (4th Cir. 1962). *See also* Smith v. Louisville Ladder Co., 237 F.3d 515 (5th Cir. 2001) (applying Texas law); Johnson v. Colt Industries Operating Corp., 797 F.2d 1530 (10th Cir. 1986) (applying Kansas law).

[136] Hood v. Ryobi America Corp., 181 F.3d 608 (4th Cir. 1999) (applying Maryland law); Pottle v. Up-Right, Inc., 628 A.2d 672 (Me. 1993); Johnson v. Harley-Davidson Motor Co. Group. Inc., 2004 Iowa App. LEXIS 344 (Iowa Ct. App. 2004).

[137] 398 F.3d 640 (7th Cir. 2005) (applying Illinois law). For other examples, see *Torsiello v. Whitehall Laboratories, Division of Home Products Corp.*, 398 A.2d 132 (N.J. Super. Ct. 1979) (the plaintiff took eight aspirin tablets a day for 14 months to relieve the pain of arthritis; as a result of the prolonged use, he suffered an attack of gastrointestinal hemorrhaging, that was diagnosed as "GI bleeding secondary to aspirin gastritis"); *Michael v. Warner/Chilcott*, 579 P.2d 183 (N.M. Ct. App. 1978) (the plaintiff developed kidney failure after using sinus tablets daily for eight years).

[138] *Id.* at 641.

In affirming the district court's grant of summary judgment to the manufacturer, the Seventh Circuit stated that the warning against prolonged
use was adequate since it was "unequivocal":[139] "the plain, clear and unambiguous language of the warning states: 'Do not use this product for more
than 3 days.' Period. . . .Moreover, the warning clearly informs users to: 'Stop
use and ask a physician if symptoms persist.' The warning was clear."[140] In
addition, the court held that the warning was adequate even though it did
not warn that the product could cause permanent nasal tissue damage and
had a risk of habituation since a manufacturer need not warn of all possible consequences of failing to follow a warning.[141]

With the growing linguistic diversity in the United States, some cases
have raised the question of whether the content of a warning was adequate if it was only in English.[142] Courts have deferred to the requirements of state and federal statutes to determine whether such warnings
were adequate. In *Ramirez v. Plough, Inc.*,[143] the mother of a four-month-
old child gave him a nonprescription aspirin manufactured by the defendant
to relieve the symptoms of his cold. Although the label stated that the
dosage for a child under two years old was "as directed by doctor," the
mother did not consult a doctor before giving her child the aspirin. Over a
two day period, she gave the child three tablets. When she finally took her
child to the hospital, a doctor advised her to give the child nonprescription
medicines that did not contain aspirin. However, she disregarded the advice
and continued to give her child aspirin. The child later developed Reye's syndrome, resulting in severe neurological damage, including cortical blindness,
spastic quadriplegia, and mental retardation. In her suit against the drug
manufacturer, the child alleged negligence because the manufacturer distributed the product with warnings in English only. The California Supreme
Court, however, affirmed summary judgment in favor of the manufacturer,
holding that it had no duty to provide warnings in Spanish since applicable
state and federal statutes required warnings to be only in English.[144] The
court felt that deciding if and when warnings or other information should
be in a language other than English was a task for which legislative and
administrative agencies were better suited.[145]

Where a manufacturer provides a warning, it is entitled to assume that
users and consumers will read it and follow it.[146] Thus, even if a warning

---

[139] *Id.* at 642.

[140] *Id.*

[141] *Id.*

[142] *See* Torres-Rio v. LPS Laboratories, Inc., 152 F.3d 11 (1st Cir. 1998).

[143] 863 P.2d 167 (Cal. 1993).

[144] *Id.* at 173-174.

[145] *Id.* at 174-175.

[146] E.R. Squibb & Sons, Inc. v. Cox, 477 So.2d 963 (Ala. 1985).

was inadequate, courts usually will bar the plaintiff from recovering if it can be shown that he or she failed to read the warning.[147] That was the situation in *Ramirez* where the plaintiff asserted an alternative basis of liability that the label in English provided defective warnings of the risks of giving young children aspirin. The California court also rejected that argument because the plaintiff's mother "neither read nor obtained translation of the product labeling. Thus, there is no conceivable causal connection between the representations or omissions that accompanied the product and plaintiff's injury."[148] Similarly, in *Daniel v. Ben E. Keith Co.*,[149] the plaintiff was unable to recover on her failure-to-warn claim against the manufacturer of a chlorine bleach product. The plaintiff there was injured when her coworker mistakenly used the defendant's bleach to clean deep fat fryers in the restaurant where they worked. Adding the bleach to the fryer caused the bleach to boil, producing chlorine gas. The plaintiff inhaled the chlorine gas, which caused her to suffer from Reactive Airway Dysfunction Syndrome. The plaintiff brought suit against the defendant, alleging that their failure to warn of the risks of chlorine bleach caused her injuries.[150] The jury found for the defendant, and the plaintiff appealed. Amongst other issues, the plaintiff argued that the court erred by not giving an instruction to the jury regarding the heeding presumption.[151]

The Tenth Circuit, applying Oklahoma law, affirmed the decision of the district court and the findings of the jury. The court noted the rule that there is a rebuttable presumption that the users of a product will read and heed an adequate warning. In *Daniel*, however, the defendant successfully rebutted that presumption. The defendant elicited testimony from the plaintiff's coworker that on the morning of the accident, "he was in a hurry and did not look at the label."[152] It was because he failed to look at the label that he mistakenly used bleach instead of fryer cleaner. Because the plaintiff's coworker completely ignored the product's label, "any presumption that a different warning would have been heeded disappeared, and plaintiffs continued to carry the burden of proving that the allegedly inadequate warning caused her injury."[153] Thus, the Tenth Circuit ruled that the district court properly refused to give a heeding presumption instruction.

---

[147] Jones v. Amazing Products, Inc., 231 F. Supp. 2d 1228 (N.D. Ga. 2002).

[148] *Ramirez*, 863 P.2d at 177.

[149] 97 F.3d 1329 (10th Cir. 1996).

[150] *Id.* at 1331.

[151] *Id.*

[152] *Id.* at 1333.

[153] *Id.*

§ 7.05 POST-SALE DUTY TO WARN OR RECALL

[A] *Post-Sale Duty to Warn*

Although every state recognizes a duty on the part of a manufacturer to warn consumers or users of dangers it knew about or should have known about at the time of the sale of a product, this duty traditionally did not extend past the sale. However, more than half of the states now also recognize a duty on a manufacturer to warn users and consumers in some situations of dangers that come to its attention after the sale of the product.[154] The underlying goal of requiring both pre- and post-sale warnings is the same: reduce the chance of injury by equalizing the information between the manufacturer and consumers about product risks. However, while the rationale for both duties is identical, the parameters in which they are applied are different.

For states recognizing a post-sale duty to warn, the duty may arise in two situations: first, when the manufacturer becomes aware of a defect that makes the product unreasonably dangerous and that condition was unknown to the seller at the time of sale but was discovered after the sale,[155] and, second, when the danger comes to the attention of the manufacturer as a result of advancements in the state of the art, with which it is expected to stay current.[156] An early example of a court recognizing such a duty to warn in such a situation is *Comstock v. General Motors Corp.*,[157] in which an automobile manufacturer learned of brake problems only weeks after releasing several of its 1953 models but failed to take action to warn buyers of the defect. The Michigan court extended its rule requiring manufacturers to warn of dangers known at the time of sale by holding that "a like duty to give prompt warning exists when a latent defect which makes the product hazardous to life becomes known to the manufacturer shortly after the product has been put on the market."[158]

---

[154] For examples, see *Bryant v. Giacomini*, S.P.A., 2005 U.S. Dist. LEXIS 23347 (N.D. Tex. 2005) (Texas recognizes a post-sale duty to warn where the manufacturer regains some significant control over the product and where a manufacturer assumed a post-sale duty and then did not use reasonable means to discharge that duty); *Patton v. Hutchinson Wil-Rich Manufacturing Co.*, 861 P.2d 1299 (Kan. 1993) (drug manufacturers); *Walton v. Avco Corp.*, 610 A.2d 454 (Pa. 1992) (limited post-sale duty to warn). *See also* Cigna Insurance Co. v. Oy Saunatec, Ltd., 241 F.3d 1 (1st Cir. 2001) (applying Massachusetts law); Densberger v. United Technologies Corp., 125 F. Supp. 2d 585 (D. Conn. 2000) (applying Connecticut law); Hodder v. Goodyear Tire & Rubber Co., 426 N.W.2d 826, 833 (Minn. 1988); Smith v. Ontario Sewing Machine Co., 548 S.E.2d 89 (Ga. Ct. App. 2001).

[155] *See* Padilla v. Black & Decker Corp., 2005 U.S. Dist. LEXIS 4720 (E.D. Pa. 2005) (applying Pennsylvania law); Mercer v. Pittway Corp., 616 N.W.2d 602 (Iowa 2000).

[156] Cover v. Cohen, 461 N.E.2d 864 (N.Y. 1984).

[157] 99 N.W.2d 627 (Mich. 1959).

[158] *Id.* at 634. *See also* Gregory v Cincinnati, Inc., 538 N.W.2d 325 (Mich. 1995).

Most states hold that there may be a post-sale duty to warn whether the plaintiff brought the claim in negligence or strict liability. However, states that recognize a post-sale duty to warn use a negligence analysis based on a "reasonableness standard" that takes a variety of factors into consideration in determining when and to whom a post-sale warning must be given, as well as the nature of the warning.[159] Although a crucial factor is whether the manufacturer had sufficient notice that the product posed a risk of serious harm,[160] the analysis is dependent on the facts in each case and includes: (1) the nature of the harm that may result unless notice is given; (2) the likelihood that harm will occur; (3) the number of persons who must be warned; (4) the economic burden on the manufacturer of identifying and notifying product users; (5) the nature of the industry; (6) the type of product involved; (7) the number of product units manufactured or sold; and (8) steps taken other than giving of notice to correct the problem.[161] In limited situations, section 10 of the Restatement (Third) also imposes a post-sale duty to warn. The section uses a "reasonable person" test to determine when a post-sale warning should be given and sets out four conditions that would lead a "reasonable person" to provide such a warning:

(a) One engaged in the business of selling or otherwise distributing products is subject to liability for harm to persons or property caused by the seller's failure to provide a warning after the time of sale or distribution of a product if a reasonable person in the seller's position would provide such a warning.

(b) A reasonable person in the seller's position would provide a warning after the time of sale if:

(1) the seller knows or reasonably should know that the product poses a substantial risk of harm to persons or property; and

(2) those to whom a warning might be provided can be identified and can reasonably be assumed to be unaware of the risk of harm; and

(3) a warning can be effectively communicated to and acted on by those to whom a warning might be provided; and

(4) the risk of harm is sufficiently great to justify the burden of providing a warning.[162]

---

[159] Lovick v. Wil-Rich, 588 N.W.2d 688 (Iowa 1999).

[160] Post-sale accidents involving the product are one factor that may provide a manufacturer with the notice required to create a post-sale duty to warn. See Cover v. Cohen, 461 N.E.2d 864 (N.Y. 1984).

[161] Patton v. Hutchinson Wil-Rich Manufacturing Co., 861 P.2d 1299, 1314-15 (Kan. 1993). See also Padilla v. Black & Decker Corp., 2005 U.S. Dist. LEXIS 4720 (E.D. Pa. 2005) (applying Pennsylvania law); Cover, 461 N.E.2d 864.

[162] RESTATEMENT (THIRD) OF TORTS: PRODUCTS LIABILITY § 10 (1998). See Lovick, 588 N.W.2d 688.

Regardless of the factors, however, courts exempt manufacturers from warning an owner who has purchased a product second-hand. Such a person becomes part of a universe of people too large and too diffuse for manufacturers and sellers to identify.[163]

Despite the trend toward recognizing a post-sale duty to warn, a few jurisdictions have rejected imposing such a duty. Generally, the states that do not recognize a post-sale duty to warn believe that requiring the duty would inject negligence principles into strict liability claims when products are defective and would eliminate the requirement under strict liability that the defect existed before the manufacturer sold the product. In *Collins v. Hyster Co.*,[164] the Illinois Appellate Court reasoned that "the law does not contemplate placing the onerous duty on manufacturers to subsequently warn all foreseeable users of products based on increased design or manufacture expertise that was not present at the time the product left its control."[165] In addition, even states that recognize a post-sale duty to warn, hold that the duty does not apply where the danger is open and obvious or the consumer is a sophisticated user of the product.

[B] *Product Recalls*

[1] Judicially Mandated Product Recalls

In addition to alleging that a manufacturer has a post-sale duty to warn of a danger that came to its attention after the product left its control, some plaintiffs have asserted that a manufacturer had a duty to recall and retrofit a product, after its sale, with a safety device. Unless mandated by a statutes, however, courts have rejected imposing such an obligation on manufacturers.[166] Although most of the cases have dealt with the issue briefly in a motion for summary judgment, the Illinois Appellate Court, in *Modelski v. Navistar International Transportation Corp.*,[167] set out its reasons for holding there was no duty in detail. In *Modelski* the plaintiff alleged that the manufacturer was negligent in failing to retrofit a tractor, after its sale, with a safety device that would have eliminated the danger created by the unexpected loss of the bolts on the battery box cover. However, the Illi-

---

[163] Lewis v. Ariens Co., 751 N.E.2d 862 (Mass. 2001).

[164] 529 N.E.2d 303 (Ill. App. Ct. 1988).

[165] *Id.* at 306.

[166] *See* Morales v. E.D. Etnyre & Co., 382 F. Supp. 2d 1285 (D. N.M. 2005) (applying New Mexico law); Padilla v. Black & Decker Corp., 2005 U.S. Dist. LEXIS 4720 (E.D. Pa. 2005) (applying Pennsylvania law); Eberts v. Kawasaki Motors Corp., U.S.A., 2004 U.S. Dist. LEXIS 1294 (D. N.D. 2004) (applying North Dakota law); Flock v. Scripto-Tokai Corp., 2001 U.S. Dist. LEXIS 23885 (S.D. Tex. 2001) (applying Texas law); Zychowski v. A.J. Marshall Co., Inc., 590 N.W.2d 301 (Mich. Ct. App. 1998).

[167] 707 N.E.2d 239 (Ill. App. Ct. 1999).

nois court held that, in the absence of a statutory obligation or voluntary undertaking, the manufacturer had no duty to recall or retrofit the product to remedy a danger of which it did not know, nor should have known. According to the court, its holding was in keeping with the position taken by most state courts.[168]

> The consequences of imposing upon manufacturers an extrastatutory duty to recall and retrofit used products to incorporate post-sale state of the art designs would be the equivalent of mandating that manufacturers insure their products will always comply with current safety standards. This we are unwilling to do. If such a continuing duty is to be imposed, it is legislature that is better suited to the task. In a legislative setting, due consideration can be given to the type of products to which such a duty would apply and to whether a statute of repose should be enacted to limit the potentially indefinite duration of the duty.[169]

The holding of the court in *Modelski* is supported by § 11 of the Restatement (Third) which deals with the "Liability of Commercial Product Seller or Distributor for Harm Caused by Post-Sale Failure to Recall Product." According to the Restatement:

> One engaged in the business of selling or otherwise distributing products is subject to liability for harm to persons or property caused by the seller's failure to recall a product after the time of sale or distribution if:
>
> (a) (1) a governmental directive issued pursuant to a statute or administrative regulation specifically requires the seller or distributor to recall the product; or
>
>   (2) the seller or distributor, in the absence of a recall requirement under Subsection (a)(1), undertakes to recall the product; and
>
> (b) the seller or distributor fails to act as a reasonable person in recalling the product.[170]

In support of this limited duty to recall a product, comment *a* to § 11 speaks of the burdens that the recall of a product places on manufacturers.

---

[168] *See* Horstmyer v. Black & Decker, (U.S.), Inc., 151 F.3d 765 (8th Cir. 1998) (applying Missouri law); Tabieros v. Clark Equipment Co., 944 P.2d 1279 (Haw. 1999); Gregory v. Cincinnati Inc., 538 N.W.2d 325 (Mich. 1995); Patton v. Hutchinson Wil-Rich Manufacturing Co., 861 P.2d 1299 (Kan. 1993).

[169] *Id.* at 247.

[170] RESTATEMENT (THIRD) OF TORTS: PRODUCTS LIABILITY § 11 (1998). For a critique of § 11, see James T. O'Reilly, *Product Recalls and the Third Restatement: Consumers Lose Twice from Defects in Products and in the Restatement*, 33 U. MEM. L. REV. 833 (2003).

Duties to recall products impose significant burdens on manufacturers. Many product lines are periodically redesigned so that they
become safer over time. If every improvement in product safety
were to trigger a common-law duty to recall, manufacturers would
face incalculable costs every time they sought to make their product
lines better and safer.[171]

[2] Legislative Product Recalls

Although courts have refused to impose a general duty to recall products
whose defects become known only after sale, a number of government agencies have the power to impose product recalls. Among these agencies are the
Consumer Protection Safety Commission ("CPSC"), the Federal Trade Commission ("FTA"), the Food and Drug Administration ('FDA"), and the
National Highway Traffic Safety Administration (NTSA"). Because of the
scope of the authority and importance of the CPSC to attorneys who represent manufacturers and sellers in products liability actions, this subsection examines briefly Consumer Product Safety Act ("CPSA")[172] as an
example of scope and procedure of legislative recalls.

Under § 2064(d) of the CPSA,[173] a manufacturer, distributor, or retailer
of a consumer product distributed in the United States that receives information which "reasonably" supports a conclusion that one of its products
contains a defect that "could" create a "substantial product hazard"[174] or create "an unreasonable risk of serious injury or death"[175] must inform the
Consumer Product Safety Commission ("CPSC") of the defect.[176] The CPSA
does not define terms such as "defect," "substantial product hazard," "unreasonable risk," or "serious injury." The reporting requirements of the CPSA
are implemented by regulations adopted by the CPSC.

Defect: The regulations state that the term "defect" includes the dictionary or commonly accepted meaning of the word. Thus, a defect is a

---

[171] *Id.* at cmt. *a*.

[172] 15 U.S.C.S. §§ 2051-2084 (2005). The CPSA was enacted by Congress in 1972. The
CPSC has jurisdiction over a "consumer product" which is defined as "any article, or component
part thereof, produced or distributed (i) for sale to a consumer for use in or around a permanent or temporary household or residence, a school, in recreation, or otherwise, or (ii) for the
personal use, consumption or enjoyment of a consumer in or around a permanent or temporary
household or residence, a school, in recreation, or otherwise." *Id.* § 2052(a)(1).

[173] *Id.* § 2064(d).

[174] 15 U.S.C. § 2064(b)(2).

[175] *Id.* § 2064(b)(3).

[176] Although the legal obligation to report is placed upon the manufacturer, the distributor, and the retailer, they may agree among themselves who will file the report and who will
be responsible for the recall. If the other parties know that the CPSC has been informed,
they do not have to file a second report.

fault, flaw, or irregularity that causes weakness, failure, or inadequacy in form or function.[177] A defect may result from an error in the design or manufacture of a product. In addition, the regulations state that

> a product may contain a defect even if the product is manufactured exactly in accordance with its design and specifications, if the design presents a risk of injury to the public. A design defect may also be present if the risk of injury occurs as a result of the operation or use of the product or the failure of the product to operate as intended. A defect can also occur in a product's contents, construction, finish, packaging, warnings, and/or instructions. With respect to instructions, a consumer product may contain a defect if the instructions for assembly or use could allow the product, otherwise safely designed and manufactured, to present a risk of injury.[178]

Substantial product hazard: The regulations define "substantial product hazard" as either (1) A failure to comply with an applicable consumer product safety rule, which failure creates a substantial risk of injury to the public, or (2) A product defect which (because of the pattern of defect, the number of defective products distributed in commerce, the severity of the risk, or otherwise) creates a substantial risk of injury to the public.[179]

Unreasonable risk: The regulations set out the following explanation of what constitutes an unreasonable risk:

> In determining whether a product presents an unreasonable risk, the firm should examine he utility of the product, or the utility of the aspect of the product that causes the risk, the level of exposure of consumers to the risk, the nature and severity of the hazard presented, and the likelihood of resulting serious injury or death.[180]

Serious injury: The regulations provide the following guidance with those events that constitute a serious injury:

> The Commission believes that the term includes not only the concept of "grievous bodily injury," defined at § 1115.12(d), but also any other significant injury. Injuries necessitating hospitalization which require actual medical or surgical treatment, fractures, lacerations requiring sutures, concussions, injuries to the eye, ear, or internal organs requiring medical treatment, and injuries necessi-

---

[177] 16 C.F.R. § 1115.4.

[178] *Id.*

[179] *Id.* § 1115.2(a).

[180] *Id.* § 1115.6(b).

tating absence from school or work of more than one day are examples of situations in which the Commission shall presume that such a serious injury has occurred.[181]

If the CPSC determines that the product contains a defect that creates a "substantial product hazard" or an "unreasonable risk," it may require the recall of the product and the submission of a corrective action plan covering all brands of the product that have the same design and manufacturing process. In some cases, the CPSC has held that, although a report was filed, no defect or "unreasonable risk" was involved. In about a third of the cases, the CPSC permits a company to monitor the problem rather than conduct a recall, if it is unclear that there actually is a "substantial product hazard" or an "unreasonable risk." In order to encourage companies to report possible defects, the CPSC provides a voluntary fast track recall under which there is no preliminary determination by the CPSC as to whether the product is defective as defined under the CPSA. A fast track recall under the CPSC regulations means that neither the government nor the company concedes that there was an "substantial product hazard" or "unreasonable risk." This is of value to companies because the recall cannot be cited in private litigation as evidence of negligence. In addition, a fast track recall promotes a more cooperative voluntary recall with the CPSC.

Typically, the CPSC imposes monetary civil penalties on companies that "knowingly" fail to report instances that it considers would have required reporting and recall actions. The civil penalties cannot exceed $8,000 for each violation and a maximum of $1,825,000 (effective January 1, 2005 and subject to an inflation adjustment) for any series of violations. The CPSC also may impose criminal penalties. However, criminal penalties are not pursued unless the company has been warned previously by the CPSC.

§ 7.06 THE LEARNED INTERMEDIARY DOCTRINE

[A] *Origin and Scope of the Learned Intermediary Doctrine*

The purpose of products liability law is to place the cost of injuries caused by products that are "unreasonably dangerous" on the manufacturers or suppliers of those products.[182] At the same time, however, some products, such as prescription drugs, may be unavoidably unsafe yet not be unreasonably dangerous because they provide a great benefit to a large number of people. In order to encourage the production of prescription drugs, the drafters of § 402A included an exception to the rule of strict liability for manufacturers of prescription drugs from strict liability provided that the

---

[181] *Id.* § 1115.6(c).

[182] Hill v. Searle Laboratories, 884 F.2d 1064 (8th Cir. 1989).

drugs are "properly prepared and accompanied by proper directions and warnings."[183]

Although manufacturers are protected from strict liability for "properly prepared" prescription drugs if they provide "proper directions and warnings," section 402A does not state to whom the "directions and warnings" must be given. Although products liability law generally requires that warnings be given to the "ultimate user or consumer" of the product, courts in almost every state have created an exception for prescription drugs in the form of the "learned intermediary doctrine."[184] This doctrine provides that prescription drug manufacturers satisfy their duty to warn if they provide complete, accurate, and timely warnings to proscribing physicians, or other health professionals who may prescribe their products, of the risks or contraindications associated with their drugs of which they know or should have reason to know.[185] The doctrine applies both to strict liability and negligence claims.[186]

Courts have given a number of reasons for the learned intermediary doctrine: patients rely on their physician's advice and warnings for prescription drugs; drug manufactures lack effective means to communicate the specific risks to each patient; the ordinary consumer is unable to understand complex medical warnings while a doctor can; imposing a duty to warn patients would interfere with the physician-patient relationship.[187] However, the primary rationale behind the doctrine is the assumption that physicians or other health professionals, as the persons who prescribe the drugs, are a "learned intermediary" between the manufacturer and the consumers. As such, they are in the best position to give an individualized warning to their patients, based upon the physicians' knowledge of their patients and the inherent risks of the drugs, which are likely to be complex

---

[183] *See* RESTATEMENT (SECOND) OF TORTS § 402A cmt. *k* (1965).

[184] *See* Ehlis v. Shire Richwood Inc., 367 F.3d 1013 (8th Cir. 2004) (the doctrine applies or is recognized in forty-eight states); Thom v. Bristol-Myers Squibb Co., 353 F.3d 848 (10th Cir. 2003) (forty-five jurisdictions have adopted the doctrine in prescription drug cases); Ellis v. C.R. Bard, Inc., 311 F.3d 1272 (11th Cir. 2002) (the doctrine is nearly universal); Vitanza v. Upjohn Co., 778 A.2d 829 (Conn. 2001) (the doctrine applies in forty-five jurisdictions). For a list of jurisdictions that have adopted the learned intermediary doctrine, see *Larkin v. Pfizer, Inc.*, 153 S.W.2d 758, 767-768 (Ky. 2004).

[185] Ehlis v. Shire Richwood, Inc., 367 F.3d 1013 (8th Cir. 2004); Edwards v. Basel Pharmaceuticals, 933 P.2d 298 (Okla. 1997); McEwen v. Ortho Pharmaceutical Corp., 528 P.2d 522 (Or. 1974). Using their medical judgment, physicians then have a duty to convey the warning to their patients. Kirk v. Michael Reese Hospital & Medical Center, 513 N.E.2d 387 (Ill. 1987).

[186] *See* Reyes v. Wyeth Laboratories, 498 F.2d 1264 (5th Cir. 1974); Hoffman v. Sterling Drug, 485 F.2d 132 (3d Cir. 1973); Stevens v. Parke, Davis & Co., 107 Cal. Rptr. 45 (Cal. 1973).

[187] Larkın v. Pfizer, Inc., 153 S.W.3d 758, 763-764 (Ky. 2004). *See also* Bernard J. Garbutt III and Melinda E. Hofmann, *Recent Developments in Pharmaceutical Products Liability Law: Failure to Warn, the Learned Intermediary Defense, and Other Issues in the New Millennium*, 58 FOOD DRUG L.J. 269, 272-73 (2003).

and vary in the effects they have on users.[188] As a medical expert, the pre-scribing physician can take into account the propensities of the drug as well as the susceptibilities of the patient and weigh the benefits of any medication against its potential dangers. The choice the physician makes is an individualized medical judgment based on a knowledge both of the patient and the drug.[189]

Although the learned intermediary concept has been recognized since the late 1940s,[190] it was not until 1966, in *Sterling Drug v. Cornish*[191] that a court first used the term "learned intermediary" when the Eight Circuit recognized that a "purchaser's doctor is a learned intermediary between the purchaser and the manufacturer."[192] In recent years, court have extended the doctrine from prescription drugs to include prescription medical implants and devices as well.[193] Discussing a cardiac pacemaker, the Fourth Circuit stated:

> The decision to prescribe a cardiac pacemaker involves precisely the sort of individualized medical balancing contemplated by the drug exception. Unlike polio vaccines, pacemakers are not dispensed indiscriminately in mass clinics, but instead are prescribed only after a physician balances the individual's needs against the known risks. Indeed, expert testimony in the present case indicated that each pacemaker candidate presents different problems requiring individualized professional judgments about lead models and gen-erator units.[194]

This evolution is reflected in the Restatement (Third). Although §§ 6(a) and 6(b) hold manufacturers of prescription drugs and medical devices liable if their products are defective in their design, manufacture or inad-equate warnings, sections 6 (c) and 6(d) codify the learned intermediary doc-trine in § 6:

> (c) A prescription drug or medical device is not reasonably safe due to defective design if the foreseeable risks of harm posed by the

---

[188] Stone v. Smith, Kline & French Laboratories, 731 F.2d 1575 (11th Cir. 1984); Jacobs v. Dista Prods. Co., 693 F. Supp. 1029 (D. Wyo. 1988).

[189] *See* Vitanza v. Upjohn Co., 778 A.2d 829 (Conn. 2001).

[190] *See* Marcus v. Specific Pharmaceuticals, 77 N.Y.S.2d 508 (N.Y. 1948). *See also* Ozlem A. Bordes, *Article: The Learned Intermediary Doctrine and Direct-to-Consumer Advertising: Should the Pharmaceutical Manufacturer Be Shielded From Liability?* 81 U. DET. MERCY L. REV. 267 (2004).

[191] 370 F.2d 82 (8th Cir. 1966).

[192] *Id.* at 85.

[193] *See* Ellis v. C.R. Bard, Inc., 311 F.3d 1272, 1280 (11th Cir. 2002); Willett v. Baxter Inter-national, Inc., 929 F.2d 1094 (5th Cir. 1991); Phelps v. Sherwood Med. Indus., 836 F.2d 296 (7th Cir. 1987).

[194] Brooks v. Medtronic, Inc., 750 F.2d 1227, 1232 (4th Cir. 1984)

drug or medical device are sufficiently great in relation to its foreseeable therapeutic benefits that reasonable health-care providers, knowing of such foreseeable risks and therapeutic benefits, would not prescribe the drug or medical device for any class of patients.

(d) A prescription drug or medical device is not reasonably safe due to inadequate instructions or warnings if reasonable instructions or warnings regarding foreseeable risks of harm are not provided to:

(1) prescribing and other health care providers who are in a position to reduce the risks or harm in accordance with the instructions or warnings.[195]

Although the learned intermediary doctrine answers the question of who must provide a warning about prescription drugs, it does not address the issue of when a drug manufacturers must warn physicians, what constitutes an adequate warning, and any exceptions to the doctrine. Those issues have been left to the courts.

[B] *When a Warning Must be Given to Physicians*

The learned intermediary doctrine applies only to prescription drugs and medical devices.[196] Manufacturers do not have to provide warnings to physicians for over-the-counter drugs and medical devices because the rationales supporting the doctrine do not apply when a physician does not individually balance the risks involved in a patient using a particular product.[197] The doctrine also applies only to warning physicians about drugs' known dangerous propensities.[198] However, since manufacturers are held to the standard of an expert in their field, they have a continuing duty to keep informed of scientific developments that affect the safety of their products and to notify physicians of risks they discover from the use of their products.[199] Manufacturers may have a duty to warn physicians of very rare, idiosyncratic, adverse reactions to their products if the potential harm is likely to be severe.[200] In warning physicians, the manufacturer must use methods that are reasonably calculated to bring the dangers to their attention.[201]

---

[195] RESTATEMENT (THIRD) OF TORTS: PRODUCTS LIABILITY §§ 6(c) and 6(d)(1) (1998). *See also* RESTATEMENT (THIRD) OF TORTS: PRODUCTS LIABILITY § (2) cmt. *i* and § 6(d)(1) cmt. *b*.

[196] Reyes v. Wyeth Laboratories, 498 F.2d 1264 (5th Cir. 1974).

[197] In the case of nonprescription drugs and devices, the manufacturer has a duty to provide the warning directly to the purchaser of the product.

[198] Kirk v. Michael Reese Hospital and Medical Center, 513 N.E.2d 387 (Ill. 1987).

[199] Proctor v. Davis, 682 N.E.2d 1203 (Ill. App. Ct. 1997).

[200] *See* Wright v. Carter Prods., 244 F.2d 53 (2d Cir. 1957) (applying New York law); Tomer v. American Home Prods. Corp., 368 A.2d 35 (Conn.1976); Crocker v. Winthrop Laboratories, 514 S.W.2d 429 (Tex. 1974).

[201] McEwen v. Ortho Pharmaceutical Corp., 528 P.2d 522 (Or. 1974).

A corollary of the learned intermediary doctrine is the principle that the manufacturer of a prescription drug or medical device does not have a duty to warn physicians of risks that are well known to the medical community. However, if there is any question of whether the drug manufacturer's knowledge is superior to that of the medical community, it is an issue for the jury to decide.[202]

[C] *Adequacy of the Warning*

Under the learned intermediary doctrine, a manufacturer is not liable if it provides adequate warnings to prescribing physicians or other health professionals.[203] In order to constitute an adequate warning, courts have adopted varying forms of a reasonableness standard.[204] According to the California Supreme Court, this "infuses some negligence concepts" into the strict liability claim.[205] Some courts also have held that an otherwise adequate warning may become inadequate if a drug manufacturer over-promotes a drug to physicians.[206]

Although whether a warning is adequate usually is a question for the trier of fact,[207] courts are likely to hold that a warning to physicians is adequate as a matter of law when the warning is clear, accurate, and unambiguous.[208] In *Thom v. Bristol-Myers Squibb*,[209] the Tenth Circuit listed five factors for determining whether a warning is adequate as a matter of law: (1) the warning must adequately indicate the scope of danger; (2) the warning must reasonably communicate the extent or seriousness of harm that could result from misuse of the drug; (3) the physical layout of the warning must adequately alert a reasonably prudent person of the dangers; (4) a simple directive may be inadequate if it fails to detail possible consequences due to failure to follow it; and, (5) the means to convey the warning must be adequate.[210] Warnings provided by drug manufacturers may be inadequate

---

[202] Hansen v. Baxter Healthcare Corp., 764 N.E.2d 35 (Ill. 2002).

[203] Pittman v. Upjohn Co., 890 S.W.2d 425 (Tenn. 1994). *See* Brown v. Glaxo, Inc., 790 So. 2d 35 (La. Ct. App. 2000) (a misleading oral statement by a pharmaceutical sale representative may supersede an otherwise adequate written warning to a physician).

[204] *See* Stahl v. Novartis Pharmaceuticals Corp., 283 F.3d 254, 267 (5th Cir. 2002) (applying Louisiana law); Ralston v. Smith & Nephew Richards, Inc., 275 F.3d 965, 974 (10th Cir. 2001) (applying Kansas law).

[205] Carlin v. Superior Court, 962 P.2d 1347, 1350 (Cal. 1996).

[206] *See* Salmon v. Parke, Davis, & Co., 520 F.2d 1359 (4th Cir. 1975); Stevens v. Parke, Davis & Co., 507 P.2d 653 (Cal. 1973); Whitley v. Cubberly, 210 S.E.2d 289 (N.C. Ct. App. 1974).

[207] Bukowski v. CooperVision Inc., 592 N.Y.S.2d 807, 807 (N.Y. 1993); Thom v. Bristol-Myers Squibb Co., 353 F.3d 848, 853 (10th Cir. 2003); MacDonald v. Ortho Pharmaceuticals, 475 N.E.2d 65, 71 (Mass. 1985).

[208] Stahl v. Novartis Pharmaceuticals Corp., 283 F.3d 254, 267 (5th Cir. 2002).

[209] 353 F.3d 848 (10th Cir. 2003).

[210] *Id.* at 852.

even though all government regulations and requirements were met in the production and marketing of the drug and in the changes to the literature.[211] In addition, if a manufacturer does not change a warning it knows is widely disregarded, a jury may infer that the warning was insufficient.[212]

In *Swayze v. McNeil Laboratories*,[213] the Fifth Circuit addressed the appropriate methods of informing a learned intermediary. The court stated that drug manufacturers use three methods for disseminating information about the benefits and dangers of their products: (1) printed warnings and detailed information on packet inserts enclosed in packages containing the drug; (2) publication of identical warnings in the Physician's Desk Reference (PDR), a "dictionary" of drugs routinely relied upon by physicians; and (3) the dispatch of "detail men," who are part salespersons and part educators, to speak with practicing physicians in their offices. The court ruled that if the warnings provided to health care practitioners, through the PDR, package inserts, and detail men, were adequate, then the drug was not unreasonably dangerous, and the manufacturer's conduct was neither unreasonable nor negligent.[214]

Courts have held that even a package insert, which had been specifically approved by the Food and Drug Administration and published in the Physicians' Desk Reference, does not, as a matter of law, relieve the manufacturer of its obligation to communicate an adequate warning to the users of a dangerous drug, where it was alleged that the approved insert did not adequately warn of potential dangers to users.[215]

[D] *Causation*

In addition to showing that a drug manufacturer provided an inadequate warning about a prescription drug or medical device, a plaintiff also must show that the inadequate warning was a substantial cause of the injury.[216] A majority of states hold that, if the plaintiff proves that the warning was inadequate, there is a rebuttable presumption that an adequate warning

---

[211] *See* Yarrow v. Sterling Drug, 263 F. Supp. 159, 162 (D.S.D. 1967); Stegall v. Catawba Oil Co., 133 S.E.2d 138 (N.C. 1963).

[212] Incollingo v. Ewing, 282 A.2d 206 (Pa. 1971).

[213] 807 F.2d 464 (5th Cir. 1987).

[214] *Id.* at 471. *See also* Tatum v. Schering Corp., 795 F.2d 925 (11th Cir. 1986); Jacobs v. Dista Prods. Co., 693 F. Supp. 1029 (D. Wyo. 1988). State and federal courts have been uniform in holding that the PDR is the recognized authority to which doctors turn to obtain adverse reaction and precaution information respecting prescription drugs. *See* United States v. Schuster, 777 F.2d 264 (5th Cir. 1985); Stanton v. Astra Pharmaceutical, 718 F.2d 518 (3d Cir. 1983); DeLuryea v. Winthrop Laboratories, 697 F.2d 222 (8th Cir. 1983).

[215] Bristol-Myers Co. v. Gonzales, 561 S.W.2d 801 (Tex. 1978).

[216] Erony v. Alza Corp., 913 F. Supp. 195, 200 (S.D.N.Y. 1995); Williams v. Lederle Laboratories, 591 F. Supp. 381, 386 (S.D. Ohio 1984).

would have been heeded had one been given.[217] However, if the drug manufacturer can prove that an adequate warning would not have changed the
doctor's decision to prescribe a particular drug, the drug manufacturer is not
liable due to lack of causation.[218] Thus, a majority of courts have held that
a manufacturer's inadequate warnings were not the proximate cause of
the plaintiff's injuries where the prescribing physician failed to read the
manufacturer's warnings. In such cases, the doctor's negligence constituted
an intervening cause.[219]

[E] *Exceptions to the Learned Intermediary Doctrine*

Section 6(d)(2) of the Restatement (Third) limits the applicability of the
learned intermediary doctrine by providing that manufacturers must warn
the patient directly "when the manufacturer knows or has reason to know
that health-care providers will not be in a position to reduce the risks of
harm in accordance with the instructions or warnings." The drafters created
this limitation to the learned intermediary doctrine because existing case
law supported the idea that warnings should be given directly to patients
when a manufacturer knows a health care provider will not act as a learned
intermediary.[220] However, the drafters of the Restatement (Third) refrained
from taking a position on what other exceptions to the learned intermediary doctrine courts should adopt, leaving it to developing case law.[221] Over
the years, courts have adopted four major exceptions to the learned intermediary doctrine.

[1] Mass Immunization

Although a manufacturer's duty to warn of the risks of prescription
drugs usually extends only to the physician, if the manufacturer knows or
should know that the drug will be sold, distributed, or administered without the intervention of individualized medical judgment to balance the
risks, as in a mass immunization, the duty to warn may run directly to the

---

[217] Garside v. Osco Drug Inc., 976 F.2d 77, 81 (1st Cir. 1992); Ralston v. Smith & Nephew
Richards, Inc., 275 F.3d 965, 977 (10th Cir. 2001).

[218] Ehlis v. Shire Richwood, Inc., 367 F.3d 1013 (8th Cir. 2004); Motus v. Pfizer Inc., 358 F.3d
659, 661 (9th Cir. 2004).

[219] Hall v. Elkins Sinn, Inc., 2004 U.S. App. LEXIS 12255 (5th Cir. 2004); Thom v. Bristol-
Myers Squibb Co., 353 F.3d 848 (10th Cir. 2003).

[220] *See* RESTATEMENT (THIRD) OF TORTS: PRODUCTS LIABILITY § 6 cmt. *e* (1998).

[221] *Id*. For a discussion of situations where the learned intermediary doctrine is not applicable, see *Vitanza v. Upjohn Co.*, 48 F. Supp. 2d 124 (D. Conn. 1999); *Edwards v. Basel Pharmaceuticals*, 933 P.2d 298 (Okla. 1997).

product user.[222] In *Reyes v. Wyeth*,[223] an eight-month-old child received an oral polio vaccination from a health clinic and two weeks later was diagnosed with polio. The Fifth Circuit held that the learned intermediary doctrine did not insulate the manufacturer from liability and that the manufacturer had a duty to warn the ultimate consumer of risks involved in taking the vaccination.[224] The court reasoned that the rationale behind the learned intermediary doctrine vanished because the manufacturer had reason to know that a physician would not make an individual balancing of the risks and benefits before administering the vaccine.[225]

Courts have limited the applicability of the mass immunization exception by providing that the exception does not apply in situations where a physician-patient relationship exists.[226] Thus, where a physician administers a vaccination to his patient, the learned intermediary doctrine still applies. In *Niemiera v. Schneider*,[227] the parents of a child who suffered a disabling convulsive episode which left him brain damaged brought an action against a physician, a hospital, and the manufacturer of the vaccine alleged to have caused the episode. The New Jersey Supreme Court held that the learned intermediary doctrine relieved the manufacturer of a duty to warn the parents directly of the vaccine's potentially dangerous side effects, since the role of the physician required an exercise in medical judgment concerning when and under what circumstances the vaccine should be administered.

---

[222] *See* Davis v. Wyeth Laboratories, 399 F.2d 121 (9th Cir. 1968) (applying Montana law). However, in *Brazzell v. United States*, 788 F.2d 1352 (8th Cir. 1986) (applying Iowa law), the Eighth Circuit held that a doctor's participation in administering the swine flu vaccine did not overcome the manufacturer's duty to warn the ultimate consumer, since vaccination program was designed to be at emergency pace, which gave physicians little opportunity to investigate the vaccine they were administering. *See also* Hurley v. Lederle Laboratories, 863 F.2d 1173 (5th Cir. 1988).

[223] Reyes v. Wyeth Laboratories, 498 F.2d 1264 (5th Cir. 1974) (applying Texas law).

[224] *Id.* at 1276.

[225] *Id.* at 1269. The situation in *Reyes* is now covered by the National Childhood Vaccine Injury Act of 1986 which provides in part:

> No vaccine manufacturer shall be liable in a civil action for damages arising from a vaccine-related injury or death associated with the administration of a vaccine after October 1, 1988, solely due to the manufacturer's failure to provide direct warnings to the injured party (or the injured party's legal representative) of the potential dangers arising from the administration of the vaccine manufactured by the manufacturer.

[226] Hurley v. Lederle Laboratories, 863 F.2d 1173, 1179 (5th Cir. 1988); Niemiera v. Schneider, 555 A.2d 1112 (N.J. 1989).

[227] 555 A.2d 1112.

[2] Oral Contraceptives and Contraceptive Devices

Some states have also carved out an exception to the learned intermediary doctrine for oral contraceptives and contraceptive devices.[228] Unlike most other prescription drugs, contraceptives generally are not therapeutic, curative, or diagnostic. Their use usually is initiated by the patient rather than the physician. A woman's heightened participation in the decision-making process as to whether she wants a specific contraceptive encourages manufacturers of contraceptives to pursue public relations campaigns directed towards potential users. Plaintiffs argue that this outreach to the ultimate consumer justifies an exception to the learned intermediary rule. In *MacDonald v. Ortho Pharmaceutical Corp.*,[229] the Massachusetts Supreme Judicial Court adopted an exception for oral contraceptives saying that, unlike other prescription drugs where patients play a passive role in determining what is prescribed to them, the patient usually plays an active role in determining what form of birth control she will use. The doctor's role as a learned intermediary is lessened because women may take oral contraceptives for an extended period of time without seeing their doctor and do not necessarily have to consult their physicians before every refill.[230]

The question of whether a manufacturer must provide a direct warning to consumers also has been raised in a number of cases involving intrauterine devices (IUDs). Although a few courts have treated IUDs like oral contraceptives,[231] the majority of courts hold the learned intermediary doctrine applies to them.[232] These courts opine that there is no reason to believe that the learned intermediary doctrine applies with any less force to a case involving the use of a prescription device than it does to a case involving a prescription drug. The physician performs an individualized balancing of the benefits and risks to the patient before prescribing the device. The doctor's prescription for the device is followed by periodic checkups and physician-patient consultations. Thus, the doctor is no less a learned intermediary

---

[228] Gurski v. Wyeth-Ayerst Div. Of American Home Products Products Corp., 953 F. Supp. 412 (D. Mass. 420) (applying Massachusetts law); Stephens v. G.D. Searle & Co., 602 F. Supp. 379 (E.D. Mich. 1985). *See* Yonni D. Fushman, *Perez v. Wyeth Labs., Inc.: Toward Creating a Direct-to-Consumer Advertisement Exception to the Learned Intermediary Doctrine*, 80 B.U.L. REV. 1161, 1167 (2000) (the oral contraceptives exception is less prevalent than the mass immunization exception).

[229] 475 N.E.2d 65 (Mass. 1985).

[230] Stephens v. G.D. Searle & Co., 602 F. Supp. 379 (E.D. Mich. 1985).

[231] *See* Hill v. Searle Laboratories, 884 F.2d 1064, 1071 (8th Cir. 1989); MacDonald v. Ortho Pharmaceutical Corp., 475 N.E.2d 65 (Mass. 1985); Odgers v. Ortho Pharmaceutical Corp., 609 F. Supp. 867 (E.D. Mich. 1985) (applying Michigan law).

[232] *See* Beyette v. Ortho Pharmaceutical Corp., 823 F.2d 990 (6th Cir. 1987); Allen v. G.D. Searle & Co., 708 F. Supp. 1142 (D. Or. 1989); Lacy v. G.D. Searle & Co., 567 A.2d 398, 398 (Del. 1989); Tetuan v. A.H. Robins Co., 738 P.2d 1210 (Kan. 1987); Terhune v. A.H. Robins Co., 577 P.2d 975 (Wash. 1978).

between the manufacturer of the IUD and the patient than a physician who prescribes oral contraceptives. As with prescription drugs, the manufacturer of an IUD must give timely and adequate warnings to the medical profession of any dangerous side effects from the use of the device.

[3] FDA Mandate

A third exception to the learned intermediary doctrine, recognized only in Oklahoma, applies where the FDA has mandated direct warnings be provided to patients.[233] In *Edwards v. Basel Pharmaceuticals*,[234] an FDA mandate required that prescription nicotine patches be accompanied by warnings to the physician as well as to the ultimate consumer. The Oklahoma Supreme Court held that when the FDA requires manufacturers to issue warnings directly to the patient, the "manufacturer is not automatically shielded from liability by properly warning the prescribing physician."[235] In addition, the court found that the manufacturer does not necessarily satisfy its duty to warn the consumer simply by complying with minimum FDA warning requirements.[236]

[4] Direct-to-Consumer Advertising

A fourth exception to the learned intermediary doctrine results from the growth of direct-to-consumer advertising for drugs and medical devices.[237] Several courts have alluded to the fact that direct-to-consumer advertising by manufacturers has lessened the role of the learned intermediary.[238] The Restatement (Third) also notes that arguments have been made in support of adopting an exception when manufacturers advertise a prescription drug in the mass media.[239] However, only the New Jersey Supreme Court explic-

---

[233] *See* Catherine A. Paytash, *Note: The Learned Intermediary Doctrine and Patient Package Inserts: A Balanced Approach to Preventing Drug-Related Injury*, 51 STAN. L. REV. 1343, 1353 (1999).

[234] 933 P.2d 298 (Okla. 1997).

[235] *Id.* at 303.

[236] *Id.*

[237] *See* Sheryl Calabro, *Breaking the Shield of the Learned Intermediary Doctrine: Placing the Blame Where It Belongs*, 25 CARDOZO L. REV. 2241, 2255 (2004).

[238] *See* Hill v. Searle Laboratories, 884 F.2d 1064, 1071 (8th Cir. 1989) (the learned intermediary doctrine should not apply to IUDs, in part because the manufacturer marketed the product to women); Garside v. Osco Drug, Inc., 764 F. Supp. 208, 211 (D.C. Mass 1991) (in addition to the mass immunization and oral contraceptives exception, "in an appropriate case, the advertising of a prescription drug to the consuming public may constitute a third exception to the learned intermediary rule"); Stephens v. G.D. Searle & Co., 602 F. Supp. 379, 380 (E.D. Mich. 1985) (differentiated oral contraceptives from other drugs by stating that manufacturers use "zealous marketing practices" to encourage women to specifically request birth control drugs).

[239] RESTATEMENT (THIRD) OF TORTS: PRODUCTS LIABILITY §6d cmt. *e* (1998).

itly has adopted a direct-to-consumer advertising exception to the learned intermediary doctrine.[240] The court felt that when manufacturers advertise directly to consumers the rationales behind the learned intermediary doctrine do not apply because the advertising does not preserve the doctor-patient relationship, indicates that drug manufacturers do have the means to communicate with patients, and indicates that the information is not too complex to convey to consumers.[241] Thus, manufacturers that advertise their prescription drugs and medical devices directly to consumers must provide adequate warnings to consumers.

---

[240] Perez v. Wyeth, 734 A.2d 1245 (N.J. 1999). *See* Fushman, *supra* note 228. See, however, *In Re Norplant Products Liability Litigation*, 165 F.3d 374 (5th Cir. 1999) and *Lennon v. Wyeth-Ayerst Laboratories, Inc.*, 779 A.2d 1228 (Pa. Super. Ct. 2001) which rejected adopting a direct-to-consumer advertising exception.

[241] *Perez*, 734 A.2d at 1255.

Chapter 8

PROBLEMS OF PROOF: DEFECT AND CAUSATION

SYNOPSIS

§ 8.01 INTRODUCTION

In every products liability case, the plaintiff faces a number of problems of proof. In a strict liability action, one of the most difficult elements to establish is that the product was in a "defective condition unreasonably dangerous" when it left the manufacturer's control. In a negligence action, the hardest issue for a plaintiff to prove usually is that the defect in the product was the result of conduct by the manufacturer or seller that fell below the required standard of care. In addition, even if the plaintiff establishes that the product was in a "defective condition unreasonably dangerous" or that the manufacturer was negligent, he or she also must prove that there was a causal connection between the condition of the product or the negligence and the injuries or damages.[1] Courts often use the term "proximate cause" to describe this connection, although causation analysis involves two separate and very different concepts: cause-in-fact and proximate (or legal) cause.[2] This chapter examines the methods a plaintiff can use to prove that a product was defective. It also analyzes some of the issues that a plaintiff may face in establishing that the defect was the cause-in-fact and proximate cause of the injury or damage.

§ 8.02 PROOF OF A DEFECT

[A] *Direct and Circumstantial Evidence*

Whether a claim is based on negligence or strict liability, the foundation of a plaintiff's cause of action is proof of the existence of a defect in the product at the time it left the control of the manufacturer or seller. Without such proof, the manufacturer or seller is entitled to summary judgment[3] or a directed verdict.[4] A plaintiff may prove that a product was defective either by direct evidence or by circumstantial evidence from which reasonable inferences of a defect may be drawn.[5] Direct evidence usually takes the form of the allegedly defective product itself and/or the testimony of an expert who has examined the product and who offers an opinion on the product's

---

[1] Sisson v. Hatteras Yachts, Inc., 1989 U.S. Dist. LEXIS 10842 (N.D. Ill. 1989) (applying Indiana law); Virgil v. "Kash n' Karry" Service Corp., 484 A.2d 652 (Md. Ct. Spec. App. 1984).

[2] E.J. Stewart, Inc. v. Aitken Products, Inc., 607 F. Supp. 883 (E.D. Pa. 1985) (applying Pennsylvania law); Mitchell v. Gonzales, 819 P.2d 872, 876 (Cal. 1991).

[3] Humphreys v. General Motors Corp., 839 F. Supp. 822 (N.D. Fla. 1993) (applying Florida law); Parsons v. Ford Motor Co., 85 S.W.3d 323 (Tex. App. 2002).

[4] Wernimont v. International Harvestor Corp., 309 N.W.2d 137 (Iowa Ct. App. 1981).

[5] Tweedy v. Wright Ford Sales, Inc., 357 N.E.2d 449 (Ill. 1976); Lauder v. Teaneck Volunteer Ambulance Corp., 845 A.2d 1271 (N.J. Super. Ct. App. Div. 2004); Motley v. Fluid Power of Memphis, Inc., 640 S.W.2d 222 (Tenn. Ct. App. 1982).

design, manufacture, or warnings.[6] In a manufacturing defect case, the defect in the product usually results from faulty materials or faulty assembly of the parts.[7] The presence of the product permits the parties and their experts to compare its condition with the requirements specified in the design or with similar products of the same model manufactured by the defendant.[8] In a design defect case, the plaintiff's expert witnesses often will compare the product with similar products from other manufacturers in an attempt to show that there was a reasonable alternative design to the one used by the manufacturer and that it would have been safer. This will require the experts used by the plaintiff and the defendant to testify about technological feasibility, cost, and the likelihood of consumer acceptance of an alternative design.[9]

Because a determination of whether a product was defective cannot be based on conjecture or speculation, direct evidence is the desired means of proof. However, direct evidence is not required to establish a *prima facie* case for a defect. This is because, in some cases, the plaintiff is unable to identify the specific defect due to the destruction or loss of the product that caused the injuries.[10] In other cases, the product may be available but the plaintiff may be unable to identify a specific defect in it.[11] In cases where the absence of direct evidence prevents the plaintiff from proving the specific defect in the design or manufacture of the product, the plaintiff can rely on the facts and circumstantial evidence of the accident to argue that a reasonable jury could conclude that the product was defective.[12] Circumstantial evidence has been defined as "the proof of certain facts and circumstances in a given case from which the jury may infer other connected facts which usually and reasonably follow according to the common experience of mankind."[13] An example of the types of circumstantial evi-

---

[6] Pouncey v. Ford Motor Co., 464 F.2d 957 (5th Cir. 1972) (applying Alabama law). In some cases, a defect may be established by a direct eyewitness of the product malfunction. In such cases, expert testimony is not necessary to defeat a motion for summary judgment. Perez-Trujillo v. Volvo Car Corp., 137 F.3d 50 (1st Cir. 1998) (applying Puerto Rican law).

[7] Willis v. Floyd Brace Co., Inc., 309 S.E.2d 295 (S.C. Ct. App. 1983); Harris v. Bardwell, 373 So.2d 277 (La. Ct. App. 1979).

[8] Keeler v. Richards Manufacturing Co., Inc., 817 F.2d 1197 (5th Cir. 1987) (applying Texas law). For a discussion of the inspection process for defective products, see § 8.02(C)[1].

[9] The role of expert witnesses is discussed in § 8.03.

[10] In *Greene v. B.F. Goodrich Avionics Systems*, 409 F.3d 784 (6th Cir. 2005) (applying Kentucky law), the plaintiff alleged that a defective gyroscope caused a helicopter crash in which her husband, the pilot, died. Since the vertical gyroscopes were destroyed in the crash, there was no direct evidence of their failure. The plaintiff was able to introduce circumstantial evidence that would allow the jury to infer a design or manufacturing defect in the product. *See also* Lindsay v. McDonnell Douglas Aircraft Corp., 460 F.2d 631 (8th Cir. 1972) (an admiralty suit) (airplane crashed in the ocean and never was recovered).

[11] *See* Motley v. Fluid Power of Memphis, Inc., 640 S.W.2d 222 (Tenn. Ct. App. 1982).

[12] *See* Worsham v. A.H. Robbins Co., 734 F.2d 676 (11th Cir. 1984) (applying Florida law); Ford Motor Co. v. Gonzales, 9 S.W.3d 195 (Tex. App. 1999).

[13] Pace v. McClow 458 N.E.2d 4, 8 (Ill. App. Ct. 1983).

dence that can lead to the inference of a product defect is *Daniel v. Indiana Mills & Manufacturing, Inc.*,[14] in which the plaintiff was injured when a truck he was driving jackknifed and left the highway. The plaintiff alleged that his injuries resulted when his seat belt failed, causing him to be thrown from the truck during the accident. On appeal from a jury verdict in favor of the plaintiff, the manufacturer of the seat belt assembly argued that the plaintiff failed to produce sufficient evidence to prove: (1) the seatbelt was worn and released during the accident, (2) he was wearing his seatbelt, or (3) he did not unlatch it himself during the accident to avoid becoming trapped with the flammable gasoline tanker he was pulling. The Missouri appellate court held that the jury could infer the existence of a defect in the seatbelt from five types of circumstantial evidence: testimony from the plaintiff and any witnesses; testimony of medical personnel who treated the plaintiff at the scene of the accident; the circumstances of the accident; testimony from experts about the seatbelt and the accident; tests duplicating the conditions of the accident.[15]

In some states, the use of circumstantial evidence to draw an inference of a product defect is known as the "general defect" or "indeterminate defect" theory.[16] Other states use a variation of this called "malfunction theory."[17] Under this theory, a plaintiff must present sufficient evidence that: (1) the product malfunctioned; (2) the plaintiff used the product in a manner intended or reasonably expected by the manufacturer; and (3) there were no other reasonable secondary causes of the defect.[18] An example of the malfunction theory is *Dominquez v. Bohn Ford, Inc.*,[19] in which the Louisiana Supreme Court held that the failure of brakes on a van to function within a few weeks after its purchase created a *prima facie* case that the van was defective and that the defect existed when the product left the manufacturer's control. There also was no evidence of abnormal use of the van during the time the plaintiff had driven it. Underlying all of these theories of circumstantial evidence for establishing an inference that a product was defective is the idea that "common experience indicates that certain

---

[14] 103 S.W.3d 302 (Mo. Ct. App. 2003).

[15] *Id.* at 309-310.

[16] In *Riley v. De'Longhi Corp.*, 2000 U.S. App. LEXIS 27082 (11th Cir. 2000) (applying Maryland law), the court determined that a product defect could be inferred from circumstantial evidence by analyzing five factors: (1) expert testimony as to possible causes; (2) the occurrence of the accident a short time after the sale; (3) same accidents in similar products; (4) the elimination of other causes of the accident; and (5) the type of accident that does not happen without a defect.

[17] *See* Edic v. Century Products Co., 364 F.3d 1276 (11th Cir. 2004) (applying Florida law); Ducko v. Chrysler Motors Corp., 639 A.2d 1204 (Pa. Super. Ct. 1994).

[18] Booth v. Black & Decker, Inc., 166 F. Supp. 2d 215, 220 (E.D. Pa. 2001) (applying Pennsylvania law).

[19] 483 So.2d 934 (La. 1986).

accidents do not occur absent some defect," and that an inference of a defect under specific circumstances should be permitted.[20]

There are other types of circumstantial evidence that may or may not be admissible to prove that a product was defective. Federal courts and most states follow the common law "subsequent repairs" doctrine and exclude evidence of subsequent remedial measures, at least when such evidence is offered to establish fault on the part of the manufacturer.[21] However, courts permit plaintiffs to present evidence of prior accidents or similar occurrences to show the unreasonably dangerous condition of a product.[22] Evidence of similar post-accident occurrences or injuries involving the same product also is admissible to refute testimony from a defense witness that the design of a product was not defective.[23] Evidence of either prior accidents or subsequent accidents usually is proper if, at the relevant times, the product involved was in substantially the same condition and the accidents were sufficiently similar.[24]

When using circumstantial evidence, a plaintiff is not required to negate all possible causes other than a defect. However, in order to establish a *prima facie* case when there is no direct evidence, the plaintiff must present evidence that tends to negate other reasonable causes, such as misuse or alteration, and justifies the jury inferring the probability of a defect.[25] An

---

[20] Williams v. Smart Chevrolet Co., 730 S.W.2d 479, 482 (Ark. 1987). *See also* Heaton v. Ford Motor Co., 435 P.2d 806, 808 (Or. 1967) (if a product fails in unusual, unexpected circumstances, "the inference is that there was some sort of defect, a precise definition of which is unnecessary"); Crump v. MacNaught P.T.Y. Ltd., 743 S.W.2d 532, 535 (Mo. Ct. App. 1987) (common sense suggests handles do not usually fly off pumps); Bombardi v. Pochel's Appliance & TV Co., 518 P.2d 202, 204 (Wash. Ct. App. 1975) (common sense would lead jury to conclude that television set was defective because it caught on fire).

[21] *See* the Federal Rules of Evidence, Rule 407 (2005):

> When, after an injury or harm allegedly caused by an event, measures are taken that, if previously taken, would have made the injury or harm less likely to occur, evidence of the subsequent measures is not admissible to prove negligence, culpable conduct, a defect in a product, a defect in a product's design, or a need for a warning or instruction. This rule does not require the exclusion of evidence of subsequent measures when offered for another purpose, such as proving ownership, control or feasibility of precautionary measures, if controverted, or impeachment.

FED. R . EVID. 407. This rule has been adopted as part of numerous state rules of evidence. Duchess v. Langston Corp., 769 A.2d 1131, 1139 n. 9 (Pa. 2001).

[22] Mercer v. Pittway Corp., 616 N.W.2d 602 (Iowa 2000); Knitz v. Minister Machine Co., 1987 Ohio App. LEXIS 5828 (Ohio Ct. App. 1987). The defendant also may introduce evidence of the lack of prior accidents if it can show that the same product was used under conditions substantially similar to those in which the plaintiff used the product. *See* McKenzie v. S K Hand Tool Corp., 650 N.E.2d 612 (Ill. App. Ct. 1995).

[23] Koehn v. R.D. Werner Co., 809 P.2d 1045 (Colo. Ct. App. 1990); Bass v. Cincinnati, Inc., 536 N.E.2d 831 (Ill. App. Ct. 1989).

[24] Johnson v. Ford Motor Co., 988 F.2d 573 (5th Cir. 1993) (applying Mississippi law); Mercer, 616 N.W.2d 602.

[25] *See* Yielding v. Chrysler Motor Co., 783 S.W.2d 353 (Ark. 1990); Motley v. Fluid Power of Memphis, Inc., 640 S.W.2d 222 (Tenn. Ct. App. 1982).

inference of a defect cannot be drawn simply from evidence that the product failed and an injury resulted.[26] Instead, the evidence must be sufficient to make a defect reasonably probable and more probable than any other theory based on the evidence.[27] Circumstantial evidence that relates to whether an inference of a defect can be drawn includes the product's age, the product's purpose, the expected useful life of the product, the occurrence of the accident a short time after the sale, and the maintenance of the product before the accident.[28] In most cases, the longer a product has been out of the manufacturer's control and the older that it is, the more likely that someone else or some other factor was responsible for the product's failure. The key to whether the circumstantial evidence is sufficient is whether the jury, which must weigh all the evidence presented to it and determine what evidence offers the more plausible explanation of the events that cause the plaintiff's injuries, properly can draw an inference that the product was defective in its design, manufacture or lack of warnings.

[B] *Res Ipsa Loquitur and "An Inference of a Product Defect"*

In negligence cases, the burden of proof is difficult where the plaintiff has been injured but has no direct evidence of the events that led to the accident. To help the plaintiff meet the burden of establishing a *prima facie* case and avoid summary judgment, courts use the doctrine of *res ipsa loquitur*, which literally means "the thing speaks for itself."[29] Res ipsa loquitur is not a cause of action or a theory of liability. Instead, it is a method of circumstantial evidence for proving that a product was defective. However, since the mere fact of an accident is not enough to create an assumption that a product was defective, res ipsa loquitur requires the plaintiff to prove that: (1) the accident was one that ordinarily does not occur in the absence of negligence[30] and (2) the defendant had exclusive management and control of the product that caused the injury.[31] Whether res ipsa loquitur is applica-

---

[26] Hernandez v. Nissan Motor Corp., 740 S.W.2d 893 (Tex. App. 1987).

[27] Scanlon v. General Motors Corp., 326 A.2d 861 (N.J. 1974); Wernimont v. International Harvester, Inc., 309 N.W.2d 137 (Iowa Ct. App. 1981).

[28] Harrison v. Bill Cairns Pontiac of Marlow Heights, Inc., 549 A.2d 385 (Md. Ct. Spec. App. 1988); Shramek v. General Motors Corp., 216 N.E.2d 244 (Ill. App. Ct. 1966).

[29] The first products liability case to use res ipsa loquitur was *Escola v. Coca Cola Bottling Co.*, 150 P.2d 436 (Cal. 1944) in which the California Supreme Court held that the plaintiff could use the doctrine to establish a prima facie case of a manufacturer's breach of duty.

[30] Parsons v. Ford Motor Co., 85 S.W.3d 323 (Tex. App. 2002).

[31] Stadtherr v. Elite Logistics, Inc., 2002 U.S. Dist. LEXIS 9701 (D. Kan. 2002) (applying Kansas law); Austin v. Mitsubishi Electronics America, Inc., 966 F. Supp. 506 (E.D. Mich. 1997) (applying Michigan law); Williams v. American Medical Systems, 548 S.E.2d 371 (Ga. Ct. App. 2001). Some courts do not apply the "exclusive control" requirement literally. *See* Condiff v. R.D. Werner Co., Inc., 2003 U.S. Dist. LEXIS 14288 (E.D. La) (applying Louisiana law); Harrison v. Bill Cairns Pontiac of Marlow Heights, Inc., 549 A.2d 385 (Md. Ct. Spec. App. 1988).

ble in a particular case is a question of law that must be decided by the court.[32] If the court decides that the doctrine of res ipsa loquitur is applicable, it then is the jury's function to weigh the evidence and to determine whether the circumstantial evidence of negligence has been overcome by any proof offered by the manufacturer. Because res ipsa loquitur is a rule of circumstantial evidence, the jury is permitted but not compelled to find for the plaintiff.[33] Any presumption raised by res ipsa loquitur in favor of the plaintiff will give way to contrary proof offered by the manufacturer. Such proof may consist of testimony about its due care in the design or manufacture of the product or proof that the accident was caused by the plaintiff's misuse of the product or by a third person.

Although res ipsa loquitur is used in products liability cases based on negligence, the vast majority of courts have held that the doctrine is not applicable in strict liability cases. The reasons for this were set out by the New Jersey Supreme Court in *Myrlak v Port Authority*[34] in which the plaintiff was injured when a chair he was using at work collapsed. No one other than the plaintiff saw the accident and there was no evidence that the chair had been misused by the plaintiff or anyone else. However, the chair was not used exclusively by the plaintiff. The plaintiff brought suit against the manufacturer of the chair based on strict liability and alleging a manufacturing defect and a failure to warn. However, at trial, the plaintiff's expert was unable to identify a specific defect in the chair or even to state that a defect had caused the accident. The New Jersey Supreme Court rejected the use of res ipsa loquitur in cases based on strict liability saying that it was a rule of evidence that allows a plaintiff in a negligence case to meet its requirement of showing that the defendant breached its duty of care. Strict liability, however, is a theory of allocating responsibility regardless of the manufacturer's fault.

Although most courts have rejected the use of res ipsa loquitur in strict liability cases, the Restatement (Third) permits circumstantial evidence to support an inference of a product defect in such cases. According to § 3 of the Restatement:

> It may be inferred that the harm sustained by the plaintiff was caused by a product defect existing at the time of sale or distribution, without proof of a specific defect, when the incident that harmed the plaintiff:
>
> > (a) was of a kind that ordinarily occurs as a result of a product defect; and

---

[32] Gould v. Motel 6 Operating L.P., 2005 Wash. App. LEXIS 244 (Wash. Ct. App. 2005); Nutting v. Northern Energy, 874 P.2d 482 (Col. Ct. App. 1994).

[33] McGuire v. Stein's Gift & Garden Center, 504 N.W.2d 385 (Wis. Ct. App. 1993).

[34] 723 A.2d 45 (N.J. 1999).

(b) was not, in the particular case, solely the result of causes other than product defect existing at the time of sale or distribution.[35]

Section 3, which is based on res ipsa loquitur, permits the jury to draw two inferences: (1) that the harmful incident was caused by a product defect, and (2) that the defect was present when the product left the manufacturer's control. In contrast, res ipsa loquitur creates a single inference that the defendant breached its duty of care. Despite this difference, section 3 parallels the elements of res ipsa loquitur requirements that (1) the product was in the defendant's exclusive control at the time of the accident and (2) the defect occurred before the product left the control of the manufacturer. These elements can be satisfied through direct or circumstantial evidence as well as by evidence that negates causes other than product defect. In addition, even those states that hold that res ipsa loquitur is not applicable to a strict products liability action have recognized that the inferences and principles that form the core of res ipsa loquitur "merely instantiates the broader principle, which is as applicable to a products case as to any other tort case, that an accident can itself be evidence of liability[,] . . . if it is reasonably plain that the defect was not introduced after the product was sold."[36]

Because § 3 of the Restatement (Third) has its origins in res ipsa loquitur, the drafters of the section were aware of the parallel between drawing an inference of negligence in an appropriate case and drawing an inference of a product defect under similar circumstances. The section was adopted to "set forth the formal requisites for drawing an inference" in some product defect cases.[37] Thus, section 3 of the Restatement (Third) does in a strict liability case what res ipsa loquitur does in a negligence case.

[C] *Product Testing and Spoliation of Evidence*

[1] Product Testing

If the product that allegedly caused the plaintiff's injuries was not destroyed in the accident, the plaintiff and the defendant will want to conduct thorough tests on it before trial to determine whether it was defective and whether it was the product that caused the injuries. Although product testing is expensive, it is a critical means of determining whether the product was defective and, if so, whether it could have been a cause of the plain-

---

[35] RESTATEMENT (THIRD) OF TORTS: PRODUCTS LIABILITY § 3 (1998).

[36] Welge v. Planters Lifesavers Co., 17 F.3d 209, 211 (7th Cir. 1994). *See also* Williams v. Smart Chevrolet Co., 730 S.W.2d 479 (Ark. 1987); Lang v. Federated Department Stores, 287 S.E.2d 729, 731 (Ga. Ct. App. 1982).

[37] RESTATEMENT (THIRD) OF TORTS: PRODUCTS LIABILITY § 3 cmt. *a* (1998).

tiff's injuries. However, before either side can conduct tests on the product (which usually is in the physical control of the plaintiff), it is necessary for the parties to draft, agree upon, and sign an "Inspection Protocol," i.e., a memorandum setting out the ground rules for the inspection. Because of the importance of product testing to all parties, the sensitive nature of the testing, and the potential for disagreements, it is necessary to have as detailed an Inspection Protocol as possible. Although the specific provisions of each Inspection Protocol will differ depending upon the nature of the accident, the particular product, and where the testing is conducted, a sample protocol is set out below.

1. The inspection shall begin at 9:00 a.m. on every workday and shall end at 6:00 p.m. unless the Team Leaders agree to a continuation.

2. The inspection shall recess for lunch from 12:00 p.m. — 1:00 p.m. Team Leaders may adjust lunchtime as necessary to the prompt completion of the task.

3. The monitor cameras, if used, shall continue without interruption during lunch.

4. No work shall be performed at the scene during lunch.

5. [The plaintiff's attorney or law firm] or its representatives shall act as host.

6. The systematic investigation of [the product or the scene of the accident] precludes "jumping ahead" to facilitate a particular goal of an interested party.

7. Each party shall be allowed one photographer who shall take their photographs and then the video shall be taken using the same method. The photographers shall perform the task as a team. After the initial documentation of [the product or the scene of the accident] by a photographer designated by each party is completed, other representatives of the parties then may photograph or video [the product or scene of the accident] as they believe necessary.

8. The goal is to photograph [the product or the scene of the accident]. Photographs of the parties shall be avoided if at all possible. Before photographing a party, it is appropriate to give notice and opportunity to move out of the photograph.

9. All parties shall have the right to engage their own engineers, scientists, chemists, or other professionals.

10. The parties shall properly identify themselves and sign the "Scene Poster."

11. Each party shall recognize a single Team Leader who shall represent his/her party in Protocol matters such as Team Leader meetings.

12. Only the Team Leaders, their representative or attorney shall be allowed to voice the position of their client.

13. There shall be a Team Leader meeting to discuss issues or concerns. Any participating party may attend the Team Leader meeting. Only the Team Leaders, attorney, or client shall be authorized to speak during this meeting.

14. Any video camera used shall not record audio. The master tape shall have no audio.

15. A single copy of all photographs and videotapes taken during the evidence inspection shall be exchanged between the parties without charge to the parties. Additional photographs can be acquired by request and compensation to their parties. This exchange does not include monitor tapes.

16. This Protocol is addressed to a [product or scene of the accident] investigation, i.e., Phase I Analysis. If it becomes necessary to conduct a more detailed examination of the [product or scene], a Phase II Analysis will be coordinated by the attorneys or claim representatives.

17. Task Protocols shall be used as necessary.

18. The Task Protocol documents the basic steps, rationale, and goal of the task. Each Team Leader must approve the Task Protocol before the task is attempted. All team Leaders must be notified before the evaluation is executed so that they may be present during the event.

19. Only a single Task Protocol can be undertaken during the same time period except as agreed upon by all Team Leaders.

20. Once documented by all parties and with an approved Task Protocol, the specific Interested Parties may assist with the manipulation or movement of their products.

21. Samples shall be numbered sequentially. There shall be no duplication of evidence numbers.

22. [Product Liability, Inc.] has been retained to receive evidence secured by the parties. Any evidence secured by interested parties shall be immediately transmitted to [Product Liability, Inc.].

23. Parties shall secure evidence they select.

24. Parties shall be responsible for their own safety.

25. Parties all bring all necessary tools for the completion of their investigation.

26. No sample, artifact, or item of evidence may be secured in violation of applicable criminal laws. The parties are responsible for verifying proper licensing of their representatives.

27. The evidence shall remain in the custody of [Product Liability, Inc.]. An "evidence list" shall be provided to each party before the scene investigation is complete.

28. Once all the evidence has been secured, it shall not be inspected without notice to all of the parties.

29. Any measurements taken must not be destructive.

30. There shall be no evidence secured without notice to the Team Leaders.

31. The surface of the evidence must not be altered. Such alteration would include, but not be limited to scratching, cutting, or wiping surface coating without a Task protocol being established first.

32. Any tests not delineated within the Protocol document must first have a written protocol submitted to the Team Leaders for approval.

33. By signature to this Protocol all parties agree to allow any other participating party to observe each test and inspection at [the site of the testing].

34. There shall be no surreptitious recordings of any type.

35. Any change in the established Protocol shall require unanimous agreement.

36. Participants using recording devices to document personal notes shall make diligent effort to maintain custody and control of their recorders.

37. Participants shall give notice before using recording devices.

38. Investigators, engineers, and other participants must adhere to all applicable criminal laws.

[2] Spoliation of Evidence

Although both the plaintiff and defendant want to conduct tests on any product involved in an accident that may lead to litigation, in some situations the product is lost, destroyed, or altered before it is possible to exam-

ine it.[38] This may be the result of intentional or negligent conduct. Thus, if the plaintiff has control of the product, it is important that he or she retain it and make sure that the product is not discarded, lost, destroyed, or altered before the manufacturer has an opportunity to conduct tests on it. Similarly, manufacturers should have a formal product retention policy to establish a uniform means by which items involved in product liability cases are stored. If not, plaintiffs and manufacturers risk an allegation of spoliation.

Spoliation consists of the destruction, mutilation, alteration, or concealment of evidence relevant to litigation that will affect adversely the ability of a plaintiff or defendant to prove the claim or defense.[39] Although claims of spoliation arise most often in cases involving documents or medical records, they also may be an issue in products liability cases, particularly those based on claims of manufacturing defects. If the plaintiff alleges that his or her damages were caused by a design defect and the product is not available or has been altered, another product of the same model can be tested. However, if the basis of the claim is a manufacturing defect, the loss, destruction, or alteration of the product will harm the ability of the plaintiff or the defendant to prove their case since it is unlikely that another product with the same "manufacturing defect" can be found.

The question for courts since the mid-1980s has been whether to treat spoliation as an independent tort subject to an award of damages or to deal with it through judicial sanctions. Currently, courts in about half-a-dozen states expressly recognize a cause of action in tort for intentional[40] and/or negligent[41] spoliation of evidence. One court that has recognized a cause of action in tort for spoliation of evidence is the Florida appellate court.[42] According to that court, a spoliation claim requires proof of six elements: (1) the existence of a potential civil action; (2) the legal or contractual duty to preserve evidence which is relevant to the potential civil action; (3) destruction of that evidence; (4) a significant impairment of the ability

---

[38] See *Hirsch v. General Motors Corp.*, 628 A.2d 1108 (N.J. Super. Ct. 1993), in which the plaintiffs' insurance company inspected their automobile that had been damaged severely by a fire. However, the day after the insurance company declared the automobile a "total loss," but before the defendants had an opportunity to test it, the automobile was given to a salvage company. *See also* Brown v. Stone Manufacturing Co., 660 F. Supp. 454 (S.D. Miss. 1986); Drayton v. Jiffee Chemical Corp., 395 F. Supp. 1081 (N.D. Ohio 1981); Kambylis v. Ford Motor Co., 788 N.E.2d 1 (Ill. App. Ct. 2003).

[39] *See* Goff v. Harold Ives Trucking Co., Inc., 27 S.W.3d 387 (Ark.2000).

[40] *See* Hazen v. Municipality of Anchorage, 718 P.2d 456 (Alaska 1986); Hirsch v. General Motors Corp., 628 A.2d 1108 (N.J. Super. Ct. 1993).

[41] *See* Holmes v. Amerex Rent-A-Car, 180 F.3d 294 (D.C. Cir. 1999); St. Mary's Hospital, Inc. v. Brinson, 685 So.2d 33 (Fla. Dist. Ct. App. 1996). For a list of states that recognize a cause of action for spoliation, see *Fletcher v. Dorchester Mutual Insurance Co.*, 773 N.E.2d 420, 424 (Mass. 2002).

[42] Continental Insurance Co. v. Herman, 576 So.2d 313 (Fla. Dist. Ct. App. 1990).

to prove the lawsuit; (5) a causal relationship between the evidence destruction and the inability to prove the lawsuit, and (6) damages.[43] Although many states do not recognize a common law duty to preserve evidence, the Illinois Supreme Court, in *Boyd v. Travelers Insurance Co.*,[44] held that such a duty may arise by agreement, a contract, a statute, a special circumstance, or the defendant's voluntary assumption of a duty by affirmative conduct. Under this test, a "special circumstance" includes a party's knowledge of pending litigation or reasonable knowledge that specific evidence may be relevant to anticipated litigation.[45] The assumption of a duty to preserve evidence may result from a company's voluntary adoption of a product retention policy that creates a duty that otherwise would not exist.

The vast majority of courts that have considered spoliation have declined to treat it as a tort.[46] Among the reasons given by the courts for their refusal is that sanctions for discovery violations already exist and that the costs and burdens that would be imposed on courts outweigh the benefits of permitting a tort claim for spoliation.[47] Instead of treating spoliation as a tort, these courts rely on the traditional judicial sanctions of (1) dismissal of the action; (2) barring the spoliator from using evidence about the product acquired before its destruction; (3) jury instructions permitting it to infer that the missing evidence would have been unfavorable to the party responsible for its loss.[48] However, under a test adopted by a number of courts, the trial court judge must analyze three factors in determining what sanctions to impose because of spoliation of evidence: (1) the degree of fault of the party who altered or destroyed the evidence; (2) the degree of prejudice suffered by the opposing party; and (3) the availability of a lesser sanction

---

[43] *Id.* at 315.

[44] 652 N.E.2d 267 (Ill. 1995). *See also* Denton v. Northeast Illinois Regional Commuter Railroad Corp., 2004 U.S. Dist. LEXIS 7234 (N.D. Ill. 2004) (applying Illinois law).

[45] Kambylis v. Ford Motor Co., 788 N.E.2d 1 (Ill. App. Ct. 2003). *See also* Hirsch v. General Motors Corp., 628 A.2d 1108 (N.J. Super. Ct. 1993).

[46] *See* MetLife Auto & Home v. Joe Basil Chevrolet, Inc., 807 N.E.2d 865 (N.Y. 2004); Lueter v. California, 115 Cal. Rptr. 2d 68 (Cal. Ct. App. 2002). For lists of states that do not recognize a cause of action for spoliation, see *Fletcher v. Dorchester Mutual Insurance Co.*, 773 N.E.2d 420, 424 n. 9 (Mass. 2002) and *Timber Tech Engineered Building Products v. The Home Insurance Co.*, 55 P. 3d 952, 954 n. 5 (Nev. 2002).

[47] Cedars-Sinai Medical Center v. Superior Court, 954 P.2d 511 (Cal. 1998); Reilly v. D'Errico, 1994 Conn. Super. LEXIS 2450 (Conn. Super. Ct. 1994).

[48] Workman v. AB Electrolux Corp., 2005 U.S. Dist. LEXIS 16306 (D. Kan. 2005) (applying Kansas law); Davis v. Ford Motor Co., 375 F. Supp. 2d 518 (S.D. Miss. 2005) (applying Mississippi law); Aetna Life and Casualty Co. v. Imet Mason Contractors, 707 A.2d 180 (N.J. Super. Ct. App. Div. 1998); Kirkland v. New York City Housing Authority, 666 N.Y.S. 2d 609 (N.Y. App. Div. 1997). Fed.R.Civ.P. 37(b)(2) gives federal courts the authority to enter sanctions for discovery abuses. But see *Stringer v. Packaging Corporation of America*, 815 N.E.2d 476 (Ill. App. Ct. 2004), in which the court denied judicial sanctions where the product was discarded by a co-worker of the plaintiff while the plaintiff was in the hospital and without his knowledge.

that will protect the opposing party's rights and deter future similar conduct.[49]

§ 8.03 EXPERT WITNESSES

[A] *Introduction*

The complexity of modern products frequently makes it difficult for juries (and judges) to determine whether they were defective. The question turns on the intricacies of the design and manufacture of the products and when and what type of warnings should be given concerning their use. The answer may require a knowledge of such diverse topics as chemistry, the principles and materials of construction, engineering, medicine, and pharmacology. As a result, evidence supporting or challenging an allegation that a product was defective may mean little or nothing to the trier of fact without the assistance of expert testimony.[50] The findings and opinions of experts not only help the trier of fact decide whether the product was defective, they also are crucial in establishing whether the defect was the cause of the plaintiff's injuries.[51] Although expert testimony is not required in every products liability case,[52] the crucial role that it plays in most cases requires an understanding of three important questions: (1) What are the standards for the admissibility of expert testimony? (2) What are the qualifications for an expert? (3) What is the permissible scope of expert testimony? In federal courts, expert testimony is governed by Rules 702 through 706 of the Fed-

---

[49] Schmid v. Milwaukee Electric Tool Corp., 13 F.3d 76 (3d Cir. 1994) (applying Pennsylvania law); Lafayette Insurance Company v. CMA Dishmachines, 2005 U.S. Dist. LEXIS 8026 (E.D. La. 2005) (applying Louisiana law); Tracy v. General Motors Corp., 524 S.E.2d 879 (W. Va. 1999); Trevino v. Ortega, 969 S.W.2d 959 (Tex. 1998). In deciding whether a party is entitled to a jury instruction directing a spoliation inference, the court in *Veloso v. Western Bedding Supply Co.*, 281 F. Supp. 2d 743, 746 (D. N.J. 2003), a products liability case involving documents allegedly lost by the defendants, stated that four factors are necessary: (1) the evidence must be under the adverse party's control; (2) there must be intentional suppression or withholding of the evidence (i.e., there is no inference where the evidence was lost or accidently destroyed); (3) the evidence must be relevant; and (4) it must have been reasonably foreseeable at the time the document was created that it later would be discoverable.

[50] For a detailed discussion of expert testimony, see PAUL C. GIANNELLI, UNDERSTANDING EVIDENCE Chs. 24–25 (2003); GLEN WEISSENBERGER & JAMES J. DUANE, WEISSENBERGER'S FEDERAL EVIDENCE Ch. 7 (4th ed. 2001).

[51] For two examples of cases that could not be decided without expert testimony, see *Allison v. McGhan Medical Corp.*, 184 F.3d 1300 (11th Cir. 1999) (whether the plaintiff's complex medical problems were caused by silicon breast implants); *Blanchard v. Eli Lilly & Co.*, 207 F. Supp. 2d 308 (D. Vt. 2002) (whether murder/suicide was caused by antidepressant drug). *See also* Derienzo v. Trek Bicycle Corp., 376 F. Supp. 2d 537 (S.D. N.Y. 2005) (applying New York law).

[52] Flight International v. Allied Signal, 1995 U.S. App. LEXIS 15599 (9th Cir. 1995) (applying California law); Harrell Motors, Inc. v. Flanery, 612 S.W.2d 727 (Ark. 1981); Atkins v. GMC, 725 N.E.2d 727 (Ohio Ct. App. 1999).

eral Rules of Evidence.[53] Since almost all states have adopted a similar approach to expert testimony, this section examines the issues of expert testimony in products liability cases by focusing on the Federal Rules.

[B] *The Standards for the Admissibility of Expert Testimony*

The most controversial question surrounding expert testimony is: What are the standards for its admissibility? At the present time, there are two principal tests for the admission of expert evidence: the *Frye* test and the *Daubert* test.

[1] The *Frye* Test

Over the years, many federal and state courts have based their decision whether to admit the testimony of experts on *Frye v. United States*.[54] In that case, the United States Court of Appeals for the District of Columbia stated:

> Just when a scientific principle or discovery crosses the line between the experimental and demonstrable stages is difficult to define. Somewhere in this twilight zone the evidential force of the principle must be recognized, and while courts will go a long way in admitting expert testimony deducted from a well-recognized scientific principle or discovery, the thing from which the deduction is made must be sufficiently established to have gained general acceptance in the particular field in which it belongs.[55]

One commentator has written that the *Frye* test is designed to accomplish six goals. These are:

> (1) ensure that a minimal reserve of experts exist who can critically examine the validity of a scientific determination in a particular case, (2) promote a degree of uniformity in decision, (3) avoid the interjection of a time consuming and often misleading determination of the reliability of a scientific technique in litigation, (4) assure that scientific evidence introduced will be reliable . . . and thus relevant, (5) provide a preliminary screening to protect against the natural inclination of the jury to assign significant weight to scientific techniques presented under circumstances where the trier of fact is in a poor position to place an accurate evaluation upon reli-

---

[53] *See* GLEN WEISSENBERGER & JAMES J. DUANE, FEDERAL RULES OF EVIDENCE: RULES, LEGISLATIVE HISTORY, COMMENTARY AND AUTHORITY (2001 & Supp. 2005-06). For a detailed discussion of Rules 702 to 706, see JACK B. WEINSTEIN & MARGARET A. BERGER, WEINSTEIN'S EVIDENCE MANUAL STUDENT EDITION Ch. 13 (7th ed. 2005).

[54] 293 F. 1013 (D.C. Cir. 1923).

[55] *Id.* at 1014.

ability, and (6) impose a threshold standard of reliability, in light of the fact that cross-examination by opposing counsel is unlikely to bring inaccuracies to the attention of the jury.[56]

In practice, the *Frye* test means that novel techniques of product testing that have not been peer reviewed and gained "general acceptance" within the particular scientific community are inadmissible. Only when the procedures have gained such acceptance are they admissible. Critics point out, however, that *Frye* does not provide judges with guidelines as to what constitutes "general acceptance" in a particular scientific community and does not permit judges to keep up with the rapid changes in scientific fields.[57] Because of these criticisms, the federal courts and more than half of the states no longer use the *Frye* standard. However, the states that continue to follow *Frye* are among those with the largest populations: California, Florida, Illinois, New York, New Jersey, Michigan, and Pennsylvania. Thus, while *Frye* no longer applies in federal courts and in the majority of the states, it continues to be the test for the admissibility of expert testimony in the states with the most products liability litigation.

[2] The *Daubert* Test

In 1975 Congress finally adopted the Federal Rules of Evidence. The version of Rule 702 of the Rules that was in effect from 1975 to 2000 defined an expert and the situations when expert testimony was admissible. Although the Rule was meant to expand the admissibility of evidence, it did not set out any standards for evaluating its admissibility. As a result, federal and state courts continued to use the *Frye* test of "general acceptance" in the relevant scientific community. However, the Supreme Court adopted a different test for federal courts in 1993 with its decision in *Daubert v. Merrell Dow Pharaceuticals, Inc.,*[58] a products liability case involving a claim that the birth defects of two children had been caused by their mother's prenatal ingestion of the prescription drug Bendectin. The defendant drug manufacturer argued that the affidavits, submitted by the plaintiffs' medical experts to establish a causal connection between Bendectin and the children's birth defects, were inadmissible because they did not meet the *Frye* test.[59] The Supreme Court, however, held that the adoption of Federal Rules of Evidence in 1975 superceded *Frye* as the basis for the admission of

---

[56] MICHAEL GRAHAM, CLEARY & GRAHAM'S HANDBOOK OF ILLINOIS EVIDENCE § 702.4, at 565 (6th ed. 1994).

[57] For a critical discussion of *Frye*, see Robert J. Goodwin, *Fifty Years of Frye of Alabama: The Continuing Debate Over Adopting the Test Established in* Daubert v. Merrell Dow Pharmaceuticals, Inc., 35 CUMB. L. REV. 231 (2005); Clark Hedger, Daubert *and the States: A Critical analysis of Emerging Trends*, 49 ST. LOUIS U. L.J. 177 (2004).

[58] 509 U.S. 579 (1993).

[59] *Id.* at 583-584.

scientific evidence.[60] According to the Court, there is nothing in the text of the Federal Rules or in the drafting history of Rule 702 that gives any indication that the "general acceptance" test of *Frye* is a necessary precondition for the admission of scientific evidence.[61] The Court also felt that the "general acceptance" test conflicted with the liberal language of Rule 402 of the Federal Rules of Evidence which states: "All relevant evidence is admissible, except as otherwise provided. . . .Evidence which is not relevant is inadmissible."[62]

Although the Federal Rules of Evidence replaced *Frye*, the Supreme Court stated that does not mean that the Federal Rules do not place limits on the admissibility of scientific evidence.[63] The Court held that, under Rule 104(a) of the Federal Rules of Evidence, dealing with questions of admissibility generally, a judge must make a preliminary assessment as to whether the underlying reasoning or methodology of the proposed testimony is scientifically valid and properly can be applied to the facts at issue.[64] When faced with potential expert scientific testimony, the trial judge no longer uses a single "general acceptance" test as in *Frye*. Instead, the Court stated that the judge must ask a series of questions such as:

- Can the theory or technique be tested and has it been tested?

- Has the theory or technique been subjected to peer review and publication?

- In the case of a particular scientific technique, what was the known or potential error rate discovered during the testing?

- What is the "general acceptance" of the theory or technique within the relevant scientific community?[65]

As a result of *Daubert*, a witness must do more than establish an area of expertise to qualify as an expert. The witness must substantiate his or her conclusions and opinions with scientific or technical findings that meet the case's criteria for relevance and reliability.[66] While the jury is free to reach judgments on the scientific evidence that the witness presents and the judge permits it to consider, the role of the judge is that of an initial "gatekeeper." The judge's job is to keep evidence from the jury if it is not sufficient to help a reasonable juror reach a conclusion. An indication of the attrac-

---

[60] *Id.* at 587.

[61] *Id.* at 587-89.

[62] *Id.* at 588.

[63] *Id.* at 589.

[64] *Id.* at 592-93. *See also* Bitler v. A.O. Smith Corp., 400 F.3d 1227 (10th Cir. 2004); Masters v. Hesston Corp., 291 F.3d 985 (7th Cir. 2002).

[65] *Daubert*, 509 U.S. at 593-594. For an example of the application of these factors in another products liability case, see *Miller v. Pfizer, Inc.*, 356 F.3d 1326 (10th Cir. 2004).

[66] Huey v. United Parcel Service Inc., 165 F.3d 1084 (7th Cir. 1999).

tiveness of this approach to the admission of expert testimony is that more than half of the states have adopted *Daubert* or some variation of it since 1993.

[3] *Daubert* and Opinion Testimony

In products liability cases, an expert witness' opinion testimony frequently is crucial in establishing whether a product was defective and whether it was the cause of the plaintiff's injuries. In *General Electric Co. v. Joiner*,[67] the plaintiff alleged that his lung cancer was "promoted" by his exposure to chemical PCBs in the workplace.[68] Although the plaintiff's experts sought to rely on animal studies linking PCBs to cancer in mice, the Supreme Court held that the district court judge did not abuse his discretion in holding that the studies were not a sufficient basis for the experts' opinions that the plaintiff's cancer was caused by exposure to the PCBs. Of importance to the use of opinion testimony in products liability cases was the Court's holding that, just because an expert has an opinion does not mean that the court has to admit it. According to the Court: "A court may conclude that there is simply too great an analytical gap between the data and the opinion proffered."[69] Just as the willingness of an expert to testify does not create the necessary link between certain *alleged* scientific data and the admissibility of the expert's opinion based on this data, the presence of the necessary link between the data and the proffered opinion may require the admission of the opinion.

[4] The Scope of *Daubert*

For purposes of products liability cases, the most important question raised by *Daubert* was whether the decision applies to all expert testimony or only to scientific expert testimony. In 1999 the Supreme Court answered that question, holding in *Kumho Tire Co. Ltd. v. Carmichael*[70] that the *Daubert* "gatekeeping" duties of district court judges apply to all expert testimony, not just to scientific testimony. This means that everyone in a products liability case whose testimony is presented as that of an expert is subject to challenge on the *Daubert* factors.

In *Kumho Tire*, the plaintiffs brought a products liability suit against a tire manufacturer and its distributor as the result of a tire blow out which caused a minivan to overturn. The plaintiffs based a significant part of their case on the deposition of a "tire failure analyst" who would testify that,

---

[67] 522 U.S. 136 (1997).

[68] Joiner v. General Electric Co., 864 F. Supp. 1310, 1312 (N.D. Ga. 1989).

[69] 522 U.S. at 146.

[70] 526 U.S. 137 (1999).

in his opinion, a manufacturing or design defect caused the tire to blow out and the vehicle to overturn. His opinion was based on a visual and tactile inspection of the tire and upon the theory that, in the absence of at least two of four specific, physical symptoms indicating tire abuse, the tire failure was of the sort that occurred when there was a defect.[71] The tire manufacturer sought to exclude the testimony on the ground that his methodology failed to satisfy Rule 702 of the Federal Rules of Evidence.[72] Although the Eleventh Circuit held that *Daubert* was limited to scientific testimony and that, since the testimony of the plaintiffs' expert was skill- or experience-based, it was not subject to *Daubert*,[73] the Supreme Court reversed. According to the Court, the obligation to ensure that expert testimony is not only relevant but reliable applies to the testimony of engineers and to other experts who are not scientists.[74] The Court gave a number of reasons for its holding. First, the language of Rule 702 does not distinguish between "scientific" knowledge and "technical" or "other specialized" knowledge[75] This is because it is the word "knowledge" in Rule 702, not the words that modify it, that establishes a standard for evidentiary reliability.[76] *Daubert* referred only to "scientific" knowledge because that was the nature of the expertise in the case.[77] Second, Rules 702 and 703 give all expert witnesses, not just "scientific" ones testimonial latitude unavailable to other witnesses on the assumption that their opinion will have a reliable basis in the knowledge and experience of the discipline.[78] Finally, the Court felt that it would be difficult, if not impossible for judges to administer a gatekeeping system that depended upon a distinction between "scientific" knowledge and "technical" or "other specialized' knowledge since there is no clear dividing line between the two types.[79] Thus, all expert witnesses in products liability cases now are subject to the *Daubert* factors in the admissibility of their testimony.[80]

---

[71] *Id*. at 143–45.

[72] *Id*. at 145.

[73] Carmichael v. Samyang Tire, Inc., 131 F.3d 1433 (11th Cir. 1997).

[74] Kumho Tire, 526 U.S. at 147.

[75] *Id*.

[76] *Id*.

[77] *Id*. at 147- 148.

[78] *Id*. at 148.

[79] *Id*.

[80] It is the responsibility of the parties to present expert testimony, where necessary, that meets the *Daubert* requirements for admissibility. *See* Weisgram v. Marley Co., 528 U.S. 440 (2000).

[5] The District Court Judge as "Gatekeeper"

The Supreme Court's trilogy of *Daubert*, *Joiner*, and *Kumho Tire* created a new framework for determining the admissibility of expert testimony.[81] In response to those decisions, Rule 702 of the Federal Rules of Evidence was amended in 2000.[82] The current Rule "reflects" the broad latitude the Supreme Court has given to district court judges to determine the admissibility of expert testimony. Under Rule 702 and the *Daubert* trilogy, district court judges must act as "gatekeepers" for the admission of expert testimony. The purpose of this role is to prevent what one court has called "speculative, unreliable expert testimony" from being presented to the jury under the "mantle of reliability" that attaches to the label "expert testimony."[83] Under *Daubert* and its progeny, the trial court judge, as the "gatekeeper," makes a "preliminary assessment of whether the reasoning or methodology underlying the [expert] testimony is scientifically valid and of whether that reasoning or methodology can be applied to the facts at issue."[84] This requires the judge to conduct an inquiry to ensure that the testimony or evidence is both reliable and relevant.[85]

[a] Reliability

The first task facing a district court judge is to evaluate whether the expert's proposed testimony has a reliable basis in the expert's discipline.[86] This requires an examination of whether the expert's opinion are based on the "methods and procedures of science" or are "subjective belief or unsupported speculation."[87] In order to meet the test for reliability, the expert must have "'good grounds' for his or her belief."[88] However, reliability does

---

[81] Truck Insurance Exchange v. MagneTek, Inc., 360 F.3d 1206, 1209 (10th Cir. 2004).

[82] Rule 702, as amended in 2000, provides:

If scientific, technical, or other specialized knowledge will assist the trier of fact to understand the evidence or to determine a fact in issue, a witness qualified as an expert by knowledge, skill, experience, training, or education, may testify thereto in the form of an opinion or otherwise, if (1) the testimony is based upon sufficient facts or data, (2) the testimony is the product of reliable principles and methods, and (3) the witness has applied the principles and methods reliably to the facts of the case.

FED. R. EVID. 702.

[83] McCorvey v. Baxter Healthcare Corp., 298 F.3d 1253, 1256 (11th Cir. 2002).

[84] Daubert v. Merrell Dow Pharmaceuticals, 509 U.S. 579, 592-593 (1993). *See* In re Silica Products Liability Litigation, 2005 U.S. Dist. LEXIS 14581 (S.D. Tex. 2005).

[85] *See* Unrein v. Timesavers, Inc., 394 F.3d 1008, 1011 (8th Cir. 2005) ("There is no single requirement for admissibility as long as the proffer indicates that the expert evidence is reliable and relevant.").

[86] Bitler v. A.O. Smith Corp., 400 F.3d 1227 (10th Cir. 2005).

[87] Calhoun v. Yamaha Motor Corp., U.S.A., 350 F.3d 316, 321 (3d Cir. 2003) (*quoting Daubert,* 509 U.S. at 590).

[88] *Id.*

not require the plaintiff to prove that the expert is "undisputably correct."[89] Instead, the plaintiff's burden is to show that the "method employed by the expert in reaching the conclusion is scientifically sound."[90]

To determine reliability, the Supreme Court in *Daubert* suggested that the district court consider four factors. These factors remain relevant after the adoption of amended Rule 702.[91] However, the *Daubert* factors are not definitive or exhaustive and a judge has wide discretion in making a determination of an expert's reliability.[92] Depending on the issue, the expert's particular expertise, and the subject of the expert's testimony, these factors may or may not be applicable in determining reliability.[93] According to the Supreme Court in *Kumho Tire*, "[f]ailure to consider one, or even any, of these factors . . . will not be dispositive of a district court's failure to fulfill its gatekeeping role."[94] Instead, the inquiry into an expert's reliability "is meant to be flexible and fact specific, and a court should use, adapt, or reject *Daubert* factors as the particular case demands."[95]

Although the judge evaluates the reliability of an expert's testimony, the gatekeeper role is not intended to replace the role of the jury. The "believ-ability or persuasiveness" of the testimony remains a matter for the trier of fact and the judge cannot exclude an expert because he or she believes one expert is more persuasive than another expert.[96] According to the Fifth Circuit, *Daubert* makes it clear that " '[v]igorous cross-examination, presentation of contrary evidence, and careful instruction on the burden of proof are the traditional and appropriate means of attacking shaky but admissible evidence.' "[97] Thus, in exercising its role as gatekeeper, a district court judge cannot transform a *Daubert* hearing into a trial on the merits.[98]

[b] Relevance

The second part of the *Daubert* test requires the district court judge to determine whether the proposed testimony is relevant to the issue in question. As stated in the Federal Rules of Evidence, relevant evidence "means evidence having any tendency to make the existence of any fact that is of consequence to the determination of the action more probable or less prob-

---

[89] Mitchell v. Gencorp, Inc., 165 F.3d 778, 781 (10th Cir. 1999).

[90] *Id.*

[91] Guy v. Crown Equipment, 394 F.3d 320 (5th Cir. 2004).

[92] Bitler v. A.O. Smith Corp., 400 F.3d 1227 (10th Cir. 2005).

[93] Pipitone v. Biomatrix, Inc., 288 F.3d 239 (5th Cir. 2002).

[94] Kumho Tire v. Carmichael, 526 U.S. 137, 152 (1999).

[95] *Id.* at 141. *See also Piptone*, 288 F.3d at 245 ("It is a fact-specific inquiry.").

[96] Rink v. Cheminova, Inc., 400 F.3d 1286, 1287 (11th Cir. 2005).

[97] *Pipitone*, 288 F.3d at 250.

[98] *Id.*

able than it would be without the evidence."[99] *Daubert* described the consideration of relevant evidence as one of "fit."[100] Thus, even if the expert's evidence satisfies the test for reliability, it may not have a sufficient bearing on the issue in the case to justify a determination that it has relevant "fit."[101] In addition, if an expert offers only an "equivocal opinion," and "does not make any fact more or less probable," the testimony will be held irrelevant and inadmissible.[102]

The district court judge's discretion as to relevance also applies to the admissibility of experimental tests as evidence in products liability cases.[103] When the science underlying an expert testimony is sound, the expert usually will not need testing to establish reliability under *Daubert*. However, if an expert proposes a theory that modifies well-established knowledge about regularly occurring phenomenon, the importance of testing in determining the reliability of the expert's testimony will "be at its highest."[104] A district court judge can exclude relevant evidence if its probative value is "substantially outweighed" by its likelihood to confuse the issue or mislead the jury.[105] This is an issue when a party introduces evidence that attempts to reconstruct an accident or evidence to show an example of the product. Courts will construe the evidence to determine if it is "sufficiently close in appearance to the original accident to create the risk of misunderstanding by the jury."[106] To avoid the exclusion of accident reconstruction evidence, the party may need to show a "substantial similarity in circumstances" between the reconstruction and the original accident.[107] In contrast, a party may introduce evidence that simply illustrates "general scientific principles" without a showing of substantial similarity in circumstances.[108] However, a court may admit an expert's experimental test into evidence to demonstrate an event could occur, if it is necessary as a basis for the expert's opinion that the event occurred during the accident.[109]

---

[99] FED. R. EVID. 401.

[100] Daubert v. Merrell Dow Pharmaceuticals, Inc., 509 U.S. 579, 591 (1993).

[101] Garlinger v. Hardee's Foodsystems, Inc., 2001 U.S. App. LEXIS 18559 (4th Cir. 2001).

[102] Pipitone, 288 F.3d at 245.

[103] McKnight v. Johnson Controls, Inc., 36 F.3d 1396 (8th Cir. 1994).

[104] Bitler v. A.O. Smith Corp., 400 F.3d 1227, 1235-1236 (10th Cir. 2004).

[105] *See* Fireman's Fund Ins. Co. v. Canon U.S.A., Inc., 394 F.3d 1054 (8th Cir. 2005); Jodoin v. Toyota Motor Corp., 284 F.3d 272 (1st Cir. 2002).

[106] Jodoin v. Toyota Motor Corp., 284 F.3d 272, 278-279 (1st Cir. 2002).

[107] *Id.* at 278.

[108] *Id.*

[109] Nemir v. Mitsubishi Motors Corp., 381 F.3d 540, 544 (6th Cir. 2004).

[6] Review of the District Court Decision

Under *Daubert*, evaluating the reliability and relevance of expert testimony is entrusted to the district court judge who has "wide discretion" both in deciding how to assess and determine an expert's reliability. An appellate court will give the district court judge "considerable leeway" in exercising its discretion.[110] An appellate court reviews *de novo* whether the district court judge properly admitted or excluded expert testimony,[111] and the standard of review is abuse of discretion.[112]

[C] *The Qualifications for an Expert*

In order to strengthen the credibility of some witnesses and to permit them to give opinion testimony about the cause of the injuries, plaintiffs and defendants in products liability actions seek to qualify them as *experts*.[113] Rule 702 of the Federal Rules of Evidence states that a witness may be "qualified as an expert" if the witness has "scientific, technical, or other specialized knowledge" that "will assist the trier of fact to understand the evidence or to determine a fact in issue."[114] This determination is made by the trial court judge after listening to the qualifications of the person and appellate courts will affirm the decision to admit or exclude expert testimony unless the decision was "manifestly erroneous."[115] State rules define the qualifications for an expert witness in much the same way as the Federal Rules of Evidence. For example, Illinois Supreme Court Rule 220 provides that

> an expert is a person who, because of education, training or experience, possesses knowledge of a specialized nature beyond that of the average person on a factual matter material to a claim or defense in pending litigation and who may be expected to render an opinion within his expertise at trial.

---

[110] Rink v. Cheminova, Inc., 400 F.3d 1286, 1291 (11th Cir. 2005). *See also* Norris v. Baxter Healthcare Corp., 397 F.3d 878, 883 (10th Cir 2005) ("we recognize the wide latitude a district court has in exercising its discretion to admit or exclude expert testimony.").

[111] Bitler v. A.O. Smith Corp., 400 F.3d 1227 (10th Cir. 2004).

[112] *Rink*, 400 F.3d at 1291 (*citing* Kumho Tire Co. v. Carmichael, 526 U.S. 137, 152 (1999).

[113] In selecting a person to testify as an expert, the attorneys for the plaintiff and the defendant want someone who has the time to devote to the case, with whom they are comfortable working, and who knows how to communicate with members of a jury in a language they can understand.

[114] FED. R. EVID. 702. This standard for admissibility is followed by the states as well. For an example, see Rule 702 of the Michigan Rules of Evidence. As a corollary, expert testimony will be excluded if it relates to an issue or fact that can be derived from common sense, common experience, the trier of fact's own perception, or simple logic. *See* Taylor v. Illinois Central R.R. Co., 8 F.3d 584 (7th Cir. 1993).

[115] General Electric Co. v. Joiner, 522 U.S. 136, 142 (1997).

Although there are no federal or state rules that explicitly require expert testimony, courts have stated that such testimony is required to assist the trier of fact when the issue "cannot be determined by common knowledge and experience."[116] Thus, expert testimony is necessary when the subject matter of an inquiry is such that only a person with particular skills or experience in the area is capable of forming an opinion. The test for the competency of an expert witness is whether the witness has the "special expertise" to entitle his or her opinion to go to a jury.[117] "Special expertise" is interpreted liberally and does not depend on the person being a member of a particular profession. Instead, courts look at a number of factors in assessing whether a person is qualified as an expert. These include not only the broad categories of education, training and experience, but also such factors as education in particular areas, attendance at related continuing education programs, teaching experience, publications and professional organization memberships. In *Calhoun v. Yamaha Motor Corp., U.S.A.*,[118] the plaintiff's fourteen-year-old daughter was killed while riding a jet ski manufactured by the defendant. The plaintiff, who alleged a design defect in the jet ski's accelerating mechanism, offered an expert to testify that the jet ski's accelerating mechanism was not as safe as other alternative designs. The expert was "a lieutenant for San Diego's Marine Safety Services for sixteen years," "had extensive experience with jet skis," and had conducted "aquatic related accident investigations."[119] The defendants sought to exclude the expert's testimony because he lacked "formal education or training in engineering...or human factors."[120] However, the Virginia court allowed his testimony about "how jet skis operate," the differences between defendant's jet ski and other brands and models, and how each type of "various accelerating mechanisms" works.[121]

Although background, education, and training usually qualify an expert as having general knowledge to testify about general matters, "specific knowledge" is required to support a specific opinion.[122] Thus, in *Calhoun*, the appellate court found that the expert had "no education or experience in product design of jet skis or accelerating mechanisms," and held that he "had neither the general background nor the specific knowledge to support his proffered testimony that the 'squeeze finger throttle' was less safe than other designs."[123] In addition, an expert witness cannot offer testimony on

---

[116] Wilson v. Stilwill, 309 N.W.2d 898, 907 (Mich. 1981).

[117] Callahan v. Commonwealth, 379 S.E.2d 476, 478 (Va. Ct. App. 1989).

[118] 350 F.3d 316 (3d Cir. 2003).

[119] *Id.* at 321.

[120] *Id.* at 323.

[121] *Id.*

[122] *Id.* at 322.

[123] *Id.* at 324.

matters "outside" his or her "area of expertise." In *Calhoun*, the plaintiff offered a second expert to testify that the jet ski's warnings were inadequate. The expert had "a bachelor's degree in naval architecture and marine engineering, as well as higher degrees in other fields," and had "worked with the Navy and the Department of Defense and served as an accident reconstruction consultant with a focus on marine engineering and boat accidents."[124] The court upheld the exclusion of the expert's testimony finding that, "in contrast to his background in naval architecture and marine engineering" which allowed him to testify generally about mechanical issues, "he possessed no expertise with regard to warning design."[125]

[D] *The Permissible Scope of Expert Testimony*

Once a witness is qualified as an expert, the final question for courts is: What is the permissible scope of the expert's testimony? Rule 702 of the Federal Rules of Evidence states that an expert may testify "in the form of an opinion or otherwise." Rule 704 gives broad scope to such testimony by stating that opinion testimony "otherwise admissible is not objectionable because it embraces an ultimate issue to be decided by the trier of fact." Thus, in addition to giving opinion testimony, an expert is given special latitude to testify based upon certain hearsay and third-party observations that normally would not be admissible.

§ 8.04 CAUSE-IN-FACT

[A] *Introduction*

A *prima facie* case of negligence or strict liability requires proof of more than the existence of a defect in the product. The plaintiff also must establish, with reasonable certainty, that the defect was, in fact, the cause of his or her injuries or damages.[126] While, in many cases, this is not difficult, with some products causation presents serious problems. For example, proving that a particular drug or chemical caused the plaintiff's injury requires expert medical testimony, while proving that a defect in a machine was the cause of the injuries may require engineering evidence. In reply, the manufacturer or seller will offer its own expert testimony and may argue that the injuries were caused by factors unrelated to the condition of the product. Normally, cause-in-fact is a question for the jury.[127] However, when

---

[124] *Id.*

[125] *Id.*

[126] For an analysis of the historical development causation, see *Union Pump Co. v. Allbritton*, 898 S.W.2d 773, 777-779 (Tex. 1995) (Cornyn, J., concurring opinion). Under § 15 of the RESTATEMENT (THIRD), "[w]hether a product defect caused harm to persons or property is determined by the prevailing rules and principles governing causation in tort."

[127] Reynolds v. Strauss Veal, Inc., 519 N.E.2d 226 (Ind. Ct. App. 1988).

the material facts are undisputed and there can be no difference in the judgment of reasonable persons as to the inferences to be drawn from them, cause-in-fact becomes a question of law and the court may grant summary judgment or direct a verdict for the plaintiff or the defendant.[128]

This section examines three issues that can arise in establishing the necessary causal connection between the product defect and the plaintiff's injuries: (1) What tests do the parties and courts use to prove causation? (2) How can the plaintiff establish causation if he or she does not know the identity of the manufacturer or seller of the product? (3) Can a plaintiff establish the necessary causal connection between the product and an injury that has not yet occurred?

[B] *"But For" and "Substantial Factor" Tests*

In order to determine whether a product was the cause-in-fact of the plaintiff's injury, courts use two tests: the *but for* test (sometimes referred to as a *sine qua non* test) and the substantial factor test. Under the *but for* test, "an act is a factual cause of an outcome if, in the absence of the act, the outcome would not have occurred."[129] Thus, the plaintiff must show that his or her injury would not have occurred without the defect in the product. An example of the use and effect of this test in a products liability case is *Gordon v. Goldman Brothers*,[130] Inc., in which a novice hiker was injured when he slipped on the side of a steep hill. The hiker brought suit against the manufacturer and retailer of the boots he was wearing at the time of the accident, alleging breach of warranty, negligence, and strict liability failure to warn. In dismissing the complaint, the New York court stated:

> Assuming that the boots in question were not designed for use on rocky or mountainous terrain, the circumstances of the accident do not on their face establish that the boots were in any way responsible for the fall. Noticeably missing from the plaintiffs' papers is any expert's affidavit or other evidence attesting to the fact that different boots might have prevented the accident.[131]

---

[128] See *Tiner v. General Motors Corp.*, 909 F. Supp. 112, 119 (N.D.N.Y. 1995) (applying New York law) in which the court granted summary judgment when the plaintiff "wholly failed to show her injuries were caused or enhanced by any defect in the air bag" in her automobile. *See also* Wright v. St. Mary's Medical Center of Evansville, Inc., 59 F. Supp. 2d 794 (S.D. Ind. 1999) (applying Indiana law).

[129] RESTATEMENT (THIRD) OF TORTS: PRODUCTS LIABILITY (Liability for Physical Harm) § 26 (2005). *See also* Rudeck v. Wright, 709 P.2d 621, 628 (Mont. 1985) ("The defendant's conduct is a cause of the event if the event would not have occurred but for that conduct; or conversely, the defendant's conduct is not a cause of the event, if the event would have occurred without it.") *and* John D. Rue, *Note: Returning to the Roots of the Bramble Bush: The "But For" Test Regains Primacy in Causal Analysis in the American Law Institute's Proposed Restatement (Third) of Torts*, 71 FORDHAM L. REV. 2679 (2003).

[130] 515 N.Y.S.2d 39 (N.Y. App. Div. 1987).

[131] *Id.* at 40.

While the *but for* test can be used in many cases to determine what, in fact, has occurred, the idea of a single cause of an injury is not appropriate in the complex society of the 21st century. Instead, an injury is more likely to have multiple or concurring causes. Application of the *but for* test in such a case relieves both tortfeasors of liability on the ground that *but for* the conduct of one, the incident would still have occurred.[132] For these reasons, most states now accept the definition of causal connection set out in § 431 of the Restatement (Second) of Torts: "The actor's negligent conduct is a legal cause of harm to another if (a) his conduct is a substantial factor in brining about the harm . . ."[133] According to one court, the phrase "substantial factor" "denotes that the defendant's conduct has such an effect in producing the harm as to lead the trier of fact, as a reasonable person, to regard it as a cause, using that word in the popular sense."[134] The substantial factor test has been criticized as not going far enough and as being too general. However, courts and commentators appear convinced that "substantial factor" is a phrase sufficiently intelligible to furnish an adequate guide in instructions to juries and that it is neither possible nor desirable to reduce it to any more specific terms.[135]

In most products liability cases, the issues faced by plaintiffs and defendants in proving and disproving factual causation are no different from those in other torts cases. Plaintiffs and defendants will rely on expert witnesses and any questions of causation will turn on the admissibility and believability of their testimony. However, in cases involving drugs and medical devices,[136] some states require plaintiffs to prove two forms of causation: general causation and specific causation.[137] What is required to prove general and specific causation in medical cases is illustrated by *Norris v. Baxter Heathcare Corp.*,[138] in which the plaintiff alleged that she suffered a systemic disease that was caused by a silicone gel breast implant. In upholding the grant of summary judgment in favor of the manufacturer of the implant, the Tenth Circuit stated that, in silicone breast implant litigation, a plaintiff must show both general and specific causation. "Gen-

---

[132] Rutherford v. Owens-Illinois, Inc., 941 P.2d 1203 (Cal. 1997).

[133] *See, e.g.,* Donaldson v. Central Illinois Public Service Corp., 767 N.E.2d 314 (Ill. 2002); Bockrath v. Aldrich Chemical Corp., 980 P.2d 398 (Cal. 1999); Union Pump Co. v. Allbritton, 898 S.W.2d 773 (Tex. 1995).

[134] Clark v. Leisure Vehicles, Inc., 292 N.W.2d 630, 635 (Wis. 1980).

[135] Bidar v. Amfac, Inc., 669 P.2d 154 (Haw. 1983).

[136] Easter v. Aventis Pasteur, Inc., 358 F. Supp. 574 (E.D. Tex. 2005) (applying Texas law).

[137] *See* REFERENCE MANUAL ON SCIENTIFIC EVIDENCE 336 (Federal Judicial Center 2d ed. 2000). According to the Kansas Supreme Court, proof of general causation ordinarily is required only in mass tort litigation with large existing epidemiological records. *See* Kuhn v. Sandoz Pharmaceuticals, Corp., 14 P.3d 1170 (Kan. 2000). However, in *Donaldson v. Central Illinois Public Service Corp.*, 767 N.E.2d 314 (Ill. 2002), the Illinois Supreme Court stated that Illinois law does not define causation in terms of "generic" or "specific" causation. Instead, a plaintiff must prove "cause in fact" and "legal cause."

[138] 397 F.3d 878 (10th Cir. 2005) (applying Colorado law).

eral causation" requires proof that the product is capable of causing a particular injury, disease, or condition in the general population. "Specific causation" focuses on whether the substance caused the particular plaintiff's injury. To establish specific causation in a case involving drugs, the plaintiff must present expert testimony showing "a specific train of medical evidence connecting the illness to the product."[139] One method of determining specific causation is differential diagnosis, a process whereby doctors experienced in diagnostic techniques provide testimony, after physical examinations, taking medical histories, and reviewing clinical and laboratory tests, countering other possible causes.[140] Since the plaintiff in *Norris* presented no epidemiological evidence of any causal connection between silicone breasts implants and systemic disease, the court held that the product could not have caused the plaintiff's injuries.[141]

Proof of general and specific causation also may be required in cases not involving drugs or medical devices.[142] In *McCoy v. Whirlpool Corp.*,[143] the plaintiffs brought a strict liability suit alleging manufacturing defects against the manufacturer of a dishwasher which caught on fire, destroying their home and killing their daughter. The district court judge held that, on the issue of general causation, the plaintiffs were required to show that a manufacturing defect that caused excessive resistance heating in the door latch switch assembly was a scientifically plausible cause of a fire in the brand of dishwasher they had purchased. On the issue of specific causation, the plaintiffs had to show that excessive resistance heating due to one of the two alleged defects in their machine raised the temperature high enough to cause the specific fire. Since the plaintiffs did not present sufficient evidence of general causation, the district court judge granted the manufacturer's motion for judgment as a matter of law.

[C] *Establishing the Identity of the Manufacturer*

In addition to proving that the defective product was the cause-in-fact of the injuries, the plaintiff also must establish that the defendant was the manufacturer or supplier of that product. It is not sufficient to identify a defendant as one of several manufacturers or suppliers of the product that caused the injury. In order to establish the necessary causal connection between the defendant and the injury, the plaintiff must establish that the defendant, in fact, manufactured or supplied the defective product.[144] The

---

[139] Newton v. Roche Laboratories, Inc., 243 F. Supp.2d 672, 682 (W.D. Tex. 2002).

[140] *See* Westberry v. Gislaved Gummi AB, 178 F.3d 257 (4th Cir. 1999); Hines v. Conrail, 926 F.2d 262 (3d Cir. 1991).

[141] 397 F.3d at 881.

[142] Smith v. General Motors Corp., 376 F. Supp. 2d 664 (W.D. Va. 2005) (seatbelt).

[143] 379 F. Supp. 2d 1187 (D. Kan. 2005) (applying Kansas law).

[144] Mulcahy v. Eli Lilly & Co., 386 N.W.2d 67, 76 (Iowa 1986).

failure to do so will result in summary judgment for the defendant.[145] An example of the problems a plaintiff can face in identifying the manufacturer of an allegedly defective product, particularly if there has been a long delay between the date of the accident and the date of filing suit, is *Moore v. Mississippi Valley Gas Co.*,[146] in which the plaintiff's daughter was burned badly when she fell into a bathtub full of hot water in 1989. By the time the plaintiff filed suit against the defendant/manufacturer of water heaters in 1996, her landlord had replaced and discarded the one involved in the accident. There were no witnesses who could identify the make, model, or manufacturer of the allegedly defective hot water heater. The only evidence of any involvement by the defendant/manufacturer was a sales invoice stating that Cornelius Williams, who had lived at the address of the accident, had purchased a 40-gallon hot water heater, Serial # 0181M17815 in 1981. However, the receipt did not indicate at what address that hot water heater was installed. Williams had since died and the company that installed the hot water heater no longer existed. Since the defendant/manufacturer did not have the opportunity to identify, inspect, or test the water heater involved in the accident, no one was certain whether the 1981 hot water heater was the defendant's. Thus, the Mississippi court refused to leave the issue to the jury's speculation or conjecture and granted summary judgment.

In *Moore* part of the problem was that the plaintiff waited seven years to bring her claim, even though she was aware of her daughter's injury and the cause of it. However, in cases involving products such as drugs, asbestos, or lead paint, the plaintiff may not know that he or she has a claim because the harmful effects may not become evident for decades. An example of this were the DES cases where the plaintiffs were the daughters of women who took the drug in the early 1950s. At the time, DES was a generic drug and a large number of manufacturers had produced the drug. By the time the plaintiffs brought their suits in the 1970s, the specific manufacturers of the DES taken by their mothers often were unknown or had gone out of business, making it impossible for the plaintiffs to identify their manufacturer of the DES taken by their mothers during their pregnancies more than two decades earlier. In *Sindell v. Abbott Laboratories*,[147] the California Supreme Court developed a new approach to the problem by basing liability on a market share theory that apportions liability among the defendant manufacturers of a fungible product based on their respective shares of the relevant market, unless a particular defendant can prove that it did not manufacture the product that caused the plaintiff's injuries.[148] In order to establish market share liability under *Sindell*, a plaintiff must show: (1) the

---

[145] Brown v. Stone Manufacturing Co., 660 F. Supp. 454, 458 (S.D.Miss. 1986).

[146] 863 S.2d 43 (Miss. 2003).

[147] 607 P.2d 924 (Cal. 1980).

[148] *Id.* at 937.

injury causing product is fungible; (2) the inability to identify the manufacturer is not due to the plaintiff's own action or inaction; and (3) the plaintiff has joined the manufacturers of a "substantial share" of the product market. Although market-share liability initially attracted wide-spread attention, the majority of courts now have rejected it.[149] In *Smith v. Eli Lilly & Co.*,[150] the Illinois Supreme Court referred to market share liability as a "radical departure" from the traditional tort principle of causation.[151] The Restatement (Third) lists the cases and articles on both sides of the question.[152]

In recent years, a new series of cases involving lead paint have raised the same issue as in the DES cases: the inability of the plaintiffs, due to no fault of their own, to identify the manufacturer of the paint in their building. As in the post-*Sindell* DES cases, most courts have rejected the use of the market share liability theory to establish causation.[153] However, in a controversial decision, the Wisconsin Supreme Court, in *Thomas v. Mallett*,[154] extended the risk-contribution theory it adopted for DES cases[155] to a minor who suffered lead poisoning as a result of ingesting lead-based paint from homes in which he lived but was unable to identify the precise producer of the white lead carbonate pigment he ingested because of its generic nature.

[D] *Exposure to Risk of Future Injury*

The challenge for plaintiffs in most products liability cases is to draw the necessary causal connection between the defective product and their existing injuries. However, in some cases, plaintiffs allege that, although the product has not caused them any present injury, it has created an increased risk for harm in the future. Claims alleging an increased risk of future harm usually result from the use or exposure to one of three types of prod-

---

[149] *See, e.g.,* Sutowski v. Eli Lilly & Co., 696 N.E.2d 187 (Ohio 1998); Shackil v. Lederle Laboratories, 561 A.2d 511 (N.J. 1989). For courts that have accepted market share liability, see *Hymowitz v. Eli Lilly & Co.*, 539 N.E.2d 1069 (N.Y. 1989); *Collins v. Eli Lilly Co.*, 342 N.W.2d 37 (Wis. 1984); *Martin v. Abbott Laboratories*, 689 P.2d 368 (Wash. 1984).

[150] 560 N.E.2d 324 (Ill. 1990).

[151] *Id.* at 334.

[152] RESTATEMENT (THIRD) OF TORTS: PRODUCTS LIABILITY § 15 cmt. c (1998).

[153] *See, e.g.,* Santiago v. Sherwin Williams Co., 3 F.3d 546 (1st Cir.1993); Jefferson v. Lead Paint Industries, 930 F. Supp. 241 (E.D. La. 1996) (applying Louisiana law); Abbasi v. Paraskevoulakos, 718 N.E.2d 181 (Ill. 1999); Brenner v. American Cyanamid Co., 699 N.Y.S.2d 848 (N.Y. App. Div. 1999).

[154] 701 N.W.2d 523 (Wis. 2005).

[155] Collins v. Eli Lilly Co., 342 N.W.2d 37 (Wis. 1984).

ucts: asbestos,[156] drugs,[157] and medical devices.[158] In these cases, plaintiffs often make three allegations in their complaints: (1) the product was defective and unreasonably dangerous; (2) the product places the plaintiff at a substantially greater risk of a specific future harm; and (3) the increased risk of future harm requires current and future medical testing and monitoring.[159]

Plaintiffs in increased risk of future harm cases must present evidence that establishes, with "reasonable probability," that the product increased the risk of a specific future medical problem.[160] An example of the issues involved in these cases is *Mauro v. Raymark Industries, Inc.*,[161] in which the plaintiff worked as a repairman and plumber-steamfitter from 1964 until the mid-to-late 1970s. In 1981 the plaintiff discovered, as the result of a physical examination, that, although his lungs were "normal" at the time, his exposure to asbestos during his employment might increase his risk of developing lung cancer. That was because he had bilateral thickening of both chest walls and calcification of the diaphragm.[162] In the plaintiff's action against the manufacturer of the asbestos, the trial court judge charged the jury that it could award the plaintiff damages for his present medical condition, the cost of medical surveillance, and for his emotional distress. Proof of an increased risk of cancer requires expert testimony and, in *Mauro*, the plaintiff's expert testified that there was a "high probability" that the plaintiff had "an increased risk" of contracting cancer during his lifetime.[163] However, the expert was unable to testify that it was "probable" that plaintiff would contract cancer, and the statistical studies the expert wanted to use to show a correlation between asbestos-related disease and cancer were excluded because they were not referred to during discovery or in the witnesses expert report. Since there was no evidence in the record of the likelihood that plaintiff would contract cancer, the judge refused to submit the increased risk claim to the jury.[164] The New Jersey Supreme Court affirmed the trial court's decision, stating that "prospective damages are not recoverable unless they are reasonably probable to occur."[165]

---

[156] Herber v. Johns-Manville Corp., 785 F.2d 79 (3d Cir. 1986); Mauro v. Raymark Industries, Inc., 561 A.2d 257 (N.J. 1989).

[157] In re Propulsid Products Liability Litigation, 208 F.R.D. 133 (E.D. La. 2002).

[158] Sutton v. St. Jude Medical S.C., Inc., 2005 U.S. App. LEXIS 18013 (6th Cir. 2005) (applying Tennessee law); In re St. Jude Med., Inc. Silzone Heart Valves Products Liability Litigation, 2004 U.S. Dist. LEXIS 13965 (D. Minn. 2004).

[159] Sutton, Inc., 2005 U.S. App. LEXIS 18013 at *7.

[160] *See* Coll v. Sherry, 148 A.2d 481, 486 (N.J. 1959).

[161] 561 A.2d 257 (N.J. 1989).

[162] *Id*. at 258.

[163] *Id*.

[164] *Id*. at 259–260.

[165] *Id*. at 261.

Mauro followed the approach taken by the majority of courts that requires the plaintiff to prove the increased risk of future harm as a reasonable medical probability. One way of establishing this is with statistical studies evidence comparing the plaintiff's future risk of the specific harm with those who were not exposed to the product.[166] However, many commentators have urged recognition of a cause of action for an enhanced risk of future harm where the risk is less than probable. In *Mauro*, the New Jersey Supreme Court reviewed a number of the articles taking that position[167] as well as the arguments in favor of and opposed to recognizing enhanced-risk damages.[168] Although not a products liability case, the Illinois Supreme Court, in *Dillon v. Evanston Hospital*,[169] came down on the side of those who argue that the reasonable probability standard is too stringent when it held that a plaintiff can recover for an increased risk of future harm, even if the injury is improbable. However, the amount of damages must reflect the probability of the occurrence of the future injury.

Plaintiffs in increased risk cases may seek two types of damages. As in the *Dillon* case, they may treat the anticipated harm as the injury and seek damages based on the statistical probability of the harm occurring in the future. In *Herber v. Johns-Manville Corp.*,[170] a case also involving an increased risk of cancer as the result of exposure to asbestos in the workplace, the plaintiff argued that the increase in risk was an element of the damage he already had suffered and should be considered in the calculation of his damage award. According to the plaintiff, he should receive an amount equal to the amount that a person having an asbestos-caused cancer would receive, reduced proportionately to reflect the probability that he would not develop cancer.[171] However, even with expert testimony such a determination is very speculative. Thus, in addition, or in the alternative, plaintiffs may view their injury as the cost of future periodic medical testing and monitoring in order to detect the future physical harm.[172] In order to recover

---

[166] In *Sutton v. St. Jude Medical S.C., Inc.*, 2005 U.S. App. LEXIS 18013 (6th Cir. 2005), the plaintiff alleged an increased risk of harm from a medical device inserted in his chest after bypass surgery when compared with persons who underwent traditional surgery. The Sixth Circuit accepted the allegation as true and remanded the case.

[167] *Id.* at 264–267.

[168] *Id.* at 266.

[169] 771 N.E.2d 357 (Ill. 2002).

[170] 785 F.2d 79 (3d Cir. 1986) (applying New Jersey law).

[171] *Id.* at 82. The Third Circuit in *Herber* refused to permit the plaintiff to litigate the issue of increased risk on the ground that he did not present evidence of the required medical probability of future cancer.

[172] *See* Friends for All Children Inc. v. Lockheed Aircraft Corp., 746 F.2d 816 (D.C. Cir. 1984). However, in *Metro-North Commuter Railroad v. Buckley*, 521 U.S. 424 (1997), the Supreme Court held that a plaintiff can not recover costs for medical monitoring in a Federal Employers' Liability Act case on the basis that there was a lack of support in the common law. For a discussion of medical monitoring in products liability cases, see *Sutton v. St. Jude Medical S.C., Inc.*, 2005 U.S. App. LEXIS 18013, at *9–*22 (6th Cir. 2005).

these costs, plaintiffs must establish a number of elements: (1) exposure to a defective product; (2) creating a significantly increased risk of future harm; (3) an existing monitoring procedure that makes detection of the future harm possible; (4) the monitoring procedure is different from the normally recommended procedure in the absence of the exposure; (5) the monitoring is reasonably necessary in light of current scientific principles.[173] Recovery for medical monitoring for future harm is recognized by a number of states.[174] One state that is opposed to medical monitoring is Louisiana which has enacted a statute preventing plaintiffs from recovering such damages. According to the statute: "Damages do not include costs for future medical treatment, services, surveillance, or procedures of any kind unless such treatment, services, surveillance, or procedures are directly related to a manifest physical or mental injury or disease."[175]

§ 8.05 PROXIMATE CAUSE

[A] *Introduction*

Proof that the defendant's product was defective and the cause-in-fact of the plaintiff's injury does not mean necessarily that the defendant will be held liable for the plaintiff's injuries. As in other areas of tort law, it still is necessary to establish that the product was the "proximate cause" or "legal cause" of the injuries.[176] A plaintiff must establish proximate cause in all products liability actions: negligence, strict liability,[177] and misrepresentation.[178] Proximate cause is not an issue of "causation" since there is no question that the product, in fact, caused the plaintiff's injuries. Instead, proximate cause is a policy question: How far should the legal responsibility of a manufacturer or seller extend for a defective product that, in fact, has caused harm?[179] The answer to this question is one of the most debated in tort law and, over the years, has produced a number of different

---

[173] *See* Redland Soccer Club v. Department of the Army, 696 A.2d 137, 145–146 (Pa. 1997).

[174] *See* Barnes v. American Tobacco Co., 161 F.3d 127, 139 n. 11 (3d Cir. 1998); Gibbs v. E.I. DuPont De Nemours & Co., 876 F. Supp. 475 (W.D.N.Y. 1995).

[175] LA. CIV. CODE. ANN. art. 2315 (2003).

[176] *See* Schultz v. Hennessy Indus., Inc., 584 N.E.2d 235 (Ill. App. Ct. 1991).

[177] *See* Price v. Blaine Kern Artista, Inc., 893 P.2d 367 (Nev. 1995).

[178] *See* Hollenbeck v. Selectone Corp., 476 N.E.2d 746 (Ill. App. Ct. 1985).

[179] In *Caputzal v. Lindsay Co.*, 222 A.2d 513, 517 (N.J. 1966), the New Jersey Supreme Court said that the answer to the question was based "upon mixed considerations of logic, common sense, justice, policy and precedent." *See* E.J. Stewart, Inc. v. Aitken Products, Inc., 607 F. Supp. 883 (E.D. Pa. 1985) (applying Pennsylvania law); Lear Siegler, Inc. v. Perez, 819 S.W.2d 470 (Tex. 1991); Anderson v. Dreis & Krump Manufacturing Corp., 739 P.2d 1177 (Wash. Ct. App.,1987). For an overview of proximate cause, see *Symposium: Legal Cause: Cause-in-Fact and the Scope of Liability for Consequences*, 54 VAND. L. REV. 941 (2001).

approaches. Most courts now hold that a defect in a product was the proximate cause of the plaintiff's injuries if the cause was "foreseeable in light of the attending circumstances" and was "the natural and probable consequence" of the defective product.[180] Foreseeability does not require that the manufacturer or seller should have foreseen the precise risk or exact result that occurred. Instead, the essential factor is that the defendant should have anticipated the general kind of consequences that occurred.[181] Similarly, whether the injury was the "natural and probable consequence" of a defect in the product requires consideration of any intervening or superceding causes such an product misuse or alteration and whether those causes were foreseeable.[182] The effect of proximate cause is to limit the responsibility of a manufacturer or seller for the consequences of defective products and prevent strict liability from becoming absolute liability.[183] This section examines three tests courts have used to determine how far legal responsibility should extend.

[B] *Foreseeability*

Foreseeability is the most often cited factor in determining proximate cause. Issues of foreseeability arise in a variety of contexts: foreseeability of the plaintiff; foreseeability of the use of the product; foreseeability of the harm; and foreseeability of intervening factors. For example, because of the abolition of privity in negligence and strict liability actions, the liability of a manufacturer or seller extends not only to users and consumers of the product[184] but also to foreseeable bystanders injured by a product.[185] However, even if the manufacturer owed a duty to the plaintiff, the manufacturer or seller may allege that it is not legally responsible for the plaintiff's particular injury because it was the result of a use of the product that was not foreseeable. Courts speak of a manufacturer having a duty to produce products that are safe when used for their "intended purpose"[186] or

---

[180] White v. Ford Motor Co., 312 F.3d 998, 1006 (9th Cir. 2002) (applying California law). *See also* Wright v. Abbott Labs., Inc., 259 F.3d 1226 (10th Cir 2001) (applying Kansas law); DiCarlo v. Keller Ladders, Inc., 211 F.3d 465 (8th Cir. 2000) (applying Missouri law).

[181] Petition of Kinsman Transit Co., 338 F.2d 708 (2d Cir. 1964); Timmons v. Ford Motor Co., 982 F. Supp. 1475 (S.D. Ga. 1997) (applying Georgia law).

[182] Buckley v. Bell, 703 P.2d 1089 (Wyo. 1985); Lopez v. Entwistle Co., 520 A.2d 849 (N.J. Super Ct. 1986).

[183] Helene Curtis Industries, Inc. v. Pruitt, 385 F.2d 841 (5th Cir. 1967).

[184] In duty to warn cases, for example, courts state that the warning must be sufficient to adequately protect all foreseeable users of the product from any hidden dangers presented by it. *See* Whitehead v. St. Joe Lead Co., 729 F.2d 238 (3rd 1984); Freas v. Prater Construction Corp., 573 N.E.2d 27 (Ohio 1991).

[185] Peck v. Ford Motor Co., 603 F.2d 1240 (7th Cir. 1979) (applying Indiana law); Rivers v. Great Dane Trailers, Inc., 816 F. Supp. 1525 (M.D. Ala. 1993) (applying Florida law).

[186] Port Authority of New York and New Jersey v. Arcadian Corp., 189 F.3d 305 (3d Cir. 1999) (applying New Jersey law). *But see* Winnett v. Winnett, 310 N.E.2d 1 (Ill. 1974) (the scope of a farm forage wagon's intended use did not include its use by a four-year-old child).

for a "reasonably foreseeable purpose."[187] However, the "intended" or "foreseeable" use of a product depends upon the specific facts and circumstance of each case. Statements by courts as to what was the "intended purpose" or a "reasonably foreseeable purpose" of a product was in previous cases is of little help in predicting what courts will do in the future.

Because foreseeability is fact specific, it is only possible to provide an example of facts that have led a court to conclude that the use of a product was foreseeable. An illustration of the extent of the foreseeable intended use of a product is *Ayers v. Johnson & Johnson Baby Products Co.*,[188] in which the parents of a 15-month-old baby brought a product liability action against the manufacturer of baby oil after the baby swallowed the oil and suffered brain damage aspiration. The parents alleged that if they had known of the risks of the product, they would have treated it more carefully.[189] The Washington Supreme Court concluded the parents had presented sufficient evidence of causation and inadequacy of warnings on the bottle of baby oil to support the jury's verdict in their favor. The evidence included testimony from the mother that "she made a practice of reading labels on products" and shelved dangerous products high out of the reach of her 15-month-old twins. The mother also testified that, besides placing dangerous products out of reach, she specifically told her teenage daughters to keep their purses away from the twins if their purses contained anything that could harm a baby.[190] The court held that the jury was entitled to infer that, if the parents had known of the dangers of aspiration, they would have treated the baby oil with the same caution they used with other items they recognized as highly dangerous, and that "had they done so, the accident would never have occurred," concluding that the evidence of causation presented to the jury was sufficient to sustain the jury's verdict.[191] According to the court:

> What makes baby oil unique, and what is the *sine qua non* of our decision, is that baby oil is intended for use *on babies*. When he drank the oil, David Ayers was acting in conformity with the behavior to be expected of any 15-month-old child. It is this kind of predictable infant behavior which necessitates that consumers and parents be alerted to the dangers of a product promoted for use on babies.[192]

The misuse of a product also may be the proximate cause of an injury if it was reasonably foreseeable.[193] As with other aspects of foreseeability,

---

[187] Frey v. Montgomery Ward & Co., 258 N.W.2d 782, 788 (Minn. 1977).

[188] 818 P.2d 1337 (Wash. 1991).

[189] *Id.* at 1341.

[190] *Id.* at 1340–1341.

[191] *Id.* at 1341.

[192] *Id.* at 1343.

[193] Morales v. American Honda Motor Co., 71 F.3d 531 (6th Cir. 1995); Belleville v. Rockford Mfg. Group, Inc., 172 F. Supp. 2d 913 (E.D. Mich. 2001); Palmer v. Avco Distributing Corp., 412 N.E.2d 959 (Ill. 1980).

whether the misuse of a product was foreseeable is fact specific and, as a result, generally is a matter for the jury to decide,[194] unless there is no evidence from which a jury reasonably could find the required causal connection between the use or the misuse of the product and the resulting injuries. An example both of the misuse of a product and a situation where that misuse was so unforeseeable that the court did not leave the issue to the jury is *Port Authority of New York and New Jersey v. Arcadian Corp.*,[195] in which the plaintiff sued the manufacturers of ammonium nitrate used by terrorists to make the explosive device used in the bombing of the World Trade Center in February, 1993. The plaintiff brought the action in negligence and strict liability alleging that the product was defective because of the failure to add anti-explosive properties to it. The district court granted the manufacturers' motion to dismiss under Rule 12(b)(6) of the Federal Rule of Civil Procedure, holding that the misuse of the fertilizer for use in the bomb was not foreseeable. The fact that the manufacturers knew of the possibility that fertilizer products could be or had been used as components in bombs did not save the claim since it showed only "subjective foreseeability." According to the court, what was required was an "objective foreseeability determination."

> No jury reasonably could conclude that one accidental explosion 50 years ago, one terrorist act in this country almost 30 years ago, and scattered terrorists incidents throughout the world over the course of the last 30 years would make an incident like the World Trade Center bombing anything more than a remote or theoretical possibility.[196]

Proximate cause extends not only to the foreseeable uses of a product but also to the foreseeable risks of harm from those uses. However, because the foreseeable use of a product and the foreseeable harm resulting from that use are closely tied, the Oregon Supreme Court, in *Newman v. Utility Trailer & Equipment Co., Inc.*,[197] used two hypotheticals involving a shovel to illustrate difference between the two. In the first hypothetical, a person used a shovel to prop open a heavy door. Because of the way the shovel was designed, it was not capable of holding the door open and it slammed shut, crushing the person's hand. The court said the manufacturer of the shovel would not be liable for the person's injury since it was not reasonably foreseeable that the shovel would be used in that manner. In the second hypothetical, the shovel was used to dig a ditch, and, while it was being used for that purpose, the blade struck a rock in the soil and a piece of steel from the

---

[194] Sanders v. Lull International, Inc., 411 F.3d 1266 (11th Cir. 2005) (applying Florida law); Heatherly v. Alexander, 421 F.3d 638 (8th Cir. 2005) (applying Nebraska law).

[195] 991 F. Supp. 390 (D.N.J. 1997) (applying New Jersey law), *aff'd* 189 F.3d 305 (3rd Cir. 1999) (applying New Jersey law).

[196] *Id.* at 402–403.

[197] 564 P.2d 674 (Or. 1977).

blade flew up and injured user's eye. In that situation, the manufacturer or seller would be assumed to have had knowledge of the risk of injury to the user caused by the use of the shovel. Since the shovel was being used for a purpose for which it was manufactured, the liability of the manufacturer would extend to the harm that a reasonable manufacturer knew or should have known was presented by the shovel.[198] That knowledge is assumed regardless of whether the particular manufacturer actually "foresaw or reasonably should have foreseen the danger."[199] It also is immaterial that the manufacturer could not foresee the precise manner or anticipate the particular chain of events that resulted in plaintiff's injury.[200] The plaintiff would be entitled to recover for the harm actually suffered, even though the extent of the injuries were more severe than manufacturer could have foreseen and even if the injuries were aggravated by plaintiff's "predisposition or weakness."[201]

[C] *Natural and Probable Consequences*

In approaching proximate cause, the focus is on the effect of the defect on the circumstances surrounding the accident. The question is whether the plaintiff's injury was a "natural and probable consequence" of the defect in the design or manufacture of the product or the failure to warn about the dangers associated with the use of the product. This becomes an issue when, after a product has left the control of the manufacturer or seller, an intervening act results in an injury to the plaintiff.[202] In order for the intervening act to break the causal connection, the intervening act must have been independent of the defective product, adequate by itself to cause the plaintiff's injury, and not reasonably foreseeable by the manufacturer.[203] In other words, the intervening act must become the superceding cause by being the new proximate cause of the injury.[204]

An intervening cause may result from actions of the plaintiff or a third party. Although an intervening act will not become a superceding cause if it was foreseeable,[205] it is not necessary that the precise injury was foresee-

---

[198] Id. at 675–676.

[199] *Id.* at 677. *See also* Green v. Smith & Nephew AHP, Inc., 629 N.W.2d 727 (Wis. 2001).

[200] Katz v. Swift & Co. 276 F.2d 905 (2d Cir 1960) (applying New York law); Stazenski v. Tennant Co., 617 So.2d 344 (Fla. App. Ct. 1993); Greenfield v. Suzuki Motor Co. Ltd. 776 F.Supp. 698 (E.D.N.Y.1991); Anderson v. Dreis & Krump Mfg. Corp., 739 P.2d 1177 (Wash. Ct. App. 1987).

[201] Poplar v. Bourjois, Inc., 80 N.E.2d 334, 337 (N.Y. 1948).

[202] Wallace v. Owens-Illinois, Inc., 389 S.E.2d 155 (S.C. Ct. App. 1989); Dugan by Dugan v. Sears, Roebuck & Co., 454 N.E.2d 64 (Ill. App. Ct. 1983).

[203] Hurt v. Coyne Cylinder Co., 956 F.2d 1319 (6th Cir. 1992) (applying Tennessee law); Kuras v. International Harvester Co., 820 F.2d 15 (1st Cir. 1987) (applying Rhode Island law); Tapp v. Blackmore Ranch, Inc., 575 N.W.2d 341 (Neb. 1998).

[204] Rossell v. Volkswagen of America, 709 P.2d 517 (Ariz. 1985).

[205] Woodling v. Garrett Corp., 813 F.2d 543 (2d Cir. 1987) (applying New York law).

able.[206] In *Wallace v. Owens-Illinois, Inc.*,[207] the intervening cause of the injury was the plaintiff's actions. In that case, the plaintiff was opening a glass soft drink bottle in his kitchen when it exploded because of a defect in its manufacture. Pieces of glass and the liquid contents of the bottle fell on the floor. However, the explosion did not injure the plaintiff. He left the kitchen and returned about five minutes later to clean up the floor. In the course of cleaning up, the plaintiff got liquid on the smooth leather soles of his bedroom slippers, which caused him to slip, fall and suffer bodily injuries. The South Carolina appellate court held that the plaintiff's intervening actions did not break the chain of causation and become a superceding cause. Instead, the explosion created a hazardous condition on the kitchen floor and the plaintiff's attempt to clean up the spill was a normal and foreseeable response to the situation. The fact that his actions may have been negligent did not eliminate the defendants' liability since the plaintiff's negligence is not a question of proximate causation but of contributory negligence.[208]

The same approach is taken by courts if the intervening cause was the act of a third party. In *Price v. Blaine Kern Artista, Inc.*,[209] the plaintiff was an entertainer who wore a caricature mask of George Bush manufactured by the defendant covering his entire head. He alleged he was injured when a patron pushed him causing the weight of the mask to injure his neck as he fell to the ground. The plaintiff claimed the mask was defective due to the absence of a safety harness to support his head and neck. The manufacturer argued that the act of the patron in pushing the plaintiff was an intervening, superceding cause of the injuries. However, the Nevada Supreme Court said that the risk of the fall and the resulting strain on the plaintiff's head and neck were within the realm of risks that should have been considered and addressed by the manufacturer in the design of the product. Thus, the initial cause of the plaintiff's fall was not important, considering that it was foreseeable that, among the users of the defendant's products, some would fall for a variety of reasons.[210]

Manufacturers often allege that the alteration of the product by the plaintiff or a third party constituted an superceding cause of the injury. As with other types of intervening acts, an alteration of product that was reasonably foreseeable by the manufacturer is not a superseding cause.[211] However, an alteration of a product that reasonably could not have been

---

[206] Achin v. Begg Tire Center, 694 F.2d 226 (10th Cir. 1982) (applying New Mexico law).

[207] 389 S.E.2d 155 (S.C. Ct. App. 1989).

[208] *Id.* at 157 (It is not the "quality" of plaintiff's actions but their foreseeability that determines proximate cause. The test is the probable consequences reasonably to be anticipated, not "character" of subsequent or intervening events.).

[209] 893 P.2d 367 (Nev. 1995).

[210] *Id.* at 370. *See also* Anderson v. Dreis & Krump Mfg. Corp., 739 P.2d 1177, 1186 (Wash. Ct. App. 1987).

[211] *Anderson*, 739 P.2d at 1184.

anticipated is a superseding cause.[212] An example of a product alteration that was an intervening act is *Rios v. Niagara Machine & Tool Works*,[213] in which a punch press was manufactured without any safety devices. After purchasing the machine, the plaintiff's employer installed a safety device that failed, resulting in the plaintiff's injury. The Illinois Supreme Court held that whatever unreasonably dangerous condition existed when the punch press left the manufacturer's control was corrected by the employer's alteration.[214] Thus, in determining whether the alteration was sufficient to relieve the manufacturer of liability, the focus is on whether the plaintiff's injury was caused by a defective condition in the original product or by an unforeseeable subsequent alteration.[215]

[D] *Cause vs. Condition*

Another method of determining the scope of a manufacturer's liability is based on a distinction between the *cause* of the injury and a *condition* that permitted the injury to occur. The *cause* of an injury is that which actually produced it. However, if the defect in the product simply created a condition by which an injury was made possible by some subsequent, independent act of a third party, the creation of the condition was not a proximate cause of the injury.[216] According to one court:

> A circumstance is a condition if the forces set in operation by the defendant have come to rest in a position of apparent safety and some new force intervenes. . . .Relevant factors include the kind of hazard that was created, its gravity, its relation in time and space to the injury, and whether the defendant could reasonably foresee that an injury would be a likely result of his conduct.[217]

Two cases illustrate the use of the cause/condition distinction to hold that a defect in a product was not the proximate cause of the plaintiff's injuries. In *Union Pump Co. v. Allbritton*,[218] the defendant's pump caught fire and, two hours after the fire was extinguished, the plaintiff was injured walking across a pipe rack wet with water and foam from the fire. The Texas Supreme Court held that the pump fire did no more than create the condition that made the plaintiff's injuries possible. The court concluded

---

[212] Hood v. Ryobi America Corp., 181 F.3d 608 (4th Cir. 1999) (applying Maryland law); McDaniel v. French Oil Mill Machine Co., 632 So. 2d 1146 (Ala. 1993).

[213] 319 N.E.2d 232 (Ill. 1974).

[214] *Id.* at 236.

[215] Medina v. Air-Mite Devices, Inc., 515 N.E.2d 770 (Ill. App. Ct. 1987).

[216] *See* Port Authority of New York and New Jersey v. Arcadian Corp., 189 F.3d 305 (3d Cir. 1999) (applying New Jersey law).

[217] First Springfield Bank & Trust v. Galman, 702 N.E.2d 1002, 1007 (Ill. App. Ct. 1998).

[218] 898 S.W.2d 773, 776 (Tex.1995).

"that the circumstances surrounding her injuries are too remotely connected with Union Pump's conduct or pump to constitute a legal cause of her
injuries." Similarly, in *Kleen v. Homak Manufacturing Co., Inc.*,[219] a 15-year-
old broke into his father's locked gun safe, removed a gun and shot himself.
The Illinois Appellate Court held that the suicide was entirely the boy's
own decision and was not foreseeable by the gun safe manufacturer. The
court found that the allegedly defective condition of the gun safe provided a
condition that allowed the boy access to the gun but did not cause his suicide.

---

[219] 749 N.E.2d 26 (Ill. App. Ct. 2001).

Chapter 9

DEFENSES

SYNOPSIS

§ 9.01 INTRODUCTION

In a products liability action, a manufacturer or seller may raise a number of defenses.[1] Many of these defenses are based on the specific requirements for negligence, strict liability, or a state's products liability statute. In a strict liability action, for example, the plaintiff has the burden of proving all of the elements of § 402A: (1) the plaintiff was injured by a "product"; (2) the product was in a "defective condition unreasonably dangerous" at the time it left the defendant's control; (3) the defendant was a "seller" of the product; (4) the plaintiff was a "user or consumer" of the product; (5) the plaintiff suffered physical injury or property damage; and (6) the defect in the product was the cause-in-fact and proximate cause of the plaintiff's injury or damage. Since a claim will fail if the manufacturer or seller can show that the plaintiff did not prove any one of those essential elements, the starting point for the defense of a strict liability action is § 402A itself.[2]

In addition to the defenses based on the specific requirements of negligence and strict liability, a manufacturer or seller in a product liability action has a number of other potential defenses. Some of these defenses, such as where the danger created by the product was "open and obvious," the product was "unavoidably dangerous," or the product was "state of the art," were discussed in the chapters dealing with the different types of product defects. This chapter examines five broad categories of defenses available in products liability actions. First, the manufacturer or seller may base its defense on the plaintiff's conduct. In addition to the defenses of contributory negligence and assumption of the risk, this category includes alteration and misuse of the product. Second, the defendant may show that its status gives it immunity from the plaintiff's products liability suit against it. Such immunity is found in state workers' compensation statutes and in the government contractor defense. Third, the manufacturer or seller may show that the plaintiff failed to file the lawsuit within the time period required by the statute of limitations, the statute of repose, or the useful safe life of the product. Fourth, the manufacturer or seller may allege that the product's conformity with governmental or industry safety standards bars liability. Finally, the manufacturer or seller may show that a federal statute preempts the state product liability claim. Most of these defenses are

---

[1] In a few situations, a manufacturers or seller also may assert an immunity from liability. *See* the Protection of Lawful Commerce in Arms Act of 2005 (Public Law No. 109-9) (giving gun makers, dealers, and distributors immunity from civil lawsuits by cities and individuals seeking to hold them liable for the unlawful use of guns by third persons) and the Biomaterials Access Assurance Act of 1998 (21 U.S.C. §§1601-1606) (governs products liability suits against raw materials and bulk component suppliers to medical device manufacturers).

[2] Similarly, the starting point for the defense of a negligence action are the four requirements of that tort: (1) a duty; (2) a breach of that duty; (3) personal injury or property damage; and (4) a causal connection between the breach of the duty and the plaintiff's injury or damage. The failure to prove any one of these elements will result in a decision for the defendant.

a complete bar to a plaintiff's recovery. However, in the case of the conduct-based defenses of contributory negligence, assumption of risk, and misuse, whether the defense bars the plaintiff's recovery or reduces the amount of the plaintiff's damages depends on whether the particular state has adopted comparative fault and whether the action is based on negligence or strict liability.

§ 9.02 CONDUCT-BASED DEFENSES

[A] *Introduction*

At common law, conduct on the part of a plaintiff that amounted to contributory negligence, assumption of risk, alteration, or misuse of a product was a total bar to recovery. However, since the 1960s, almost every state has adopted some form of comparative fault that has changed the effect that some of the conduct-based defenses have on the plaintiff's recovery. Depending on the state and on the particular type of conduct, these defenses either may bar the plaintiff's recovery or they may reduce the amount of the plaintiff's damages based upon the percentage of his or her fault. Since the adoption of comparative fault has not lessened the importance of the plaintiff's conduct as a defense in a products liability action, this section analyzes contributory negligence, assumption of risk, alteration, and misuse of a product separately and then examines the various forms of comparative fault and their effect upon recovery.

[B] *Contributory Negligence*

At common law, a plaintiff's contributory negligence was a complete bar to recovery in a negligence action.[3] Contributory negligence consists of conduct on the part of the plaintiff that "falls below the standard to which he should conform for his own protection, and which is a legally contributing cause co-operating with the negligence of the defendant in bringing about the plaintiff's harm."[4] Unlike the defense of misuse, which involves the plaintiff's deliberate use of a product in a manner that was unintended or unforeseeable by the manufacturer, a plaintiff is contributorily negligent when he or she fails to take reasonable care for the proper use of a product, fails to discover the defect in the product, or fails to take steps to guard

---

[3] Butterfield v. Forrester, 103 Eng. Rep. 926 (K.B. 1809). The *Butterfield* rule entered American law in *Smith v. Smith*, 18 Mass. 621 (2 Pick.) (1824). *See* John Wade, *Comparative Negligence — Its Development In The United States And Its Present Status In Louisiana*, 40 LA. L. REV. 299 (1980).

[4] RESTATEMENT (SECOND) OF TORTS § 463 (1965). *See also* § 464 which applies the reasonable person standard in contributory negligence cases.

against the defect once it is discovered.[5] The almost universal acceptance of contributory negligence as a bar to recovery in the early 1960s,[6] even when the plaintiff's fault was slight when compared to the defendant's, was one of the reasons that led to the adoption of strict liability for products liability cases. According to comment n of § 402A:

> Since the liability with which this Section deals is not based upon negligence of the seller, but is strict liability, the rule applied to strict liability cases (§ 524) applies. Contributory negligence of the plaintiff is not a defense when such negligence consists merely in a failure to discover the defect in the product, or to guard against the possibility of its existence.[7]

In the early years of § 402A, the effect of contributory negligence was one of the defining differences between negligence and strict liability in products liability actions. In negligence cases contributory negligence remained a bar to the plaintiff's recovery,[8] subject to some limited exceptions such as the extreme youth of the plaintiff[9] or a statute creating the defendant's duty.[10] In contrast, courts ignored a plaintiff's contributory negligence in strict liability actions when it consisted of the failure to discover the defect in the product or to guard against the possibility of its existence.[11] However, as part of broadening the scope of tort liability in the late 1960s and early 1970s that led to the adoption of strict liability for products liability cases, courts and legislatures began to abandon contributory negligence as a complete bar to recovery in negligence cases and to create a system of "comparative negligence." As a result, all but five jurisdictions[12] now have adopted, either by legislation or judicial decision, some form of comparative fault under which the plaintiff's negligence is not necessarily an absolute bar to recovery in negligence cases. Instead, the jury determines the percentage of the plaintiff's negligence and the defendant's negligence in order

---

[5] Jimenez v. Sears Roebuck & Co., 904 P.2d 861, 865 (Ariz. 1995); General Motors v. Saint, 646 So.2d 564, 568 (Ala. 1994).

[6] Section 467 of the RESTATEMENT (SECOND) OF TORTS, adopted in 1965, states that "the plaintiff's contributory negligence bars recovery against a defendant whose negligent conduct would otherwise make him liable to the plaintiff for the harm sustained by him."

[7] RESTATEMENT (SECOND) OF TORTS § 402A cmt. n (1965).

[8] See Parris v. M.A. Bruder & Sons, Inc., 261 F. Supp. 406 (E.D. Pa. 1966); Reed v. Carlyle & Martin, Inc., 202 S.E.2d 874 (Va. 1974).

[9] See Porter v. United Steel & Wire Co., 436 F. Supp. 1376 (N.D. Iowa 1977) (applying Iowa law).

[10] See Zerby v. Warren, 210 N.W.2d 58 (Minn. 1973).

[11] McCown v. International Harvester Co., 342 A.2d 381 (Pa. 1975); Williams v. Brown Manufacturing Co., 261 N.E.2d 305 (Ill. 1970).

[12] Alabama, the District of Columbia, Maryland, North Carolina, and Virginia have not adopted comparative fault and make the plaintiff's contributory negligence a complete bar to recovery. See Reid v. Washington Overheard Door, Inc., 122 F. Supp. 2d 590 (D. Md. 2000).

to decide whether the plaintiff can recover and, if so, the amount damages he or she should receive.

The adoption of comparative negligence forced states to consider whether, in cases based on strict liability, they should continue to follow comment *n* and ignore the plaintiff's contributory negligence or to take a plaintiff's contributory negligence into consideration in determining liability and damages. Some courts have refused to import comparative negligence into cases based on strict liability.[13] Among the reasons for their hesitation are the language of comment *n* to § 402A, the perceived difficulty of comparing the plaintiff's negligence with the defendant's strict liability for the product defect, and the feeling that it was not appropriate to use negligence principles in strict liability cases.[14] Despite these concerns, however, the majority of states now treat the plaintiff's ordinary negligence as a factor to be taken into consideration in apportioning liability and in determining the amount of damages in strict liability cases as well as those based on negligence.[15] This approach is contained in the Connecticut products liability statute which states that "[i]n causes of action based on strict tort liability, contributory negligence or comparative negligence shall not be a bar to recovery."[16] The statute then provides that "the comparative responsibility of, or attributed to, the claimant, shall not bar recovery but shall diminish the award of compensatory damages proportionately, according to the measure of responsibility attributed to the claimant."[17]

The type of conduct that will reduce a plaintiff's recovery in a products liability case is illustrated by *General Motors Corp. v. Saint*.[18] In that case, a woman was injured when the automobile she was driving hit a low shoulder on a road, went out of control, and hit a tree. The woman sued General Motors, claiming that the car was not crashworthy because its seat belt assembly failed to protect her adequately from the enhanced injuries she suffered in the accident. Specifically, she alleged that the seat belt's "comfort feature," which General Motors designed and installed in its cars, allowed extensive slack to develop and, as a result, caused the seat belt not

---

[13] Two states that refuse to admit evidence concerning a plaintiff's ordinary contributory negligence in a strict liability are Oregon (Hernandez v. Barbo Machinery Co., 957 P.2d 147 (1998)) and Pennsylvania (Kimco Development v. Michael D's Carpet, 637 A.2d 603 (Pa. 1993)).

[14] *See* Bowling v. Heil Co., 511 N.E.2d 373 (Ohio 1987); Beshada v. Johns-Manville Products Corp., 447 A.2d 539 (N.J. 1982); Sheehan v. Anthony Pools, 440 A.2d 1085 (Md. Ct. Spec. App. 1982).

[15] See *Whitehead v. Toyota Motor Corp.*, 897 S.W.2d 684, 691-692 (Tenn. 1995), for a list of the "overwhelming majority of states [that] have adopted the view that comparative fault should apply to products liability actions based on strict liability." The RESTATEMENT (THIRD) also states that a "strong majority" of courts now apply comparative negligence principles in strict products liability cases. *See* RESTATEMENT (THIRD) OF TORTS: PRODUCTS LIABILITY § 17 cmt. *a* (1998).

[16] CONN. GEN. STAT. § 52-572l (1991).

[17] *Id.* § 52-572o(a).

[18] 646 So. 2d 564 (Ala 1994).

to restrain properly the occupant.[19] The Alabama Supreme Court reversed a jury verdict in favor of the woman. According to the court, there was evidence from the woman's own expert that she was aware of the slack and allowed it to remain in her seat belt when wearing it. General Motors foresaw the danger that would result from someone's doing so and warned against it in its owner's manual. The court held that a jury could find that, although the woman did not use her seat belt in an unintended or unforeseen manner, she nonetheless was negligent in failing to use reasonable care in wearing it. The court remanded the case, saying that General Motors was entitled to a jury charge on contributory negligence.[20]

[C] *Assumption of Risk*

Like contributory negligence, assumption of risk was a complete bar to a plaintiff's recovery in a negligence action at common law.[21] Courts recognize two types of assumption of risk. Primary or express assumption of risk arises where the "parties have voluntarily entered a relationship in which plaintiff assumes well-known, incidental risks."[22] As a condition of the relationship, plaintiffs often sign a written agreement in which they expressly assume some or all of the risks of the relationship.[23] In products liability cases, primary assumption of risk often involves persons injured while engaging in sporting activities.[24] Secondary or implied assumption of risk is defined as "a type of contributory negligence where the plaintiff voluntarily encounters a known and appreciated hazard created by the defendant without relieving the defendant of his duty of care with respect to such hazard."[25] Although the drafters of § 402A felt that courts should ignore a plaintiff's ordinary contributory negligence in determining liability and damages, they took a different position concerning secondary or implied assumption of risk. According to comment *n*:

> [T]he form of contributory negligence which consists in voluntarily and unreasonably proceeding to encounter a known danger, and commonly passes under the name of assumption of risk, is a defense under this Section as in other cases of strict liability. If the user or

---

[19] *Id.* at 565.

[20] *Id.* at 568.

[21] Nally v. Charbonneau, 362 A.2d 494 (Conn. 1975); Murphy v. Steeplechase Amusement Co., 166 N.E. 173 (N.Y. 1929).

[22] Olson v. Hansen, 216 N.W.2d 124, 127 (Minn. 1974).

[23] *See* Neumann v. Gloria Marshall Figure Salon, 500 N.E.2d 1011 (Ill. App. Ct. 1986) (a woman who was injured by an exercise machine at a health club had signed a contract with the health center containing an exculpatory clause). The ability of a manufacturer or seller to disclaim liability for personal injuries is well-established.

[24] *See, e.g.*, Westlye v. Look Sport, Inc., 22 Cal. Rptr. 2d 781 (Cal. Ct. App. 1993).

[25] *See, e.g.*, Andren v. White-Rodgers Company, 465 N.W.2d 102, 104 (Minn. Ct. App. 1991).

consumer discovers the defect and is aware of the danger, and nevertheless proceeds unreasonably to make use of the product and is injured by it, he is barred from recovery.[26]

Although the drafters of § 402A were willing to permit primary or express assumption of risk to remain a defense in strict liability actions, section 18 of the Restatement (Third) also takes the position that "contractual exculpations, oral or written, do not bar or reduce otherwise valid products liability claims against sellers or other distributors of new products fo harm to persons."[27]

Contained within comment n to § 402A are both the definition of assumption of risk and the three elements that a manufacturer or seller must show to establish both primary and secondary assumption of risk.[28] First, courts hold that the plaintiff must have had knowledge of the particular risk or danger in the product. It is not sufficient for the defendant to show simply that the plaintiff was aware generally that the product exposed him or her to danger. Instead, the defendant must prove that the plaintiff was aware of the specific defect which caused his injury. Second, the plaintiff must have understood the unreasonably dangerous risk created by the product. Finally, the plaintiff must have chosen voluntarily and unreasonably to use the product after discovering the defect and its danger.[29] Thus, unlike contributory negligence, which is based on a showing that the plaintiff failed to use ordinary care in dealing with the product and does not require that the plaintiff was aware of the risk or even have thought about it, assumption of risk requires that the plaintiff knew, understood, and voluntarily accepted the specific danger created by the product.

An example of the application of the three requirements for assumption of risk is *Haugen v. Minnesota Mining & Manufacturing Co.*,[30] in which the plaintiff was blinded when the grinding wheel on which he was working exploded and a piece from the wheel struck him in the eye. The Washington appellate court affirmed the trial court's finding for the plaintiff and held that the jury instructions given by the trial court were proper. The instruction read:

> It is not enough to bar recovery . . . on the defense of assumption of the risk that the plaintiff knew that there was a general danger connected with the use of the product, but rather it must be shown that

---

[26] RESTATEMENT (SECOND) OF TORTS § 402A cmt. n (1965). Many states continue to treat assumption of risk as a complete defense both in negligence and strict liability actions. *See* Dillinger v. Caterpillar, Inc., 959 F.2d 430 (3d Cir. 1992) (applying Pennsylvania law).

[27] RESTATEMENT (THIRD) OF TORTS: PRODUCTS LIABILITY § 18 (1998).

[28] Walk v. Starkey Machine, Inc., 180 F.3d 937 (8th Cir. 1999) (applying Minnesota law); Little v. Liquid Air Corp., 37 F.3d 1069 (5th Cir. 1994); Ellsworth v. Sherne Lingerie, Inc., 495 A.2d 348 (Md. 1985).

[29] Bowen v. Cochran, 556 S.E.2d 530 (Ga. Ct. App. 2001).

[30] 550 P.2d 71 (Wash. Ct. App.1976).

the plaintiff actually knew, appreciated, and voluntarily and unreasonably exposed himself to the specific defect and danger which
caused his injuries.[31]

Although the court in *Haugen* allowed the manufacturer to raise assumption of risk, courts are divided over whether a worker can "voluntarily"
assume a risk of injury from a product in the workplace. Some courts take
the position that the exposure to the risk is not voluntary when it occurs in
the workplace even if workers could have chosen not to do their job.[32] Other
courts, however, view the employees' voluntary exposure to a known risk in
the workplace as assumption of risk.[33]

The test for determining whether the plaintiff assumed the risk is subjective rather than objective.[34] It is the particular plaintiff's understanding
and appreciation of the danger presented by the product that must be
assessed, rather than that of the reasonably prudent person under similar
circumstances. In making this determining, the jury is entitled to assess all
of the facts and is not required to accept the plaintiff's testimony that he or
she was unaware of the danger if, in light of all of the evidence, the plaintiff could not have been unaware of the hazard. In making that determination, the plaintiff's age, experience, knowledge, and understanding, as
well as the obviousness of the defect and the danger it poses, are relevant
factors for the jury to consider.[35] The application of the subjective test in
product liability cases is illustrated by *Thomas v. Kaiser Agricultural Chemicals*[36] in which the plaintiff suffered an eye injury when liquid nitrogen fertilizer sprayed into his face while he was attempting to fill a fertilizer
applicator. His injury occurred after he inadvertently opened the air pressure relief valve on the applicator, which released pent-up pressure and the
remaining liquid nitrogen. The plaintiff alleged that the machine contained
a defective attachment called an adaptor. He testified that he had read the
conspicuous and detailed warning label cautioning users to bleed off all
the air pressure in the tank before refilling the applicator. However, he
attempted to refill the applicator without verifying that the air pressure
gauge read zero as the instructions directed. The Illinois Supreme Court
held that the plaintiff assumed the risk only if he was actually aware of the

---

[31] *Id.* at 74. But see *Lonon v. Pep Boys, Manny, Moe & Jack*, 538 A.2d 22 (Pa. Super. Ct.
1988), for a decision approving "general" assumption of risk.

[32] Cremeans v. Willman Henderson Manufacturing Co., 566 N.E.2d 1203 (Ohio 1991);
Suter v. San Angelo Foundry & Machine Co., 406 A.2d 140 (N.J. 1979).

[33] Byrne v. SCM Corp., 538 N.E.2d 796 (Ill. App. Ct. 1989).

[34] Walsh v. Emergency One, Inc., 26 F.3d 1417 (7th Cir. 1994) (applying Illinois law); Zahrte
v. Sturm, Ruger & Co., 203 Mont. 90 (Montana 1983). This differs from contributory negligent
where juries apply the objective reasonable person standard in judging the plaintiff's conduct.

[35] Moran v. Raymond Corp., 484 F.2d 1008 (7th Cir. 1973); Johnson v. Clark Equipment Co.,
547 P.2d 132 (Ore. 1976); Staymates v. ITT Holub Industries, 527 A.2d 140 (Pa. Super. Ct.
1987).

[36] 407 N.E.2d 32 (Ill. 1980).

defective nature of the product and appreciated its unreasonably dangerous condition but voluntarily chose to act in disregard of the danger.[37] The court found insufficient evidence of such awareness, despite the plaintiff's eighteen years as a farmer, because he had used the particular machine only once before.

[D] *Alteration or Modification of a Product*

Under warranty, negligence, and strict liability theories, a manufacturer is liable for a defect in a product that existed at the time the product left its control. At the same time, the plaintiff has the burden of proving that the product "was expected to, and did, reach the user without substantial change in the condition in which it was sold."[38] In some cases, however, the buyer alters or modifies the product after purchase. An alteration or modification occurs when

> a person or entity other than the product seller changes the design, construction, or formula of the product, or changes or removes warnings or instructions that accompanied or were displayed on the product. "Alteration or modification" of a product includes the failure to observe routine care and maintenance, but does not include ordinary wear and tear.[39]

In order for a manufacturer to succeed on the alteration defense, it must establish four elements:[40] (1) there was a substantial alteration or modification of the product; (2) the alteration or modification occurred after it left the manufacturer's control; (3) the alteration or modification was the proximate cause of the plaintiff's injury;[41] and (4) the alteration or modification was not made with the manufacturer's express or implied consent and was not reasonably foreseeable.[42]

The fact that a product was altered by the buyer after the sale does not necessarily relieve the manufacturer of liability.[43] Instead, the alteration in the product must have been "substantial."[44] What constitutes a substantial

---

[37] *Id.* at 36.

[38] RESTATEMENT (SECOND) OF TORTS § 402A (1965).

[39] IDAHO CODE § 6-1405(4)(a) (2004). *See also* KY. REV. STAT. § 411.320(2) (1992). These sections are taken from the Model Uniform Products Liability Act § 112(D)(1).

[40] Islam v. Modern Tour, Inc., 2004 U.S. Dist. LEXIS 19768 (S.D.N.Y. 2004) (applying New York law); Tober v. Graco Children's Products, 2004 U.S. Dist. LEXIS 18254 (S.D. Ind. 2004) (applying Indiana law).

[41] Smock Materials Handling Co. v. Kerr, 719 N.E.2d 396 (Ind. Ct. App. 1999).

[42] Skurnowicz v. Ryder Transportation Serves, 2000 U.S. Dist. LEXIS 9667 (E.D. Pa. 2000) (applying Pennsylvania law); Ritter v. Emerson Elec. Co., 1996 U.S. Dist. LEXIS 13925 (E. D. Mich. 1996) (applying Michigan law).

[43] Johnson v. Niagara Machine & Tool Co., 555 So.2d 88 (Ala. 1989).

[44] *See* Almazan v. CTB, Inc., 2000 U.S. Dist. LEXIS 21434 (W. D. Tex. 2000) (applying Texas law); Banner Welders, Inc. v. Knighton, 425 So.2d 441 (Ala. 1982).

alteration is left to the legislatures and courts to decide. North Dakota, for example, states that the alteration or modification must have "changed the purpose, use, function, design, or intended use or manner of use of the product from that for which the product was originally designed, tested, or intended."[45] Thus, a change in a product that does not affect its operation is not a substantial alteration.[46]

Before a court can make the determination that the alteration was substantial, it must decide whether the design or manufacture of the product was defective before its alteration. If the product was not defective when it left the control of the manufacturer or seller, but became so because of the alteration, then the alteration was substantial and the manufacturer is not liable.[47] The alteration, rather than the design or manufacture, made the product more dangerous than a consumer would expect the product to be.[48] However, if the product was defective when it left the manufacturer's control and there was a substantial modification after the sale, then it is a question of fact whether the original defect or the subsequent modification was the cause of the plaintiff's injuries.

In order to succeed on an alteration defense, a manufacturer must show not only a substantial alteration or modification after the product left its control, it must prove that the change "proximately caused the claimant's harm."[49] For most courts, this showing of a causal connection between the modification of the product and the injury is the heart of the alteration defense.[50] Connecticut, for example, requires proof that the injury would not have occurred "but for" the alteration in the product.[51]

Finally, a manufacturer will not be able to succeed on the alteration defense if the changes were made according to the manufacturer's instructions or specification or with its express or implied consent. In addition, a modification or alteration that was part of the anticipated use of the product is considered foreseeable and is not sufficient to apply the alteration defense.[52] The more difficult an alteration or modification is to make, the

---

[45] N.D. REV. STAT. § 28-01.3-03 (2005 Supp.).

[46] Banner Welders, Inc. v. Knighton, 425 So.2d 441, 450 (Ala. 1982).

[47] Amatulli v. Delhi Construction Corp., 571 N.E.2d 645 (N.Y. 1991).

[48] See the discussion of the "substantial" requirement in *Hiner v. Deere and Co., Inc.*, 340 F.3d 1190, 1198-1199 (10th Cir. 2003) (applying Kansas law).

[49] IDAHO CODE § 6-1405(4)(b) (2004).

[50] *See* KY. REV. STAT. § 411.320(2) (1992) (the alteration or modification must have been "a substantial cause of the occurrence that caused injury or damage to the plaintiff").

[51] *See* Potter v. Chicago Pneumatic Tool Co., 694 A.2d 1319, 1339 (Conn. 1997). *See also* Halsey v. A.B. Chance Co., 695 So. 2d 607 (Ala. 1997).

[52] IDAHO CODE § 6-1405(4) (2004); Hall v. Porter Paints Store, 2004 U.S. Dist. LEXIS 19590 at *23 (S.D. Ind. 2004) (applying Indiana law) ("The modification or alteration of a product must be independent of the expected use of the product in order for the modification or alteration defense to apply.").

less foreseeable it is to the manufacturer.[53] Thus, where a manufacturer was aware that heavy-equipment users sometimes installed twelve-volt accessories in their machines made the installation of a twelve-volt harness a foreseeable alteration.[54] Courts determine the foreseeability of an alteration by examining the design of the product in light of its "intended and reasonably foreseeable uses, modifications, or alterations."[55] An example of this is *Monsanto Co. v. Reed*[56] in which the Kentucky Supreme Court held that a chemical manufacturer was not liable for injuries to salvage employees because their exposure to the chemicals resulted from an alteration of the product outside of the scope of intended use.

[E] *Misuse of the Product*

In addition to contributory negligence, assumption of risk, and alteration of a product, a manufacturer or seller also may not be liable if the plaintiff misused the product that caused the injuries or damage. What distinguishes misuse from the other conduct-based defenses, both in negligence and strict liability cases, is that the majority of states treat proof of the absence of misuse as an element of the plaintiff's case instead of requiring the defendant to plead misuse as an affirmative defense.[57] For those states taking the majority position, misuse goes to the issue of causation, and proof by the plaintiff that the product was used in an objectively foreseeable manner is necessary to establish that a defect in the product, rather than misuse, was the cause of the injury or damages.[58] Whether part of the plaintiff's case or an affirmative defense, misuse of a product that is not reasonably foreseeable is a bar to recovery.[59] Misuse that is foreseeable either is not a defense or is included in states' comparative fault schemes where the misuse contributed to the plaintiff's injuries.[60]

---

[53] *See* Bates v. Richland Sales Corp., 803 N.E.2d 977, 985 (Ill. App. Ct. 2004) (because the removal of a roll bar required employees to cut through eight bolts and electrical wires as well as use a hoist to lift the heavy bar from the front-end loader, the alteration was substantial and unforeseeable).

[54] Welch Sand & Gravel, Inc. v. O & K Trojan, Inc., 668 N.E.2d. 529, 534 (Ohio Ct. App. 1995).

[55] *Id.* at 533.

[56] 950 S.W.2d 811 (Ky. 1997).

[57] *See, e.g.,* Jurado v. Western Gear Works, 619 A.2d 1312 (N.J. 1993); Hughes v. Magic Chef, Inc., 288 N.W.2d 542 (Iowa 1980); Moran v. Faberge, Inc., 332 A.2d 11 (Md. Ct. Spec. App. 1975). For a decision treating misuse as an affirmative defense, see *Tellez-Cordova v. Campbell*, 29 Cal. Rptr. 3d 744 (Cal. Ct. App. 2004).

[58] *See* Madona v. Harley Davidson, Inc., 708 A.2d 507 (Pa. Super. Ct. 1998); Rogers v. Toro Manufacturing Co., 522 S.W.2d 632 (Mo. Ct. App. 1975).

[59] Andrews v. Harley-Davidson, Inc., 796 P.2d 1092 (Nev. 1990).

[60] Smith v. Ingersoll-Rand Co., 14 P.2d 990 (Alaska 2000); Jimenez v. Sears, Roebuck & Co., 904 P.2d 861 (Ariz. 1995); Elliott v. Sears, Roebuck & Co., Inc., 642 A.2d 709 (Conn. 1994); Deere & Co. v. Grose, 586 So.2d 196 (Ala. 1991).

Statutes, courts, and the Restatement define misuse as the use of a product by the plaintiff "in a way not reasonably foreseeable by the manufacturer or seller"[61] that was a cause of the plaintiff's injury or damages.[62] Under this definition, there is no misuse simply because the plaintiff used the product in a way that the manufacturer did not intend (i.e., inattention, carelessness or foreseeable misuse). Instead, the manufacturer must show that the plaintiff's injuries were caused by a misuse that was not foreseeable, i.e., that the plaintiff intentionally used the product in a way that was not reasonably related to its intended uses.[63] The Restatement (Third) also defines the scope of liability for design defects and defects due to inadequate warnings in terms of "the foreseeable risks of harm posed by the product."[64] According to comment *m* to § 2:

> Subsections (b) and (c) impose liability only when the product is put to uses that it is reasonable to expect a seller or distributor to foresee. Product sellers and distributors are not required to foresee and take precautions against every conceivable mode of use and abuse to which their products might be put. Increasing the costs of designing and marketing products in order to avoid the consequences of unreasonable modes of use is not required.[65]

It is the use of the product in a manner that is not reasonable for the seller to expect that separates misuse from contributor negligence and assumption of the risk. In *O.S. Shapley Co. v. Miller*,[66] the Arizona Supreme Court distinguished the three forms of conduct by defining contributory negligence as the "[f]ailure to discover a defect in the product which the plaintiff should, if he was reasonably diligent, have discovered." The court went on to state that, "notwithstanding the discovery of such a defect, [if] the plaintiff nevertheless uses the article" the conduct is assumption of the risk. Finally, the court said that the plaintiff's use of a product "for

---

[61] Rahmig v. Mosley Manufacturing Co., 412 N.W.2d 56, 74 (Neb. 1987). *See also* COL. REV. STAT. ANN. § 13-21-402.5 (2005). According to comment *h* to § 402A:

> A product is not in a defective condition when it is safe for normal handling and consumption. If the injury results from abnormal handling, as where a bottled beverage is knocked against a radiator to remove a cap; or from abnormal preparation for use, as where too much salt is added to food; or from abnormal consumption, as where a child eats too much candy and is made is, the seller is not liable.

[62] Hoey v. Textron, 1993 Conn. Super. LEXIS 2781 (Conn. Super. Ct. 1993).

[63] Venezia v. Miller Brewing Co., 626 F.2d 188 (1st Cir. 1980); Romito v. Red Plasic, Inc., 44 Cal. Rptr. 834 (Ca. Ct. App. 1995); Heil Co. v. Grant, 534 S.W.2d 916 (Tex. App. 1978). In addition, a plaintiff's alteration or modification of a product in a way that, although foreseeable, goes against the express warnings of the manufacturer, also may be misuse that bars recovery. *See* Prince v. B.F. Ascher Co., Inc., 90 P. 3d 1020 (Okla. 2004).

[64] RESTATEMENT (THIRD) OF TORTS: PRODUCTS LIABILITY §§ 2(b) and 2(c) (1998).

[65] *Id.* at cmt. *m*.

[66] 447 P.2d 248, 253 (Ariz. 1968).

certain purposes or in a manner not reasonably foreseen by the manufacturer is misuse."[67]

Because the use of each product is different and many products have more than one foreseeable use, it is impossible for courts to set out a formula for determining what uses of a product are and are not "reasonably foreseeable." An example of a use that a court held was foreseeable is *Ellsworth v. Sherne Lingerie*,[68] in which the plaintiff was severely burned when the nightgown she was wearing ignited as a result of its coming in contact with a burner on the stove in her kitchen. The plaintiff brought an action based in breach of warranty, negligence, and strict liability against the manufacturer.[69] At the time of the accident, the plaintiff admitted that she was wearing the nightgown inside out and that the two pockets were protruding. At trial, the defendant argued that the plaintiff's use of the gown "in effect draping it over a hot burner for an appreciable period of time, cannot seriously be considered a reasonably foreseeable manner of use."[70] However, the Maryland appellate court held that, while the plaintiff's use of the nightgown may have been careless, it was reasonably foreseeable that loosely fitting clothes such as a nightgown occasionally will be worn inside out and thus could come in contact with a stove while worn in the kitchen (which also was foreseeable).[71] Thus, the court concluded that her use of the product was reasonably foreseeable.[72]

A number of misuse cases involve foreseeable misuse of a product by persons for whom the product was not intended. For example, in a long line of cases involving disposable cigarette lighters, courts have sought to determine whether manufacturers must include childproof latches on their products, even though they are intended to be used only by adults. Even though the number of accidents involving children makes the risk of their setting fires foreseeable, most courts hold that manufacturers do not have a duty to design a product intended for adults in a way that will make it safe for children just because it is foreseeable that the product might fall into the hands of children.[73]

---

[67] *Id.* at 253.

[68] 495 A.2d 348 (Md. Ct. Spec. App. 1985).

[69] *Id.* at 351.

[70] *Id.*

[71] *Id.* at 356-357.

[72] For other cases holding that the misuse was foreseeable, see *Chronister v. Bryco Arms*, 125 F. 3d 624 (1997) ("defendant may not escape liability on grounds of misuse or abnormal use if the actual use proximate to the injury was objectively foreseeable."); *Threats v. General Motors, Corp.*, 890 S.W. 2d 327 (Mo. Ct. App. 1994) (since speeding, although illegal, is foreseeable, the manufacturer should have designed the automobile airbag to deploy in such circumstances).

[73] *See, e.g.*, Hernandez v. Tokai Corp., 2 S.W.3d 251 (Tex. 1999).

[F] *Comparative Fault*

Although a few states adopted comparative negligence as early as the middle of the 19th century,[74] the doctrine did not become widespread until the early 1970s. As of 2005, all but five jurisdictions — Alabama, the District of Columbia, Maryland, North Carolina, and Virginia — had adopted some form of comparative fault, either by legislation or judicial decision.[75] Many states go beyond simply comparing the plaintiff's negligence with that of the defendant and weigh the fault of the plaintiff when it consists of assumption of the risk or alteration of the product.[76] States also take the fault of the plaintiff into account in assessing damages when the defendant is strictly liable.[77] A few states also have incorporated misuse of the product into their comparative fault systems.[78] The effect of these statutes and decisions is to ease the harsh effect of contributory negligence under which any degree of fault on the part of a plaintiff barred recovery.

Comparative fault takes one of two different forms.[79] First, about one-third of the states have adopted "pure" comparative fault, either for all theories of recovery or only for negligence or strict liability cases. For these states, the pure comparative fault is the only system that truly apportions damages according to the relative fault of the parties.[80] An example of pure comparative fault is the New York statute which provides that, in actions for personal injury, property damage, and wrongful death,

> the culpable conduct attributable to the claimant or to the decedent including contributory negligence or assumption of risk, shall not bar recovery, but the amount of damages otherwise recoverable shall be diminished in the proportion which the culpable con-

---

[74] *See* Galena & Chicago Union Ry. v. Jacobs, 20 Ill. 478 (Ill. 1858). However, in 1885 Illinois returned to contributory negligence. Calumet Iron & Steel Co. v. Martin, 3 N.E. 456 (Ill. 1885).

[75] For a discussion of comparative fault in products liability cases, see Richard C. Henke, *Comparative Fault in Products Liability: Comparing California and New Jersey*, 19 T.M. COOLEY L. REV. 301 (2002).

[76] See IDAHO CODE § 6-1405(4)(b) which states that, when a product seller proves that the product was altered and the alteration was the cause of the plaintiff's injuries, "the claimant's damages shall be subject to reduction or apportionment to the extent that the alteration or modification was a proximate cause of the harm." However, the North Dakota code makes alteration a bar to a plaintiff's recovery. N.D. CENT. CODE § 28-01.3-03 (2005 Supp.).

[77] Whitehead v. Toyota Motor Corp., 897 S.W.2d 684 (Tenn. 1995).

[78] For example, see *Jimenez v. Sears Roebuck & Co*, 904 P.2d 861 (Ariz. 1995), in which the Arizona Supreme Court held that comparative fault principles apply to the defense misuse of a product in a strict liability action, and N.D. CENT. CODE § 32.03.2 (1991).

[79] For a summary of the different approaches to "comparative responsibility," see RESTATEMENT (THIRD) OF TORTS: PRODUCTS LIABILITY (Apportionment of Liability) § 7 Reporters' Notes (2000).

[80] *See* Alvis v. Ribar, 421 N.E.2d 886, 898 (Ill. 1981).

duct attributable to the claimant or decedent bears to the culpable conduct which caused the damages.[81]

Under the New York statute, and in other states that use the pure form of comparative fault, plaintiffs who are 1%, 50% or even 99% at fault for their injuries, whether resulting from contributory negligence or assumption of risk, recover the amount of their damages less the percentage of their fault. In *Ocampo v. Paper Converting Mach. Co.*,[82] the plaintiff was maintaining and inspecting an aluminum foil interfolder machine when her hair became caught in the machine, resulting in a portion of her scalp being torn from her head. In a suit against the manufacturer of the machine, the jury found that the plaintiff's damages for medical care, pain and suffering, disfigurement and loss of normal life totaled $6.1 million. In apportioning responsibility for the plaintiff's injuries, the jury concluded that she was 8% responsible, the manufacturer of the machine was 67% responsible, and the plaintiff's employer was 37% responsible. The jury reduced the plaintiff's total damages by her percentage of fault (8%).

Second, the majority of states that have adopted comparative fault use one of two forms of the "modified rule." Under the modified rule, the amount of the plaintiff's damages is reduced by the percentage of his or her fault. However, unlike the pure form of comparative fault, if the plaintiff's fault exceeds a stated percentage of the total fault, the plaintiff is barred from recovering any damages. There are two forms of modified comparative fault. First, about a dozen states follow what is referred to as the "50% rule" under which the plaintiff's fault is a complete bar to recovery if the plaintiff was 50% or more at fault. This means that, if the fact-finder determines that the plaintiff and defendant each were 50% at fault, the plaintiff is barred from all recovery. However, if a plaintiff is found to be less than 50% at fault, the award is reduced by the percentage of the plaintiff's fault. An example of this form of comparative fault is the Arkansas statute which states, in part:

(1) If the fault chargeable to a party claiming damages is of a lesser degree than the fault chargeable to the party or parties from whom the claiming party seeks to recover damages, then the claiming party is entitled to recover the amount of his damages after they have been diminished in proportion to the degree of his own fault.

(2) If the fault chargeable to a party claiming damages is equal to or greater in degree than any fault chargeable to the party or parties from whom the claiming party seeks to recover damages, then the claiming party is not entitled to recover such damages.[83]

---

[81] N.Y. C.P.L.R. § 1411 (McKinney 1997).

[82] 2005 U.S. Dist. LEXIS 17107 (N.D. Ill. 2005).

[83] ARK. CODE ANN. § 16-64-122 (Michie 2005 Supp.).

Under the second form of modified comparative fault, the "more than 50% rule," the plaintiff's contributory fault will be a complete bar to recovery only if it exceeds that of the defendant. An example of this approach is the Illinois statute which states:

> In all actions on account of bodily injury or death or physical damage to property based on . . . product liability based on strict tort liability, the court shall instruct the jury in writing that the defendant shall be found not liable if the jury finds that the contributory fault of the plaintiff is more than 50% of the proximate cause of the injury or damage for which recovery is sought.[84]

Under this form of comparative fault, if the fact-finder determines that the plaintiff and defendant were each 50% at fault, the plaintiff still recovers 50% of his or her damages.[85] An example of the "more than 50% rule" is *Tidemann v. Nadler Gold Co.*,[86] in which the plaintiff was severely injured when a golf cart that she was attempting to operate suddenly lurched forward and crashed into a garage door. The plaintiff's strict liability theory was dismissed as a matter of law, but her negligence claim went to the jury. The jury returned a verdict in which it apportioned 82% of the fault for the accident to the plaintiff and 18% to the defendant that had reconditioned and sold the gold cart. Since the plaintiff's fault for the accident was more than 50%, she recovered no damages.

The Restatement (Third) does not follow comment *n* to § 402A. Instead, section 17 adopts the position followed by the majority of states and does not distinguish between contributory negligence, assumption of risk, alteration, and misuse as defenses. According to the section:

> A plaintiff's recovery of damages for harm caused by a product defect may be reduced if the conduct of the plaintiff combines with the product to cause the harm and the plaintiff's conduct fails to conform to generally applicable rules establishing appropriate standards of care.[87]

§ 9.03 STATUS-BASED DEFENSES

[A] *Employer Immunity*

[1] Employer Liability to Employees

According to the Bureau of Labor Statistics, 5,559 persons were killed and over 4.4 million persons suffered injuries or illnesses in workplace inci-

---

[84] 735 ILL. COMP. STAT. 5/2-1116 (2004).

[85] *See* General Motors Corp. v. Sanchez, 997 S.W.2d 584 (Tex. 1999).

[86] 224 F.3d 719 (7th Cir. 2000) (applying Illinois law).

[87] RESTATEMENT (THIRD) OF TORTS: PRODUCTS LIABILITY § 17 (1998).

dents in the U.S. in 2003.[88] Although many of these deaths and injuries resulted from falls, fires, homicides, and vehicle accidents, a large number of the accidents involved machine tools, such as punch presses, drills, saws, and meat cutters, and exposure to harmful substances such as chemicals and asbestos. Many of the victims of these accidents or their survivors were able to bring negligence or strict liability suits against the manufacturers of the machines or the harmful substances. However, every state has adopted a workers' compensation statute that bars "employees" who suffer injuries "arising out of" and "in the course of employment" from bringing tort suits against their employers.[89] In the place of the common law right of employees to sue their employers, workers' compensation statutes establish an administrative system of no-fault liability for employers that removes the defense of the workers' contributory negligence and imposes statutory limits on the amount injured employees may recover.[90] These statutes not only provide compensation for medical care and lost income to workers and death benefits to the families of workers killed "in the course of employment" (although, in many cases, in a lower amount that they could recover in a tort action), they also give immunity to employers from lawsuits brought by workers. The procedure and compensation provided by the workers' compensation statutes are the exclusive remedy for all claims against employers, subject to limited exceptions. Although those exceptions vary among the states, one example is the California worker's compensation statute which, after stating that it is "the sole and exclusive remedy of the employee or his or her dependents against the employer,"[91] provides that an employee, or his or her dependents in the case of death, may bring a tort action for damages against the employer in three situations:

> (1) Where the employee's injury or death is proximately caused by a willful physical assault by the employer. (2) Where the employee's injury is aggravated by the employer's fraudulent concealment of the existence of the injury and its connection with the employment. . . . (3) Where the employee's injury or death is proximately caused by a defective product manufactured by the employer and sold, leased, or otherwise transferred for valuable consideration to

---

[88] U.S. Department of Labor, Bureau of Labor Statistics, Injuries, Illnesses, and Fatalities, http://bls.gov./iif/home.htm (last visited August 9, 2005).

[89] For examples, see 820 ILL. COMP. STAT. 305/1 *et. seq.* (2004); N.J. STAT. ANN. § 34:15-8 (2000). *See also* Marshall v. H. K. Ferguson Co., 623 F. 2d 882 (4th Cir. 1980) (under the Virginia Workmens' Compensation Act, the employer was immune from any common law action by an employee injured on the job).

[90] Participation in the workers' compensation system is mandatory in every state except Texas, which permits employers to choose whether or not to provide workers' compensation, although public employers and employers that enter into a building or construction contract with a governmental entity must provide workers' compensation to their employees.

[91] CAL. LAB. CODE § 3602(a) (2003).

an independent third person, and that product is thereafter provided for the employee's use by a third person.[92]

California also permits an exception to the exclusive remedy provision of its workers' compensation statute where the injury or death resulted from the employer's knowing removal of, or failure to provide, a guard on a power press.[93]

Another exception to the exclusive remedy provisions is the "dual capacity" or "dual persona" doctrine. Under this doctrine, an employer may be liable in tort to an injured employee if, in addition to acting in its capacity as the employer, the employer operates in a second capacity that places on it obligations independent of those imposed upon it as an employer.[94] In order to invoke the doctrine, an employee must show that the employer acted in two distinct capacities and that he or she was injured as a result of conduct in which the employer engaged while acting in its capacity other than that of employer.[95] However, where the duties of the employer under both capacities are intertwined to the extent that its conduct in the second capacity cannot be held to create obligations unrelated to its capacity as an employer, the dual capacity doctrine is inapplicable.[96] Despite the attention that it has received, the dual capacity doctrine is recognized only by about half-a-dozen states. The two states that initially adopted it, California and Ohio, since have rejected it.[97]

In recent years the exclusive remedy provision has been challenged on constitutional grounds.[98] The only successful case has been *Smothers v. Gresham Transfer*,[99] in which an employee claimed that his respiratory problems were work-related. When the employee was denied worker's compensation, the Oregon trial court permitted him to bring a negligence action against his employer. In upholding the employee's suit, the Oregon Supreme Court held that, because the state's workers' compensation statute provided the exclusive remedy for all work-related injuries, the statute violated

---

[92] *Id.* § 3602(b). *See also* Rainer v. Union Carbide Corp., 402 F.3d 608 (6th Cir. 2004) (applying Kentucky law); Perry v. Heavenly Valley, 209 Cal. Rptr. 771 (Cal. Ct. App. 1985).

[93] *Id.* §4558 (2003).

[94] For discussion of the dual capacity exception, see *Gerrish v. Savard*, 739 A.2d 1195 (Vt. 1999); *Dyke v. St. Francis Hospital*, 861 P.2d 295 (Okla. 1993). For a rejection of the dual capacity doctrine, see *Corr v. Willamette Industries, Inc.*, 713 P.2d 92 (Wash. 1986).

[95] For an example of the dual capacity doctrine, see *Rosales v. Verson Allsteel Press Co.*, 354 N.E.2d 553 (Ill. App. Ct. 1976).

[96] McCormick v. Caterpillar Tractor Co., 423 N.E.2d 876 (Ill. 1981).

[97] See *Bell v. Industrial Vangas, Inc.*, 637 P.2d 266 (Cal. 1981), which was overturned by legislation (CAL. LAB. CODE § 3602(a), (2003)) and *Mercer v. Uniroyal, Inc.*, 361 N.E.2d 492 (Ohio Ct. App. 1976), which was rejected by *Schump v. Firestone Tire and Rubber Co.*, 541 N.E.2d 1040 (Ohio 1989).

[98] In *Engel v. Workers' Compensation Appeals Board*, 1998 Cal. LEXIS 4199 (Cal. 1998), the California Supreme Court denied a petition to review the constitutionality of that state's workers' compensation act.

[99] 23 P.3d 333 (Or. 2001).

the state constitution. The court found that the exclusive remedy provision's bar to employer liability violate the remedy clause of the Oregon constitution which provides that "every [person] shall have remedy by due course of law for injury done him in his person, property, or reputation."[100]

[2] Employer Liability to Third Parties

Employees injured in the course of employment are barred by workers' compensation laws from suing their employers in negligence or strict liability for their injuries. If the employees were injured by machinery or a work-place substance, they will sue the manufacturer of the product. However, the manufacturer may bring a third-party action against the employer seeking indemnification or contribution.[101] Such claims by the manufacturer may be based on allegations that the employer failed to provide the employee with a safe working environment, failed to adequately instruct the employee on how to use the product, failed to adequately supervise the employee while using the product, or failed to maintain the product properly.[102] However, the vast majority of states extend the immunity of the employer from torts suits by its employees to include immunity from claims for contribution by third-parties for contribution.[103] Only one state, New York, permits a defendant to recover unlimited contribution from negligent employers. In addition, a few states allow limited contribution from the employer.[104] In Illinois, for example, the Contribution Act[105] requires employers to contribute to tort judgments when they are found to be responsible for any part of an employee's injuries. However, the amount that an employer can be required to contribute is limited to the amount of its statutory liability under the state's workers' compensation statute.[106]

---

[100] OREGON CONSTITUTION, art. 1, § 10.

[101] *See* Coello v. Tug Manufacturing Corp., 756 F. Supp. 1258; (W.D. Mo. 1991) (applying Missouri law).

[102] *See* Ocampo v. Paper Converting Machine Co., 2005 U.S. Dist. LEXIS 17107 (N.D. Ill. 2005) (applying Illinois law).

[103] *See, e.g.,* Oaklawn Jockey Club v. Pickens-Bond Construction, 477 S.W.2d 477 (Ark. 1972).

[104] *See* Kotecki v. Cyclops Welding Corp., 585 N.E.2d 1023 (Ill. 1991); Lambertson v. Cincinnati Corp., 257 N.W.2d 679 (Minn. 1977).

[105] 740 ILL. COMP. STAT. 100/0.01 (2004).

[106] *See* Kotecki v. Cyclops Welding Corp., 585 N.E.2d 1023 (Ill. 1991).

[B] *Government Contractor Defense*

[1] Framework for the Defense

The government contract defense provides an affirmative defense in products liability cases by extending the immunity given to the federal government for discretionary functions under the Federal Tort Claims Act[107] to contractors that manufacture equipment for the federal government. The framework for the government contractor defense was laid out by the Supreme Court in *Boyle v. United Technologies Corp.*,[108] in which a Marine helicopter crashed off the Virginia coast during a training exercise. Although Boyle, the copilot, survived the impact of the crash, he was unable to escape from the helicopter and drowned. His father brought an action against the manufacturer of the helicopter, alleging that it had defectively designed the copilot's emergency escape-hatch system since the hatch opened out instead of in. Although there is no federal legislation specifically giving immunity to government contractors, the Supreme Court held that there are a few situations involving "uniquely federal interests" where state law may be preempted and replaced by federal law prescribed by the courts.[109] According to the Court, the procurement of equipment by the United States is an area of uniquely federal interest.[110] However, rather than give government contractors a blanket immunity from liability, the Court formulated a "government contractor defense." Under this defense, state law imposing liability for design defects in military equipment is displaced where: (1) the United States approved reasonably precise specifications for the product; (2) the product conformed to those specifications; and (3) the supplier warned the United States about dangers in the use of the product known to the supplier but not to the United States.[111] In *Boyle*, the Court held that the state-imposed duty of care, as an asserted basis for a contractor's liability, was in direct conflict with the duty imposed by the government contract and thus the state tort law had to be displaced.

[2] The Three Prongs of the Defense

The first prong of the government contractor defense set out in *Boyle* requires a showing that the government "approved reasonably precise specifications" for the product. Courts have interpreted the term "approved" as requiring actual review and evaluation of the specifications for the equip-

---

[107] 28 U.S.C. §§ 1346(b), 2671-2678, 2680.

[108] 487 U.S. 500 (1988).

[109] *Id*. at 504-505.

[110] *Id*. at 505-507.

[111] *Id*. at 512.

ment rather than simply a "rubber stamp."[112] The approval must constitute a "discretionary function" of the government, which is defined as government acts involving "the use of policy judgment."[113] Courts have reinforced the importance of actual review, stating that only "genuine consideration and informed judgment satisfies the first prong of *Boyle*."[114] The requirement that the specifications be "reasonably precise" means that the government will exercise its discretion over "significant details and all critical design choices" unless it approves only general guidelines; the contractor then will have discretion over design choices.[115] On the other hand, the government is not required to instruct the manufacturer on how to make the product and can approve a design for which it provided no input.[116]

The second prong of the government contractor defense requires a manufacturer to establish that the product conformed to the reasonably precise specifications approved by the government. In *Elmore v. Rockwell Automation*,[117] a Postal Service worker suffered a severe injury when his arm became entangled in a mail conveyer system. The worker brought suit against the builder of the conveyer system and the subcontractor that provided its electrical control boxes. The defendants relied on the government contractor defense, asserting that the conveyor system conformed to government specifications.[118] However, the worker offered expert testimony that the system violated Occupational Safety and Health Administration (OSHA) safety guidelines, that the machine did not have a warning where it was required, and that the emergency stop button was too far from the nip point. Since conformity with OSHA guidelines was a requirement in the Postal Service's specifications, the district court denied the defendants' motion for summary judgment based on the government contractor defense.[119]

The third prong of the government contractor defense requires proof that the contractor warned the United States government about known dangers associated with the use of the product.[120] Under this prong, the con-

---

[112] *See* Trevino v. General Dynamics Corp., 865 F.2d 1474, 1480 (5th Cir. 1989).

[113] *Id.*

[114] Haltiwanger v. Unisys Corp., 949 F. Supp. 898, 902-903 (D.D.C. 1996).

[115] *Trevino*, 865 F.2d at 1481. *See also* Kerstetter v. Pacific Scientific Co., 210 F.3d 431, 438 (5th Cir. 2000) ("'the reasonably precise' standard is satisfied so long as the specifications address, in reasonable detail, the product design feature, alleged to be defective"); Bailey v. McDonnell Douglas Corp., 989 F.2d 794, 799 (5th Cir. 1993) (specifications need not address the specific defect alleged, just the specific feature).

[116] *Trevino*, 865 F.2d at 1480.

[117] 306 F. Supp. 2d 751 (N.D. Ill. 2004).

[118] *Id.* at 753.

[119] *Id.*

[120] *See* Haltiwanger v. Unisys Corp., 949 F. Supp. 898, 904 (D.D.C. 1996); Niemann v. McDonnell Douglas Corp., 721 F. Supp. 1019, 1028 (S.D. Ill.1989).

tractor must disclose information when the government knows less about the danger than the contractor. However, a contractor is not required to warn about latent defects, only those about which it has actual knowledge.[121] The party asserting the government contract defense must prove either that "the contractor lacked actual knowledge of the danger or that the government was independently aware of the defect" in order to demonstrate that the government was as aware of the danger as the contractor.[122] Thus, "if the government was already independently aware of a risk and chose to act regardless of the knowledge, [a] defendant may still employ the government contractor defense without further warning the government."[123]

In *Boyle*, the Supreme Court applied the government contractor defense in the context of a design defect. Federal courts are split as to whether the defense applies only to design defects or to manufacturing defects as well.[124] In *Bailey v. McDonnell Douglas Corporation*,[125] for example, the Fifth Circuit held that the defense its not limited to design defect claims. The court stated that the defense will apply when the three conditions laid out in *Boyle* are satisfied with respect to "the particular product feature upon which the claim is based."[126] Many courts also have held the defense applies to failure to warn claims.[127] In *Kerstetter v. Pacific Scientific Company*,[128] the Fifth Circuit held that, since the Navy knew of the danger of the uncommanded seat release on the T-34C aircraft's pilot restraint system, the contractor did not have a duty to warn it of that danger. In addition, even if the government was unaware of the defect, a contractor's failure to warn the government about latent defects would not preclude the use of the defense.[129] In *Densberger v. United Technologies*,[130] the Second Circuit held

---

[121] Kerstetter v. Pacific Scientific Co., 210 F.3d 431 (5th Cir. 2000).

[122] *Haltiwanger*, 949 F. Supp. at 904; Niemann v. McDonnell Douglas Corp., 721 F.Supp. 1019, 1028 (S.D. Ill.1989).

[123] Stout v. Borg-Warner Corp. 933 F.2d 331, 336-337 (5th Cir. 1991).

[124] *See, e.g.*, Mitchell v. Lone Star Ammunition, Inc., 913 F.2d 242 (5th Cir. 1990) (the defense only applies in cases of defective design); Bentzlin v. Hughes Aircraft Co., 833 F. Supp. 1486 (C.D. Cal. 1993) (the defense applies to manufacturing defect claims); Torrington Co. v. Stutzman, 46 S.W.3d 829 (Tex. 2000) (upholding refusal to submit the defense to the jury because the defect originated in the product's manufacture, not in its design).

[125] 989 F.2d 794 (5th Cir. 1993).

[126] *Id.* at 801-802.

[127] In *Tate v. Boeing Helicopters*, 55 F.3d 1150, 1157 (6th Cir. 1995), the court outlined the elements a contractor must establish in a failure to warn case: (1) the federal government exercised its discretion and approved any warnings; (2) the contractor's warnings conformed to those approved by the government; and (3) the contractor warned the government of any dangers known to the contractor but not to the government. *See also* Emory v. McDonnell Douglas Corp., 148 F.3d 347 (4th Cir. 1998); Oliver v. Oshkosh Truck Corp., 96 F.3d 992 (7th Cir. 1996).

[128] 210 F.3d 431 (5th Cir. 2000).

[129] *Id.* at 436.

[130] 297 F.3d 66 (2d Cir. 2002).

that a helicopter manufacturer was liable in negligence for deaths arising out of the company's post-sale failure to warn the Army that its helicopter could become uncontrollable. According to the court, the government contractor defense makes sense only if the government limited the warnings that the contractor was permitted to give to the users. However, in *Densberger*, the manufacturer failed to warn the Army of the problems with the helicopter, not the pilots. Thus, the defense did not apply and the survivors were permitted the brings their action.

[3] Expansion of the Defense

Although the government contractor defense once was limited to manufacturers and suppliers that did business with the government, Congress expanded the defense and gave it new importance in 2002 with the enactment of the Homeland Security Act. Contained within that Act is the Support Anti-Terrorism by Fostering Effective Technologies Act of 2002 (the "Safety Act"),[131] under which the Secretary of the Department of Homeland Security can designate certain products as "qualified anti-terrorism technology."[132] These include "any product, equipment, service, device, or technology designed, developed, modified, or procured for the specific purpose of preventing, detecting, identifying, or deterring acts of terrorism or limiting the harm such acts might otherwise cause."[133] If a claim arises from an act of terrorism when "qualified anti-terrorism technology" has been used in defense against the terrorism, there is a federal cause of action.[134] In addition, the Act creates a rebuttable presumption that the government contractor defense applies to the sellers of these technologies.[135] However, in a change from the past application of the defense, the presumption applies not only when a plaintiff's claims arises from the sale of the technology to the federal government but also when the sale was to private parties.[136] Before the presumption arises, the Secretary, who has the exclusive responsibility for reviewing and approving anti-terrorism technology, must certify that the technology: (1) will perform as intended; (2) conforms with the seller's specifications; and (3) is safe for use as intended.[137]

---

[131] 6 U.S.C. § 441-444.

[132] *Id.* § 441(b).

[133] *Id.* § 444(1).

[134] *Id.* § 442.

[135] *Id.* § 442(d)(1).

[136] *Id.*

[137] *Id.* 442(d)(2).

§ 9.04 TIMES-BASED DEFENSES

[A] *Statutes of Limitations*

Every state has enacted a statute of limitations that establishes specific time limits for filing products liability actions based on warranty, negligence, and strict liability. These statutes provide an affirmative defense that the manufacturer or seller must plead. These statutes are an attempt to strike a balance between giving injured plaintiffs adequate time to bring their claims and the need to protect manufacturers and sellers by making sure that the evidence and witnesses' memories are fresh. If a defendant fails to raise the defense, the action will proceed.

The time periods set out in the statutes of limitations vary from state to state and depend on whether the claim is for personal injury, property damage, or wrongful death. They can as short as one year, as in Kentucky,[138] Louisiana,[139] and Tennessee,[140] or as long as six years, as in Maine,[141] Minnesota,[142] and North Dakota.[143] However, the most common limitation periods are four years for breach of warranty actions[144] and two or three years for negligence[145] and strict liability[146] claims.

In most states, the statute of limitations begins to run from the date "the cause of action accrues." Usually, this is the date on which the personal injury or property damage occurred. However, because that can frustrate the goal of giving the injured plaintiff adequate time to bring his or her claim, courts have held that the running of the statute of limitations may be tolled by certain situations. Thus, if a child is injured by a defective product, the statute is tolled during the period that he or she is a minor.[147] In addition, courts in most states have created some form of a discovery rule.[148] Under this rule, the statute of limitations does not begin to run until

---

[138] KY. REV. STAT. ANN. §§ 413.140(1)(a) (Michie 1992) (personal injury); 413.180 (Michie 1992) (wrongful dealth and survival actions).

[139] LA. CODE CIV. PROC. ANN. art. 3492 (1998).

[140] TENN. CODE ANN. § 28-3-104(b) (2000) (personal injury).

[141] ME. REV. STAT. ANN. tit. 14, § 752 (2003) (personal injury).

[142] MINN. STAT. ANN. § 541.05. Subd. 1 (2000) (personal injury or property damage).

[143] N.D. CENT. CODE § 28-01-16(5) (1991).

[144] *See, e.g.*, FLA. STAT. ANN. § 95.11(3)(k) (2002).

[145] *See, e.g.* GA. CODE ANN. § 9-3-33 (1982) (two years) *and* MD. CODE ANN., CTS. AND JUD. PRO. § 5-101 (2002) (three years).

[146] *See, e.g.*, N.J. STAT. ANN. § 2A:14-2 (2000) (two years) *and* MISS. CODE ANN. § 15-1-49 (2003) (three years).

[147] *See* Cox v. McDonnell-Douglas Corp., 665 F.2d 566 (5th Cir.1982) (applying Texas law); Miles v. S.C. Johnson & Son, Inc., 2001 U.S. Dist. LEXIS 12904 (N.D. Ill. 2001).

[148] *See* John's Heating Service v. Lamb, 46 P.2d 1024 (Alaska 2002); Lawhon v. L.B.J. Institutional Supply, Inc., 765 P.2d 1003 (Ariz. Ct. App. 1988).

the plaintiff knows, or reasonably should have known, of an injury and knows or reasonably should have known that the injury was caused by the wrongful action of another.[149] Although in most products liability cases, plaintiffs will know of the injury at the time of the accident, the discovery rule can be important in cases involving drugs, medical implants, or exposure to substances such as asbestos where plaintiffs may not know that they have suffered legal damage. In *Sawtell v. E.I. DuPont De Nemours and Co.*,[150] the plaintiff claimed that the defendant manufactured polymers inappropriately used in temporomandibular joint prostheses causing a foreign body reaction that resulted in bone degeneration, extreme pain and five operations. The district court granted summary judgment on the basis of New Mexico's three year statute of limitations and the Tenth Circuit affirmed. Based on the facts of the case, the court found undisputed evidence that the plaintiff had enough facts to make out the elements of her products liability cause of action and should have known the specific cause of her injuries before the statute of limitations expired.

[B] *Statutes of Repose*

In addition to statutes of limitation, states in the late 1960s began to enact statutes of repose. Regardless of when the cause of action accrued, these statutes bar a plaintiff's claim unless it is brought within a specific number of years from the date the defendant manufactured or sold the product.[151] These statutes have been criticized as unfair to plaintiffs,[152] since they may bar claims before they have arisen, and challenged on constitutional grounds.[153] As a result, more than 30 states do not have statutes of repose. In those states that do, the goal of the statute is the same as with statutes of limitations: give plaintiffs time to prepare their claims while giving manufacturers and sellers certainty that, after a specific period of time, they will not have to worry about suits involving their products.[154]

Among the states that have adopted statutes of repose, the statutes are state specific and the time varies greatly. In Illinois, for example, the statute

---

[149] *See* Martin v. Arthur, 3 S.W.3d 684 (Ark. 1999); Nolan v. Johns-Manville Asbestos, 421 N.E.2d 864 (Ill. 1981).

[150] 22 F.3d 248 (10th Cir. 1994) (applying New Mexico law).

[151] *See* McGovern, *The Variety, Policy and Constitutionality of Product Liability Statutes of Repose*, 30 Am. U.L. Rev. 579 (1981).

[152] *See* Comment, *Due Process Challenges to Statutes to Repose*, 40 Sw. L.J. 997 (1986).

[153] The constitutionality of most state statutes of repose has been upheld. *See, e.g.,* Barwick v. Celotex Corp., 736 F.2d 946 (4th Cir. 1984) (upholding the constitutionality of the North Carolina statute) *and* McIntosh v. Melroe Co., 729 N.E.2d 972 (Ind. 2000) (upholding the constitutionality of the Indiana statute). However, a number of statutes have been struck down as violating state constitutions. For examples, see *Dickie v. Harmers Union Oil Co.*, 611 N.E.2d 168 (N.D. 2000); *Hazine v. Mongomery Elevator Co.*, 861 P.2d 625 (Ariz. 1993); and *Kennedy v. Cumberland Engineering Co.*, 471 A.2d 195 (R.I. 1984).

[154] Goad v. Celotex Corp., 831 F.2d 508 (4th Cir. 1987) (applying Texas law).

of repose states that, a "product liability action based on the doctrine of strict liability in tort" must be commenced "within 12 years from the date of first sale, lease or delivery of possession by a seller or 10 years from the date of first sale, lease or delivery of possession to its initial user, consumer, or other non-seller, whichever period expires earlier."[155] However, North Carolina has the shortest statute of repose: six years.[156] Some states also limit the application of their statutes of repose. For example, although Connecticut has no general statute of repose, a statute of repose bars all claims arising out of workplace accidents brought more than 10 years after the date the seller parted with possession of the product.[157] Georgia's statute of repose does not apply to failure to warn claims,[158] actions in negligence against manufacturers of products implicated in birth defects, or actions against manufacturers that arise out of negligence.[159] In Massachusetts and Minnesota, states without a statute of repose in products liability actions, some products liability claims still may be subject to the states' statutes of repose applicable to tort actions arising out of improvements to real property.[160] The Texas statute of repose expressly does not apply to electronic products.[161]

[C] *Useful Shelf-Life*

In 2005 DaimlerChrysler and Ford Motor Company began advising their automobile and truck customers: "Tires and spare tire should be replaced after six years, regardless of the remaining tread. Failure to follow this warning can result in sudden tire failure. You could lose control and have an accident resulting in serious injury or death."[162] The companies were responding to research that suggested tires can degrade rapidly as they get older, regardless of how much they are used. This raises the question of whether, independently of the statute of repose, a manufacturer has a defense that the product has exceeded its "useful safe life."[163]

---

[155] 735 ILL. COMP. STAT. 5/13-213(b) (1996). Although § 5/13-213(b) contains a ten-year statute of repose, *Davis v. Toshiba Machine Co., America*, 710 N.E.2d 399 (Ill. 1999), held that an action can be filed within two years of the injury as long as the injury occurred within the statute of repose, regardless of whether the statute of repose has expired.

[156] *See* N.C. GEN. STAT. § 1-50(a)(6) (2003); Vogl v. LVD Corp., 514 S.E.2d 113 (N.C. Ct. App. 1999).

[157] CONN. GEN. STAT. § 52-577a(c) (1991).

[158] Chrysler Corp. v. Batten, 450 S.E.2d 208 (Ga. 1994).

[159] GA. CODE ANN. § 51-1-11(c) (1982); Vickery v. Waste Management of Georgia, Inc., 549 S.E.2d 482 (Ga. 2001).

[160] MASS. GEN. LAWS ANN. ch. 260, § 2B (2004); Minn. Stat. Ann. § 541.051 (2000).

[161] TEX. CIV. PRAC. & REM. CODE ANN. § 16.012 (Vernon 2002).

[162] "Chrysler: Change Tires after 6 Years," *The Detroit News*, May 27, 2005, http://www.detnews.com/2005/autoinsider/0505/27/C01-195417.htm.

[163] *See* Charles E. Cantu, *The Useful Life Defense: Embracing the Idea That All Products Eventually Grow Old and Die*, 80 NEB. L. REV. 1 (2001).

The source of useful safe life analysis is the Model Uniform Product Liability Act (MUPLA), created by the Department of Commerce in 1979.[164] Section 110(A)(1) of the Act states that "a product seller shall not be subject to liability to a claimant for harm under this Act if the product seller proves by a preponderance of the evidence that the harm, was caused after the product's 'useful safe life' had expired."[165] The Act states that the "useful safe life" of a product begins "at the time of delivery of the product and extends for the time during which the product would normally be likely to perform or be stored in a safe manner."[166] The Act then sets out a number of factors that help determine whether a product's useful safe life has expired. These include: (1) the amount of "wear and tear" to which the product has been subject; (2) the effect of deterioration from the user, similar users, and from climate or other conditions under which the product was used or stored; (3) the normal practices of the user, similar users, and the product seller with respect to the circumstances, frequency, and purposes of the product's use, and with respect to repairs, renewals, and replacements; (4) any representations, instruction, or warnings made by the product seller concerning proper maintenance, storage, and use of the product or the expected useful safe life of the product; and (5) any modification or alteration of the product by a user or third party.[167]

Statutes of repose and the concept of useful safe life are similar in that they provide a period of time beyond which a manufacturer or seller will not be liable for a product. However, useful life statutes are more advantageous to plaintiffs since that they are more flexible and do not contain the rigid periods of time imposed by statutes of repose. For example, instead of a fixed statute of repose, Idaho provides that a manufacturer or seller is not liable for harm if it can prove that the harm occurred after the product's "useful safe life" had expired.[168] The statute states, however, that the manufacturer can be liable if it expressly warranted the product for a longer period of time. For claims involving harm caused more than ten years after the time of the delivery of the product, there is a rebuttable presumption that the harm was caused after the useful safe life expired. Kansas also has a useful life statute that is almost identical to the one in Idaho.[169] However, the Kansas statute lists the five factors in the MUPLA to help the fact-finder determine whether the product's safe life has expired.[170] In Washington, the useful safe life statute has many similarities to those in other states as

---

[164] 44 FED. REG. 62,714 (1979).

[165] *Id.* at 62,732.

[166] *Id.*

[167] *Id.*

[168] IDAHO CODE § 6-1403(1) (2004).

[169] KAN. STAT. ANN. § 60-3303 (1994); Hiner v. Deere & Co., 161 F. Supp. 2d 1279 (D. Kan. 2001) (applying Kansas law).

[170] KAN. STAT. ANN. § 60-3303(a) (1994).

well as a few important differences.[171] Although a product seller generally is not liable for harm after the product's useful safe life has expired, it may be liable if: (1) it told the buyer the product had a longer warranty than the useful safe life; (2) it intentionally misrepresented facts about the product or concealed information about it and such conduct led to the plaintiff's injury; or (3) the injury was caused by exposure to a defective product, which the plaintiff received and used for the first time within the product's safe life but the harm did not manifest itself until after the safe life had expired. In addition, the Washington statute states that if the injury occurred more than twelve years after the buyer received the product, there is a presumption that the useful safe life had expired.[172]

§ 9.05 GOVERNMENT AND INDUSTRY SAFETY STANDARDS

In products liability cases, plaintiffs often attempt to show that the manufacturer or seller was negligent per se or that the product was unreasonably dangerous by reference to government and industry safety standards. Similarly, manufacturers frequently attempt to rebut allegations of negligence and product defectiveness by relying on those same standards.

[A] *Government Safety Standards*

In addition to the standards imposed by negligence and strict liability, manufacturers of products as diverse as airplanes, automobiles, drugs, food, and toys are subject to state and federal statutes and administrative regulations intended to promote product safety. These regulations may apply to the design, inspection, testing, manufacture, labeling, warnings, or instructions for use of the product. In negligence cases, a violation of a government regulation results in a finding that the manufacturer was negligent *per se*, helping the plaintiff to establish a *prima facie* case of negligence.[173] This approach first was articulated in *Martin v. Herzog*[174] when Judge Benjamin Cardozo stated that the "unexcused omission" of a statutory requirement was "more than some evidence of negligence. It *is* negligence in itself . . . Jurors have no dispensing power by which they may relax the duty."[175] This position was adopted by the Restatement (Second) of Torts which states: "The unexcused violation of the legislative enactment or an administrative regulation which is adopted by the court as

---

[171] WASH. REV. CODE § 7.72.060(1) (1992).

[172] *Id.* § 7.72.060(2).

[173] *See* Baxley v. Fischer, 134 S.E.2d 291 (Va. 1964).

[174] 126 N.E. 814 (N.Y. 1920).

[175] *Id.* at 815 (emphasis in the original).

defining the standard of conduct of a reasonable man, is negligence in itself."[176] Thus, if a manufacturer is found to have violated a statute or regulation, the questions for the jury are: (1) was the statute or regulation in effect at the time of the sale of the product? (2) was the plaintiff within the class of persons intended to be protected by the statute or regulation? (3) was the violation of the statute or regulation a cause of the plaintiff's injury? and (4) was the violation of the statute an "excused omission"?[177]

A manufacturer also may raise compliance with a government statute or regulation as a defense to an allegation that its product was defective.[178] Although, in negligence cases, the fact that a product complied with an applicable statute is evidence that the product was not defective, it is not conclusive and does not shield a manufacturer from liability.[179] One reason for this is that government standards are considered to be a minimum standard for a product and, in some situations, the product is expected to meet more than that minimum standard. The Restatement (Second) of Torts, for example, states that "[c]ompliance with a legislative enactment or an administrative regulation does not prevent a finding of negligence where a reasonable man would take additional precautions."[180] In strict liability actions, a few states also hold that compliance with government standards is relevant but not conclusive as to whether the product was defective.[181] However, the majority of states hold that compliance with a government regulation should not be considered "where the product's condition and consumer expectations are the central inquiries and liability may be imposed regardless of the degree of care exercised by the manufacturer."[182] Some states have codified a rebuttable presumption that a product is not in a defective condition if it is in "conformity with government standards established for that industry."[183]

---

[176] RESTATEMENT (SECOND) OF TORTS § 288B (1965).

[177] Although Judge Cardozo did not discuss when an omission of a statute might be excused, § 288A of the RESTATEMENT (SECOND) OF TORTS lists five situations when a "violation is excused."

[178] See Symposium: Regulatory Compliance as a Defense to Products Liability, 88 GA. L.J. 2049 (2000).

[179] Woodell v. Proctor & Gamble Manufacturing Co., 1999 U.S. Dist. LEXIS 12850 (N.D. Tex. 1999) (applying Texas law); Abadie v. Metropolitan Life Insurance Co., 784 So.2d 46 (La. Ct. App. 2001); Barry v. Don Hall Laboratories, 642 P.2d 685 (Or. Ct. App. 1982).

[180] RESTATEMENT (SECOND) OF TORTS § 288C (1965).

[181] See Lorenz v. Celotex Corp., 896 F.2d 148 (5th Cir. 1990) (applying Texas law).

[182] Bailey v. V & O Press, 770 F.2d 601, 607-609 (6th Cir. 1985) (applying Ohio law). See also Harsh v. Petroll & Hac, 840 A.2d 404 (Pa. 2003).

[183] See N.D. CENT. CODE § 28-01.3-09 (2005). North Dakota also provides that there is a "disputable presumption" that aircraft and aircraft component parts are not defective if they are "in compliance with (a) Government standards established for that product." N.D. CENT CODE § 28-01.4-02 (2005). See also COLO. REV. STAT. § 13-21-403 (2005); FLA. STAT. ANN. § 768.1256 (2005); IND. CODE § 34-20-5-1 (1998).

The Restatement (Third) now applies in strict liability cases the same position taken by the majority of states in negligence cases toward the noncompliance and compliance with safety statutes and regulations. Section 4, which applies "[i]n connection with liability for defective design or inadequate instructions or warnings," states:

    (a) a product's noncompliance with an applicable product safety statute or administrative regulation renders the product defective with respect to the risks sought to be reduced by the statute or regulation; and

    (b) a product's compliance with an applicable product safety statute or administrative regulation is properly considered in determining whether the product is defective with respect to the risks sought to be reduced by the statute or regulation, but such compliance does not preclude as a matter of law a finding of product defect.[184]

[B] *Industry Standards*

In addition to government safety regulations, there are numerous industry standards for the design and use of products.[185] Compliance with these standards and with the custom in the industry is an issue in design defect cases more often than those involving manufacturing defects and the failure to warn. Although industry standards and custom do not have the force of law, courts tend to treat them in the same way that they view government standards. Thus, in a negligence case, if the manufacturer did not comply with an industry standard for the design of the product, the trier of fact may find that it breached its duty of care to the plaintiff. Conversely, manufacturers introduce evidence of their compliance with industry standards and custom in the hope of showing that they acted like reasonable manufacturers in the selection of the design and thus met the requirement of due care.[186] However, as with government regulations, compliance with industry standards and custom, while evidence of what is the reasonable standard in the industry in negligence cases, does not conclusively establish the standard of care the manufacturer is expected to meet.[187] If an indus-

---

[184] RESTATEMENT (THIRD) OF TORTS: PRODUCTS LIABILITY § 4 (1998).

[185] Among these are the American National Standards Institute (ANSI) codes and the Underwriter Laboratories (UL) Standards.

[186] Bragg v. Hi-Ranger, Inc., 462 S.E.2d 321 (S.C. Ct. App. 1995); Westinghouse Electric Corp. v. Nutt, 407 A.2d 606 (D.C. Ct. App. 1979).

[187] Masters v. Heeston Corp., 291 F.3d 985 (7th Cir. 2002) (applying Illinois law); McKee v. Cutter Laboratories, Inc., 866 F.2d 219 (6th Cir. 1989) (applying Kentucky law); Condos v. Musculoskeletal Transplant Foundation, 208 F. Supp. 2d 1226 (D. Utah 2002) (applying Utah law); Dunn v. Wixom Brothers, 493 So.2d 1356 (Ala. 1986); Vis v. Cushman, Inc., 638 N.W.2d 393 (Wis. Ct. App. 2001).

try has adopted careless methods, it is not permitted to set its own uncontrolled standard.[188] Similarly, although compliance with industry standards is used in negligence cases, is not admissible in strict liability cases[189] Courts feel that such evidence injects negligence concepts into strict liability where the focus is on the product and not on the manufacturer's conduct.[190]

§ 9.06 PREEMPTION

[A] *Introduction*

In 2000 a group of peanut farmers in western Texas sprayed their crops with a pesticide manufactured by Dow Agrosciences. Although the chemical killed the weeds, it also stunted the growth of their crops, resulting in millions of dollars in losses. The farmers notified Dow of their intent to sue for false advertising, breach of warranty, and fraudulent trade practices under the Texas Deceptive Trade Practices Act (DTPA), on the grounds that they were misled by the retailers of the pesticide and were not warned that it was harmful in soils with high pH levels. In response, Dow filed a declaratory judgment action in federal court, asserting that the farmers' claims expressly or impliedly were pre-empted by Federal Insecticide, Fungicide, and Rodenticide Act (FIFRA).[191] The farmers then counterclaimed, alleging strict liability, negligence, fraud, breach of warranty, and a violation of the Texas DTPA. The district court granted Dow's motion for summary judgment on the grounds that the claims expressly were pre-empted by § 136v(b) of the FIFRA which provides that states "shall not impose or continue in effect any requirements for labeling or packaging in addition to or different from those required under this subchapter."[192] The Fifth Circuit affirmed, saying that FIFRA overrides state laws that either directly or indirectly impose different labeling requirements.[193] In June 2004 the Supreme Court granted certiorari in *Bates v. Dow Agrosciences* and agreed to decide whether the farmers' claims of defective design, defective manufacture, negligent testing, and breach of express warranty were preempted by FIFRA.[194]

Although the question of when a federal statute preempts state common law has become a frequent source of litigation and scholarly attention, it was not until 1992 that the Supreme Court began to address the issue in the con-

---

[188] Jones v. Hutchinson Manufacturing, Inc., 502 S.W.2d 66, 70 (Ky. Ct. App. 1973).

[189] *See* Grimshaw v. Ford Motor Co., 174 Cal. Rptr. 348, 378 (Cal. Ct. 1981) ("In a strict products liability case, industry custom or usage is irrelevant to the issue of defect.").

[190] *See* Blacker v. Oldsmobile Division, General Motors Corp., 869 F. Supp. 313 (E.D. Pa. 1994) (applying Pennsylvania law).

[191] 7 U.S.C. § 136.

[192] Dow Agrosciences, LLC v. Bates, 205 F. Supp. 2d 623 (N.D. Tex. 2002).

[193] Dow Agrosciences, LLC v. Bates, 332 F.3d 323 (5th Cir. 2003).

[194] Bates v. Dow Agrosciences, LLC, 2004 U.S. LEXIS 4598 (2004).

text of products liability cases.[195] Because the decisions still are evolving, they are difficult to reconcile, making preemption the most confusing of all of the defenses in products liability cases. The basis of the power of the federal government to preempt state products liability laws is the Supremacy Clause of the Constitution which provides that the "Constitution and the Laws of the United States . . . shall be the supreme Law of the Land; and the Judges in every State shall be bound thereby, any Thing in the Constitution or Laws of any State to the Contrary notwithstanding."[196] As a result, when a state law conflicts with a federal law, the state law is "without effect.[197] However, the Supremacy Clause itself conflicts with the traditional powers of the states to regulate and to decide disputes involving their citizens. Because of the concern for state powers, the Supreme Court in 1947 instructed federal courts that state police powers were not to be superceded by federal law unless "that was the clear and manifest purpose of Congress.[198] Despite these concerns about interfering with state regulatory powers, a number of product-related federal statutes contain preemption provisions. In addition to FIFRA, preemption clauses can be found in such diverse legislation as the Public Health Cigarette Smoking Act of 1969,[199] the Federal Hazardous Substances Act,[200] and the Medical Device Amendments to the Food, Drug and Cosmetic Act.[201] In recent years, courts also have sought to determine the extent to which the federal preemption provisions bar state common law products liability actions.

Federal preemption of state product liability cases would not be as controversial if it was limited to situations where Congress or a federal agency clearly stated its express intent to preempt state law. However, in *Louisiana Public Service Commission v. FCC*,[202] the Supreme Court set out the three different ways in which a federal statute preempts a state law:

> Pre-emption occurs when Congress, in enacting a federal statute, expresses a clear intent to preempt state law, when there is outright or actual conflict between federal and state law, where compliance with both federal and state law is in effect physically impossible, where there is implicit in federal law a barrier to state regulation, where Congress has legislated comprehensively, thus occupying an entire field of regulation and leaving no room for the states to supplement federal law, or where the state law stands as an obstacle to the

---

[195] Cipollone v. Liggett Group, Inc., 505 U.S. 504 (1992).

[196] U.S. CONST., art. VI. cl.2.

[197] Maryland v. Louisiana, 451 U.S. 725, 746 (1981).

[198] Rice v. Santa Fe Elevator Corp., 331 U.S. 218, 230 (1947).

[199] 15 U.S.C. § 1334(b).

[200] 15 U.S.C. § 1261.

[201] 21 U.S.C. § 360(k).

[202] 476 U.S. 355 (1986).

accomplishment and execution of the full objectives of Congress. Preemption may result not only from action taken by Congress itself; a federal agency acting within the scope of its congressionally delegated authority may preempt state regulation.[203]

Contained within the *Louisiana Public Service Commission* opinion are the three situations in which federal preemption applies in products liability cases: (1) where Congress expressly has preempted state action (express preemption); (2) where Congress has implemented a comprehensive regulatory scheme in an area, removing the entire field from state regulation (field preemption); or (3) where state action conflicts with federal law (conflict preemption).

[B] *Express Preemption*

When Congress chooses expressly to preempt state law, the question for courts is whether the challenged state law is one the federal statute intends to preempt. An example of statutory language designed to preempt state laws is § 136v(b) of FIFRA which provides that states "shall not impose or continue in effect any requirements for labeling or packaging in addition to or different from those required under this subchapter." The problem for the Court with this section in *Bates* was to determine the meaning of the term "requirements" imposed by a state. Some courts have held that "requirements" includes only state legislative "requirements,[204] while other courts have interpreted the term to include common-law tort claims as well.[205]

The Supreme Court first confronted the issue of whether or not common-law tort claims could be expressly preempted in *Cipollone v. Liggett Group, Inc.*,[206] where the Court found that the preemption provision in the Public Health Cigarette Smoking Act of 1969 was broad enough to preclude common law tort actions as well as state statutes.[207] Lower courts faced with the task of construing preemption provisions similar or identical to the one in *Cipollone* also have found common law claims to be preempted.[208] However, in *Medtronic, Inc. v. Lohr,* [209] the Supreme Court held

---

[203] *Id.* at 368-369. *See also* Lorillard Tobacco Co. v. Reilly, 533 U.S. 525, 541 (2001): "State action may be foreclosed by express language in a congressional enactment, by implication from the depth and breadth of a congressional scheme that occupies the legislative field, or by implication because of a conflict with a congressional enactment."

[204] *See* Oja v. Howmedica, Inc., 111 F.3d 782 (10th Cir. 1997).

[205] *See* Martin v. Medtronic, Inc., 254 F.3d 573 (5th Cir. 2001); Kemp v. Medtronic, 231 F.3d 216 (6th Cir. 2000); Mitchell v. Collagen Corp., 126 F.3d 902 (7th Cir. 1997).

[206] 505 U.S. 504 (1992).

[207] *Id.* at 521-522.

[208] *See* Taylor AG Industries v. Pure-Gro, 54 F.3d 555 (9th Cir. 1995) (construing the Federal Insecticide, Fungicide, and Rodenticide Act); Busch v. Graphic Color Corporation, 662 N.E.2d 397 (Ill. 1996) (construing the Federal Hazardous Substances Act).

[209] 518 U.S. 470 (1996).

that the preemption provision in § 360(k) of the Medical Device Amendments to the Food, Drug and Cosmetic Act[210] bars state requirements with respect to medical devices that are different from or in addition to specific federal requirements, but does not preclude common law actions based on a breach of the general duties imposed on every manufacturer of products placed in the stream of commerce.[211] The Court in *Medtronic* refused the plaintiff's invitation to hold that common law duties are never "requirements" within the meaning of section 360(k) and that the section, therefore, never preempts common law action. The Court did not respond directly to the plaintiff's request for two reasons:

> First, since none of the . . . [plaintiff's] claims is pre-empted in this case, we need not resolve hypothetical cases. . . . Second, given the critical importance of device specificity in our (and the FDA's) construction of section 360K, it is apparent that few, if any common-law duties have been preempted by this statute. It will be rare indeed for a court hearing a common-law cause of action to issue a decree that has "the effect of establishing a substantive requirement for a specific device." Until such a case arises, we see no need to determine whether the statute explicitly pre-empts such a claim.[212]

Thus, under *Cipollone* and *Medtronic*, Congress has the power expressly to preempt common-law claims. However, courts must read the federal statute's preemption language with care to determine exactly which common-law claims are preempted and which claims can stand.

It was against the backdrop of *Cipollone* and *Medtronic* that the Supreme Court decided *Bates v. Dow Agrosciences* in April 2005.[213] The Court noted that unlike the language in the *Cipollone* preemption clause, FIFRA's preemption clause only prohibits requirements that are "in addition to or different from" the labeling and packaging requirements of FIFRA.[214] The Court stressed further that nothing in the statute "preclude[s] States from imposing different or additional *remedies*, but only different or additional *requirements*."[215] Thus, it held that common-law "rules that require manufacturers to design reasonably safe products, to use due care in conducting appropriate testing of their products, to market products free of manufacturing defects, and to honor their express warranties . . . do not qualify as requirements for 'labeling or packaging'"[216] and were not preempted. The

---

[210] 21 U.S.C. § 301.

[211] 518 U.S. at 500-502.

[212] *Id.* at 502-503.

[213] 2005 U.S. LEXIS 3706 (2005).

[214] *Id.* at * 29.

[215] *Id.* at * 31.

[216] *Id.* at * 25.

Court further explained that although the defendant's express warranty was written on their label, the cause of action for breach of warranty only sought to enforce the defendant's voluntary contractual commitment that was created when they made their warranty. However, that did not resolve all of the plaintiff's claims. The Court said it had insufficient information to determine whether the Texas definition of fraud imposed a broader duty on the defendant than the requirement in FIFRA that labels can not have false or misleading statements. If so, the Texas' common-law would, in fact, impose an additional requirement on the defendant. Thus, the Court remanded the plaintiffs' claims for fraud and negligent failure to warn to the court of appeals to determine whether or not Texas's common-law duties were equivalent to the FIFRA misbranding standards.[217]

[C] *Field Preemption*

Even in the absence of explicit language in a federal statute intended to preempt state law on a subject, federal preemption still may be implied. Courts recognize that implied preemption takes two forms: field preemption and conflict preemption. Field preemption occurs when the "scheme of federal regulation [is] so pervasive as to make reasonable the inference that Congress left no room for the States to supplement it."[218] In deciding whether there is any room left for state regulation, courts look to the pervasiveness of the federal scheme of regulation, the federal interest at stake, and the danger of frustration of federal goals in making the determination as to whether a challenged state law can stand.

Although field preemption is important in other areas of the law, it has not been the subject of extensive analysis in products liability cases. An example of a court finding no field preemption in a products liability case is *Pinney v. Nokia Inc.*,[219] in which the Fourth Circuit held that five class action lawsuits brought by plaintiffs who alleged they were exposed to unsafe levels of radio frequency radiation from using wireless telephones should be heard by the state courts where they originated, because there was no federal subject-matter jurisdiction. Although Congress enacted § 332 of the Federal Communications Act[220] to ensure the development of an infrastructure necessary to provide wireless services, the court said the Act does not occupy the legislative field of wireless communications so thoroughly as to create a reasonable inference that Congress meant to leave no room for the states to supplement it.[221]

---

[217] *Id.* at * 42.

[218] Fidelity Federal Savings & Loan Association v. De la Cuesta, 458 U.S. 141, 153, (1982). *See also* English v. General Electric Co., 496 U.S. 72 (1990); Rice v. Santa Fe Elevator Corp., 331 U.S. 218 (1947); Choate v. Champion Home Builders Co., 222 F.3d 788 (10th Cir. 2000).

[219] 402 F.3d 430 (4th Cir. 2005).

[220] 47 U.S.C. § 151.

[221] 402 F.3d at 459.

A rare example of a federal statute that occupies an entire field of regulation in products liability cases is the Federal Locomotive Inspection Act (FLIA).[222] The precursor to the FLIA was the Locomotive Boiler Inspection Act. As early as 1926, the Supreme Court ruled in *Napier v. Atlantic Coast Line Railroad Company* that Congress intended to occupy the entire field of locomotive regulation.[223] The original Boiler Inspection Act only covered the boiler on a train's locomotive. The Supreme Court noted, however, that in 1915 the Act was modified to "include the entire locomotive and tender and all parts and appurtenances thereof."[224] This language, in conjunction with the authority given to the Interstate Commerce Commission to "prescribe requirements and establish rules to secure compliance" convinced the Court that the Boiler Inspection Act, as amended, occupied the entire field of locomotive safety.[225] Thus, state laws in Georgia and Wisconsin with specific certain safety features were preempted by the Boiler Inspection Act. Subsequently, the Boiler Inspection Act was replaced with the FLIA, which also occupies the entire field of locomotive regulation.[226]

[D] *Conflict Preemption*

The most common form of implied preemption is conflict preemption. Conflict preemption occurs where a state law conflicts with a federal statute or regulation, or when the state law frustrates the purposes of Congress in enacting the legislation. The Supreme Court has explained that

> even where Congress has not completely displaced state regulation in a specific area, state law is nullified to the extent that it actually conflicts with federal law. Such a conflict arises when compliance with both federal and state regulations is a physical impossibility, or when state law stands as an obstacle to the accomplishment and execution of the full purposes and objectives of Congress.[227]

Thus, state regulations that have not been preempted explicitly by Congress still may be preempted. Such preemption will occur both when it is "a physical impossibility" to comply with both state and federal law, and when "the state law stands as an obstacle to the accomplishment of the full purposes and objectives of Congress."[228]

---

[222] 49 U.S.C. § 20701.

[223] 272 U.S. 605, 613 (1926).

[224] *Id.* at 608.

[225] *Id.* at 608-09.

[226] *See* GMC v. Kilgore, 853 So.2d 171 (Ala. 2002).

[227] Hillsborough County v. Automated Med. Labs., 471 U.S. 707, 713 (1985).

[228] *Id.*

It is within implied conflict preemption, and specifically obstacle preemption, that the Supreme Court, in *Geier v. American Honda Motor Co.*,[229] held that state tort suits for failure to provide airbags conflicted with the purposes of Federal Motor Vehicle Safety Standard 208 (FMVSS 208). FMVSS 208 was adopted by the Department of Transportation under the powers given to it by the National Traffic and Motor Vehicle Safety Act.[230] The Act contained a saving clause which provided that "compliance with a federal safety standard does not exempt any person from any liability under common law."[231] The Court held, however, that conflict preemption may exist even when Congress includes a saving clause so that state liability is not expressly preempted by the federal statute.[232] To hold otherwise, the Court said, would allow the law "to destroy itself."[233] The Court then considered the validity of the plaintiff's common law action, which sought to hold the defendant liable for failing to install air bags in its 1987 Honda Accord. The Court noted that the Department of Transportation enacted FMVSS 208 to encourage a gradual introduction of a variety of passive restraint systems into the marketplace. The plaintiffs' action, however, would have required all automobile manufacturers to install airbags in all of their automobiles in 1987. Such a requirement would have been "an obstacle to the variety and mix of devices that the federal regulation sought."[234] Thus, the Court ruled that the plaintiffs' action was preempted by FMVSS 208.[235]

Conflict preemption can occur when a state action would conflict with the policies motivating a federal safety regulation. In *Sprietsma v. Mercury Marine*,[236] the Supreme Court confronted the issue of whether conflict preemption exists when a federal agency has decided *not* to issue a safety regulation. In *Sprietsma*, the plaintiff's wife was killed in a boating accident when she was struck by the propeller on an outboard motor manufactured by the defendant. The plaintiff filed a complaint alleging that the motor was an unreasonably dangerous product because it did not have a propeller guard. The defendant argued that the plaintiff's claims were preempted by the Federal Boat Safety Act of 1971 (FBSA).[237] Specifically, the defendant argued that, because the Coast Guard had considered and rejected a regu-

---

[229] 529 U.S. 861 (2000). *See* Susan Raeker-Jordan, *A Study in Judicial Slight of Hand: Did Geier v. American Honda Motor Co. Eradicate the Presumption Against Preemption?* 17 BYU J. Pub. L. 1 (2002).

[230] 15 U.S.C. § 1381 (1988) (current version at 49 U.S.C. § 30101 (1995)).

[231] 529 U.S. at 868.

[232] *Id.* at 869.

[233] *Id.* at 872.

[234] *Id.* at 881.

[235] *Id.*

[236] 537 U.S. 51 (2002).

[237] 46 U.S.C. §§ 4301-4311.

lation that would have required propeller guards on motorboats, state law would conflict with the Coast Guard's regulations if common law claims for failing to install a propeller guard were permitted. However, the Supreme Court rejected the defendant's argument and held that the FBSA did not preempt the plaintiff's common law tort claims.[238] The Court noted that the Coast Guard did not decide that "as a matter of policy, the States . . . should not impose some version of propeller guard regulation, and it most definitely did not reject propeller guards as unsafe."[239] Instead, the Coast Guard declined to issue a regulation because of the economic problems of retrofitting millions of boats and because there was no single motor guard that could be fitted to all outboard motors. Thus, the Court reasoned that the Coast Guard did not "convey an 'authoritative' message of a federal policy against propeller guards," but rather "left the door open for a jury to rule that "some type of propeller guard should have been installed on this particular kind of boat equipped with respondent's particular type of motor."[240] Thus, there was no conflict preemption, and the Court permitted the plaintiff to pursue his common law claims against the defendant.[241]

---

[238] 537 U.S. at 65.

[239] *Id.* at 67.

[240] *Id.*

[241] The Court, in separate sections of its opinion, also ruled that the plaintiffs claims were not expressly preempted, nor was there implied field preemption. *See* 537 U.S. at 62 (no express preemption because Congress only preempted state laws and regulations); and 537 U.S. at 68 (the FBSA does not occupy the field of safety regulation for recreational boats).

Chapter 10

DAMAGES

SYNOPSIS

§ 10.01 INTRODUCTION

The goal of all plaintiffs in products liability cases is to recover compensation for the personal injury and/or property damage they have suffered, and may suffer in the future, as the result of defective products. As in all cases involving personal injury and property damage, there are two broad categories of damages plaintiffs may recover in products liability lawsuits: compensatory and punitive. The goal of compensatory damages is to compensate plaintiffs not only for the medical expenses, lost wages, and dam-

age or destruction of property caused by the defective product but also for non-economic injuries such as pain and suffering, loss of enjoyment of life, and emotional distress. However, if the only loss a plaintiff suffers is the damage or destruction of the product itself or economic loss from the failure of the product to perform as expected, the economic loss doctrine limits recovery to an action for breach of warranty.[1] Since defective products sometimes also cause death, the beneficiaries of a decedent may seek compensation for their economic and non-economic losses under a wrongful death statute. Finally, punitive damages are available in certain products liability actions as a means of punishing manufacturers or sellers for misrepresentation or for conduct that showed a reckless disregard for the safety of others.

§ 10.02 COMPENSATORY DAMAGES

The purpose of compensatory damages is to reimburse the plaintiff for losses caused as a result of the defendant's tortuous conduct. This goal is an integral part of all of the sections of the Restatements governing products liability. Sections 388, 390, 392, 395, 397, 398 of the Restatement (Second) of Torts, which deal with the liability in negligence of persons who supply goods for the use by others, state that a supplier is liable for the "physical harm" caused by its product. The comments to those sections make it clear that "physical harm" includes both bodily harm and property damage. Similarly, section 402A provides that the seller of a defective product in a strict liability action is liable for the "physical harm . . . caused to the ultimate user or consumer, or to his property." Finally, section 1 of the Restatement (Third) states that "[o]ne engaged in the business of selling or otherwise distributing products who sells or distributes a defective product is subject to liability for harm to persons or property caused by the defect."[2] Although all of the Restatement sections allow an injured person to recover damages for personal injury and property damage, they do not discuss the specific types and amount of the damages that a plaintiff can recover. Those issues are left to the legislatures and to the courts to determine.

[A] *Damages for Personal Injury*

[1] General Damages and Special Damages

In a products liability action, the types of damages the plaintiff may recover for personal injury and the principles governing their recovery are the same as those in all breach of contract and tort lawsuits. However, the

---

[1] Because damages for breach of warranty are covered in Chapter 2, this chapter will discuss only damages brought under the theories of negligence and strict liability.

[2] Comment *d* to § 1 of the RESTATEMENT (THIRD) states that the section "applies only to harm to persons or property." Economic loss is governed by § 21 of the RESTATEMENT (THIRD).

specific categories of those damages vary from state to state.[3] One example of the range of compensatory damages is contained in the Illinois Pattern Jury Instructions[4] which, in the appropriate situation, permits a plaintiff to recover one or more of eight types of damages for personal injury.

- The disfigurement resulting from the injury.[5]

- The disability experienced (and reasonably certain to be experienced in the future) or

- The loss of normal life experienced (and reasonably certain to be experienced in the future).[6]

- The increased risk of future harm resulting from the injury.[7]

- The pain and suffering experienced (and reasonably certain to be experienced in the future) as a result of the injuries.[8]

- The emotional distress experienced (and reasonably certain to be experienced in the future).[9]

- The reasonable expense of necessary medical care, treatment, services received (and the present cash value of the reasonable expenses of medical care, treatment, and services reasonably certain to be received in the future).[10]

- The value of (time) (earnings) (profit) (salaries) (benefits) lost and the present cash value of the (time) (earnings) (profits) (salaries) (benefits) reasonably certain to be lost in the future.[11]

---

[3] One category of damages that varies among the states is "loss of enjoyment of life" or "hedonic damages." These damages are meant to compensate a plaintiff for the loss of enjoyment of activities that he or she once valued but can no longer participate in because of the injuries, such as the inability to continue participating in organized sports. States often include such damages as part of loss of enjoyment of life or pain and suffering. However, most states do not recognize hedonic damages as a separate category of damages. For a discussion of hedonic damages, see *Saia v. Sears, Roebuck and Co.*, 47 F. Supp. 2d 141 (D. Mass. 1999) (applying Massachusetts law); *Loth v. Truck-A-Way Corp.*, 70 Cal. Rptr. 2d 571 (Cal. Ct. App. 1998).

[4] ILLINOIS PATTERN JURY INSTRUCTIONS (CIVIL) (2005 ed.).

[5] *Id.* at No. 30.04.

[6] *Id.* at No. 30.04.01.

[7] *Id.* at No. 30.04.03.

[8] *Id.* at No. 30.05.

[9] *Id.* at No. 30.05.01.

[10] *Id.* at No. 30.06.

[11] *Id.* at No. 30.07.

- The reasonable expense of necessary help which has been required as a result of the injury (and the present cash value of such expense reasonably certain to be required in the future).[12]

Traditionally, courts have divided these compensatory damages into two broad categories — general damages and special damages — each with its own pleading and proof requirements. General (or noneconomic) damages are those that are difficult to calculate in terms of money. These include disfigurement, disability, pain and suffering, and emotional distress. Since an objective amount cannot be awarded for general damages, the plaintiff does not have to plead or prove a specific amount in order to recover. Special (or economic) damages, on the other hand, are those economic losses that are a direct result of the injury. Special damages include the plaintiff's medical expenses (past and future), lost earnings and earning capacity (past and future), and the cost of repair or value of replacement of property that has been damaged or destroyed. Since it is possible to quantify these damages by presenting bills and receipts (or, in the case of future medical expenses or future lost wages, with the help of expert testimony), the plaintiff must plead and prove their specific amount in order to recover.

An example of the types and amount of compensatory damages that a jury may award in a products liability suit is *Anderson v. Sears, Roebuck & Co.*,[13] in which the plaintiff's home was destroyed completely by a fire that was ignited by a defective heater. In addition to the property loss, the plaintiff and her infant daughter were burned severely, resulting in multiple permanent injuries to the daughter. The plaintiff brought suit against the manufacturer and the retailer of the heater. The jury returned a verdict in favor of the plaintiffs for $2 million. In response to a post-trial motion that the damages were excessive, the district court judge held that the award of $600,000 for the child's past physical and mental pain was not unreasonable.[14] The child suffered extensive burns over a large portion of her body that required a number of hospitalizations, four operations and skin grafts, and resulted in a number of infections including pneumonia. The judge felt that the most tragic aspect of the case was the mental and emotional trauma suffered by the child at an age that is crucial to a child's psychological and personality formation.[15] The judge also upheld the jury's award of: $750,000 for the future physical and mental pain that the child would undergo;[16] $250,000 for future medical expenses including lifetime treatment and counseling by plastic surgeons, psychiatrists and sociologists;[17]

---

[12] *Id.* at No. 30.09.

[13] 377 F. Supp. 136 (E.D. La. 1974) (applying Louisiana law).

[14] *Id.* at 138-139.

[15] *Id.*

[16] *Id.* at 139.

[17] *Id.*

$330,000 for the permanent loss of earning capacity;[18] and up to $1,100,000 for permanent disability and disfigurement.[19]

[2] Present Cash Value

Personal injury awards usually are paid to a plaintiff in a present lump-sum amount rather than in installments over a number of years. Because some types of special damages that a jury may award will not occur until a future date (i.e., future medical expenses, future wage losses), it is necessary for it to discount them to their "present cash value" in order to avoid giving the plaintiff a windfall. [20] This is because, due to inflation, money received in one year is worth more than the same dollar amount received ten or twenty years in the future. "Present cash value" is defined in as "the sum of money needed now, which, when added to what that sum may reasonably be expected to earn in the future, will equal the amounts of the [expenses] [earnings] [benefits] at the times in the future when [the expenses must be paid] [or] [the earnings (benefits) would have been received]."[21]

Courts usually do not become involved in determining the actual present cash value of an award. It is for the parties to produce expert testimony, usually from economists, to project the total amount of those future economic damages for the trier of fact.[22] Since jury instructions usually do not state how inflation should be considered in projecting future losses or how to deal with anticipated future increases in the injured person's earnings, these also are matters for the parties and expert testimony in determining present value.[23] Finally, the parties must suggest to the trier of fact the appropriate percentage rate that should be used in discounting future damages. State statutes either are silent on this matter or are vague as to the amount. The Alaska statute, for example, speaks only of investment at "long-term future interest rates in the best and safest investments."[24]

---

[18] *Id.* at 139-140.

[19] *Id.* at 140.

[20] Estate of Shinholster v. Annapolis Hospital, 685 N.W.2d 275 (Mich. 2004); Wagner v. Union Pacific R.R., 642 N.W.2d 821 (Neb. Ct. App. 2002). Some states hold that future damages for noneconomic damages such as pain and suffering, loss of a normal life and loss of society are not reduced to present value. *See* Andrade v. Pangborn Corp., 2004 U.S. Dist. LEXIS 22704 (N.D. Cal. 2004) (applying California law); Friedman v. C & S Car Service, 527 A.2d 871 (N.J. 1987).

[21] ILLINOIS PATTERN JURY INSTRUCTIONS (CIVIL) No. 34.02 (2005 ed.).

[22] For detailed discussions of the methods of reducing future damages to present value, see *Jones & Laughlin Steel Corp. v. Pfeifer*, 462 U.S. 523 (1983); *Kaczkowski v. Bolubasz*, 421 A.2d 1027 (Pa. 1980); *Stringham v. United Parcel Service, Inc.*, 536 N.E.2d 1292 (Ill. App. Ct. 1989).

[23] Culver v. Slater Boat Co., 722 F.2d 114 (5th Cir. 1983).

[24] ALASKA STAT. § 09.17.040(b) (Michie 2004).

[3] Collateral Source Rule

In a personal injury case, some of a plaintiff's economic losses, such as medical expenses and lost wages, may be covered by insurance policies, social security, workers' compensation, pension benefits, or the plaintiff's employer. However, under the "collateral source rule," the defendant is barred from introducing evidence that the plaintiff received any benefits from sources independent of the defendant.[25] One purpose of the rule is to prevent the jury from being influenced or distracted in its determination of liability or damages by evidence that the plaintiff was receiving some form of compensation.[26] More importantly, there is a feeling that, if the defendant was responsible for the losses, it should not be relieved of paying compensation because the plaintiff had the foresight to purchase insurance or because some other source paid the plaintiff's expenses.[27]

As part of their tort reform legislation, approximately half of the states have enacted legislation either permitting defendants to introduce evidence of collateral sources of benefits[28] or directing their court to reduce the plaintiff's award by the amount of such benefits.[29] The principal reason for this is the belief that the plaintiff should not be compensated twice for the same injury. Thus, many of the states that have abolished or limited the collateral source rule provide that such evidence is not applicable to collateral benefits paid under federal programs, insurance policies paid for by the plaintiff, pensions, or where a right of subrogation exists.[30]

[4] Loss of Consortium

Although most products liability suits involve a claims for compensation by the person who was injured by the defective product, states also permit the spouse of an injured person to recover for loss of consortium.[31] Loss of

---

[25] Jurgensen v. Smith, 611 N.W.2d 439 (N.D. 2000).

[26] Simmons v. Hoegh Lines, 784 F.2d 1234 (5th Cir. 1986). *See also* Kenneth S. Abraham, *What Is A Tort Claim? An Interpretation of Contemporary Tort Reform*, 51 MD. L. REV. 172, 190-193 (1992).

[27] Gurliacci v. Mayer, 590 A.2d 914 (Conn. 1991); Helfend v. Southern California Rapid Transit Dist., 465 P.2d 61 (Cal. 1970).

[28] *See, e.g.,* IDAHO CODE § 6-1606 (Michie 2004); IND. CODE § 34-44-1-2 (1998); and N.Y. C.P.L.R. § 45-4545 (McKinney 2005).

[29] *See, e.g.,* COLO. REV. STAT. § 13-21-111.6 (2005); CONN. GEN STAT. § 52-225a (1991). For a history of the collateral source rule, including the different approaches taken by statutory modification, see *Perreira v. Rediger*, 778 A.2d 429 (N.J. 2001).

[30] *See, e.g.,* ALASKA STAT. 9.17.070 (Michie 2004) *and* OR. REV. STAT. § 31.580 (2003).

[31] In August 2005, a jury in Texas found the pharmaceutical company Merck & Co. liable for the death of a man who took the painkiller Vioxx. The jury awarded the man's widow $24 million for mental anguish and loss of companionship. Merck stated it would appeal. *See also* Baughn v. Eli Lilly & Co., 356 F. Supp. 2d 1177 (D. Kan. 2005) (applying Kansas law); Lillebo

consortium is an injury to the marital relationship and damages are intended to compensate the spouse for the loss of society, affection, assistance, and sexual relations caused by the injury. Although spouses may recover for loss of their consortium and for the consortium of their children,[32] the majority of states refuse to permit children to recover for the loss of consortium of a parent in personal injury cases.[33] The courts have given a number of reasons for their position: (1) uncertainty as to the scope of the class of plaintiff to whom the action would be available; (2) the additional economic burden placed on the public; (3) fear of multiplicity of lawsuits; (4) the difficulty in assessing damages; (5) the possibility of double recovery; and (6) the feeling that the issue is one for the legislature to resolve.[34]

[B] *Damages for Pain and Suffering*

The categories of special damages are capable of exact measurement or of an estimate with the help of expert witnesses. The categories of general damages, however, are much more difficult to calculate since they involve noneconomic loss. Because of the staggering amounts that juries sometimes award, the most controversial category of noneconomic damages is pain and suffering.[35] The traditional arguments in favor of such damages are that they console the victim, indicate the victim's interest in the integrity of his/her person, and provide a fund from which to pay attorney fees. Since there is no standard by which a jury can determine objectively the "value"

---

v. Zimmer, Inc., 2005 U.S. Dist. LEXIS 2563 (D. Minn. 2005) (applying Minnesota law); Timms v. Verson Allsteel Press Co., 520 F. Supp. 1147 (N.D. Ga. 1981) (applying Georgia law); Schreiner v. Fruit, 519 P.2d 462 (Alaska 1971).

[32] For an analysis of the law involving filial consortium and a list of the 31 states that recognize it, see *Hancock v. The Chattanooga Hamilton County Hosp. Authority*, 54 S.W.3d 234 (Tenn. 2001).

[33] For cases rejecting a cause of action by a child for the loss of a parent's consortium, see *Kershner v. Beloit Corp.*, 611 F. Supp. 943 (D. Me. 1985) (applying Maine law); Taylor v. Beard, 104 S.W.3d 507 (Tenn. 2003); *Lewis v. Rowland*, 701 S.W.2d 122 (Ark. 1985); *Siciliano v. Capitol City Shows, Inc.*, 475 A.2d 19 (N.H. 1984); *Gaver v. Harrant*, 557 A.2d 210 (Md. Ct. Spec. App. 1989). However, some states permit a child to recover for their loss of parental consortium in personal injury actions. *See* Roberts v. Williamson, 111 S.W.3d 113 (Tex. 2003); Hipbschman v. Prudhoe Bay Supply, Inc., 734 P.2d 991 (Alaska 1987).

[34] *See* Jennifer C. Parker, *Comment: Torts — Taylor v. Beard: The Tennessee Supreme Court Declines Adoption of a Cause of Action for Loss of Parental Consortium in Personal Injury Cases* 34 U. Mem.L.Rev. 737 (2004).

[35] In *McDougald v. Garber*, 536 N.E.2d 372 , 374-375 (N.Y. 1989), the New York Court of Appeals stated: "An economic loss can be compensated in kind by an economic gain; but recovery for non-economic losses such as pain and suffering and loss of enjoyment of life rests on the 'legal fiction that money damages can compensate for a victim's injury.'...We accept this fiction, knowing that although money will neither ease the pain nor restore the victim's abilities, this device is as close as the law can come in its effort to right the wrong. We have no hope of evaluating what has been lost, but a monetary award may provide a measure of solace for the condition created."

of the plaintiff's pain and suffering and since witnesses may not express their subjective opinion on the matter, some courts permit counsel for the plaintiff and the defendant to suggest to the jury a total amount of damages for the pain the plaintiff has suffered in the past and is likely to suffer in the future.[36] The problem with this method, however, is that there is no objective basis for such any suggestion because the "value" of the pain and suffering is only an estimate by both sides.

In order to provide the jury some guidance in determining the damages for pain and suffering, about half of the states permit a plaintiff's attorney to "suggest" to the jury that the plaintiff's damages for pain and suffering be measured in terms of a specific dollar amount for a specific period of time.[37] This method, known as the *"per diem"* or *"unit-of-time"* approach, asks the jury to think about the plaintiff's injury in terms of "$x" per day. The jury then is asked to multiply that amount by the number of days of the plaintiff's pain and suffering.[38] In making its determination, the jury can consider evidence of the plaintiff's age and life expectancy.

Many states prohibit use of the *per diem* approach to calculate damages for pain and suffering.[39] In *Caley v. Manicke*,[40] the Illinois Supreme Court held that although it is permissible, during closing arguments, for counsel to suggest to the jury a total amount to compensate for pain and suffering, it is improper for counsel to suggest a formula, such as an award of a specific sum *per diem* to calculate those damages.[41] The court held that pain and suffering has no commercial value to which a jury can refer in determining damages and that the *per diem* approach produces an illusion of certainty.[42] According to the court, the *per diem* formula, rather than encouraging reasonable and practical consideration, tends to discourage such consideration.

Whether a court uses the *per diem* method or permits counsel to suggest a total amount of damages for pain and suffering, the determination of such damages is left to the jury so long as there is adequate believable evi-

---

[36] *See* Allison v. Stalter, 621 N.E.2d 977 (Ill. App. Ct. 1993).

[37] Debus v. Grand Union Stores, 621 A.2d 1288 (Vt. 1993); Vanlandingham v. Gartman, 367 S.W.2d 111 (Ark. 1963); Jones v. Hogan, 351 P.2d 153 (Wash. 1960).

[38] For a discussion of the per diem approach for arguing damages for pain and suffering, see *Faught v. Washam*, 329 S.W.2d 588, 601-04 (Mo. 1959). For examples of the per diem approach, see *Westbrook v. General Tire & Rubber Co.*, 754 F.2d 1233 (5th Cir. 1985); *Worsley v. Corcelli*, 377 A.2d 215 (R.I. 1977); *Jones v. Hogan*, 351 P.2d 153 (Wash. 1960); *Giant Food Inc. v. Satterfield*, 603 A.2d 877 (Md. Ct. Spec. App. 1992).

[39] The use of mathematical formulas in calculating pain and suffering damages was rejected by California's Supreme Court in *Beagle v. Vasold*, 417 P.2d 673 (Cal. 1966). *See also* Meyers v. Southern Builders, Inc., 7 S.W.3d 507 (Mo. Ct. App. 1999).

[40] 181 N.E.2d 206 (Ill. 1962).

[41] *Id.* at 208.

[42] *Id.*

dence to support the award. Expert testimony may be needed to support a plaintiff's claim that such damages are reasonably certain to occur in the future. In addition, a plaintiff can offer photographic evidence as proof of the nature and extent of the pain and suffering, as well as day-in-the-life videotapes.[43] Juries also may consider the plaintiff's own testimony and the testimony of family and friends about symptoms of pain and suffering they have witnessed in determining the amount of damages to award.[44]

[C] *Damages for Emotional Distress*

[1] The Impact Rule

Another form of noneconomic damages that plaintiffs may seek in products liability actions is emotional distress. Although plaintiffs occasionally allege intentional infliction of emotional distress,[45] most claims are based on negligent infliction of emotional distress. When the person who alleges negligent infliction of emotional distress was the user or consumer of the product, states follow the "impact rule" and require the person to establish that the emotional distress was caused by physical injury resulting from the defective product.[46] The reasons for the common law rule requiring physical injury as a prerequisite for an award for emotional distress were stated by the Texas Supreme Court:

> [M]ental anguish, standing alone, is too subtle and speculative to be measured by any known standard; mental anguish and its consequences are so intangible and peculiar and vary so much with the individual that they cannot reasonably be anticipated, hence they fall without the boundaries of any reasonably proximate causal connection with the act of the defendant; a "wide door" might thereby be opened not only to fictitious claims but to litigation over trivialities and mere bad manners as well; and finally, since mental anguish can exist only in the mind of the injured party, not only its

---

[43] Bannister v. Noble, 812 F.2d 1265 (10th Cir. 1987) (applying Oklahoma law); Ellingwood v. Stevens, 564 So. 2d 932 (Ala. 1990); Jones v. City of L.A., 24 Cal. Rptr. 2d 528 (Cal. Ct. App. 1993).

[44] *See* Swift v. State Farm Mut. Auto. Ins. Co., 796 F.2d 120 (5th Cir. 1986) (applying Louisiana law); Delph v. Jenkins, 1987 Ohio App. LEXIS 8708 (Ohio Ct. App. 1987).

[45] RESTATEMENT (SECOND) OF TORTS, § 46 (1965). For a case in which damages for intentional infliction of emotional distress were alleged, but were not successful, in a products liability suit, see *Vietnam Association for Victims of Agent Orange / Dioxin v. Dow Chemical Co. (In re "Agent Orange" Products Litigation)*, 2005 U.S. Dist. LEXIS 3644 (E.D.N.Y. 2005).

[46] *See* Ball v. Joy Technologies, Inc., 958 F.2d 36 (4th Cir. 1991) (applying Virginia and West Virginia law); Pope v. Rollins Protective Services Co, 703 F.2d 197 (5th Cir. 1983) (applying Texas law); Schwarz v. National Van Lines, 375 F. Supp. 2d 690 (N.D. Ill. 2005) (applying Illinois law); Zeigler v. Fisher-Price, Inc., 261 F. Supp. 2d 1047 (N.D. Iowa 2003) (applying Iowa law).

extent but its very existence can be established only by the word of the injured party, in the absence of some objective injury.[47]

A number of emotional distress cases in products liability have resulted from finding foreign objects in food or drink products.[48] An example of what constitutes "physical injury" in those cases is *Kroger Co. v. Beck*,[49] in which the plaintiff was eating a piece of steak when she felt a sharp pain in the back of her throat. When she vomited, she found that it contained an inch-long piece of a hypodermic needle used for injecting animals. The Indiana appellate court affirmed an award of damages for her emotional distress even though the injury did not require medical treatment or cause permanent physical problems. According to the court, the award was justified by her physical reaction and anxiety over what could have happened if she had swallowed the needle and her resulting aversion to eating meat.

In recent decades, products liability cases have included claims of emotional distress from the threat or fear of future disease, such as AIDS or cancer. Although most courts refuse to permit recovery in the absence of present symptoms[50] or, in some cases, a "serious" or "reasonable probability" that the injury will occur,[51] some courts do permit recovery for emotional distress from the fear of contracting AIDS if the plaintiff can show actual exposure to the HIV virus.[52] Courts also deny recovery of damages for emotional distress for the fear of future injury from the use of a product. In *Khan v. Shiley Incorporated*,[53] the plaintiff, who was the recipient of an artificial heart valve, brought an action against the manufacturer of the valve alleging emotional and physical distress upon learning the valve was within a group being recalled due to a propensity to fracture. In denying relief from what the plaintiff described as, "the constant threat of imminent death or other serious physical injury and the anxiety, fear and emotional distress that results [from the defective valve],"[54] the California appellate court

---

[47] Harned v. E-Z Finance Co., 254 S.W.2d 81, 85 (Tex. 1953).

[48] *See* Palmer v. Nan King Restaurant, Inc., 798 A.2d 583 (N.H. 2002); Ellington v. Coca Cola Bottling Co., Inc., 717 P.2d 109 (Okla. 1986); Chambley v. Apple Restaurants, Inc., 504 S.E.2d 551 (Ga. Ct. App. 1998); Way v. Tampa Coca Cola Bottling Co., 260 So.2d 288 (Fla Dist. Ct. App. 1972).

[49] 375 N.E.2d 640 (Ind. Ct. App. 1978).

[50] Metro-North Commuter Railroad Co. v. Buckley, 521 U.S. 424 (1997) (asbestos); Southern Bakeries, Inc. v. Knipp, 852 So. 2d 712 (Ala. 2002) (asbestos); Payton v. Abbott Laboratories, 437 N.E.2d 171 (Mass. 1982) (DES).

[51] *See* Gideon v. Johns-Mansville Sale Corp., 761 F.2d 1129 (5th Cir. 1985) (applying Texas law); McCafferty v. Centerior Service Co., 983 F. Supp. 715 (N.D. Ohio 1997); Sullivan v. Combustion Engineering, 590 A.2d 681 (N.J. Super. Ct. 1991).

[52] Johnson v. American National Red Cross, 578 S.E.2d 106 (Ga. 2003); Hagen v. Coca-Cola Bottling Co., 804 So.2d 1234 (Fla. 2001).

[53] 266 Cal. Rptr 106 (Cal. Ct. App. 1990).

[54] *Id.* at 108.

stated that "a cause of action does not presently exist under any theory premised on the *risk* the valve *may* malfunction in the future."[55] The court held that, as long as the valve continued to function, the recipient stated no cause of action under strict liability, negligence, or breach of warranty.[56]

[2] Medical Monitoring

Because courts are reluctant to permit recovery for emotional distress caused by the fear of future disease or injury, plaintiffs who have been exposed to a product or a drug increasingly seek compensation for medical monitoring. A medical monitoring award covers the costs of periodic medical examinations to track the long-term effects of the plaintiff's use of a drug or medical device or exposure to chemicals.[57] In *Mauri v. Raymark*,[58] the plaintiff was unable to recover for the enhanced risk of contracting cancer due to exposure to asbestos because he did not present evidence establishing the future occurrence of cancer was a reasonable medical probability. The New Jersey Supreme Court, however, upheld the right of plaintiffs to recover medical surveillance expenses. In its opinion, the court discussed the reasons for permitting medical monitoring and the requirements that the plaintiff must establish.

> [W]e hold that the cost of medical surveillance is a compensable item of damages where the proofs demonstrate, through reliable expert testimony predicated upon the significance and extent of exposure to chemicals, the toxicity of the chemicals, the seriousness of the diseases for which individuals are at risk, the relative increase in the chance of onset of disease in those exposed, and the value of early diagnosis, that such surveillance to monitor the effect of exposure to toxic chemicals is reasonable and necessary. In our view, this holding is thoroughly consistent with our rejection of plaintiffs' claim for damages based on their enhanced risk of injury. That claim seeks damages for the impairment of plaintiffs' health, without proof of its likelihood, extent, or monetary value. In contrast, the medical surveillance claim seeks reimbursement for the specific dollar costs of periodic examinations that are medically

---

[55] *Id.* at 112.

[56] The court, however, reversed the grant of summary judgment for the manufacturer on the deceit count, saying that it was not dependent on the value malfunctioning. *Id.* at 112-113.

[57] For a discussion of medical monitoring, see *In re Paoli R.R. Yard PCB Litigation*, 916 F.2d 829, 849-852 (3d Cir. 1990); *Cook v. Rockwell International Corp.*, 755 F. Supp. 1468 (D. Colo. 1991). However, in *Metro-North Commuter R.R. v. Buckley*, 521 U.S. 424 (1997), the Supreme Court held that a plaintiff exposed to asbestos could not recover for medical monitoring in an FELA case.

[58] 561 A.2d 257 (N.J. 1989).

necessary notwithstanding the fact that the extent of plaintiffs' impaired health is unquantified.[59]

Because medical monitoring can extend over a number of years, it can be expensive for defendants, particularly in class action suits or suits involving multiple plaintiffs. An example of this is *Burns v. Jaquays Mining Corp.*,[60] in which 56 residents of land adjacent to an asbestos-producing mill brought suit against the mill owner to recover for subclinical asbestos-related injuries. The residents, none of whom was diagnosed as having asbestosis, sought damages for the increased risk of developing cancer or other asbestos-related diseases and for the emotional distress caused by the knowledge and fear of these impending developments. The Arizona court held that subclinical asbestos-related injury was not sufficient to constitute the actual loss or damage required to support a cause of action. The court refused to award damages for the fear of contracting asbestos-related diseases in the future without some showing of bodily injury. However, the court awarded the residents damages for "medical surveillance" of the development of cancer and other asbestos-related diseases. The court, citing policy considerations behind awarding such expenses, stated that such damages were:

> consistent with the important public health interest in fostering access to medical testing for individuals whose exposure to toxic chemicals creates an enhanced risk of disease. . . .The availability of a substantial remedy before the consequences of plaintiff's exposure are manifest may also have the beneficial effect of preventing or mitigating serious future illnesses and thus reduce the overall costs of the responsible parties.[61]

[3] Bystanders

States take a variety of approaches to determining when a bystander is entitled to recover damages for emotional distress resulting from witnessing the injury or death of a third person caused by a defective product. Most courts limit recovery to those bystanders who can prove that they were within the "zone of danger."[62] Under this standard, "a bystander who is in the zone of physical danger and who, because of the defendant's negligence, has reasonable fear for his own safety, is given a right of action for physical injury or illness resulting from emotional distress."[63] Although a

---

[59] *Id.* at 263 (*quoting* Ayers v. Jackson Township, 525 A.2d 287, 312-313 (N.J. 1987)). The Utah Supreme Court set out eight similar requirements that a plaintiff must prove to recover medical monitoring costs in *Hansen v. Mountain Fuel Supply Co.*, 858 P.2d 970 (Utah 1993).

[60] 752 P.2d 28 (Ariz. Ct. App. 1987).

[61] *Id.* at 33 (*quoting* Ayers v. Township of Jackson, 525 A.2d 287, 311 (N.J. 1987)).

[62] *See* Rickey v. Chicago Transit Authority, 457 N.E.2d 1 (Ill. 1983).

[63] *Id.* at 5.

bystander is not required to suffer physical impact or injury from the defective product, the bystander must have been in such proximity to the accident that there was a high risk that he or she would suffer physical impact.

Although the majority of states have adopted the zone of danger test for bystanders, some states have confined it to negligence and have not extended it to strict liability. In *Pasquale v. Speed Products Engineering*,[64] the plaintiff and his wife were watching an automobile race when parts from one of the cars flew into the stands, struck the wife and killed her. Despite the plaintiff's severe emotional trauma at witnessing his wife's death, the Illinois Supreme Court held that fault is an indispensable element in an action for infliction of emotional distress. Since strict liability is not based upon fault, the court held that the manufacturer should not be liable for inflicting emotional distress.

Despite the limitation on recovery for emotional distress in *Pasquale*, about half of the states have moved beyond the "zone of danger" test and permit bystanders to recover for negligent infliction of emotional distress under a foreseeability test.[65] In *Dillon v. Legg*,[66] the California Supreme Court held that damages for mental distress could be recovered if the distress was a reasonably foreseeable result of the tortfeasor's conduct.[67] The court set out three factors to determine whether the injury was foreseeable:

(1) Whether the plaintiff was located near the scene of the accident as contrasted with one who was a distance away from it. (2) Whether the shock resulted from a direct emotional impact upon the plaintiff from the sensory and contemporaneous observance the accident. (3) Whether plaintiff and the victim were closely related, as contrasted with an absence of any relationship or the presence of only a distant relationship.[68]

Although many states have adopted some form of the *Dillon* foreseeability guidelines for recovery for emotional distress of bystanders, few courts have had the opportunity to apply those guidelines in products lia-

---

[64] 654 N.E.2d 1365 (Ill. 1995).

[65] *See* Pearsall v. Emhart Industries, Inc., 599 F. Supp. 207 (E.D. Pa. 1984) (applying Pennsylvania law).

[66] 441 P.2d 912 (Cal.1968). In *Dillon*, a mother was permitted to state a claim for emotional distress from witnessing the death of her child as a result of a motorist's alleged negligent driving. As a bystander, the mother was not in the "zone of danger" nor was she threatened personally with bodily harm. However, she allegedly that, as a result of witnessing the fatal accident, she "sustained great emotional disturbance and shock and injury to her nervous system which caused her great physical and mental pain and suffering." *Id.* at 914.

[67] *Id.* at 921.

[68] *Id.* at 920.

bility cases.[69] A case that did apply the *Dillon* test is *Culbert v. Sampson's Supermarket, Inc.*,[70] in which a mother became emotionally distressed after witnessing her infant child gag and choke on foreign substance contained in a jar of baby food. The Maine Supreme Judicial Court rejected the "zone of danger" theory, adopted the *Dillon* test, and held that a "bystander may recover damages for serious mental distress foreseeably resulting from a witnessing another person harmed by the tortfeasor's negligent act."[71]

Some courts have avoided the difficulties of choosing between the "zone of danger" test and the *Dillon* test by characterizing the plaintiff as a "user" of the product rather than as a "bystander." An example of this is *Gnirk v. Ford Motor Company*,[72] in which a child drowned when his mother's car rolled backwards as she was attempting to open a fence gate. The mother brought an action against Ford for the emotional distress of witnessing the death of her son caused by the allegedly defective park mechanism. She claimed the accident caused her great depression, insomnia, permanent psychological injury, and physical illness.[73] The district court viewed the mother as a "user" of Ford's product and not as a "bystander."[74] As such, Ford owed the mother an independent duty not to harm her.[75] In recognizing the fine line distinguishing physical from emotional injury, the court stated that Restatement (Second) of Torts § 436A, comment *c*,[76] was a reasonable guide for determining whether the mother suffered bodily injury proximately caused by emotional disturbance inflicted by Ford.[77] The court

---

[69] For a state that has adopted *Dillon*, see *Walker v. Clark Equipment*, 320 N.W.2d 561 (Iowa 1982). The court in Clark found "no qualitative difference, once liability is found, between recoveries under theories of negligence, strict liability or warranty. Once a defendant is found liable a plaintiff should recover all damages cognizable under the law and supported by the evidence." *Id.* at 563.

[70] 444 A.2d 433 (Me. 1982).

[71] *Id.* at 438. See also *Shepard v. Superior Court*, 142 Cal. Rptr. 612 (Cal. Ct. App. 1977), in which, after being side-swiped by another car, the rear car door popped open, throwing a brother and sister onto highway. The court held that the parents and brother stated a cause of action against the automobile manufacturer for damages from witnessing the sister being run over and killed by another car.

[72] 572 F. Supp. 1201 (D. S.D. 1983) (applying South Dakota law).

[73] *Id.* at 1202.

[74] *Id.*

[75] *Id.* at 1203.

[76] RESTATEMENT (SECOND) OF TORTS § 436 A, comment *c* states:

> [Emotional distress] accompanied by transitory, non-recurring physical phenomena, harmless in themselves, such as dizziness, vomiting, and the like, does not make the actor liable where such phenomena are in themselves inconsequential and do not amount to any substantial bodily harm. On the other hand, long continued nausea or headaches may amount to physical illness, which is bodily harm; and even long continued mental disturbance, as for example in the case of repeated hysterical attacks, or mental aberration, may be classified by the courts as illness, notwithstanding their mental character.

[77] 572 F. Supp. at 1204-1205.

denied Ford's motion for summary judgment and remanded the case to determine whether the mother could establish a case on the issue of whether she sustained bodily injury proximately caused by the alleged emotional disturbance inflicted by Ford. If successful, the mother also would be entitled to recover damages for her emotional distress. However, few courts have followed the approach used in *Gnirk*.[78]

[D] *Limitations on Noneconomic Damages*

Many states place no limitations on the amount of noneconomic damages that a plaintiff may recover in a products liability case. However, because of the uncertainty of noneconomic damages in general, and damages for pain and suffering in particular, about half of the states have enacted some form of legislative limitation on them.[79] While many of these statutory caps on noneconomic damages apply only in medical malpractice cases,[80] a number of them apply in all cases, including products liability cases. The form and amount of these limitations vary greatly. Some states, for example, simply place a limit on the total amount a plaintiff can recover for pain and suffering[81] or for all noneconomic damages in personal injury cases.[82] However, other states either have a variable limit or permit the amount of recovery for noneconomic damages to be raised in certain situations. Idaho, for example, limits noneconomic damages to $400,000 with adjustments based on the state's average annual wage.[83] Colorado imposes a $250,000 cap on noneconomic damages but permits the court to increase the amount to $500,000 if it finds "clear and convincing evidence" to do so.[84] Alaska states that noneconomic damages may not exceed the greater

---

[78] For two other cases that treated the plaintiff as the "user" of the produce, see *Bray v. Marathon Corp.*, 588 S.E.2d 93 (S.C. 2003); *Kately v. Wilkinson*, 195 Cal. Rptr. 902 (Cal. Ct. App. 1983). For a case that distinguished *Gnirk* and held that the plaintiff was not a "user," *see Staub v. Fisher and Paykel Health Care*, 990 P.2d 384 (Utah 1999).

[79] Tort reform legislation and caps on damages have been challenged in state courts on constitutional grounds. State supreme courts have upheld some limitations while striking down others. *See* Fairfax Hospital Systems v. Nevitt, 457 S.E.2d 10 (Va. 1995); Brannigan v. Usitalo, 587 A.2d 1232 (N.H. 1991).

[80] Missouri, for example, limits noneconomic damages to $350,000 but only in medical malpractice cases. MO. REV. STAT. § 538.210 (2005). Illinois limits noneconomic damages against physicians to $500,000 and against hospitals to $1,000,000. However, some of those caps have been struck down as violating state constitutions. *See* Ferdon v. Wisconsin Patients Compensation Fund, 2005 Wisc. LEXIS 401 (Wis. 2005).

[81] Kansas limits pain and suffering damages to $250,000 (KAN. STAT. ANN. § 60-19a01 (2004)) while Hawaii raises the limit to $375,000 (HAW. REV. STAT. § 663-8.7 (2002)). *See* Samsel v. Wheeler Transportation Services, 789 P.2d 541 (Kan. 1990).

[82] Maryland limits all noneconomic damages in personal injury cases to $350,000 (MD. CODE ANN. CTS. & JUD. PROC. § 11-108 (2002)) while Mississippi raises the limit to $1,000,000 in non-health care provider cases (MISS. CODE ANN. § 11-1-60 (2002)).

[83] IDAHO CODE § 6-1603 (Michie 2004).

[84] COLO. REV. STAT. § 13-21-102.5 (2005).

of \$400,000 or \$8,000 multiplied by the years of the plaintiff's life expectancy. However, if the plaintiff suffers severe permanent injury, the amount increases to the greater of \$1 million or \$25,000 times the years of the plaintiff's life expectancy.[85] Ohio restricts noneconomic loss to \$250,000 or three times the amount of economic loss, not to exceed \$350,000 per plaintiff or \$500,000 per occurrence. The Ohio cap is not applicable, however, in cases of catastrophic injury, which is defined as injury resulting in "permanent and substantial physical deformity, loss of use of a limb or loss of a bodily organ system"[86] or "a permanent physical functional injury that permanently prevents the injured person from being able to independently care for self and perform life sustaining activities."[87]

[E] *Wrongful Death and Survival Actions*

When a person is killed by a defective product, the claim for compensation must be brought under the state's wrongful death statute.[88] These statutes have been adopted in every state in response to the common law doctrine that a cause of action dies with the victim or the wrongdoer. As a result, no action for wrongful death can be brought outside of the statutes. Wrongful death actions raise difficult valuation problems and the amount of the award of damages varies from state to state.

A wrongful death action is brought by the personal representative of the deceased person in order to recover compensation for the economic and noneconomic losses suffered by the decedent's relatives as a result of the death.[89] The personal representative must bring the action for the benefit of a specific class of beneficiaries, usually limited to the surviving spouse, children, parents, and siblings. There are two principal elements of compensation in a wrongful death action. The first is the reasonable expectation of the financial contributions the decedent would have made to the beneficiaries had he or she not died. This amount is based upon what the decedent earned in the past, the amount the decedent spent on his or her own personal expenses, what the decedent contributed to the beneficiaries in the past, and the earning capacity of the decedent. A court also may consider the decedent's age, heath, life expectancy, and habits of work and thrift in

---

[85] ALASKA STAT. § 9.17.010 (Michie 2004).

[86] OHIO REV. CODE ANN. § 2315.19(B)(3)(a) (Anderson 2005).

[87] *Id.* § 2315.19(B)(3)(b).

[88] For examples of wrongful death statutes, see DEL. CODE ANN. tit. 10, §§ 3721-3725 (1999); 740 ILL. COMP. STAT. 180/1-180/2.2 (2004); KY. REV. STAT. ANN. § 411.130 (1992); TENN. CODE ANN. § 20-5-113 (2002); WIS. STAT. § 895.04 (1997).

[89] For examples of products liability suits brought under wrongful death acts, see *Rivera v. Philip Morris, Inc.*, 395 F.3d 1142 (9th Cir. 2005) (applying Nevada law); *Palmer v. Volkswagen of America, Inc.*, 2005 Miss. LEXIS 21 (Miss. 2005); *General Motors Corp. v. Hebert*, 501 S.W.2d 950 (Tex. App. 1993).

determining the amount he or she would have contributed to the beneficiaries.

In recent years, states have expanded the scope of recovery in wrongful death actions to include noneconomic items. A spouse, for example, is entitled to compensation for the loss of the services, society, affection, and sexual relations the deceased spouse would have contributed if he or she lived.[90] In addition, when the wrongful death involves a parent, the surviving children can recover the value of their parent's companionship, love, and affection.[91] If the decedent left young children, this also includes the value of the instruction, moral training, and supervision of education the decedent might have been expected to give the children had he or she lived. Although parents can recover wrongful death damages for the loss of services of a child, there is disagreement whether surviving parents also may recover for their loss of the child's society and companionship.[92] States also permit the recovery of funeral expenses as a part of a wrongful death action. However, punitive damages are not available in a wrongful death action.[93]

Since wrongful death statutes limit recovery to the losses suffered by the beneficiaries, states have enacted separate survival acts permitting any cause of action the decedent had at the time of his or her death to survive the death.[94] These statutes, which can be brought along with a wrongful death action,[95] are a response to the common law which does not permit a tort action to survive the death of the victim or the tortfeasor. In a survival action, the legal representative of the decedent brings an action for the economic and noneconomic damages suffered by the decedent between the date of the injury and the date of death. Thus, any products liability action that the decedent could have brought had he or she lived survives the death, and any damages that are awarded are for the benefit of the decedent's estate.[96] The damages recoverable in a survival action include the decedent's

[90] *See* Klein v. Sears, Roebuck & Co., 608 A.2d 1276 (Md. Ct. Spec. App. 1992). A claim for loss of consortium can be made only by husbands and wives who were legally married at the time of the injury. It does not permit recovery for the loss an ex-spouse. Doerner v. Swisher International, Inc., 272 F.3d 928 (7th Cir. 2001) (applying Indiana law).

[91] Guilani v. Guiler, 951 S.W.2d 318 (Ky. 1997); Hall v. Gillins, 147 N.E.2d 352 (Ill. 1958).

[92] For a decision permitting loss of society of a minor child, see *Bullard v. Barnes*, 468 N.E.2d 1228 (Ill. 1984). For a decision refusing to permit a claim by parents for the loss of companionship arising out of injury to their child, see *Siciliano v. Capitol City Shows, Inc.*, 475 A.2d 19 (N.H. 1984).

[93] Eisert v. Greenberg Roofing & Sheet Metal Co., 314 N.W.2d 226 (Minn. 1982).

[94] For an example of such laws, see the Pennsylvania Survival Act (42 PA. CONS. STAT. § 8302 (1998)) which states simply: "All causes of action or proceedings, real or personal, shall survive the death of the plaintiff or of the defendant, or the death of one or more joint plaintiffs or defendants." *See also* 755 ILL. COMP. STAT. 5/27-6 (2004); TENN. CODE ANN. § 20-5-102 (2002).

[95] *See* Peltz v. Sears, Roebuck and Co., 367 F. Supp. 2d 711 (E.D. Pa. 2005) (applying Pennsylvania law).

[96] Estate of Merrill v. Jerrick, 605 N.W.2d 645 (Wis. Ct. App. 1999).

medical expenses, conscious pain and suffering, lost earnings, and the damage or loss of the decedent's property.

[F] *Damage to Property*

Finally, a plaintiff in a products liability suit may recover compensation for the damage or destruction of real or personal property caused by the defective product. The measure of compensation in products liability cases is the same as in other cases. If the property is destroyed, the plaintiff is entitled to the value of the property at the time of its destruction.[97] In cases where the property was not destroyed totally, but where the damage is not capable of being repaired, the measure of damages is the difference between the reasonable value of the property before and after the damage. If the damaged personal property can be repaired, the measure of damages is the cost of those repairs plus the amount of the difference in the value of the property, if the value of the property after repair is less than its value before it was damaged.[98]

§ 10.03 ECONOMIC LOSS DOCTRINE

Of particular importance in products liability actions are cases where the plaintiff claims only "economic loss." Economic loss is defined as "damages for inadequate value, costs of repair or replacement of the defective product, or consequent loss of profits — without any claim of personal injury or damage to other property."[99] Such loss includes "the diminution in value of the product because it is inferior in quality and does not work for the general purposes in which it was manufactured and sold."[100] Under the "economic loss doctrine," a plaintiff whose only damages are injury to the product itself cannot recover in negligence or strict liability. Instead, the plaintiff is limited to an action for breach of warranty.[101] The rationale behind the doctrine, which is followed by almost every state both in con-

---

[97] Harman & Conway v. Nucor Corp., 1989 Ky. App. LEXIS 127 (Ky. Ct. App. 1989).

[98] Behrens v. W. S. Bills & Sons, Inc., 283 N.E.2d 1 (Ill. App. Ct. 1972).

[99] Casa Clara Condominium Ass'n, Inc v. Charley Toppino & Sons, Inc., 620 So.2d 1244, 1246 (Fla. 1993) (quoting Note, *Economic Loss in Products Liability Jurisprudence*, 66 COLUM. L. REV. 917, 918 (1966)).

[100] *Id.* at 1246 (*quoting* Comment, *Manufacturers' Liability to Remote Purchasers for "Economic Loss" Damages — Tort or Contract?*, 114 U. PA. L. REV. 539, 541 (1966).

[101] *See* Reed v. Central Soya Co., 621 N.E.2d 1069 (Ind. 1993); Moorman Manufacturing Co. v. National Tank Co., 435 N.E.2d 443 (Ill. 1982); Mid-Continent Aircraft Corp. v. Curry County Spraying Service, 572 S.W.2d 308 (Tex. 1978). Some states make an exception to the economic loss rule for claims based on misrepresentation. *See* Guardian Construction Co. v. Tetra Tech Richardson, Inc., 583 A.2d 1378 (Del. Super. Ct. 1990).

sumer and commercial transactions, is that damage to the product itself means simply that customer received "insufficient product value."[102]

The starting point for the economic loss doctrine in products liability cases is *Seely v. White Motor Co.*,[103] in which the purchaser of a defective truck sued for damages to the truck and for lost profits from his inability to use it in his hauling business. The California Supreme Court allowed the purchaser to recover against the manufacturers for breach of express warranty. The court, however, refused to allow recovery on the theory of strict liability.[104] Since there was no personal injury or damage to property other than to the product itself, the court held that strict liability was not designed "to undermine the warranty provisions of the Uniform Commercial Code but, rather, to govern the distinct problem of physical injuries."[105]

The vast majority of states follow the economic loss doctrine as articulated in *Seely*.[106] However, a few states permit an exception based on a distinction between a disappointed consumer and an endangered one. Alaska, for example, has held that a plaintiff may recover economic loss in strict products liability if the "defective product creates a situation potentially dangerous to persons or other property, and loss occurs as a result of that danger. . . ."[107] A mid-flight engine failure caused by a defective product is an example of a "potentially dangerous" situation in which economic loss is recoverable.[108] Georgia permits recovery for economic loss when a "sudden and calamitous event" not only causes damages to the product but poses an unreasonable risk of injury to persons and other property.[109] Similarly, the Iowa Supreme Court has held that a consumer can sue the manufacturer in tort if the damage to the property resulted from a "sudden or dangerous occurrence."[110] In addition to this exception, a few other states permit recovery of economic loss in negligence[111] or arising out of consumer (as opposed to commercial) transactions.[112]

---

[102] Oceanside at Pine Point Condominium Owners Association v. Peachtree Doors, Inc., 659 A.2d 267, 270 (Me. 1995). *See also* Progressive Insurance Co. v. General Motors Corp., 749 N.E.2d 484 (Ind. 2001).

[103] 403 P.2d 145 (Cal. 1965).

[104] *Id.* at 145.

[105] *Id.* at 149.

[106] For a review of these cases, see *Alloway v. General Marine Industries, L.P.*, 695 A.2d 264, 270-271 (N.J. 1997).

[107] Northern Power & Engineering Corp. v. Caterpillar Tractor Co., 623 P.2d 324, 329 (Alaska 1981). *See also* Morris v. Osmose Wood Preserving, 667 A.2d 624 (Md. 1995) ("serious, and unreasonable risk of death or personal injury").

[108] *Id.*

[109] Vulcan Materials Co. v. Driltech, Inc., 306 S.E.2d 253, 257 (Ga. 1983).

[110] American Fire and Casualty Co. v. Ford Motor Co., 588 N.W.2d 437, 439 (Iowa 1999).

[111] Berg v. General Motors Corp., 555 P.2d 818 (Wash. 1976).

[112] Rosseau v. K.N. Construction, Inc., 727 A.2d 190 (R.I. 1999).

In 1986 the United States Supreme Court reviewed the roles of tort and contract law in a case involving economic loss in *East River Steamship Corporation v. Transamerica Delaval, Inc.*[113] In *East River*, the plaintiffs, who were the charterers of four ships, sued the manufacturer of the turbines installed in the ships in negligence and strict liability, alleging that the turbines were defectively designed. The plaintiffs claimed that the damage to the turbines entitled them to compensation for the cost of repairs and for lost income while the ships were out of service. The Supreme Court adopted an approach similar to *Seely*, holding that "a manufacturer in a commercial relationship has no duty under either a negligence or strict products liability theory to prevent a product from injuring itself."[114] The Court stated that when a product injures only itself, "the reasons for imposing a tort duty are weak and those for leaving the party to its contractual remedies are strong."[115] The Court's decision has been very influential on state courts in their interpretation of the economic loss rule.[116]

In support of its holding, the Supreme Court reviewed the policy considerations in favor of the application of the economic loss doctrine to commercial transactions. The Court first stressed the importance of maintaining the historical distinction between tort law and contract law. According to the Court, tort liability is concerned primarily with safety and protects society's interest in freedom from harm, regardless of any agreement between the parties.[117] When a person is injured "the cost of an injury and the loss of time or health may be an overwhelming misfortune" that one person is not prepared to meet.[118] Conversely, a contractual duty arises from society's interest in the performance of promises and traditionally has been concerned with the fulfillment of reasonable economic expectations. When the only damage is to the product itself, the commercial user loses the value of the product, risks dissatisfied customers who find the product fails to meet their needs, or experiences increased costs in performing a service; all losses which can be insured.[119] As a result, the Court found that the tort concern with safety is reduced when an injury is only to the product itself.[120] In addi-

---

[113] 476 U.S. 858 (1986). Although *East River* was decided under admiralty law, included in its holding was that admiralty law incorporates general principles of product liability law.

[114] *Id.* at 871.

[115] *Id.*

[116] *See* Mt. Lebanon Personal Care Home, Inc. v. Hoover Universal Inc., 276 F.3d 845 (6th Cir. 2002) (applying Kentucky law); Casa Clara Condominium Association, Inc. v. Charley Toppino & Sons, Inc., 620 So.2d 1244, 1246 (Fla.1993); Oceanside At Pine Point Condominium Owners Association v. Peachtree Doors, Inc., 659 A.2d 267 (Me. 1995).

[117] East River Steamship Corporation v. Transamerica Delaval, Inc., 476 U.S. 858, 871 (1986).

[118] *Id.*

[119] *Id.*

[120] *Id.*

tion, "the increased cost to the public that would result from holding a manufacturer liable in tort for injury to the product itself is not justified."[121]

The Court also emphasized that damage to the product itself is best understood in terms of warranty since the product did not meet the consumer's expectations.[122] According to the Court, "maintenance of product value and quality is precisely the purpose of express and implied warranties."[123] A consumer's claim of a non-working product can be brought as a breach-of-warranty action, or the consumer can reject the product, or revoke its acceptance, and sue for breach of contract.[124] The Court found that when a product causes economic disappointment by not meeting a purchaser's expectations, the resulting failure to receive the benefit of the bargain is a core concern of contract law, not tort law.

Included in the Court's policy considerations governing the economic loss rule were the parties' freedom to allocate economic risk by contract. The Court stated that contract law, and specifically warranty law, is better suited for commercial controversies because "the parties may set the terms of their own agreements."[125] The economic loss doctrine encourages the party best situated to assess the risk of economic loss (usually the purchaser) to assume, allocate, or insure against that risk. For example, a manufacturer may be in a better position to absorb the risk of loss from physical injury or property damage, but a purchaser may be better situated to absorb the "risk of economic loss caused by the purchase of a defective product."[126] In addition, "the manufacturer can restrict its liability, within limits, by disclaiming warranties or limiting remedies."[127] In exchange, the Court reasoned, the purchaser pays less for the product.[128] Thus, the Court found that commercial situations are best regulated by warranty law because they generally do not involve large disparities in bargaining power and the parties are free to allocate the risk through contract.[129]

Finally, the Supreme Court emphasized that warranty law has built-in boundaries and restraints on liability, in contrast to tort actions which may

---

[121] *Id.* at 872.

[122] *Id.*

[123] *Id. See* U.C.C. § 2-313 (express warranty), § 2-314 (implied warranty of merchantability), and § 2-315 (warranty of fitness for a particular purpose).

[124] *Id. See* U.C.C. §§ 2-601, 2-608, 2-612.

[125] *East River*, 476 U.S. at 872-873.

[126] Seely v. White Motor Co., 403 P.2d 145 (Cal. 1965).

[127] *East River*, 476 U.S. at 872-873.

[128] *Id.* at 873.

[129] Many state courts follow *East River* in commercial transactions and preclude tort actions when a product damages only itself. *See* Alloway v. General Marine Industries, L.P., 695 A.2d 264 (N.J. 1997); Cooperative Power Association v. Westinghouse Elec. Corp., 493 N.W.2d 661 (N.D. 1992); Koss Construction v. Caterpillar Inc., 960 P.2d 255 (Kan. Ct. App. 1998).

subject the manufacturer to limitless damages. "In products liability law," the Court reasoned, "where there is a duty to the public generally, forseeability is an inadequate brake . . . Permitting recovery for all foreseeable claims for purely economic loss could make a manufacturer liable for vast sums."[130] As a result, the Court found that it would be extremely difficult for a manufacturer to account for the expectations of all persons who may encounter its product. Warranty law, in contrast, places limitations on liability based on privity and the requirement of foreseeability of consequential damages as a result of breach.[131] The application of warranty law to commercial losses was necessary to prevent manufacturers from being liable for damages unknown and unlimited in scope.

In addition to state courts and the Supreme Court, the economic loss rule also is supported by § 21 of the Restatement (Third). This section codifies the economic loss rule in products liability actions and provides that:

> For purposes of this Restatement, harm to persons or property includes economic loss if caused by harm to:
>
> (a) the plaintiff's person; or
>
> (b) the person of another when harm to the other interferes with an interest of the plaintiff protected by tort law; or
>
> (c) the plaintiff's property other than the defective product itself.

This section sets out the limitations courts have placed on the application of products liability law to various forms of economic loss.[132]

Although the economic loss doctrine prevents recovery of compensation in negligence or strict liability, a plaintiff can use negligence, strict liability, and warranty theories when the product causes damage to "other property."[133] One problem for courts has been defining what constitutes "other property." The Supreme Court discussed the scope of "other property" in the context of component parts in *Saratoga Fishing Co. v. J.M. Martinac & Co.*,[134] in which the primary purchaser of a ship added to a skiff, a fishing net and spare parts. The vessel, with the added parts, then was sold to the plaintiff. An engine room fire, partially caused by a faulty hydraulic system, led to the sinking of the ship. The plaintiff brought a products liability suit against the manufacturer of the hydraulic system and the company that

---

[130] *East River*, 476 U.S. at 874.

[131] *Id.*

[132] *See* Flowers v. Viking Yacht Co., 840 A.2d 291, 294-295 (N.J. 2003); Bay Breeze Condominium Association, Inc. v. Norco Windows, Inc., 651 N.W.2d 738, 743 (Wis. Ct. App. 2002).

[133] *East River*, 476 U.S. at 871. *See* 2-J Corporation v. Tice, 126 F.3d 539 (3d Cir. 1997) (applying Pennsylvania law); A.J. Decoster Co. v. Westinghouse Electric Corp., 634 A.2d 1330 (Md. 1994).

[134] 520 U.S. 875 (1997).

built the vessel. The Court concluded that when a manufacturer places an item into the stream of commerce by selling it to an initial user, that item is the "product itself."[135] Items added to the product by the initial user are "other property" and the initial user's sale of the product to a subsequent user does not change these characterizations. The Court held that the initial user's added equipment constituted "other property" within the meaning of the *East River* doctrine, allowing the plaintiff to recover damages for its destruction.

§ 10.04 PUNITIVE DAMAGES

[A] *Introduction*

In August 2005 a jury of seven men and five women in Angleton, Texas, decided a products liability action brought against the pharmaceutical company Merck by a woman who alleged that her husband's death from a heart attack in 2001 was caused by taking the prescription painkiller Vioxx.[136] By a 10-2 vote, the minimum required under Texas law to find a defendant liable, the jury awarded the woman $450,000 in economic damages for her husband's lost income, $24.5 million for her mental anguish and loss of companionship, and $229 million in punitive damages.[137] Despite the jury's verdict, a Texas statute automatically limits the amount of punitive damages the woman can recover to $1.6 million. However, for supporters and critics of punitive damages, the verdict is another example either of a jury sending a message to a large corporation that its reckless conduct will not be tolerated or of a jury that was out of control and harming business and the country with its verdict.

One reason for the controversy over the verdict in the Vioxx case is that, in all but five states,[138] plaintiffs are eligible to recover, in certain situations, punitive damages in addition to their compensatory damages. Punitive damages, also referred to by courts as "exemplary damages,"[139] are intended to punish defendants as well as to deter them and others who might engage in the same type of conduct in the future.[140] Traditionally, punitive damages

---

[135] *Id.* at 879.

[136] At the time of the case, more than 4200 state and federal Vioxx-related lawsuits were pending in the United States.

[137] "Jury Calls Merck Liable in Death of Man on Vioxx," *N.Y. Times*, August 20, 2005, at A1. Merck has stated that it will appeal the verdict.

[138] Three states (Nebraska, New Hampshire, and Washington) prohibit punitive damages entirely while two other states (Louisiana and Massachusetts) permit punitive damages only when authorized by a specific statute.

[139] *See* Pacific Mutual Life Insurance Co. v. Haslip, 499 U.S. 1, 7 (1991).

[140] Smith v. Wade, 461 U.S. 30, 54 (1983) ("Punitive damages are awarded in the jury's discretion 'to punish [the defendant] for his outrageous conduct and to deter him and others like

were a matter solely for the common law. In recent years, however, the Supreme Court and many state legislatures have placed constitutional and statutory limitations and guidelines on the award of punitive damages. As a result, three questions surround punitive damages in products liability cases: (1) what must a plaintiff prove in order to recover punitive damages; (2) what limitations, if any, are there on the amount of punitive damages a plaintiff can receive; and (3) what limitations does the Constitution place on the award of punitive damages? The first question is governed by state statutes and common law. In order to answer the second question, it is necessary to look at the legislation adopted in many states that places caps and other restrictions on the amount of punitive damage a plaintiff can receive.[141] Finally, the Supreme Court has addressed the third question in a number of cases and has set out "guideposts" for the review of punitive damages awards to help lower courts determine what ratios of punitive to compensatory damages meet the requirements of the Due Process clause.[142]

[B] *Conduct and Standard of Proof Required for Punitive Damages*

Although the states vary widely in the amount of punitive damages they permit a plaintiff to recover in a products liability action, there is general agreement on the type of conduct required of a defendant before punitive damages may be awarded and on the standard of proof required of that conduct.[143] Typical of the type of conduct required for punitive damages is the statement of the New Mexico Supreme Court that, since the purpose of punitive damages is to punish wrongdoing, the plaintiff must prove that the defendant's behavior rose to "a willful, wanton, malicious, reckless, oppressive, or fraudulent" level.[144] This standard also is used in products liability cases. The Connecticut products liability statute, for example, states that a plaintiff may be awarded punitive damages in a products liability action if "the harm suffered was the result of the product seller's reckless disregard for the safety of product users, consumers or others who were injured by the product."[145] Courts have interpreted this to mean that punitive damages

---

him from similar conduct in the future.' RESTATEMENT (SECOND) OF TORTS § 908(1) (1979). The focus is on the character of the tortfeasor's conduct — whether it is of the sort that calls for deterrence and punishment over and above that provided by compensatory awards."

[141] For a "Fifty-One Jurisdiction Survey of Punitive Damages," see Michael L. Rustad, *The Closing of Punitive Damages' Iron Cage*, 38 LOY. L.A. L. REV. 1297, 1370 - 1419 (2005).

[142] *See* State Farm Mutual Automobile Insurance Co. v. Campbell, 538 U.S. 408 (2003); BMW of North America, Inc. v. Gore, 517 U.S. 559 (1996).

[143] According to the RESTATEMENT (SECOND) OF TORTS § 908 (1979), "[p]unitive damages may be awarded for conduct that is outrageous, because of the defendant's evil motive or his reckless indifference to the rights of others."

[144] Clay v. Ferrellgas, Inc., 881 P.2d 11, 14 (N.M. 1994).

[145] CONN. GEN. STAT. § 52-240b (2004).

require a showing of reckless disregard for the rights of others and intentional and wanton violations of those rights.[146] Similarly, the Kansas Supreme Court has stated that punitive damages are permissible in products liability cases "whenever the elements of fraud, malice, gross negligence, or oppression mingle in the controversy."[147]

Since punitive damages have a quasi-criminal nature, thirty states require the plaintiff to prove the defendant's conduct with a higher standard of "clear and convincing evidence."[148] This standard is contained in the Mississippi punitive damages statute, which also sets out the required conduct: "Punitive damages may not be awarded if the claimant does not prove by clear and convincing evidence that the defendant against whom punitive damages are sought acted with actual malice, gross negligence which evidences a willful, wanton, or reckless disregard for the safety of others, or committed actual fraud."[149] The "clear and convincing" standard is a compromise between "a preponderance of the evidence" usually required in civil cases and the higher standard of "beyond a reasonable doubt" used in criminal law.

An example of a products liability case where the manufacturer's conduct resulted in the award of punitive damages is *Grimshaw v. Ford Motor Co.*[150] In *Grimshaw*, a driver rear-ended a stalled 1972 Ford Pinto, causing it to burst into flames. The plaintiff, a 13-year-old passenger in the Pinto, suffered severe and permanent disfiguring burns to his face and body. The plaintiff sued Ford Motor Company for negligence and strict liability, claiming that Ford was aware from crash tests that the Pinto contained a design defect that would cause the passenger area to catch fire in the event of a rear-end collision.[151] A jury awarded the plaintiff $2.5 million in compensatory damages and $125 million in punitive damages.[152] On Ford's motion for a new trial, the judge required the plaintiff to remit all but $3 million of the punitive award as a condition for the denial of the motion.[153] However, Ford appealed, claiming that punitive damages were statutorily and constitutionally impermissible in products liability cases, and that no evidence supported the jury's finding of malice.[154]

---

[146] Ames v. Sears, Roebuck & Co., 514 A.2d 352 (Conn. App. Ct. 1986) (*quoting* Collens v. New Canaan Water Co., 234 A.2d 825 (Conn. 1967)).

[147] Tetuan v. A.H. Robins Co., 738 P.2d 1210, 1239 (Kan. 1987).

[148] *See, e.g.,* FLA STAT. § 768.73 (2004); GA. CODE ANN. § 51-12-5.1 (2003); N.C. GEN STAT. § 10-15(b) (2003): OKLA. STAT. ANN. tit. 23, § 9.1 (2005). Colorado requires that the proof "beyond a reasonable doubt." COLO. REV. STAT. § 13-21-102 (2001).

[149] MISS. CODE. ANN. § 11-1-65(4) (2005).

[150] 174 Cal. Rptr. 348 (Cal. Ct. App. 1981).

[151] *Id.* at 363.

[152] *Id.* at 358.

[153] *Id.*

[154] *Id.* at 380.

Ford argued that the world "malice" as used in § 3294 of the California Civil Code[155] was intended to apply only to traditional tort claims, and not to products liability actions.[156] However, the California appellate court rejected that argument, citing the state's long-standing allowance of punitive damages at common law, and defining "malice" as used in the California Civil Code as "conduct evincing 'a conscious disregard of the probability that the actor's conduct will result in injury to others.' "[157] Stating that the primary purpose of punitive damages is to punish "conduct evincing callous and conscious disregard of public safety by those who manufacture and market mass produced articles," and defending punitive damage awards as "the most effective remedy for consumer protection against defectively designed mass produced articles," the court refused to find any statutory impediment to the award of punitive damages.[158] The court concluded that, because Ford knew of the defect and could have remedied it at a small per-car cost, it had acted with the required malice.[159] Finding the trial judge's calculation of punitive damages was "fair and reasonable," the court upheld the $3.5 million punitive damage award.[160]

[C] *Statutory Controls on Punitive Damage Awards*

Once the plaintiff has shown that the defendant's conduct met the standard required for punitive damages, the next question is: What limitations, if any, are there on the amount of punitive damages that the plaintiff can receive? This is the most controversial issue concerning punitive damages. Half of the states place no legislative or common law cap on the amount of punitive damages a trier or fact may award.[161] However, as a result of tort reform efforts, twenty states now place some statutory limitations on the amount of punitive damages a plaintiff can recover. These limitations, which apply to all cases, fall into three broad categories. First, a few states impose an absolute cap on the amount of punitive damages. Georgia, for example, limits punitive damages to $250,000 unless the plaintiff can show that the defendant acted with the specific intent to harm, not a situation found in products liability cases.[162] Similarly, Virginia limits an award of

---

[155] "In an action for the breach of an obligation not arising from contract, where it is proven by clear and convincing evidence that the defendant has been guilty of oppression, fraud, or malice, the plaintiff, in addition to the actual damages, may recover damages for the sake of example and by way of punishing the defendant." CAL. CIV. CODE § 3294(a) (2005).

[156] 174 Cal. Rptr. at 381.

[157] *Id.*

[158] *Id.* at 383.

[159] *Id.* at 385.

[160] *Id.* at 391.

[161] These states include California, Illinois, Minnesota, Missouri, New York, and Pennsylvania.

[162] GA. STAT. ANN. § 51-12-5.1 (2003).

punitive damages to $350,000.[163] A second group of states limits an award of punitive damages to a multiplier of the amount of compensatory damages. Connecticut[164] and Ohio,[165] for example, restrict the amount of punitive damages to twice the amount of the compensatory damages. A third approach to limiting punitive damages is to use a multiplier of compensatory damages along with an absolute cap. This is the most widely used method of imposing a cap on punitive damages. Although the multipliers and absolute amounts vary among the states,[166] one example of this approach is Florida which limits an award of punitive damages to the greater of three times the amount of compensatory damages or $500,000. The limit rises to the greater of four times the compensatory damages or $2,000,000 if the defendant's conduct was motivated by unreasonable financial gain.[167] A variation of this is the Kansas approach that limits punitive damages to the lesser of a defendant's annual gross income or $5 million.[168] The most complex formula for punitive damages in products liability cases was adopted by Mississippi in 2004.[169] Under the sliding scale used in the state's statute, punitive damages are limited to $20 million for a defendant with a net worth of more than $1 billion; $15 million for a defendant with a net worth between $750 million and $1 billion; $5 million for a defendant with a net worth of more than $500 million but not more than $750 million; $3.75 million for a defendant with a net worth of more than $100 million but not more than $500 million; $2.5 million for a defendant with a net worth of more than $50 million but not more than $100 million; and 2% of the defendant's net worth for a defendant with a net worth of $50 million or less.

Some states limit punitive damages by procedural methods rather than by caps. Illinois, for example, prohibits a plaintiff from requesting punitive damages in the complaint. Instead, after a plaintiff files the complaint, he or she must move to amend the complaint to seek punitive damages.[170] The decision whether or not punitive damages are appropriate for the jury in the case to consider is in the discretion of the trial judge.[171] Other states reverse the approach and let the jury decide whether punitive damages

---

[163] VA. CODE ANN. § 8.01-38.1 (Michie 2000).

[164] CONN. GEN. STAT. ANN. § 52-240b (2000).

[165] OHIO REV. CODE ANN. § 2315.21(D)(2)(a) (2005).

[166] For example, in Indiana punitive damages are limited to three times the amount of compensatory damages or $50,000 (IND. CODE § 34-51-3-4 (1998)); in North Carolina, it is the greater of three times the amount of compensatory damages or $250,000 (N.C. GEN. STAT. §§ 1D-25(b) (2003)); in New Jersey, it is the greater of five times the amount of compensatory damages or $350,000 (N.J. STAT. ANN. § 2A:15-5.14 (2000)).

[167] FLA. STAT. § 768.73(1) (2004).

[168] KAN. STAT. ANN. § 60-3702 (1994).

[169] MISS. CODE ANN. § 11-1-65(3)(a) (2004 Supp.).

[170] 735 ILL. COMP. STAT. 5/2-604.1 (2004).

[171] Schenker v. Chicago Title & Trust Co., 470 N.E.2d 1264 (Ill. App. Ct. 1984).

are appropriate in the case and then leave it to the judge to determine the amount.[172] In doing so, the Kansas Supreme Court has stated that the trial judge must base the award of punitive damages on "the actual damages sustained, the actual damage award, the circumstances of the case, the evidence presented, the relative positions of the plaintiff and the defendant, and the defendant's financial worth."[173]

Another procedural method designed to limit the amount of punitive damages is to bifurcate the trial, with the jury first determining the question of liability and whether punitive damages are appropriate and a second proceedings to determine the amount of punitive damages.[174] Eighteen states either require such bifurcated proceedings or permit the parties to request them. Other states limit the amount of punitive damages that the plaintiff can recover by requiring that a certain percentage of the award be paid to the state or a designated beneficiary.[175] About half-a-dozen states have adopted what is referred to as the "FDA defense" to punitive damages.[176] Under these statutes, a pharmaceutical company is not liable for punitive damages if its product complies with FDA standards.

In addition to the statutory limitations placed on punitive damages, every state subjects a jury's award to review, first by the trial judge, and then on appeal. The trial judge may set aside a punitive damages award if it is excessive as a matter of law or is so grossly disproportionate as to raise the presumption that it was the product of passion or prejudice. An award of punitive damages also is subject to review on appeal. In deciding whether an award is excessive, the California court in *Grimshaw* stated that four factors should be weighed: (1) the degree of reprehensibility of the defendant's conduct; (2) the wealth of the defendant; (3) the amount of compensatory damages; and (4) an amount which would serve as a deterrent effect of like conduct by defendant and others.[177] These factors also are reflected in the Restatement (Second) of Torts which sets out three factors that a trier of fact can consider in making its calculation of punitive damages: (1) the

---

[172] *See* Connecticut (CONN. GEN. STAT. § 52-240b (1999)) and Kansas (KAN. STAT. ANN. § 60-3702(a) (1994)).

[173] Tetuan v. A.H. Robins Co., 738 P.2d 1210, 1239 (Kan. 1987).

[174] For examples, see Alaska (ALASKA STAT. § 09.17.020(b) (Michie 2003)); California (CAL. CIV. CODE § 3294(a) (1997)); OHIO REV. CODE ANN. § 2315.21(B)(1) (2005 Supp.); and Utah (UTAH CODE ANN. § 78-18-1 (2004 Supp.)).

[175] Indiana law, for example, requires plaintiffs who receive punitive damage awards to deposit 75% of the award in a violent crime victim's compensation fund. IND. CODE § 34-51-3-6 (1998). Missouri requires that plaintiffs deposit 50% of punitive damage awards into a state tort victim's compensation fund. MO. REV. STAT. § 537.675(2) (2000). For other examples, see ALASKA STAT. § 09.17.020(j) (Michie 2003 Supp.)); GA. CODE ANN. § 51-12-5.1(e)(2) (2003)); IOWA CODE ANN. § 668A.1 (1998); UTAH CODE ANN. § 78-18-1 (2004 Supp.).

[176] For examples, see ARIZ. REV. STAT. § 12-701(A)(1) (2003) and COLO. REV. STAT. § 13-64-302.5(5)(a) (2001).

[177] Grimshaw v. Ford Motor Co., 174 Cal. Rptr. 348, 388 (Cal. Ct. App. 1981).

character of the defendant's act; (2) the nature and extent of the harm; and (3) the defendant's wealth.[178]

[D] *The Constitutionality of Punitive Damages*

Although punitive damages once were a matter solely for state legislatures and the courts, they now are a frequent source of constitutional litigation. The basis for much of this litigation is the Due Process clause of the Fourteenth Amendment which prohibits states from depriving any person of "life, liberty, or property, without due process of law."[179] In the case of punitive damage awards, the Supreme Court has stated that "the Due Process Clause of the Fourteenth Amendment prohibits the imposition of grossly excessive or arbitrary punishments on a tortfeasor."[180] Since the mid-1980s, the Court has addressed the constitutionality of punitive damages on a number of occasions and has set out guidelines for awarding such damages. Although none of these Supreme Court cases has involved defective products, the decisions govern the award of punitive damages in products liability cases.

Until 1996 the Supreme Court deferred to state law when examining the constitutionality of punitive damage awards.[181] In *Browning-Ferris Industries of Vermont, Inc. v. Kelco*,[182] for example, the Court held that the Excessive Fines clause of the Eighth Amendment "does not apply to awards of punitive damages in cases between private parties."[183] The Court also refused to set any guidelines for the award of punitive damages, stating that their regulation was a matter "of state, and not federal, common law."[184] Two years later, the Court again refused to hold the amount of a punitive damages award unconstitutional, finding instead that the awards "rationally advance the State's interest in minimizing fraud."[185] As long as a punitive damages award was reasonable and not "grossly excessive," the Court was willing to uphold it.[186]

---

[178] RESTATEMENT (SECOND) OF TORTS § 908(2) (1979). *See also* Franz v. Calaco Development Corp., 818 N.E.2d 357, 371 (Ill. App. Ct. 2004).

[179] U.S. Const. amend. XIV, § 1.

[180] State Farm Mutual Automobile Insurance Co. v. Campbell, 538 U.S. 408, 415-16 (2003).

[181] *See* Michael P. Allen, *The Supreme Court, Punitive Damages and State Sovereignty*, 13 GEO. MASON L. REV. 1 (2004).

[182] 492 U.S. 257 (1989).

[183] *Id.* at 261.

[184] *Id.* at 279.

[185] Pacific Mutual Life Insurance Co. v. Haslip, 499 U.S. 1, 15 (1991) (While admitting that individual awards could "jar one's constitutional sensibilities," the Court declined to establish any framework for the calculation of punitive damages.).

[186] TXO Production Corp. v. Alliance Resources Corp., 509 U.S. 443, 465-66 (1993) (A $10 million punitive damage award was acceptable under Fourteenth Amendment procedural and

The Supreme Court made its first attempt to impose limits on punitive damages in *BMW of North America, Inc. v. Gore*.[187] In *Gore*, an auto buyer purchased a new BMW automobile that, as a result of BMW's policy of not disclosing damage under a certain percentage of the car value, had been painted to cover minor body damage. This reduced the value of the car by approximately 10%, and, for that, the Alabama jury awarded the buyer $4,000 in compensatory damages and $4 million dollars in punitive damages, a 1000 to 1 ratio, "based on a determination that [BMW's] nondisclosure policy constituted 'gross, oppressive or malicious' fraud."[188] The Alabama Supreme Court reduced the award to $2 million, an amount that still was 500 times the amount of the compensatory damages.[189] The Supreme Court granted certiorari to "illuminate 'the character of the standard that will identify unconstitutionally excessive awards' of punitive damages."[190] In its opinion, the Court set out three "guideposts" to help lower courts determine the constitutionality of punitive damages awards: (1) the degree of reprehensibility; (2) the ratio of actual harm as demonstrated by the compensatory damages to the punitive damages; and (3) the sanctions imposed by the state legislature for similar misconduct.[191]

Applying the guideposts to the facts of *Gore*, the Court held that the punitive damage award was unconstitutional. First, BMW's conduct was not reprehensible. The harm to the buyer was purely economic and the Court found none of the "deliberate false statements, acts of affirmative misconduct, or concealment of evidence of improper motive" present, as it is in cases where courts uphold substantial punitive damages awards.[192] Second, in light of the lack of reprehensibility, a punitive damages award of more than four hundred times the compensatory damages was not within a constitutionally acceptable range.[193] Finally, $2 million dollars was a significantly larger dollar amount than what was permitted by state statute to punish similar wrongdoing.[194]

The Supreme Court's most recent attempt to clarify when punitive damages awards are excessive under the Due Process clause is *State Farm Mutual Automobile Insurance Co. v. Campbell*.[195] In *Campbell*, a driver

---

substantive due process. The Court stated that substantive due process may impose an upper limit on a punitive damage award, but declined to impose a "bright line" rule, instead encouraging courts to use a standard of "general concern of reasonableness.").

[187] 517 U.S. 559 (1996).

[188] *Id.* at 564-65.

[189] *Id.* at 567.

[190] *Id.* at 568.

[191] *Id.* at 575, 580, 583.

[192] *Id.* at 577, 579.

[193] *Id.* at 583.

[194] *Id.* at 584.

[195] 538 U.S. 408 (2003).

insured by State Farm was involved in an automobile accident that resulted in another driver's death and a third driver's permanent disability. Despite advice to the contrary, State Farm refused to settle the claim for the policy limits of $50,000, and, at trial, a jury returned a judgment against the plaintiff for $186,000. Although State Farm eventually agreed to pay the entire judgment, the plaintiff brought suit against the company "alleging bad faith, fraud, and intentional infliction of emotional distress."[196] The Utah appellate court reduced the trial jury's award of $2.6 million in compensatory damages and $145 million in punitive damages. The Utah Supreme Court analyzed the award under the three guideposts set out in *Gore* and reinstated the original award.[197] The Supreme Court granted certiorari and held that the Utah Supreme Court was in "error to reinstate the jury's $145 million punitive damages award."[198]

In examining the facts in *Campbell*, the Court reaffirmed and clarified the three *Gore* guideposts. First, courts must analyze the reprehensibility of an act by considering the following: (1) the nature of the harm; (2) whether the conduct "evinced an indifference to or a reckless disregard of the health or safety of others;" (3) the financial vulnerability of the plaintiff; (4) whether the act was an isolated incident or repeated occurrence; and (5) and whether "the harm was the result of intentional malice, trickery, or deceit, or mere accident."[199] While State Farm's actions were not laudable, they were not so reprehensible that the state's interest in deterring similar conduct could not have been achieved by a more modest punitive damages award.[200]

In its discussion of the ratio guidepost, the Court declined to adopt bright-line rules on what constitutes a constitutional ratio of punitive to compensatory damages. Instead, the Court stated that "in practice, few awards exceeding a single-digit ratio between punitive and compensatory damages, to a significant degree, will satisfy due process."[201] However, as the Court stated in *Gore*, in cases of extremely reprehensible conduct, punitive damages of multiple-digit ratios can survive constitutional scrutiny, as long as the punitive damage award is "reasonable and proportionate to the amount of harm to the plaintiff and to the general damages recovered."[202] In *Campbell*, the ratio of punitive to compensatory damages was 145 to 1, which, when considered in light of the nature of the act, was constitutionally disproportionate.[203]

---

[196] *Id*. at 414.

[197] *Id*. at 415.

[198] *Id*. at 418.

[199] *Id*. at 419.

[200] *Id*. at 420.

[201] *Id*. at 425.

[202] *Id*. at 425-26.

[203] *Id*. at 426-28.

In analyzing the third *Gore* guidepost, statutory penalties for similar misconduct, the Court in *Campbell* cautioned against using "the civil process to assess criminal penalties that can be imposed only after the heightened protections of a criminal trial have been observed, including, of course, its higher standards of proof."[204] The possibility that the act of a tortfeasor might lead to criminal punishment does not automatically justify an award of punitive damages. Because Utah's statutory fine for fraud was $10,000, the punitive damage award of $145 million did not meet the test set out in the third *Gore* guidepost.

Shortly after it decided *Campbell*, the Supreme Court vacated and remanded four products liability cases for further reconsideration of the awards of punitive damages. These cases provide little guidance as to how courts will apply *Gore* and *Campbell* when analyzing other punitive damage awards. However, the decisions do show an attempt to bring awards of punitive damages within the constitutional guidelines concerning ratios and what may be considered. In *Bocci v. Key Pharmaceuticals Inc.*,[205] the Oregon appellate court had to determine the appropriate punitive damages award for the failure of a pharmaceutical company to provide the plaintiff with adequate information concerning the potential toxicity of a certain drug, resulting in permanent brain damage. The court concluded on remand that, while a 45 to 1 ratio was "clearly in excess of the single-digit neighborhood that the Court has suggested lies at the outer edge of constitutionality," a 7 to 1 punitive damages award was constitutionally permissible.[206] Similarly, on remand in *Romo v. Ford Motor Co.*,[207] the California appellate court held that if the plaintiffs agreed to remit all of the punitive damages judgment except $23,723,287, approximately a 5 to 1 ratio, the punitive damages judgment would be modified and affirmed in that amount. However, if they did not agree to the remittitur, the punitive damages judgment would be reversed and the case would be remanded for a new trial on the amount of the punitive damages. In *Sand Hill Energy, Inc. v. Ford Motor Co.*,[208] a products liability suit against a truck manufacturer, the Kentucky appellate court initially reduced the trial court's $20 million damage award to $15 million in light of the relationship between the defendant's conduct and the plaintiff's injury.[209] On remand from the United States Supreme Court, the Kentucky Supreme Court found that the jury had considered the manufacturer's conduct on a nationwide scale in arriving at the punitive damages award. The court ordered a new trial on the amount

---

204 *Id.* at 428.

205 76 P.3d 669 (Or. Ct. App. 2003).

206 *Id.* at 675.

207 6 Cal. Rptr. 3d 793 (Cal. Ct. App. 2003).

208 83 S.W.3d 483 (Ky. Ct. App. 2002).

209 *Id.* at 496.

of punitive damages since the jury instructions contained no limitation on extraterritorial punishment as required by *Campbell*.[210] In *Williams v. Philip Morris Inc.*,[211] a wrongful death action against a cigarette manufacturer, the jury awarded the plaintiff $800,000 in compensatory damages and $79.5 million in punitive damages. On remand from the Supreme Court, the Oregon appellate court held that the punitive damages award was "reasonable and proportionate to the wrong inflicted on decedent and the public of this state" and did not violate due process under the *Gore* guideposts.[212]

§ 10.05 PRE-JUDGMENT AND POST-JUDGMENT INTEREST

If a jury awards a plaintiff damages in a products liability case, the plaintiff may be entitled to recover pre-judgment and post-judgment interest on the award. Whether a plaintiff is able to recover interest on an award, as well as the amount of the interest, is governed by statutes that vary from state to state.

The controversy over awarding interest on damages awards centers on prejudgment interest. The rationale behind prejudgment interest is to ensure that plaintiffs are compensated fully for the loss of the use of the money due them as damages between the date their claim arose and the date of judgment.[213] When interest rates are high or where large sums of money are involved, plaintiffs often argue that defendants attempt to stall their cases in order to use the money for as long as possible. Defendants, however, counter that plaintiffs are the ones who delay in order to demonstrate additional pain and suffering, as well as complications from their injuries, and that an award of prejudgment interest penalizes them and overcompensates plaintiffs. Thus, both supporters and opponents of prejudgment interest cast their arguments in terms of preventing delays in litigation, and promoting efficiency and settlements, and fairness to the plaintiff or defendant.

Every state permits prejudgment interest and most provide that it is applicable to all damages. Some states, however, limit prejudgment interest to amounts that were liquidated or ascertainable at the time of the loss. The states also differ as to the starting point from which prejudgment interest begins to accrue in breach of warranty and tort actions. Among these are the date of the injury;[214] the date the suit was filed;[215] a stated

---

[210] Sand Hill Energy, Inc. v. Smith, 142 S.W.3d 153 (Ky. 2004).

[211] 92 P.3d 126 (Or. Ct. App. 2004).

[212] *Id.* at 146.

[213] City of Milwaukee v. Cement Division, National Gypsum Co., 515 U.S. 189 (1995).

[214] *See* HAW. REV. STAT. § 636-16 (2002); S.D. CODIFIED LAWS § 21-1-13.1 (Michie 2003).

[215] *See* OKLA STAT. tit 12, § 727E (2000).

number of days after a written demand is rejected;[216] or at the discretion of the court or jury.[217] Finally, the amount of pre-judgment interest varies from a specific amount (the most common method)[218] to a one using the Federal Reserve discount rate,[219] the prime rate,[220] or the U.S. Treasury Bill rate.[221] In addition, more than a dozen states have made prejudgment interest part of their tort reform packages in recent years. Most of this legislation deals with the amount of the prejudgment interest rate and the date on which prejudgment interest begins to accrue. While most states also do not permit plaintiffs to recover prejudgment interest on punitive damages,[222] a few states have held that it is recoverable.[223]

Post-judgment interest is less controversial. Like prejudgment interest, it is meant to prevent delay and to compensate a plaintiff for the lost use of money because of delay. However, the argument for post-judgment interest is stronger because the money on which the plaintiff seeks interest already has been awarded to the plaintiff by the court. Every state permits the award of post-judgment interest, either from the date of the verdict[224] or from the date of judgment.[225] The amount of post-judgment interest also is set by state statutes and varies greatly. As with prejudgment interest, most statutes set the interest rate at a specific amount[226] or at a specific percentage above the Federal Reserve's discount rate.[227]

§ 10.06 JOINT AND SEVERAL LIABILITY

As products liability litigation becomes increasingly complex, many cases involve more than one defendant, i.e., a component part manufacturer, the manufacturer of the finished product, the retailer of the product. Traditionally, a finding that multiple defendants were liable resulted in them being "jointly and severally liable," i.e., each defendant was responsible for the entire amount of the damages suffered by the plaintiff, regardless of its

---

[216] *See* MO. REV. STAT. § 408.040(2) (2001).

[217] *See* VA. CODE ANN. § 8.01-382 (Michie 2000).

[218] *See* ARK. CODE ANN. § 16-65-114(a) (Michie 1987); MONT. CODE ANN. § 27-1-210(1) (2003).

[219] *See* ALASKA STAT. § 09.30.070(a) (Michie 2004) (3% above the discount rate).

[220] *See* GA. CODE ANN. § 7-4-12 (2004) (prime rate rate plus 3%).

[221] *See* IOWA CODE § 668.13 (1998) (constant maturity index plus 2%); NEB. REV. STAT. § 45-103 (2005) (1% above the Treasury Bill rate).

[222] *See* ALASKA STAT. § 9.30.070 (Michie 2004); IND. CODE § 34-51-4-3 (1998); OHIO REV. CODE. ANN. § 2315.21(D)(3) (2005 Supp.).

[223] Werremeyer v. K.C. Auto Salvage Co., 134 S.W.3d 633 (Mo. 2004).

[224] *See* IND. CODE § 24-4.6-1-101 (1996); TENN. CODE ANN. § 47-14-122 (2001).

[225] *See* CAL. CIV. PROC. CODE § 685.020(a) (West 1987); 735 ILL. COMP. STAT. 5/2-1303 (2004).

[226] *See* MONT. CODE ANN. § 25-9-204, 205(1) (2003) (10% per annum).

[227] *See* ALASKA STAT. § 09.30.070 (2004).

actual responsibility for the damages. As a result, "the injured person may sue one or all of the tortfeasors to obtain a recovery for his injuries; the fact that one of the tortfeasors is impecunious or otherwise immune from suit does not relieve another tortfeasor of his liability for damage which he himself has proximately caused."[228]

Joint and several liability grew out of situations where the defendants acted in concert, concurrently, or successively to bring about the plaintiff's injuries.[229] Commentators and courts offered three principal rationales for holding each defendant liable potentially for the entire amount of the damages in these cases: (1) each of the defendants caused the plaintiff's injuries; (2) joint and several liability relieves the plaintiff of having to identify and to sue each person responsible for the injury in order to receive full compensation; and (3) if one (or more) of the defendants is unable to pay the damages, the remaining defendants should be responsible so that the innocent plaintiff receives the full amount awarded by the jury or judge.[230] However, critics of joint and several liability point to the possibility that a defendant who is only slightly responsible for the plaintiff's damages may be required to pay the entire amount because of the financial inability of other defendants whose percentage of the responsibility is much greater.[231] These critics argue that, instead, liability should be apportioned among the defendants based upon their share of the liability for the damage. Critics also point to strict liability cases which are not based upon any showing of fault on the part of the defendant. Joint and several liability results in a defendant who is strictly liable being held responsible for other defendants who also are strictly liable or who actually are at fault.

As a result of these criticisms, almost forty states have made some changes in their laws governing joint and several liability in recent years. The result is that the state laws governing joint and several liability and contribution among tortfeasors now are so state-specific that it is impossible to make anything more than broad generalizations about them. Among the approaches adopted by the states are four principal ones. First, a number of states have abolished joint liability, either entirely or selectively. In these states, defendants no longer are individually liable for the entire amount of the plaintiff's damages. Instead, a judgment must be entered against each defendant on the basis of several liability according to each defendant's relative percentage of fault.[232] However, if one of the potential defendants is immune from liability to the plaintiff, some states hold that

---

[228] Richards v. Owens-Illinois, Inc., 60 Cal. Rptr. 2d 103, 108 (Cal. 1997) (*quoting* American Motorcycle Association v. Superior Court, 578 P.2d 899, 904 (Cal. 1978)).

[229] F. JAMES, F. HARPER AND O. GRAY, 2 THE LAW OF TORTS, § 10.1 (2d ed. 1986).

[230] *See* William L. Prosser, *Joint Torts and Several Liability*, 25 CAL. L. REV. 413 (1936); John Henry Wigmore, *Joint-Tortfeasors and Severance of Damages; Making the Innocent Party Suffer Without Redress*, 17 ILL. L. REV. 458 (1923); Woods v. Cole, 693 N.E.2d 333 (Ill. 1998).

[231] Stevenson v. Keene Corp., 603 A.2d 521 (N.J. Super Ct. 1992).

[232] *See* ALASKA STAT. § 09.17.080 (Michie 2003 Supp.); COLO. REV. STAT. § 13-21-111.5 (2001).

the trier of fact must exclude it when determining the relative percentage of the total fault.[233] Second, some states apply joint and several liability only if the defendant's fault is more than a specific percentage of the total fault. If the defendant's fault is below the required amount, it is severally liable.[234] Third, other states provide that, if one of the tortfeasors is insolvent, its share is reapportioned among the solvent defendants and the plaintiff in proportion to their respective percentage of the fault.[235] Finally, some states retain joint and several liability for economic damages but apply several liability for non-economic losses.[236]

---

[233] WASH. REV. CODE § 4.22.070(1) (2005). *See also* Geurin v. Winston Industries, Inc., 316 F.3d 879 (9th Cir. 2002) (applying Washington law).

[234] *See* TEX. CIV. PRAC. & REM. CODE § 33.013(b)(c) (Vernon 2004-2005 Supp.).

[235] *See* OR. REV. STAT. § 31.610(3) (2003).

[236] *See* CAL. CIV. CODE § 1431.2(a) (1997).

Chapter 11

RESEARCH AND PRACTICE IMPLICATIONS OF CHOICE OF THEORY

SYNOPSIS

§ 11.01 INTRODUCTION

There are a series of real world considerations that consistently attend products liability litigation, requiring focused attention by counsel for either side of the particular case involved. All litigation, regardless of kind, is an exercise in attempting to prove a set of historical facts upon which legal responsibility may or may not be eventually imposed. It is the same in civil as in criminal law. The plaintiff or state proffers facts, disputed in part by the respondent, from a typically circumscribed point in the history of the defendant and/or the victim of a crime. Did the defendant run the stop sign and cause the collision with the plaintiff's vehicle that resulted in two deaths? Did Martha Stewart have certain insider information and subsequently lie about to federal prosecutors? Did defendant threaten a bank teller with harm to get money on a certain day? Did the defendant in a stalking prosecution engage in a historical pattern of behavior sufficient to meet the statutory requirements?

In most litigation in American courts, the past history of importance is usually quite limited in time, as the above examples illustrate. Some litigation such as anti-trust, sexual or age discrimination, or stock fraud, often involve a more extensive examination into a defendant's past business history. Even in the latter cases, however, the period of history that may be arguably relevant to the issues is generally not decades long. Products liability investigation and preparation, however, typically involve the investigation of decades of science, industry development, government regulatory activities and the research development, production and marketing of a products liability defendant.

Products liability litigation is grounded in the range of sophisticated policy considerations discussed in Part I of this book. It is, perhaps, more than
any other area of tort practice, inseparable from the litigation process itself.
Accordingly, it involves all of the intricacies of modern civil procedure, discovery practice, evidence theory and trial technique. Tort litigation, of which
products liability litigation is a major component, essentially second-guesses
the judgment of the defendant individual, doctor, hospital, company or
other institution in taking or failing to take the specified actions set forth
in each count of the complaint. Products litigation, centered as it is in the
decisions of international companies heavily invested in science and global
economics, necessarily requires extensive scientific and technical research,
close examination of international manufacturing and marketing structures and an understanding of the document production process of the
company involved. As a result, the pre-filing, filing, pre-trial investigation
and discovery issues associated with twenty-first century products liability
litigation involves an enormous investment of time and money on the part
of plaintiff and defense counsel. This is a considerably more difficult undertaking than that typically encountered in more focused tort litigation such
as negligence or even in the more scientifically sophisticated medical malpractice case.

Chapters 1-10 analyzed the history of products liability and provided
detailed discussions of the current theories used to channel any particular
litigation. Each of the liability theories and their policy bases that were considered in Chapters 1 through 10 focus on disparate activities within the
defendant corporation over some period of time in its manufacturing history.
When chosen by a party to forward and channel a products liability claim,
each of these theories, while broadly based and policy driven, are nonetheless inextricably centered in a searching examination by plaintiff and
defense counsel of significant historical scientific and business-related
materials. Depending on the product and the specific theory of liability
used to focus the investigation, counsel can be involved in an investigative
span of a quarter of a century or longer. While discovery requests for excessively extensive periods may be denied as unreasonable or irrelevant, courts
will typically allow decades long discovery if the complexity or age of the
product history warrants it. [1]

It is at the complaint stage that legal theory enters and serves as the
major catalyst in the process of structuring the products litigation. The
rules of civil practice necessitate the encapsualization of the basic facts
and require the plaintiff to state how he wishes the court or jury to officially

---

[1] *See* In re John Crane Inc., 2003 Tex. App. LEXIS 9684 (Tex. App. 2003). Here, the request,
as written, required John Crane to produce documents related to acquisitions spanning 86
years of asbestos-related business. The court ruled that the burden imposed on John Crane was
far out of proportion to any benefit to the plaintiff. In its discovery response, John Crane
acknowledged that it did not contest responsibility for the sales of asbestos-containing materials of any of its predecessors; therefore, the court ruled, plaintiff's justification for seeking
the documents was rendered moot.

characterize the defendant's conduct, here, whether it be negligence, breach of warranty, strict liability or misrepresentation. The routine post-complaint processes of motion practice, discovery and pre-trial motions-in-limine are no different in products liability cases. This preliminary unofficial labeling of liability counts sets in motion the plethora of litigation-related rules which determine the manner and pace at which the problem is to be channeled through the process to eventual resolution. In turn, the conceptual defect mode(s) used to characterize the actual case facts — manufacturing defect, misrepresentation, failure to instruct, failure to warn or overall design defect — also trigger a host of discovery rules that will determine the documentary center of the litigation. [2]

Experienced products litigators acknowledge that as a base line precondition to success, the plaintiff must answer three essential questions: (1) did the defect or defects alleged in the complaint cause the claimed death or injury? (2) was the defendant aware of the risk that allegedly materialized and caused the claimed damage? [Was it even a risk according to scientific and related statistical theory?] (3) what, if anything, did the defendant company do about the alleged risk of its products once it was aware of it?

The answer to each of these questions, in turn, involves the examination of a significant amount of historical data involving the following broad subjects: (1) scientific literature addressed to important aspects of the science underlying the suspect product [Cancer causing potential of the suspect pharmaceutical's basic ingredients or the the findings of certain tests to determine the failure rate of metals at varying stress levels]; (2) the historical and contemporary corporate members of the industry of which the defendant is a member; (3) comparative analyses of the design or chemical formulation of competing products in America and internationally; (4) the warnings and instructions history of any such products; (5) government agency regulatory efforts as regards the suspect product category, and (6) the documentary history of the defendant's development, testing, production, marketing and post-marketing of the suspect product or similar product lines.

§ 11.02 THE SCOPE OF PRODUCTS LIABILITY LITIGATION

As noted, the products liability theories discussed in Part I of this book each have their own, typically extensive, scientific, regulatory and company documentary references in the life of the defendant company. While

---

[2] *See* Terrence F. Kiely, *The Art of the Neglected Obvious In Products Liability Cases: Some Thoughts On Llewellyn's The Common Law Tradition*, 25 DEPAUL L. REV. 914, 921 (1975). *See generally* TERRENCE F. KIELY, SCIENCE AND LITIGATION: PRODUCTS LIABILITY IN THEORY AND PRACTICE (CRC Press 2002).

the basic overriding corporate organizational processes, inter-industry, are generally the same, each corporation, with regard to each product nonetheless have its own body of state of the art materials and internal corporate standard operating procedures and product-focused documentation that will serve as the basis for hard fought discovery and trial.

Regardless of the particular products liability theory chosen to channel the litigation, there are a series of initial questions that must be addressed in this type of case. Although a particular theory, such as a failure to warn or instruct defect setting, has its own very focused research goals for both sides to the dispute, there is a wide area of knowledge to be determined across theoretical lines. At the outset of every product liability litigation, the lawyer-researcher, whether plaintiff or defendant, is required to address a wide range of questions that must be satisfactorily answered through the course of pre-filing research and investigation. Defense counsel has the initial advantage of ready access to most of the materials only available to plaintiff counsel after hard fought discovery. Nonetheless the learning curve is the same for individual trial counsel and consumes considerable time and effort.

Answering these questions will require many hours of study of sources normally unfamiliar to those other than experienced specialists in the products field. Even then, new products and industries will invariably raise a host of new questions. Whether a plaintiff or defense lawyer, counsel will require answers to the majority of the following questions:

Initial Questions in Products Liability Litigation

[1] Is there an identifiable defect that was remediable prior to or subsequent to the original manufacture?

[2] Is the problem essentially one of manufacture, packaging, instructions, warnings or design?

[3] Is it a combination of several of them?

[4] How is the product manufactured [engineered product, pharmaceutical, chemical]?

[5] What is its physical makeup or chemical ingredients?

[6] How do its design and materials composition compare to competing products in the same market?

[7] What companies are involved in supplying materials or component parts?

[8] What other companies are involved in the vertical chain of distribution of this product?

[9] Is a foreign corporation involved? [Manufacturer, distributor, retailer?]

[10] Has there been a sale of the manufacturer creating a successor liability problem?

[11] How do the product's instructions and warnings compare to competing products given the apparent risks involved?

[12] What is the price differential among similar products with enhanced safety features?

[13] What share of the market does this product have?

[14] What does the authoritative literature say about this arguable defect or range of defects?

[15] Is the alleged defect well documented in authoritative sources?

[16] Has the defendant company ignored clearly expressed and authoritative concerns about this alleged defect?

[17] Do all competing products have the same basic problem to a greater, same or lesser degree?

[18] What are the leading authoritative journals in this area?

[19] Who are the recognized individual authorities?

[20] What are the in–house statistics regarding the potential for product failure and resultant projections regarding death or injury?

[21] What are the publicly available statistics regarding the potential for product failure and resultant projections regarding death or injury?

[22] Were there or are there government regulations in effect or proposed that have a direct bearing on, or can be used by analogy concerning the product under scrutiny?

[23] Have there been government imposed recalls or defect investigations in the past?

[24] Is there company documentation available in agency files that are accessible prior to discovery through a Freedom of Information Act request?

[25] Has there been a concerted effort by the industry and/or this defendant to alter or impede safety regulations?

[26] How do existing or proposed performance standards compare to thinking in the scientific community regarding the relevant performance feature?

[27] Is there a good argument for government agency preemption as a basis for dismissal of the litigation?

[28] How is the defendant manufacture organized over the period of the target product's life in the company?

[29] How long have they been involved in this business and this product line or similar products?

[30] Have they or do they manufacture, distribute or sell this product in foreign countries or nation communities such as the European Community?

[31] Are the products liability laws different in each of those countries or groupings?

[32] How does a products liability case proceed in such jurisdictions? Is there any provision for pre-trial discovery similar to those available in the United States?

[33] Are there international treaties that govern any aspect of this litigation that may effect the efforts of plaintiff and defense counsel?

[34] Has this defendant and product been involved in previous litigation?

These and a host of other questions face the products litigator at the beginning of each products case undertaking. It is the goal of this section of the book to address the practice aspects of each of the inquiries set out above. Once the litigation is joined and discovery begins, a host of additional questions will arise and also be addressed in the subsequent chapters.

§ 11.03 THE MAJOR RESEARCH TASKS IN PRODUCTS LIABILITY LITIGATION

The choices made from the theories of liability analyzed in Part I will substantially influence the extent that specific research and preparation factors come into play. Set out below is a detailed checklist of the major work product subjects and routine activities involved in representing a client in a products liability case.

Prefiling Product-Related Research Responsibilities

[1] Lengthy time frames for conducting prefiling research and discovery (typically 10-25 years or in some recent instances such as asbestos, as many as 50 years).

[2] Extensive scientific and technical investigation of the authoritative sources regarding the type of product line and specific aspect of the product involved in the case.

[3] Extensive investigation of the industry wherein the defendant does business and its organizational history in relation to the subject product or product line.

[4] Comparative product analyses, to include domestic and foreign manufacture, distribution or sales.

[5] Extensive investigation of past, present and future regulatory activity affecting the subject product or product lines in the relevant industry.

[6] Mastering the defendant company's document producing processes (SOP's) respecting the design, testing, production, marketing and post-marketing activities, including record retention policies for paper and digital records.

[7] The intricacies of company document retention and destruction policies and their system for electronic storage of records.

[8] Discovery planning and the issuance of interrogatories, document requests and depositions.

[9] The ongoing issue of motions for discovery enforcement.

[10] The issuance of protective orders.

[11] The international/domestic business organizations issues increasingly involved in litigation with multi-national corporations.

[12] International treaties relative to service of process, damage caps, and foreign discovery [or the lack of it by national law].

[13] Language/translation issues.

§ 11.04 RESEARCH TIME FRAMES

It is important to note at the outset that the period of historical research that is relevant to any particular case will vary according to the reason it is being conducted. There are typically three such research periods in a products liability case:

[A] **Broad-based pre-filing investigative research** [How long has this product or chemical been used commercially? Has the relevant scientific community addressed any health related concerns? Has there been any effort by governmental units to regulate any aspect of the commerce for this ingredient or product? Have there been prior lawsuits regarding this product?]

[B] **Discovery research** [In what period in the documentary history of the defendant company may a plaintiff justifiably seek information by way of interrogatories, document requests or depositions?]

[C] **Trial** evidence [What are the selected periods of defendant's design, testing, production, marketing and post-marketing product history that will need to be addressed in plaintiff's effort to prove the case?]

The central initial decision in the entire investigative and research aspects of the case is to approximate the chronological period or periods

within which to seek out scientific, industry, regulatory and company information. This decision will eventually result in the historical period or time
frame within which the plaintiff will ask the court for discovery and eventually the jury to assess the appropriateness of defendant corporation's
conscious business decisions.

For solely *investigative purposes* counsel may choose any period considered of background importance for purposes of scientific, industry, regulatory and company research. However, the selection of a relevant and
manageable time frame *for discovery* purposes requires considerable
thought and will be the subject of heated pre-trial motions to expand or limit
the period. The discovery time frame will, in turn, have great bearing on the
historical period within which evidence will be accepted at trial. It must be
emphasized here, that the typical time frame for products liability cases is
15-20 years, with periods as long as 50 years in certain settings such as
asbestos litigation. Initial discovery skirmishes will eventually result in a
court-imposed time period perceivably too long for defendant and too short
for plaintiff.

The introduction of a drug or manufactured item into the marketplace is
the result of more than a few years of investigation, testing and careful
planning by the defendant company. Often a new product in a marketing
sense — i.e., a new line of sports-utility vehicles — utilizes existing technology for the materials of the new product. In automotive design for example, manufacturers typically recycle existing axles, door locks, engines or
other technological components. Retooling is expensive, time-consuming
and usually unnecessary. Most engineered products are rarely made of
whole cloth. It is characteristic that the broad outlines of new or improved
products are manufactured by pre-existing technology both in the company
and the industry worldwide. However, it is the case that new pharmaceuticals and products from the chemical industry often are made of new
designs and ingredients.

The task for the products litigator is to determine the relevant historical
antecedents of the case product in state-of-the-art literature, industry publications, government agency filings and the defendant company's internal
files. As will be discussed in Chapters 16 through 19, the susceptibility of
similar product data is always a very large bone of contention.[3] For example, knowledge of the limits of certain ball-joint technology that is used
across defendant's pickup truck lines would seem to be fair game in a case
based upon a catastrophic failure during the range of intended uses of the
vehicle. Defense counsel are sensitive to this problem and are constantly
cautioned to take preemptive, if questionable, steps to minimize or eliminate
it. As recently noted in a products defense attorney publication:

---

[3] *See* Bradley C. Nahrstadt, "Narrowing The Scope Of Discovery For Substantially Similar
Products," *Practical Litigator*, November 2004, at 38.

Products Liability actions are not easy cases to prepare, nor are they easy cases to try. More often than not, such cases involve complex industrial or consumer products, monumental amounts of documents, intricate theories of liability and defense, and horrific injuries. Defense counsel must make sense of a variety of complex issues and present a coherent, cohesive, and streamlined theory of defense to the jury. Obviously, the defense attorney who is successful in preventing the introduction of "extraneous" issues to the jury will be far ahead of the game in terms of limiting the scope of the case and concentrating the jury's focus on the salient legal issues. One of the most successful ways of limiting the introduction of "extraneous" issues is to prevent the plaintiff's attorney from finding out about them during the course of discovery. The purpose of this article is to discuss various strategies that may be employed by defense counsel to narrow the scope of discovery requests seeking information regarding other products manufactured by a products liability defendant and to discuss relevant case law in which the court has been asked to decide whether a defendant should be compelled to provide information regarding other products.[4]

The clear-cut demarcation identification of relevant discovery time frames routinely cannot be had until the conclusion of discovery depositions, often resulting in supplemental requests for documentation.[5]

It is plaintiff's responsibility to throw down the timing gauntlet by initiating an historical period in the life of the defendant company by indicating over what period of years her discovery requests are to extend. An example would be an interrogatory requesting the test numbers of all pickup truck ball-joint stress tests for the years 1990-2005. This 15-year period would initiate defense relevancy arguments objecting to the length of time over which the information is being requested. Interrogatories are the usual place for the time frame arguments to begin and such arguments resurface at all ensuing phases of discovery. Chapter 19, Protective Orders and Discovery Enforcement, will discuss this process in depth.

Consequently, a key purpose and goal of prefiling investigation and research is to mark out the years in the past history of state-of-the-art, regulatory and company life that will arguably have discovery relevance, shedding light on the good judgment, or absence of it, of the conscious design choices engaged in by the defendant in getting the product into the hands of the targeted consumers. It is important to note here, that the concept of *relevancy* in discovery is considerably broader than that utilized in determinations of the admissibility of trial evidence. This is a point that

---

4 *Id.*

5 The Catch-22 in the process is that counsel is unable to effectively engage in prefiling research or discovery without some fairly firm idea of just what those time frames may be. *See* Kiely, *supra* note 2, at 245.

plaintiff counsel often fail to emphasize and one that defense lawyers at times pass over in discovery enforcement debates.

The definition of relevance is provided by Rule 401 of the Federal Rules of Evidence. That provision defines relevant evidence as follows: "Relevant evidence' means evidence having any tendency to make the existence of a fact that is of consequence to the determination of the action more probable or less probable than it would be without the evidence." By referencing this broad standard and providing for the free discovery of data that may be reasonably calculated to lead to the discovery of such, the federal courts have mandated a liberal discovery scheme.

As noted by Justice Powell of the United States Supreme Court, writing for a unanimous court in *Oppenheimer Fund, Inc. v. Sanders*, 437 U.S. 340, 351(1978):

> The key phrase in this definition — 'relevant to the subject matter involved in the pending action' — has been construed broadly to encompass any matter that bears on, or that reasonably could lead to other matter that could bear on, any issue that is or may be in the case. (citations omitted). . . . Consistently with the notice-pleading system established by the Rules, discovery is not limited to issues raised by the pleadings, for discovery itself is designed to help define and clarify the issues.(citation omitted). Nor is discovery limited to the merits of a case, for a variety of fact-oriented issues may arise during litigation that are not related to the merits.

A request for discovery should be considered relevant if there is any possibility that information sought may be relevant to the subject matter of the action. Discovery is not limited to formally admissible evidence because its primary purpose is to formulate, define and narrow issues to be tried, increase the chances for settlement, and give each party the opportunity to inform himself of the facts that may come out at trial.[6] As stated in the 1984 case of *Chubb Integrated-Systems Ltd. v. National Bank of Washington, et al.*[7]:

> . . . Whether this information is found to be admissible at trial has little bearing on the issue of discoverability. Rule 26(b) makes a clear distinction between information that is relevant to the subject matter for pretrial discovery and the ultimate admissibility of that information at trial.[8]

---

[6] Detweiler Bros., Inc. v. John Graham & Co., 412 F. Supp. 416 (E.D. Wash. 1976); Duplan Corp. v. Deering Milliken, Inc., 397 F. Supp. 1146 (D.S.C.1974); Carlson Companies, Inc. v. Sperry & Hutchinson Co., 374 F. Supp. 1080 (D. Minn. 1974); Sylgab Steel & Wire Corp. v. Imoco-Gateway Corp., 357 F. Supp. 659 (N.D. Ill. 1973).

[7] 103 F.R.D. 52 (D.D.C. 1984.)

[8] *Id.* at 59.

Admissibility at trial is not the yardstick of permissible discovery.[9] The relevancy of the information sought also bears directly on the issue of whether discovery requests are burdensome. If the requested material is relevant, no matter the volume, it must be produced. The initial focal point to determine the actual scope of this broadly-interpreted concept is the plaintiff's complaint. As noted in the leading case of *Rosenberg v. Johns-Manville Corp.*: "The detail in the complaint specifies the necessary relevance of the interrogatories. . . . The burden now falls upon GAF, the party resisting discovery, to clarify and explain its objections and to provide support therefor." [10] The allegations of the complaint serve to determine the broad subject matters involved in the case, and relevance is to be measured, not according to the specific issues raised by the pleadings, but rather, by reference to such subject matters.[11]

The distinction between the scope of relevancy for discovery and trial admissibility purposes is a substantial one. The fixing of time frames in discovery requests, in turn, has a significant bearing on the admissibility of evidence at trial. Fed. R. Civ. P. 26(b)(1) provides that materials subject to review in the discovery process are much broader, since the materials accessible in discovery are all materials that are relevant in an evidentiary sense plus those likely to lead to the discovery of relevant evidence. The latter concept allows for far reaching examination of materials in defendant's possession or control.[12] Nonetheless, this expansive view of discovery relevancy is tempered by the provision that discovery may be limited by the court if it determines that: (i) the discovery sought is unreasonably cumulative or duplicative, or is obtainable from some other source that is more convenient, less burdensome, or less expensive; (ii) the party seeking discovery has had ample opportunity by discovery in the action to obtain the information sought; or (iii) the burden or expense of the proposed discovery outweighs its likely benefit. . . ."[13]

Courts have recognized that while it is true that relevance in discovery is broader than that required for admissibility at trial, "the object of inquiry must have some evidentiary value before an order to compel disclosure of

---

[9] *See* Rosenberg v. Johns-Manville Corp., 85 F.R.D. 292 (E.D. Pa. 1980); Chubb Integrated Sys. v. National Bank of Washington, 103 F.R.D. 52 (1984). *See also* FED. R. CIV. P. 26 (b)(1) advisory committee's note, 1970 Amendment.

[10] 85 F.R.D. at 297.

[11] Smith v. F.T.C., 403 F. Supp. 1000 (D. Del.1975).

[12] *Id.* The discovery rules are accorded a broad and liberal treatment to affect their purpose of adequately informing litigants in civil trials. Herbert v. Lando, 441 U.S. 153 (1979). Nevertheless, discovery does have "ultimate and necessary boundaries," Oppenheimer Fund, Inc. v. Sanders, 437 U.S. 340, 351 (1978) (*quoting* Hickman v. Taylor, 329 U.S. 495, 507 (1947)), and "it is well established that the scope of discovery is within the sound discretion of the trial court." Coleman v. Am. Red Cross, 23 F.3d 1091, 1096 (6th Cir. 1994).

[13] FED. R. CIV .P. 26(b)(2).

otherwise inadmissible material will issue."[14] Further, the information must be "reasonably calculated to lead to the discovery of admissible evidence."[15] Courts have also recognized that "the legal tenet that relevancy in the discovery context is broader than in the context of admissibility should not be misapplied so as to allow fishing expeditions in discovery."[16] Therefore, discovery methods will be limited by the Court if it determines that the discovery sought is unreasonably cumulative or duplicative.[17]

§ 11.05 CRITERIA FOR SELECTION OF TIME FRAMES

The choice of investigative and eventually, discovery and evidentiary time frames, involves a complex mix of factors, especially plaintiff's choice of the available theoretical defect categories. Actual defect allegations involving communications between the public and the company, such as instructions and warnings run the gamut from the decision to publish those communications up to the date of the alleged injury. Time frames for those defect types can run for many years, depending upon how long the product has been on the market. Many popular pharmaceuticals such as Percodan or familiar household products such as Drano may serve as examples. Overall design defect cases involve time frames extending from the date the particular design was officially adopted up to the date of the alleged injury.

Accordingly, scientific, industry, governmental and internal corporate data is fair game for discovery and the subject of intense discovery motion practice. The typically voluminous state of the art materials are readily available to the litigators who are aware of how to locate them and how to absorb what they have to offer. The self-education of both plaintiff and defense counsel is an ever present fact of life in these cases no matter how much funding is available for expert witness assistance.

The preliminary study engaged in by products litigators will familiarize the lawyers with the location and extent of relevant primary source materials and introduce them to the terminology and general outlines of the relevant technology and industry involved. Because of their centrality to the entire products liability undertaking, the subject of investigative and trial admissibility time frames will be noted throughout the remainder of this

---

[14] Zenith Elec. Corp. v. Exzec, Inc., 1998 U.S. Dist. LEXIS 215, at *8 (N.D. Ill. 1998) (*quoting* Piacenti v. Gen. Motors Corp., 173 F.R.D. 221, 223 (N.D.Ill.1997)).

[15] *Id.*

[16] *Id.*

[17] FED. R. CIV. P. 26(b)(2)(i). *See* Volvo Trucks North America, Inc. v. Crescent Ford Truck Sales, 2006 U.S. Dist. LEXIS 5811 (E.D. La. 2005). Relevancy for discovery purposes is extremely broad. The information sought need not be admissible in court in order to be relevant. Rather, the relevancy burden is met if the party can show that the information sought "appears reasonably calculated to lead to the discovery of admissible evidence."

book. Set out below is a capsule summary of the remaining chapters of Part II of this book.

Chapter 12. Researching the Products Case, will address the identification of the theoretical defect mode [Manufacturing defect? Failure to instruct? Failure to Warn? Overall design defect? Misrepresentation?]; identification of the precise scientific defect [defectively designed ball joints in trucks resulting in loss of a wheel]; and the quantitative [significant adverse reaction or product failure reports]and qualitative extent of the scientific defect's harm [the injury pattern, while infrequent, is of a devastating nature] over the various research and investigative periods.

Chapter 13. The Expert Witness, discusses the early task of determining expert witness needs by category case-wide. This potentially involves experts in the relevant areas of science, government regulation, the profile of the entire industry, the history of the named defendant(s)' research and development, testing programs, production, marketing and/or advertising, and damages. The chapter will also discuss considerations in choosing expert witnesses, and using expert witnesses for pretrial, discovery and trial purposes.

Chapter 14. Products Liability and Discovery, addresses the key topics of discovery relevancy v. trial relevancy, duties of full and ongoing disclosure, the general discovery rules as related to products liability settings, relevancy in relation to case investigative time frames, relevancy as applied to the discovery of a company's historical materials as they relate to its industry relations, research and development testing, their interaction with regulatory agencies, their particular manufacturing processes. The chapter also addresses the general topic of destructive testing; categorizing case information needs over the desired historical period in the history of the company, the drafting of discovery documents, and the crucial new expansion and increasing complexity of electronic discovery.

Chapter 15. Drafting the Complaint and Discovery Focus, analyzes important aspects of the complaint drafting process, such as the judicial education function, the controlling relation between the product defect allegations and discovery and the subject of proximate cause.

Chapter 16. Interrogatories and Request to Admit Facts, will focus on the purpose of interrogatories in products liability cases, the introduction by plaintiff of preliminary discovery time frames, the categorization of interrogatories and their relationship to document requests, statutory limitation on the initial number of interrogatories, supplemental interrogatories, the organization and specificity of interrogatories, and an introduction to discovery objections and enforcement.

Chapter 17. Requests to Produce Documents, will discuss the purpose of document requests in product liability cases, the refinement of the discovery request period, the categorization of document requests, supplemental requests for documentation, the organization and specificity of doc-

ument requests, objections to document requests and some thoughts on objections to requests and motions to enforce discovery.

Chapter 18. Discovery and Evidence Depositions, analyzes the scope of discovery and evidence depositions, the choice of deponents, the basis for objections in discovery or evidence depositions, and the trial use of discovery and evidence depositions.

Chapter 19. Protective Orders and Discovery Enforcement, provides discussions of trade secrets and other bases for the imposition of a protective order, trial relevancy v. discovery relevancy and the enforcement of discovery rights.

Chapter 12

RESEARCHING THE PRODUCTS CASE

SYNOPSIS

§ 12.01 INTRODUCTION

There are four broad evidentiary clusters that serve as plaintiff counsel's focal points for the preparation of a product liability case:

1. Information potentially demonstrating corporate knowledge of product defects and feasible alternative designs.

2. Socially unacceptable management decisions in light of such knowledge.

3. Proof that one or more of the identified defects in fact caused the death or injury to the client.

4. Proof that one or more of the feasible alternative designs, warnings or instructions would have minimized or eliminated such death or injury.

Defense counsel must examine the same body of information to build a case for responsible, defect-free design, testing, manufacturing and marketing by its corporate client.

This undertaking involves the gathering and analysis of large amounts of data from without and within the defendant corporation. Much of this information is often difficult technical data. A substantial amount of the internal company documents received via discovery will reflect the internal processes of the corporation in all stages of manufacture from design to the inventory shelf. Plaintiff lawyers must compete with substantially superior investigative, expert witness and law firm staff typically available to the corporate defendant. Nonetheless, defense counsel faces the same daunting learning curve experienced by plaintiff. Both sides must face the considerable task of making sense of all of these documents to a series of motion judges, and most importantly, a trial judge and jury.

A very considerable amount of the *pre-filing* state-of-the-art literature required by counsel is available through public, often cost-free sources. The contemporary explosion of information sites on the Internet makes that research task less onerous every day. In addition to the broad availability of technical literature in engineering, pharmaceuticals and chemistry, substantial data sources on regulatory activity is available even without a Freedom of Information Act Request. Large amounts of preliminary industry corporate information are also accessible from a number of web-based sources.

The greatest amount of information reviewed by counsel will yield its primary value in respect to its *investigative importance*. What does this information tell me about this technology, industry or corporation that I did not know before? In what directions does it point for additional research? Hard choices must be made at the conclusion of research and discovery to convert the massive accumulation of data into a controllable as well as communicable case for jury consumption. The bulk of the information that counsel will marshal most likely will not be admissible at trial under the rules of evidence, but has great value in forwarding written discovery and evidence depositions. Accordingly, counsel must be able to determine the unique value that each item of information will have to both the investigation and formal legal requirements of the planned lawsuit. This dual perspective will be referenced throughout the remainder of this work.

§ 12.02 THE RANGE OF WORK AREAS IN PRODUCTS LIABILITY LITIGATION

A simple graphic can illustrate the basic nature of pre-filing and pre-trial products liability research:

PRETRIAL PRODUCT-RELATED RESEARCH

Products Liability Research Related Information Sources

EXTERNAL DATA [Pre-Filing Research]	INTERNAL COMPANY DATA [Discovery]
1. State-of-the-Art Literature	1. Design Documents
2. Industry Custom	2. Testing Documents
3. Regulatory Activity	3. Production Documents
4. Injury History	4. Marketing Documents
5. Litigati0n History	5. Post-Marketing Documents

BASIC RESEARCH ISSUES

1. What mechanical or chemical or pharmacological aspect of defendant's product actually caused the plaintiff's death or injury?

2. How did it do that?

3. Was the defendant aware of that injury-producing potential? When?

4. Could the defendant have done something to have eliminated or minimized that risk and still have aggressively competed in its chosen markets?

5. If it could have, why didn't it?

Set out below is a detailed checklist of the major work product subjects and routine activities involved in representing a client in a products liability case.

Prefiling Product-Related Research Responsibilities

[1] Lengthy time frames for conducting prefiling research and discovery (typically 10-25 years or in some recent instances such as asbestos, as many as 50 years).

[2] Extensive scientific and technical investigation of the authoritative sources regarding the type of product line and specific aspect of the product involved in the case.

[3] Extensive investigation of the industry wherein the defendant does business and its organizational history in relation to the subject product or product line.

[4] Comparative product analyses, to include domestic and foreign manufacture, distribution or sales.

[5] Extensive investigation of past, present and future regulatory activity affecting the subject product or product lines in the relevant industry.

[6] Mastering the defendant company's document producing processes (SOP's) as respects the design, testing, production, marketing and post-marketing activities, including record retention policies for paper and digital records.

[7] The intricacies of company retention and destruction policies and their system for electronic storage of records, especially e-mails.

[8] Discovery planning and the issuance of interrogatories, document requests and depositions.

[9] The ongoing issue of motions for discovery enforcement.

[10] The issuance of protective orders.

[11] The international/domestic business organizations issues increasingly involved in litigation with multi-national corporations.

[12] International treaties relative to service of process, damage caps, and foreign discovery [or the lack of it by national law].

[13] Language/translation issues.

§ 12.03 DUAL ASPECTS OF RESEARCH DATA

It is important in every aspect of product research that counsel maintain a dual perspective toward each item of information gathered and analyzed. Those two considerations are the *investigative* and *legal* significance of each item of information gathered. The bulk of materials examined will have only investigative significance — i.e., what does this tell me about the development and injury-producing potential of the product? Where does it lead me in furthering the pre and post filing research effort? How does it help to interpret documents sought or received in the discovery stage of the case? How do case experts value this information?

In terms of *legal significance*, does this item of information aid, in whole or in part, to establish one or more of the essential elements of the complaint. Does it establish knowledge of risk or the lack of it? Does it go toward establishing a feasible alternative design? Does it show that any such alternative is a subsequent remedial measure and thus required to be excluded from evidence? Does it help establish proximate cause?

All research serves an investigative function, however slight. Some small portion of it will constitute proof necessary to get to a jury. A considerable task at the end of the research period is making the hard choice of documents to use at trial from the mountain of materials gathered through pre-trial research and discovery.[1]

§ 12.04 RESEARCH POINTS OF REFERENCE

The suspect product is normally one of a generic type of manufactured good produced in an industry which draws on an existing body of technology and business practices. In the broad scientific divisions of product creation-engineering, pharmaceuticals and chemicals, products have been and will continue to be produced on a vast scale. The associated scientific, industry and manufacturing literature is substantial and varied, ranging from highly sophisticated journals to books, newsletters and symposia papers. Many specific product industries or particular product lines or precise technological issues such as pain killers, infant car seats, pesticides, auto rollover protection and the like are often subject to some form of government regulation. Each of these regulatory efforts will yield important documents of keen interest to plaintiff and defense counsel. In addition, with respect to the design feature under scrutiny, there may be an injury producing history, which in turn may provide important data for study and later introduction in evidence.

Each of these areas for inquiry involves extensive amounts of literature, documentary submissions and corporate documents that must be located and reviewed. As noted above, the greatest part of the relevant data sought may be found in sources outside of the defendant corporation. The multi-year generation of internal corporate documentation addressing the design, testing, production and marketing of the product may only be reviewed following difficult and long-term discovery efforts.

§ 12.05 IDENTIFICATION OF THE THEORETICAL DEFECT TYPE

The initial task for both plaintiff or defense counsel is to settle on just what it is that was actually wrong with the suspect product in common sense terms. Was there some flaw in the product unit that caused the injury not present in other units sold by the defendant? Was the client injured by the product packaging and not the product itself? Is it a question of misleading instructions or inadequate or non-existent warnings? Is there something wrong with the basic design of the product in a particular respect? Prior to purchase, was the client misled by some material misrepresentation

---

[1] This important issue is addressed in discussed in Chapter 17, Requests to Produce Documents and Chapter 19, Protective Orders, Discovery Enforcement, and Motions-In-Limine.

about the product that he relied upon to his detriment? Are more than one of these problems involved?[2]

Regardless of the broad classification of actual case product defects alleged in a count of a products complaint, there are only seven *theoretical categories* within which any particular litigation can be described:

- **Unit defect** [One unit that was defective or flawed]

- **Packaging Defects** [The access to the product is allegedly dangerous, not the product itself]

- **Instructions Defects** [The instructions for use are inadequate or confusing resulting in potential injury to the user]

- **Warnings Defects** [The manufactured good, pharmaceutical or chemical has no warnings specific to the alleged risk of injury or contains misleading or insufficient warning]

- **Overall Design Defects** [Some feature, aspect, or component to all the products in the line of which the suspect product is a member, has a design flaw that effects all units of like manufacture]

- **Misrepresentation** [The consumer justifiably relied upon a false or misleading statement of fact about product's features made in advertising or other marketing literature]

- **Breach of Warranty** [Failure to meet actual or implied warranties as to performance and safety][3]

These theoretical, non-fact-specific defect types, determine the reach of prefiling research, and in large part determine the limits of discovery and the acceptability of trial evidence. Each of these generic defect types has unique research requirements and the typical products litigation will often involve one or more of them alleged concurrently. The discussion to follow will focus on several basic pre-filing research points that will help to center and guide the entire research undertaking.

§ 12.06 IDENTIFYING THE PRODUCT'S INJURY-PRODUCING ASPECT

In products cases grounded in each type of defect category, it is obvious that any real injury was *caused* by some physical aspect of the product itself, although the legal responsibility may arise from the company's *facilitation of that event,* by its allegedly poor manufacturing methods, mis-

---

[2] Typically a product liability complaint involves at least one of the defects in addition to a failure to warn. Product shortcomings are generally classified in legal parlance as being either manufacturing or design defects. *See* Chapter 15, Drafting the Complaint and Discovery Focus.

[3] *See* OWEN & PHILLIPS, PRODUCTS LIABILITY (2005).

leading instructions for use, faulty warnings, risky design choices, or fraudulent misrepresentation.[4] It is clear that the failure to warn about the potential dangers of the drug Vioxx cannot cause any physical injury to anyone, nor can a faulty design of an automobile part or a pharmaceutical or chemical composition cause cancer. The products liability policy discussed throughout Chapters 1 through 10 supplies the basic rationale for allowing this type of litigation. The law asks if the defendant company *facilitated* any such injury by encouraging the consumer's use in the face of any of the defect types discussed. The actual, physical or biological cause of the injury is not within the company's control, and is never the central issue in modern products liability litigation.[5] What *is always at issue* is the extent and manner of the defendant's *facilitation of* death or injury resulting from its associating the consumer with the product with established risks of injury flowing from defective designs or communications, via instructions and/or warnings.

Whenever someone is injured or killed through their interaction with a manufactured item, pharmaceutical or chemical, there arises the preliminary inference that some aspect of the product was flawed, individually or, more often, generically to all units of the product. Examples would be failed ball joints on several models of pickup trucks resulting in the loss of a wheel during travel; confusing instructions for use of paint removers resulting in asphyxiation; inadequate warnings as to heart problems resulting from the ingestion of painkillers for arthritis. Once counsel has estimated the precise technical cause of the injury-producing event, the general category or categories of defects within which the case falls, must be decided upon. Depending upon the particular theoretical defect type involved in the case, the actual biological, engineering or chemical aspects of the product will have varying degrees of importance to the litigation.[6]

---

[4] See discussion in Chapter 8, Causation.

[5] The *Parlodel* litigation may serve as an example, where defendant manufacturer argues that the chemical brocriptomine, a central component of its anti-lactation drug Parlodel was biologically incapable of causing brain aneurysms in young mothers. The central factual issue in the seminal *Daubert* case was whether the ingredients of the drug Bendectin could cause fetal malformations in the group of expectant mothers who ingested the drug. *See, e.g.*, 19 No. 7 Andrews Pharmaceutical Litig. Rep. 8.

Questioning the credibility of causal evidence offered by a woman who says her use of the lactation suppressant Parlodel led her to suffer a stroke, a federal judge in Greensboro, N.C. declared the data inadmissible and granted defendant Sandoz Pharmaceuticals Corp.'s motion for summary judgment. Dunn v. Sandoz Pharmaceuticals Corp., 275 F. Supp. 2d 672 (M.D.N.C. 2003).

[6] *See* JAMES A. HENDERSON, JR. & AARON D. TWERSKI, PRODUCTS LIABILITY: PROBLEMS AND PROCESS (5th ed. 2004); DAVID G. OWEN, PRODUCTS LIABILITY LAW HORNBOOK (2005).

§ 12.07 THE EXTENT OF THE ALLEGED INJURIES TO CONSUMERS

Once the underlying biological, structural or chemical contributors of the injury have been tentatively identified, it must be estimated how extensive the problem has been for consumers of the suspect or comparable products. Outside of the individual unit case, the real world extent of the problem can have a dramatic bearing on the success or failure of the lawsuit. When the legal focus is on a design, instructions or warnings aspect for an entire line of goods, a relatively insignificant injury history makes it difficult to prove that the product was in a "defective condition unreasonably dangerous." While the broader based design defect category of cases do balance numerous factors in the effort to judge the social acceptability of defendant's conscious design choices, the cold figures delineating the product's injury history are often the decisive point in the analysis. This is particulary so in drug cases.[7]

§ 12.08 THE SERIOUSNESS OF THE ALLEGED INJURIES TO CONSUMERS

An equally important area of research is the determination of just how serious any injuries are flowing from the alleged defects. The honored liability theorem of Judge Learned Hand balancing the forseeabilityof harm against the seriousness of the harm if it does occur, and the efforts required to minimize or eliminate it comes into play here.[8]

An injury profile of a severe magnitude can counterbalance a statistically low injury occurrence record. In instances where an actor can foresee statistically insignificant, but catastrophic injuries potentially materializing from his acts or omissions, the law has always required that the party best able to minimize or eliminate the risk take precautions not normally required of the reasonably prudent person.[9] The policy base of product liability law adds support to this famous modern legal maxim.

§ 12.09 STATE-OF-THE-ART COMMENTARY ON THE ALLEGED DEFECTS AND INJURIES

A primary pre-filing research task once the specific scientific defect has been tentatively identified and the range of the alleged injuries in terms of

---

[7] *See* TERRENCE F. KIELY, SCIENCE AND LITIGATION: PRODUCTS LIABILITY IN THEORY AND PRACTICE 237 (CRC Press 2002).

[8] "Possibly it serves to bring this notion into relief to state it in algebraic terms: if the probability be called P; the injury, L; and the burden, B; liability depends upon whether B is less than L multiplied by P: i.e., whether $B < PL$." United States v. Carroll Towing Co., 159 F.2d 169, 173 (2d Cir. 1947).

[9] *Id.*

magnitude and severity preliminarily estimated, is to establish the level at which the relevant scientific authorities have even acknowledged that a problem actually exists. Equally important is the determination of the extant literature that addresses efforts to minimize or eliminate the risks allegedly associated with the suspect product. This research constitutes the foundation of what is referred to as the "state of the art" investigations, which focuses on historical developments and materials *outside* the life of the defendant company. This broad literature ranges from highly specialized engineering, pharmaceutical, chemical and medical journals, to industry trade association journals, newsletters and popular publications available in chain bookstores, such as recreational vehicle magazines. This latter type of publication exists in and around all consumer product areas and often provides highly relevant information such as alternative design products providing greater safety. Stabilizing bars for recreational vehicles to prevent unit sway and chain saw guards are examples.

Product litigators, with or without the initial advice of experts, must determine the identity and availability of the key books, journals, other publications, databases and websites considered authoritative in the field. These can be specific to a select topic such as the large number of text and journals devoted to discrete areas such as diabetes, heart, lung, kidney and anasthesia, [10] or prestigious journals more general in nature such as Lancet,[11] The New England Journal of Medicine[12] or The Journal of the American Medical Association (JAMA).[13]

It is important to realize that the authoritative sources that need to be consulted to resolve the defect-injury issue are rarely product, and on occasion, not even industry specific. Available websites and databases are numerous and incredibly comprehensive.

§ 12.10 GOVERNMENT REGULATION OF THE DEFENDANT'S INDUSTRY

The majority of the nation's major industries are subject to some degree of government regulation through the activities of a number of federal agencies. There are a group that loom above most products cases in one degree or another, regulating the introduction of a product to the market, such as the Food and Drug Administration (FDA)[14] or mandate performance standards for existing technology, such as the National Highway Safety

---

[10] See the extensive listing of medical journals provided free at http://www.freemedicaljournals.com/.

[11] http://www.thelancet.com/.

[12] http://content.nejm.org/.

[13] http://jama.ama-assn.org/.

[14] http://www.fda.gov/.

Administration (NHTSA)[15] for automobiles, the Environmental Protection Agency (EPA)[16] for industrial emissions or the Consumer Product Safety Commission (CPSC)[17] for consumer goods, such as bicycles or shower door glass. It is unusual in the present time to come across a manufactured good that is not subject, in some respect, to a proposed or existing federal agency regulation.

The issuance of a proposed performance standard by an agency is one of the most important investigative finds in the early stage of products liability research. Crash tests required by NHTSA to determine the resistance to fires resulting from rear end collisions or seat belt integrity in a relatively small and light weight vehicle such as the GEO may serve as an example.[18] These proposed regulations typically require some level of performance from the targeted products in an industry — i.e., zero fuel leakage following a 30-mile per hour rear end collision of the targeted vehicle into a flat laboratory barrier or actual vehicle at 30 miles an hour. (NHTSA) Strength tests for architectural glass used in shower doors (CPSC) are another early example. The proposed performance level may be a certain co-effient of friction on backyard pool slides to prevent injuries to small children (CPSC) or a specified level of mercury emissions from industrial stacks. (EPA)

These proposed regulations are important in several respects to product litigators focused on the same performance range:

(A) The very issuance of the proposal assumes that the companies within the affected industry are not currently meeting the proposed performance level and the tentative belief of the agency that such level can and should be met.

(B) The typical 90-day or longer period within which the industry can respond to the need and/or specifics of any proposal typically prompts the issuance of a large body of internal company documents directed towards all aspects of the ability, inability or lack of agreement that any such performance levels are necessary or economically or technologically feasible. Do we currently achieve the proposed performance level? If not, why not? Can we achieve it if eventually required by agency action finalizing the proposed rule? What design changes are needed to achieve this level of performance? What about the economic feasibility? Does

---

[15] http://www.nhtsa.gov/.

[16] http://www.epa.gov/.

[17] http://www.cpsc.gov/.

[18] *See, e.g.*, Reports Accepted During October 2004 For FY 2003 Test . . . 33. 208. Occupant Crash Protection. Vehicle-19. TEST. 34. 209. NEO GEN CX3V9VM1203. . . . www.nhtsa.dot.gov/cars/testing/comply/monthly/2004/statrept.0412.doc - 2005-02-09.

the cost outweigh the benefits to the company? The documents issued in-house in these regulatory contacts are often some of the most telling in the discovery and trial stages of the case.

(C) These documents are discoverable inasmuch as they typically address the very defect issue involved in the litigation. This is not to say they are easily discoverable, since company defendants will quite properly oppose any such submission on relevancy, privilege and other grounds.[19]

(D) Defendants often take the position that if there was no existing agency performance standard then the court should rule as a matter of law that they complied with any and all government regulation and hence no defect can be found. Contemporary case law, however, is clear that agency performance standards are to be considered minimum standards only and do not eliminate a consumer's right to bring an action for injuries under negligence or strict liability arising out of design features which are the actual subject of a regulation.[20]

In cases where the industry members have complied with a mandated agency performance standard, such as windshield retention standards in auto collisions, or a set of mandated instructions or warnings in the pharmaceutical or chemical industry, it tends to shift the case analysis to the subject regulation as *the* "reasonable" standard. This argument has been found wanting many more times that not and is an understandable item in all contemporary state and federal products liability reform proposals.[21]

The difficulty here is that often the proposed performance standards are, indeed, merely minimal safety considerations that perhaps should have been designed to a higher level by the manufacturers themselves. The requirements that automobile windshields do not fly out or door locks not fail and allow doors to open in highway crash situations are two simple examples.[22]

---

[19] See Chapter 19, Protective Orders, Discovery Enforcement, and Motions-In-Limine, for a detailed discussion of the objection to discovery and the accompanying motions to enforce discovery.

[20] This is a position of long standing. *See, e.g.*, Usery v. Tamiami Trail Tours, Inc., 531 F.2d 224 (5th Cir. 1976). *See also, Evidence as to Compliance or Noncompliance with Federal Safety Laws or Standards*, 63B AM. JUR. 2d *Products Liability* § 2022 (2005).

[21] Corporations which have made a significant investment in time, manpower and money to comply with the standard, quite understandably argue that the standard is equivalent to *the* reasonable standard which should end the case, at least as respects the alleged defect that is addressed by the regulation.

[22] Federal Motor Vehicle Safety Standard 212 (FMVSS 212) provides requirements for retention of the windshield. FMVSS 219 provides requirements for intrusion into the windshield. *See* http://www.nhtsa.dot.gov/.

Industries are given the opportunity to comment on proposals and to provide issue opposing position papers and supporting documentation to the issuing agency. Unless classified as privileged by the agency, these historical materials are generally available to plaintiff counsel, even prior to filing suit, through a Freedom of Information Act request.[23]

§ 12.11 THE HISTORY OF THE INDUSTRY REACTION TO THE SCIENTIFIC PROBLEM

All products under scrutiny in these cases are typically designed, manufactured and marketed within an industry of like-minded manufacturing concerns. The aerospace industry, automobile industry, electronics industry, pharmaceutical industry and the chemical industry are the major players that provide the technical and managerial backdrop to the lion's share of all individual products litigation. There are common technologies and common concerns among these large groupings of companies in addition to keen competitive issues. Each industry has several industry-wide associations that keep track of the activities of state and federal regulators and legislatures that may effect their members. The cooperation in these industries is as keen as the competition.[24]

It is within this industry context that the idea of comparative product analysis has its research value. There is a considerable commonality of design in such industries as the automobile industry. It is of value to determine early the differences, if any, among the design under study in the case at hand and the same design feature in the competition. This will extend to the precise technology, such as the stability of automobile door locks and windows in highway crash settings to the instructions, warnings and other communicative aspects of the marketing of such products. This is especially the case for foreign manufacture and sale of the same product. International requirements for warnings and even basic design features can often veer sharply from United States domestic manufacture.

While conformity to industry custom is not legally equivalent to due care, the fact that all participants in an industry follow identical protocols for select design features, such as fuel system integrity[25] or seat belt or airbag

---

[23] *See* http://www.usdoj.gov/04foia/. Each federal agency is responsible for meeting its FOIA responsibilities for its own records. A list of principal FOIA contacts at federal agencies is available from this site. The Act has provisions allowing for confidentiality of certain classes of company data heretofore submitted to an agency during an investigation. *See* Janene Boyce, *Disclosure Of Clinical Trial Data: Why Exemption 4 Of The Freedom Of Information Act Should Be Restored*, 2005 DUKE L. & TECH. REV. 3 (2005).

[24] See The Directory of Associations, a comprehensive source of information on professional, business, and trade associations, 501(c) non-profit organizations, chambers of commerce, and other charity and community institutions, at http://www.marketingsource.com/associations/.

[25] Fuel System Integrity refers to design features aimed at keeping the fuel inside the gas tank, thus minimizing fuel-fed fires in automobile collisions.

technology, make it very difficult to maintain that an alternative design should have been adopted by an individual industry member. Often referred to as the "everybody was doing it" defense, it is nonetheless a very powerful argument. Initially, it requires the plaintiff to challenge the decisions of highly trained and respected scientists and business executives. It also casts the plaintiff's proposed alternative in an isolated spot with a considerable uphill battle to convince a jury to buck an entire industry as well as the state and federal governments that had failed to require any higher performance or design standards.

Fortunately for plaintiffs, other manufacturers, as well as the named corporation, often manufacture similar lines of goods in different models of the base product line such as automobiles, space heaters and power saws, that make use of different levels of technology resulting in higher safety performance. It is easy to see $150, $350 and $500 space heaters and the variance in their design and on-board safety features such as automatic shut off and denser grill openings. In such instances, plaintiff is provided with an in-house comparative product demonstration of a feasible alternative design.

The issue of a corporation's right to participate in various market levels with accompanying variances in safety, is a multifaceted one and is the subject of many policy debates. Nonetheless, a solid basis for establishing the feasibility of an alternate package, instruction, warning or design, is that either the defendant itself or others in the industry have actually incorporated it in a product line. This in turn, raises the appropriateness of the application of the evidence rule prohibiting the introduction of subsequent remedial measures.[26]

Comparative product analysis thus necessitates close familiarity with the industry of which the defendant is a part and detailed understanding of the technology of comparable or competing products. Not only does this research demonstrate the relevant industry's position as to the alleged scientific problem, but may reveal a concerted industry endeavor to hinder or eliminate an alleged safety-prone design methodology. Product industry research is an essential aspect of product liability research.

---

[26] FEDERAL RULE OF EVIDENCE 407. Subsequent Remedial Measures.

When, after an injury or harm allegedly caused by an event, measures are taken that, if taken previously, would have made the injury or harm less likely to occur, evidence of the subsequent measures is not admissible to prove negligence, culpable conduct, a defect in a product, a defect in a product's design, or a need for a warning or instruction. This rule does not require the exclusion of evidence of subsequent measures when offered for another purpose, such as proving ownership, control, or feasibility of precautionary measures, if controverted, or impeachment.

§ 12.12 STUDY OF DEFENDANT CORPORATION'S ORGANIZATION AND MANUFACTURING PROCESSES

In the typical scenario, where the defendant is a major corporation, plaintiff and defense counsel face the daunting task of following the operational string through the labyrinth of the company's document production and decision-making processes. While defense counsel has a distinct advantage in this often herculean effort, both counsel must nonetheless determine the key dates and the identity of the offices, departments, sections and major committees involved in the central design decisions that are the basis of the allegations in the complaint. In what years and from what office, department, committee or individual was relevant documentation of a wide variety of types issued and accompanying decisions made?

A business phenomenon that can befuddle litigators seeking to locate and identify relevant offices, departments, sections, committees and committee personnel, is that as the world of science and marketing changes so do the nomenclature and function of the organizational structures of the corporations that adopt and make use of such changes. This means that a department or office playing an active role in one period of the development and marketing of a product may disappear in an ensuing period. It is important to understand that corporate defendants are under no obligation to educate plaintiff counsel about the changes to the company over the years. It is plaintiff's obligation to study the relevant markets, theories of corporate organizations and track changes in the targeted defendant.

As an example, the shifting emphasis in the automobile industry to compact and sub-compact cars in the late 1960s, significantly changed the nomenclature of the corporate entities charged with the new ventures and manufacturing operational entities in the several competing companies. New departments such Light Vehicle Development Offices began to replace traditional functional units, putting the outsider litigant at a distinct disadvantage in efforts to locate document generating units for discovery purposes. In cases where the investigative time frame is considerable, this provides defense counsel with potent opportunities to impede discovery based on the plaintiff's counsel's incorrect use of corporate nomenclature when requesting historical documents.[27]

---

[27] *See* Terrence F. Kiely, *The Paper Chase: Organization and Analysis of Corporate Documents in a Product Case*, 22 TRIAL 105 (1986).

§ 12.13 THE DEVELOPMENT OF THE CORPORATE DEFENDANT'S REACTION TO THE ALLEGED SCIENTIFIC DEFECT

The central issue in products liability litigation is whether the defendant ignored clear risks of injury to consumers in conscious design choices in the face of economically and technically feasible alternatives in their instructions, warnings, overall design or through flat out misrepresentation. The plaintiff in a products case must initially realize that the famous "smoking gun" rarely surfaces. Alleged corporate failings will occur, if at all, in the course of the company's ordinary business processes. It may appear at the end of a case that a defendant ignored clear warning signs in their pre-production clinical trials, or metal fatigue or crash tests that, in balance, should have been acted upon for the benefit of future consumers. Standard operating procedures (SOPs) more often tell the tale in products cases, not an outrageously irresponsible document stressing money over safety.[28]

The complete internal organization of modern corporations is considered, quite properly, as a trade or business secret or privileged information. Corporations understand that the more information a competitor has about their organizational structure and nomenclature, the closer they are to knowing what is being developed and planned for their domestic or foreign markets. This concern is in addition to concerns over discovery requests in products liability litigation. The detailed, routine internal processes of a corporation in planning, designing, testing and marketing a product are multifaceted, sometimes following routine, trackable stages, and sometimes not. Line responsibilities for decision-making often veer from standard operating procedures by the assignment of functional responsibility to one or more units for specific project purposes. Nothing nefarious about that, but it makes for discovery nightmares for plaintiff or defense lawyers trying to lay out a clear paper trail.[29]

Getting from point A to point Z is the result of assembling a road map from disparate pieces of a company's total document generation over the period of the case discovery time frame and whatever public documents, such as annual reports that are usually accessible. There are typically thousands of documents that may be arguably relevant to the investigation by counsel. In major actions such as the recent cigarette or Vioxx litigation there can be up to a million documents placed in Multi-district litigation document depositories. The harsh reality of the trial aspect of products liability litigation is that only a handful of such documents will be used at trial,

---

[28] This is not to say that such documents do not periodically surface. This is especially the case with the modern phenomenon of e-mail. See Chapter 14, Products Liability and Discovery, for a discussion of recent developments in electronic discovery.

[29] *See* KIELY, SCIENCE AND LITIGATION, *supra* note 7, at Chapter 7, Science and Business Documentation.

following a rigorous document review and selection process.[30] The entire document discovery process is one of the most time-consuming and frustrating aspects of products liability case preparation.

§ 12.14 PRIOR LITIGATION, SETTLEMENTS, OR CASE FILINGS

An important initial research step is to determine the existence of appellate decisions, prior litigation verdicts, case settlements or current case filings. Lawyers for either side of the issue can provide tremendous assistance to the neophyte in narrowing research issues and identifying relevant information sources, key areas of the scientific literature, expert witnesses and the like. In addition to plaintiff and defense information sharing organizations, such as the plaintiff's American Trial Lawyers Association (ATLA)[31] and the Defense Research Institute (DRI)[32] directed to defense counsel, there are numerous services available on Lexis/Nexis and Westlaw and law libraries that track appeals, trials, verdicts, and settlements in products liability cases.[33] Both organizations, in addition to offering expert witness databases and referrals to other lawyers sharing the same or similar interests, provide listings of verdicts, settlements and products liability filings.

§ 12.15 MATERIALS SUPPLIERS AND COMPONENT PART MANUFACTURERS INFORMATION SOURCE CATEGORIES

Determining who are the suppliers of materials and component parts to the defendant company is an important research obligation. Intermediary parties, in addition to being potential defendants, can be a fertile source of important documentary evidence, especially in instances where the materials or component parts are made to precise specifications by the defendant. Common practice is to name all material suppliers and component parts manufacturers. The considerable cost and annoyance to these entities is an unfortunate by product of the inability of plaintiffs to get needed informa-

---

[30] See Chapter 17, Requests to Produce Documents, for a more detailed discussion of document rating and selection criteria.

[31] See http://www.atla.org/.

[32] See http://www.dri.org/.

[33] For example, Lexis provides the following services:

Jury Verdicts and Settlements, Combined; What's It Worth? A Guide to Personal Injury Awards and Settlements; Mealey's Jury Verdicts and Settlement Report; National Jury Verdict Review & Analysis; National Law Journal Annual Verdict and Settlement Review; Verdicts, Settlements and Tactics and Jury Verdicts by Jurisdiction.

tion aside from discovery rights. In some instances the alleged defects do stem from failings on the part of one or more of these middle-men.[34]

§ 12.16 LIBRARY COLLECTIONS

A very valuable source of bibliographic information is available free of charge from a growing number of Internet accessible university library database networks such as OCLC. These systems allow the user to search through the collections of groups of university libraries on title, author, and in some instances, subject matter. These library networks are a tremendous source of bibliographic information. In increasing numbers, these systems are accessible, and free of charge to alumni or student clerks. Products litigators should determine what online alumni privileges are available from the various general and law libraries of firm members. These resources are expanding at a great rate and alumni should keep current as to what free research tools are available to them. A simple Yahoo or Google search will yield extensive listings of public and private libraries arranged by topic. It is relatively easy to locate specialized collections where needed information can be had.[35]

§ 12.17 GOVERNMENT DATABASES

There is a enormous amount of information available to the public at little or no cost, that is contained in United States government agency sponsored and maintained websites and database systems. At the present time there are numerous and varied websites offering information from every federal government agency. The Louisiana State University LSU Libraries maintain a Federal Agencies Directory,[36] divided by executive, legislative, judicial, independent and quasi-independent websites that currently references over 1100 sites, each offering information of great interest to products litigators.

Several of the government sponsored databases of greatest importance to the products litigator, such as the Medline system, produced by the National Library of Medicine, and the National Technical Information Service, are easily accessible for cost-free bibliographic searches. The Medline collection currently numbers ten million bibliographic references in the areas of medicine, bio-medicine and health. It is accessible free of charge through the

---

[34] A Google or Yahoo search on "materials suppliers" returns literally thousands of company names and websites organized by product type or industry.

[35] For example, a very small portion of a Yahoo search on libraries yielded Public Libraries (5327); Academic Libraries (515); Business Libraries (26); Digital Libraries (84); Librarians (28); Professional Resources (140); Library and Information Science (332); National Libraries (48); Archives; Arts Libraries; Commercial Library Services; Conferences (10); Countries (26); Environmental Libraries; Government Documents and Health Libraries.

[36] http://www.lib.lsu.edu/gov/fedgov.html.

Internet at the National Institutes of Heath's (NIH) National Library of Medicine website[37] which provides links to PubMed (biomedical journal information), Medline Plus (health and drug information) and the Household Products Database (health and safety information on household products). The Medline system is one of the most productive of the vast array of government information websites available free of charge to the public.

The FedWorld website, maintained by the United States Department of Commerce links to the massive National Technical Information Service database which is the largest central resource for government-funded scientific, technical, engineering, and business related information available today. Here you will find information on more than 600,000 information products covering over 350 subject areas from over 200 federal agencies. FedWorld also links to FirstGov, allowing search access to over 30 Million Government Web Pages covering Government R&D Reports and numerous science and technical sites.[38]

The Government Printing Office website[39] provides access to all publications of the Unites States government from all three branches of the federal government, including an extensive list of official federal resources available on GPO Access.[40]

CRISP (Computer Retrieval of Information on Scientific Projects) is a searchable database of federally funded biomedical research projects conducted at universities, hospitals, and other research institutions. The database, maintained by the Office of Extramural Research at the National Institutes of Health, includes projects funded by the National Institutes of Health (NIH), Substance Abuse and Mental Health Services (SAMHSA), Health Resources and Services Administration (HRSA), Food and Drug Administration (FDA), Centers for Disease Control and Prevention (CDCP), Agency for Health Care Research and Quality (AHRQ), and Office of Assistant Secretary of Health (OASH). Users, including the public, can use the CRISP interface to search for scientific concepts, emerging trends and techniques, or identify specific projects and/or investigators. [41]

§ 12.18 BOOKS AND PERIODICALS

Books, scientific and technical journals, consumer magazines and industry newsletters, are the primary sources of pre-trial non-corporate information in products cases. The great bulk of these publications are available

---

[37] http://www.nlm.nih.gov/.

[38] See SciTech Resources at http://www.scitech.gov/, which provides easy access to key government science and technology web sites.

[39] http://www.gpo.gov/.

[40] The University of North Texas Libraries also maintains a website called the Government Information Connection, which provides links to a wide variety of state, federal and foreign government agency information cites. *See* http://www.library.unt.edu/govinfo/default.htm.

[41] http://crisp.cit.nih.gov/.

in selected university or public library collections as well, in increasing numbers, on a free or minimal fee base on the Internet. There are very few, if any, scientific or other specialty journals that are not available to the litigator prior to trial. The Library of Congress is an excellent early source for information on medical, pharmaceutical, engineering or chemical books in print.[42] The very comprehensive Bowker Books In Print database is available in public and private libraries and is the most comprehensive book listing on the Internet and in print form.[43] The OCLC service, available in most public, university and private libraries provides access to books from the Americas, Europe and Asia.

All litigators, especially small firms, should have all partners and associates check the alumni library privileges of their respective universities and law schools. These are often substantial and can provide readily available and focused free research sources.

§ 12.19 DIALOG INFORMATION SERVICES

The Dialog Information Services System is the grandaddy of database collections and is still the premier system to use for serious scientific or technical research. Dialog is a massive collection of the online databases of thousands of information services, available through a common search language.[44] This massive collection of searchable databases covers virtually every world data source in the broad areas of business, intellectual property, science and technology, news and trade journals and all aspects of market research. Many of the hundreds of available databases are bibliographic in nature, but an increasing number are offered full-text.

Descriptive *Dialog Bluesheets* are written guides for the use of every database on the Dialog® service. They contain detailed instructions on search techniques for the special features of each database, including file description, subject coverage, date range, update frequency, sources of the data, and the origin of the information. On the Bluesheet you will also find a sample record that shows what you can expect to obtain when you perform a search in the database. A most important part of the Bluesheets are the Search Options section, where you see the field labels that you can use to focus or narrow your search, as well as examples of how to use them online. Bluesheets on the Web are updated regularly and reflect the most current database information available.

---

[42] http://www.loc.gov/.

[43] *See* http://www.booksinprint.com/bip/.

[44] http://www.Dialog.com/.

The Dialog website[45] provides complete listings of all its bibliographic and full text sources which may be downloaded for private research examination. There is virtually nothing in print in multiple languages that is not accessible via the Dialog system. In addition to bibliographic cites, Dialog provides and increasing number of full-text articles for download. Both Lexis and Westlaw provide gateways to this terrific resource.

§ 12.20 POPULAR PUBLICATIONS

Popular print publications such as monthly magazines or bi-annual editions address a great variety of subjects of interest and value to the products litigator at the early stage of pretrial investigation and research. Many of them are also currently available online on the Internet.[46] Extensive listings of trade association publications are easily located on the Internet, for download or tracking in library holdings or reprint services.[47] In the home products area alone there are hundreds of magazines covering an amazing variety of subjects that contain valuable investigative leads, from infant car seats, strollers, toys, flammable fabric clothing concerns, bicycle and other protective headwear, etc. There are also numerous publications devoted to recreational vehicles, camping equipment, firearms, pesticides, and the like. Many of these publications conduct annual reviews and comparisons of the product categories they cover, including comparative product specifications.

Consumer oriented publications such as Consumer Reports, which have perspectives on a wide variety of products, usually provide comparative product reviews that are of special interest to product litigators. The Gale Group Magazine Database, available on Dialog and directly from Gale, provides current and retrospective news from more than 400 popular magazines on such subjects as consumer behavior, media trends, popular culture, political opinion, leisure activities, and contemporary lifestyles. Gale Group Magazine Database also contains large collections of entertainment reviews and ratings of books, films, theater, concerts, hotels, and restaurants. This database is ideal for searchers who need background material and a variety of perspectives to supplement any business search. Gale Group Magazine Database includes indexes and abstracts for 400 publications and the full text for more than 250 magazines.

---

[45] *See* http://www.Dialog.com. An additional several hundred databases are available on the DataStar System for commercial access via a Thomson/Dialog portal to more than three hundred databases in diverse areas including news, business, medicine, and healthcare. *See* www.datastarweb.com/.

[46] See the extensive subject listing at the NewsDirectory website located at http://newsdirectory.com/listmag.php.

[47] *Id.*

These publications also typically carry a considerable number of advertisements for alternative technology that reflects on the feasibility of feasible alternative designs, and thereby may provide significant investigative leads. Advertisments for stabilizing bars to minimize recreational vehicles' rolling motion or products increasing power tool safety may serve as examples.

These publications invariably list the various trade associations involved in the industry's purposes, a quick reference for litigators. There are thousands of trade associations, big and small, which are a tremendous source of information and further investigative leads. Each trade association publishes a journal and often industry newsletters, easily located in many public and university libraries and on the Internet.[48] In some instances, such as the automobile, aerospace, pharmaceutical and chemical industries, the trade association serves as an investigator and depository of injury statistics and serves as an important force in the industry efforts to minimize or eliminate proposed government agency performance or design regulations.

Finally, these popular publications have new product announcements, trade show and upcoming conference dates and other details of potential value to products litigators. It is a good idea for counsel to subscribe to all of the popular publications addressing the product type and industry in litigation.

§ 12.21 ACADEMIC AND PROFESSIONAL JOURNALS

The peer-reviewed studies and articles published in academic and professional journals, such as *The Lancet* or the *New England Journal of Medicine*, constitute the heart of the state-of-the-art literature. It is the grist for the expert witness' mill in establishing and supporting the scientific reliability of expert opinion. They also establish the outlines of what was considered the state-of-the-art in design, research and manufacture during the relevant period of the defendant corporation's history at issue. The number, variety and variances in quality and academic or professional reputation of these publications are enormous. Since peer-reviewed studies[49] are one of the primary items on the Supreme Court's short list of factors to be used to assess the reliability of a science underlying an expert's opinion[50] it is essential that products counsel identify the premier journals in the scientific field involved in the case. [51]

---

[48] *See, e.g.,* Newsletter Access, located at http://www.newsletteraccess.com/directory.php.

[49] The whole subject of peer-review and just what it is and is not from a scientific and ethical basis is a current concern world-wide as more information is emerging about ghost authors, financial entanglements and other serious ethical issues. *See* KIELY, SCIENCE AND LITIGATION, *supra* note 7, at Chapter 3, Science and Peer Review, 77-131.

[50] See Chapter 13, The Expert Witness, for a discussion of the famous *Daubert* criteria for determining scientific reliability for purposes of allowing expert opinion testimony.

[51] Research librarians and expert witnesses can provide this list, although counsel should always be satisfied of its solidity based on their own inquiries.

The Elsevier and Blackwell health and science publishers[52] maintain websites searchable by medical or other health related subjects and will return information about the journals considered key to their field. These websites are excellent and a great source for litigators' initial investigation into the body of authoritative state-of-the-art publications.

§ 12.22 ACADEMIC AND PROFESSIONAL ANNUAL MEETINGS AND SPECIAL CONFERENCES

A routine task for products litigators should be the location of schedules of academic and professional annual meetings and special conferences, both domestic and international, which address the scientific issues involved in the case. This is readily obtained on Dialog on the Internet through a Google search. Often these listings provide the titles of papers to be presented and the credentials of the participants. In addition to learning the nature of the concerns of the experts in the field, these papers are usually available for download in English shortly after their presentation. These conference source sites also typically go back two to three years, so the identity of recent conference papers can be readily assessed. These conference paper listings also provide early leads on the identity of potential expert witnesses or fodder for the deposition or cross-examination of an opposing expert.[53]

§ 12.23 RESEARCH IN PROGRESS AND GRANTS

A products liability case, depending upon its complexity, can often last for periods up to five years or more. During that period the world of science and technology proceeds apace. Ongoing research of interest or crucial to one or the other of the sides in the case may become finalized, published and available for study and use. While it is not possible to identify all research in progress, there are sources available to provide interested parties with basic information on a variety of ongoing scientific research. This has been accomplished by the publication of the identity of the recipients of government and private research fund grants. This information is available in

---

[52] *See* http://journals.elsevierhealth.com/ and http://www.blackwellpublishing.com/.

[53] The AllConferences website, located at http://www.allconferences.com/ is a directory focusing on conferences, conventions, trade shows, exhibits, workshops, events and business meetings. Inside Conferences is produced by the British Library. The database contains details of all papers given at every congress, symposium, conference, exposition, workshop, and meeting received at the British Library Document Supply Centre (BLDSC) since October 1993. Each year over 16,000 proceedings are indexed, covering a wide range of subjects published as serials or monographs. Over 500,000 bibliographic citations for individual conference papers are be added annually. Most records are in English, with many languages represented in the source documents. *See also* http://www.medicalconferences.com/.

both print and database form from commercial vendors such as Dialog and various free or low-cost Internet sites.[54]

The Federal Research In Progress (FEDRIP) website[55] provides access to information about ongoing federally funded projects in the fields of the physical sciences, engineering, and life sciences. The ongoing research announced in FEDRIP is an important component to the technology transfer process in the U.S. FEDRIP's uniqueness lies in its structure as a non bibliographic information source of research in progress. Project descriptions generally include: project title, keywords, start date, estimated completion date, principal investigator, performing and sponsoring organizations, summary, and progress report. Record content varies depending on the source agency.

Federal agencies that contribute to FEDRIP include the Department of Agriculture (AGRIC Subfile); Department of Energy (ENRGY Subfile); Department of Veterans Affairs (VA Subfile); Environmental Protection Agency (EPA Subfile); Federal Highway Administration (FHWA Subfile); National Institutes of Health (CRISP Subfile); NASA (NASA Subfile); National Science Foundation (NSF Subfile); U.S. Geological Survey (USGS Subfile); National Institute of Standards and Technology (NBS Subfile); Nuclear Regulatory Commission (NRC Subfile); and the Small Business Innovation Research (SBIR Subfile). A modest annual fee can provide access to this very important body of current information about research in progress in fields of great interest to products litigators.

Foundation and other non-governmental grants information can be accessed through Dialog in the Foundation Grants Index[56] and GRANTS files.

§ 12.24 STATISTICAL PUBLICATIONS AND DATA BANKS

Statistics comprise a very important component in the development, testing, production and marketing of a wide variety of products in every field. The very question of whether a risk of cancer or heart problems is associated with the use of a pharmaceutical requiring a warning is grounded in statistical theory and various statistical analytical models. The fact that a risk of cancer or heart attack or other medical anomaly may occur does not in itself mandate the issuance of a drug or chemical warning. The manufacturer has the right to base that decision on the statistical probabilities or percentages of occurrence and may not be required to warn for incidents below a set percentage.

---

[54] *See* http://www.dialog.com.

[55] http://grc.ntis.gov/fedrip.htm.

[56] http://fdncenter.org/.

The whole idea of the practical application of products liability theory is often grounded in some aspect of the statistical incident projections. All industries use one or more statistical models to estimate risks and their accompanying level of responsibilities. It is incumbent on products litigators to familiarize themselves with the statistical databases and system used by the government, national and international health research bodies, and the industry and company under scrutiny.

There are three basic aspects of statistical materials that counsel must separate out for study: the standards applied to the collection of the data used to generate the statistics, the statistical methodology applied to such data, and finally, the figures themselves.

The data bank may have been collected using criteria that do not allow for a complete or accurate analysis of the issues of importance to the case. This can seriously distort the reality behind the statistics. There are a bewildering number of statistical theories that may be applied to data. Counsel will need to become conversant with the range of statistical methodologies arguably available for use with such data so as to determine the possibility of results at variance with the actual figures under study. Finally, the results themselves must be checked against the actual method used to create them, to determine their accuracy within that methodology. The Internet is an excellent source for the identification of health statistics and projections. The federal government has a significant collection of readily accessible collections of statistics ranging from automobile fatalities to the carcinogenic risks from chemicals and other industrial artifacts.

The FedStats website[57] provides topic links from A to Z, statistical profiles of States, counties, cities, Congressional Districts, and Federal judicial districts, statistics by geography from U.S. agencies with international comparisons, a statistical reference shelf of published collections of statistics available online including the Statistical Abstract of the United States, a search feature going across agency websites, a listing of websites listed alphabetically with descriptions of the statistics they provide and links to their websites, contact information, and key statistics. It also provides an extensive listing of federal agencies by subject and selected agency online databases, such as the NIH National Cancer Institute's statistics[58] or the Fatal Accident Reporting System (FARS) data maintained by the National Highway Traffic Safety Administration [Statistics and Analysis].[59]

---

[57] http://www.fedstats.gov/.

[58] http://www.nci.nih.gov/statistics/.

[59] http://www-nrd.nhtsa.dot.gov/.

§ 12.25 MATERIALS, DESIGN, AND PERFORMANCE STANDARDS

Every product of whatever type is designed, tested and manufactured according to some set of standards, whether issued by international, national or industry standards setting bodies. The American National Standards Institute (ANSI)[60] or the American Society for Testing Materials (ASTM)[61] are examples of the more prestigious standards issuing organizations. The lion's share of manufactured products in America are produced with strict adherence to national standards for products, although not mandatory. There are published standards for a bewildering number of products ranging from laboratory test tubes to garden hose nozzles. It is important to be familiar with any relevant standards, the standards issuing entity, as well as the proposed standards constantly being issued by them. The current and proposed standards provide a ready frame of reference when establishing the reasonableness of a suspect design. Since these bodies are often funded by an industry, the committies are typically staffed by representatives of the companies engaged in the manufacture of products referenced by a set of standards.

The National Institute of Standards and Technology (NIST)[62] founded in 1901 is a non-regulatory federal agency within the U.S. Commerce Department's Technology Administration. NIST's mission is to develop and promote measurement, standards, and technology to enhance productivity, facilitate trade, and improve the quality of life. Computer databases maintained by the National Center for Standards and Certification Information (NCSCI) provides detailed information on over 270,000 government and private materials, design and performance standards.

Accessing and mastering these public and private standards is important in several key respects. Initially, they provide basic background information on the actual standards utilized or considered to be appropriate for the industries they address. Accordingly, these standards provide counsel with a means of assessing the extent to which he will be required to counter defense arguments based on conformity to industry custom at various stages over the preparation and trial of the case. Often, the testing methodology utilized by a target defendant closely follows the guidelines set forth in one of these standards. The publications of these bodies are also an entre to

---

[60] The American National Standards Institute (ANSI) is a private, non-profit organization (501(c)(3) that administers and coordinates the U.S. voluntary standardization and conformity assessment system. *See* http://www.ansi.org/.

[61] http://www.astm.org/.

[62] http://www.nist.gov/.

additional state-of-the-art materials that must eventually be identified, located and studied.

These bodies of standards are under continual review and thus counsel can determine the latest authoritative perspectives on the processes covered by them. Also, in cases involving new technology or products, these standards setting bodies will often promulgate preliminary proposed standards issuing from committees or sub-committees researching materials and performance testing issues relating to them. This provides counsel with a body of data highlighting the technological priorities set by these important industry organizations relative to the product or processes of concern to counsel.[63]

§ 12.26 CONSUMER INTEREST GROUPS AND ASSOCIATED PUBLICATIONS

The Consumer Product Safety Commission (CPSC) website[64] provides extensive and up-to-date listings of products recalls, safety news and the CPSC's work in the area of voluntary safety standards. The CPSC also provides many safety reports on various product groupings, including all-terrain vehicles, bicycles, child safety, children's furniture, clothing safety, crib safety and SIDS reduction, electrical safety, home heating equipment, household products safety, older consumers safety, outdoor power equipment safety, playground, pool and Spa safety and a wide variety of recreational products. The CPSC is a powerful regulatory agency whose investigative files, generally available under FOIA requests as with most other agencies, often is a primary source of data in products cases involved with consumer goods. The Federal Trade Commission's Consumer Page is also a helpful resource.[65]

Large and influential consumer interest organizations also provide a wealth of information of interest to the product litigator. These groups range from substantial entities such as the Center for Auto Safety,[66] the Insurance Institute for Highway Safety, [67] and Public Citizen,[68] to federally funded government organizations such as the Center for Disease Control[69] and the National Institutes of Health.[70] There are, in addition, thousands

---

[63] See the extensive testing data supplied by Underwriters Laboratory at http://www.ul.com/.

[64] http://www.cpsc.gov/.

[65] See http://www.ftc.gov/ftc/consumer.htm.

[66] http://www.autosafety.org/.

[67] http://www.iihs.org/.

[68] http://www.citizen.org/. (Safer drugs advocacy.)

[69] http://www.cdc.gov/.

[70] http://www.nih.gov/.

of smaller consumer interest groups addressing virtually every area of consumer concern, ranging from toddler clothing and toys, sports equipment, dietary supplements and the like.

Each year numbers of new websites appear providing general information, government contact sites and phone numbers, pamphlets and chat rooms. The larger organizations publish magazines available online and in public and university periodical collections. Consumers Union, publisher of Consumer Reports,[71] is an independent, nonprofit testing and information site that is a comprehensive source for unbiased advice about products and services, personal finance, health and nutrition, and other consumer concerns. Products litigators are able to check on international consumers organizations at the Consumers International site.[72] Listing of all state consumer agencies are also available that contain a wealth of information of interest to products litigators.[73]

§ 12.27 PROFESSIONAL AND TRADE ASSOCIATIONS AND ORGANIZATIONS

Identifying the professional organizations whose members have been historically involved in the study and development of the technology of interest to counsel is another important investigational goal. These organizations are a focal point for the professional activities of their members and generally publish one or more journals addressing current technological matters of interest to that membership and the industries that they serve. For example, one of the more important state-of-the-art data sources in automobile products litigation is the Journal of the Society of Automotive Engineers[74]. Professional organizations and related publications exist for virtually every area of technology of interest to the products litigator. In addition to the technical studies published by these organizations, they are also a primary research source for information relating to private performance and materials standards, addressing virtually every aspect of the product type under study. The membership of most organization's and association's technical committees and sub-committees is generally composed of industry representatives. This is an important focal point for detailed cross-referencing of state-of-the-art and company documents received in the course of discovery.

---

[71] http://www.consumerreports.org/main/home.jsp. See also their Consumer WebWatch page at http://www.consumerwebwatch.org/.

[72] http://www.consumersinternational.org/.

[73] http://www.ifg-inc.com/StateAgencies.html. (Excellent and extensive listing.)

[74] http://www.sae.org/servlets/index.

Two standard references, The Encyclopedia of Associations[75] (Detroit: Gale Research Co.) and the Yearbook of International Associations (Brussels: Union of International Associations) list national and international organizations by subject matter and include in many instances their annual conferences, meetings and publications. A simple Google search on professional associations will bring up a number of comprehensive listings sites.

§ 12.28 TRADE ASSOCIATIONS

In addition to the more academically oriented professional associations noted above, each industry normally has one or more trade associations. Trade association publications address a variety of practical issues such as industry economics, government regulation, public relations and other more purely marketing concerns affecting its membership. There are a large number of such associations, ranging from very powerful bodies such as the Automotive Manufacturers Association or the Pharmaceutical Manufacturers [76] organizations that represent concentrated industries, to a variety of smaller bodies which serve the interests of broad-based multi-member industries such as the electronics industry.

Trade associations, like professional associations, generally publish journals, newsletters or other materials that can be of great value to the products litigator. The practical ramifications of technological innovations or government regulation are often the subject matter of these publications. They provide a ready source of historical information as well as current industry thinking on those important issues. They are also a repository of valuable investigative leads on contemporary state-of-the-art source materials referenced throughout them. A very important aspect of trade association activity is the gathering of statistical data on a wide variety of subjects of interest to the product litigator.

Collections of injury data and profiles related to industry product lines are often made by these bodies. This latter information can be of inestimable value not only as a source of investigative material but on the central issue of corporate knowledge of defect itself. In less concentrated industries, these statistical collections may be the primary basis upon which a particular company could determine the extent of any risk potential associated with its product. Even in highly concentrated industries, these trade associations often serve as repositories of data generated by its members, providing them with a clear assessment of the danger associated with a design parameter common to the total membership.

Additional data collections and statistics may exist on materials availability and costs. They often contain position papers addressed to govern-

---

[75] http://www.infoplease.com/ipa/A0004878.htm.

[76] *See* http://www.phrma.org/.

ment agencies on the industry's behalf arguing for the elimination or reduction in performance levels of proposed agency regulations. All of these materials are informative and in some instances, central to the successful completion of case preparation. In some instances, the volume or nature of trade association information gathering and dissemination may be such that they should be seriously considered as a named defendant.

A publication entitled Encyclopedia of Associations provides a comprehensive geographical listing of the nations's trade associations. The Dialog System also provides detailed listings of such materials as well as abstracts and, in some instances, full text of the journals published by them. Commercial sites currently provide extensive fee-based searches for trade associations.[77]

§ 12.29 PATENTS

Patent research is highly complex and should be only attempted after counsel has a solid grounding in the technical and industry context of the technology under investigation. Patents provide a wealth of detailed technical information about a particular design as well as information on generically similar designs. An additional value of the patent research is to learn whether or not the target defendant actually holds the patent on what counsel feels are feasible alternative designs that were not implemented by it.

Patent research may be conducted in major public libraries as well as the DIALOG commercial databases.[78] The Patent Office database contains complete abstracts of all patents issued since 1970. This is very time consuming and difficult research. Counsel is well advised to seek expert assistance in this effort.

§ 12.30 COMPANY RESEARCH

Conducting thorough prefiling company research is important in several key respects. It is essential to the final determination of the pool of potential defendants and the eventual selection of named parties. This will require a search through the research sources to be discussed below to determine the existence of parent companies, subsidiaries and holding companies. It will also be necessary to determine the possible sale of one of the defendants in the pool to estimate whether or not a successor liability problem exists. The identity of all component parts and materials suppliers and participants in the vertical chain of distribution must also be determined before case planning and complaint drafting can be effectively begun.

---

[77] *See, e.g.,* http://www.marketingsource.com/associations/.

[78] *See* http://www.uspto.

Chapters 14 through 17 will analyze in detail how essential prefiling company research is to the entire discovery process. It is important to note here that maximum results in accessing defendant's internal documentation cannot be achieved without it. To complete counsel's comparative product analyses, he must determine the existence of generically similar product lines within the target defendant as well as that of similar product lines manufactured by competitors. Defendant's market share and assets are crucial to the punitive damage count.

The source material to be discussed below will identify some of the basic company research sources available to the litigator prior to initiating discovery.

All companies, foreign and domestic, are required by the Securities and Exchange Commission to file registration statements, periodic reports, and other forms electronically through EDGAR.[79] This source is a good start to gather preliminary information about a company in products liability litigation. Commercial, but cost-effective commercial services are also readily available through Dialog or comprehensive business information research websites such as D&B's Hoover's website.[80]

§ 12.31 ANNUAL REPORTS

Annual reports are an excellent, readily accessible source with which to determine the broad outlines of a corporation's business activity and its organizational structure. Annual reports, in some instances going back decades, are normally available for study at most large public and university libraries. They are also accessible through the Dialog System in its PTS ANNUAL REPORTS ABSTRACTS and the ICC British Company Annual Reports. While these abstracts are very useful, it is often important to give a close reading of the entire series of reports once a selection has been made. A very useful website is AnnualReports.com, whose free service allows users to review an annual report in an easy and convenient manner.

Annual reports generally provide broad based information on corporate divisions, major offices, boards of directors, earnings and major purchases and divestments. They often list the names of top level managers and central staff committees as well. The close examination of annual reports will provide a solid context for ensuing detailed investigation of the target defendant in the type of publications referenced below.

---

[79] http://www.sec.gov/edgar.shtml.

[80] http://www.hoovers.com/free/.

§ 12.32 DIRECTORY OF CORPORATE AFFILIATIONS

D&B, The Dunn and Bradstreet Directory of Corporate Affiliations "Who Owns Whom"[81] available on Dialog, is a worldwide company directory file that links a company to its corporate family, showing the size of the corporate structure, family hierarchy, and key information on the parent company, headquarters, branches, and subsidiaries worldwide. Corporate family structure information is provided in one easy-to-read online record.

It is also accessible through the Lexis/Nexis Information website,[82] where you can research corporate hierarchies ("who owns whom") to the seventh level — starting with as little information as a brand name. The D&B Directory of Corporate Affiliations™ database covers more than 180,000 of the most prominent parent companies, affiliates, subsidiaries, and divisions worldwide to help users to research corporate ownership. This directory of corporate affiliations covers companies listed on the major exchanges, the Fortune 1000 and a large selection of both privately owned and traded-over-the counter companies. The first section lists over 4000 parent companies, including high level managers, divisions, subsidiaries and affiliates. A second section cross-references over 45,000 divisions, subsidiaries and affiliates to their parent company set out in section one. Similar information and cross-referencing is provided for parent corporations located in foreign countries.

§ 12.33 THOMAS REGISTER OF AMERICAN MANUFACTURERS

The Thomas Register of American Manufacturers (NY: Thomas Pub.Co. Annual), is another valuable tool, especially with respect to initiating comparative product analyses. This seven-volume print set lists companies by the category of product that they manufacture. Volume Seven contains a brand name and product index. This is a readily available reference source, now available on the Internet, allowing for a quick introduction to the companies and products involved in the industry under investigation.[83]

§ 12.34 FOREIGN CORPORATIONS

It is becoming increasingly the case that the products litigator is faced with the problem of accessing information on a party defendant who is a foreign corporation. Several standard reference tools, periodically updated, can greatly assist in that task.

---

[81] http://library.dialog.com/bluesheets/html/bl0522.html.

[82] http://www.lexisnexis.com/dca/.

[83] http://www.thomasnet.com/.

Jane's Major Companies of Europe[84] provides company listings by country and type of business as well as directors and subsidiaries. It is available in most public and university libraries. Moody's International Manual has listings for over 3000 foreign corporations which cover company history, subsidiaries, offices, directors and financial status.

The New York Public Library maintains a website providing information on directories of foreign manufacturers doing business in the United States.[85]

§ 12.35 SUMMARY

Prefiling research must be tailored to the specific industry, product and design feature of concern to the litigator. The materials in this chapter are intended to point the product litigator in the right direction and highlight those areas and focal points within them that will serve as the most efficacious guidelines for this very time-consuming but vital aspect of case preparation. The subject of products liability research will be a continuing one throughout the remainder of this book.

§ 12.36 APPENDIX: PRODUCTS LIABILITY INTERNET RESEARCH SITES

APPENDIX
Researching Products Liability Cases
Websites Listing

[Each of the sites listed below, such as the Food and Drug Administration (FDA), National Institutes of Health (NIH) or the Center for Disease Control (CDC) sites, will provide many related links. For that reason we have not set out all of the related sites.]

PHARMACEUTICAL INFORMATION

• **VIRTUAL LIBRARY PHARMACY**

http://www.pharmacy.org/

• **PHARMWEB**

http://www.pharmweb.net/

---

[84] (London: Macdonald and Jane's Publishers, 1979-)

[85] Worldwide Business Directories (http://www.nypl.org/research/sibl/directories/namerica.htm). This is a guide to general business directories covering geographic areas around the world held by the Science, Industry and Business Library, located at 188 Madison Ave., at 34th St. in Manhattan. These lists include coverage of International Directories, North America, Europe, Asia and the Pacific, the Middle East, Latin America, the Caribbean, and Africa.

- **THE PHARMACEUTICAL RESEARCH AND MANUFACTURERS OF AMERICA [PHRMA]**

http://www.phrma.org/

- **PHARMACEUTICAL ON-LINE**

http://www.pharmaceuticalonline.com/content/homepage/default

ENGINEERING INFORMATION

- **GLOBALSPEC ENGINEERING SEARCH DATABASE**

http://www.globalspec.com/ProductFinder/FindProducts?query=chemical%20manufactur

- **WWW VIRTUAL LIBRARY SEARCH PAGE**

http://vlib.org/

- **YAHOO ENGINEERING CATEGORIES**

http://dir.yahoo.com/Science/Engineering/

- **ELSEVIER ENGINEEERING DATABASES**

http://www.ei.org/

- **EEVL TECHNICAL LITERAURE**

http://www.eevl.ac.uk/lit_searching.html

- **ENGINEERING INFORMATION**

http://www.ei.org/

CHEMICAL INFORMATION

- **CHEMICAL MANUFACTURERS VIRTUAL LIBRARY**

http://www.globalspec.com/

- **CHEMICAL INDUSTRIES DIRECTORIES**

http://www.liv.ac.uk/Chemistry/Links/chemcomps1.html

- **CHEMICAL PRODUCTS REGISTER**

http://www.chemicalregister.com/

- **CHEMICAL SCIENCE AND TECHNOLOGY LABORATORY**

http://www.cstl.nist.gov/

- **AMERICAN CHEMICAL SOCIETY**

http://www.chemistry.org/portal/a/c/s/1/home.html

MEDICINE AND HEALTH INFORMATION

- **FOOD AND DRUG ADMINISTRATION (FDA)**

http://www.fda.gov/

- **OCCUPATIONAL SAFETY AND HEALTH ADMINISTRATION (OSHA)**

http://www.osha.gov/

- **NATIONAL CENTER FOR HEALTH PROMOTION AND DISEASE PREVENTION (VA)**

http://www.nchpdp.med.va.gov/

- **NATIONAL CENTER FOR COMPLEMENTARY AND ALTERNATIVE MEDICINE (NCCAM)**

http://nccam.nih.gov/

- **MEDLINE PLUS**

http://medlineplus.gov/

- **YAHOO HEALTH & MEDICINE**

http://dir.yahoo.com/Health/Medicine/

- **ARCHIVES OF INTERNAL MEDICINE**

http://archinte.ama-assn.org/

- **NATIONAL HEART, BLOOD AND LUNG INSTITUTE**

http://www.nhlbi.nih.gov/index.htm

- **WORLD HEALTH ORGANIZATION**

http://www.who.int/en/

- **NATIONAL INSTITUTE OF ALLERGY AND INFECTIOUS DISEASES**

http://www3.niaid.nih.gov/

- **AMERICAN MEDICAL ASSOCIATION**

http://www.ama-assn.org/

- **ELSEVIER HEALTH JOURNALS**

http://journals.elsevierhealth.com/

- **BLACKWELL MEDICAL JOURNALS**

http://www.blackwellpublishing.com/

- **FREE ACCESS TO MEDICAL JOURNALS**

http://www.freemedicaljournals.com/

CLINICAL TRIALS

- **CLINICAL TRIALS. GOV**

http://www.clinicaltrials.gov/

- **CENTERWATCH CLINICAL TRIALS LISTING**

http://www.centerwatch.com/

- **VERITAS MEDICINE**

http://www.veritasmedicine.com/index.cfm

- **SOCIETY FOR CLINICAL TRIALS**

http://www.sctweb.org/

- **MEDLINE PLUS — CLINICAL TRIALS**

http://www.nlm.nih.gov/medlineplus/clinicaltrials.html

- **APPLIED CLINICAL TRIALS [EU]**

http://www.actmagazine.com/appliedclinicaltrials/

- **NATIONAL CANCER INSTITUTE — CLINICAL TRIALS**

http://www.cancer.gov/clinicaltrials

- **TRIALS CENTRAL [Must See]**

http://www.trialscentral.org/

- **CURRENT CONTROLLED TRIALS**

http://www.controlled-trials.com/

BIOMEDICAL INFORMATION

- **MEDWEB EMORY UNIVERSITY**

http://www.medweb.emory.edu/MedWeb/

- **AMERICAN INSTITUTE FOR MEDICAL AND BIOLOGICAL ENGINEERING**

http://www.aimbe.org/

- **BIOPHYSICAL SOCIETY**

http://www.biophysics.org/

- **BIOMEDICAL ENGINEERING ONLINE**

http://www.biomedical-engineering-online.com/

- **BIOMECHANICS WORLDWIDE**

http://www.per.ualberta.ca/biomechanics/bwwframe.htm

- **INTERNATIONAL FEDERATION FOR MEDICAL AND BIOLOGICAL ENGINEERING**

http://www.ifmbe.org/

- **WILEY INTERSCIENCE**

http://www3.interscience.wiley.com/cgi-bin/home

- **WHITEHEAD INSTITUTE FOR BIOMEDICAL RESEARCH**

http://www.wi.mit.edu/research/papers.html

- **INSTITUTE OF BIOMEDICAL SCIENCE**

http://www.ibms.org/

- **KAROLINSKA INSTITUTET [EU]**

http://www.mic.ki.se/Other.html

- **MEDSCAPE MEDICAL CONFERENCE LISTINGS**

http://www.medscape.com/conferencedirectory/Default

- **FOUNDATION FOR BIOMEDICAL RESEARCH**

http://www.fbresearch.org/

- **BIOMEDICAL ENGINEERING NETWORK**

http://www.bmenet.org/BMEnet/

- **BIOMEDICAL ENGINEERING SOCIETY**

http://www.bmes.org/

- **GENETESTS**

http://www.geneclinics.org/

- **HUMAN GENOME PROJECT: MEDICINE AND THE NEW GENETICS**

http://www.ornl.gov/sci/techresources/Human_Genome/medicine/
medicine.shtml

- **CENTER FOR MEDICAL GENETICS**

http://research.marshfieldclinic.org/genetics/Default.htm

- **AMERICAN BOARD OF MEDICAL GENETICS**

http://www.abmg.org/

- **BIOMED CENTRAL**

http://www.biomedcentral.com/

- **OFFICE OF SCIENTIFIC AND TECHNICAL INFORMATION**

http://www.osti.gov/

- **NATIONAL TECHNICAL INFORMATION SERVICE**

http://www.ntis.gov/

- **NATIONAL SCIENCE FOUNDATION**

http://www.nsf.gov/

- **NATIONAL HUMAN GENOME RESEARCH INSTITUTE**

http://www.genome.gov/

- **NATIONAL INSTITUTE OF BIOMEDICAL IMAGING AND BIO-ENGINEERING**

http://www.nibib1.nih.gov/

FEDERAL GOVERNMENT SOURCES

- **FEDERAL MINE SAFETY AND HEALTH REVIEW COMMISSION**

http://www.fmshrc.gov/

- **ENVIRONMENTAL PROTECTION AGENCY (EPA)**

http://www.epa.gov/

- **NATIONAL INSTITUTES OF HEALTH (NIH)**

http://www.nih.gov/

- **NATIONAL CENTER ON MINORITY HEALTH AND HEALTH DISPARITIES (NCMHD)**

http://www.ncmhd.nih.gov/

- **NATIONAL EYE INSTITUTE**

http://www.nei.nih.gov/

- **NATIONAL INSTITUTE OF DIABETES & DIGESTION & KIDNEY DISEASES**

http://www.niddk.nih.gov/

- **UNITED STATES DEPARTMENT OF HEALTH AND HUMAN SERVICES**

http://www.hhs.gov/

- **CENTER FOR BIOLOGICS EXAMINATION AND RESEARCH**

http://www.fda.gov/cber/

- **OFFICE OF PUBLIC HEALTH AND SAFETY**

http://www.osophs.dhhs.gov/ophs/

- **OFFICE OF THE SURGEON GENERAL**

http://www.surgeongeneral.gov/

- **NATIONAL INSTITUTE OF DENTAL AND CRANIOFACIAL RESEARCH**

http://www.nidcr.nih.gov/

- **AGENCY FOR HEALTH CARE RESEARCH AND QUALITY (AHRQ)**

http://www.ahrq.gov/

- **AGENCY FOR TOXIC SUBSTANCES AND DISEASE REGISTRY (ATSDR)**

http://www.atsdr.cdc.gov/atsdrhome.html

- **AIRFORCE AIR SAFETY CENTER**

http://afsafety.af.mil/

- **NATIONAL LIBRARY OF MEDICINE**

http://www.nlm.nih.gov/

- **OFFICE OF OCCUPATIONAL SAFETY AND HEALTH**

http://www1.va.gov/vasafety/

- **OFFICE OF INSPECTOR GENERAL**

http://www.oig.doi.gov/

- **UNITED STATES PATENT AND TRADEMARK OFFICE**

http://www.uspto.gov/

- **GOVERNMENT ACCOUNTABILITY OFFICE — REPORTS**

http://www.gpoaccess.gov/gaoreports/index.html

- **OFFICE OF NAVAL RESEARCH — SCIENCE AND TECHNOLOGY**

http://www.onr.navy.mil/sci_tech/engineering/331_physical/default.asp

- **NATIONAL TRANSPORTATION SAFETY BOARD (NTSB)**

http://www.ntsb.gov/

- **NATIONAL HIGHWAY TRAFFIC SAFETY ADMINISTRATION [NHTSA]**

http://www.nhtsa.dot.gov/

- **SMITHSONIAN INSITUTION**

http://www.si.edu/

- **LIBRARY OF CONGRESS**

http://www.loc.gov/

- **NATIONAL CENTER FOR STATISTICS AND ANALYSIS [NHTSA/DOT]**

http://www-nrd.nhtsa.dot.gov/departments/nrd-30/ncsa/

- **FATALITY ANALYSIS REPORTING SYSTEM (FARS)-WEB-BASED ENCYCLOPEDIA**

http://www-fars.nhtsa.dot.gov/

- **NHTSA RESEARCH AND DEVELOPMENT**

http://www-nrd.nhtsa.dot.gov/

- **NHTSA-OFFICE OF DEFECTS INVESTIGATION**

http://www-odi.nhtsa.dot.gov/cars/problems/recalls/recallsearch.cfm

- **FHWA/NHTSA NATIONAL CRASH ANALYSIS CENTER (NCAC)**

http://www.ncac.gwu.edu/

- **LSU LIBRARIES FEDERAL AGENCIES DIRECTORY**

http://www.lib.lsu.edu/gov/fedgov.html

- **CONSUMER PRODUCTS SAFETY COMMISSION (CPSC)**

http://www.cpsc.gov/

- **FEDWORLD GOVERNMENT INFORMATION**

http://www.fedworld.gov/

- **FEDERAL FOOD SAFETY INFORMATION**

http://www.foodsafety.gov/

- **FOOD SAFETY INFORMATION CENTER**

http://www.nalusda.gov/foodsafety/

- **FOOD SAFETY AND INSPECTION SERVICE (FSIS)**

http://www.fsis.usda.gov/

- **ANIMAL AND PLANT HEALTH INSPECTION SERVICES (APHIS)**

http://www.aphis.usda.gov/

- **TOXICOLOGY DATA NETWORK (TOXNET)**

http://toxnet.nlm.nih.gov/

- **COMPUTER RETRIEVAL OF INFORMATION ON SCIENTIFIC PROJECTS (CRISP)**

http://crisp.cit.nih.gov/

- **UNIVERSITY OF NORTH TEXAS GOVERNMENT INFORMATION DATABASE**

http://www.library.unt.edu/govinfo/subject/catsindx.html

- **FEDSTATS-FEDERAL STATISTICAL DATA**

http://www.fedstats.gov/

- **CENTERS FOR DISEASE CONTROL AND PREVENTION (CDC)**

http://www.cdc.gov/

- **NATIONAL CANCER**

http://www.cancer.gov/

- **HEALTH RESOURCES AND SERVICES ADMINISTRATION**

http://www.hrsa.gov/

- **NATIONAL CENTER FOR HEALTH STATISTICS (NCHS)**

http://www.cdc.gov/nchs/

- **BUREAU OF LABOR STATISTICS**

http://www.bls.gov/

- **U.S. GOVERNMENT PRINTING OFFICE**

http://www.gpo.gov/

- **GPO ACCESS**

http://www.gpoaccess.gov/index.html

STANDARDS ORGANIZATIONS

- **AMERICAN NATIONAL STANDARDS INSTITUTE (ANSI)**

http://www.ansi.org/

- **NATIONAL INSTITUTE OF STANDARDS AND TECNOLOGY (NIST)**

http://www.nist.gov/

- **AMERICAN NATIONAL STANDARDS INSTITUTE (ANSI)**

http://www.ansi.org/

- **ASTM INTERNATIONAL-STANDARDS WORLDWIDE (ASTM)**

http://www.astm.org/cgi-bin/SoftCart.exe/index.shtml?E+mystore

COMPANY INFORMATION

- **SEC FILINGS AND FORMS (EDGAR)**

http://www.sec.gov/edgar.shtml

- **HOOVER'S COMPANY INFORMATION**

http://www.hoovers.com/free/

- **DIALOG INFORMATION SYSTEM BLUE SHEETS**

http://library.dialog.com/bluesheets/

- **ANNUAL REPORTS GALLERY**

http://www.reportgallery.com/

- **D&B — WHO OWNS WHOM**

http://library.dialog.com/bluesheets/html/bl0522.html

- **DIRECTORY OF CORPORATE AFFILIATIONS**

http://www.lexisnexis.com/dca/

- **THOMASNET COMPANY INFORMATION**

http://www.thomasnet.com/

Chapter 13
THE EXPERT WITNESS

SYNOPSIS

§ 13.01 EXPERT WITNESSES: PRE-TRIAL CONSIDERATIONS

There are a wide variety of factors that are involved in the area of the initial pretrial use of expert witnesses in products liability cases. Set out below is a brief discussion of the most important basic pretrial considerations with regard to expert witness.

[A] *Analyzing Expert Witness Needs*

[1] Determining Expert Witness Needs

The question of expert witness requirements should be analyzed from the dual perspectives of counsel's legal and investigative needs since the expert often has much to offer in the purely investigative aspects of case preparation. Such choices are often one of the most difficult due to counsel's initial unfamiliarity with the range of state of the art, regulatory and corporate issues involved in the case. Several categories of experts need not be utilized until counsel is ready to initiate discovery, while others need not be called upon to any significant degree until the case approaches trial. The ever present need to control expert witness costs requires close planning regarding the actual uses of the expert. The following sections will address several considerations that should enter into the decision to engage an expert or experts. It is also important to note that experts may not be easily substituted later in the case and case planning requires an early and solid relationship.

[2] Categorizing Expert Witness Needs

The preliminary research on the broad state-of-the-art context of the case will point toward the specific technical areas generally involved in cases of the type under review. In any products case, state of the art, regulatory and corporate information are central concerns. The key legal and technical issues are those specifically related to defect, feasible alternative design and proximate causation As preliminary legal, state of the art, regulatory, industry and company research advance, the general outlines of the specific research areas central to the case will emerge. In a case involving a disintegrating ball-joint on a pickup truck resulting in the loss of a wheel, where is the technical ball-joint theoretical literature to be located? Is the National Highway Traffic Safety Administration the primary regulatory agency? How do I access information about industry trade associations and the company itself?

Counsel for both sides may initially determine that the following categories of expertise may be required: general automotive design; ball joint system design and materials selection in particular; automobile crash testing methodology; metallurgy; accident reconstruction; National Highway Traffic Safety Administration regulatory processes; corporate documentation and decision-making processes; corporate accounting principles; and statistical analyses. Once the scope of expert witness categories has been estimated, counsel should then make a determination of what additional specialized expertise, if any, may be required by the particular facts of the case under investigation. Considerable attention must also be given to experts in the damages area, which will involve medical expertise and economists and often, statisticians on the issue of future damages.

[B] *Choosing the Expert Witness*

[1] Expert Witness Research Sites

The Internet provides an amazing number of websites devoted to the listing of expert witnesses in every area of possible interest to products liability litigators. Many are free of charge, others like that of fee-based listings[1] such as the service of the plaintiff's bar American Trial Lawyers Association (ATLA)[2] provide names of firms with past experience with the experts of interest. Sites such as Expert Law[3] break experts down by area such as automobile products cases.[4]

[2] Expert Witness Clearing Houses

In addition to the numerous websites providing expert witness location and resumes, there are a number of expert witness corporations that provide extensive, multi-tiered expert services and the latest system support laboratories and equipment.[5]

[3] ATLA Exchange and DRI

The ATLA Exchange is a legal research service available to ATLA plaintiff lawyers. The Exchange provides contacts with lawyers with previous experience in similar cases and those who are currently or have recently utilized the type of expert being sought. The Exchange also provides current information on product recalls and provides leads to procuring depositions, court documents, case abstracts, CLE materials, experts, Law Reporter Court Document sets, and a wealth of other information such as Injury Collections, Abstract Sets, and Ultimate Document Sets.

---

[1] *See, e.g.,* The Leading Global Source, http://www.LECG.com; JurisPro Expert Witnesses, http://www.JurisPro.com; Expert Pages, http://expertpages.com; Expert Witness Directory, http://ExpertWitness.com; Martindale-Hubbell's Directory, http://www.martindale.com/resources; http://www.matcoinc.com; http://www.lawyersandsettlements.com; http://www.romingerlegal.com; http://www.legal-database.com. There are many more listings on the Internet resulting from an "expert witnesses" Google search.

[2] http://www.atla.org/.

[3] http://www.expertlaw.com/experts/Products/.

[4] http://www.expertlaw.com/experts/Products/Automotive.html.

[5] A good example is Packer Engineering, http://www.packereng.com/index.cfm, providing sophisticated expert witness services in the areas of aerospace, automotive, bioengineering, building technology, chemical engineering, electrical engineering, electronics, engineering mechanics, explosions, fires, human factors, machinery, materials engineering, mechanical engineering, safety engineering, and structural engineering.

The Defense Research Institute[6] (The Voice of the Defense Bar) provides similar services to the defense bar, and as does ATLA, is affiliated with state and local support groups[7] for product liability defense counsel.

[4] Lexis and Westlaw Listings

The LexisNexis legal research system[8] provides extensive access to the leading expert witness listing sources. Their Combined Verdicts, Settlements and Expert Directories, Expert Witness Directories, include expert4law, LA County Bar Association Expert Witness Dir, ALM Experts New England Directory, JurisPro Expert Witness Directory, ALM Experts New Jersey Directory, ALM Experts Legal Expert Pages, ALM Experts New York Directory, Martindale-Hubbell(R) Law Directory — Experts & Services, ALM Experts Southeastern Directory, ALM Experts Mid-Atlantic Directory Source, ALM Experts Southwestern Directory and the ALM Experts Mid-Western Directory.

The Westlaw legal research system provides access to a full range of expert witness sources. Its database listings include (WLD-EXPERTS), Expert Witness Resumes (EXPTRESUME), Expert Witness Journal (EXP-WITJ), Profiler — Profiles of Expert Witnesses (PROFILER-EW), Data-monitor Expert View (DATAMEXPVIEW), ExpertNet (EXPNET), Expert Witnesses in Civil Trial (EXPWIT-CIV), and Expert Witness Checklists (EXPWITC).

[C] *Organizational Factors*

In addition to the interview with the prospective expert, counsel should definitely consult with attorneys who are currently using or have used the expert. Counsel should also be sure to consult attorneys with whom the expert has worked who are not on the expert's list of formal references. Such attorneys can provide invaluable insights into virtually every area of concern to the product litigator faced with the difficult task of engaging a particular expert witness. Of primary concern are whether he is a sole practitioner, the extent of his staff support, the nature and modernity of his specialized equipment, his preferred method of approach and his current workload and accessibility.

---

[6] http://www.dri.org. This is the major counterpart to ATLA, which serves the community of plaintiff personal injury litigators.

[7] *See also* The Federation of Defense and Corporate Council, http://www.thefederation.org, The International Association of Defense Council, http://www.iadclaw.org, and The Federation of Defense & Corporate Counsel (FDCC), http://www.thefederation.org/professional development.

[8] http://www.lexis.com.

There has been a dramatic change in the nature of expert witness involvement in product liability cases over the past several decades resulting from the rapid development of expert witness service corporations of increasing size and complexity. This has resulted in the attendant displacement of the sole practitioner or several member firm as the primary players in the preparation and trial of the products case. Accordingly, an initial discussion of the advantages and disadvantages of the sole practitioner versus the expert witness service organization is in order. It should first be recalled that counsel may not have a choice due to his or her being the first to bring a suspect product type to litigation. In those areas, the fields of expertise may be such that the large expert witness organizations are simply unable or unwilling to supply or sub-contract with an individual possessed of sufficient background to meet counsel's broad requirements. Admittedly, this hypothetical situation is becoming a rare phenomenon, due to expert witness service organizations constantly expanding the range of experts working for them.

A sole practitioner may be unacceptable due to a lack of technical facilities with which to compete with the most recent scientific methods for product and occurrence evaluation. The increasingly hierarchical nature of expert witness service corporations, with their highly refined areas of responsibility, wealth of scientific equipment, extensive support staffs and expanding areas of expertise, put great strain upon the sole practitioner in attempts to compete with the well financed and supported corporate defendant.[9]

There are definite advantages to using the sole practitioner if counsel is confident that he has the technological capability and experience to counter the expertise provided by a large expert witness service corporation. There is an opportunity to develop a personal relationship and shared commitment to the case and the client, important factors often sorely lacking when utilizing the services of an assigned employee of a large expert witness corporation. There is also the possibility of more flexible fee and payment modes.

---

[9] *See* TERRENCE F. KIELY, SCIENCE AND LITIGATION: PRODUCTS LIABILITY IN THEORY AND PRACTICE 268 (CRC Press 2002). Another potential drawback to the utilization of the sole practitioner is the problem of accessibility. In addition to the increasing technological inadequacies of the sole practitioner, there is the important factor of available time as a central consideration. The sole practitioner, especially in the fields relevant to engineered products, has little or no backup support and — if effective in their field — are generally constantly on the go, studying accident sites and product units across the country. Their unavailability in instances where time is of the essence can have harmful and at times long lasting negative effects on the prosecution of a products case. *Id.*

[D] *Categories of Experts*

Expert testimony is the centerpiece of a products liability case. Automotive engineers, consumer products designers, pharmacologists, chemists and medical device designers are just a few of the type of experts typically involved in products litigation. Aside from the obvious technical expert witnesses, there are often a range of non-technical experts that are required to address complex issues resulting from the complexity of modern manufacturing processes. Such non-technical witnesses will include experts in management principles and corporate processes, regulatory agency procedures and policy, statisticians, corporate accountants and marketing and advertising experts.

Formal company systems for integrating safety in design, company protocols for cooperating with or fending off regulatory measures, the statistical models used to determine if a statistical risk is equivalent to a risk that must be considered in manufacture and marketing, internal corporate accounting factors that assign "costs" that may not be actually reflected in a showroom or market price, and drafts of advertising proposals and marketing campaign analyses may each require explanatory expertise at trial. For example, the Vioxx litigators will show keen interest in discussions had in the company about whether statistical data required the company to include or ignore any concerns over risk of heart attacks in their warnings insert or advertising. A complex series of corporate decision-making processes may require expertise to unravel it for a jury. In an SUV rollover case, discussions of the wording of brochures or the content of television advertising spots may require emphasis or explanation. Costs will affect the use of non-technical experts, but they should be considered as research progresses.

In addition to technical experts giving opinions, experts are often employed as narrative experts only, to explain the history and basics of the science involved in the case.

§ 13.02 PLAINTIFF REQUIRED TO PRESENT EXPERT TESTIMONY

In *Rosenberg v. Otis Elevator Co.*,[10] a 2004 New Jersey opinion, invitees brought an action against an elevator company, who both manufactured and maintained the subject elevator, and the building owner after they were injured when elevator in which they were riding dropped three floors. The Superior Court, Law Division, Ocean County, granted summary judgment in favor of the elevator company and the building owner. The Appellate Division reversed and remanded.

---

[10] 841 A.2d 99 (N.J. Super. App. Div. 2004).

The appellate court ruled that the jurors did not require expert testimony to address the issue whether the elevator company and the building owner met their duty to invitees. The court held that judicial evaluation of the need for expert testimony in a products liability case should take account of the complexity of evidence related to the instrumentality involved in an accident, rather than simply focusing on whether the instrumentality is complex.

Likewise, in *Jones v. Toyota Motor Sales USA, Inc.*, No. 03-1397 (3d Cir. March 22, 2004), the court ruled that under Pennsylvania law, a tow tractor operator was required to produce expert evidence in order to support his products liability claim against the manufacturer under crashworthiness doctrine based on lack of operator restraints, despite the operator's contention that the concept of providing belt or restraint to bilateral open-sided machine was not beyond comprehension of ordinary lay persons, where the issue required consideration of engineering, medical, and biomechanical analysis that was not within know-how of ordinary layperson.

§ 13.03 THE LEGAL REQUIREMENTS OF EXPERT TESTIMONY

Although forensic scientists in criminal cases are required to conduct a variety of science-based tests and report and interpret their findings,[11] this has not been the practice in civil law products liability cases. For one thing, the scientific testimony in those cases typically references some generic design, instructions or warnings issues that was pre-existent to the occurrence giving rise to the case. In addition, the purposes in doing any such case-science would be distinctly different from that supporting scientific inquiry in a criminal case. The issue of whether the drug Parlodel can cause brain aneurysm in a products liability lawsuit, is quite different from the forensic issue of whether blood, semen, hair or fiber expert testimony may be used to link a defendant to a crime scene in a rape-homicide prosecution.

Experts in products liability cases, including those engaged by defendant companies, do not typically conduct actual scientific work for the case proper, but rather base their opinions on previously published scientific material. Nobel Prize winner Stanley Miller referred to articles or opinions based on other articles as merely *paper science,*[12] as opposed to hard fought work in research laboratories. It is quite likely that expert testimony by way of *paper science* is what will continue to be the basis of the

---

[11] *See* TERRENCE F. KIELY, FORENSIC EVIDENCE: SCIENCE AND THE CRIMINAL LAW (CRC Press, 2d ed. 2006).

[12] *See* KIELY, *supra* note 9, at 55. See also *ATLA's Litigating Tort Cases*, A. Russell Smith, Chapter 14, Discovery Strategy and Privileges (2004), for a good recent summary of the various *Daubert* related issues; Robert C. Morgan & Ashe P. Puri , *Expert Witnesses and Daubert Motions*, 5 SEDONA CONF. J. 15 (2004); Douglas Hanna & Paul R. Ferreira, EXPERT WITNESS OVERVIEW A COMMON SENSE APPROACH, 229-AUG. N.J. LAW 11 (2004).

expert witnesses' contribution to the products liability process. Indeed, in some cases, such as the questioning of the adequacy of 1960s titanium alloy foundry techniques central to the Iowa DC-10 crash filings and discovery, any other requirement may very well be both technological and economic impossibilities. Where the questioned science or engineering practice or allegedly inadequate instructions or warnings are susceptible to some actual investigation by the expert what, if anything should be required other than the expert's bare opinion?[13]

The controlling evidence rule governing the admissibility of expert testimony in products liability litigation is Federal Rule of Evidence 702 (or its equivalents under state law[14]) which provides:

> If scientific, technical, or other specialized knowledge will assist the trier of fact to understand the evidence or to determine a fact in issue, a witness qualified as an expert by knowledge, skill, experience, training, or education, may testify thereto in the form of an opinion or otherwise, if (1) the testimony is based upon sufficient facts or data, (2) the testimony is the product of reliable principles and methods, and (3) the witness has applied the principles and methods reliably to the facts of the case.[15]

---

[13] Recently, efforts have been made to ostracize errant experts from their respective professional organizations. *See* Terry Carter, M.D., *With A Mission: A Physician Battles Against Colleagues He Considers Rogue Expert Witnesses*, 90-AUG. A.B.A. J. 41 (2004).

[14] *See generally* PAUL C. GIANNELLI, UNDERSTANDING EVIDENCE (2d ed. LexisNexis 2006), Chapter 24 Expert Testimony: FRE 702,704, 706. This is an excellent general treatise on modern evidence law.

[15] It is the position of both state and federal courts that plaintiffs must present some expert testimony as a minimal requirement to prove a product design defect. *See, e.g.,* Burgad v. Jack L. Marcus, Inc., 345 F. Supp. 2d 1036 (D.N.D. 2004) (In light of the absence of any expert testimony as to whether vendor of sports bra breached any standard of care in its design and manufacture of the bra, whether the bra was defective, unsafe, or unreasonably dangerous, or whether there was any causal connection between any design defect and plaintiff's injuries, vendor of sports bra was not liable in negligence, under North Dakota law, to purchaser allegedly burned while wearing the garment. As a general rule, a plaintiff is required to prove a product defect through an expert witness.); Jones v. Toyota Motor Sales USA, Inc., No. 03-1397 (3d Cir. March 22, 2004) (Under Pennsylvania law, tow tractor operator was required to produce expert evidence in order to support his products liability claim against manufacturer under crashworthiness doctrine based on lack of operator restraints, despite operator's contention that concept of providing belt or restraint to bilateral open-sided machine was not beyond comprehension of ordinary lay persons, where issue required consideration of engineering, medical, and biomechanical analysis that was not within know-how of ordinary layperson.). *But see* Rosenberg v. Otis Elevator Co., 841 A.2d 99 (N.J. Super. App. Div. 2004) (Invitees brought action against elevator company, who both manufactured and maintained elevator, and building owner after they were injured when elevator in which they were riding dropped three floors. Judicial evaluation of the need for expert testimony in a products liability case should take account of the complexity of evidence related to instrumentality involved in an accident, rather than simply focusing on whether the instrumentality is complex.).

The famous Daubert case and its progeny, centered in Rule 702, have been discussed in detail in Chapter 8, Problems of Proof: Defect and Causation.[16] It is the purpose of the ensuing discussion to examine the very practical issue of recent court pronouncements on the actual presentation of expert opinions and feasible alternative design testimony.

§ 13.04 EXPERT TESTIMONY NOT SUPPORTED BY RELIABLE SCIENCE

In *Goodyear Tire & Rubber Co. v. Rios*,[17] a widow brought a products liability action against a tire manufacturer alleging that the tire contained a manufacturing defect and failure to warn defect. The 229th Judicial District Court, Duval County, Alex W. Gabert, J., entered judgment on jury verdict in favor of plaintiff and against manufacturer in the amount of $40 million. The appellate court reversed , holding that plaintiff's tire expert's testimony regarding cause of tire failure was not reliable evidence of whether a manufacturing defect existed. The expert's opinion was based only on visual and tactile testing of tire, and no evidence indicated that other experts used same methodology to determine that a manufacturing defect existed, as opposed to a defect caused by the use and abuse of tire over time. Additionally, the expert did not refer to any article or publication that specifically supported his approach.

The plaintiffs offered the testimony of two experts to establish the existence of a manufacturing defect, Robert Ochs and John Crate. Goodyear asserted that the testimony of these experts provided no evidence of a manufacturing defect because the experts were either unqualified or their opinions were not reliable. The court ruled that to be reliable, the expert's testimony must be grounded in scientific method and procedure such that it amounts to more than subjective belief or unsupported speculation. The Texas Supreme Court had enumerated a list of *Daubert*-type factors to determine the reliability of expert testimony, including: (1) the extent to which the theory has or can be tested; (2) the extent to which the technique relies upon subjective interpretation of the expert; (3) whether the theory has been subjected to peer review and publication; (4) the technique's potential rate of error; (5) whether the underlying theory or tech-

---

[16] See *Seeley v. Hamilton Beach / Proctor-Silex, Inc.*, 349 F. Supp. 2d 381 (N.D.N.Y. 2004), where homeowners sued a toaster manufacturer for negligence, strict products liability, and breach of warranties, seeking to recover damages for which they were not compensated by their insurer due to fire that allegedly resulted from toaster malfunction. The manufacturer moved to preclude testimony of the homeowners' proposed expert witness. The case, in the process of denying the defendant's motion, provides a very detailed discussion of the *Daubert* and *Kumho Tire* cases in the context of engineering expertise. See also *Cooper Tire & Rubber Co. v. Mendez*, 155 S.W.3d 382 (Tex. App. 2004) for an even more extensive discussion of the basic *Frye, Daubert,* and *Kumho Tire* requirements.

[17] 143 S.W.3d 107 (Tex. App. 2004).

nique has been generally accepted as valid by the relevant scientific community; and (6) the nonjudicial uses that have been made of the theory or technique.[18]

On appeal, the manufacturer defendant contended that the expert's opinions were not reliable because none of the *Robinson/Daubert* factors were satisfied, and that Ochs offered nothing to establish the reliability of "his naked opinion." Ochs's opinion was based on demonstrable facts, which he observed either by touch or visually. He stated that tire manufacturers use certain failure analysis techniques and principles to adjust warranty claims, including (1) examination of the tire's exposed surfaces to determine the tire's condition, (2) whether those conditions included abuse, and (3) an examination of exposed surfaces to identify the surface's characteristics so that the characteristics can be related back to mechanisms such as abrasion or polishing. He testified there were a number of generally accepted explanations for the type of separation that occurred in this tire, including (1) the circumstances under which the tire was used, (2) the operation of the tire in a overdeflected state due to either underinflating the tire for a given load or using proper inflation but applying an excessive load, (3) impact or trauma that causes a local fracture or failure of components in the belt that expands into a greater separation, (4) any of these conditions coupled with a manufacturing or design defect, (5) a design or manufacturing defect alone, or (6) operating the tire at an excessively high speed. He said his opinion was based on his experience, training, and background, as well as documents describing surface conditions and relating these conditions to materials used in construction of the tire. [19]

Despite the tire's age and condition, Ochs concluded that the tread separation resulted from a manufacturing defect. He testified the tire separated because of a lack of adhesion between the brass cable and the rubber over the cable, which he explained as follows. Poor adhesion allows the brass plating on the cable to separate from the rubber, which results in the cable ceasing to be part of the tire's structure. The cable separates, resulting in cracking and polishing of the cables. Exposed cable wires, the color of steel instead of brass, indicates polishing, i.e., that the brass has been rubbed away and this was the beginning of the separation. The separation continues through the spread of the tire, resulting in enough of an area opening up so that the tread and upper belt, through centrifugal force, begin to lift away from the lower belt and carcass of the tire. Ochs admitted he had never seen the specifications for this tire, he conducted no tests on the tire other than visual and tactile, and he was not relying on any of the docu-

---

[18] *See* E.I. du Pont de Nemours & Co. v. Robinson, 923 S.W.2d 549, 557 (Tex. 1995). However, in *Gammill v. Jack Williams Chev., Inc.*, 972 S.W.2d 713, 726 (Tex. 1998), the court held that the *Robinson* factors do not always apply to expert testimony because they do not always fit. "Experience alone may provide a sufficient basis for an expert's testimony in some cases, but it cannot do so in every case."

[19] *Rios*, 143 S.W.3d at 113-114.

ments in a "museum" that contains various information about tire failures.[20]

Goodyear asserted that Ochs's purely visual and tactile test was unreliable because his technique was entirely subjective. The court disagreed, observing that the issue was "not the reasonableness *in general* of a tire expert's use of a visual and tactile inspection to determine what caused the tire's tread to separate from its steel-belted carcass."[21] Instead, the court stated, "it [is] the reasonableness of using such an approach, along with [the expert's] particular method of analyzing the data thereby obtained, to draw a conclusion regarding *the particular matter to which the expert testimony was directly relevant.*"[22] Here, the court noted, as in that matter concerned the likelihood that a defect in the tire caused its tread to separate from its carcass. Also here, the relevant issue was whether the expert could reliably determine the cause of this tire's separation.

The court found that the analysis employed by the Court applied here. Ochs attempted to rule out other possible causes for the tread separation. However, the issue concerns Ochs's use of visual/tactile inspection to conclude that a manufacturing defect was present without any evidence in the record indicating that other experts in the industry use Ochs's methodology (the existence of steel wires with little to no coverage of rubber) to determine that a manufacturing defect exists, as opposed to a defect caused by the use and abuse of the tire over time. Ochs did not refer to any article or publication that specifically supported his approach. For these reasons, his testimony was not reliable and, therefore, amounted to no evidence of a manufacturing defect.[23] Goodyear argued that plaintiff expert John Crate was not qualified to render an opinion because he had no experience with tires outside the litigation setting. He also had no experience, education, or training in tire design, manufacture, or forensic analysis of tire treads.

Crate was a research scientist at the Georgia Institute of Technology in Atlanta, Georgia. He had a bachelor's degree in chemistry and a master's degree in polymer science and engineering. He received his master's degree in 2000. In the summer of 1991 before he began work at the Institute, he worked as an analytical chemist, which he did for about ten years, analyzing the failure of polymeric products and rubber. Although Crate's background included research generally into the adhesion properties of various materials, the court noted, none of his experience was specific to tires. He had no background in tires, and did not consider himself an expert on them. He admitted that the vast amount of his experience in failure analysis has been related to products other than tires. He had tested a tire only once, to determine the presence of foreign substances. None of the texts upon which

---

[20] *Id.* at 114

[21] *Id.* (*quoting* Kumho Tire Co. v. Carmichael, 526 U.S. 137, 153-54 (1999)).

[22] *Kumho Tire*, 526 U.S. at 154.

[23] *Rios*, 143 S.W.3d at 115.

he relied to give his opinion in this case were specific to tires. Instead, the court observed, the focus of the texts were adhesion, failure, and fracture surfaces generated on various surfaces.[24]

He had never done any studies to determine the effects of aging, puncture holes, torn or damaged beads, patched tires, and overloaded tires. Although his background may have enabled Crate to discuss adhesion failures generally, he was not qualified to opine on the specifics of the actual subject matter for which he was called to testify: whether the Rios's tire failed because of an adhesion defect present at the time of manufacture. Accordingly, the court held that Crate was not qualified as an expert in the field of tire failure analysis; therefore, his testimony amounts to legally insufficient evidence of a manufacturing defect.[25]

§ 13.05 TESTING ALTERNATIVES IN UNIT DEFECT CASES

Short of requiring expert witnesses to unrealistically replicate high tech laboratories to test their opinions, just what can post-*Daubert* trial courts require the testifying expert to do other than closely review the state of the art literature and come up with a supportable opinion? This issue is the latest twist in the progression of the *Daubert* principles through the *Joiner* and *Kumho Tire* progression.[26]

This requirement in design defect cases must be distinguished from cases alleging a unit defect case, where the defect allegation refers only to the specific unit used by the plaintiff. An example would be a skateboard with a defective wheel attaching apparatus not typical of the product line. The distinction was discussed in the recent decision of *The Hartford Insurance Company v. Broan-Nutone LLC*,[27] a subrogation action arising from a fire originating in an apartment stove. The court addressed the issue of requiring experts who proffer an alternative design in a design defect case to present evidence that it was tested. The court observed that given the importance of testing alternative designs when alleging a design defect, plaintiffs have failed to provide sufficient evidence to support a claim under that theory. However, the court noted, plaintiffs' response to the motion for summary judgment indicated that they were actually alleging a manufacturing defect, not a design defect. Therefore, the importance of testing an alternative design did not apply, since Hartford and State Farm alleged there was a failure specific to the product that gave rise to the alleged injury — an electrical malfunction in the range hood due to improper wiring

---

[24] *Id.*

[25] *Id.*

[26] *See* Chapter 8, Problems of Proof: Defect and Causation.

[27] 2004 U.S. Dist. LEXIS 6765 (N.D.Ill. 2004).

by defendant. The experts' opinions finding the origin of the fire to be the range hood and the cause of the fire to be an electrical malfunction in the hood, certainly supported plaintiffs' allegations. The lack of testing by Agosti and Anderson did not render their opinions inadmissible.

In design defect cases, where some aspect of the manufacture and sale of the product is singled out but is common to all product units, current judicial rulings are expecting something more than a bare opinion from an expert that a feasible alternative design was available to the manufacturer. A recent trend, originating in the Seventh Circuit Court of Appeals, is requiring that the expert, before he will be allowed to proffer an opinion on a safer alternative design, present evidence that any such alternative was *actually tested* by the expert. Courts have not been specific about just what any *testing* might consist of. Obviously it would be impossible to require an expert to maintain a state-of-the-art research and design facility or to engage in independent drug or chemical research in order to proffer an opinion about safer alternative warnings. In failure to warn or instruct cases, is submission to standards setting groups, or existing federal or state regulatory agencies for approval a realistic requirement? On the other hand, simple justice would seem to require that costly corporate research and development efforts of product manufacturers not be adequately challenged on the basis of a bare opinion by an expert. This issue does not arise in manufacturing defect cases, where the existence of an alternative design does not arise.[28]

§ 13.06 TESTING ALTERNATIVES IN DESIGN DEFECT CASES

This very practical post-*Daubert* question was recently addressed in the 2005 federal district court opinion in the case *Phillips v. The Raymond Corporation*,[29] where, following the removal of a worker's products liability action against a forklift manufacturer, the parties moved to strike the opposing party's experts. The federal district court ruled that a mechanical engineer's testimony regarding an alternate rear door design for a doorless stand-up forklift was inadmissible, but that a biomechanical engineer's testimony was admissible for the limited purpose of determining how a worker sustained his leg injuries. The latter opinion, however, was not admissible to determine what the mechanism of worker's injury would have been if the

---

[28] *See also* Allstate Ins. Co. v. Maytag Corp., 1999 U.S. Dist. LEXIS 5083 (N.D. Ill. 1999) (*quoting* Cummins v. Lyle Industries, 93 F.3d 362, 369 (7th Cir.1996)) ("[T]esting is not 'an absolute prerequisite to the admissibility of expert testimony'.") The Seventh Circuit has emphasized that a court's inquiry into the reliability of an expert's opinion should be flexible and that the factors of reliability listed in *Daubert* should not be viewed as an exhaustive list. *See Bourelle v. Crown Equipment Corp.*, 220 F.3d 532, 536 (7th Cir. 2000); *United States v. Vitek Supply Corp.*, 144 F.3d 476, 485 (7th Cir.1998)

[29] 364 F. Supp. 2d 730 (N.D. Ill. 2005).

forklift was equipped with mechanical engineer's alternative design feature. The action arose out of an accident in which one Phillips was involved while working on a forklift manufactured by Raymond.[30]

Phillips and Raymond sought to introduce the testimony of two experts each. Each party moved to strike the opposing party's experts.

Phillips was employed at the Jewel Food Stores warehouse in Melrose Park, Illinois and was operating a stand-up forklift in connection with his normal work duties. He was driving a Model 31i forklift manufactured by Raymond, which was a stand-up, rear-entry forklift. The forklift had a doorless opening in the back of the forklift through which the driver of the forklift would pass when entering or leaving the machine. Phillips claims that during his shift, while traveling in reverse, he unknowingly struck a "wood chip" with a wheel of the forklift. Given the small size of the forklift's wheels, the wood chip became pinned between the wheel and the floor, jamming the wheel's ability to revolve. Consequently, Phillips alleged, the forklift stopped suddenly, and he was ejected from the forklift onto the floor through the uncovered opening in the back of the forklift. Phillips landed in the path of the forklift. Although the forklift has a "dead-man pedal," which must be depressed for the forklift to be able to move (rendering it impossible, at least theoretically, to have a pilotless, runaway forklift), the forklift's momentum carried it over the lower portion of Phillips's right leg. As a result of this trauma, doctors had to amputate Phillips's leg below the knee.

Phillips alleged that the forklift was unreasonably dangerous because there was a satisfactory alternate design, specifically a latching-rear door, which would have safeguarded Phillips from the foreseeable event of being thrown from the open operator's compartment when the forklift stopped suddenly and forcefully.

Phillips retained and offered John Sevart ("Sevart") and Dr. Y King Liu ("Liu") as experts. Sevart was a mechanical engineer who, among other things, has designed and tested rear entry forklifts, in particular, a latching-rear door that he maintains should have been present on the Raymond 31i forklift. Dr. Liu was a biomechanical engineer whose purpose was to testify about the "mechanism" or physics behind Phillips's injury and what the mechanics (or lack thereof) would have been had the forklift had a rear door.

Raymond's motion to strike any testimony alleged that Liu was unqualified to offer opinions relevant to a stand-up forklift and that both Sevart and Liu could offer nothing more than their subjective beliefs as to the cause of this accident, and propose the addition of John Sevart's allegedly

---

[30] Counts One and Three asserted that Raymond was strictly liable for Phillips's injury, while Counts Two and Four asserted that Raymond was negligent in its maintenance and sale of the forklift. Raymond successfully petitioned to remove the case from the Circuit Court of Cook County in April 1999.

safer alternative design, *which each speculates would have prevented the accident.*[31]

Raymond retained Edward Caulfield ("Caulfield"), a mechanical engineer, and Dr. Catherine Ford Corrigan ("Corrigan"), a biomechanical engineer, to support its contentions that the latching-rear door was not a viable or beneficial alternative design.

The court noted that governed the admission of expert testimony:

> If scientific, technical, or other specialized knowledge will assist the trier of fact to understand the evidence or to determine a fact in issue, a witness qualified as an expert by knowledge, skill, experience, training, or education, may testify thereto in the form of an opinion or otherwise if (1) the testimony is based upon sufficient facts or data, (2) the testimony is the product of reliable principles and methods, and (3) the witness has applied the principles and methods reliably to the facts of the case.

The court observed that an expert must possess sufficient specialized expertise to render his opinion on the topic reliable, as required by *Daubert.*[32] Of specific importance, the court found that an expert's competence in the general field at issue must extend to his specific testimony on the matter before the Court.[33] Once a court determines that an individual is qualified to be considered an expert, the *Raymond* court continued, it must apply a two-step analysis to determine whether the expert's opinion is admissible. First, a district court must ascertain whether the expert's testimony is reliable, and second, the court must determine whether the evidence assists the trier of fact in understanding the evidence or determining a fact in issue.[34] The question of admissibility, the court noted, asks whether "there is simply too great an analytical gap between the data and the opinion proffered."[35]

In order for the opinion to be considered scientific, and thus admissible, the court set out the familiar famous criteria to determine the question set forth in the 1993 U.S. Supreme Court opinion in *Daubert v. Merrell Dow Pharmaceuticals.*[36] The testimony must:

---

[31] Raymond's motion was substantially based on the Seventh Circuit's decision in *Dhillon v. Crown Controls Corp.*, 269 F.3d 865, 867-870 (7th Cir. 2001), which affirmed the exclusion of Sevart's testimony in a similar case.

[32] *See also* United States v. Allen, 390 F.3d 944, 949 (7th Cir. 2004) (discussing Rule 702)

[33] *See* Ty, Inc. v. Pub. Int'l., Ltd., No. 99 C 5565, 2004 WL 2359250, at *5 (N.D. Ill. Oct. 19, 2004); *accord* Carroll v. Otis Elevator Co., 896 F.2d 210, 212 (7th Cir. 1990).

[34] *See, e.g.,* Riach v. Manhattan Design Studio, No. 00 C 5883, 2001 U.S. Dist. LEXIS 15480, at *9 (N.D. Ill. Sept. 25, 2001) (*quoting Daubert*, 509 U.S. at 590); *see also* Walker v. Soo Line R.R. Co., 208 F.3d 581, 587 (7th Cir. 2000)

[35] General Elec. v. Joiner, 522 U.S. 136, 146 (1997).

[36] 509 U.S. 579 (1993).

(1) be based upon sufficient facts or data; (2) be the product of reliable principles and methods; and (3) come from a witness who has applied the principles and methods reliably to the facts of the case. Factors that may illuminate the analysis include: (1) whether the theory or technique can be and has been verified by the scientific method through testing; (2) whether the theory or technique has been subject to peer review and publication, (3) the known or potential rate of error of the technique, and (4) whether the theory or technique has been generally accepted by the relevant scientific community. These factors are merely guides, however, and do not serve as a series of prerequisites; their applicability depends on the particular facts and circumstances of each case. Nonetheless, a court must focus on the principles and methodology, not on the substance generated by the methodology — the latter is the province of the jury.[37]

The court observed that a subset of *Daubert*-type expert cases concern alternate designs, where a party claims that a manufacturer should be liable because a safer, alternate design existed at the time of the accident than the one employed by the defendant's product. Alternative design cases, the court noted, often require potential experts to take into account certain factors, including the degree to which the alternative design is compatible with existing systems; the relative efficiency of the two designs; the short and long term maintenance costs associated with the alternative design; the ability of the purchaser to service and to maintain the alternative designs; the relative cost of installing the two designs; and the effect, if any, that the alternative design would have on the price of the machine.[38] Many of these alternative considerations, the *Raymond* court observed, are product- and manufacturer-specific and cannot be reliably determined without testing.[39]

The court began by examining expert Sevart's methodology. Sevart's expertise and methodology were extensively questioned in the Seventh Circuit, namely in *Dhillon v. Crown Controls Corp.*[40] In *Dhillon,* the court noted, the Seventh Circuit affirmed the trial court's exclusion of Sevart in a strict liability and negligence action, arising out of injuries sustained in a forklift accident, similar to this case. Sevart's proffered testimony and methodology were almost identical to his methodology and testimony in the *Phillips* case. His testimony was to the effect that the defendant's forklift was improperly designed because it did not come with a latching-rear door.[41]

---

[37] *Raymond* at *3. *See also Daubert*, 509 U.S. at 590-91.

[38] *See* Cummins v. Lyons Indus., 93 F.3d 362, 369 (7th Cir. 1996).

[39] *See* Dhillon v. Crown Controls Corp., 269 F.3d 865, 870 (7th Cir. 2001).

[40] 269 F.3d 865 (7th Cir. 2001).

[41] The *Phillips* court observed that in the *Dhillon* case, the Seventh Circuit was troubled by Sevart's utter lack of testing and professional rigor, *Dhillon,* 296 F.3d at 869-70, the fact that

The Phillips court found efforts by plaintiff to overcome Sevart's problems in *Dhillon* unavailing.[42] The court noted two unsuccessful attempts. The court found that the existence of a single patent application was not helpful to Phillips, as it was not indicative of any meaningful acceptance within a relevant scientific or design community. The Crown forklift with a rear door presented as a working alternative design the court observed, was for freezers only and not for general warehouse use. None of the trade magazines offered by Phillips discussed *latching*-rear doors, nor did they indicate that the rear doors are standard or non-optional features.[43] The manual presented, which was an *operator's manual* and not any design analysis, had no apparent relevance as related to forklift design. None of the materials presented, individually or collectively, would suggest that the sensible course was to depart from the path set forth in *Dhillon*.

As to the reliability of Sevart's methodology in concluding that Raymond's design was defective, the court noted several factors against acceptance by the court:

> Notwithstanding Sevart's rejection by the Seventh Circuit in *Dhillon*, Sevart performed no new tests for the instant case, instead relying on the tests previously criticized because they were done after Sevart reached his conclusions about the rear-door forklift. In addition, Phillips's briefs only discussed the conclusions of the tests, not their underlying methodology. Furthermore, Phillips's discussion of the egress time for a latching-rear door is misplaced, as escape is only one small, tangential issue. (D.E. 95 at 9-10.) To the extent it is relevant to Phillips's briefing, it may be that in this one

---

the tests he did were performed on a different type of forklift *after* Sevart formed his conclusions, *id.* at 870, and that Sevart did not perform any of the *Cummins* analysis for alternate design cases, *id.* at 870-71. Furthermore, Sevart did not favorably subject his methodology to any peer review and publication, nor could Sevart establish that his design had been accepted for general application by any manufacturer, regulatory body, or standards organization. *Id.*

[42] Phillips unsuccessfully attempts to overcome *Dhillon*'s damaging pronouncements. To attempt to refute Sevart's prior lack of general acceptance (his proposed design appears to have been overwhelming rejected by virtually everyone), Phillips cites to several publications and entities that purportedly support Sevart's assertion that latching-rear doors are generally accepted as necessary. He cites to the Swedish Board of Occupational Safety and Health, an unnamed patent applicant, a 1989 edition of a forklift operator's manual, trade magazines, ten (unnamed) forklift manufacturers who "provide a rear post or rear door at [sic] standard equipment," an uncited report from 1977, and the fact that Crown, another forklift manufacturer, makes a forklift with a rear door. (D.E. 95 at 5-6.) Finally, Phillips maintains that the American National Standards Institute's ("ANSI") overwhelming rejection of Sevart's proposed design is based on bias and fear, since the chairman of the committee "is a Raymond employee and 28 of the 31 members are employees of . . . entities who have a vested financial interests in resisting mandatory improvements for forklifts." *Id.* at 5.

[43] As for the "ten forklift manufacturers," alleged to have adopted Sevart's general design idea, the court found that claim *imprecise and unhelpful*, because they include forklifts with a "rear post," which was not at issue, and it was unclear how many, if any, of the ten manufacturers offered rear doors as opposed to rear posts. *Raymond Corporation*, at *4.

regard the latching-rear door does not make the forklift more dangerous, but that does not mean that a forklift without a latching-rear door is inherently unsafe or less safe overall than a forklift with a latching door.[44]

Simply put, the court concluded that Sevart had not persuaded it that any of the *Daubert* factors were met:

> There is no apparent peer review or publication of Sevart's methods. Sevart's "analysis" amounts to little more than a series of foregone and conclusory assertions that are not supported by serious documentation, peer review, or acceptable testing. Furthermore, Sevart's method did not include any testing to indicate whether his design would be feasible, and he never created or tested a prototype or other tangible demonstration of his design. Sevart's testing also appears to treat a rear door and a rear guard or post as interchangeable without any substantiation or justification. Additionally, Sevart did not conduct any new tests after the Seventh Circuit's decision in *Dhillon*, and in *Dhillon* the Court concluded that all his previous tests had occurred after he had already made up his mind about a rear door forklift design. It is difficult to understand how Sevart could seek to testify under such circumstances. Sevart also did not abide by the steps he himself believed a design engineer should take before reaching an opinion concerning a marketable and safe design.[45]

Moreover, the court continued, Sevart's methodology and design had not been generally accepted, and in fact, had been overwhelmingly and resoundingly rejected by the only design community discussed and he had not established that any other manufacturer offered his design as a standard feature.[46]

§ 13.07 QUALIFICATIONS TO TESTIFY AT TRIAL

The decision the case of *Phillips v. The Raymond Corporation*,[47] also addressed the important issue of an expert's qualifications to give a particular opinion, while otherwise acceptable as an expert in the general area of science or technology involved. The court next turned to the proffered testimony of the biomedical engineer Dr. Y King Liu. Dr. Liu was retained to address two points: (1) the mechanism of injury to Phillips as a result of the accident as it occurred and (2) what the extent and mechanism, if any, of Phillips's injury would have been had the forklift had a latching-rear door

---

[44] *Raymond Corporation* at *6.

[45] *Id.* at *8.

[46] *See* Cummins v. Lyons Indus., 93 F.3d 362, 369 (7th Cir. 1996).

[47] 364 F. Supp. 2d 730 (N.D. Ill. 2005).

of the type promoted and endorsed by Sevart. After reviewing the relevant information, the Court concluded that Dr. Liu could testify concerning the first issue, but he could not do so regarding the second, as it was derivative of the excluded Sevart testimony.

Raymond argued that although Liu was an experienced biomechanical engineer, he was not qualified to give testimony in this forklift design case because his expertise did not "fit" the facts of the present case. The court rejected this argument, finding that Dr. Liu was, in fact, perfectly qualified. He was a professor of biomechanical engineering, was the founder and president of the University of Northern California, and had testified at over 100 depositions or trials:

> While Liu may not have thorough experience with injuries resulting from forklifts, his knowledge and experience as a biomechanical engineer is enough for him to testify on the mechanics of the injury in this case. Liu need not be an expert in the specific machine involved with an injury if, taking the circumstances of the injury as true, he uses an appropriate methodology to discuss the extent and manner of the injury.[48]

Having determined that Liu was a qualified expert, the Court focused on whether his specific testimony was reliable. Raymond argued that Liu's testing was improperly "designed for the courtroom" since it discussed what the likely injuries would be when a body was ejected from a forklift, as opposed to replicating the facts of the case to determine whether a person would actually be ejected. The court held that Liu did not address whether Phillips reasonably could fall out of a forklift as he contends, but rather what would happen to a person if he were ejected from the forklift. Raymond was free to argue at trial that the jury should not put much weight in Liu's study since its results do not adequately shed light on the instant case before the trier of fact.

Raymond next argued that Liu's testimony was unreliable because it had not been the subject of any peer review or publication. This absence, however, was not determinative on the facts of this case. The court noted that the particular tests performed by Liu were specialized to the facts of this case as alleged by Phillips and thus were not worthy of industry-wide analysis or peer review. Without a further explanation of the connection between lack of publication and reliability *in this case,* the court could not determine the extent to which this factor had on the reliability of the methodologies used by Liu.

However, the court noted, it appeared that the potential rate of error of Liu's calculations were unknown, which weighed against admissibility:

> Apparently, for Liu to be able to determine the rate of error for his tests (thus helping to make them scientifically valid), he would

---

[48] *Raymond Corporation* at *8.

have had to engage in a "retrospective analysis." Liu did not conduct such a "retrospective analysis." Thus, Liu cannot provide a potential rate of error. This cuts against admissibility.[49]

An additional factor undercutting the admissiblity of Lilly's testimony was the Daubert factor that the science upon which the opinion was based was generally accepted in the scientific community. Phillips argued that Liu's testing met all the standards of the Society of Automotive Engineers (SAE) and the International Organization for Standardization (ISO), asserting that "the testing performed by Dr. Liu has been accepted in the industry as the gold standard in evaluating the biomechanical forces on the human body in crashes. (Appendix A1)." The court observed that nonetheless, Dr. Liu provided nothing more than his own opinion as to the acceptability of his own tests. It would have been helpful, the court observed, if Phillips had demonstrated what the SAE or ISO standards were, noting that unsubstantiated testimony, such as presented here, did not ensure that the experts's opinion had a reliable basis in knowledge and experience of his discipline.[50]

Nevertheless, the *Phillips* court, emphasizing that district courts were not hidebound to the *Daubert* factors, concluded that Dr. Liu's tests were very basic, using straightforward (albeit somewhat intuitive) procedures to arrive at a general conclusion, regardless of whether they are actually "the gold standard." While concluding that Phillips should have better supported his allegation that Liu's methods were in accordance with the "gold standard of the industry," given the simplicity of the issue to be addressed and the tests Liu conducted, the court found Liu passed the *Daubert* standard for the limited purpose of determining, in his opinion, how Phillips sustained his leg injuries.[51]

Since Liu's tests were sufficiently reliable, albeit barely, the Court turned to the second admissibility prong: determining whether the testimony can help the trier of fact to understand the evidence. The Court concluded that the trier of fact may or may not agree with his view of how Phillips injured his leg, but that it would be up to the trier of fact to assess, in light of the flaws Raymond believes it has identified, what significance to place on Dr. Liu's testimony.

In contrast, the Court did not find Liu's testimony relevant with regards to his second charge: determining what the mechanism of Phillips's injury would have been if the forklift was equipped with Sevart's latching-rear door. The court held that since the ultimate issue and all germane tests were

---

[49] *Raymond Corporation* at *9.

[50] *See* Deimer v. Cincinnati Sub-Zero Prods., Inc., 58 F.3d 341, 345 (7th Cir. 1995). *See also* Chapman v. Maytag Corp., 297 F.3d 682, 688 (7th Cir. 2002).

[51] *Raymond Corporation* at *9.

premised on and relied on Sevart's findings and proposals, which had been found to be inherently unreliable and inadmissible, it would be affirmatively unhelpful for Liu to offer testimony discussing tests on an essentially non-existent alternative design. Therefore, Raymond's motion to strike Liu's testimony was granted with regard to any statements he might make concerning hypothetical injuries (or lack thereof) relating to Sevart's testimony and design. Raymond's motion was denied as to Liu's explanation of the mechanism of Phillips's actual injury in the case with the Raymond forklift.

Phillips then moved to exclude Raymond Corporation expert witnesses Dr. Catherine Ford Corrigan and Dr. Edward Caulfield.

Raymond sought to introduce the testimony of Dr. Catherine Ford Corrigan, a biomechanical engineer, to evaluate, from a biomechanical perspective, the nature of Phillips's injuries, the mechanism of his injury and the occupant kinematics to reconstruct the accident. She would also analyze the biomechanical issues surrounding the existence of a rear door for the Raymond 31i-DR45, the type of forklift involved in Phillips's accident. On the first basic qualifications issue, background, and specialized training and experience, Dr. Corrigan passed with flying colors:

> Corrigan's qualifications entitled her to testify about the two afore-mentioned areas. Corrigan had a Ph.D. in medical engineering, after participating in a combined doctoral program at Harvard and the Massachusetts Institute of Technology ("MIT"), and she also obtained a masters degree in mechanical engineering from MIT. She is currently the Principal Engineer in the Biomechanics Practice at Exponent Failure Analysis Associates, where she specializes in human tolerance, occupant kinematics, bone and fracture mechanics, and rigid body mechanics. She also serves as a visiting Lecturer at Princeton University. In addition to being member of various biomechanical societies, Corrigan is a reviewer for the Journal of Biomechanics. She has also published multiple articles concerning bone mechanics and the mechanism of injuries.[52]

Given this extensive experience, the court concluded, Corrigan was qualified, overall, to testify about Phillips's injury and related biomechanical issues.

As far as the acceptability of her particular opinions in the instant case, the court then turned to the reliability of the scientific methodology used to support her opinions. The court noted that Corrigan reviewed roughly twenty-nine categories of documents that were sent to her, including accident statements, the reports of Sevart and Liu, diagrams of the accident site, other experts' inspection and testing notes, various regulations, photos and testing data from Dr. Liu's testing, and Phillips's medical records and radiographs. The court found that Dr. Corrigan was qualified to analyze

---

[52] *Id.* at *10.

these documents given both her education and her extensive training in radiological anatomy. She had also, through her associates, inspected and took measurements of two exemplar Model 31i forklifts, using this information to study the geometry of the Raymond forklift and how it interacted with injury mechanisms. Furthermore, the court observed, Dr. Corrigan reviewed a considerable amount of medical literature. On the issue of the alternative design of a rear door, the court observed, Dr Corrigan used computer simulations and historical testing of stand-up rear entry forklifts regarding alternative designs. Finally, the court concluded, she had applied all this information to this case using her experience, training, knowledge, and understanding of principles of human tolerance, biomechanics and physics in order to reach her conclusions.[53]

Phillips objected on the basis that, as opposed to adopting any specific, scientifically valid, biomechanical method, Corrigan relied on mere "background and experience" and impermissible factors, thus rendering Corrigan's opinion nothing more than *ipse dixit*. The Court respectfully disagreed:

> First, the process of analyzing assembled data while using experience to interpret the data is not illicit; an expert need not actively conduct his or her own tests to have a valid methodology. Thus, Corrigan's review of others' human testing was a valid methodology that legitimately led to her conclusion that the operator, under the same or similar circumstances described by Phillips, could not have been forcibly ejected from the forklift.[54]

> Second, Phillips maintains that Corrigan failed to engage in an objective analysis by improperly reaching opinions on witnesses' credibility, namely by concluding that the version of events Phillips alleges did not and could not have happened. However, it was not improper for Corrigan to have subjected Phillips's version of the facts to a rigorous analysis. Coming to her conclusion, Corrigan relied on objective analysis, test results, and medical records. As a result, she came to a conclusion at odds with Phillips's testimony and theory of the case. This version may or may not be accepted by the jury, and Phillips is certainly free to attempt to undermine Dr. Corrigan by cross-examining her. But Phillips's objection to Corrigan was not well taken. Finally, Phillips questioned the accuracy of Corrigan's conclusions. However, the miscalculations and inaccu-

---

[53] *Id.* at *11.

[54] *Id.* The court cited *Clark v. Takata Corp.*, 192 F.3d 750, 758 (7th Cir.1999) (holding that either "hands-on testing" or "review of experimental, statistical, or other scientific data generated by others in the field" may suffice as a reasonable methodology upon which to base an opinion).

racies Phillips contends he has identified go to the weight of the evidence and not its admissibility. They are not a basis to exclude Corrigan.[55]

Phillips next sought to exclude Dr. Edward Caulfield, President and Chief Technical Officer of Packer Engineering, Inc., retained to investigate Phillips's accident and to assist with relevant technical issues. Specifically, Caulfield reviewed the background file, conducted multiple inspections and analyses of the accident site, and conducted multiple tests of forklifts and human tolerance. He concluded that the design and manufacture of the Raymond forklift did not cause the accident.[56]

As far as basic qualifications to give any opinion, Dr. Caulfield was found to be more than qualified to testify as an expert. He had a Ph.D. in Theoretical and Applied Mechanics from the University of Illinois and served as an assistant professor in the Department of Mechanical Engineering at the University of Illinois. He had twenty-five years of industrial experience, had published multiple articles, and had served and been qualified as an expert many times.[57]

Most relevant to the instant motion the court determined were three general categories of tests Caulfield conducted: (1) five tests and an informal survey in 1987 whose purpose was to "quantify and measure" the injury levels "if a person were to go off a dock in a forklift and stayed with the machine during the off the dock event and not step off"; (2) a 2000 test essentially identical to the one Caulfield conducted in 1987; and (3) a test in 2003 designed to replicate Phillips's accident scenario to "determine whether relative displacement of the operator . . . occurred as a result of collisions" with wooden objects on the floor.

Phillips argued that Caulfield's survey was unreliable and inadmissible, arguing the survey did not pass *Daubert* scrutiny. However, the court noted, Phillips's invocation of *Daubert* was misplaced, in that Raymond did not submit the survey, nor did Caulfield conduct the survey, to demonstrate any statistical significance. Rather, the court noted, its purpose was simply as generic background information, one piece of information that helped Caulfield form his opinions with regard to the 1987 testing as a whole. Raymond also had not claimed, and would not attempt, to offer the survey as a statistically conclusive sample.[58]

---

[55] *Raymond Corporation* at *12.

[56] *Raymond Corporation* at *12.

[57] *Id*. at *13.

[58] Phillips also argued that the 1987 and 2000 tests were unreliable, claiming that Caulfield failed to consider certain facts (such as human reaction time), relied heavily on the allegedly infirm survey, did not subscribe to an acceptable methodology, and that the tests did not sufficiently fit the facts of the case. The court noted that Phillips provided no factual support for his assertion that the survey played a commanding role in the 1987 test or that that the

As far as the tests utilized by Caulfield, the court found that they were in fact relevant. That the 1987 and 2000 tests concerned step off or off-the-dock accident while the instant case did not, was not material. When taking into account an alternative design, such as a latching-rear door, the district court noted, the Seventh Circuit required that the parties should be cognizant of the entire impact of the new design,[59] Off-the-dock accidents appear to be a foreseeable occurrence in the industry, and thus should factor into any consideration of the net benefit of a new design. In sum, the court concluded:

> Caulfield's methods and results were discernible, clear, and rooted in real science. Put differently, they were empirically testable and "intellectually rigorous."[60] As such, they were unlikely to give the jury a misguided impression, especially since Phillips could question vigorously Caulfield's results as he saw fit, and Raymond will almost certainly try to bolster Caulfield's testimony by demonstrating how the figures are allegedly calculated correctly. This was all a matter of the weight of the testimony, not its admissibility. Consequently, Phillips's motion to strike Caulfield's testimony was denied.[61]

In *Clark v. Safety-Kleen Corp.*,[62] a 2004 New Jersey Supreme Court decision, an auto mechanic brought a defective design and inadequate warning products liability action against the manufacturer of a carburetor cleaner after he used the cleaner and developed an infection in a cut on his finger, which subsequently led to loss of substantial function in the finger. The Supreme Court held that a research chemist was sufficiently qualified to give expert testimony regarding basic toxicological effects that cresylic acid, which was contained in cleaner, had on human skin; that the research chemist's opinion testimony, in which the chemist testified how cresylic acid got into mechanic's skin, was admissible; and that a research chemist's testimony, that hospitals do not typically have access to apparatuses to determine nature or chemical composition of an irritant that gets into an open wound, was also admissible.

The question in the case centered on the admissibility of testimony from non-physicians regarding medical causation in a products liability action. The New Jersey Supreme Court ruled that the admissibility of testimony from non-physicians regarding medical causation in a products liability action will depend on the facts and on the non-physician's qualifications. As

---

entire test was somehow meaningfully tainted so as to render Caulfield's testimony inadmissible. Furthermore, Phillips's quarrels with Caulfield's inclusion or rejection of certain factors or calculations (such as grip strength), implicated his conclusions and were thus properly left for exploration through cross-examination. *Id.* at *13.

[59] Cummins v. Lyons Indus., 93 F.3d 362, 369 (7th Cir. 1996).

[60] *Citing Kumho Tire*, 526 U.S. at 139, 152 (1999).

[61] *Raymond Corporation* at *14.

[62] 845 A.2d 587 (N.J. 2004).

in any case involving the admissibility of such testimony, the preliminary requirements are that she must be sufficiently qualified by education, knowledge, training, and experience in the specific field of science, and she must possess a demonstrated professional capability to assess the scientific significance of the underlying data and information, to apply the scientific methodology, and to explain the bases for the opinion reached.[63]

Here the court found that a proffered research chemist was sufficiently qualified to give expert testimony regarding basic toxicological effects that cresylic acid, which was contained in carburetor cleaner used by auto mechanic, had on human skin. The chemist testified that he had engaged in research relating to various chemicals and worked with cresylic acid and observed the damage that it could do to human tissue. The chemist testified to the scientific materials that he consulted in preparation for the case and stated that they were the types of data an expert in his field would rely on in formulating an opinion.[64]

A similar result was had in *Smalls v. Pittsburgh-Corning Corp.*,[65] a Pennsylvania decision, where a former employee who in course of employment prior to retirement handled valve-packing products containing asbestos, filed a personal injury lawsuit against defendant/former employer, claiming asbestos-related injuries. The court found that the expert was a board-certified as pulmonary specialist and could testify about relationship between breathing asbestos and development of asbestos-related disease. The court also allowed the testimony by the expert that "Each and every breath of asbestos fibers is [a] significant and substantial contributing factor to the asbestos related disease that Mr. Smalls has."[66]

In *Nemir v. Mitsubishi Motors Corp.*, 381 F.3d 540 (6th Cir. 2004), a driver who was injured in an automobile accident brought a products liability suit against automobile manufacturers, alleging that the seatbelt

---

[63] *See* FED. R. EVID. 702.

[64] *See also* Cottrell, Inc. v. Williams, 596 S.E.2d 789 (Ga. Ct. App. 2004). (Engineer whose education, training and experience had familiarized him with the flammability rating of glass cleaner kept by driver in his truck cab properly was permitted to testify as expert and to offer an opinion about that flammability rating in a products liability action brought by truck driver, who alleged that a fire in his truck cab was triggered by wire hanger coming in contact with exposed switch that auto equipment manufacturer had installed in cab.)

[65] 843 A.2d 410 (Pa. Super. Ct. 2004).

[66] See also, *Bitler v. A.O. Smith Corp.*, 391 F.3d 1114 (10th Cir. 2004), where the victim of a propane gas water heater explosion brought products liability action in state court against water heater manufacturer and installer of heater and propane piping. The 10th Circuit upheld a verdict against the manufacturer, finding that a fire investigator's proffered testimony, namely, that the water heater was source of the explosion, was based on sufficiently reliable methodology, and that an accident investigator's proffered testimony that gas leak was caused by copper sulfide contamination on water heater's safety valve seat was also reliable. The court also found that evidence of prior accidents involving unscreened safety valves was admissible, notwithstanding fact that the safety valve involved in the instant explosion contained a mesh screen.

was defectively designed and that dashboard seatbelt light failed to warn him that seatbelt was only partially latched. The Sixth Circuit Court of Appeals held that a protective order prohibiting driver's counsel from unilaterally contacting any of manufacturer's complaining consumers was not warranted; that the District Court's failure to rule on driver's motion for sanctions against manufacturer for obstructing discovery required remand, that the testimony of the driver's automotive safety engineer was admissible, and that the driver was erroneously prevented from introducing relevant impeachment evidence.

The plaintiff's automotive safety engineer's testimony about his testing of seat belt latching mechanism was relevant, and therefore admissible. The engineer's method of testing mechanism, i.e., purposeful manipulation of buckle at varying speeds and angles, was appropriate for his conclusion that defective mechanism caused driver's injuries.

The court also found that the plaintiff was entitled to call court-appointed expert to testify in the case. The expert's testimony would have corroborated plaintiff's automotive safety engineer's testimony that the defective seat belt latching mechanism caused the driver's injuries, and that even infrequent partial latching of mechanism could constitute a serious defect would have bolstered weight afforded to engineer's research, which found partial engagement in two out of 20 attempts.

The driver was erroneously prevented from introducing relevant impeachment evidence when, as the driver attempted to impeach manufacturer's expert by confronting him with excerpt from a book co-authored by another expert retained by manufacturer the court instructed him to save such questioning for authoring expert's upcoming testimony, and then precluded such questioning on ground that it was outside scope of authoring expert's direct testimony, where excerpt was offered to impeach earlier-testifying expert, not to have him comment on authoring expert's upcoming testimony.[67]

§ 13.08 SOURCES REASONABLY RELIED UPON BY EXPERTS IN THE FIELD

In the 2004 South Dakota opinion in *First Premier Bank v. Kolcraft Enterprises, Inc.*,[68] an infant's guardian ad litem brought claims against manufacturer of a playpen for defective and unreasonably dangerous design and failure to warn, resulting in the infant's severe burns from fire. Also challenged was the product's use of foam pads which were not fire retardant. The trial court entered judgment on the jury's verdict for manufacturer.

---

[67] *See* FED. R. EVID. 706. See also Cottrell, Inc. v. Williams, 596 S.E.2d 789 (Ga. Ct. App. 2004).

[68] 686 N.W.2d 430 (S.D. 2004).

The South Dakota Supreme Court ruled that a playpen manufacturer's expert could base his opinion in the underlying products liability action, that dropping of cigarette or knocking off of cigarette ash when the infant was placed in playpen was most likely cause of the fire, on the fact that infant's parents smoked, regardless of whether their smoking habits were admissible as evidence or were instead inadmissible hearsay. The fact that residents of the dwelling smoked was evidence of a type an expert could reasonably rely upon to form an opinion regarding the cause of a fire.

The fact that the fire inspector had ruled out cigarette butts as an ignition source for fire in playpen, because he could not find any cigarette butts in children's bedroom after the fire and because burn characteristics for playpen were inconsistent with cigarette ignition, did not preclude playpen manufacturer's expert from forming opinion, that the dropping of a cigarette or knocking off of cigarette ash when infant was placed in playpen was the most likely cause of the fire. The court found that the manufacturer's expert was not required to begin and end his analysis with the fire inspector's premise, but was instead was free to use his expertise to reach his own conclusion.

Peggy and Ken Boone, the infant's parents, were both smoking in the home on the day of the fire. Defendant Kolcraft established to the court's satisfaction that improper disposal of cigarettes was "a way of life in the Boone household." Photographs showed extensive smoking, overflowing ashtrays, and the improper disposal of cigarettes on windowsills and on floors. Terry Flakus, the Fire Inspector for Sioux Falls, however, ruled out cigarettes altogether as an ignition source because he could not find any cigarette butts in the children's bedroom after the fire, and the burn characteristics were inconsistent with a cigarette ignition. Based on that conclusion, plaintiff argued that no reliable foundation existed from which Kolcraft's expert, Robert Wargin, could state that careless cigarette smoking could have been the cause of the fire. Defense expert Wargin studied the burn patterns and other evidence and concluded that the point of origin for the fire was not the Playard, defendant's product, but some item within the playpen. Based on this conclusion, he could not rule out cigarette smoking as a cause of the fire. He found that the fire originated inside the playpen.[69]

In examining the Playard, he concluded that the playpen pad and fiberboard bottom showed that the fire was from the top down and not from under the playpen. Major fuel material for the fire consisted of pillows, a quilted comforter, a blanket, and clothing draped over the playpen. He believed that the urethane foam inside the playpen pad was not responsible for the spread of the fire. Less than thirty percent of both the pad and fiberboard bottom were consumed in the ten-minute fire. Finally, he deduced, through "process of elimination, the dropping of a cigarette or

---

[69] *Id.* at 445.

knocking off of cigarette ash when Daniel was placed in the Playard is the most likely cause of the fire." In sum, the court concluded, Wargin declined to begin and end his analysis on Inspector Flakus's premise that cigarette smoking was not the cause. The court found that Wargin was free to do so, and Kolcraft was free to present his opinion because there were sufficient facts to support it.

Plaintiff next contended that Wargin's testimony did not suffice to prove proximate cause. The court first noted that plaintiff, not Kolcraft, had the burden of proving proximate cause and that Wargin's testimony was offered to refute plaintiff's claim that the Playard was the source of the fire. Plaintiff raised the question of whether under a analysis, Wargin could have properly based his opinion on evidence of smoking in the Boone apartment?[70] The court noted that the question was whether a *plaintiff's* expert could testify when the methodology used was not generally accepted in the relevant scientific community, reasoning that proposed testimony must be supported by appropriate validation — i.e., "good grounds," based on what is known.[71] The focus, the *Daubert* court ruled, must be solely on principles and methodology, not on the conclusions that they generate. The present court noted that the *Daubert* court stated that vigorous cross-examination, presentation of contrary evidence, and careful instruction on the burden of proof are the traditional and appropriate means of attacking shaky but admissible evidence and that those conventional devices, rather than wholesale exclusion under an uncompromising "general acceptance" test, were the appropriate safeguards where the basis of scientific testimony meets the standard of Rule 702.[72]

The South Dakota court found that Wargin's testimony fit squarely within the Supreme Court's "traditional and appropriate means" of assailing plaintiff's expert testimony:

> Plaintiff would seemingly have us declare that one expert's opinion is invulnerable. Plaintiff argues that because other experts did not draw a definitive conclusion about the origin of the fire, one defense expert must be precluded from testifying on other causes of the fire. By his own testimony, Inspector Flakus must have initially considered the possibility of a cigarette causing the fire. He conducted a layer search of the burned area. During this search he attempted to locate possible causes. He stated that he did not find a cigarette butt; therefore, he believed careless cigarette disposal did not start the fire. Wargin did not stop with that hypothesis. He did not have the benefit of searching the area immediately after the fire. However, this does not mean that he had to accept all of Inspector

---

[70] Daubert v. Merrell Dow Pharmaceuticals, Inc., 509 U.S. 579 (1993).

[71] *Id.* at 590.

[72] *Id.*

Flakus's conclusions based on that search. He was free to use his expertise to reach his own conclusions. To Wargin, the absence of a cigarette butt only proved that a cigarette butt was not found.[73]

Federal Rule of Evidence 703 provides:

The facts or data in the particular case upon which an expert bases an opinion or inference may be those perceived by or made known to him at or before the hearing. If of a type reasonably relied upon by experts in the particular field in forming opinions or inferences upon the subject, the facts or data need not be admissible in evidence.[74] Here, the court ruled, the statute allowed Wargin to base his opinion on the fact that the Boones smoked, whether their smoking habits were admissible as evidence or were inadmissible hearsay. The only qualification was that the fact must be reasonably relied upon by other experts in the field. Surely, the *Kolcraft* court found, the fact that the residents of the apartment smoked was a reasonable basis from which to infer that smoking *may* have caused a fire. This inference was no less reasonable than an inference drawn by fire inspector Flakus that smoking *could not* have caused the fire because there was no evidence of smoking in a particular room despite evidence of smoking everywhere else in the apartment.[75]

---

[73] *First Premier Bank*, 686 N.W.2d at 445.

[74] *Id*. at 447.

[75] *Id*.

Chapter 14

DRAFTING THE COMPLAINT
AND DISCOVERY FOCUS

SYNOPSIS

§ 14.01 INTRODUCTION

It is not the purpose of this chapter to analyze the development and nuances of strict liability theory. That broad subject is comprehensively addressed in Chapters 1 through 10 in this book. This chapter will, instead, focus on the practical questions faced by plaintiff counsel in initiating a product liability lawsuit. A selection of Sample Complaints will illustrate the transition from products liability theory analysis to products liability litigation. In particular, it will stress the ongoing effect that decisions made in the initial filings have on each ensuing step in case preparation, especially during the discovery process. It is essential to realize that the acts or omissions of any named corporate defendant alleged as warranting negligence or strict liability findings, are to be proven, if at all, somewhere in a massive body of corporate documentation. This documentation will be accessible in relevant portions, during the discovery process, depending on the artfulness with which the complaint counts are drafted. There is a close relationship between the specific factual allegations of the complaint and the potential discovery of their documentary counterparts in corporate archives.

§ 14.02 STANDARD ALLEGATIONS IN THE PRODUCTS CASE

It is important that counsel realize the controlling importance of the complaint in the pre-trial process. A clearly drafted, technically correct complaint is one of the major keys to successful discovery, motions in limine and trial practice. During the entire pre-trial period and the course of the trial itself, this document will serve as the court's primary basis for deciding a wide variety of crucial issues.

The propriety of plaintiff's interrogatories, requests to admit fact, requests for documentation and defendant's motions in limine, are all resolved by reference to the language of the plaintiff's complaint. The same holds true for all proffers of evidence made by counsel during the trial of the case. Counsel can rest assured that corporate defense lawyers will go through the complaint with a fine-toothed comb searching for weaknesses with which to frustrate undeserved discovery or otherwise dampen plaintiff's efforts.

It is appropriate here to analyze the stock allegations that are present in any product liability case involving any product under any available theory of design liability. The following allegations may be tailored to counsel's specific product, company and occurrence facts:

(1) The defendant manufacturer was in the business of designing, producing, and marketing product lines of the type involved on, prior to and subsequent to the occurrence date, and in fact designed produced, and marketed the product unit at issue.

(2) The middleman (distributor-wholesaler-retailer) was in the business of distributing, wholesaling, or retailing product lines of the type involved on, prior to and subsequent to the occurrence date, and in fact distributed, wholesaled or retailed the product unit at issue.

(3) The plaintiff purchased the unit at the bottom of the vertical chain or came in contact with the unit by way of someone who did purchase it.

(4) The product unit was, when received by the purchaser and at the time of the occurrence, in substantially the same condition as when it left the hands of the manufacturer.

(5) The defendant manufacturer, distributor, wholesaler, or retailer had a duty to use due care in the design, manufacture, and marketing of such product so as not to expose purchasers or foreseeable users to an unreasonable risk of harm, and that such duty ran to the plaintiff as purchaser and/or foreseeable user.

(6) The defendant manufacturer, distributor, wholesaler, or retailer had an obligation to refrain from placing in the stream of commerce products which were in a defective condition unreasonably dangerous to purchasers and/or foreseeable users of such products and that such obligation was owed to plaintiff as purchaser and/or foreseeable user.

(7) The defendant breached the duty of care owed to plaintiff in one or all of the specified respects or placed in the stream of commerce the suspect product that was in a defective condition unreasonably dangerous in one or all of the specified respects.

(8) A statement that at all relevant times the plaintiff was using the product for its intended purpose.

(9) A brief description of the injury-producing event and injury and an allegation that such injury was a direct and proximate result of the aforementioned breaches of defendant's duty of care or corporate obligation.

(10) Ad damnum clause of statement of jurisdictional amount, as appropriate.

These allegations, with the important exception of item 7, are standard in products cases and need little other than minor factual adjustments to meet the needs of a particular case. The factual allegations of those subparagraphs constituting item 7, however, are the heart of plaintiff's case. Each serve as a separate basis for recovery. They are determinative of the extent of the discovery and the admissibility of the defect evidence that plaintiff offers at the trial.

§ 14.03 SAMPLE COMPLAINT: PRESSURIZED BEVERAGE CANISTER

The sections to follow will analyze the drafting of a hypothetical four-count product liability complaint directed against four manufacturers resulting from the explosion of a pressurized beverage container that resulted in the loss of an eye by an employee of a soft drink distributor.

In this factual scenario, plaintiff John Denton, an employee of the Benton Brothers Beverage Company, was leaning over a pallet of empty containers in the process of releasing the remaining pressure and removing the beverage identification labels, prior to the containers' sterilization and reuse down the line. As he was doing this, one of the containers nozzle fittings exploded next to his head, resulting in the loss of Denton's eye.

The first defendant is the The Fremantle Tire & Rubber Company, the primary manufacturer of the complete pressurized beverage container. The second defendant is the Polymer Plastic Corporation, the manufacturer of

the plastic cap or closure that struck plaintiff's eye as a result of the explosion. The third defendant is the Apex Grinding Company, manufacturer of the pressure release or relief mechanism for incorporation into the stainless steel beverage canister involved herein. Finally, the fourth defendant is the Premier Plastic Corporation, manufacturer of a plastic material known as BasicPro V56-77, that was incorporated into the plastic cap or closure on the pressurized stainless steel beverage canister involved in the *Denton* case.

The complaint here contains two counts against each defendant: negligence and strict liability. The complaint example is reduced here for ease of illustration and example. Products liability complaints typically plead multiple counts grounded in the products theories discussed in detail in Part I of this book. Sample paragraphs will be given to cover each of the standard allegations in such complaints set out below. Extended treatment will be given to the allegations of product defect and their centrality in the hard-fought discovery process.

§ 14.04 DISTRIBUTIVE CHAIN

The allegations necessary to adequately identify the defendants' participation in the vertical chain of distribution are simply stated by examining selections from the Sample Complaint of *Denton v. The Freemantle Tire and Rubber Company et al.*:

- On and prior to January 29, 2001, defendant, **THE FREMANTLE TIRE & RUBBER COMPANY**, designed, manufactured, maintained, assembled, distributed and sold a pressurized stainless steel beverage canister, which was offered for sale to the public, a unit of which is the pressurized stainless steel beverage canister involved in this case.

- On and prior to January 29, 2001, defendant, **POLYMER PLASTIC COMPANY**, located in Cuyahoga Falls, Ohio, designed, manufactured, maintained, assembled, distributed and sold plastic caps or closures for installation in pressurized stainless steel beverage canisters, an individual unit of which caps or closures was installed in the pressurized stainless steel beverage canister involved in this case.

- On and prior to January 29, 2001, defendant, **APEX GRINDING COMPANY**, located in Mogadore, Ohio, designed, manufactured, maintained, assembled, distributed and sold a pressure release or relief mechanism for incorporation into stainless steel beverage canisters, an individual unit of which mechanism was installed in the pressurized stainless steel beverage canister involved in this case.

- On and prior to January 29, 2001, defendant, **PREMIER PLAS-TIC CORPORATION**, designed, manufactured, maintained, assembled, distributed and sold a plastic material known as BasicPro V56-77, for incorporation into the plastic cap or closure on pressurized stainless steel beverage canisters, which plastic was incorporated into the plastic cap or closure on the pressurized stainless steel beverage canister involved in this case.

§ 14.05 ABSENCE OF ALTERATION OR MODIFICATION

In order to meet the requirement of Section 402A of the Restatement of Torts (2d) and (3d) that the product at the time of the injury was in substantially the same condition as when it left the hands of the "seller," an optional pleading might state:

- That no changes or alterations were made to said canister or any of its component parts prior to its purchase by plaintiff's employer or John Denton or anyone on their behalf prior to or on the date of January 29, 2001, and that said pressurized canister was in substantially the same condition on such date as when it and its component parts left the hands of the Defendant Freemantle Tire and Rubber Company.

§ 14.06 DEFENDANT'S DUTY OR OBLIGATION

A statement of defendant's responsibility to foreseeable consumers, users and bystanders is essential in a negligence count and appropriate in a count based on strict liability.

[NEGLIGENCE]

- The Defendants The FREMANTLE TIRE & RUBBER COMPANY, POLYMER PLASTIC COMPANY, APEX GRINDING COMPANY, and PREMIER PLASTIC CORPORATION, and each of them owned a duty of due care in the design, testing, manufacture and marketing of the aforesaid pressurized beverage canister involved in this cases or any of its component parts such as the plastic caps or closures, pressure release or relief mechanisms, for installation in pressurized stainless steel beverage canisters, or a plastic material known as BasicPro V56-77, used in any component part, to avoid unreasonable risk of death or injury to purchasers or foreseeable users of such pressurized beverage canisters. Said duty was owed to Plaintiff John Denton as a foreseeable purchaser or user of said canister.

[FAILURE TO WARN]

- The Defendants The FREMANTLE TIRE & RUBBER COMPANY, POLYMER PLASTIC COMPANY, APEX GRINDING COMPANY, and PREMIER PLASTIC CORPORATION, and each of them breached a duty of

due care to Plaintiff John Denton in that said canister was not reasonably safe in that defendants, and each of them, failed to provide adequate warnings of the dangers involved in the handling of said canister, including, but not limited to the over pressurization of the canister and the resultant shattering or exploding of the plastic closure or cap or other portions of said canister.

[STRICT LIABILITY VERSION]

• The Defendants The FREMANTLE TIRE & RUBBER COMPANY, POLYMER PLASTIC COMPANY, APEX GRINDING COMPANY, and PREMIER PLASTIC CORPORATION, and each of them, at all relevant times mentioned herein, had an obligation to refrain from placing in the stream of commerce products which were in a defective condition unreasonably dangerous to foreseeable purchasers and users of their products, and to instruct and warn such users as to any such conditions. This obligation extended to the design, testing, manufacture and marketing of the aforesaid pressurized beverage canister involved in this cases or any of its component parts such as the plastic caps or closures, pressure release or relief mechanisms, for installation in pressurized stainless steel beverage canisters, or a plastic material known as BasicPro V56-77, used in any component part, to avoid risk of death or injury to purchasers or foreseeable users of such pressurized beverage canisters. Said duty was owed to Plaintiff John Denton as a foreseeable purchaser or user of said canister.

[FAILURE TO WARN]

• The Defendants The FREMANTLE TIRE & RUBBER COMPANY, POLYMER PLASTIC COMPANY, APEX GRINDING COMPANY, and PREMIER PLASTIC CORPORATION, and each of them breached an obligation to Plaintiff John Denton in that said canister was not reasonably safe for its intended use in that defendants, and each of them, failed to provide adequate warnings of the dangers involved in the handling of said canister, including, but not limited to the over pressurization of the canister and the resultant shattering or exploding of the plastic closure or cap or other portions of said canister.

§ 14.07 INTENDED USE

A statement that the product was being used for its intended purpose is required under both negligence and strict liability theories:

• That at all relevant times herein, Plaintiff John Denton was using said pressurized beverage canister for the purposes for which it was intended by Defendants.

§ 14.08 INJURY-PRODUCING EVENT

A brief statement of the injury-producing event, is required. These paragraphs should contain sufficient information to sketch the outlines of the occurrence without binding plaintiff to fine points of detail that could be problematic as judicial admissions later in the case.

• Plaintiff John Denton, while an employee of the Benton Brothers Beverage Company, was leaning over a pallet of empty pressurized beverage containers in the process of releasing the remaining pressure and removing the beverage identification labels, prior to the containers sterilization and reuse down the line. As he was doing this one of the nozzle fittings exploded next to his head, resulting in the loss of Denton's eye. The container was manufactured in whole or part by the Defendants The FREMANTLE TIRE & RUBBER COMPANY, POLYMER PLASTIC COMPANY, APEX GRINDING COMPANY, and PREMIER PLASTIC CORPORATION, and each of them.

§ 14.09 BREACH OF DUTY OR OBLIGATION: SETTING OUT THE DEFECT MODES

These sub-paragraphs inform both the court and defense counsel what it is that plaintiff deems is wrong with the suspect product and how that defect caused Plaintiff's injury. As such, these allegations must be carefully drawn to reach a balance between the absence of any true description of product failings and a too-detailed description of them that may later limit plaintiff's full discovery efforts and evidentiary submissions at trial.

The allegations must set forth the basic defect modes involved in the case in clear terms. Allegations cannot be restricted to broad general allegations that the product was not "properly designed," was not "safe," was "defective," was not "adequately tested," or that defendant "failed to issue proper warnings or instructions." Allegations such as these are of little assistance to a court in attempting to determine the precise extent of plaintiff's right to examine internal corporate documents or whether to grant comprehensive defense motions in limine.

[FREEMANTLE TIRE AND RUBBER COMPANY]

• On and before January 29, 2001, and at the time the aforesaid canister left the control of defendant, THE FREMANTLE TIRE & RUBBER COMPANY, the canister was in a defective condition unreasonably dangerous in one or all of the following respects:

　　a. Said canister was not reasonably safe in design due to the substantial risk that the plastic closure or cap on said canister would shatter or explode;

b. Said canister was not reasonably safe in design due to inadequate pressure release or relief mechanisms to prevent the shattering or exploding of the plastic closure or cap or other portions of said canister;

c. Said canister was not reasonably safe in design due to inadequate mechanisms to prevent the over pressurization of said canister, thereby creating the risk of the shattering or exploding of the plastic closure or cap or other portions of said canister;

d. Said canister was not reasonably safe in that defendant, failed to provide adequate warnings of the dangers involved in the handling of said canister, including, but not limited to the over pressurization of the canister or the shattering or exploding of the plastic closure or cap or other portions of said canister.

[POLYMER PLASTIC COMPANY]

• On and before January 29, 2001, and at the time the aforesaid canister left the control of defendant, POLYMER PLASTIC COMPANY, the plastic cap or closure manufactured by defendant was in a defective condition unreasonably dangerous in one or all of the following respects:

a. Said plastic cap or closure was not reasonably safe in design due to the substantial risk that it would shatter or explode after being installed for purposes of capping or closing the pressurized stainless steel beverage canister involved in this case.

b. Said plastic cap or closure was not reasonably safe in design due to inadequate materials strength to withstand the over pressurization of said canister, thereby creating the risk of the shattering or exploding of the plastic cap or closure;

c. Said plastic cap or closure was not reasonably safe in that defendant, failed to provide adequate warnings of the dangers involved in the handling of said canister, including, but not limited to the over pressurization of such canister or the shattering or exploding of the plastic cap or closure or other portions of said canister.

[APEX GRINDING COMPANY]

• On and before January 29, 2001, and at the time the aforesaid canister left the control of defendant, APEX GRINDING, the aforesaid pressure release or relief mechanism was in a defective condition unreasonably dangerous in one or all of the following respects:

a. Said pressure release or relief mechanism was not reasonably safe in design due to inadequate pressure relief mechanisms to prevent the shattering or exploding of the plastic closure or cap or other portions of said pressure release mechanism;

b. Said pressure release or relief mechanism was not reasonably safe in design due to inadequate mechanisms to prevent the over pressurization

of said canister, thereby creating the risk of the shattering or exploding of the plastic closure or cap or other portions of said canister;

c. Said pressure release or relief mechanism was not reasonably safe in that defendant, failed to provide adequate warnings of the dangers involved in the handling of said pressure release or relief mechanism, including, but not limited to over pressurization of such canister or the shattering or exploding of the plastic closure or cap or other portions of said canister.

[POLYMER PLASTIC CORPORATION]

• On and before January 29, 2001, and at the time the aforesaid BasicPro V56-77 plastic left the control of defendant, the aforesaid BasicPro V56-77 plastic was in a defective condition unreasonably dangerous in one or all of the following respects:

a. Said BasicPro V56-77 plastic was not reasonably safe in design, when incorporated into caps or closures for pressurized beverage canisters, due to defendant's failure to provide adequate materials strength to prevent the shattering or exploding of the plastic cap or closure on pressurized beverage canister of the type involved in this case;

b. Said BasicPro V56-77 plastic was not reasonably safe in that defendant, failed to provide adequate warnings of the dangers involved in the utilization of said plastic for the manufacture of pressurized beverage canister caps or closures, including, but not limited to the over pressurization of such canister or the shattering or exploding of the plastic cap or closure.

§ 14.10 PROXIMATE CAUSE

The proximate cause allegation, linking the breach of duty or obligation to the occurrence facts, ties together all of the preceding allegations of the complaint.

• As a proximate result of one or all of the aforesaid conditions, plaintiff, JOHN DENTON, suffered and in the future will continue to suffer injuries of a personal and pecuniary nature.

§ 14.11 PUNITIVE DAMAGES

The punitive damage count is grounded in the callous and reckless manner in which defendant disregarded known risks to consumers. It is tied to the particular corporate failings alleged in the formal negligence and strict liability counts that precede it. The essential ingredients of a punitive damage count are a substantial risk of knowledge of serious risk and utter indifference to consumer safety in light of such risk. It is also grounded in improper motives, such as financial gain, in failing to instruct, warn or

properly design. A growing number of states have statutes controlling the allowance of a punitive damages count in a products liability case.

[PUNITIVE DAMAGES]

1. That plaintiff realleges, reaffirms and incorporates by reference herein, each and every allegation contained in Counts I-IV of this complaint.

2. That at all times mentioned herein, Defendants FREMANTLE TIRE & RUBBER COMPANY, POLYMER PLASTIC COMPANY, APEX GRINDING COMPANY, and PREMIER PLASTIC CORPORATION, and each of them, knew of the defective and dangerous conditions of the pressurized beverage container and its component parts and other defects as aforesaid. Defendants and each of them, were aware of their duties and obligations to consumers to provide safe products to them and/or warn such consumers of all known dangerous and defective conditions of said product.

3. Despite the Defendants' knowledge of the dangerous and defective conditions inherent in the Freemantle pressurized beverage container, Defendants and each of them callously, recklessly, willfully and wantonly failed to take appropriate steps to remedy the defects in said container or to warn Plaintiff of said dangers. Plaintiff alleges that the failure of the Defendants, and each of them, to remedy said defects and/or failure to warn consumers was solely the result of their desires for financial gain.

4. Plaintiff alleges that Defendants, and each of them, mass produced their respective products and that Defendants and each of them, knew of the numerous defective and dangerous conditions in said canisters. Despite their knowledge of said defects, and despite the extremely high risk of injury to user of such canisters, Defendants, and each of them, callously, recklessly, willfully and wantonly disregarded the state-of-the-art literature regarding safer designs, adequate testing, safer materials selection and safer construction methods.

5. It is further alleged that the aforesaid callous, reckless, willful and wanton acts and omissions by Defendants, and each of them, were the proximate cause of the injuries to Plaintiff John Denton as stated.

6. Plaintiff therefore asks for exemplary and punitive damages in an amount sufficient so that an example will be made of these Defendants, and each of them, in order to promote safety and to provide an incentive for Defendants and others so situated to engage in safer design, testing, production and marketing practices.

§ 14.12 SAMPLE COMPLAINT: STANDUP FORKLIFT TRUCK

The next scenario involves a worker seriously injured while operating a forklift truck at his place of employment. The forklift allegedly failed to

properly brake and the absence of a rear guard rail resulted in his leg being smashed against a post in the factory.

Count I (Strict Liability)

Plaintiff, JOHN HUSSEY, complaining of defendant, THE STOCKLIFT CORPORATION, a foreign corporation, (hereinafter referred to as STOCK-LIFT), states:

1. On and prior to August 1, 2002, defendant, THE STOCKLIFT COR-PORATION, (hereinafter referred to as STOCKLIFT), designed, manufactured, maintained, assembled, distributed and sold a certain product commonly known as a Stocklift Pacer Model 60 standup forklift, which was offered for sale to the public.

2. On and prior to August 1, 2002, defendant, STOCKLIFT placed the aforesaid forklift into the stream of commerce.

3. On August 1, 2002, plaintiff, JOHN HUSSEY, was operating said forklift on the premises of Matoon Distribution Company located at 5000 Proviso Drive, in the City of Matoon Park, County of Cook, State of Illinois.

4. On August 1, 2002, while the plaintiff, JOHN HUSSEY, was operating said forklift in the course of his duties for the Matoon Distribution Company, said forklift failed to stop its forward motion, resulting in the crushing of plaintiff's leg between the forklift and a concrete pillar.

5. On and before August 1, 2002, and at the time the aforesaid forklift left the control of defendant, STOCKLIFT, the forklift was in a defective condition unreasonably dangerous in one or all of the following respects:

a. Said forklift was not reasonably safe in design due to the substantial risk that the acceleration and braking systems in said forklift could malfunction;

b. Said forklift was not reasonably safe in that defendant, STOCK-LIFT, provided inadequate braking mechanisms which failed to stop said fork lift when the braking mechanism was engaged;

c. Said forklift was not reasonably safe in that defendant, STOCK-LIFT, failed to provide an expanded deck or other extension to the operator's platform to prevent the operator from being crushed in the event of collision with or intrusion by stationery objects.

d. Said forklift was not reasonably safe in that defendant, STOCK-LIFT, failed to provide a metal or other sufficiently strong gate across the back of the operator's platform to prevent the operator from being crushed in the event of collision with or intrusion by stationery objects.

e. Said forklift was not reasonably safe in that defendant, STOCK-LIFT, failed to provide adequate width or depth for the operator's platform to allow the operator to adequately operate said forklift in emergency situations.

f. Said forklift was not reasonably safe in that defendant, STOCK-LIFT, failed to provide adequate posts or other protective features around the operator's platform to prevent the operator from being crushed in the event of collision with or intrusion by stationary objects.

g. Said forklift was not reasonably safe in that defendant, STOCK-LIFT, failed to provide adequate warnings of the dangers involved in the operation of said forklift.

6. As a proximate result of one or all of the aforesaid conditions, plaintiff, JOHN HUSSEY, suffered and in the future will continue to suffer injuries of a personal and pecuniary nature.

WHEREFORE, plaintiff, JOHN HUSSEY, asks judgment against the defendant, THE STOCKLIFT CORPORATION, a foreign corporation, in a sum in excess of FIFTEEN THOUSAND DOLLARS ($15,000.00).

Count II

(Negligence)

Plaintiff, JOHN HUSSEY, complaining of defendant, THE STOCKLIFT CORPORATION, a foreign corporation, (hereinafter, referred to as STOCK-LIFT), states:

1. On and prior to August 1, 2002, defendant, STOCKLIFT, designed, manufactured, maintained, assembled, distributed and sold a certain product commonly known as a Stocklift Pacer model 60 standup forklift, which was offered for sale to the public.

2. On and prior to August 1, 2002, defendant, STOCKLIFT, placed the aforesaid forklift into the stream of commerce.

3. On August 1, 2002, plaintiff, JOHN HUSSEY, was operating said forklift on the premises of Matoon Distribution Company located at 5000 Proviso Drive, in the City of Matoon Park, County of Cook, State of Illinois.

4. On August 1, 2002, while the plaintiff, JOHN HUSSEY, was operating said forklift in the course of his duties for the Matoon Distribution Company, said forklift failed to stop its forward motion, resulting in the crushing of plaintiff's leg between the forklift and a concrete pillar.

5. On and before August 1, 2002, defendant, STOCKLIFT, had a duty to exercise due care in the design, testing, production and marketing of the Stocklift Pacer Model 60 forklift truck, which duty extended to plaintiff JOHN HUSSEY a forseeable user of said forklift.

6. That on and before August 1, 2002, defendant, STOCKLIFT, through its duly authorized agents and employees, breached the duty of care owed to plaintiff JOHN HUSSEY and was negligent in one or all of the following respects:

a. Said forklift was not reasonably safe in design due to the substantial risk of risk that the acceleration and braking systems in said forklift could malfunction;

b. Said forklift was not reasonably safe in that defendant, STOCK-LIFT, provided inadequate braking mechanisms which failed to stop said fork lift when the braking mechanism was engaged;

c. Said forklift was not reasonably safe in that defendant, STOCK-LIFT, failed to provide an expanded deck or other extension to the operator's platform to prevent the operator from being crushed in the event of collision with or intrusion by stationery objects.

d. Said forklift was not reasonably safe in that defendant, STOCK-LIFT, failed to provide a metal or other sufficiently strong gate across the back of the operator's platform to prevent the operator from being crushed in the event of collision with or intrusion by stationery objects.

e. Said forklift was not reasonably safe in that defendant, STOCK-LIFT, failed to provide adequate width or depth for the operator's platform to allow the operator to adequately operate said forklift in emergency situations.

f. Said forklift was not reasonably safe in that defendant, STOCK-LIFT, failed to provide adequate posts or other protective features around the operator's platform to prevent the operator from being crushed in the event of collision with or intrusion by stationery objects.

g. Said forklift was not reasonably safe in that defendant, STOCK-LIFT, failed to provide adequate warnings of the dangers involved in the operation of said forklift.

7. As a proximate result of one or all of the foregoing negligent acts or omissions, plaintiff, JOHN HUSSEY, suffered and will continue to suffer injuries of a personal and pecuniary nature.

WHEREFORE, plaintiff, JOHN HUSSEY, asks judgment against defendant, THE STOCKLIFT CORPORATION, a foreign corporation, in a sum of money in excess of FIFTEEN THOUSAND DOLLARS ($15,000.00).

Chapter 15

PRODUCTS LIABILITY AND DISCOVERY

SYNOPSIS

---

§ 15.01 INTRODUCTION

The discovery process is one of the most challenging stages in products liability litigation. The plaintiff must access large amounts of information from within the defendant company's files in order to prove her case. Complaints grounded in allegations of defectively designed packaging or products as well as those centered in failure to instruct or warn and misrepresentation, require the review of thousands of documents generated over periods ranging from ten to fifty years. The discovery effort requires

detailed planning and careful drafting of discovery requests.[1] In every products liability litigation there is a great disparity between the very limited information that may be provided by the plaintiff in discovery and that of the corporate defendant. Corporate defendants always possess considerable amounts of information in the form of corporate documents generated over years of corporate life pursuant to standard operating procedures.

Chapters 16 through 18[2] will discuss the products liability-focused aspects of interrogatories, requests to admit facts, requests for production of documents and depositions. It is the purpose of the present chapter to provide an overview of the civil discovery processes in state and federal courts, which is essential to garner a competent understanding of products liability theory and practice. Discovery requests are quite properly vigorously opposed by defense counsel and contested discovery motions are a common feature of these cases. Chapter 19, Protective Orders, Discovery Enforcement, and Motions-In-Limine will discuss the discovery enforcement aspect of products litigation in detail.

Discovery planning is central to the successful prosecution of any litigation. It is essential in product liability cases. The innate difficulty of tracking the stages in the progress of a product over a multi year time frame and the significant amount of documentation attendant to such, require a concentrated discovery effort.

The standard and most utilized discovery tools are interrogatories, requests to admit fact or the genuineness of documents, the request for the production of documents, and discovery and evidence depositions. Each

---

[1] For an introductory overview of federal and state products liability discovery planning, see, JAMES A. LOWE & MARK L. WAKEFIELD, AMERICAN LAW OF PRODUCTS LIABILITY, PART 16. PRACTICE, CHAPTER 66. PLAINTIFF'S PRETRIAL PRACTICE: PREPARING A DISCOVERY PLAN; INTERROGATORIES. See also AMERICAN LAW REPORTS, INDEX TO ANNOTATIONS: DISCOVERY: PRODUCTS LIABILITY, covering ALR2d, ALR3d, ALR4th, ALR5th, ALR6th, ALR Fed., and ALR Fed.2d (2005).

[2] See, *infra*, Chapter 16, Interrogatories and Requests to Admit Fact, Chapter 17, Requests to Produce Documents, and Chapter 18, Discovery and Evidence Depositions.

state[3] as well as the federal courts[4] have a series of quite similar discovery provisions that are aimed at channeling discovery utilizing those devices.[5]

---

[3] The Illinois Discovery Rules are typical:

Rule 26 - General Provisions Governing Discovery; Duty of Disclosure

Rule 27 - Depositions Before Action or Pending Appeal

Rule 28 - Persons Before Whom Depositions May be Taken

Rule 29 - Stipulations Regarding Discovery Procedure

Rule 30 - Depositions Upon Oral Examination

Rule 31 - Depositions Upon Written Questions

Rule 32 - Use of Depositions in Court Proceedings

Rule 33 - Interrogatories to Parties

Rule 34 - Production of Documents and Things and Entry Upon Land for Inspection and Other Purposes

Rule 35 - Physical and Mental Examinations of Persons

Rule 36 - Requests for Admission

Rule 37 - Failure to Make Disclosure or Cooperate in Discovery: Sanctions

[4] The Federal Rules are very close to state provisions:

Rule 26 - General Provisions Governing Discovery; Duty of Disclosure

Rule 27 - Depositions Before Action or Pending Appeal

Rule 28 - Persons Before Whom Depositions May be Taken

Rule 30 - Depositions Upon Oral Examination

Rule 31 - Depositions Upon Written Questions

Rule 32 - Use of Depositions in Court Proceedings

Rule 33 - Interrogatories to Parties

Rule 34 - Production of Documents and Things and Entry Upon Land for Inspection and Other Purposes

Rule 35 - Physical and Mental Examinations of Persons

Rule 36 - Requests for Admission

Rule 37 - Failure to Make Disclosure or Cooperate in Discovery: Sanctions

[5] In a rare case, prefiling discovery may be obtained to identify a person who may be responsible for damages in the anticipated litigation but has yet to be identified.

See, e.g., Illinois Supreme Court Rule 224. Discovery Before Suit to Identify Responsible Persons and Entities:

(i)   A person or entity who wishes to engage in discovery for the sole purpose of ascertaining the identity of one who may be responsible in damages may file an independent action for such discovery.

(ii) The action for discovery shall be initiated by the filing of a verified petition in the circuit court of the county in which the action or proceeding might be brought or in which one or more of the persons or entities from whom discovery is sought resides. The petition shall be brought in the name of the petitioner and shall name as respondents the persons or entities from whom discovery is sought and shall set forth: (A) the reason the proposed discovery is necessary and (B) the nature of the discovery sought and shall ask for an order authorizing the petitioner to obtain such discovery. The order allowing the petition will limit discovery to the identification of responsible persons and entities and where a deposition is sought will specify the name and address of each person to be examined, if known, or, if unknown, information sufficient to identify eachperson and the time and place of the deposition.

Many states require a case management conference at the onset of a case as a means of policing the flow and problems involved.[6] The same requirement exists under the Federal Rules of Civil Procedure.[7]

---

[6] The Illinois provision may serve as a typical example:

Illinois Supreme Court Rule 218. Pretrial Procedure.

(a) Initial Case Management Conference. Except as provided by local circuit court rule, which on petition of the chief judge of the circuit has been approved by the Supreme Court, the court shall hold a case management conference within 35 days after the parties are at issue and in no event more than 182 days following the filing of the complaint. At the conference counsel familiar with the case and authorized to act shall appear and the following shall be considered:

(1) the nature, issues, and complexity of the case;

(2) the simplification of the issues;

(3) amendments to the pleadings;

(4) the possibility of obtaining admissions of fact and of documents which will avoid unnecessary proof;

(5) limitations on discovery including:

(i)　the number and duration of depositions which can be taken;

(ii)　the area of expertise and the number of opinion witnesses who can be called; and

(iii)　deadlines for the disclosure of opinion witnesses and the completion of written discovery and depositions;

(6) the possibility of settlement and scheduling of a settlement conference;

(7) the advisability of alternative dispute resolution;

(8) the date on which the case should be ready for trial;

(9) the advisability of holding subsequent case management conferences; and

(10) any other matters which may aid in the disposition of the action.

[7] Federal Rule 26. General Provisions Governing Discovery; Duty of Disclosure.

(f) Meeting of Parties; Planning for Discovery.

Except in actions exempted by local rule or when otherwise ordered, the parties shall, as soon as practicable and in any event at least 14 days before a scheduling conference is held or a scheduling order is due under Rule 16(b), meet to discuss the nature and basis of their claims and defenses and the possibilities for a prompt settlement or resolution of the case, to make or arrange for the disclosures required by subdivision (a)(1), and to develop a proposed discovery plan. The plan shall indicate the parties' views and proposals concerning:

(1) what changes should be made in the timing, form, or requirement for disclosures under subdivision (a) or local rule, including a statement as to when disclosures under subdivision (a)(1) were made or will be made;

(2) the subjects on which discovery may be needed, when discovery should be completed, and whether discovery should be conducted in phases or be limited to or focused upon particular issues;

(3) what changes should be made to limitations on discovery imposed under these rules or by local rule, and what other limitations should be imposed; and

(4) any other orders that should be entered by the court under subdivision (c) or under Rule 16(b) and (c).

The federal system requires opposing counsel to submit a variety of important information even without a formal request by opposing counsel.[8] The federal rules, as all state discovery schemes, require the responding party to seasonably update discovery previously answered, a requirement rarely, if ever, complied with by the parties, especially products litigators.[9] It is the intention of discovery provisions that the parties themselves provide full disclosure, more a fond wish rather than current routine practice.[10]

---

[8] Federal Rule 26. General Provisions Governing Discovery; Duty of Disclosure.

  (a) Required Disclosures; Methods to Discover Additional Matter.

    (1) Initial Disclosures. Except to the extent otherwise stipulated or directed by order or local rule, a party shall, without awaiting a discovery request, provide to other parties:

    (A) the name and, if known, the address and telephone number of each individual likely to have discoverable information relevant to disputed facts alleged with particularity in the pleadings, identifying the subjects of the information;

    (B) a copy of, or a description by category and location of, all documents, data compilations, and tangible things in the possession, custody, or control of the party that are relevant to disputed facts alleged with particularity in the pleadings;

    (C) a computation of any category of damages claimed by the disclosing party, making available for inspection and copying as under Rule 34 the documents or other evidentiary material, not privileged or protected from disclosure, on which such computation is based, including materials bearing on the nature and extent of injuries suffered; and

    (D) for inspection and copying as under Rule 34 any insurance agreement under which any person carrying on an insurance business may be liable to satisfy part or all of a judgment which may be entered in the action or to indemnify or reimburse for payments made to satisfy the judgment.

Unless otherwise stipulated or directed by the court, these disclosures shall be made at or within 10 days after the meeting of the parties under subdivision (f). A party shall make its initial disclosures based on the information then reasonably available to it and is not excused from making its disclosures because it has not fully completed its investigation of the case or because it challenges the sufficiency of another party's disclosures or because another party has not made its disclosures.

[9] A party is under a duty seasonably to amend a prior response to an interrogatory, request for production, or request for admission if the party learns that the response is in some material respect incomplete or incorrect and if the additional or corrective information has not otherwise been made known to the other parties during the discovery process or in writing.

[10] Illinois Supreme Court Rule 201. General Discovery Provisions:

  (1) Full Disclosure Required. Except as provided in these rules, a party may obtain by discovery full disclosure regarding any matter relevant to the subject matter involved in the pending action, whether it relates to the claim or defense of the party seeking disclosure or of any other party, including the existence, description, nature, custody, condition, and location of any documents or tangible things, and the identity and location of persons having knowledge of relevant facts. The word "documents," as used in these rules, includes, but is not limited to, papers, photographs, films, recordings, memoranda, books, records, accounts, communications and all retrievable information in computer storage.

It is important to note at the outset that without adequate prefiling research and analysis,[11] the only party involved in the case who has detailed knowledge of the nature and extent of the manufacturing information is the corporate defendant. The greatest amount of time and frustration encountered by plaintiff's counsel in preparing these cases occurs in the discovery process. It is important to note that in general terms counsel has only one opportunity to conduct discovery. While plaintiff counsel has the right to supplemental discovery after study of the materials received pursuant to the original issuance of discovery requests, she does not have the prerogative of starting over if the original discovery requests were inadequately analyzed and poorly written. In addition to showing an example of superficial preparation, it can get discovery off on a wrong track that cannot be easily corrected.

§ 15.02 THE PURPOSES AND REACH OF DISCOVERY

PRETRIAL PRODUCT-RELATED RESEARCH

BASIC RESEARCH ISSUES

1. **What mechanical or chemical or pharmacological aspect of defendant's product actually caused the plaintiff's death or injury?**

2. **How did it do that?**

3. **Was the defendant aware of that injury-producing potential? When? Through what sources?**

4. **Could the defendant have done something to have eliminated or minimized that risk and still have aggressively competed in its chosen market?**

5. **If it could have, why didn't it?**

PRODUCTS LIABILITY RESEARCH
RELATED INFORMATION SOURCES

EXTERNAL DATA [Pre-Filing Research]	**INTERNAL COMPANY DATA** [Discovery Tools]
1. State-of-the-Art Literature	**1. Design**
2. Industry Custom	**2. Testing**
3. Regulatory Activity	**3. Production**
4. Injury History	**4. Marketing**
5. Litigation History	**5. Post-Marketing**

---

[11] *See* Chapter 12, Researching the Products Case.

Set out below are selections from the general discovery rules of the United States Courts and a state court, Illinois, as illustrative of the statutory measures that will channel and control the extensive effort undertaken in products liability pretrial discovery.

[A] *Illinois Supreme Court Rule 201. General Discovery Provisions*

(1) Full Disclosure Required. Except as provided in these rules, a party may obtain by discovery full disclosure regarding any matter relevant to the subject matter involved in the pending action, whether it relates to the claim or defense of the party seeking disclosure or of any other party, including the existence, description, nature, custody, condition, and location of any documents or tangible things, and the identity and location of persons having knowledge of relevant facts. The word "documents," as used in these rules, includes, but is not limited to, papers, photographs, films, recordings, memoranda, books, records, accounts, communications and all retrievable information in computer storage.

(2) Privilege and Work Product. All matters that are privileged against disclosure on the trial, including privileged communications between a party or his agent and the attorney for the party, are privileged against disclosure through any discovery procedure. Material prepared by or for a party in preparation for trial is subject to discovery only if it does not contain or disclose the theories, mental impressions, or litigation plans of the party's attorney. The court may apportion the cost involved in originally securing the discoverable material, including when appropriate a reasonable attorney's fee, in such manner as is just.

[B] *FRCP 26. General Provisions Governing Discovery; Duty of Disclosure*

(b) Discovery Scope and Limits. Unless otherwise limited by order of the court in accordance with these rules, the scope of discovery is as follows:

(1) In General. Parties may obtain discovery regarding any matter, not privileged, which is relevant to the subject matter involved in the pending action, whether it relates to the claim or defense of the party seeking discovery or to the claim or defense of any other party, including the existence, description, nature, custody, condition and location of any books, documents, or other tangible things and the identity and location of persons having knowledge of any discoverable matter. The information sought need not be admissible at the trial if the information sought appears reasonably calculated to lead to the discovery of admissible evidence.

(2) Limitations. By order or by local rule, the court may alter the limits in these rules on the number of depositions and interrogatories and

may also limit the length of depositions under Rule 30 and the number of requests under Rule 36. The frequency or extent of use of the discovery methods otherwise permitted under these rules and by any local rule shall be limited by the court if it determines that:

(i) the discovery sought is unreasonably cumulative or duplicative, or is obtainable from some other source that is more convenient, less burdensome, or less expensive;

(ii) the party seeking discovery has had ample opportunity by discovery in the action to obtain the information sought; or

(iii) the burden or expense of the proposed discovery outweighs its likely benefit, taking into account the needs of the case, the amount in controversy, the parties' resources, the importance of the issues at stake in the litigation, and the importance of the proposed discovery in resolving the issues. The court may act upon its own initiative after reasonable notice or pursuant to a motion under subdivision (c).

§ 15.03 THE DISCOVERY TOOLS

The discovery tools set out below are essentially the same whether issuing from Congress or a state legislature. The basic set of discovery tools are written interrogatories, requests for the production of documents and depositions. The sections to follow will provide selections from the relevant rules and proceed to discuss each of them in the context of products liability litigation. It bears reminding that the choice of legal theory from among the body of products law discussed in Chapters 1-10 will control how discovery plays out in any litigation.

§ 15.04 INTERROGATORIES

[A] FRCP Rule 33 — Interrogatories to Parties

(a) Availability. Without leave of court or written stipulation, any party may serve upon any other party written interrogatories, not exceeding 25 in number including all discrete subparts, to be answered by the party served or, if the party served is a public or private corporation or a partnership or association or governmental agency, by any officer or agent, who shall furnish such information as is available to the party. Leave to serve additional interrogatories shall be granted to the extent consistent with the principles of Rule 26(b)(2). Without leave of court or written stipulation, interrogatories may not be served before the time specified in Rule 26(d).

(b) Answers and Objections.

(1) Each interrogatory shall be answered separately and fully in writing under oath, unless it is objected to, in which event the objecting party

shall state the reasons for objection and shall answer to the extent the interrogatory is not objectionable.

(2) The answers are to be signed by the person making them, and the objections signed by the attorney making them.

(3) The party upon whom the interrogatories have been served shall serve a copy of the answers, and objections if any, within 30 days after the service of the interrogatories. A shorter or longer time may be directed by the court or, in the absence of such an order, agreed to in writing by the parties subject to Rule 29.

(4) All grounds for an objection to an interrogatory shall be stated with specificity. Any ground not stated in a timely objection is waived unless the party's failure to object is excused by the court for good cause shown. (5) The party submitting the interrogatories may move for an order under Rule 37(a) with respect to any objection to or other failure to answer an interrogatory.

(c) Scope; Use at Trial. Interrogatories may relate to any matters which can be inquired into under Rule 26(b)(1), and the answers may be used to the extent permitted by the rules of evidence.

An interrogatory otherwise proper is not necessarily objectionable merely because an answer to the interrogatory involves an opinion or contention that relates to fact or the application of law to fact, but the court may order that such an interrogatory need not be answered until after designated discovery has been completed or until a pre-trial conference or other later time.

(d) Option to Produce Business Records. Where the answer to an interrogatory may be derived or ascertained from the business records of the party upon whom the interrogatory has been served or from an examination, audit or inspection of such business records, including a compilation, abstract or summary thereof and the burden of deriving or ascertaining the answer is substantially the same for the party serving the interrogatory as for the party served, it is a sufficient answer to such interrogatory to specify the records from which the answer may be derived or ascertained and to afford to the party serving the interrogatory reasonable opportunity to examine, audit or inspect such records and to make copies, compilations, abstracts or summaries. A specification shall be in sufficient detail to permit the interrogating party to locate and to identify, as readily as can the party served, the records from which the answer may be ascertained.

§ 15.05 REQUESTS TO PRODUCE DOCUMENTS

[A] FRCP Rule 34 — Production of Documents and Things and Entry Upon Land for Inspection and Other Purposes

(a) Scope. Any party may serve on any other party a request.

(1) to produce and permit the party making the request, or someone acting on the requestor's behalf, to inspect and copy, any designated documents (including writings, drawings, graphs, charts, photographs, phone records, and other data compilations from which information can be obtained, translated, if necessary, by the respondent through detection devices into reasonably usable form), or to inspect and copy, test, or sample any tangible things which constitute or contain matters within the scope of Rule 26(b) and which are in the possession, custody or control of the party upon whom the request is served; or

(2) to permit entry upon designated land or other property in the possession or control of the party upon whom the request is served for the purpose of inspection and measuring, surveying, photographing, testing, or sampling the property or any designated object or operation thereon, within the scope of Rule 26(b).

(b) Procedure. The request shall set forth, either by individual item or by category, the items to be inspected, and describe each with reasonable particularity. The request shall specify a reasonable time, place, and manner of making the inspection and performing the related acts. Without leave of court or written stipulation, a request may not be served before the time specified in Rule 26(d).

§ 15.06 REQUESTS TO ADMIT FACTS OR THE GENUINENESS OF DOCUMENTS

[A] FRCP Rule 36 — Requests for Admission

(a) Request for Admission. A party may serve upon any other party a written request for the admission, for purposes of the pending action only, of the truth of any matters within the scope of Rule 26(b)(1) set forth in the request that relate to statements or opinions of fact or of the application of law to fact, including the genuineness of any documents described in the request. Copies of documents shall be served with the request unless they have been or are otherwise furnished or made available for inspection and copying. Without leave of court or written stipulation, requests for admission may not be served before the time specified in Rule 26(d).

Each matter of which an admission is requested shall be separately set forth. The matter is admitted unless, within 30 days after service of the request, or within such shorter or longer time as the court may allow or as the parties may agree to in writing, subject to Rule 29, the party to whom the request is directed serves upon the party requesting the admission a written answer or objection addressed to the matter, signed by the party or by the party's attorney. If objection is made, the reasons therefor shall be stated. The answer shall specifically deny the matter or set forth in detail the reasons why the answering party cannot truthfully admit or deny the matter. A denial shall fairly meet the substance of the requested admission,

and when good faith requires that a party qualify an answer or deny only a part of the matter of which an admission is requested, the party shall specify so much of it as is true and qualify or deny the remainder. An answering party may not give lack of information or knowledge as a reason for failure to admit or deny unless the party states that the party has made reasonable inquiry and that the information known or readily obtainable by the party is insufficient to enable the party to admit or deny. A party who considers that a matter of which an admission has been requested presents a genuine issue for trial may not, on that ground alone, object to the request; the party may, subject to the provisions of Rule 37(c), deny the matter or set forth reasons why the party cannot admit or deny it.

§ 15.07 DEPOSITIONS

[A] FRCP Rule 30 — Depositions Upon Oral Examination

(a) When Depositions May be Taken; When Leave Required.

(1) A party may take the testimony of any person, including a party, by deposition upon oral examination without leave of court except as provided in paragraph (2). The attendance of witnesses may be compelled by subpoena as provided in Rule 45.

(2) A party must obtain leave of court, which shall be granted to the extent consistent with the principles stated in Rule 26(b)(2), if the person to be examined is confined in prison or if, without the written stipulation of the parties,

(A) a proposed deposition would result in more than ten depositions being taken under this rule or Rule 31 by the plaintiffs, or by the defendants, or by third-party defendants;

(B) the person to be examined already has been deposed in the case; or

(C) a party seeks to take a deposition before the time specified in Rule 26(d) unless the notice contains a certification, with supporting facts, that the person to be examined is expected to leave the United States and be unavailable for examination in this country unless deposed before that time.

§ 15.08 RELEVANCY IN THE DISCOVERY PROCESS

In addition to similar discovery tools, the state and federal discovery schemes share a common philosophy of discovery as to what materials are discoverable and the ongoing duties and obligations of the litigants during this crucial stage. The central idea in both systems is the concept of relevancy.

The legal standard used to determine the information available to the parties in the course of discovery is stated in Federal Rule of Civil Procedure 26(b)(1):

> . . . Parties may obtain discovery regarding any matter, not privileged, which is relevant to the subject matter involved in the pending action, whether it relates to the claim or defense of any party, including the existence, description, nature, custody, condition and location of any books, documents, or other tangible things and the identity and location of persons having knowledge of any discoverable matter. It is not ground for objection that the information sought will be inadmissible at the trial if the information sought appears reasonably calculated to lead to the discovery of admissible evidence.[12]

The definition of relevance is provided by Federal Rule of Evidence 401, which defines relevant evidence as information having any tendency to make the existence of a fact that is of consequence to the action more probable or less probable than it would be without it.[13] Hence, by providing for the discovery of data that may *be reasonably calculated to lead to* formally admissible evidence both federal and state courts have fashioned a very liberal discovery format.

As noted by Justice Powell of the United States Supreme Court, writing in 1978 for a unanimous court in *Oppenheimer Fund, Inc. v. Sanders*:[14]

> . . . The key phrase in this definition — "relevant to the subject matter involved in the pending action" — has been construed broadly to encompass any matter that bears on, or that reasonably could lead to other matter that could bear on, any issue that is or may be in the case.[15] Consistently with the notice-pleading system established by the Rules, discovery is not limited to issues raised by the pleadings, for discovery itself is designed to help define and clarify the issues. Nor is discovery limited to the merits of a case, for a variety of fact-oriented issues may arise during litigation that are not related to the merits.[16]

A request for discovery should be considered relevant if there is "any possibility" that information sought may be relevant to the subject matter of the action. The primary focal point to determine the actual scope of discovery relevancy is the plaintiff's complaint. As noted in the leading case of *Roesberg v. Johns-Manville Corp*:[17]

---

[12] FED. R. CIV. P. § 26(b)(1).

[13] FED. R. EVID. 401.

[14] 437 U.S. 340 (1978).

[15] *Id.* (*citing* Hickman v. Taylor, 329 U.S. 495, 501 (1947)).

[16] *Hickman*, 329 U.S. at 500-501.

[17] 85 F.R.D. 292, 296-297 (E.D. Pa. 1980).

. . . The detail in the complaint specifies the necessary relevance of the interrogatories. . . . The burden now falls upon GAF, the party resisting discovery, to clarify and explain its objections and to provide support therefor. . . .[18]

The allegations of each count in the complaint determine the broad subject matters involved in the case. However, relevance is to be measured, not strictly according to the specific fact issues raised by the pleadings, but by reference to the broader logical parameters of those facts.[19]

Arguments over the application of this liberal interpretation of relevancy in the discovery process are at the center of most pre-trial motions seeking to limit plaintiff's requests, whether in time or subject matter or both.[20] More recent cases, while emphasizing that discovery does indeed have limits,[21] tend to follow the open interpretation of Justice Powell.[22]

---

[18] *Id.* at 297

[19] Smith v. F.T.C., 403 F. Supp. 1000 (D. Del. 1975).

[20] *See* Chapter 19, Protective Orders, Discovery Enforcement, and Motions-In-Limine.

[21] *See* Rule 26. General Provisions Governing Discovery; Duty of Disclosure:

(1) In General. Parties may obtain discovery regarding any matter, not privileged, which is relevant to the subject matter involved in the pending action, whether it relates to the claim or defense of the party seeking discovery or to the claim or defense of any other party, including the existence, description, nature, custody, condition and location of any books, documents, or other tangible things and the identity and location of persons having knowledge of any discoverable matter. The information sought need not be admissible at the trial if the information sought appears reasonably calculated to lead to the discovery of admissible evidence.

(2) Limitations. By order or by local rule, the court may alter the limits in these rules on the number of depositions and interrogatories and may also limit the length of depositions under Rule 30 and the number of requests under Rule 36. The frequency or extent of use of the discovery methods otherwise permitted under these rules and by any local rule shall be limited by the court if it determines that:

(i) the discovery sought is unreasonably cumulative or duplicative, or is obtainable from some other source that is more convenient, less burdensome, or less expensive;

(ii) the party seeking discovery has had ample opportunity by discovery in the action to obtain the information sought; or

(iii) the burden or expense of the proposed discovery outweighs its likely benefit, taking into account the needs of the case, the amount in controversy, the parties' resources, the importance of the issues at stake in the litigation, and the importance of the proposed discovery in resolving the issues. The court may act upon its own initiative after reasonable notice or pursuant to a motion under subdivision (c).

[22] *See, e.g.,* J.W. v. B.B., 700 N.W.2d 277 (Wis. Ct. App. 2005); In re Estate of Mechanic, 2005 WL 1384122; Kirk v. Ford Motor Co., 116 P.3d 27 (Idaho 2005); In re TIG Ins. Co., 2005 WL 1903841; City of King City v. Community Bank of Central California, 2005 Cal. LEXIS 13081 (Cal. 2005). Virtually all cases addressing this point cite and/or quote the language of Justice Powell in the *Oppenheimer* case.

In re Kevin Silva v. Basin Western Inc.,[23] involved a trial court order compelling the production of information regarding insurance reserves and settlement authority in a personal injury claim. The question of whether insurance reserves and settlement authority fell within the scope of discovery was a question of first impression in Colorado requiring the court to explore the nature of insurance reserves and settlement authority to determine whether such information was reasonably calculated to lead to admissible evidence in a personal injury action and thus discoverable.

The court noted that this question was to be resolved by reference to Colorado Rules of Civil Procedure 26(B)(1), which provided that:

> [P]arties may obtain discovery regarding any matter, not privileged, which is relevant to the subject matter involved in the pending action, whether it relates to the claim or defense of the party seeking discovery or to the claim or defense of any other party, including the existence, description, nature, custody, condition and location of any books, documents, or other tangible things, and the identity and location of persons having knowledge of any discoverable matter. The information sought need not be admissible at trial if the information sought appears reasonably calculated to lead to admissible evidence.[24]

The court emphasized that relevancy for purposes of discovery was not the same as relevancy for admissibility of evidence at trial.[25] Section 26(b)(1) permitted parties to obtain "discovery regarding any unprivileged, relevant matter that 'relates to the claim or defense of the party seeking discovery or to the claim or defense of any other party if it is reasonably calculated to lead to the discovery of admissible evidence. Further, it is not a proper ground for objection that the information sought will be inadmissible at trial if the information appears reasonably calculated to lead to the discovery of admissible evidence. The court observed that while the law generally favored discovery, the scope of discovery was not limitless. The need for discovery must be balanced by weighing a party's right to privacy and protection from harassment against the other party's right to discover information that is relevant. Thus, the information sought through discovery must be relevant to the subject matter of the action and reasonably calculated to lead to the discovery of admissible evidence.[26]

---

[23] 47 P. 3d 1184 (Colo. Sp. Ct. 2002).

[24] COLO. R. CIV. P. 26(B)(1).

[25] *See* Williams v. Dist. Court, 866 P.2d 908, 911 (Colo. 1993); Kerwin v. Dist. Court, 649 P.2d 1086, 1088 (Colo. 1982).

[26] *Silva*, 47 P.3d at 1188 n. 5.

§ 15.09 SETTING THE DISCOVERY TIME FRAME

The actual periods of history within which discovery is to be conducted is not an issue until plaintiff files his first set of interrogatories. Until that time, prefiling technical, agency and company research is strictly a matter of personal choice in conducting whatever preliminary investigative goals that have been set. Discovery, however, requires that plaintiff indicate the years in the life of the company over which documentation is to be forthcoming from the defendant corporation.

Initial defense objections to plaintiff's discovery requests are typically centered in the excessive number of years over which information is requested. The primary theoretical basis for objection lies in the alleged irrelevancy of requested materials generated by defendant in years preceding and following the model year or date of manufacture of the product unit involved in the case. Extensive time frame requests also prompt objections based on the burdensome nature of lengthy multi-year interrogatories and requests for documents.

The problem from the perspective of products liability defense lawyers was simply put in a recent article by a defense attorney:

> THE PROBLEM. Every defense attorney who has ever handled a products liability action is all too familiar with the unbelievably broad discovery requests propounded by plaintiffs' attorneys. More often than not, plaintiffs' attorneys serve defense counsel with interrogatories or requests for production of documents which request volumes of information regarding not only the product at issue, but other products that have also been manufactured by the defendant. These interrogatories and requests for production of documents often request information regarding the design, manufacture, production, distribution, and sale of any product the defendant has ever manufactured which is remotely similar (or in some cases not even remotely similar) to the product which the plaintiff claims caused his or her injury. [27]
>
> When faced with such expansive discovery requests, defense counsel must take a restrictive, conservative approach to providing information to plaintiff's counsel regarding products other than the product at issue in that particular case. The reasons for serious, aggressive attempts by defense counsel to limit the amount and type of information supplied about the manufacture of other products should be obvious. Evidence regarding other products, including evidence of problems encountered with other products, if admitted into evidence during the course of a trial, can confuse the

---

[27] Bradley C. Nahrstadt, *Narrowing The Scope Of Discovery For Substantially Similar Products*, 15 No. 6 PRAC. LIT. 37, 38 (2004).

jury and may lead it to wrongly conclude that the product at issue is defective. In addition, the more negative information the plaintiff's attorney can present to the jury about the defendant's products, the more likely it is that the jury will return a plaintiff's verdict based not on quality, but quantity. Most importantly, improper introduction of damaging evidence concerning other products manufactured by the defendant can make the difference between a plaintiff's verdict and a defense verdict, an award of punitive damages as opposed to only compensatory damages, or a moderate compensatory damage award and an excessive compensatory damage award.[28]

This standard response to time frame and subjects of initial discovery filed by plaintiffs sets the stage for the intense motion practice involving discovery enforcement, protective orders and motions-in-limine. These periods are often unavoidably extensive due to the nature of the suspect product or technology at issue. For example, in asbestos cases, a time frame going back as far as 40 years may be necessary to responsibly prepare the litigation. In other cases such as those involving Firestone tires and SUV rollovers, where the basic design has remained constant, counsel may legitimately argue for a time frame that begins a decade or more earlier when the product was originally developed and widely used in similar product lines. The manufacturer's experience with a component item such as ball joints on an entire line of pickup trucks is fair game in a case questioning the design of a ball-joint system.[29]

A common objection in the course of products liability cases is that the plaintiff's requests are unduly broad in both chronology and subject matter, resulting in irrelevant and burdensome requestsThis issue was recently addressed in the case of *State ex rel. Ford Motor Co. v. Nixon*.[30]

Roy Dietiker, a former employee of Ford, filed a worker's compensation suit against Ford and a products liability suit against multiple other defendants for allegedly having been exposed to defective products containing asbestos while working for Ford that resulted in him contracting lung cancer. These two lawsuits were ongoing at the time of Dietiker's death from the cancer, and discovery in these suits had been obtained from Ford. After Dietiker's death, his relatives filed a wrongful death action against Ford, and discovery requests were served in this third lawsuit. Plaintiffs sought information and documents regarding every product containing asbestos that was ever manufactured, sold or distributed by Ford in its 102-year history without limitation as to locality or as to the specific products to which Dietiker was allegedly exposed. Ford did not comply with the dis-

---

[28] *Id.*

[29] *See Durango Ball Joint Woes Persist* [CBS News], http://www.cbsnews.com/stories/2004/03/03/eveningnews/main603833.shtml.

[30] 160 S.W.3d 379 (Mo. 2005).

covery requests in this action, and the trial court issued an order to compel production.

Ford claimed that the discovery requests in the wrongful death action were overbroad and unduly burdensome because there were no geographical, time or subject matter restrictions in the discovery requests. Ford also argued that discovery should be limited to the products-related claims, because the court lacks jurisdiction over the employment-related claims. Finally, Ford asserted that the discovery requests were duplicative because counsel was the same in all of these cases and had already received many of the requested materials.

The court held that discovery without temporal, geographic or subject matter limitation was overbroad. It also noted that discovery already obtained by counsel from other ongoing cases between the same parties provided a means to lessen the burden of duplicate discovery requests on Ford.[31]

Here, the trial court abused its discretion when ordering Ford to comply with all of Dietiker's discovery requests. Adhering to Rule 56, the trial court was ordered to vacate its order to compel and limit discovery to the reasonable parameters of the petition allowing discovery of relevant and temporal subject matter that has not already been discovered. The trial court was ordered to establish a factual record of individual challenges to discovery materials and issue protective orders when required.

§ 15.10 DEFECT CATEGORY AND TIME FRAMES

The primary consideration on the question of determining the beginning and end points for investigative research and discovery is the generic type or types of defect involved in the case. Each defect type has a fairly clear period of history associated with it that bears directly on the issue of relevancy in both a discovery and evidentiary sense.

During prefiling research counsel for both sides should follow whatever historical leads may be found with respect to the science, technology, industry, regulation and the company under investigation. Becoming acquainted with the general areas where any such data may be found is one of the most important goals for the products litigator. It will provide a feel for the scientific, governmental and business context of the litigation and facilitate identification of the range of relevant issues that may be involved. Once accomplished, counsel may then be able to isolate those points in time in the life of the defendant corporation when state-of-the-art material and internal company documents addressing central technological and manufacturing issues were likely generated.

---

[31] *Id.* at 381.

Another important discovery goal is the education of a range of judges who will be involved in resolving key pretrial complaint process and discovery in the litigation. Whether a contested motion judge or trial judge, the reality is that they are normally totally unfamiliar with the scientific, industry, regulatory or company aspects of the nascent litigation. Hence, judicial education is a primary goal for both plaintiff and defense counsel.

§ 15.11 TIME FRAMES IN UNIT DEFECT CASES

The unit defect case involves the most restrictive time frame, which usually commences from the date that plaintiff purchased a unit of the product up to the date of the injury. This is the only category of defect where strict liability truly exists. Here, the product unit with which the client had contact is flawed in a real sense. Due to this flaw or defect, the unit is dangerously different from the other units in the same line manufactured by the defendant. In most instances the flaw can be identified with some precision and the product unit isolated from the general line of similar goods manufactured by the defendant.[32]

In this category of defect, true strict liability principles control the information flow in the trial. In these settings, the basic public policy underpinnings of strict liability have full force and effect. The time, effort and money spent by defendant to prevent mismanufactured units from reaching the inventory shelf, the inherent merits of its design or its relative position when examined in reference to the state of the art, are all irrelevant to the analysis.[33]

Plaintiff need to prove the flaw or defect in their unit, absence of alterations or modifications, use within the anticipated range of intended uses of the product and proximate causation. The legal focus is the single offending product unit. The defendant's production of the defective unit provides the frame of reference that reflects the defective nature of this unit. The relevant time frame in the unit manufacturing defect case is the period of time from the date that the suspect product was manufactured and left the hands of the manufacturer, up to the date of the date of the injury producing event.

This does not mean that lawyers for the plaintiff are relieved of an obligation to engage in product research relative to the basic design, materials composition and production of the product. That data is needed to determine if the case product unit is truly a defective unit. The extensive time frame over which technical research must be conducted in the typical design category case is not present here. The right or wrong of defendant's conscious

---

[32] TERRENCE F. KIELY, SCIENCE AND LITIGATION: PRODUCTS LIABILITY IN THEORY AND PRACTICE 342 (CRC Press 2002).

[33] *Id.*

design choices prior to marketing the good have no bearing on the overriding issue of the integrity of the offending product unit.[34]

§ 15.12 TIME FRAMES IN DESIGN DEFECT CASES

In products liability cases centered in the *design* categories [Packaging, Overall Design, Instructions, and Warnings] the inception of the time frame is typically the point when the earliest references in the authoritative literature to the technology or design feature involved in the case are found. The time frame begins at that period and arguably ends at the point in company history when the specifications for the suspect design were frozen and production authorized. As we have seen that can be and often is a decades long period of scientific, industry, regulatory and corporate history. Warnings related to the use of the pain killer Percodan, for example, can go back to the early 1950s. A significant amount of science has come and gone over such a period that would reflect on the manufacturer's knowledge of potentially dangerous side-effects. The same can be said for potential problems associated with attention deficit drugs such as Ritalin[35] or a wide range of current anti-depression medications.[36]

There are three important focal considerations in estimating investigative, discovery and trial time frames in cases centered within one of the design defect categories:

1. The model year of the product unit or the year of the introduction of a drug or chemical with their respective sets of instructions and warnings.

2. Whether the suspect design, component instructions or warnings have been utilized in earlier years or in earlier model year offerings of the same or comparable product lines in the United States or foreign markets.

3. The period of time over which the technology or instruction or warning in the case has been addressed in the state of the art literature and/or been adopted or utilized in the industry within which defendant does business.

These three areas provide a wide but manageable set of boundaries for pretrial research of the type discussed in Chapter 12, Researching the Products Case. While the model year of the suspect unit may be an arguably terminal date in the manufactured product design case, it is by no means

---

[34] *See, e.g.,* O'Brien v. Muskin Corp., 463 A.2d 298 (N.J. 1983).

[35] *FDA Probing ADHD Drug Side Effects. Ritalin, Concerta Possibly Linked to Psychiatric Problems,* http://www.msnbc.msn.com/id/8403762.

[36] See the FDA letter requiring increased warnings of suicide for sellers of antidepressants, http://www.fda.gov/cder/drug/antidepressants/SSRIlabelChange.htm.

determinative of the inception of the relevant time frame. In instances of a technology basic to an industry, such as the design of automobile door locks or gas tanks, of which the offending unit is a result, the relevant historical time frame can be extensive. Accordingly, relevant state of the art materials and internal company records often antedate the model year of the suspect unit by several years.

In the design defect counts, plaintiff is necessarily challenging the propriety of defendant's conscious design choices for the entire line of goods of which the offending unit is a member. The company, being considered an expert, is deemed to have constructive knowledge of the findings of all authoritative literature in its fields of research and development.[37] Plaintiffs can also argue for the discovery of documents addressing *subsequent* technological developments to the extent they indicate the existence of a feasible alternative design prior to the point in time when the specifications of the suspect design were fixed for production purposes.[38]

§ 15.13 TIME FRAMES IN FAILURE TO INSTRUCT OR WARN CASES

Cases centered in allegations of failure to properly instruct in the safe use of a manufactured article or in allegations of failure to warn of risks and side-effects in prescription drug settings, constitute a large part of the products liability litigation in American state and federal courts. In these cases, the time frame for investigative and discovery research typically runs from the initial development of the item to the date of the injury-producing event. This is because the legal focus is on the absence or inadequacy of the instruction or warning accompanying the product, and thus the heart of the case lies in defendant's knowledge of danger. Prior to release of the product into the stream of commerce, any such knowledge would be had from study of the relevant scientific literature and any knowledge gained from studying commercial uses of the design feature allegedly raising the risk. The end point of the time frame is the date of the injury-producing event. The defendant manufacturer's obligation to adequately warn or instruct is an ongoing one over the course of the product's market life. Such duty does not depend upon any internal corporate guidelines as to finalization of product specifications for production purposes.

---

[37] Lindsay v. Ortho Pharmaceutical Corp., 637 F.2d 87 (2d Cir. 1980).

[38] *See* D.L. v. Heubner, 329 N.W.2d 890 (Wis.1983); Schelbauer v. Butler Mfg. Co., 673 P.2d 743 (Cal. 1984). Additionally, some courts hold that the traditional ban against the admissibility of subsequent remedial measures has no applicability to strict liability cases. Sanderson v. Steve Snyder Enterprises, 196 Conn. 134 (1985); Holmes v. Sahara Coal Company, 475 N.E.2d 1383 (Ill. App. Ct. 1985); Caprara v. Chrysler Corporation, 417 N.E.2d 545 (N.Y. 1981).

In these cases, the legal and factual focus is on the defendant's opportunities for determining product risks and acting responsibly in light of them. The recent concern and litigation over the adequacy of warnings about heart attacks for users of Merck Corporation's Vioxx pain killer is an excellent example of the this point. All scientific information, whether internal or external to the defendant company that demonstrates the possibility of gaining knowledge is subject to discovery and admissible at trial. This would include all testing and related documentation on the basic design feature at issue in the case generated after the release of the suspect unit for sale. In cases of products such as basic automotive features such as axles or prescription drugs that experience little or no change after their initial production, amount of discoverable post-production data can be substantial.[39]

§ 15.14 TIME FRAMES IN MISREPRESENTATION CASES

In the 402B or misrepresentation case,[40] the start of the relevant discovery time frame, as with all design cases, begins with the first inklings in the literature relative to the design feature under scrutiny. Since the risks involved stem from some design flaw typically lies at the heart of the defendant's misstatement, it logically determines the starting point for analysis.

In determining the end point of the time frame in misrepresentation cases, the same considerations as pertain to instruction and warning cases apply. In all three instances, the focus is on the form and nature of communications that were made to the consumer in marketing literature as opposed to technological considerations proper. In the misrepresentation case, however, the time frame is generally considered to be terminated at the date of purchase, inasmuch as the central legal focal point is justifiable reliance on a misstated inducement to buy. Accordingly, the terminal point of the time frame can be substantially shorter than in counts grounded in failure to instruct or warn.

§ 15.15 ORGANIZATION AND DRAFTING OF DISCOVERY REQUESTS

Interrogatories and requests to produce documents seek information from the same corpus of internal documents in the possession of the defendant. Interrogatories seek very specific answers to questions tailored to elicit the organizational structure of the defendant, the names and titles of

---

[39] *See* Robert B. Patterson, *Products Liability: The Manufacturer's Continuing Duty to Improve His Product or Warn of Defects After Sale*, 62 ILL. B.J. 92 (October 1973); LaBelle v. McCauley Indus. Corp., 649 F.2d 46 (1st Cir.1981).

[40] See Chapter 3, Misrepresentation, for a detailed analysis of this category of products liability litigation.

committee members, the names of groups, offices, department and sections, wherein the decisions of interest to plaintiff were processed and finalized. Requests for the Production of Documents address the same corpus of corporate documentation and should be planned with a consistent organizational method and terminology.

There are a series of corporate activities that may serve as the organizational focal points bases for the actual drafting of discovery requests, whether interrogatories or document requests:

1. The case time frames.

2. The routine corporate phases over the case time frame(s) from the idea stage to the inventory shelf and the document types typically generated in any one of such phases. Design, Testing, Production, Marketing and Post-Marketing are typical stages over the course of product development and manufacture.

3. The identifiable activities occurring within any one phase in that overall process. The early Design phase will generate documents that tend to cross lines since designers, technicians, financial personnel, labor supervisors and marketing staff all add input to the design details and prospects for government regulatory problems, competition and the like.

4. The types of documents likely generated at any one point in time as a result of such activities. The Testing period of a product will obviously generate documents distinctly different from those concerned with the overall marketing and distributorship planning.

5. The offices, departments, sections, committees and key personnel involved in those document generating functions.

Initially planning requests around those broad aspects of the manufacture of a product will provide a structured approach to discovery that lends itself to consistent responses to the inevitable objections to any broad-based discovery requests. Concentrating on routine document generating processes over designated time periods and grounding requests in the document types logically associated with the defect modes involved in the case, provides organizational clarity. This clarity substantially minimizes the defendant's opportunities to divert the court's attention from the underlying documentary reality of the case. Discovery requests obtained from form books not only make for a very poor impression, but are simply inadequate. Closely considered customized requests are the most effective devices for achieving success in these cases.[41]

---

[41] See KIELY, *supra* note 32, at 347-348.

§ 15.16 INADVERTENT DISCLOSURE IN DISCOVERY

The issues involved in instances of inadvertent production of privileged documents in discovery are not new. Complex litigation involving the increased use of photocopy machines, facsimile transmission, electronic mail, and other technologies have resulted in a significant increase in these cases, in which parties contend that their privileged information has inadvertently been disclosed to opponents. The courts vary as to whether they will find a waiver in such circumstances, whether they will remedy the situation, and, if a waiver is to be found, the scope of such waiver. The problem of inadvertent discovery has come to the fore in very recent days due to the great attention being paid to the phenomenon of electronic discovery. Two recent annotations address the important issues involved and the range of judicial solutions under federal and state law.[42]

A survey conducted by the ABA Digital Evidence Project, a working group of the Section of Science and Technology Law, reported that 12 percent of respondents found that privileged information was inadvertently produced during the gathering and subsequent production of electronic evidence.[43]

§ 15.17 ELECTRONIC DISCOVERY

As noted by author Jason Krause in a recent ABA Journal article:

> It's mainly a matter of volume. The discovery phase of a trial can involve millions of pages of documents from e-mail, word processing, instant messaging, handheld devices or even deleted data that has been recovered and restored.

> The chair of the ABA's Digital Evidence Project, attorney George Paul of Phoenix, notes that the handling of privileged documents is one of the most controversial aspects of proposed new civil procedure rules. Proposed rule 26(b)5(B) includes a clawback provision that would apply to any type of document involved in discovery.

---

[42] *See* Annotation, *Waiver Of Evidentiary Privilege By Inadvertent Waiver Of Evidentiary Privilege By Inadvertent Disclosure — Federal Law*, 159 A.L.R. FED. 153 (For several years, courts and commentators have debated vigorously whether and to what extent an inadvertent release of privileged information should be construed as a waiver of evidentiary privilege under federal law); Annotation, *Waiver Of Evidentiary Privilege By Inadvertent Disclosure — State Law*, 51 A.L.R. 5TH 603; PAUL R. RICE, ATTORNEY-CLIENT PRIVILEGE IN THE UNITED STATES, SECOND EDITION [Database updated April 2005], Chapter 9, § 9:70 Waiver, F. *Exceptions to Waiver by Voluntary Disclosure. See also* Anita Ramasastry, *The Proposed Federal E-Discovery Rules: While Trying to Add Clarity, the Rules Still Leave Uncertainty*, http://writ.news.findlaw.com/ramasastry/20040915.html.

By far, the greatest number of judicial discussions of *inadvertent discovery* are had in criminal cases involving issues of plain view search claims by the state or federal government. This is a quite distinct problem from the topic when centered in discovery in complex civil cases.

[43] *See* Jason Krause, *Porous Privilege: Lawyers Struggle to Keep Work Product, Legal Advice Secret in Electronic Discovery*, 91-AUG. A.B.A.J. 61 (2005).

Under the proposed rule, if one side were to claim a document is privileged after producing it to opposing counsel, the side that received the document would have to return, sequester or destroy the document and retrieve any copies that it distributed, pending a court ruling on the document's admissibility.

Privileged documents, including inadvertently produced documents, are now handled according to different rules and standards in each jurisdiction.[44]

In today's current litigation climate the greatest number of important documents in large-scale products liability cases are to be found in electronically generated emails, word processed documents, or spreadsheets.[45] The electronic archiving of corporate information is nothing new to litigators seeking corporate records. The most significant aspect of the current obsession with electronic discovery is really centered in e-mails, including those that were deleted but are still accessible by software and hard drive examinations.[46] The new catch phrase *data forensics* has been coined to describe the processes involved in the crucial mining of electronic data on a wide variety of corporate computer-related equipment.[47]

---

[44] *Id.* at 62.

[45] *See LPT Virtual Roundtable: A Goldmine of Electronic Discovery Expertise: A Conversation Among Veterans of Electronic Discovery Battles*, http://www.abanet.org/lpm/lpt/articles/ftr07041.html. (Interesting and wide-ranging discussion by seasoned lawyers in the fields of complex litigation and electronic discovery.)

[46] *See* Carole Longendyke, *SEEK AND FIND: Data Forensics Brings CSI to Your Office*, 24 No. 4 LEGAL MGMT. 20 (2005). (Data forensics in your office may not hold the same allure as the forensic sciences that deal with blood evidence, fingerprints, DNA and fiber analysis, but your trace data are relevant and useful in investigations. Administrators need to be aware of what their systems capture and store — and how that information can be used.)

[47] Data forensics is the collection, preservation, analysis and presentation of evidence found on electronic devices. In contrast to traditional crime scene investigation that involves the collection of fingerprints, blood, fibers, etc., at the scene of the crime, the "crime scene" in the data forensic investigation is typically a computer or other electronic device. *Id.* at 20.

There is a growing body of books,[48] practice literature,[49] and websites[50] devoted to this relatively new and complex litigation phenomenon. All of them seek to address the problem of attempting, let alone adequately completing electronic discovery. The problem is especially acute in product liability cases involving a product with international sales over a multi-year time frame.[51] The recent cigarette and Vioxx cases will serve as good examples. There are and will be several million paper and electronic sources subject to identification, retrieval and analysis over the course of those litigations.

In addition to the categories of documents traditionally associated with various types of manufactured products such as engineered goods, chemicals or pharmaceuticals, counsel must also be concerned with the identification of the defendant's computer systems, e-mail programs, digital archives and a host of other minutiae not typically associated with an already burdensome discovery workload. It is clear that a respondent's limitation of discovery to hard copies will no longer suffice.[52] Areas which would be the subject of interrogatories and document requests would include the names and current company position if any of all personnel with authority for the use of computers or management of data systems, identification of all computers currently in use and those no longer in use but

---

[48] See PAUL R. RICE, ELECTRONIC EVIDENCE: LAW AND PRACTICE (ABA 2005); MICHELE C.S. LANGE & KRISTIN NIMSGER, ELECTRONIC EVIDENCE AND DISCOVERY: WHAT EVERY LAWYER SHOULD KNOW (ABA 2004); MICHAEL R. ARKFELD, ELECTRONIC DISCOVERY AND EVIDENCE (Ring-bound) (Law Partner Publishing 2003).

[49] See Monique C.M. Leahy, J.D., *Recovery and Reconstruction of Electronic Mail as Evidence*, 41 AM. JUR. 3D 1 (POF) (American Jurisprudence Proof of Facts) [Database updated June 2005]; Symposium on Proposed Change to FRCP Federal Rule of Civil Procedure; Ken Withers, *Two Tiers And A Safe Harbor: Federal Rulemakers Grapple With E-Discovery*, 51-SEP. FED. LAW. 29 (2004); Patrick R. Grady, *Discovery of Computer Stored Documents and Computer Based Litigation Support Systems: Why Give Up More Than Necessary*, 14 J. MARSHALL COMPUTER & INFO. L. 523, 539 (1996); Richard L. Marcus, *Confronting the Future: Coping with Discovery of Electronic Material*, 64 LAW & CONTEMP. PROBS. 253, 253 (2001); LANGE & NIMSGER, *supra* note 48, at 30-40; Kenneth J. Withers, *Computer Based Discovery in Federal Civil Litigation*, 2000 FEDERAL COURTS LAW REVIEW 2 (October 2000).

[50] See the excellent and extensive collection of e-discovery materials collected by Kenneth J. Withers, *Annotated Case Law and Further Reading on Electronic Discovery* [Updated March 10, 2004], http://www.kenwithers.com. (This website is maintained by Ken Withers of the Federal Judicial Center, but is unofficial. It contains articles on electronic discovery, sets of PowerPoint slides and text from judicial education and bar association seminars on electronic discovery, and additional resources.) *See also* Kroll-Ontrack, http://www.krollontrack.com/LawLibrary/. (Commercial e-discovery company.)

[51] See Kenneth J. Withers, *Computer Based Discovery in Federal Civil Litigation*, 2000 FEDERAL COURTS LAW REVIEW 2 (October 2000). This is an excellent guide to navigating the initial conferences in cases heavily invested in various forms of electronic discovery. *See also* Lorie J. Marco & Katie M. Connoly, *Electronic Records: What To Look And Ask For (With Glossary)*, 15 No. 2 PRAC. LITIGATOR 39 (2004).

[52] See Zubulake v. UBS Warburg, 217 F.R.D. 309 (S.D.N.Y. 2003) (despite defendant's offer of 100 pages of hard copy e-mails, further electronic production was required).

accessible; all software systems such as networks, databases, spreadsheets, graphics, wordprocessors, e-mail programs, tape and digital archival systems and programs, telecommunications and internet software and systems and all data storage and retrieval capabilities for current and warehoused hardware and software.[53]

The costs of retrieval of data from retired hard drives and older archival programs, let alone current documents and e-mails can be staggering. The recent cigarette and Vioxx litigations may serve as example of cases where literally millions of documents are potentially involved. This reality has resulted in a number of recent articles examining the topic of cost-shifting and cost-sharing in such cases.[54] A series of decisions known as the *Zubulake* cases, addresses a wide range of cost-shifting issues, and are considered authoritative references on the subject.[55]

---

[53] Kroll Ontrack provides a comprehensive set of Sample Interrogatories for use in the federal district courts. *See* Kroll OnTrack, Sample Interrogatories, http://www.krollontrack.com/practicaltools/Interrogatory_mailer.pdf. The complete starter set, free of charge, includes Rule 16(c) Pretrial Conference Agenda for Computer-Based Discovery, Sample Preservation letter — to client, Sample Preservation letter — to opponent or 3rd party, Sample Fed. R. Civ. P. 30(b)(6) Deposition Notice, Sample E-Discovery Interrogatories and a Sample Motion to Compel Electronic Discovery.

[54] *See, e.g.,* Mohammad Iqbal, *The New Paradigms Of E-Discovery And Cost-Shifting. Determining Who Pays for Electronic Discovery*, 72 DEF. COUNS. J. 283 (July 2005). This is an excellent, comprehensive article setting out all of the issues involved in the move towards cost allocations in electronic discovery, with a very useful arrangement and summary of the key cases. *See also* Michele C.S. Lange, *Who Should Pay For Electronic Discovery?*, 48-FEB. B.B.J. 14 (2005); Shira A. Scheindlin & Jeffery Rabkin, *Electronic Discovery in Federal Civil Litigation: Is Rule 34 up to the Task?* 41 B.C. L. REV. 327, 368. (2000); Virginia Llewellyn, *Electronic Discovery Best Practices*, 10 RICH. J.L. & TECH. 51. (2004). *See also* Toshiba America Electronic Components v. The Superior Court of Santa Clara County, 124 Cal. App. 4th 762, 21 Cal. Rptr. 3d 532 (2004) (The court concluded that proper cases may require the demanding party to pay retrieval expenses. The determination of a proper case is a factual matter best left to the discretion of the trial court.).

[55] There are five *Zubulake* decisions, two dealing with cost-shifting, two with sanctions, and one unrelated to e-discovery.

- Zubulake I, May 13, 2003: Zubulake v. UBS Warburg, 217 F.R.D. 309 (S.D.N.Y. 2003) (stating legal standards for determining cost-shifting for producing emails stored on backup tapes);

- Zubulake II, May 13, 2003: Zubulake v. UBS Warburg, 230 F.R.D. 290 (S.D. N.Y. 2003) (denying release of deposition transcript to securities regulators);

- Zubulake III, July 24, 2003: Zubulake v. UBS Warburg, 216 F.R.D. 280 (S.D.N.Y. 2003) (allocating backup tape restoration costs between parties);

- Zubulake IV, October 22, 2003: Zubulake v. UBS Warburg, 220 F.R.D. 212 (S.D. N.Y. 2003) (ordering sanctions against UBS for violating its duty to preserve evidence); and

- Zubulake V, July 20, 2004: Zubulake v. UBS Warburg, 229 F.R.D. 422 (S.D. N.Y. 2004) (imposing sanctions). *See* Iqbal, *supra* note 54.

In Zubulake IV,[56] the court noted a distinction between accessible electronic evidence, such as evidence on hard drives, servers, optical disks, magnetic tapes, or removable media, and inaccessible electronic evidence, such as evidence on a backup tape or erased, fragmented, or damaged data. As to accessible evidence, the court said the cost of production should presumptively remain with the responding party, just as with conventional paper discovery. The court treated inaccessible evidence differently. It held that costs of production could be apportioned depending on the following seven factors, in order of importance:

(1) the extent to which the request is specifically tailored to discover relevant information;

(2) the availability of such information from other sources;

(3) the total cost of production compared to the amount in controversy;

(4) the total cost of production compared to the resources available to each party;

(5) the relative ability of each party to control costs and its incentive to do so;

(6) the importance of the issue at stake in the litigation; and

(7) the relative benefits to the parties of obtaining the information.[57]

The Zublake and other cases have utilized the idea of sampling to avoid undue expense and delay to estimate whether producing a larger volume of electronic evidence is worth the cost, and, if so, which party should pay for the effort. In sampling settings the requesting party highlights a small selection of electronic data for the producing party to restore and submit for inspection, typically from difficult to access sources such as backup tapes and discontinued archival systems, where restoration and production costs are routinely high. The court will then evaluates the sample and craft an appropriate production and cost-allocation order, based on whatever multi-factor test the court considers appropriate.[58]

---

[56] Zubulake v. UBS Warburg, 217 F.R.D. 309 (S.D.N.Y. 2003).

[57] *Id. See also* David K. Isom, *Electronic Discovery Primer For Judges*, FED. COURTS L. REV. (February 2005). (Excellent and comprehensive.)

[58] Jonathan M. Redgrave Erica J. Bachmann, *Cost-Shifting in Electronic Discovery*, 50-DEC. FED. LAW. 31 (2003). A good recent summary of the key issues and suggested guidelines for action can be found in *The Sedona Principles: Best Practices Recommendations & Principles for Addressing Electronic Document Production* (March 2003), http:// www.thesedonaconference.org/publicationshtml. See http://www.thesedonaconference.org/wgs for more information on The Sedona Conference and its working groups.

A steady stream of very thoughtful articles and conference materials are becoming available online. They range from comprehensive, related articles, in *Trial Magazine*[59] to the recent publication of the Sedona Conference[60]

---

[59] *See Electronic Evidence*, TRIAL, October 2005. *See also*:

Gathering digital data

Richard J. Arsenault & John Randall Whaley

(In the digital age, it's not enough to know what documents or information to ask for in discovery. You also need to know what kind of computer system the defendant is using to store those documents, how the system works, and how to frame your requests. A clear, specific preservation letter and detailed requests for production will ensure that you get exactly what you need.)

A practical guide to e-mail discovery

Craig Ball

(Do you know the difference between IMAP and POP? Or whether it matters if the opposing party uses Gmail or Hotmail? With e-mail replacing communication that used to happen over the phone, in person, or by letter, these digital missives are an essential target of discovery.)

Electronic evidence in everyday cases

William S. Friedlander & Mark A. Buchanan

(Digital evidence can play a role in almost any type of lawsuit. A search through electronic records might reveal a deceitful spouse in a matrimonial case. And an employment case might turn up a "smoking gun" showing an intent to retaliate.)

Make the most of e-data experts

Keith L. Altman

(When it comes to electronic data, two heads are definitely better than one. Match your subject-matter expert with a hands-on technical expert who can search the defendant's database, find hidden information, or run specialized queries.)

Can this photo be trusted?

Edward J. Imwinkelried

(Digital cameras produce pictures that are easy to work with; computer technology can change the colors, sharpnesss, or other elements of a photo. But this ease of alteration also means that photos produced as evidence may not be what they seem. Here's how to recognize when your opponent's digital photos may be misleading, and how to use your own digital images to best effect.)

Ethics in the era of electronic evidence

Christopher D. Wall

(Electronic records are fairly new to litigation, so you may not have had a chance to brush up on the ethics involved in this type of discovery. What do the federal rules and bar codes of conduct say about your e-discovery obligations? And how can you make sure that you—and your opponent—are fulfilling your duties? High-tech tools like online document repositories can help.)

[60] The Sedona Conference exists to allow leading jurists, lawyers, experts, academics and others, at the cutting edge of issues in the area of antitrust law, complex litigation, and intellectual property rights, to come together — in conferences and mini-think tanks (Working Groups) — and engage in true dialogue, not debate, all in an effort to move the law forward in a reasoned and just way. The documents currently available from the Sedona Conference may be acccessed at http://www.thesedonaconference.org/.

Principles for Electronic Document Production.[61] The latter are receiving increased attention in the growing literature addressed to the pressing problems in products liability and other areas of complex litigation.

---

[61] The Sedona Conference Principles for Electronic Document Production:

1. Electronic data and documents are potentially discoverable under FED. R. CIV. P. 34 or its state law equivalents. Organizations must properly preserve electronic data and documents that can reasonably be anticipated to be relevant to litigation.

2. When balancing the cost, burden, and need for electronic data and documents, courts and parties should apply the balancing standard embodied in FED. R. CIV. P. 26(b)(2) and its state law equivalents, which require considering the technological feasibility and realistic costs of preserving, retrieving, producing, and reviewing electronic data, as well as the nature of the litigation and the amount in controversy.

3. Parties should confer early in discovery regarding the preservation and production of electronic data and documents when these matters are at issue in the litigation, and seek to agree on the scope of each party's rights and responsibilities.

4. Discovery requests should make as clear as possible what electronic documents and data are being asked for, while responses and objections to discovery should disclose the scope and limits of what is being produced.

5. The obligation to preserve electronic data and documents requires reasonable and good faith efforts to retain information that may be relevant to pending or threatened litigation. However, it is unreasonable to expect parties to take every conceivable step to preserve all potentially relevant data.

6. Responding parties are best situated to evaluate the procedures, methodologies, and technologies appropriate for preserving and producing their own electronic data and documents.

7. The requesting party has the burden on a motion to compel to show that the responding party's steps to preserve and produce relevant electronic data and documents were inadequate.

8. The primary source of electronic data and documents for production should be active data and information purposely stored in a manner that anticipates future business use and permits efficient searching and retrieval. Resort to disaster recovery backup tapes and other sources of data and documents requires the requesting party to demonstrate need and relevance that outweigh the cost, burden, and disruption of retrieving and processing the data from such sources.

9. Absent a showing of special need and relevance a responding party should not be required to preserve, review, or produce deleted, shadowed, fragmented, or residual data or documents.

10. A responding party should follow reasonable procedures to protect privileges and objections to production of electronic data and documents.

11. A responding party may satisfy its good faith obligation to preserve and produce potentially responsive electronic data and documents by using electronic tools and processes, such as data sampling, searching, or the use of selection criteria, to identify data most likely to contain responsive information.

12. Unless it is material to resolving the dispute, there is no obligation to preserve and produce metadata absent agreement of the parties or order of the court.

13. Absent a specific objection, agreement of the parties or order of the court, the reasonable costs of retrieving and reviewing electronic information for produc-

§ 15.18 SUMMARY

Chapters 16 through 18 will address the subject of discovery in greater detail by analyzing the theory and practice for interrogatories, requests for admission of fact, requests for documentation and depositions. Chapter 19 will discuss objections to discovery, protective orders and motions-in-limine.

---

tion should be borne by the responding party, unless the information sought is not reasonably available to the responding party in the ordinary course of business. If the data or formatting of the information sought is not reasonably available to the responding party in the ordinary course of business, then, absent special circumstances, the costs of retrieving and reviewing such electronic information should be shifted to the requesting party.

14. Sanctions, including spoliation findings, should only be considered by the court if, upon a showing of a clear duty to preserve, the court finds that there was an intentional or reckless failure to preserve and produce relevant electronic data and that there is a reasonable probability that the loss of the evidence has materially prejudiced the adverse party.

Chapter 16

INTERROGATORIES AND REQUESTS TO ADMIT FACTS

SYNOPSIS

§ 16.01 INTRODUCTION

This chapter focuses on the general structure and style of interrogatories in products liability cases. Examples of interrogatories in an automobile rollover case, an exploding pressurized stainless steel beverage container and a defectively designed stand-up forklift case are provided to illustrate the points made.

§ 16.02 INTERROGATORIES — STATUTORY DEFINITIONS — FEDERAL

The Federal Rules of Civil Procedure provide for the issuance and management of interrogatories in Rule 33:

FRCP Rule 33 — Interrogatories to Parties

(a) Availability. Without leave of court or written stipulation, any party may serve upon any other party written interrogatories, not exceeding 25 in number including all discrete subparts, to be answered by the party served or, if the party served is a public or private corporation or a partnership or association or governmental agency, by any officer or agent, who shall furnish such information as is available to the party. Leave to serve additional interrogatories shall be granted to the extent consistent with the principles of Rule 26(b)(2). Without leave of court or written stipulation, interrogatories may not be served before the time specified in Rule 26(d).

(b) Answers and Objections.

(1) Each interrogatory shall be answered separately and fully in writing under oath, unless it is objected to, in which event the objecting party shall state the reasons for objection and shall answer to the extent the interrogatory is not objectionable.

(2) The answers are to be signed by the person making them, and the objections signed by the attorney making them.

(3) The party upon whom the interrogatories have been served shall serve a copy of the answers, and objections if any, within 30 days after the service of the interrogatories. A shorter or longer time may be directed by the court or, in the absence of such an order, agreed to in writing by the parties subject to Rule 29.

(4) All grounds for an objection to an interrogatory shall be stated with specificity. Any ground not stated in a timely objection is waived unless the party's failure to object is excused by the court for good cause shown. (5) The party submitting the interrogatories may move for an order under Rule 37(a) with respect to any objection to or other failure to answer an interrogatory.

(c) Scope; Use at Trial. Interrogatories may relate to any matters which can be inquired into under Rule 26(b)(1), and the answers may be used to the extent permitted by the rules of evidence.

An interrogatory otherwise proper is not necessarily objectionable merely because an answer to the interrogatory involves an

opinion or contention that relates to fact or the application of law to fact, but the court may order that such an interrogatory need not be answered until after designated discovery has been completed or until a pre-trial conference or other later time.

(d) Option to Produce Business Records. Where the answer to an interrogatory may be derived or ascertained from the business records of the party upon whom the interrogatory has been served or from an examination, audit or inspection of such business records, including a compilation, abstract or summary thereof and the burden of deriving or ascertaining the answer is substantially the same for the party serving the interrogatory as for the party served, it is a sufficient answer to such interrogatory to specify the records from which the answer may be derived or ascertained and to afford to the party serving the interrogatory reasonable opportunity to examine, audit or inspect such records and to make copies, compilations, abstracts or summaries. A specification shall be in sufficient detail to permit the interrogating party to locate and to identify, as readily as can the party served, the records from which the answer may be ascertained.

§ 16.03 INTERROGATORIES — STATUTORY DEFINITIONS — STATE

State law provides a similar scheme for the issuance and parameters of the interrogatories discovery tool. Illinois Supreme Court Rule 213 may serve as an example:

Rule 213. Written Interrogatories to Parties

(a) Directing Interrogatories. A party may direct written interrogatories to any other party. A copy of the interrogatories shall be served on all other parties entitled to notice.

(b) Duty of Attorney. It is the duty of an attorney directing interrogatories to restrict them to the subject matter of the particular case, to avoid undue detail, and to avoid the imposition of any unnecessary burden or expense on the answering party.

(c) Number of Interrogatories. Except as provided in subparagraph (j), a party shall not serve more than 30 interrogatories, including sub-parts, on any other party except upon agreement of the parties or leave of court granted upon a showing of good cause. A motion for leave of court to serve more than 30 interrogatories must be in writing and shall set forth the proposed interrogatories and the reasons establishing good cause for their use.

(d) Answers and Objections. Within 28 days after service of the interrogatories upon the party to whom they are directed, the party shall serve a sworn answer or an objection to each interrogatory, with proof of service upon all other parties entitled to notice. Any objection to an answer or to the refusal to answer an interrogatory shall be heard by the court upon prompt notice and motion of the party propounding the interrogatory. The answering party shall set forth in full each interrogatory being answered immediately preceding the answer. Sworn answers to interrogatories directed to a public or private corporation, or a partnership or association shall be made by an officer, partner, or agent, who shall furnish such information as is available to the party.

§ 16.04 INTERROGATORIES — LIMITATIONS ON NUMBER

A continuing problem in organizing and drafting interrogatories are limitations placed on the number of interrogatories allowed in the first wave of discovery and whether sub-parts in a question will count against the total allowed. This issue is of considerable importance given the very large, essentially disparate areas of inquiry that are legitimate investigative targets and a general initial limit of 30 questions, including all "sub-parts. The limitation on the number of initial interrogatories was an attempt to force litigators to think about their information needs and to organize their discovery along reasonable lines. All too often in the past parties seeking answers to interrogatories would issue shotgun requests running into a hundred or more poorly considered and repetitious inquiries.[1] While such limitations may cause hardship in cases involving significant time frames, they are nonetheless becoming standard in state discovery statutes and motion practice. This is not a new development,[2] but continues to draw attention as products liability cases increase in complexity.[3] Some jurisdictions make no mention of specific numerical limits, instead allowing the courts to monitor any excesses.[4]

---

[1] See Cohn, *Federal Discovery: A Survey of Local Rules and Practices in View of Proposed Changes to the Federal Rules*, 63 MINN. L. REV.253 (1979). It is the intent of such rules to force lawyers to carefully consider the categories of information they are seeking and organize their written requests accordingly.

[2] See R. HAYDOCK & D. HERR, DISCOVERY PRACTICE 288-296 (Boston: Little, Brown & Co. 1982).

[3] See Ronald J. Berke & Andrew L. Berke, *ATLA's Litigating Tort Cases*, Chapter 16. Interrogatories (Database updated July 2004).

The practitioner must review local rules to determine the number of interrogatories allowed. Counsel must determine whether the number of interrogatories includes sub-parts, and whether, if multiple parties are represented by a single law firm, that firm is bound by the restriction.

[4] BERKE & BERKE (citing Pennsylvania Rules of Civil Procedure, Rule 4005(c) ("The number of interrogatories or of sets of interrogatories to be served may be limited as justice

A recent decision addressing the issue of interrogatory sub-parts and the limitation of the number of interrogatories is the 2002 Colorado case of *Leaffer v. Zarlengo*,[5] holding that only discrete subparts of *non-pattern* interrogatories, and not those logically or factually subsumed within and necessarily related to the primary question, need be counted toward the interrogatory limit.[6] In *Leaffer*, a patient and her spouse brought a medical malpractice and wrongful death action against physician and others, contending that patient received inadequate care during her pregnancy. The Colorado Supreme Court held that on a matter of first impression, only discrete subparts of non-pattern interrogatories counted toward the interrogatory limit, holding that the legal question of how subparts to interrogatories should be counted was issue of significant importance and presented matter of first impression.

During the discovery stage of the litigation, Petitioners served sixteen non-pattern interrogatories, among other discovery demands, to Respondents. Respondents argued that each subpart of each interrogatory should be considered a separate question. Since the Case Management Order limited the number of non-pattern interrogatories to *twenty*, Respondents separated the interrogatories into sixty separate questions, renumbered them, and advised Petitioners to choose twenty of the sixty for Respondents to answer. For example, Plaintiffs' Interrogatory No. 11 asked: *"Describe your medical training specific to the conditions of cardiomyopathy, pre-eclampsia, and high-risk pregnancies (particularly involving twin pregnancies and advanced maternal age)."* Respondents treated this interrogatory as three separate interrogatories directed to their training for each of the conditions in question.

Petitioners filed a motion to compel responses to their first set of written discovery with the trial court, arguing that pursuant to only "discrete" subparts should be counted separately. Petitioners argued that discrete subparts are those that are not "logically or factually subsumed within and necessarily related to the primary question." Therefore, Petitioners contended, none of their interrogatories contained discrete subparts; rather, any subparts focused on issues that were logically and factually related to the primary question and therefore should not be counted separately.

The court addressed the policy bases for an initial interrogatory limitation:

> We, like the federal courts that have interpreted, recognize the importance of determining how subparts should be counted. On one hand, the extensive use of subparts could defeat the numerical limit imposed by the Case Management Order unless each subpart

---

requires to protect the party from unreasonable annoyance, embarrassment, oppression, burden, or expense.").

[5] 44 P.3d 1072 (Colo. 2002).

[6] *Also see* In re SWEPI L.P., 103 S.W.3d 578 (Tex. App. 2003).

counts as a separate question; however, if each subpart counts as a separate interrogatory, then a party's fact-gathering ability might be unduly stymied or requests for an increase in the numerical limit might become automatic.[7]

The order provided in relevant part: "Any party may serve upon any other party written interrogatories, not exceeding the number, *including all discrete subparts,* set forth in the Case Management Order, to be answered by the party served. . . ." "Any pattern interrogatory and its subparts shall be counted as one interrogatory. *Any subpart* to a non-pattern interrogatory shall be considered as a separate interrogatory."

The interrogatories at issue were *non-pattern* interrogatories. The court noted that the "any subpart" language conflicted with the "all discrete subparts" language. While subsection (e) stated that "any subpart" of a non-pattern interrogatory shall be considered a separate interrogatory, subsection (a) included "all discrete subparts." The court observed that to count each subpart — irrespective of whether it is a discrete subpart — toward the interrogatory limit would lead to the absurd result of unreasonably frustrating legitimate discovery.

Examples from the case provided illustrations of this problem. Petitioners' Interrogatory No. 12 asked Respondents to "[d]escribe the occasions on which [they] have diagnosed and/or treated individuals with cardiomyopathy, including [Respondents'] role in those cases and the circumstances and outcomes of those diagnoses and/or treatments." Respondents divided this request for a description into three questions: (1) the description; (2) Respondents' role in the cases; and (3) the circumstances or outcome of the diagnoses and/or treatments. If this interrogatory had asked for no more than a description, it would have been impossible for Respondents to split it into separate questions; however, because Petitioners followed their request for a description with requests that the description contain particular information, Respondents split it into multiple inquiries.

In addition, Petitioners' Interrogatory No. 19 asked Respondents to "[d]escribe any complaints, lawsuits, grievances, license suspension revocation proceedings, reprimands, or denials of certification instituted against [them], including the name of the complainant, the nature of the complaint, and its resolution." Respondents split this request for a description into four interrogatories: (1) the description; (2) the identity of the complainant; (3) the nature of the complaint; and (4) the resolution of the com-

---

[7] *Leaffer*, 44 P.3d at 1076 (*citing* Nyfield v. Virgin Islands Tel. Corp. 200 F.R.D. 246, 247 (D.V.I. 2001)); Williams v. Bd. of County Comm'rs of the Unified Gov't of Wyandotte County, 192 F.R.D. 698, 701 (D. Kan. 2000); Safeco v. Rawstron, 181 F.R.D. 441, 443 (C.D. Cal. 2004).

[8] *Leaffer*, 44 P.3d at 1079-1080.

plaint. The court observed that the identity of the complainant and nature and resolution of the complaint were integral parts of the description itself.[8]

> As these examples make clear, to parse out each of the requests for specific details of a particular event and require that they count as separate interrogatories would penalize a litigant for requesting information that the opposing party would already reasonably be expected to provide. Indeed, to do so would force parties to create general — perhaps even vague — open-ended interrogatories, leading to absurd results and frustrating the legitimate purpose of using interrogatories to ascertain specific facts. We emphasize that "[l]egitimate discovery efforts should not have to depend upon linguistic acrobatics."[9]

Therefore, given the application of the principles of statutory construction, the court found that the only reasonable construction of subsection (e) was that its reference to "[a]ny subpart" meant "any discrete subpart."

In fact, the court observed, federal courts interpreting local rules that do not contain the "discrete subparts" language — and thus do not have the same conflict as — still have refused to necessarily count each subpart toward the interrogatory limit; instead, they have counted a subpart as part of a single question if a direct relationship exists between the specific information called for in the interrogatory.[10] This appears to be the general position of the authorities who have addressed this important discovery issue.[11]

---

[9] *Id.* (*citing* Ginn v. Gemini Inc., 137 F.R.D. 320, 322 (D. Nev. 1991)).

[10] *See* Clark v. Burlington N. R.R., 112 F.R.D. 117, 118 (N.D. Miss.1986) (interpreting local rule providing that "each subpart of a question shall be counted as a question," reasoning that the local rule was not "intended to frustrate legitimate discovery efforts," and concluding that "an interrogatory is to be counted as but a single question . . . even though it may call for an answer containing several separate bits of information, if there is a direct relationship between the various bits of information called for"). *See also Ginn,* 137 F.R.D. at 320, 322 (interpreting local rule limiting number of interrogatories to 40 "including subparts" and holding that "subparts are to be counted as part of but one interrogatory for the purposes of [the local rule] if they are logically or factually subsumed within and necessarily related to the primary question").

[11] While discrete subparts are counted separately, subparts that are related to the primary question are not. *See* 7 JAMES WM. MOORE, MOORE'S FEDERAL PRACTICE § 33.30[2] (3d ed. 1997) ("The better view is that subparts may be counted as part of one interrogatory if they are logically and necessarily related to the primary question. This approach is most consistent with the intent of the discovery rules to provide information, not hide information, within reasonable limits."); 8A CHARLES ALAN WRIGHT, ARTHUR R. MILLER, & RICHARD L. MARCUS, FEDERAL PRACTICE AND PROCEDURE § 2168.1, at 261 (2d ed. 1994) ("[A]n interrogatory containing subparts directed at eliciting details concerning the common theme should be considered a single question, although the breadth of the area inquired about may be disputable.")

§ 16.05 ORGANIZING AND DRAFTING THE INTERROGATORIES

Interrogatories in products liability cases serve as an organizational prototype for the entire discovery stage of the case. They should be structured along the chronology and phases of the development of the suspect product. There are typically five such stages:

1. **Product Design** [Concept, market, costing, facilities and labor needs, comparative product analysis, regulatory reviews, material, initial designs, alternative designs, component parts, international requirements]

2. **Product Testing** [Testing parameters, test facilities, test requests, test goals, testing for regulatory compliance, alternative design testing, comparative product testing, drafts of test reports]

3. **Product Production** [Final product specifications, production runs, design changes]

4. **Product Marketing** [Marketing goals, market test studies, advertising campaigns and documentation]

5. **Product Post-Marketing** [Adverse reaction or defect complaint reports, regulatory activity, new design, testing and marketing documentation]

Each interrogatory should be closely reviewed to estimate any opportunity that defense counsel may have to refuse to answer on the grounds of relevancy, vagueness, or undue hardship. The basic drafting style and focus try to limit objections to a relevancy or privilege objection. Any objections potentially based on an alleged lack of clarity in the question should be immediately eliminated during the drafting process.

§ 16.06 SAMPLE INTERROGATORIES

At this point we will examine two sets of products liability interrogatories to serve as examples of organizational and drafting considerations unique to this type of complex litigation. The first set involves a products case brought as a result of severe injuries resulting from the rollover of a jeep-type vehicle on a superhighway. The interrogatories are directed to the manufacturer of the rollover vehicle, Fourwheel Corporation and Rollbar Incorporated, manufacturer of a rollbar that was allegedly defective resulting in its collapse during the rollover. We will address the drafting of interrogatories in those cases that focus on various aspects of the product development and manufacturing process for the vehicle.

This set will be followed in turn by an examination of interrogatories in two other products cases. The first of these involves an exploding commercial pressurized stainless steel beverage container and the second looks at a case of an allegedly defectively designed standup fork lift.

§ 16.07 SAMPLE INTERROGATORIES: FOUR WHEEL CORPORATION

In this example, John Consumer was driving a Jeep CJ-5 type vehicle manufactured by the defendant Fourwheel Incorporated. When executing a sharp turn to avoid a sudden obstruction on the highway, the vehicle rolled over several times, during which the roll bar failed, striking plaintiff on the head. He was also hit by the collapse of the windshield frame and ejected from the vehicle due to the allegedly defective occupant restraint system. Fourwheel is a wholly-owned subsidiary of the Outdoors Motor Company. [See this complaint in § 14.03 et seq.]

The Plaintiff John Q. Consumer, Pursuant to Rule 33 of the Federal Rules of Civil Procedure, requests that the Defendant Fourwheel Corporation answer each of the following interrogatories fully, in writing, under oath, within thirty-three (33) days of service hereof, which interrogatories shall be deemed continuing so as to require prompt supplemental answers if the Defendant obtains or recalls further information relative thereto between the time the answers are submitted to Plaintiff and the time of trial. The answers to these interrogatories should include the knowledge and beliefs of the Defendant.

INSTRUCTIONS AND DEFINITIONS

I. "Identify" when used in reference to a person (whether individual, corporation, or other entity), means to state his or its full name, present address and present telephone number if known, and in the case of an individual, his present or last known position and business affiliation.

II. "Identify" when used in reference to a document, means to state the date and author, addressee or intended recipient, type of document, or some other means of identifying it, and its present or last known location or custodian. If such document was, but no longer is, in your possession or subject to your control, state what disposition was made of it.

III. "Document" as used herein, includes but is not limited to, all abstracts, agreements, all physical forms of correspondence, including FAX transmissions, analyses, applications, books, certificates, charter charts, computer print-outs, computer read-outs, computer tapes, contracts, diaries, PDA recorded data, drafts, drawings, estimates, films, forms, graphs, jour-

nals, letters, licenses, manuals, maps, meeting reports, memoranda, memoranda of all conversations including telephone calls, notes, orders, opinions, permits, photographs, photo-maps, plans, press releases, recordings, reports, resolutions, sketches, summaries, tapes, telegrams, texts, time records, transcripts, videotapes, writings and work papers, and any copies not identical to the original, regardless whether the documents are an original or a copy and all e-mails, whether ever sent or received or intended to be sent or received, or deleted but not destroyed or otherwise erased from any PDA, laptop, desktop or computer work station.

IV. "Person or persons" means all entities, and without limiting the generality of the foregoing, includes natural persons, joint owners, associations, companies, partnerships, joint ventures, corporations, trusts and estates.

V. The answers to these INTERROGATORIES are to include any such information requested for products sold the United States and in member nations of the European Community (EC), Asia, Africa, Mexico and Central and South America.

VI. The time period covered by these interrogatories is from 1993 to 2004

INTERROGATORY NO. 1:

State the names of the Fourwheel Corporation (hereinafter referred to as FWC) Divisions, Groups, or Offices having any responsibility for either the design, testing, production or marketing of the Fourwheel Models line of utility motor vehicles and the names of the offices, departments, sections or other functional employee groupings within such Divisions, Groups or Offices, for the years 1993 to 2004, as well as the names, title and current company position, if any, of the individual employees managing such group, office, department or section for each of the designated years.

INTERROGATORY NO. 2:

State the names of the FWC committee or committees having any responsibility for the review of and/or the making of corporate decisions regarding any aspect of the design, testing, production or marketing of the Fourwheel model line of utility motor vehicles for the years 1993-2004, as well as the names, title, and current company position, if any, of the members of such committee or committees for each of the designated years.

INTERROGATORY NO. 3:

State with particularity, the corporate relationship between Outdoors Motors Corporation and Fourwheel Corporation and Rollbar, Inc., relative to Outdoors Motors Corporation's (hereinafter referred to as OMC) ownership interest in Fourwheel Corporation and Rollbar Inc.

INTERROGATORY NO. 4:

State whether any OMC offices, departments, sections, committees or any other applicable OMC organizational entity, or individual OMC employees have, for the years 1993-2004, either participated in or exercised supervisory authority in any respect, over Fourwheel Corporation policy or decisions in regard to either the design, testing, production or marketing of the Fourwheel line of utility motor vehicles, including, but not limited to the rollbars installed in such vehicles.

INTERROGATORY NO. 5:

If the answer to Interrogatory No. 4 is in the affirmative, state:

1. The name of the office, department, section, committee, or other applicable OMC organizational entity either participating in or exercising supervisory capacity as stated, as well as the nature or subject matter of the same for each of the designated years.

2. The names, titles and current company position, if any, of the individual members of such offices, departments, sections, committees or other applicable OMC organizational entity for each of the designated years.

INTERROGATORY NO. 6:

State whether any FWC offices, departments, sections, committees or any other applicable FWC organizational entity, or individual FWC employees have, for the years 1993-2004, either participated in or exercised supervisory authority in any respect, over Rollbar Inc. policy or decisions in regard to either the design, testing, production or marketing of the Rollbar Inc. rollbars installed in Fourwheel Corporation's Fourwheel line of motor vehicles.

INTERROGATORY NO. 7:

If the answer to Interrogatory No. 6 is in the affirmative, state:

1. The name of the office, department, section, committee, or other applicable FWC organizational entity either participating in or exercising supervisory capacity as stated, as well as the nature or subject matter of the same for each of the designated years.

2. The names, titles and current company position, if any, of the individual members of such offices, departments, sections, committees or other applicable FWC organizational entity for each of the designated years.

INTERROGATORY NO. 8:

State the name of the office, department, section, committee or other applicable FWC organizational entity having any responsi-

bility for liaison with Fourwheel Corporation regarding the relationship of the Fourwheel Corporation with the National Highway Traffic Safety Administration relative to Federal Motor Vehicle Safety Standards, defect investigations, recalls or other matters involving the Fourwheel line of motor vehicles, for each of the years 1993-2004. State as well, the names, title and current company position, if any, of the individual members of such offices, departments, sections, committees or other applicable FWC organizational entity for each of the designated years.

INTERROGATORY NO. 9:

State the name of the individual or individuals employed by FWC, whether Operating Officers on the Central Staff level, Product Development or Manufacturing Group Vice-President or other applicable FWC organizational title, having primary responsibility for liaison between FWC and the National Highway Traffic Safety Administration, Federal Trade Commission or other federal regulatory agencies having jurisdiction over any aspect of the design, testing, production or marketing of the Fourwheel line of motor vehicles for the years 1993-2004.

INTERROGATORY NO.10:

State for the years 1993-2004, whether FWC has made either formal or informal responses to complaints filed with the National Highway Traffic Safety Administration or its predecessor the National Highway Traffic Safety Board or the Federal Trade Commission, alleging safety related problems with the Fourwheel line of utility motor vehicles or its advertising or promotional literature. If the answer to this interrogatory is in the affirmative, state the name of the individual or group filing such petition or complaint, the date or dates of the same and a brief description of all FWC submissions in response to such petitions or complaints.

INTERROGATORY NO. 11:

State for the years 1993-2004, whether any FWC offices, departments, sections, committees or other applicable FWC organizational entity generated engineering or styling design layouts, specifications, blueprints, models, mathematical analyses, or other renderings of original, intermediate, alternative or final designs of the Fourwheel line of utility motor vehicles, including, but not limited to designs relative to rollbar materials specification, rollbar configuration, rollbar placement and attaching apparatus; windshield framing configuration and attaching apparatus; vehicle center of gravity and track width; and occupant restraint systems

INTERROGATORY NO. 12:

State whether tests were conducted on the Fourwheel line of utility vehicles, whether on a test track or in a laboratory, to determine in whole or in part, the following:

1. Rollbar strength.

2. Rollover potential.

3. Windshield framing stability.

4. Adequacy of occupant restraint systems.

INTERROGATORY NO. 13

If the answer to Interrogatory No. 12 is in the affirmative, state:

1. The test number.

2. The test title.

3. The requesting office,department, section, committee or individual.

4. The name of the testing organization.

5. The make and model of the vehicle tested.

6. The purpose of the test.

7. The test conditions and vehicle configuration.

8. The date and the current location of every such test.

INTERROGATORY NO. 14:

State whether, for the years 1993-2004, tests were conducted by FWC or anyone on their behalf, whether conducted on a test track or in a laboratory, to determine the feasibility of alternate designs other than those eventually incorporated in the production models of the Fourwheel line of utility vehicles.

INTERROGATORY NO. 15:

If the answer to Interrogatory No. 14 is in the affirmative, state:

1. The test number.

2. The test title.

3. The requesting office,department, section, committee or individual.

4. The name of the testing organization.

5. The make and model of the vehicle tested.

6. The purpose of the test.

7. The test conditions and vehicle configuration.

8. The date and the current location of every such test.

INTERROGATORY NO. 16:

State whether FWC has ever recommended to the Fourwheel Corporation, changes in the design, materials or attaching apparatus of the rollbars installed in the Fourwheel line of utility vehicles for the years 1993-2004. If the answer is in the affirmative, state the name of FWC offices, departments,sections, committees or individuals making such recommendations, as well as the action, if any, taken by Fourwheel Corporation in response to such recommendations for each of the designated years.

INTERROGATORY NO.17:

Identify by reference to standard operating procedures number or other applicable FWC organizational designation, the record retention and record destruction policies of FWC, relative to the retention or destruction of records of all types, including but not limited to financial memoranda, engineering memoranda, test reports and customer, retailer or service representative complaints regarding the safety or performance of the Fourwheel line of utility vehicles.

INTERROGATORY NO. 18:

State whether FWC has received any notification or complaints relative to the safety of the Fourwheel line of utility vehicles, from any source, with respect to rollover problems, rollbar failure, occupant restraint systems or windshield framing materials, design and attaching apparatus. If the answer is in the affirmative, state the following for each of the years 1993-2004:

1. The total number of such complaints by reference to the above categories.

2. The name and address of the individual, group or company making such complaint.

3. The FWC office, department, section, committee or individuals processing such complaints.

INTERROGATORY NO. 19:

Identify for the years 1993-2004, all lawsuits, both pending and closed, by case title, jurisdiction, docket number, date of filing and name and address of all plaintiff's counsel, in which FWC was named as a defendant against allegations alleging a negligently or defectively designed Fourwheel utility vehicle, relative to rollover problems; rollbar failure; windshield framing, materials selection or attaching apparatus problems; occupant restraint systems prob-

lems; or failure to warn and/or instruct consumers with respect to any or all of such problems.

INTERROGATORY NO. 20:

For each lawsuit referred to in Interrogatory No. 19, state:

1. The model and model year of the vehicle and a brief statement of the alleged defects in said vehicle.

2. The name and address of the owner of such vehicle.

3. A brief description of the factual circumstances giving rise to the lawsuit.

4. A brief description of the damage alleged to such vehicle.

INTERROGATORY NO. 21:

State the name of the manufacturer of the rollbar installed in the Fourwheel model 2 utility vehicle involved in the instant action, as well as the names of all manufacturers who have manufactured rollbars for the Fourwheel line of utility vehicles for each of the years 1993-2004.

INTERROGATORY NO. 22:

State whether FWC, Fourwheel Corporation or Rollbar, Inc., or any persons acting on its behalf has inspected the Fourwheel model 2 utility vehicle involved in the instant action, with respect to the mechanical and/or physical condition of said vehicle, If the answer is in the affirmative, state the dates and location of any such inspection, the identity of the person or organization making such inspection, and whether any written reports and/ or photographs were generated as a result of such inspection.

INTERROGATORY NO. 23:

State the name and current address of each person known to FWC who was present or claims to have been present at the scene of the accident giving rise to this lawsuit, as well as the names and current addresses of any other persons known to FWC who claim to have knowledge or information regarding this occurrence.

INTERROGATORY NO. 24:

Does FWC have in its possession any statements of witnesses to this occurrence or photographs of the scene or vehicles involved? If so, state the name and current address of the individuals issuing such statements and the number and subject matter of any photographs.

INTERROGATORY NO. 25:

If FWC was covered by any policy of liability insurance effective on the date of the occurrence giving rise to this action, state the effec-

tive dates, policy number, company or companies issuing such policy or policies and the maximum coverage of any such policy for each individual and each occurrence.

§ 16.08 PLAINTIFF'S FIRST SET OF INTERROGATORIES TO DEFENDANT ROLLBAR CORPORATION

Rollbar Corporation

[Manufacturer of the rollbar installed in the jeep-type vehicle in suit]

The Plaintiff John Q. Consumer, Pursuant to Rule 33 of the Federal Rules of Civil Procedure, requests that the Defendant Rollbar, Inc. answer each of the following interrogatories fully, in writing, under oath, within thirty-three (33) days of service hereof, which interrogatories shall be deemed continuing so as to require prompt supplemental answers if the Defendant obtains or recalls further information relative thereto between the time the answers are submitted to Plaintiff and the time of trial. The answers to these interrogatories should include the knowledge and beliefs of the Defendant.

[Definitions as above]

INTERROGATORY NO. 1:

State the names of the Rollbar, Inc. Corporation (hereinafter referred to as RBI) Divisions, Groups, or Offices having any responsibility for either the design, testing, production or marketing of the Fourwheel Models line of utility motor vehicles and the names of the offices, departments, sections or other functional employee groupings within such Divisions, Groups or Offices, for the years 1993 to 2004, as well as the names, title and current company position, if any, of the individual employees managing such group, office, department or section for each of the designated years.

INTERROGATORY NO. 2:

State the names of the RBI committee or committees having any responsibility for the review of and/or the making of corporate decisions regarding any aspect of the design, testing, production or marketing of the Fourwheel model line of utility motor vehicles for the years 1993-2004, as well as the names, title, and current company position, if any, of the members of such committee or committees for each of the designated years.

INTERROGATORY NO. 3:

State with particularity, the corporate relationship between Outdoors Motors Corporation and Fourwheel Corporation and Rollbar,

Inc., relative to Outdoors Motors Corporation's ownership interest in Rollbar, Inc.

INTERROGATORY NO. 4:

State whether any Outdoors Motors Corporation offices, departments, sections, committees or any other applicable organizational entity of either, or individual employees of either have, for the years 1993-2004, either participated in or exercised supervisory authority in any respect, over Rollbar, Inc. policy or decisions in regard to either the design, testing, production or marketing of the Four-wheel line of utility motor vehicles, including, but not limited to the rollbars installed in such vehicles.

INTERROGATORY NO. 5:

If the answer to Interrogatory No. 4 is in the affirmative, state:

1. The name of the office, department, section, committee, or other applicable organizational entity of the aforesaid corporation either participating in or exercising supervisory capacity as stated, as well as the nature or subject matter of the same for each of the designated years.

2. The names, titles and current company position, if any, of the individual members of such offices, departments, sections, committees or other applicable Outdoors Motors Corporation organizational entity for each of the designated years.

INTERROGATORY NO. 6:

State whether any Fourwheel Corporation offices, departments, sections, committees or any other applicable Fourwheel Corporation organizational entity, or individual Fourwheel Corporation employees have, for the years 1993-2004, either participated in or exercised supervisory authority in any respect, over Rollbar, Inc. policy or decisions in regard to either the design, testing, production or marketing of the Rollbar, Inc. rollbars installed in the Fourwheel line of utility motor vehicles.

INTERROGATORY NO. 7:

If the answer to Interrogatory No. 6 is in the affirmative, state:

1. The name of the office, department, section, committee, or other applicable Fourwheel Corporation organizational entity either participating in or exercising supervisory capacity as stated, as well as the nature or subject matter of the same for each of the designated years.

2. The names, titles and current company position, if any, of the individual members of such offices, departments, sections, com-

mittees or other applicable Fourwheel Corporation organizational entity for each of the designated years.

INTERROGATORY NO. 8:

State the name of the office, department, section, committee or other applicable Rollbar, Inc. organizational entity having any responsibility for liaison for Rollbar, Inc. regarding the relationship of Rollbar, Inc. with the National Highway Traffic Safety Administration relative to Federal Motor Vehicle Safety Standards, defect investigations, recalls or other matters involving the Fourwheel line of motor vehicles, for each of the years 1993-2004. State as well, the names, title and current company position, if any, of the individual members of such offices, departments, sections, committees or other applicable Rollbar, Inc. organizational entity for each of the designated years.

INTERROGATORY NO. 9:

State the name of the individual or individuals employed by Rollbar, Inc., whether Operating Officers on the Central Staff level, Product Development or Manufacturing Group Vice-President or other applicable Rollbar, Inc. organizational title, having primary responsibility for liaison between Rollbar, Inc. and the National Highway Traffic Safety Administration, Federal Trade Commission or other federal regulatory agencies having jurisdiction over any aspect of the design, testing, production or marketing of the Fourwheel line of motor vehicles for the years 1993-2004.

INTERROGATORY NO. 10:

State for the years 1993-2004, whether Rollbar, Inc. has made either formal or informal responses to complaints filed with the National Highway Traffic Safety Administration or its predecessor the National Highway Traffic Safety Board or the Federal Trade Commission, alleging safety related problems with the Fourwheel line of utility motor vehicles or its advertising or promotional literature. If the answer to this interrogatory is in the affirmative, state the name of the individual or group filing such petition or complaint, the date or dates of the same and a brief description of all Rollbar, Inc. submissions in response to such petitions or complaints.

INTERROGATORY NO. 11:

State for the years 1993-2004, whether any Rollbar, Inc. offices, departments, sections, committees or other applicable Rollbar, Inc. organizational entity generated engineering or styling design layouts, specifications, blueprints, models, mathematical analyses, or other renderings of original, intermediate, alternative or final designs of the Fourwheel line of utility motor vehicles, including, but not limited to designs relative to rollbar materials specifica-

tion, rollbar configuration, rollbar placement and attaching apparatus; windshield framing configuration and attaching apparatus;
vehicle center of gravity and track width; and occupant restraint
systems.

INTERROGATORY NO. 12:

State whether tests were conducted on the Fourwheel line of utility vehicles, whether on a test track or in a laboratory, to determine in whole or in part, the following:

1. Rollbar strength.

2. Rollover potential.

3 Windshield framing stability.

4. Adequacy of occupant restraint systems.

INTERROGATORY NO. 13:

If the answer to Interrogatory No. 12 is in the affirmative, state:

1. The test number.

2. The test title.

3. The requesting office,department, section, committee or individual.

4. The name of the testing organization.

5. The make and model of the vehicle tested.

6. The purpose of the test.

7. The test conditions and vehicle configuration.

8. The date and the current location of every such test.

INTERROGATORY NO. 14:

State whether, for the years 1993-2004, tests were conducted by
Rollbar, Inc. or anyone on their behalf, whether conducted on a test
track or in a laboratory, to determine the feasibility of alternate
designs other than those eventually incorporated in the production
models of the Fourwheel line of utility vehicles.

INTERROGATORY NO. 15:

If the answer to Interrogatory No. 14 is in the affirmative, state:

1. The test number.

2. The test title.

3. The requesting office,department, section, committee or individual.

4. The name of the testing organization.

5. The make and model of the vehicle tested.

6. The purpose of the test.

7. The test conditions and vehicle configuration.

8. The date and the current location of every such test.

INTERROGATORY NO. 16:

State whether Outdoors Motors Corporation or Fourwheel Corporation have ever recommended to Rollbar, Inc., changes in the design, materials or attaching apparatus of the rollbars installed in the Fourwheel line of utility vehicles for the years 1993-2004. If the answer is in the affirmative, state the name of the Outdoors Motors or Fourwheel offices, departments,sections, committees or individuals making such recommendations, as well as the action, if any, taken by Rollbar, Inc. in response to such recommendations for each of the designated years.

INTERROGATORY NO. 17:

Identify by reference to standard operating procedures number or other applicable Rollbar, Inc. organizational designation, the record retention and record destruction policies of Rollbar, Inc., relative to the retention or destruction of records of all types, including but not limited to financial memoranda, engineering memoranda, test reports and customer, retailer or service representative complaints regarding the safety or performance of the Fourwheel line of utility vehicles.

INTERROGATORY NO. 18:

State whether Rollbar, Inc. has received any notification or complaints relative to the safety of the Fourwheel line of utility vehicles, from any source, with respect to rollover problems, rollbar failure, occupant restraint systems or windshield framing materials, design and attaching apparatus. If the answer is in the affirmative, state the following for each of the years 1993-2004:

1. The total number of such complaints by reference to the above categories.

2. The name and address of the individual, group or company making such complaint.

3. The Rollbar, Inc. office, department,section, committee or individuals processing such complaints.

INTERROGATORY NO. 19:

Identify for the years 1993-2004, all lawsuits, both pending and closed, by case title, jurisdiction, docket number, date of filing and

name and address of all plaintiff's counsel, in which Rollbar, Inc. was named as a defendant against allegations alleging a negligently or defectively designed Fourwheel utility vehicle, relative to rollover problems; rollbar failure; windshield framing, materials selection or attaching apparatus problems; occupant restraint systems problems; or failure to warn and/or instruct consumers with respect to any or all of such problems.

INTERROGATORY NO. 20:

For each lawsuit referred to in Interrogatory No.19, state:

1. The model and model year of the vehicle and a brief statement of the alleged defects in said vehicle.

2. The name and address of the owner of such vehicle.

3. A brief description of the factual circumstances giving rise to the lawsuit.

4. A brief description of the damage alleged to such vehicle.

INTERROGATORY NO. 21:

State the name of the manufacturer of the rollbar installed in the Fourwheel model 2 utility vehicle involved in the instant action, as well as the names of all manufacturers who have manufactured rollbars for the Fourwheel line of utility vehicles for each of the years 1993-2004.

INTERROGATORY NO. 22:

State whether Rollbar, Inc., or any persons acting on its behalf has inspected the Fourwheel model 2 utility vehicle involved in the instant action, with respect to the mechanical and/or physical condition of said vehicle, If the answer is in the affirmative, state the dates and location of any such inspection, the identity of the person or organization making such inspection, and whether any written reports and/ or photographs were generated as a result of such inspection.

INTERROGATORY NO. 23:

State the name and current address of each person known to Rollbar, Inc. who was present or claims to have been present at the scene of the accident giving rise to this lawsuit, as well as the names and current addresses of any other persons known to Rollbar, Inc. who claims to have knowledge or information regarding this occurrence.

INTERROGATORY NO. 24:

Does Rollbar, Inc. have in its possession any statements of witnesses to this occurrence or photographs of the scene or vehicles

involved? If so, state the name and current address of the individuals issuing such statements and the number and subject matter of any photographs.

INTERROGATORY NO. 25:

If Rollbar, Inc. was covered by any policy of liability insurance effective on the date of the occurrence giving rise to this action, state the effective dates, policy number, company or companies issuing such policy or policies and the maximum coverage of any such policy for each individual and each occurrence.

§ 16.09 SAMPLE INTERROGATORIES — PRESSURIZED STAINLESS STEEL BEVERAGE CANISTER

This set of interrogatories seeks information about the manufacture of a returned pressurized stainless steel beverage canister that exploded while being prepared for sterilization by a worker who was attempting to release the remaining pressure in the tank. Fremantle manufactured the tank. The second defendant is the Polymer Plastic Corporation, the manufacturer of the plastic cap or closure that struck plaintiff's eye as a result of the explosion. The third defendant is the Apex Grinding Company, manufacturer of the pressure release or relief mechanism for incorporation into the stainless steel beverage canister involved herein. Finally, the fourth defendant is the Premier Plastic Corporation, manufacturer of a plastic material known as BasicPro V56-77, that was incorporated into the plastic cap or closure on the pressurized stainless steel beverage canister involved in the Denton case. The sample set will be restricted to selected inquiries to the manufacturer Fremantle, although full sets would also be issued to the other noted defendants.

SAMPLE INTERROGATORIES: *Denton v. Fremantle Tire and Rubber Company*

INTERROGATORY NO. 1:

Please summarize, and identify by reference to standard operating procedures number or other applicable organizational designation, the record retention and record destruction policies, of the defendant THE FREMANTLE TIRE AND RUBBER COMPANY, relative to the retention or destruction of records of all types, including financial memoranda; sales data; test requests, test reports, test summaries, synopses and evaluations; warning decals, labels and labeling or warning or instructional related memoranda and drafts; operating instructions; consumer inquiries; warranty service of par-

ticular units; quality control documents; computer archive copies of data; communications with suppliers and distributors of stainless steel pressurized beverage canisters.

INTERROGATORY NO. 2:

Please list for the years 1975 to the present, the office or department and individual or individuals and the company position and current company position, if any, of those who had or currently have as their duties or part of their duties the accumulation and/or summarizing of internal reports, analyses, studies, tests, reviews or working papers in any form, generated by individual engineers, technicians, scientists or others, whether or not in your employ, respecting the issue of the design of or warnings respecting the normal use and handling of pressurized stainless steel beverage canisters.

INTERROGATORY NO. 3:

State, for the years 1975-1987, the names of THE FREMANTLE TIRE AND RUBBER COMPANY committee or committees having any responsibility for the review of and/or the making of corporate decisions regarding any aspect of the design, testing, production, sale or marketing of the pressurized stainless steel beverage canisters of the type involved in this lawsuit, as well as the names, title, and current company position, if any, of the members of such committee or committees for each of the designated years.

INTERROGATORY NO. 4:

Please list, for the years that you have manufactured and/or distributed the pressurized stainless steel beverage canisters of the type involved in this lawsuit, the date, title, author and journal for all published article(s) and all other published information, regardless of the date of publication, and whether or not the author is in your employ, regarding the uses, safety, and potential or actual health hazards associated with the handling of said canisters, on which you relied in the formulation of your design, labeling, warning and instructional policy as regards the manufacture, distribution and/or sale of such canisters.

INTERROGATORY NO. 5:

Please identify for the years 1975 to date, and provide current addresses, for all companies involved in the manufacture of components, assemblies, and sub-assemblies incorporated in the pressurized stainless steel beverage canisters of the type involved in this lawsuit, and briefly describe the component, assembly, or sub-assembly for each company so listed.

INTERROGATORY NO. 6:

Please state whether THE FREMANTLE TIRE AND RUBBER COMPANY is a member of any trade association that address the manufacture and/or sale of pressurized stainless steel beverage canisters or canister caps or closures, of the type involved in this lawsuit. If the answer is in the affirmative, state whether any of the officers of the defendant has or are currently serving as officers of directors of any such trade association and indicate the position held and the years in which such person has served in that capacity.

INTERROGATORY NO. 7:

For each year from 1975 to date, please state the number of units of the pressurized stainless steel beverage canisters of the type involved in this lawsuit, sold and/or distributed within the United States by the THE FREMANTLE TIRE AND RUBBER COMPANY, in which the canister cap or closure was made of plastic and those in which the canister cap was made of steel or other metal materials. Please list separately by cap material for each of the designated years.

INTERROGATORY NO. 8: [TESTING]

Please state whether any tests, experiments or other exercises have been performed on pressurized stainless steel beverage canisters of the type involved in this lawsuit, by or at the direction of THE FREMANTLE TIRE AND RUBBER COMPANY, to determine in whole or in part, the adequacy of pressure release or relief mechanisms, the adequacy and strength of plastic or metal caps or closures, or the feasibility of alternative pressure release or relief mechanisms or cap or closure designs other than those eventually manufactured and sold by the defendant.

If the answer to the foregoing is in the affirmative, for each test identify:

a. the company, person, office, or department conducting the test;

b. the person requesting the test and the date of the test;

c. the model or other identifying name of the canister being tested;

d. the purpose for which the test was conducted; and

e. the title or other identifying name for all documents relating to any such test.

Interrogatories of this type [TESTING] are directed to several important blocks of data.

Initially, they solicit information on the core testing program respecting the suspect product unit in the context of the defect

modes identified as having causal relevance to the case. Secondly, they focus on the offices, departments, sections, committees and individuals involved in that process over the case time frame. Finally, such questions lend themselves to focused argument respecting their scope in ensuing debates over defendant's obligation to respond. A question formulated along these lines should leave little doubt as to the nature of the information that it seeks and should eliminate needless argument over the essential technical context of the case towards which it is directed.

INTERROGATORY NO. 9:

For each year from 1975 through the present, please identify each model of pressurized canisters which incorporate pressure release or relief mechanisms or plastic or metal caps or closures of the type involved in this lawsuit, manufactured and/or distributed by THE FREMANTLE TIRE AND RUBBER COMPANY and the number of units of each such model distributed and/or sold for each of the designated years.

INTERROGATORY NO. 10:

Please state whether THE FREMANTLE TIRE AND RUBBER COMPANY is a party to any lawsuits, pending or closed, involving the design, manufacture, sale, or distribution of pressurized beverage canisters wherein the plaintiff was allegedly injured while handling or otherwise utilizing any such canister.

If the answer in the affirmative, state:

a. the full caption of the case;

b. the court or jurisdiction in which the case has been filed;

c. the docket number of the case;

d. the date the case was filed;

e. the model of canister involved;

f. the name and address of the opposing party's counsel; and

g. the disposition, if any, of the claims.

INTERROGATORY NO. 11:

State whether THE FREMANTLE TIRE AND RUBBER COMPANY has received any notification or complaints relative to the safety of pressurized beverage canisters of the type involved in this lawsuit, from any source, with respect to explosions of such canisters, including but not limited to the explosion or other failure, under pressure, of the plastic or metal cap or closure on such canisters. If the answer to the foregoing is in the affirmative, state:

a. The total number of such complaints by reference to the above categories.

b. The name and address of the individual, group or company making such complaint.

c. The FREMANTLE TIRE AND RUBBER office, department, section, committee or individuals processing such complaints.

INTERROGATORY NO. 12:

Has THE FREMANTLE TIRE AND RUBBER COMPANY ever offered as optional equipment for the pressurized beverage canisters of the type involved in this case with respect to pressure release or relief mechanisms or cap or closure mechanisms?

If the answer to the foregoing is in the affirmative, state separately, each of such options, the name, part number, catalog number, price and function of all items of optional equipment or features of the types specified, for each of the years 1975 to the present.

INTERROGATORY NO. 13:

Are FREMANTLE TIRE AND RUBBER COMPANY pressurized beverage containers of the type involved in this lawsuit sold in foreign countries? If the answer is in the affirmative, identify each of such countries and the years within which any such sales were made, including the present time.

INTERROGATORY NO. 14:

Identify all voluntary standards, or standards mandated by any agency of the United States government, by issuing body and standards number, that were or are followed in the design, testing, production and marketing of the type of pressurized beverage canisters involved in this lawsuit, including, but not limited to standards prepared and/or issued by the American Society of Mechanical Engineers (ASME) and/or the American National Standards Institute (ANSI).

Information relative to the defendant's relationship with federal regulatory agencies is also a primary subject for discovery. Interrogatories addressing this issue should also be concentrated along the lines of corporate organization rather than being directed towards detailed information.

§ 16.10 SAMPLE INTERROGATORIES — STANDUP FORKLIFT TRUCK

[See this complaint in § 14.12 et seq.]

INSTRUCTIONS AND DEFINITIONS (as before)

INTERROGATORY NO. 1:

Please state the full name, title, residence address, business address and telephone number of the person completing these interrogatories.

INTERROGATORY NO. 2:

Please identify, for the years 1995 to present, the offices, departments, person or persons, having primary responsibility for communications with the Occupational Safety and Health Administration of the United States government, respecting any aspect of the design, labeling, marketing, distribution, or sale of the STOCKLIFT Pacer Model 60 standup forklift truck manufactured and/or distributed by you.

INTERROGATORY NO. 3:

Please summarize, and identify by reference to standard operating procedures number or other applicable organizational designation, the record retention and record destruction policies, of the STOCK-LIFT CORPORATION, relative to the retention or destruction of records of all types, including financial memoranda; sales data; test requests, test reports, test summaries, synopses and evaluations; warning decals, labels and labeling or warning or instructional related memoranda and drafts; operating instructions; consumer inquiries; warranty service of particular units; quality control documents; computer archive copies of data; communications with suppliers and distributors of STOCKLIFT products; and communications to and from the Occupational Safety and Health Administration of the United States government and the Industrial Truck Association (ITA).

INTERROGATORY NO. 4:

Please list for the years 1995 to the present, the office or department and individual or individuals and the company position and current company position, if any, of those who had or currently have as their duties or part of their duties:

a. The accumulation and/or summarizing of internal reports, analyses, studies, tests, reviews or working papers in any form, generated by individual engineers, technicians, scientists or others, in your employ, respecting the issue of operator safety or safety design for standup forklift trucks.

b. The accumulation and/or summarizing of scientific reports, analyses, studies, tests, reviews or working papers in any form, generated by individual engineers, technicians, scientists or others, not in your employ, respecting the issue of operator safety or safety design for standup forklift trucks.

c. The accumulation and/or summarizing of scientific reports, analyses, studies, tests, reviews or working papers in any form, generated by individual engineers, technicians, scientists or others, not in your employ, respecting injuries to the operators of standup forklift trucks.

d. The preparation and the review and evaluation of the preparation of all labels, labeling, operating instructions, warnings, graphs, diagrams, drawings, illustrations or advertising or promotional material used by the STOCKLIFT Corporation in connection with the distribution and sale of the STOCKLIFT CORPORATION's line of standup forklift trucks.

e. The preparation and the review and evaluation of all standard operating procedures or other memoranda that establish, describe or otherwise address the processes respecting the literature reviews noted in sub-section (a) through (c).

INTERROGATORY NO. 5:

State the names of the STOCKLIFT CORPORATION committee or committees having any responsibility for the review of and/or the making of corporate decisions regarding any aspect of the design, testing, production, sale or marketing of the STOCKLIFT Pacer Model 60 standup forklift truck for the years 1995-2005, as well as the names, title, and current company position, if any, of the members of such committee or committees for each of the designated years.

INTERROGATORY NO. 6:

Please list, for the years that you have manufactured and/or distributed the STOCKLIFT Pacer Model 60 standup forklift truck, the date, title, author and journal for all published article(s) and all other published information, regardless of the date of publication, whether or not the author is in your employ, regarding the uses, safety, and potential or actual health hazards associated with the operation of standup forklift trucks, on which you relied in the formulation of your labeling, warning and instructional policy as regards the distribution and/or sale of the STOCKLIFT Pacer Model 60 standup forklift trucks.

INTERROGATORY NO. 7:

Please identify all companies involved in the manufacture of components, assemblies, and subassemblies incorporated in the STOCKLIFT Pacer Model 60 standup forklift trucks, and briefly describe the component, assembly, or subassembly for each company so listed.

INTERROGATORY NO. 8:

Please state whether the STOCKLIFT CORPORATION is a member of the Industrial Truck Association. If the answer is in the affirmative, state whether any of the officers of the STOCKLIFT CORPORATION have or are currently serving as officers of directors of the Industrial Truck Association and indicate the position held and the years in which such person has served in that capacity.

INTERROGATORY NO. 9:

State for the years 1995 to the present whether the STOCKLIFT CORPORATION sells standup forklift trucks to any branch of the United States military. If the answer is in the affirmative, state:

a. the branch or branches of the United States military where such units are or have been sold.

b. whether any such standup forklift trucks are built to specification of such military branch or branches.

c. the model of standup forklift truck so sold.

INTERROGATORY NO. 10:

Please state whether any copyrightable material is used in the manufacture, distribution or sale of the STOCKLIFT Pacer Model 60 standup forklift truck, including, but not limited to any and all warnings, labeling, package inserts, graphs and instructional material.

If the answer to the above is in the affirmative, then

a. state the type of work in which a copyright is claimed;

b. identify the author;

c. state the date of creation;

d. state whether the work was registered with the Copyright Office;

e. and, if the work is registered, state the Certificate of Registration number.

INTERROGATORY NO. 11:

Please state whether a patent has been claimed or is being sought in any process, machine, manufacture, composition of matter, or

new, original ornamental design incorporated in or used in the design, manufacture, or operation of the STOCKLIFT Pacer Model 60 standup forklift truck.

If the answer is in the affirmative, state:

a. The short title of the invention;

b. The full name and mailing address of the inventor;

c. The government issuing the patent;

d. The registration and file number of the patent or patent application; and

e. The full name and mailing address of any assignee of the patent.

INTERROGATORY NO. 12:

For each year from 1995 through the present, please state the number of units of the STOCKLIFT Pacer Model 60 standup forklift truck sold and/or distributed within the United States by the STOCKLIFT CORPORATION.

INTERROGATORY NO. 13:

Please state whether any tests, experiments or other exercises have been performed by or at the direction of the STOCKLIFT CORPORATION to determine the extent to which the STOCKLIFT CORPORATION line of standup forklift trucks compare in maneuverability, stability, durability or general functioning compare to standup forklift trucks manufactured by others.

If the answer to the foregoing is in the affirmative, for each test identify:

a. the company, person, office, or department conducting the test;

b. the person requesting the test and the date of the test;

c. the model or the prototype of the standup forklift truck being tested;

d. the purpose for which the test was conducted; and

e. all documents relating to the test.

INTERROGATORY NO. 14:

Please state whether any tests, experiments or other exercises have been performed by or at the direction of the STOCKLIFT CORPORATION to determine the risk of injury to operators of standup forklift trucks resulting from tipovers, intrusion of objects into the operator's platform, the collision of the forklift into stationery

objects or the failure of any of the methods employed in decreasing or stopping the forward or backward motion of the unit.

If the answer to the foregoing is in the affirmative, for each test identify:

a. the company, person, office, or department conducting the test;

b. the person requesting the test and the date of the test;

c. the model or the prototype of the standup forklift truck being tested;

d. the purpose for which the test was conducted; and

e. all documents relating to the test.

INTERROGATORY NO. 15:

Please state whether the STOCKLIFT CORPORATION has reviewed and/or had any knowledge of any tests performed by persons other than the STOCKLIFT CORPORATION to determine the risk of injury to operators of standup forklift trucks resulting from tipovers, intrusion of objects into the operator's platform, the collision of the forklift into stationery objects or the failure of any of the methods employed in decreasing or stopping the forward or backward motion of the unit.

If the answer to the foregoing is in the affirmative, for each test identify:

a. the company, person, office, or department conducting the test;

b. the person requesting the test and the date of the test;

c. the model or the prototype of the standup forklift truck being tested;

d. the purpose for which the test was conducted; and

e. all documents relating to the test.

INTERROGATORY NO. 16:

For each year from 1995 through the present, please identify each model of standup forklift truck other than the STOCKLIFT Pacer Model 60 standup forklift truck manufactured and/or distributed by the STOCKLIFT CORPORATION and the number of units of each such model distributed and/or sold.

INTERROGATORY NO. 17:

Please state whether the STOCKLIFT CORPORATION is a party to any lawsuits, pending or closed, involving the design, manufacture, sale, or distribution of the STOCKLIFT Pacer Model 60

standup forklift truck wherein the plaintiff was an operator of a Pacer Model 60, allegedly injured while operating such a forklift.

If the answer in the affirmative, state:

a. the full caption of the case;

b. the court or jurisdiction in which the case has been filed;

c. the docket number of the case;

d. the date the case was filed;

e. the nature of the cause of action;

f. the name and address of the opposing party's counsel; and

g. the disposition, if any, of the claims.

INTERROGATORY NO. 18:

For each lawsuit referred to in Interrogatory NO. 17, state:

a. The model and model year of the forklift truck and a brief statement of the alleged defects in said forklift truck.

b. The name and address of the owner of such forklift truck.

c. A brief description of the factual circumstances giving rise to the lawsuit.

d. A brief description of the damage alleged to have been caused by said defect.

INTERROGATORY NO. 19:

Please state the method for determining the identification of the manufacturing plant of a particular unit of the STOCKLIFT Pacer Model 60 standup forklift truck.

INTERROGATORY NO. 20:

Please state, for the years 1995-2001, whether any tests, experiments, design drawings, proposals, renderings or other work was conducted by you, or anyone on your behalf, to determine the feasibility of alternate designs with respect to designs, other than those actually incorporated in the STOCKLIFT Pacer Model 60 standup forklift truck manufactured, distributed and/or sold by you, with respect to the following:

a. an expanded deck or other extension to the operator's platform to prevent the operator from being crushed in the event of collision with or intrusion by stationery objects.

b. a metal or other sufficiently strong gate across the back of the operator's platform to prevent the operator from being crushed in the event of collision with or intrusion by stationery objects.

c. increased width or depth for the operator's platform to allow the operator to more safely or efficiently operate said forklift in emergency situations.

d. posts or other protective features around the operator's platform to prevent the operator from being crushed in the event of collision with or intrusion by stationery objects.

e. warnings respecting the dangers involved in the operation of said
. forklift.

INTERROGATORY NO. 21:

If the answer to Interrogatory No. 20 is in the affirmative, state:

a. The document title and date.

b. The test date and test number.

c. The requesting office, department, section, committee or individual.

d. The name of the testing organization.

e. The make and model of the prototype or standup forklift tested.

f. The purpose of the test.

g. Whether a prototype system was built.

h. The date and the current location of every such test.

INTERROGATORY NO. 22:

State whether the STOCKLIFT CORPORATION has received any notification or complaints relative to the safety of the STOCKLIFT Pacer Model 60 standup forklift truck, from any source, with respect to tipovers, intrusion of objects into the operator's platform, the collision of the forklift into stationery objects or the failure of any of the methods employed in decreasing or stopping the forward or backward motion of the unit. If the answer is in the affirmative, state the following for each of the years 1995-2001:

a. The total number of such complaints by reference to the above categories.

b. The name and address of the individual, group or company making such complaint.

c. The STOCKLIFT CORPORATION office, department, section, committee or individuals processing such complaints.

INTERROGATORY NO. 23:

State the gross profits generated by the STOCKLIFT CORPORA-
TION resulting from its manufacture, distribution and/or sale of the
STOCKLIFT Pacer Model 60 standup forklift truck for each of the
years from 1995-2001.

INTERROGATORY NO. 24:

State whether the STOCKLIFT CORPORATION maintains a pol-
icy of liability insurance. If the answer is in the affirmative state the
name of any and all liability insurance carriers, the policy number
or numbers and the limits of any such policies as to each individual
and occurrence.

INTERROGATORY NO. 25:

State the names and addresses and telephone numbers of all witnesses known to you who claim to have witnessed the events giving
rise to this lawsuit. Also please state whether you have in your possession statements of any such persons, identifying each by witness
name.

INTERROGATORY NO. 26:

Describe the name, part number, catalog number, price and function
of all items of optional equipment or features available to purchasers of the STOCKLIFT Pacer Model 60 standup forklift truck,
for the years 1995 to the present.

INTERROGATORY NO. 27:

Has the STOCKLIFT CORPORATION ever offered as optional
equipment for the STOCKLIFT Pacer Model 60 standup forklift
truck any of the following or similar equipment or features:

a. an expanded deck or other extension to the operator's platform.

b. a metal or other sufficiently strong gate across the back of the
operator's platform.

c. increased width or depth for the operator's platform.

d. posts, pillars or other protective features around the operator's
platform.

e. warnings respecting the dangers involved in the operation of said
forklift.

INTERROGATORY NO. 28:

If the answer to the foregoing interrogatory is in the affirmative,
state separately, each of such options, the name, part number, cat-

alog number, price and function of all items of optional equipment or features of the types, for the years 1995 to the present.

INTERROGATORY NO. 29:

Are STOCKLIFT Pacer Model 60 standup forklift trucks sold in foreign countries? If the answer is in the affirmative, identify each of such countries and the years within which any such sales were made, including the present time.

INTERROGATORY NO. 30:

Identify all voluntary standards, by issuing body and standards number, that are followed in the design, testing, production and marketing of STOCKLIFT CORPORATION standup forklift trucks, including, but not limited to standards prepared and/or issued by the American Society of Mechanical Engineers (ASME) and/or the American National Standards Institute (ANSI) relative to standup forklift operations and operator safety

§ 16.11 OBSERVATIONS ON SAMPLE INTERROGATORIES

The above selections of products liability interrogatories may serve as examples of a structured approach to drafting focusing primarily on the identification of the document generating processes of the corporation and the organizational and individual participants in relevant decision-making processes. Rather than seeking specific facts more appropriately and efficiently obtained through document requests and depositions, interrogatories should aim towards determining the identity of company committee work productive of relevant documents generated within the case time frame. Basic corporate organization consisting of groups, offices, departments, sections and committees allow for a consistent service of interrogatories across product lines. The answers to interrogatories in the products case can often serve as a road map through the details of potentially thousands of pages of material accessed through document requests.

§ 16.12 REQUESTS TO ADMIT FACT OR THE GENUINENESS OF DOCUMENTS

Requests to admit facts under Rule 36 (Fed.R.Civ.P Rule 36) or a state equivalent are not generally considered a major discovery tool in products liability cases.[12] For one thing there are simply too many important factual

---

[12] FRCP Rule 36 — Requests for Admission

(a) Request for Admission. A party may serve upon any other party a written request for the admission, for purposes of the pending action only, of the truth of any matters within the scope of Rule 26(b)(1) set forth in the request that relate to statements or opinions of fact or of the application of law to fact, including the genuineness of any documents described in the request. Copies of documents shall be served with the request unless they have been or are otherwise furnished or made available for inspection and copying. Without leave of court or written stipulation, requests for admission may not be served before the time specified in Rule 26(d).

Each matter of which an admission is requested shall be separately set forth. The matter is admitted unless, within 30 days after service of the request, or within such shorter or longer time as the court may allow or as the parties may agree to in writing, subject to Rule 29, the party to whom the request is directed serves upon the party requesting the admission a written answer or objection addressed to the matter, signed by the party or by the party's attorney. If objection is made, the reasons therefore shall be stated. The answer shall specifically deny the matter or set forth in detail the reasons why the answering party cannot truthfully admit or deny the matter. A denial shall fairly meet the substance of the requested admission, and when good faith requires that a party qualify an answer or deny only a part of the matter of which an admission is requested, the party shall specify so much of it as is true and qualify or deny the remainder. An answering party may not give lack of information or knowledge as a reason for failure to admit or deny unless the party states that the party has made reasonable inquiry and that the information known or readily obtainable by the party is insufficient to enable the party to admit or deny. A party who considers that a matter of which an admission has been requested presents a genuine issue for trial may not, on that ground alone, object to the request; the party may, subject to the provisions of Rule 37(c), deny the matter or set forth reasons why the party cannot admit or deny it.

The party who has requested the admissions may move to determine the sufficiency of the answers or objections. Unless the court determines that an objection is justified, it shall order that an answer be served. If the court determines that an answer does not comply with the requirements of this rule, it may order either that the matter is admitted or that an amended answer be served. The court may, in lieu of these orders, determine that final disposition of the request be made at a pre-trial conference or at a designated time prior to trial. The provisions of Rule 37(a)(4) apply to the award of expenses incurred in relation to the motion.

(b) Effect of Admission. Any matter admitted under this rule is conclusively established unless the court on motion permits withdrawal or amendment of the admission. Subject to the provision of Rule 16 governing amendment of a pretrial order, the court may permit withdrawal or amendment when the presentation of the merits of the action will be subserved thereby and the party who obtained the admission fails to satisfy the court that withdrawal or amendment will prejudice that party in maintaining the action or defense on the merits. Any admission made by a party under this rule is for the purpose of the pending

issues that are nuanced and need careful development over the course of discovery. Any use of this discovery device is sure to result in time consuming motion practice due to defense objections. They are the least utilized of available discovery devices.[13] The opportunities are great for opposing counsel to supply equivocal answers or to allege inability to admit or deny. Most importantly, any such facts that do stand admitted are generally not subject to proof at trial. This can result in gaps in the dynamic presentation of the case that must be filled by the reading of the dry admission responses themselves.[14]

---

action only and is not an admission for any other purpose nor may it be used against the party in any other proceeding.

Illinois Supreme Court Rule 216. Admission of Fact or of Genuineness of Documents

(a) Request for Admission of Fact. A party may serve on any other party a written request for the admission by the latter of the truth of any specified relevant fact set forth in the request.

(b) Request for Admission of Genuineness of Document. A party may serve on any other party a written request for admission of the genuineness of any relevant documents described in the request. Copies of the documents shall be served with the request unless copies have already been furnished.

(c) Admission in the Absence of Denial. Each of the matters of fact and the genuineness of each document of which admission is requested is admitted unless, within 28 days after service thereof, the party to whom the request is directed serves upon the party requesting the admission either (1) a sworn statement denying specifically the matters of which admission is requested or setting forth in detail the reasons why he cannot truthfully admit or deny those matters or (2) written objections on the ground that some or all of the requested admissions are privileged or irrelevant or that the request is otherwise improper in whole or in part. If written objections to a part of the request are made, the remainder of the request shall be answered within the period designated in the request. A denial shall fairly meet the substance of the requested admission. If good faith requires that a party deny only a part, or requires qualification, of a matter of which an admission is requested, he shall specify so much of it as is true and deny only the remainder. Any objection to a request or to an answer shall be heard by the court upon prompt notice and motion of the party making the request.

(d) Public Records. If any public records are to be used as evidence, the party intending to use them may prepare a copy of them insofar as they are to be used, and may seasonably present the copy to the adverse party by notice in writing, and the copy shall thereupon be admissible in evidence as admitted facts in the case if otherwise admissible, except insofar as its inaccuracy is pointed out under oath by the adverse party in an affidavit filed and served within 14 days after service of the notice.

(e) Effect of Admission. Any admission made by a party pursuant to request under this rule is for the purpose of the pending action and any action commenced pursuant to the authority of section 13-217 of the Code of Civil Procedure (Ill. Rev. Stat. 1983, ch. 110, par. 13-217) only. It does not constitute an admission by him for any other purpose and may not be used against him in any other proceeding.

[13] *See* R. HAYDOCK & HERR, *supra* note 2, at 375.

[14] *See* TERRENCE F. KIELY: SCIENCE AND LITIGATION: PRODUCTS LIABILITY IN THEORY AND PRACTICE 355-356 (CRC Press 2002).

Chapter 17

REQUESTS TO PRODUCE DOCUMENTS

SYNOPSIS

§ 17.01 INTRODUCTION

The central pretrial goal of products liability cases is the obtaining of internal working documents created and distributed by the defendant company over the course of the selected time frame. A Request for the Production of Documents, available in the federal and all state discovery schemes, provides the vehicle for this considerable discovery obligation. These requests will generally be rigorously opposed by defense counsel. The intricacies of that effort will be discussed in detail in Chapter 19, Protective Orders and Discovery Enforcement.

Discovery planning is central to the successful prosecution of any litigation. It is especially important in product liability cases. The inherent complexity of tracing the development of a product over a multi-year time frame and the large amount of corporate documentation attendant to such a process mandate an intensive discovery effort. Careful planning and thorough prefiling research are required to counter defense tactics designed to delay and frustrate discovery.

Discovery is viewed today as liberal in nature. It is believed by the courts to be the most effective way to streamline the search for the truth and to allow counsel to bring the full range of his professional skills to the analysis of the facts underlying the claim. Liberal discovery, however, cannot operate in a factual vacuum. Without adequate prefiling research and analysis, the only party involved in the case who has detailed knowledge of the nature and extent of those facts is the corporate defendant. This gives the trial court little choice but to lean towards corporate counsel's perspective as to the appropriateness of discovery requests. The greatest amount of time and frustration encountered by plaintiff's counsel in preparing these cases occurs in the discovery process. Adequate discovery is the key to a successful settlement or verdict.

It is important to recall that counsel has only one opportunity to conduct discovery. Plaintiff has the right to supplemental discovery after study of the materials received pursuant to the original issuance of discovery requests. However, he does not have the prerogative of starting fresh if the original discovery was insufficiently thought out and drafted. Getting started on the wrong foot can be fatal to the successful prosecution of these cases. It is essential that the discovery phase of product liability litigation receive close attention before any discovery requests are issued to defendant.

The material to follow will concentrate on effective strategies for both the planning and drafting of document discovery requests. Chapter 19 will address the complexities of motion practice attendant to the discovery phase of product liability litigation. Federal Rule 34 sets the conditions for such requests.

§ 17.02 THE DISCOVERY RULES — DOCUMENT PRODUCTION

Federal Rule 34 — Production of Documents and Things and Entry Upon Land for Inspection and Other Purposes[1]

(a) Scope. Any party may serve on any other party a request

(1) to produce and permit the party making the request, or someone acting on the requestor's behalf, to inspect and copy, any designated documents (including writings, drawings, graphs, charts, photographs, phono records, and other data compilations from which information can be obtained, translated, if necessary, by the respondent through detection devices into reasonably usable form), or to inspect and copy, test, or sample any tangible things which constitute or contain matters within the scope of Rule 26(b) and which are in the possession, custody or control of the party upon whom the request is served; or

(2) to permit entry upon designated land or other property in the possession or control of the party upon whom the request is served for the purpose of inspection and measuring, surveying, photographing, testing, or sampling the property or any designated object or operation thereon, within the scope of Rule 26(b).

(b) Procedure. The request shall set forth, either by individual item or by category, the items to be inspected, and describe each with reasonable particularity. The request shall specify a reasonable time, place, and manner of making the inspection and performing the related acts. Without leave of court or written stipulation, a request may not be served before the time specified in Rule 26(d).

A typical state provision is Illinois Supreme Court Rule 214:

Illinois Supreme Court Rule 214. Discovery of Documents, Objects, and Tangible Things — Inspection of Real Estate provides a typical state version of the Request for the Production of Documents.

Any party may by written request direct any other party to produce for inspection, copying, reproduction photographing, testing or sampling specified documents, objects or tangible things, or to permit access to real estate for the purpose of making surface or subsurface inspections or surveys or photographs, or tests or taking samples, or to disclose information calculated to lead to the discovery of the whereabouts of any of these items, whenever the nature, contents, or condition of such documents, objects, tangible things, or real estate is relevant to the subject matter of the action. The request shall specify a reasonable time, which shall not be less than 28 days except by agreement or by order of court, and the place and manner of making the inspection and performing the related acts. One copy of the request shall be served on all other parties entitled to notice.

A party served with the written request shall (1) produce the requested documents as they are kept in the usual course of business or organized and labeled to correspond with the categories in the request, and all retrievable information in computer storage in printed form or (2) serve upon the party so requesting written objections on the ground that the request is improper in whole or in part. If written objections to a part of the request are made, the remainder of the request shall be complied with. Any objection to the request or the refusal to respond shall be heard by the court upon prompt notice and motion of the party submitting the request. If the party claims that the item is not in his or her possession or control or that he or she does not have information calculated to lead

to the discovery of its whereabouts, the party may be ordered to submit to examination in open court or by deposition regarding such claim. The party producing documents shall furnish an affidavit stating whether the production is complete in accordance with the request.

A party has a duty to seasonably supplement any prior response to the extent of documents, objects or tangible things which subsequently come into that party's possession or control or become known to that party. This rule does not preclude an independent action against a person not a party for production of documents and things and permission to enter upon real estate.

§ 17.03 PLANNING DOCUMENT REQUESTS

There are several important considerations that the product litigator must address with respect to the planning of or responding to, requests for documents. The cases for plaintiff and defendant typically stand or fall on the timing and content of internal documents received in the course of discovery. There are several initial tasks for counsel for both sides:

1. Identifying the category of company documents that are routinely contained in corporate archives at the ensuing stages of product development, testing, production, marketing and post-marketing.

2. Determining of whether those categories of documents over the case time frame would or would not meet the discovery relevancy standard for disclosure.

3. Assessing initial objections to the requests as filed.

4. Estimating how to oppose or enforce discovery rights with respect to such documents.

5. How to organize and analyze them once the appropriate body of documents has been set.

6. How to rate the investigative or legal significance of any one document with an eye towards including it in the documentary component of defendant's or plaintiff's case-in-chief.

Corporate defendants have no legal obligation to voluntarily identify, organize and package all arguably "relevant" documentation in the course of document discovery. It is incumbent upon plaintiff counsel to assess what documents may be available, over what periods of the case time frame they may have been generated and to clearly identify them by type in succinct requests for documentation. It is also requesting counsel's burden to understand it once received and to read the materials closely for purposes of drafting supplementary requests for documents.

It is of central importance at this point in the discussion to address the topic of the types of documents routinely generated at the design, testing, production, marketing and post-marketing stages of manufacture. These are generally quite similar in related industries such as automobiles or pharmaceuticals.

§ 17.04 THE GENERATION OF CORPORATE DOCUMENTS

All commercial products are planned, tested, produced and marketed with a corporate structure that is quite comparable to other companies in the same or related industries. While there are many hypothetical ways in which any company in an industry could be organized, the reality is that they tend to follow only several classic organizational formats that have been standard for years. Radical shifts in development ideas do not typically change the manner in which things are done. The interest for products litigators here is that there is a consistency in when and how documents are generated and that a fairly similar set of steps followed. Each of these steps or stages will generate corporate documents that tend to be of like kind. The latter point is brought home by the factor of Standard Operating Procedures (SOPs) that guide the form and generic content of corporate documents. Assuming it wanted to, it would be cumbersome for a corporation to try to eliminate sensitive documents that were generated pursuant to standard operating procedures that mandate set forms of document content and distribution along well established systems of corporate communication. These organizational facts of life are of great importance in thinking about and drafting the document discovery stage of the product liability undertaking.

§ 17.05 STAGES OF DOCUMENT GENERATION

An essential pre-trial investigative task is the identification of the categories of documentation consistently generated at the various phases or sub-phase of the totality of the product development, manufacturing and marketing effort. It is also essential to get a rough sense of the system and manner in which that documentation is disseminated throughout the organization, especially today, via electronic communication protocols.

While litigation and corporate experts may vary in choice of labels, the major stages along the product development and manufacturing continuum in large corporations, are principally five: (1) Design, (2) Testing (3) Production, (4) Marketing and (5) Post-Marketing. These broad categories can be further sub-divided for document discovery purposes by a further division of the routine activities that are the primary focus of corporate energies at that point in the overall manufacture of the product.

Documents supporting or weakening the positions of plaintiff or defense counsel are going to be found in one or more of these product development and manufacture stages. Recent release of clinical trial stage documents in the VIOXX cases serve as a contemporary example. In a typical products liability case involving a multi-national corporation defense and plaintiff counsel must be prepared to organize and review many thousands of such documents in the search for those useful or dispositive at trial.

§ 17.06 SAMPLE: AUTOMOBILE MANUFACTURING PROCESSES

A rough breakdown of corporate activities in the development of a new automobile or upgraded model can serve as an example of factors useful in the planning and drafting of document requests in a products liability case. This breakdown is intended to give an idea of the stages products go through and the topics typically encountered that will generate corporate documents that must be sought in the document production phase of the litigation. As was seen in Chapter 16, interrogatories are designed to facilitate this step by eliciting detailed organization data and nomenclature that will greatly support the document production in the case.

The basic stages in any such overall product planning would routinely include the following subjects and resulting documentation.

[A] OVERALL PRODUCT PLANNING

[1] Market Feasibility Reviews

[2] Technical Feasibility Reviews

[3] Financial Feasibility Reviews

[4] Tooling Reviews

[5] Regulatory Reviews

[6] Detailed Component Reviews

[7] Prototype Testing

[8] Final Project Approvals

[B] PRODUCT DESIGN TESTING:

[1] Regulatory Certification Testing

[2] Prospective Regulatory Testing

[3] Alternative Design Testing

[4] Detailed Component Testing

[5] Production Validation Testing

[C] PRODUCT PRODUCTION RUNS:

[1] Finalization of Specifications Manuals

[2] Production Runs Documentation

[3] Quality Control Reviews

[D] PRODUCT MARKETING:

[1] Instructions and Warnings Drafting

[2] Marketing Campaigns (Domestic and International)

[3] Advertising Campaigns and Media Presentations

[4] Product Complaint Processing and Reviews

[E] PRODUCT POST-MARKETING:

[1] Post-Production Design Changes

[2] Advanced Marketing Planning

[3] Prospective Government Regulatory Activity[1]

[4] Post-Production Injury Reports

§ 17.07 OVERLAP IN DOCUMENT GENERATION

Each of the above-noted production and manufacturing steps has a separate function from the others in the long process of getting the product to market. As noted, each such phase has within it identifiable, progressive steps each of which, in turn, will normally generate routine types of documents written with predictable document formats. It is important to realize that there is a continuing overlap among the various phases and sub-phases of the product development and manufacturing process. This is

---

[1] For an excellent and detailed analysis of key topics in pharmaceutical products cases, see DOUGLAS DANNER & LARRY L. VARN, PATTERN DISCOVERY: PRODUCTS LIABILITY (3d. ed. 2003), Chapter 32, Injuries from Drug Products: D. Interrogatories.

Areas highlighted by the authors include the following:

[A] Similar Products

[B] Trade Names

[C] Tests And Inspections

[D] F.D.A.

[E] Recalls

[F] Consulting Opinions

[G] Advertising

[H] Warnings

[I] Instructions or Manuals

[J] Trade Associations

so even though each separate phase is primarily involved with a specific task, such as testing, of the total product development and manufacturing cycle. The best that can be done is to isolate within the case time frame the chronological segments *primarily involved* with design, testing, production, marketing and post-marketing. The facts of corporate life are that there will be ongoing generation of documents relating to each of those activities across chronological lines.

Product development work in particular, cannot progress in isolation from future production, marketing and regulatory concerns of the central production and manufacturing project. Accordingly, while each particular stage has specific tasks to complete, each must be considered in its own effect on the total organizational effort. Decisions on a particular design aspect of a specific model line are routinely made with an eye to other planned corporate activities that may be affected. This reality is further complicated by the fact that broad decisions, especially with respect to regulatory policy, are made across model or product category lines.

§ 17.08 DRAFTING REQUESTS FOR DOCUMENTS

As the interrogatories and requests for documentation both target the same generic category of information, they should attempt to follow the same organizational pattern and be grounded in the same areas of interest. Like interrogatories, document requests are directed towards large blocks of data composed of a variety of standard document types routinely generated in predictable stages over the case time frames. Requests pursuant to Rule 34 (Fed. R. Civ. P. Rule 34) or a state equivalent, are necessarily best made by reference to generic document types in the initial requests. Once the first wave of documents have been received and studied, supplemental requests for documents will be quite detailed and specific. The initial set however should be drafted around the defect allegations made in the complaint and corporate organizational or operational processes and mechanisms.

What follows in this chapter are three examples of products liability requests for documents. These are provided to serve as examples of a structured approach to this vital stage in the discovery process. The products and defects vary considerably, but the basic approach remains the same.

§ 17.09 SAMPLE REQUEST FOR DOCUMENTS: PRESSURIZED STAINLESS STEEL BEVERAGE CANISTERS

[Complaint set out in § 14.03]

Plaintiff John Denton requests the above named defendant, THE FREMANTLE TIRE AND RUBBER COMPANY, to produce and permit Plaintiff and his representatives to inspect and copy all documents in the possession, custody or control of the Defendant, their subsidiaries, agents or attorneys, which are relevant to the claims and defenses asserted by the parties in this matter or appear reasonably calculated to lead to the discovery of relevant information, which documents are specified more particularly to include the following:

INSTRUCTIONS AND DEFINITIONS

I. "Identify" when used in reference to a person (whether individual, corporation, or other entity), means to state his or its full name, present address and present telephone number if known, and in the case of an individual, his present or last known position and business affiliation.

II. "Identify" when used in reference to a document, means to state the date and author, addressee or intended recipient, type of document, or some other means of identifying it, and its present or last known location or custodian. If such document was, but no longer is, in your possession or subject to your control, state what disposition was made of it.

III. "Document" as used herein, includes but is not limited to, all abstracts, agreements, all physical forms of correspondence, including FAX transmissions, analyses, applications, books, certificates, charter charts, computer print-outs, computer read-outs, computer tapes, contracts, diaries, PDA recorded data, drafts, drawings, estimates, films, forms, graphs, journals, letters, licenses, manuals, maps, meeting reports, memoranda, memoranda of all conversations including telephone calls, notes, orders, opinions, permits, photographs, photo-maps, plans, press releases, recordings, reports, resolutions, sketches, summaries, tapes, telegrams, texts, time records, transcripts, video tapes, writings and work papers, and any copies not identical to the original, regardless whether the documents are an original or a copy and all e-mails, whether ever sent or received or intended to be sent or received, or deleted but not destroyed or otherwise erased from any PDA, laptop, desktop or computer work station.

IV. "Person or persons" means all entities, and without limiting the generality of the foregoing, includes natural persons, joint own-

ers, associations, companies, partnerships, joint ventures, corporations, trusts and estates.

V. The documents to be produced pursuant to this DOCUMENT REQUEST are to include any such information requested for products sold in the United States and in member nations of the European Community (EC), Asia, Africa, Mexico and Central and South America.

VI. The time period covered by these interrogatories is from 1990 to 2005.

DOCUMENTS TO BE PRODUCED

REQUEST NO. 1:

Corporate organization charts or other applicable listings of THE FREMANTLE TIRE AND RUBBER COMPANY for the years 1990 to 2005, including, but not limited to any and all Divisions, Groups, Offices, Departments, Sections, Committees or any other FREMANTLE TIRE AND RUBBER COMPANY functional employee group designations, for those employees having any responsibility for either the design, testing, production or marketing of the pressurized beverage canisters of the type involved in this lawsuit.

REQUEST NO. 2:

The names, company position or title and current company position, if any, of the Vice Presidents or managers of the above-noted THE FREMANTLE TIRE AND RUBBER COMPANY organizational entities and the members of the designated committees for each of the years 1990 to 2005.

REQUEST NO. 3:

Any and all documents, memoranda, summaries, synopses, graphs, computer printouts or other data recordations in any form, either generated or reviewed by THE FREMANTLE TIRE AND RUBBER COMPANY entities referred to above, relative to any aspect of the design, testing, production or marketing of the pressurized beverage canisters of the type involved in this lawsuit, including, but not limited to financial and engineering documents addressing pressure release or relief mechanisms and/or plastic or metal caps or closures for such canisters.

REQUEST NO. 4:

Any and all memoranda, reports, summaries, synopses, engineering or styling design layouts, specifications, blueprints, models, mathematical analyses, or other renderings as respects the original, intermediate, alternative or final designs of the pressurized beverage canisters of the type involved in this lawsuits including, but not

limited to designs relative to pressure release or relief mechanisms and/or plastic or metal caps or closures for such canisters.

REQUEST NO. 5:

Any and all final or intermediate test reports, test requests, test summaries, test synopses or test evaluations in any form, in your possession, and whether or not actually conducted by you, of tests that were conducted on pressurized beverage canisters of the type involved in this lawsuit, or any component parts thereof, including, but not limited to any such documents that address in whole or in part, pressure release or relief mechanisms and/or plastic or metal caps or closures for such canisters.

REQUEST NO. 6:

Any and all documents respecting the record retention and record destruction policies, of THE FREMANTLE TIRE AND RUBBER COMPANY, relative to the retention or destruction of records of all types, including financial memoranda; sales data; test requests, reports, summaries, synopses and evaluations; labels and labeling related memoranda and drafts; operating instructions; consumer inquiries; warranty service of particular units; quality control documents; computer archive copies of data; communications with suppliers and distributors of products; and communications to and from the Occupational Safety and Health Administration (OSHA) of the United States government.

REQUEST NO. 7:

Any and all complaints or notices of claimed injury, in any form, and all accident reports resulting from the use or handling of pressurized beverage canisters of the type involved in this lawsuits, which injury arose out of the use or handling of any such canisters.

REQUEST NO. 8:

Any and all labels, decals, operating instructions, warnings, graphs, diagrams, advertising or promotional material, letters or other communications used by the THE FREMANTLE TIRE AND RUBBER COMPANY in connection with the distribution and sale of pressurized beverage canisters of the type involved in this lawsuit, including, but not limited to correspondence with respect to the utilization of plastic or metal caps or closures incorporated in such canisters.

REQUEST NO. 9:

Any and all standard operating procedures or other memoranda that establish, describe or otherwise address the processes in the THE FREMANTLE TIRE AND RUBBER COMPANY respecting the accumulation, listing, reviewing, summarizing or synopsizing,

of scientific, professional, engineering or industry trade association literature addressing the design, testing, manufacture, distribution and/or sale of pressurized beverage canisters or other pressurized canisters in which liquids are stored.

REQUEST NO. 10:

Any and all correspondence between THE FREMANTLE TIRE AND RUBBER COMPANY and the Occupational Safety and Health Administration (OSHA) of the United States government, discussing safety issues as related to the use or handling of the type of pressurized beverage canisters involved in this lawsuit.

REQUEST NO. 11:

Any and all correspondence, reports, or memoranda of any type, exchanged between THE FREMANTLE TIRE AND RUBBER COMPANY and any trade association with respect to the subjects of pressure release or relief mechanisms and/or plastic or metal caps or closures on pressurized beverage canisters, including, but not limited to any such exchanges with the Can Manufacturers Institute, the Closure Manufacturers Association, the Industrial Metal Containers Section of the Material Handling Institute, the Beverage Machinery Manufacturers Association, and the Carbonated Beverage Institute.

REQUEST NO. 12:

Any and all documents, notes, sketches or photographs resulting from any inspection of the pressurized beverage canisters of the type involved in this lawsuit involved in the instant action, with respect to the mechanical and/or physical condition of such canister.

REQUEST NO. 13:

Any statements in any form of witnesses to this occurrence or photographs of the scene or the pressurized beverage canister involved in the occurrence giving rise to this lawsuit.

REQUEST NO. 14:

Any and all catalogs, sales brochures and other marketing literature describing, illustrating or otherwise referencing all optional equipment available for purchasers of THE FREMANTLE TIRE AND RUBBER COMPANY lines of pressurized beverage canisters, including, but not limited to pressure release or relief mechanisms and/or plastic or metal closures for such canisters.

§ 17.10 SAMPLE REQUEST FOR DOCUMENTS: JEEP-TYPE VEHICLE ROLLOVER

The Plaintiff John Q. Consumer, Pursuant to Rule 34 of the Federal Rules of Civil Procedure, requests that the Defendant Fourwheel Corporation, produce and permit Plaintiff John Q. Consumer and his representatives to inspect and copy all documents in the possession, custody or control of the Defendant, their subsidiaries, agents or attorneys, which are relevant to the claims and defenses asserted by the parties in this matter or appear reasonably calculated to lead to the discovery of relevant information, which documents are specified more particularly to include the following:

INSTRUCTIONS AND DEFINITIONS (as before)

REQUEST NO. 1:

Corporate organization charts or other applicable listings of FWC for the years 1990-2005, including, but not limited to any and all Divisions, Groups, Offices, Departments, Sections, Committees or any other FWC functional employee group designation, for those employees having any responsibility, either independently or in conjunction with offices of the Main Motors Corporation, or Rollbar, Inc., for either the design, testing, production or marketing of the Fourwheel Corporation line of utility motor vehicles.

REQUEST NO. 2:

The names, company position or title and current company position, if any, of the Vice Presidents or managers of the the above-noted FWC entities and committees for each of the years 1990-2005.

REQUEST NO. 3:

Any and all documents, memoranda, summaries, synopses, graphs, computer printouts or other data recordations in any form, either generated or reviewed by the FWC entities referred to above, relative to any aspect of the design, testing, production or marketing of the Fourwheel line of utility vehicles, for the years 1990-2005, including, but not limited to financial and engineering documents addressing center of gravity and track width design and testing; rollbar materials selection, design and testing; windshield materials selection, design and testing; and occupant restraint systems.

REQUEST NO. 4:

FWC Annual Report to stockholders for the years 1990-2005.

REQUEST NO. 5:

FWC 10K and 8K filings with the Securities and Exchange Commission for the years 1990-2005.

REQUEST NO. 6:

Any and all documents, memoranda, summaries, synopses, graphs, computer printouts or other data recordations in any form, either generated or reviewed by the FWC entities referred to above, relative to any aspect of the design, testing, production or marketing of the Fourwheel line of utility vehicles for use by the United States military, for the years 1990-2005, including, but not limited to financial and engineering documents addressing center of gravity and track width design and testing; rollbar materials selection,design and testing; windshield materials selection, design and testing; and occupant restraint systems.

REQUEST NO. 7:

FWC corporate organization charts or other applicable listings indicating the name of the office, department, section, committee or other applicable FWC organizational entity having any responsibility for liaison with Fourwheel Corporation regarding the relationship of the Fourwheel Corporation with the National Highway Traffic Safety Administration relative to Federal Motor Vehicle Safety Standards, defect investigations, recalls or other matters involving the Fourwheel line of motor vehicles, for each of the years 1990-2005. Provide as well, documents setting forth the names, title and current company position, if any, of the individual members of such offices, departments, sections, committees or other applicable FWC organizational entity for each of the designated years.

REQUEST NO. 8:

FWC corporate organization charts or other applicable listings indicating the name of the office, department, section, committee or other applicable FWC organizational entity and the name of the individual or individuals employed by FWC, having primary responsibility for liaison between FWC and the National Highway Traffic Safety Administration, Federal Trade Commission or other federal regulatory agencies having jurisdiction over any aspect of the design, testing, production or marketing of the Fourwheel line of motor vehicles for the years 1990-2005.

REQUEST NO. 9:

Any and all submissions, correspondence or other submissions, or any other formal or informal responses to complaints filed with the National Highway Traffic Safety Administration or its predecessor the National Highway Traffic Safety Board or the Federal Trade Commission, or the United States military relative to safety related allegations with respect to the Fourwheel line of utility motor vehicles or its advertising or promotional literature.

REQUEST NO. 10:

Any and all engineering or styling design layouts, specifications, blueprints, models, mathematical analyses, or other renderings of original, intermediate, alternative or final designs of the Fourwheel line of utility motor vehicles, including, but not limited to designs relative to rollbar materials specification, rollbar configuration, rollbar placement and attaching apparatus; windshield framing configuration and attaching apparatus; vehicle center of gravity and track width; and occupant restraint systems.

REQUEST NO. 11:

Any and all final or intermediate test reports, test requests, test summaries or test synopses in any form, of tests that were conducted on the Fourwheel line of utility vehicles, whether on a test track or in a laboratory, to determine in whole or in part, the following:

1. Rollbar strength.

2. Rollover potential.

3. Windshield framing stability.

4. Adequacy of occupant restraint systems.

REQUEST NO. 12:

Any and all documents respecting the record retention and record destruction policies of FWC, relative to the retention or destruction of records of all types, including but not limited to financial memoranda, engineering memoranda, test reports and customer, retailer or service representative complaints regarding the safety or performance of the Fourwheel line of utility vehicles.

REQUEST NO. 13:

Any and all complaints in any form relative to the safety of the Fourwheel line of utility vehicles, from any source, with respect to rollover problems, rollbar failure, occupant restraint systems or windshield framing materials, design and attaching apparatus.

REQUEST NO. 14:

Any and all documents, notes, sketches or photographs resulting from any inspection of the Fourwheel model 2 utility vehicle involved in the instant action, with respect to the mechanical and/or physical condition of such vehicle.

REQUEST NO. 15:

Any statements in any form of witnesses to this occurrence or photographs of the scene or vehicles involved.

§ 17.11 SAMPLE REQUEST FOR DOCUMENTS: STAND-ALONE FORKLIFT TRUCK

[Complaint set forth in § 14.12 et seq.]

Plaintiff John Hussey requests the above named defendant, The STOCK-LIFT Corporation, pursuant to Illinois Supreme Court Rules 201 and 214, to produce and permit Plaintiff and his representatives to inspect and copy all documents in the possession, custody or control of the Defendant, their subsidiaries, agents or attorneys, which are relevant to the claims and defenses asserted by the parties in this matter or appear reasonably calculated to lead to the discovery of relevant information, which documents are specified more particularly to include the following:

INSTRUCTIONS AND DEFINITIONS (as before)

REQUEST NO. 1:

Corporate organization charts or other applicable listings of The STOCKLIFT CORPORATION for the years 1990 to 2005, including, but not limited to any and all Divisions, Groups, Offices, Departments, Sections, Committees or any other STOCKLIFT CORPORATION functional employee group designations, for those employees having any responsibility for either the design, testing, production or marketing of the STOCKLIFT Pacer Model 60 standup forklift truck.

REQUEST NO. 2:

The names, company position or title and current company position, if any, of the Vice Presidents or managers of the above-noted The STOCKLIFT Corporation organizational entities and the members of the designated committees for each of the years 1990 to 2005.

REQUEST NO. 3:

Any and all documents, memoranda, summaries, synopses, graphs, computer printouts or other data recordations in any form, either generated or reviewed by the STOCKLIFT CORPORATION entities referred to above, relative to any aspect of the design, testing, production or marketing of the STOCKLIFT Pacer Model 60 forklift trucks, including, but not limited to financial and engineering documents addressing:

a. an expanded deck or other extension to the operator's platform to prevent the operator from being crushed in the event of collision with or intrusion by stationery objects.

b. a metal or other sufficiently strong gate across the back of the operator's platform to prevent the operator from being crushed in the event of collision with or intrusion by stationery objects.

c. increased width or depth for the operator's platform to allow the operator to more safely or efficiently operate said forklift in emergency situations.

d. posts or other protective features around the operator's platform to prevent the operator from being crushed in the event of collision with or intrusion by stationery objects.

e. warnings respecting the dangers involved in the operation of said forklift.

f. the deadman pedal location and function.

g. the directional speed control handle.

h. optional equipment.

i. accident statistics.

REQUEST NO. 4:

The STOCKLIFT Corporation corporate organization charts or other applicable listings indicating the name of the office, department, section, committee or other applicable The STOCKLIFT Corporation organizational entity and the name of the individual or individuals employed by The STOCKLIFT Corporation, having primary responsibility for liaison between STOCKLIFT Corporation and the Occupational Safety and Health Administration (OSHA) of the United States government or other federal regulatory agencies having jurisdiction over any aspect of the design, testing, production or marketing of the STOCKLIFT Pacer Model 60 standup forklift trucks.

REQUEST NO. 5:

Any and all memoranda, reports, summaries, synopses, engineering or styling design layouts, specifications, blueprints, models, mathematical analyses, or other renderings as respects the original, intermediate, alternative or final designs of the STOCKLIFT Pacer Model 60 standup forklift trucks including, but not limited to designs relative to:

a. the width, depth and height of the operator's platform

b. the deadman pedal

c. the directional/speed control

d. posts or other protective features around the operator's platform.

e. warnings, decals, brochures and any educational materials respecting the dangers involved in the operation of said forklift.

REQUEST NO. 6:

Any and all final or intermediate test reports, test requests, test summaries, test synopses or test evaluations in any form, in your

possession, and whether or not actually conducted by you, of tests that were conducted on STOCKLIFT standup forklift trucks, including, but not limited to Pacer Model 60 forklift trucks, that addressed in whole or in part, the risk of injury to operators of standup forklift trucks resulting from tipovers, intrusion of objects into the operator's platform, the collision of the forklift into stationery objects or the failure of any of the methods employed in decreasing or stopping the forward or backward motion of the unit.

REQUEST NO. 7:

Any and all final or intermediate test reports, test requests, test summaries, test synopses or test evaluations in any form, in your possession, and whether or not actually conducted by you, of tests that were conducted on STOCKLIFT standup forklift trucks, including, but not limited to Pacer Model 60 forklift trucks, to determine the extent to which the STOCKLIFT CORPORATION line of standup forklift trucks compare in maneuverability, stability, durability or general functioning compare to standup forklift trucks manufactured by others.

REQUEST NO. 8:

Any and all documents respecting the record retention and record destruction policies, of the STOCKLIFT CORPORATION, relative to the retention or destruction of records of all types, including financial memoranda; sales data; test requests, reports, summaries, synopses and evaluations; labels and labeling related memoranda and drafts; operating instructions; consumer inquiries; warranty service of particular units; quality control documents; computer archive copies of data; communications with suppliers and distributors of products; and communications to and from the Occupational Safety and Health Administration of the United States government.

REQUEST NO. 9:

Any and all complaints or notices of claimed injury, in any form, and all accident reports resulting from the operation of a STOCKLIFT standup forklift truck, including, but not limited to the STOCKLIFT Pacer Model 60 standup forklift trucks, which injury arose out of the operation of any such forklift truck.

REQUEST NO. 10:

Any and all labels, decals, operating instructions, warnings, graphs, diagrams, advertising or promotional material used by the the STOCKLIFT Corporation in connection with the distribution and sale of STOCKLIFT standup forklift trucks, including, but not limited to the STOCKLIFT Pacer Model 60 standup forklift truck..

REQUEST NO. 11:

Any and all standard operating procedures or other memoranda that establish, describe or otherwise address the processes in the The STOCKLIFT Corporation respecting the accumulation, listing, reviewing, summarizing or synopsizing, of scientific, professional, engineering or industry trade association literature addressing the design, testing, manufacture, distribution and/or sale of standup forklift trucks.

REQUEST NO. 12:

Any and all correspondence between the STOCKLIFT CORPO-RATION and the Occupational Safety and Health Administration (OSHA) of the United States government, respecting operator safety in the operation of standup forklift trucks, including, but not limited to:

a. an expanded deck or other extension to the operator's platform to prevent the operator from being crushed in the event of collision with or intrusion by stationery objects.

b. a metal or other sufficiently strong gate across the back of the operator's platform to prevent the operator from being crushed in the event of collision with or intrusion by stationery objects.

c. increased width or depth for the operator's platform to allow the operator to more safely or efficiently operate said forklift in emergency situations.

d. posts or other protective features around the operator's platform to prevent the operator from being crushed in the event of collision with or intrusion by stationery objects.

e. warnings respecting the dangers involved in the operation of standup forklift trucks.

f. the deadman pedal location and function.

g. the directional speed control handle.

h. optional equipment.

i. accident statistics.

j. recommended standards prepared for the American Society of Mechanical Engineers (ASME) and/or the American National Standards Institute (ANSI) relative to standup forklift operations and operator safety.

REQUEST NO. 13:

Any and all correspondence between the STOCKLIFT CORPO-RATION and the Industrial Truck Association (ITA) respecting oper-

ator safety in the operation of standup forklift trucks, including, but not limited to:

a. an expanded deck or other extension to the operator's platform to prevent the operator from being crushed in the event of collision with or intrusion by stationery objects.

b. a metal or other sufficiently strong gate across the back of the operator's platform to prevent the operator from being crushed in the event of collision with or intrusion by stationery objects.

c. increased width or depth for the operator's platform to allow the operator to more safely or efficiently operate said forklift in emergency situations.

d. posts or other protective features around the operator's platform to prevent the operator from being crushed in the event of collision with or intrusion by stationery objects.

e. warnings respecting the dangers involved in the operation of standup forklift trucks.

f. the deadman pedal location and function.

g. the directional speed control handle.

h. optional equipment.

i. accident statistics.

j. recommended standards prepared for the American Society of Mechanical Engineers (ASME) and/or the American National Standards Institute (ANSI) relative to standup forklift operations and operator safety.

REQUEST NO. 14:

Any and all documents, notes, sketches or photographs resulting from any inspection of the STOCKLIFT Pacer Model 60 standup forklift truck involved in the instant action, with respect to the mechanical and/or physical condition of such truck.

REQUEST NO. 15:

Any statements in any form of witnesses to this occurrence or photographs of the scene or STOCKLIFT Pacer Model 60 standup forklift truck involved in the occurrence giving rise to this lawsuit.

REQUEST NO. 16:

Any and all catalogs, sales brochures and other marketing literature describing, illustrating or otherwise referrencing all optional equipment available for purchasers of the STOCKLIFT CORPORATION lines of standup forklift trucks, including, but not limited to the STOCKLIFT Pacer Model 60 standup forklift truck.

REQUEST NO. 17:

Any and all correspondence between the STOCKLIFT CORPO-RATION and the Department of Defense or any branch of the United States military respecting operator safety in the operation of standup forklift trucks, including, but not limited to:

a. an expanded deck or other extension to the operator's platform to prevent the operator from being crushed in the event of collision with or intrusion by stationery objects.

b. a metal or other sufficiently strong gate across the back of the operator's platform to prevent the operator from being crushed in the event of collision with or intrusion by stationery objects.

c. increased width or depth for the operator's platform to allow the operator to more safely or efficiently operate said forklift in emergency situations.

d. posts or other protective features around the operator's platform to prevent the operator from being crushed in the event of collision with or intrusion by stationery objects.

e. warnings respecting the dangers involved in the operation of standup forklift trucks.

f. the deadman pedal location and function.

g. the directional speed control handle.

h. optional equipment.

i. accident statistics.

j. recommended standards prepared for the American Society of Mechanical Engineers (ASME) and/or the American National Standards Institute (ANSI) relative to standup forklift operations and operator safety.

§ 17.12 SUPPLEMENTAL DISCOVERY

Federal Rule of Civil Procedure 26(e) and comparable state provisions impose a continuing duty to supplement any incomplete discovery responses and correct any inaccuracies.[2] Counsel should insist on these requirements.

---

[2] *See* HAYDOCK, HERR & STEMPEL'S FUNDAMENTALS OF PRETRIAL LITIGATION (American Casebook Series®, 5th ed. 2001), Part Three, Discovery Practice: Depositions, Interrogatories, Requests for Production and Physical Examinations, Requests For Admissions, Enforcing Discovery Rights. *See also* ANATOMY OF A PERSONAL INJURY LAWSUIT: CREATIVE DISCOVERY (ATLA Press); FULL DISCLOSURE: COMBATING STONEWALLING AND OTHER DISCOVERY ABUSES (ATLA Press); SCOTT BALDWIN, FRANCIS H. HARE, JR. & FRANCIS E. MCGOVERN, PREPARATION OF A PRODUCT LIABILITY CASE (Aspen Publishers) [Latest Supplemented Date: 4/4/2005]; DANNER & VARN, *supra* note 3.

However, it is unwise to do so in lieu of comprehensive supplemental inter-rogatories and requests for documentation. It must be recalled that the right to supplemental discovery does not mean that counsel can start over fresh if defendant's submissions show serious flaws in plaintiff's original dis-covery plan.[3]

During the course of counsel's close examination of documents obtained in the initial round of discovery, many questions will appear that could not have reasonably been anticipated prior to having had the chance to organ-ize and closely read the documents. This initial review will normally reveal the existence of large amounts of additional documentation referenced therein that counsel will need to fill the documentary gaps that will be encountered in the initial document analysis. Rule 26(e) allows for supple-mental discovery and counsel should take full advantage of it.

§ 17.13 SUMMARY

Chapter 19, Protective Orders, Discovery Enforcement and Motions-In-Limine will return to the major themes of products liability discovery in the context of defense motions for comprehensive protective orders, based upon trade secrets and other objections to publication. It will also address in detail motion practice centered in discovery enforcement and requests for discovery sanctions. Requests for motions-in-limine seeking to bar certain evidence such as that considered to be subsequent remedial measures will also be discussed.

---

[3] *See* TERRENCE F. KIELY, SCIENCE AND LITIGATION: PRODUCTS LIABILITY IN THEORY AND PRAC-TICE 361-362 (CRC Press 2002).

Chapter 18
DISCOVERY AND EVIDENCE DEPOSITIONS

SYNOPSIS

§ 18.01 INTRODUCTION

Discovery depositions provide the opportunity for the requesting party to ask the corporate defendant's key personnel a series of very detailed inquiries about the design, testing, production, marketing and post-marketing phases of the product development cycle involving the product under scrutiny. Sophisticated prefiling scientific, regulatory, industry and company research sets the stage for the type of intensive discovery discussed in the preceding chapters. That effort, in turn, supplies the groundwork for discovery or evidence depositions, which serve several central purposes in the pretrial process. Gaps in the chronology of events reflected in the answers to interrogatories and requests for documents may be filled. The names and function of all relevant committees and the details about personnel involved in generating important documents may be ascertained. The defendant's interpretation of key documents can be determined, as well as the fine points of defendant's defense. The depositions of expert witnesses can provide clear knowledge of the expert's positions and the bases for them from his or her experience and the relevant scientific literature.

There is a very large and growing body of deposition guides to practice available from respected trial lawyer organizations such as the National Institute for Trial Advocacy (NITA),[1] the Defense Research Institute (DRI)

---

[1] An excellent overview and guide to the taking of depositions is provided in the National Institute for Trial Advocacy publication entitled THE EFFECTIVE DEPOSITION: TECHNIQUES AND STRATEGIES THAT WORK (Nita Practical Guide Series 2001), written by David M. Malone and

and the Association of Trial Lawyers of America (ATLA). State bar journals and specialty journals aimed at the trial lawyers are filled with deposition advice from planning to execution.[2] There are also numerous purely commercial offerings by a variety of providers in the burgeoning area of skills literature, audio-tapes and DVDs.[3] Each of the fifty state bar associations

---

Peter T. Hoffman. This volume, also available on Amazon, addresses key components of successful deposition practice. (Purposes of Taking Depositions; Advantages and Disadvantages of Depositions; Planning and Scheduling Depositions; Preparing to Take the Deposition; Questioning Techniques; Style, Organization, and Other Matters; Using Documents; Preparing the Witness to be Deposed; Defending the Deposition; Depositions for Use at Trial; Videotape Depositions; Overview of the Expert Deposition.)

See also Stuart M. Israel, *Twelve Deposition Principles, Mechanics, Strategies, And Practices, Practical Litigator* (May 2004) at 31. (This excellent article addresses 12 basic deposition principles, mechanics, strategies, and practices, including who may be deposed, when, where, and how to get them there, limitations on the number and duration of depositions, the relationship between depositions and "paper" discovery, "Rambo" litigation tactics, and "other nuts, bolts, and screws that hold the deposition process together.")

[2] There are a number of excellent contemporary articles discussing deposition practice aimed at both neophyte and veteran. They are well worth consulting. *See, e.g., Effective Depositions in Employment and Other Cases,* PRACTICAL LITIGATOR (July 2005) at 35 (There are no secrets to a good deposition, just a lot of preparation.); David S. Wachen, *Preparing Fact Witnesses for Deposition,* PRACTICAL LITIGATOR (July 2005) at 7 (With the exception of the "pros" who have been through depositions on many occasions, the typical fact witness is likely to be both curious and a little apprehensive about the deposition process. So your preparation must put the witness at ease to the extent possible. You can do this by explaining the process, who will be there, how it will happen, and what the basic rules are. Nearly all witnesses will find considerable comfort in this kind of preparation. And with the confidence that it inspires, they will be effective witnesses who will know what to say — and what not to say.) *Id.* at 11; Paul Horowitz , *Deposition Tips Your Parents Taught You,* N.Y.S. B.J. 18 (March/April 2005) (An amusing but informative article on the basic principles of communication we were supposed to absorb as children.); Association of Trial Lawyers of America (ATLA), ATLA Winter 2003 Convention Reference Materials, Advocacy Track: *Discovery Can Make Your Case — How to Do It Right, Planning and Executing Depositions* (Numerous pointed articles on all aspects of pretrial discovery applicable to products liability litigation, with a focus on planning.); Association of Trial Lawyers of America (ATLA), February, 2001 ATLA Winter Convention Reference Materials, Advocacy Track: *Getting Full Disclosure — Discovery and Depositions, Practical Aspects of Planning and Executing Depositions*; Charles H. Samel, *The Five People You Meet Preparing for Your Deposition,* 31 No. 4 LITIGATION 35 (2005) (Interesting article on preparing company executives for deposition.); Stephen M. Terrell, *Preparing Your Client for a Video Deposition,* 48-DEC. RES GESTAE 26 (December 2004); Nina Ivanichvili, *A Lawyer's Guide to Cross-Cultural Depositions,* 28-OCT. CHAMPION 38 (September/October, 2004) (Interesting and useful discussion regarding the deposition of foreign nationals, an increasing factor in products liability cases involving multi-national corporations.)

[3] See, for example, the website of the National Institute of Trial Lawyers (NITA), http://www.nita.org/, for a listing of locations for deposition planning and skills seminars and materials available for purchase. The Americal Trial Lawyers Association website and print publications provide a large amount of information about effective deposition planning and practice in the form of seminars, current and past, audio and video tapes and DVD, as well as print and digital copies of depositions actually conducted in a wide variety of product liability cases. *See* http://www.atla.org/.The Defense Law Research Site also offers a wealth of information on the effective planning and execution of depositions in products liability cases of all types at http://www.dri.org.

and the federal bar[4] also provide a steady stream of continuing legal education courses and specialty deposition training programs.[5]

§ 18.02 THE DEPOSITION RULES

The utilization of discovery and evidence depositions, as with most discovery rules, are comparable in federal and state court practice.[6] Depositions in federal courts are controlled by Federal Rule of Civil Procedure Rule 30, which provides in part:

[A] FRCP Rule 30 — Depositions Upon Oral Examination

(a) When Depositions May be Taken; When Leave Required.

(1) A party may take the testimony of any person, including a party, by deposition upon oral examination without leave of court except as provided in paragraph (2). The attendance of witnesses may be compelled by subpoena as provided in Rule 45.

(2) A party must obtain leave of court, which shall be granted to the extent consistent with the principles stated in Rule 26(b)(2), if the person to be examined is confined in prison or if, without the written stipulation of the parties,

(A) a proposed deposition would result in more than ten depositions being taken under this rule or Rule 31 by the plaintiffs, or by the defendants, or by third-party defendants;

(B) the person to be examined already has been deposed in the case; or

---

[4] See the listings of discovery related continuing legal education programs at http://www.fedbar.org/cle.html.

[5] A simple Google search on *state bar deposition* will yield hundreds of listings for deposition training and reading and viewing materials. The same result will be had when searching for interrogatories and document discovery.

[6] For depositions taken in foreign countries, see generally, George Blum, 26B C.J.S. Depositions § 26, Corpus Juris Secundum (Database updated June 2005):

Depositions may be taken in foreign countries only before persons authorized to take depositions, examine witnesses, or administer oaths therein. . .Under some statutes depositions are authorized to be taken in other jurisdictions before persons empowered to take depositions, examine witnesses, or administer oaths therein. Such depositions can be taken only by officials of the kind or class designated. In some jurisdictions, an American consul or vice consul residing in a foreign country and duly accredited there is authorized to take depositions in such country. . . . The rule that when assistance is asked of an officer of another state or country in matter of taking testimony, affidavits, or administering oaths for use in local forum, if it is performed, it is done by virtue of local and not foreign authority, applies to authority which may be extended by federal government.

(C) a party seeks to take a deposition before the time specified in Rule 26(d) unless the notice contains a certification, with supporting facts, that the person to be examined is expected to leave the United States and be unavailable for examination in this country unless deposed before that time.

(2) The party taking the deposition shall state in the notice the method by which the testimony shall be recorded. Unless the court orders otherwise, it may be recorded by sound, sound-and-visual, or stenographic means, and the party taking the deposition shall bear the cost of the recording. Any party may arrange for a transcription to be made from the recording of a deposition taken by nonstenographic means.

State court discovery schemes by and large have adopted the broad principles of the Federal Rules of Civil Procedure, which allow discovery depositions in some settings to be used as evidence at trial.[7]

§ 18.03 RELEVANCY AND DEPOSITIONS

Relevancy controls the flow of questions and answers in depositions as it does all of the discovery devices. It is important to remember that the term has an expansive meaning in discovery, including discovery depositions.[8] This principal was recently stressed in a state court context in the 2005 Illinois decision in *Tomczak v. Ingalls Memorial Hospital*,[9] where the defendant

---

[7] Illinois is the only jurisdiction in the United States that promotes separate discovery and evidence depositions:

> While many of the state discovery rules — and civil procedural rules in general — have moved toward the model of the federal rules, Illinois has stridently held onto its two-step deposition strategy. It is time to relinquish the notion that the two-step requirement serves a legitimate purpose.

> In Illinois, unless specified otherwise, a deposition is by default limited to discovery. If both discovery and evidence depositions are desired of the same witness they must be taken separately, unless the parties stipulate otherwise or the court orders otherwise upon notice and motion. This rule establishes a clear delineation between discovery depositions and evidence depositions in Illinois. *See, It's Time to Move Beyond Separate Discovery and Evidence Depositions in Illinois*, ILL. B.J., July 2004, at 344.

[8] *See* In re StarFlite Management Group, Inc., 162 S.W.3d 409 (Tex. App. 2005). (Although the scope of discovery is broad, requests must show a reasonable expectation of obtaining information that will aid the dispute's resolution; therefore, discovery requests must be reasonably tailored to include only relevant matters.); Stewart v. Colonial Western Agency, Inc., 87 Cal. App. 4th 1006, 105 Cal. Rptr. 2d 115 (2001) (Admissibility is not the test and information unless privileged, is discoverable if it might reasonably lead to admissible evidence. . . . These rules are applied liberally in favor of discovery, and (contrary to popular belief), fishing expeditions are permissible in some cases.) *See also* David Young, *A New Theory of Relativity: The Triumph of the Irrelevant at Depositions*, 36 UWLA L. REV. 56 (2005) (Discussing the wide range of opinion on the idea of "relevancy" in a discovery deposition context as opposed to a trial.).

[9] 834 N.E.2d 549 (Ill. App. Ct. 2005).

hospital contended that the circuit court abused its discretion by ordering compliance with the discovery request because the information sought was not so material or relevant as to justify the burden of securing its disclosure. The Circuit Court granted an administrators' motion to compel information related to emergency room records of nonparty patients. The hospital refused, and on its own motion, was held in contempt and fined $50 for refusal to comply. The appellate court rejected the hospital's argument based on relevancy:

> Supreme Court Rule 201(b)(1) allows a party to "obtain by discovery full disclosure regarding any matter relevant to the subject matter involved in the pending action." (citations omitted) The circuit court is afforded great latitude in determining the scope of pretrial discovery, as the concept of relevance for discovery purposes encompasses not only what is admissible at trial, but also that which may lead to the discovery of admissible evidence. (citations omitted) We will reverse a circuit court's ruling on a motion to compel discovery only where the appellant "affirmatively and clearly" shows an abuse of discretion.[10]

Here, the information requested contained neither the nonparty patients' names, nor a history of their prior or present medical conditions, treatments, or diagnoses. As such, the court concluded that the nonparty patients' identities could not be determined from the information the court ordered Ingalls to disclose. Accordingly, the court ruled that the nonparty patients' triage times, treatment times, and triage acuity designations fall outside the category of "protected health information." Moreover, the court continued, even if they were to assume arguendo that the information sought was "protected health information," they would still find that it was discoverable in the absence of a qualified protective order.[11]

Attempts by a party to stay discovery pending a motion to dismiss the complaint typically fall on deaf ears. This important issue was recently addressed in the 2005 case of *Evitts v. DaimlerChrysler Motors Corp.*,[12] where automobile owners brought a putative class action suit against automobile manufacturer and extended service contract provider alleging breach of warranty and violation of consumer protection statutes based on allegedly defective rear window defroster. The court stressed the function of discov-

---

[10] *Id.* at 556 (*citing* Dufour v. Mobile Oil Corp., 703 N.E.2d 448 (1998)).

[11] A proper reading of regulation 164.512(e)(1) shows that a qualified protective order must only be secured when a disclosure is being made in "response to a subpoena, discovery request, or other lawful process, that is not accompanied by an order of a court." 45 C.F.R. § 164.512(e)(1)(ii) (2002). Here, Ingalls was ordered by the circuit court to comply with the plaintiffs' discovery request and produce the specified information. *Ingalls*, 834 N.E.2d at 556.

[12] 834 N.E.2d 942 (Ill. App. Ct. 2005).

ery in helping the plaintiff to refine or even establish his theory of liability during the discovery process:

> Plaintiffs contended that the circuit court abused its discretion by staying discovery pending its ruling on DCMC's motion to dismiss. They argued that the court's refusal to reopen discovery in effect required them to prove their case at the pleading stage and violated Supreme Court Rule 201(a). Defendants responded that the circuit court was correct to circumscribe discovery because plaintiffs' discovery requests were overly broad and were submitted with the intent of supporting wide-ranging class action litigation, when plaintiffs' complaints were insufficient to allege their own individual claims.

The court supported plaintiff"s position, stating:

> Parties may obtain discovery by full disclosure regarding any relevant matter, even where the discovery relates to the claims of the parties seeking disclosure. (citations omitted) A circuit court has wide latitude in ruling on discovery motions, and we will not disturb such a ruling unless it constitutes a manifest abuse of discretion. A court abuses its discretion only where its ruling is arbitrary, fanciful, or unreasonable, or where no reasonable person would adopt the court's view.[13]

> . . . A circuit court may properly stay or quash a discovery request when it has sufficient information upon which to rule on a motion to dismiss. However, a court should not refuse a discovery request and grant a motion to dismiss where it reasonably appears discovery might assist the nonmoving party.[14]

The question of the bounds of relevancy in a discovery deposition was recently analyzed in the 2005 Florida case of *Sterling Casino Lines, L.P. v. Plowman-Render*.[15] There it was held that the trial court abused its discretion in admitting irrelevant evidence which impugned the character of one of Sterling's chief witnesses, the emergency medical technician who treated Plowman-Render. The questions Plowman-Render's counsel asked Gardner in his deposition concerning his alcohol-induced coma, suicide attempt, stays in a mental facility and the reason for his termination from employment with Sterling may have been appropriate in a discovery context. The court stressed that the concept of "relevancy" was broader in discovery than at trial and a party may be permitted to discover relevant

---

[13] *Id.* (*citing* Mutlu v. State Farm Fire & Casualty Co., 785 N.E.2d 951 (Ill. App. Ct. 2003)).

[14] *Id.* (*citing* Adkins Energy, LLC. v. Delta-T Corp., 806 N.E.2d 1273 (Ill. App. Ct. 2004)). The court also observed, however, that discovery is not necessary where a cause of action has not been stated.

[15] 902 So. 2d 938 (Fla. Dist. Ct. App. 2005).

evidence that would be inadmissible at trial so long as it may lead to the discovery of admissible evidence.

However, the court stated, these questions were irrelevant to the issues at trial and served simply to portray Gardner in an unfavorable light. Plowman-Render did not establish Gardner's memory had been impaired by the coma or any other medical condition. Likewise, Plowman-Render did not show any reason for delving into the specific reason for Gardner's termination from Sterling. Gardner was attempting to protect his privacy at his deposition but his refusal to answer some questions may have seemed evasive to the jury.

The credibility of witnesses was clearly crucial in this case. Plowman-Render's friends apparently did not see the incident and Dean has been diagnosed with Alzheimer's and did not testify. Thus the case came down to Plowman-Render's version of events or Gardner's and Jones' version, which were in direct conflict. These questions impugned Gardner's character and may have destroyed his effectiveness as a witness.

In these circumstances, the court concluded, Sterling was entitled to a new trial.

Similarly, in *J.W. v. B.B.*,[16] the court held that information concerning a physician's sexual orientation was not discoverable concerning a job applicants' claim that the physician failed to obtain informed consent before conducting digital-rectal exams on applicants while performing pre-employment medical examinations. The court ruled that the physician's motive or intent in conducting exams was not relevant to the dispositive inquiry of whether the applicants were provided with information that a reasonable patient would want to know before consenting to such a procedure.

§ 18.04 OBJECTIONS IN DEPOSITIONS

FRCP 30 (c) provides that [a]ll objections made at the time of the examination to the qualifications of the officer taking the deposition, to the manner of taking it, to the evidence presented, to the conduct of any party, or to any other aspect of the proceedings shall be noted by the officer upon the record of the deposition; but the examination shall proceed, with the testimony being taken subject to the objections.

Rule 30(d) (4) addresses the abuse of the deposition process, unfortunately not a rare occasion in contemporary practice:

> At any time during a deposition, on motion of a party or of the deponent and upon a showing that the examination is being conducted in bad faith or in such manner as unreasonably to annoy, embarrass, or oppress the deponent or party, the court in which

---

[16] 700 N.W.2d 277 (Wis. Ct. App. 2005).

the action is pending or the court in the district where the deposition is being taken may order the officer conducting the examination to cease forthwith from taking the deposition, or may limit the scope and manner of the taking of the deposition as provided in Rule 26(c). If the order made terminates the examination, it shall be resumed thereafter only upon the order of the court in which the action is pending. Upon demand of the objecting party or deponent, the taking of the deposition shall be suspended for the time necessary to makea motion for an order.

Facing a flurry of objections made during the course of a deposition is a very common problem in products liability cases, regardless of whether the deponent is an expert, corporate officer or other employee. There seems to be a lack of agreement as to just what is or is not objectionable, whether the question must be answered nonetheless over objection, whether the deposition may be terminated and the resumed, and a host of civility related issues. As recently noted by trial attorney David Paul Horowitz:

> There is a fair amount of disagreement over what constitutes a proper objection under particular circumstances, and what effect interposing an objection has on the witness's obligation to answer the question. There is also disagreement about what types of behavior and demeanor are appropriate for attorneys questioning and defending depositions, and what conduct on the part of the witness may be objectionable.

> Counsel may seek to have sanctions imposed for the failure of a party or witness to appear at the deposition, and may raise objections to the form or substance of questions posed. Objections may also be raised regarding the qualifications of the person officiating, the competency of a witness or the behavior of adverse counsel.

> A court will not rule on the propriety of a particular question in advance of a deposition. Instead, the question must be posed, objection taken, and then the court may rule on the question.[17]

There are differing views on this subject. While inappropriate deposition conduct may offend civility principles and be regulated, overarching discovery rules, seeking court intervention is not always desirable. As noted by Stewart Israel in his recent article, *Twelve Deposition Principles, Mechanics, Strategies, And Practices*, it may cause delay and a host of other unwanted results:

> It can be time-consuming and expensive. And often it is difficult to communicate the obstructive impact of the other side's behavior to

---

[17] *See* David Paul Horowitz, *Objections and Objectionable Conduct at Depositions*, 77-JAN. N.Y.S. B.J. 20 (2005).

someone who wasn't there, i.e., the judge. Worse, seeking court intervention often is ineffective because many judges are unable or unwilling to devote the time, effort and attention necessary to understanding discovery motions. Some are too busy. Some find discovery disputes beneath them. Some are lazy or impatient with details. Too many react to discovery motions with the a-plague-on-both-your-houses attitude or by automatically blaming the victim. Most litigators spend most of their litigating time occupied with discovery, so judges ought to spend their valuable time addressing and deciding discovery disputes, but it's a fact of life that many judges just do not like discovery disputes. So, even if you're in the right, bringing a motion to compel or for a protective order may produce judicial antipathy or worse. As noted, when you go to court on a discovery motion, you risk application of the Law of Unintended Consequences, which may result in judicial micromanagement, burdensome discovery limitations, undesirable discovery extension and expansion, merits prejudgment ("premature adjudication"), and sanctions for having the temerity to file a motion that is denied.[18]

In the last half century or more, trial lawyers' development of the discovery deposition as a central information gathering and trial support vehicle has improved dramatically. Despite occasional calls by defense-oriented authors to ensure "mum's the word",[19] discovery in general and depositions in particular have advanced towards full disclosure of relevant information. Unfortunately, some lawyers for both sides have developed quarrelsome and contentious tactics in the course of defending depositions that can seriously impede the flow of information from a witness. Courts and bar associations have made important efforts to eliminate or at least severely reduce this behavior.[20]

---

[18] Israel, *supra* note 1, at 42.

[19] *See* Nahrstadt, *Narrowing the Scope of Discovery for Substantially Similar Products*, 15 No. 6 PRAC. LIT 37, 38 (2004) (Products liability actions are not easy cases to prepare, nor are they easy cases to try. More often than not, such cases involve complex industrial or consumer products, monumental amounts of documents, intricate theories of liability and defense, and horrific injuries. Defense counsel must make sense of a variety of complex issues and present a coherent, cohesive, and streamlined theory of defense to the jury. Obviously, the defense attorney who is successful in preventing the introduction of "extraneous" issues to the jury will be far ahead of the game in terms of limiting the scope of the case and concentrating the jury's focus on the salient legal issues. One of the most successful ways of limiting the introduction of "extraneous" issues is to prevent the plaintiff's attorney from finding out about them during the course of discovery.) *Id.*

[20] *See* Valerie A. Yarashus, *Don't Let Your Opponent Disrupt Depositions,* TRIAL, November 2004, at 56. These authors cite what they feel are the most common forms of obstruction used during depositions are:

[ ] conferences to frame a witness's answer or to interrupt the proceedings

[ ] speaking objections and interjections to suggest answers or disrupt the flow of information

[ ] errata sheets to change a witness's testimony. *Id.*

In *Mora v. Saint Vincent's Catholic Medical Center of New York*,[21] the defendant, in a medical malpractice case, sought to compel the plaintiff to appear for a continued deposition and to postpone the depositions of the defendants pending the completion of the plaintiff's continued deposition. During the course of the deposition counsel for Dr. Hsu attempted to ask the plaintiff the following questions, each of which plaintiff's counsel directed her not to answer: (1) whether the plaintiff was taking any medications at the time of the deposition, (2) whether the plaintiff was on disability (i.e. Social Security Disability Insurance), and if so, when she began receiving benefits and the nature of the disability, (3) whether the plaintiff had ever filed for bankruptcy, (4) whether the plaintiff had ever been diagnosed with a psychological disorder, (5) whether the plaintiff had ever experienced palpitations, and (6) whether the plaintiff had undergone surgery prior to the surgery giving rise to this action.[22]

The court ruled that the proper procedure during the course of an examination before trial was to permit the witness to answer all questions posed, subject to objections, unless a question was clearly violative of the witness's constitutional rights or of some privilege recognized in law, or was palpably irrelevant. The reason for this maxim, the court stated, was simple: only objections to form and the technical aspects of the deposition are waived if not timely raised at the deposition.[23]

The court noted that the goal of discovery schemes was to attempt to create an environment conducive to open, expansive disclosure during the taking of a deposition. Unfortunately, the court observed, this environment was *routinely polluted* by the conduct of attorneys at depositions. Judicially unsupervised depositions had become breeding grounds for a myriad of unprofessional and dilatory conduct.[24] So profound and widespread was this behavior that a series of recent law review articles have been dedicated to highlighting its existence, and proposed regulations have been suggested to stymie its proliferation.[25]

The deposition-related conduct in the case at bar highlighted one of the "abuses" the Advisory Committee was seeking to address, namely the practice of attorneys directing witnesses not to answer questions. Initially, plaintiff's counsel did not assert that any of the blocked questions implicated

---

[21] 800 N.Y.S.2d 298 (N.Y. Sup. Ct. 2005).

[22] *Id.* at 300.

[23] *Id. (citing* 1 PAYNE & ZALAYET, MODERN NEW YORK DISCOVERY § 8.55, at 136-138 (2d ed. 2004)).

[24] *Mora*, 800 N.Y.S.2d at 301.

[25] *Id. See* Horowitz, *Objections and Objectionable Conduct at Depositions*, 77-JAN. N.Y.S. B.J. 20 (2005); Cary, *Rambo Depositions: Controlling an Ethical Cancer in Civil Litigation*, 25 HOFSTRA L. REV. 561 (1996); 2005 Report of Advisory Comm. on Civil Practice, at 90-94 (regulations aimed at curbing the practice of "speaking objections" and delineating when an attorney can direct a witness not to answer a question).

the plaintiff's constitutional rights or a privilege recognized in law. Rather, counsel essentially asserted that the blocked questions were palpably irrelevant.[26]

§ 18.05 DEPOSITION PLANNING

A primary purpose in deposing corporate staff is to fill in those gaps in the total products design, testing, production, marketing and post-marketing information already garnered by the parties. The products liability plaintiff has much to fill. Literally millions of pieces of paper are churned out over the course of a products initiation and subsequent life in the market. As noted in Chapter 17, Requests to Produce Documents, only a very small percentage of that mountain of paper is of interest to plaintiff or defense counsel, let alone relevant from a trial standpoint. What is supplied by the company in discovery is necessarily only a small, very disjointed portion of what is present in defendant's files. The phenomenon of email and ensuing electronic discovery only swells the total. Depositions in these cases require considerable preparation in the form of document organization, analysis and cross-referencing.

There are several basic goals that should be focal points for planning the depositions of corporate personnel and expert witnesses. In the broadest sense, counsel need to answer and flesh out the following points over the course of the depositions taken:

- Remaining questions about the defendant's decision-making processes as relates to the suspect product or line of product.

- Identifying the corporation's state of the art defense strategies.

- Getting the details of the defendant's response to proposed governmental regulations.

- Discovering the details of defendant's foreign operations and marketing.

- Discovering the corporate defendant's and its experts' position on the importance of individual or a related series of documents, such as testing or clinical trials.

- Identifying the defense strategy with respect to the defendant's design, testing, production, marketing and post-marketing proceeses as relates to the suspect product or line of product.

---

[26] Here, plaintiff's counsel improperly directed plaintiff not to answer defense counsel's questions as to whether plaintiff was taking any medications at the time of the deposition, whether plaintiff was receiving disability benefits, and whether plaintiff had ever filed for personal bankruptcy. Plaintiff's counsel also improperly blocked questions relating to plaintiff's general health and prior surgeries. Those questions were relevant on the issue of damages. In addition, plaintiff was directed to answer questions regarding her mental health history unless she withdrew any claims for emotional or psychological damages.

- Identifying the corporation's interpretation of key documents of all types.

- Identifying the corporation's proximate cause defenses.[27]

Preparing the depositions of corporate staff and defense experts around these broad areas will go a long way towards the resolution of most of the gaps in knowledge encountered over the course of case investigation and early discovery.

§ 18.06 DOCUMENT ORGANIZATION AND DEPOSITION PREPARATION

Depositions in the products liability case are centered on issues raised by the information received in discovery. This is especially so with documents addressing the chronological stages of the production and marketing of the product. A close review and organization of such materials is essential, both for further information and determining issues and related documentation for use at trial. There are a series of organizational and analytical focal points that need to be addressed prior to initiating case depositions:

DOCUMENT GENERATING PROCESSES AND BASIC CONTENT

- Grading the Importance of Corporate Documents

- Indexing by Nature or Type of Document

- Routine Informational Content of Documents

- Identifying Document Points of Interest/Fields

- Indexing of All Corporate Documents by Date and Subject Matters

- Indexing of All Documentary Materials: State-of-the-Art and Internal Processes

- Preparing a Glossary of Terms

---

[27] *See* TERRENCE F. KIELY, SCIENCE AND LITIGATION: PRODUCTS LIABILITY IN THEORY AND PRACTICE 362-363 (CRC Press 2002). *See also* Mark J. Evans, *Make the Most of Company-Employee Depositions*, TRIAL, November 2003, at 36:

A corporate representative will usually have experience testifying, which makes it more likely that his or her deposition will be best used for discovery purposes. It is a good idea to take these depositions as early as possible so you have time to conduct additional discovery to follow up on any answers that require more investigation.

The other group comprises company employees who are not corporate representatives. Their depositions serve an entirely different purpose. They should be conducted with the jury, not discovery, in mind. They will typically involve a narrow area of inquiry, focusing on the employee's involvement in and knowledge of events directly related to the alleged defect. They may involve knowledge of testing that showed the product was susceptible to failure, or alternative designs considered by the manufacturer. *Id.* at 37.

- Isolating Selected Activity over the Case Time Frame
- Gaps in the Generation of Documentation

INTERNAL ORGANIZATION AND STANDARD OPERATING PROCEDURES

- Requesting Offices and Department
- Requesting Individuals
- Distribution Lists
- Committees and Committee Meetings
- Key Tests or Clinical Trials
- Government Regulation
- Consumer Complaints
- Law Suits or Recalls

MATCHING THE DOCUMENTS TO LEGAL THEORY OF LIABILITY

- Knowledge of Defect
- Knowledge of Alternative Design
- Legal Theories and Relevancy
- Proximate Cause

Depositions of corporate staff[28] should only follow the organization and analysis of answers to interrogatories and the documents received after the resolution of requests for documentation.[29] The examination and organization of such materials must be accompanied by the preparation of a readily accessible database system allowing for both the rapid retrieval and cross-referrencing of names, dates, topics, meetings and other key points across the design, testing, production and marketing of the product at issue. Microsoft Access and Filemaker are the two more popular database programs used by small to medium size firms. Both are inexpensive yet powerful additions to any firm's technological arsenal, with a number of easy to

---

[28] In products cases, the most helpful depositions are often given by company employees. Don't make the mistake of using these witnesses only as fonts of discovery information. Instead, keep your eye on the ultimate goal — jury persuasion — and keep your cross-examination skills sharp. *Evans*, supra note 27, at 39.

[29] *Id.*

read guides.[30] Making the best use of available technology, such as the now common videotaping of depositions, can often yield dramatic results.[31]

Federal Rule of Civil Procedure 30(b)(6) allows a party to request that a corporation designate one or more individuals to be deposed on subject matters specified in the deposition notice. The purpose of the rule is to allow for depositions on these matters when counsel is unable to adequately identify knowledgeable individuals at the time when the deposition is requested.[32] The organization and analysis of corporate documentation will identify key personnel who were actively involved in the product development and manufacturing processes of primary concern to counsel. These are the employees who typically have the most to offer. While these persons will be well prepared by defense lawyers, they are not professional witnesses. Counsel is much more likely to gain important testimony from them than from employees whose job description includes testifying at depositions.[33]

---

[30] **Filemaker**: *See* GEOFF COFFEY & SUSAN PROSSER: FILEMAKER PRO 8: THE MISSING MANUAL (O'Reilly Media 2005); STEVEN A. SCHWARTZ & DENNIS R. COHEN: FILEMAKER PRO 7 BIBLE (Wiley 2004); STEVE SCHWARTZ, CREATING A DATABASE IN FILEMAKER PRO 8 : VISUAL QUICKPROJECT GUIDE (Visual Quickproject Series) (Peachpit Press 2005).

Microsoft Access: MICROSOFT OFFICE ACCESS 2003 STEP BY STEP: ONLINE TRAINING SOLUTIONS (Online Training Solutions, Inc. 2003); JOHN L. VIESCAS & JOHN VIESCAS: MICROSOFT OFFICE ACCESS 2003 INSIDE OUT (Microsoft Press; Bk&CD-Rom edition (August 27, 2003)); CARY N. PRAGUE, MICHAEL R. IRWIN & JENNIFER REARDON: ACCESS 2003 BIBLE, (Wiley; Bk&CD-Rom edition (October 3, 2003)).

[31] You should find a videographer who has experience working with sophisticated document cameras and presenters. This technology allows you to display the deposition document on a screen at trial while you question the witness about it. *See* Evans, *supra* note 27, at 36; Stephen M. Terrell, *Preparing Your Client For A Video Deposition*, 48-Dec. RESG 26 (Res Gestae December 2004); Andre M. Lagomarsino, *Strategic Use Of Video Depositions*,11-Jun. NEV. LAW. 8 (2003).

[32] While this and comparable state provisions have great utility in a wide variety of settings, they should as a matter of practice, be used as a last resort in product liability litigation. Most major corporations have engineers and other scientists whose sole function is to work with the legal staff in defending these cases. A primary part of their employment is to represent the corporation in 30(b)(6) depositions. While these individuals are totally familiar with all of the documentation involved in the case, they are also skilled at leading inexperienced counsel astray or providing little or no valuable information during the course of a deposition.

[33] A primary purpose of these depositions is establishing the precise chain of command for varying activities over the case time frames. It is important to track decision-making to the highest levels possible. Corporate line charts tell only part of the story. Specialized reporting formats are often at the heart of the development of new product lines. These would not normally appear on standard organization charts and are often utilized for the resolution of short term corporate goals. It is also common business practice for managers to establish various "activities," "task forces" or other functional groupings to carry out important work. Counsel must specifically identify any such organizational processes and the personnel involved to adequately assess the exact nature and extent of corporate knowledge. *See* KIELY, *supra* note 27, at 365.

§ 18.07 DEPOSING DEFENSE EXPERTS

The deposition of the defense expert is one of the most important in the entire series of depositions that will be undertaken. They not only have significant amount of information and experience but will most likely be a major defense witness at trial.[34] While estimating the technical testimonial competence of any deponent is an important goal of deposition practice, it is especially important in products liability cases. The bulk of the testimony in these depositions will revolve around the state-of-the-art and proximate cause defenses. These technical expert witnesses typically have little to offer as to the details of company's document generating and decision-making processes. Their primary goal is to establish that the defendant's packaging, instructions, warnings or overall design reflected the state of the art when examined in light of either the authoritative literature in the field or the customary practice of the industry. The other key aspect of the defense expert is to establish that the feature of defendant's product involved in the case was not the proximate cause of plaintiff's death or injury.

The deposition of the defendant's technical experts will reveal in detail the substance of the defendant's state-of-the-art, documentary and proximate cause strategies. Expert witnesses for both sides are the center of attraction in these cases, and the success of the case often stands or falls on the quality of what they say and how they say it. The manner in which the expert communicates, or as the case may be, fails to communicate important information, is often of equal value to the substance of their testimony. There is a wealth of practice-oriented literature addressing every aspect of this crucial stage of products liability discovery.[35]

---

[34] Members of defendant's technical and managerial staff deposed by plaintiff may not, and routinely are not be called to testify. Chief among the reasons for relying on experts is the in-house staff's inexperience as witnesses.

[35] See, e.g., Nahrstadt, supra note 19, at 38; George Brent Mickum IV & Luther L. Hajek, Guise, Contrivance, Or Artful Dodging?: The Discovery Rules Governing Testifying Employee Experts, 24 REV. LITIG. 301 (Spring 2005); 1 DOUGLAS DANNER & LARRY L. VARN, EXPERT WITNESS CHECKLISTS § 1:64 (3d ed.), Chapter 1, General Use of the Expert Witness, VII. Pretrial Discovery of the Expert Witness (Database updated June 2005); 2 ATLA's LITIGATING TORT CASES § 18:56, Roxanne Barton Conlin & Gregory S. Cusimano, Editors-in-Chief, Chapter 18, Depositions by Linda Miller Atkinson, § 18:56. Deposing the opposing expert — Benefits of deposing the opposing expert (Database updated July 2005); Paul Lisnek & Michael Kaufman, Depositions: Procedure, Strategy & Technique, Part III, THE DEFENDING PARTY'S PERSPECTIVE, Chapter 15, The Deposition of an Expert Witness. (Database updated September 2005); Marilyn J. Holifield, Deposing Expert Witnesses In Products Liability Cases, 12 NO. 2 PRAC. LITIGATOR 31 (March 2001); Richard D. Hailey, Know The Science Before Deposing Medical Experts, TRIAL, December 2000, at 95.

In addition to the number of sources available through the American Trial Lawyers Association (ATLA), the Defense Research Institute (DRI) provides a number of excellent articles and papers on deposing expert witnesses from the defense position. See http://www.atla.org and http://www.dri.org/.

Chapter 19

PROTECTIVE ORDERS AND DISCOVERY ENFORCEMENT

SYNOPSIS

§ 19.01 INTRODUCTION

This chapter will address two crucial areas in the entire products liability litigation undertaking: Seeking or opposing protective orders and enforcing or opposing requests for discovery. In many ways, the success or failure of these two efforts can be dispositive in these cases. The first topic to be discussed is protective orders.

A major issue that plaintiff's counsel will encounter are defense motions for a comprehensive protective order. The entry of a protective order can significantly impede counsel's efforts to achieve a detailed understanding of defendant's document generating and decision-making processes. This is because one of the major goals of such orders is to deprive plaintiff's counsel of the opportunity consult with more experienced lawyers. This consultation may take the form of document tutorials and/or the exchange of

information. Corporate concern over the sharing of information supplied in discovery with other lawyers, often a reason for increased filings against them, is a major factor in the routine requests for protective orders. The motion for a protective order has been usually deemed a disfavored motion, with the clear burden on the moving party to show some plainly important basis for the order.[1]

The question of the issuance or extent of protective orders seeking nondisclosure of material obtained in public trials has been of great concern for the long tenure of product liability litigation. The right of the public to documents issuing from public trial discovery processes and the countervailing interests of a wide variety of interested parties, including the government and industry is still very much in contention. The latest effort to resolve these complex matters is being produced by the highly thought of Sedona Conference in the The Sedona Guidelines: Best Practices Addressing Protective Orders,Confidentiality & Public Access In Civil Cases (April 2005 Public Comment Version).[2] The Sedona Conference® Working Group Addressing Protective Orders, Confidentiality and Public Access (POPA) was established to foster *some clarity and uniformity to practices involving protective orders in civil litigation, and determinations affecting public access to documents filed or referred to in court.*[3]

§ 19.02 PROTECTIVE ORDERS: THE RULES

Protective orders in U.S. Courts are governed by Federal Rule 26 General Provisions Governing Discovery which provides:

> (c) Protective Orders. Upon motion by a party or by the person from whom discovery is sought, accompanied by a certification that the movant has in good faith conferred or attempted to confer with other affected parties in an effort to resolve the dis-

---

[1] *See, e.g.,* United States v. Purdome, 30 F.R.D. 338, 341 (D.C. MO. 1962); Glick v. McKesson and Robbins, Inc., 10 F.R.D. 477 (D.C. MO. 1950); Blankenship v. Hearst Corp., 519 F. 2d 418 (9th Cir., 1975); U.S. v. International Business Machines Corp., 66 F.R.D. 186, 189 (S.D.N.Y. 1974); Davis v. Romney, 55 F.R.D. 180 (D.C. Pa. 1972); Hunter v. International Systems and Controls Corp., 51 F.R.D. 251 (D.C. Mo. 1970).

[2] 6 SEDONA CONF. J. 183 (Fall 2005). The important papers and conference produced by the Sedona Conference may be accessed online at http://www.thesedonaconference.org/.

[3] *Id.* Preliminary working assumptions are: Chapter 2. Discovery: **Principle 1.** There is no presumed right of the public to participate in the discovery process or to have access to the fruits of discovery that are not submitted to the court; **Principle 2.** A litigant has the right to disclose the fruits of discovery to non-parties, absent an agreement between the parties or an order based on a showing of good cause; **Principle 3.** A broad protective order entered under Fed. R. Civ. P 26(c) to facilitate the exchange of discovery materials does not substitute for the individualized judicial determination necessary for sealing such material, if filed with the court on a non-discovery matter; **Principle 4.** On a proper showing, non-parties should be permitted to intervene to challenge a protective order that limits disclosure of otherwise discoverable information.

pute without court action, and for good cause shown, the court in which the action is pending or alternatively, on matters relating to a deposition, the court in the district where the deposition is to be taken may make any order which justice requires to protect a party or person from annoyance, embarrassment, oppression, or undue burden or expense, including one or more of the following:

(1) that the disclosure or discovery not be had;

(2) that the disclosure or discovery may be had only on specified terms andconditions, including a designation of the time or place;

(3) that the discovery may be had only by a method of discovery other than that selected by the party seeking discovery;

(4) that certain matters not be inquired into, or that the scope of the disclosure or discovery be limited to certain matters;

(5) that discovery be conducted with no one present except personsdesignated by the court;

(6) that a deposition, after being sealed, be opened only by order of thecourt;

(7) that a trade secret or other confidential research, development, or commercial information not be revealed or be revealed only in a designated way; and

(8) that the parties simultaneously file specified documents or information enclosed in sealed envelopes to be opened as directed by the court.[4]

State discovery schemes provide similar provisions. Illinois Supreme Court Rule 201, General Discovery Provisions provides:

Protective Orders. The court may at any time on its own initiative, or on motion of any party or witness, make a protective order as justice requires, denying, limiting, conditioning, or regulating discovery to prevent unreasonable annoyance, expense, embarrassment, disadvantage, or oppression.[5]

§ 19.03 PROTECTIVE ORDERS IN PRODUCTS LITIGATION

The type of comprehensive protective orders often sought by corporate defense counsel read as follows:

---

[4] FED. R. CIV. P. 26 — General Provisions Governing Discovery.

[5] Illinois Supreme Court Rule 201. General Discovery Provisions.

1. All documents and materials which are produced and exhibited by the defendant in this action shall remain in the possession of the defendant's counsel.

2. Any and all copies of said documents and materials made by or at the incidence of the plaintiff or his attorneys, shall remain in the physical custody, possession and control of the plaintiff's attorneys, and each such item which is not admitted into evidence at trial shall be returned to the defendant's counsel at the termination of this litigation. Moreover, each such item which is admitted into evidence shall be returned to the defendant's counsel at the termination of this litigation.

3. All experts retained by the plaintiff and by the plaintiff's counsel are prohibited from making any copy of any item produced in this action by the defendant. The plaintiff, his counsel, and all experts retained by the plaintiff or by the plaintiff's counsel are prohibited from, in any fashion, distributing or disseminating any documents or materials or copies thereof produced in this action by the defendant.

4. Any and all notes, whether handwritten, typed or recorded in any form, and any copies or reproductions thereof, which are made by or at the instance of the plaintiff, his attorneys, or any experts retained by the plaintiff or by his attorneys from any documents and materials which are produced and exhibited by the defendant in this action or copies thereof shall be turned over to defendant's counsel at the termination of this litigation.

5. The plaintiff, his counsel, and all experts retained by the plaintiff or by the plaintiff's counsel are prohibited from, in any fashion, distributing or disseminating any notes, whether handwritten, typed, recorded, or reproduced in any form made from any documents and materials which are produced and exhibited by the defendant in this action, or copies thereof.

6. Any contents of any documents or materials produced in this action by the defendant which deals with or concerns any matters other than the fuel storage and delivery systems may be excised and obliterated by the defendant prior to the production of said documents and materials.

The entry of an order along the above lines can seriously detract from counsel's efforts to maximize his knowledge of corporate documents and processes.

§ 19.04 REQUIREMENT OF SPECIFIC SUPPORTIVE FACTS

As with all objections to discovery requests, the moving party here must allege specific facts in support of the motion for a protective order. A bare repetition of the statutory grounds for such orders is inadequate. The party seeking the order must demonstrate *good cause* for its issuance. A showing of good cause requires facts demonstrating that disclosure of the information "will work a clearly defined and very serious injury."[6]

§ 19.05 INFORMATION SHARING

It is an arduous task for a single plaintiff to complete discovery in a complex products liability case such as a Vioxx litigation when faced with a corporate opponent who has significantly greater resources and support staff. This is a products liability reality that has not escaped the attention of the nation's state and federal courts. In the leading case of *Williams v. Johnson & Johnson*, 50 F.R.D. 31, 33 (S.D.N.Y. 1970), the Court observed:

> In this situation (where numerous similar suits had been filed) it is at least theoretically advantageous for plaintiffs in the various suits to share the fruits of discovery. They thus reduce the time and money which must be expended to prepare for trial and are probably able to provide more effective, speedy, and efficient representation to their clients. . . . On its face, such collaboration comes squarely within the aims laid out in the first and fundamental rule of the Federal Rules of Civil Procedure. . . . Thus there is no merit to the all-encompassing contention that the fruits of discovery in one case are to be used in the case only. . . .

In rejecting defendant's bald claim that plaintiff's counsel would encourage litigation against it and otherwise seek to harass defendant, the Court stated:

> It is difficult to draw a clear line between the legitimate educative activities of any attorney and the drumming up of business from those who might otherwise settle their disputes without the entanglements of litigation. . . . It is impossible to draw that line sharply and distinctly when virtually no facts are presented to the Court. The only specific allegations defendants make in this respect is that plaintiff's attorneys may sell or may have sold the fruits of discovery in this case with other materials and information to attorneys engaged in similar cases. Without more, the charging of fees

---

[6] United States v. International Business Machines Inc., 67 F.R.D.40,46 (S.D.N.Y. 1975); Reliance Insurance Co. v. Barrons, 428 F. Supp. 200, 203 (S.D.N.Y. 1977); In re Halkin, 598 F.2d 176,186,191 (D.C. Cir. 1979).

between attorneys collaborating in similar cases and the collaboration itself both seem reasonable on their face. . . . [7]

In *Johnson Foils v. Huycke Corp.*, 61 F.R.D. 405, 410 (1973), the court echoed the ruling in Williams:

> . . . unless it can be shown that the discovering party is exploiting the instant litigation solely to assist in other litigation before a foreign forum, federal courts do allow full use of the information in other forums. . . . Indeed, there must be some evidence of bad faith in the institution of the suit on the part of the discovering party before a Court will act to limit the discovery process.

Defense arguments alleging the iniquity of information sharing are increasingly rejected by state and federal courts. In the recent case of *Earl v. Gulf & Western Manufacturing Company*, 366 N.W.2d 160 (1985), the Court of Appeals of Wisconsin, in denying defendant's motion for a protective order stated:

> The only reason advanced by Gulf & Western for the protective order is its fears that the Earls might pass the information along to other plaintiffs involved in litigation against Gulf & Western. This does not rise to the level of "good cause" for a protective order. Gulf & Western has not shown that it has a legitimate interest in denying parties to other lawsuits access to the information. If the information is irrelevant to the issues raised in those cases, it will not be admissible against Gulf & Western; if it is relevant, the other plaintiffs can discover it from Gulf & Western in any event, and their obtaining it from the Earls will save Gulf & Western the trouble and expense of producing the same information several times over. Gulf & Western argues that there is no reason why the Earls should be allowed to disseminate the information "at will" because doing so will not help their case. Gulf & Western misunderstands its burden on a motion for a protective order. The presumption is that no order is necessary; the movant must show a positive reason (i.e., "good cause") for the entry of an order. It is insufficient merely to argue that no reason exists not to issue an order.[8]

The growth of plaintiff information sharing organizations is increasingly seen by courts as a positive factor in achieving the goal of efficient dispute resolution. Corporations view information sharing among plaintiff's attorneys as a serious problem, aimed at fomenting litigation. The recent Vioxx and cigarette litigations may serve as examples. The American Trial Lawyers Association (ATLA) fosters a large number of support groups for purposes of mutual education and exchange of motions, briefs, interroga-

---

[7] *Williams*, 50 F.R.D. at 33.

[8] *Earl*, 366 N.W.2d at 165.

tories, depositions and corporate documents received in discovery.[9] The Defense Research Institute and other defense oriented groups provide similar services.

In *Patterson v. Ford Motor Company*, 85 F.R.D. 152 (D.C. Tex. 1980), defendant sought the entry of a protective order on the basis that plaintiff's counsel were members of both state and national trial lawyers associations which engaged in information sharing among its members. In denying Ford's motion, the Court stated:

> For good cause shown, this Court will make any order which justice requires to protect Ford from annoyance, embarrassment, oppression, or undue burden or expense. Rule 26(C), F.R.C.P. To show good cause, Ford asserts that counsel for Plaintiff are members of the Texas Trial Lawyers Association and the American Trial Lawyers Association, which collect and distribute information with regard to manufacturers. Such collaboration among plaintiff's attorneys would come squarely within the aims of the Federal Rules of Civil Procedure — to secure the just, speedy, and inexpensive determination of every action.[10]

§ 19.06 PROTECTION AGAINST FRAUD

An additional reason often stated by the nation's courts in refusing to accept the alleged impropriety of information sharing as a basis for the issuance of broad-based protective orders is the prevention of fraud in the discovery process.[11] The possibility of a corporate defendant falsifying responses to discovery requests by an individual claimant who has no access

---

[9] ATLA Litigation Groups in 2005, covers a wide variety of products such as Baycol, Benzene/Leukemia, Climbers and Other Diet Products: Fen-Phen, Electrical Accidents, Embolization Devices (Cyanoacrylate), Ephedra, Firearms and Ammunition, Heart Devices, Herbicides & Pesticides (including Agent Orange, Dioxin & PCB's), Hormone Therapy, Laparoscopy, Lead Paint, Orthopedic Implant Devices, Selective Serotonin Reuptake Inhibitors (Anti-Depressants including Paxil, Zoloft and Prozac), Sexual Dyfunction Drugs, Stand-up Forklifts, Vioxx/Bextra (includes all Cox-2 Inhibitor Arthritis Drugs such as Celebrex), and Zyprexa.

[10] 85 F.R.D. 152.

[11] Alleged fraud in the discovery process is addressed in FED. R. CIV. P. RULE 60, Relief from Judgment or Order:

> (b) Mistakes; Inadvertence; Excusable Neglect; Newly Discovered Evidence; Fraud, Etc. On motion and upon such terms as are just, the court may relieve a party or a party's legal representative from a final judgment, order, or proceeding for the following reasons: (1) mistake, inadvertence, surprise, or excusable neglect; (2) newly discovered evidence which by due diligence could not have been discovered in time to move for a new trial under Rule 59(b); (3) fraud (whether heretofore denominated intrinsic or extrinsic), misrepresentation, or other misconduct of an adverse party; (4) the judgment is void; (5) the judgment has been satisfied, released, or discharged, or a prior judgment upon which it is based has been reversed or otherwise vacated, or it is no longer equitable that the judgment should have prospective application; or (6) any other reason justifying relief

to other sources of information is, although apparently rare, nonetheless very real.

In the case of *Rozier v. Ford Motor Company*, 573 F. 2d 1332 (5th Cir. 1978), defendant falsified its answer to one of plaintiff's interrogatories regarding the existence of a certain document. After a verdict for defendant, the subject document came to light and plaintiff was granted a new trial. In condemning such action, the U.S. Court of Appeals for the Fifth Circuit stated:

> Through its misconduct in this case, Ford completely sabotaged the federal trial machinery, precluding the 'fair contest' which the Federal Rules of Civil Procedure are intended to secure. Instead of serving as a vehicle for ascertainment of the truth, the trial in this case accomplished little more than the adjudication of a hypothetical fact situation imposed by Ford's selective disclosure of information. The policy protecting the finality of judgments is not so broad as to require protection of judgments obtained in this manner. . . .[12]

In a similar context, in the case of *Buehler v. Whalen*, 374 N.E.2d 460 (Ill. 1978), the defendant company falsified answers to plaintiff's interrogations and otherwise failed to honestly honor requests for documents. As noted by the Illinois Supreme Court, only information sharing revealed the fraud:

> This was vital information which was withheld by defendant Ford Motor Corporation. Whalen's attorney had obtained this Ford record from some litigation other than the instant one-a sad commentary on the effectiveness of the discovery here. . . .[13]

---

from the operation of the judgment. The motion shall be made within a reasonable time, and for reasons (1), (2), and (3) not more than one year after the judgment, order, or proceeding was entered or taken. A motion under this subdivision (b) does not affect the finality of a judgment or suspend its operation. This rule does not limit the power of a court to entertain an independent action to relieve a party from a judgment, order, or proceeding, or to grant relief to a defendant not actually personally notified as provided in Title 28, U.S.C., § 1655, or to set aside a judgment for fraud upon the court. Writs of coram nobis, coram vobis, audita querela, and bills of review and bills in the nature of a bill of review, are abolished, and the procedure for obtaining any relief from a judgment shall be by motion as prescribed in these rules or by an independent action.

[12] *Rozier*, 573 F. 2d 1332 at 1346. *See also* Hesling v. CSX Transp., Inc., 396 F.3d 632 (5th Cir. 2005) (*Rozier* distinguished); Cummings v. General Motors Corp., 365 F.3d 944 (10th Cir. 2004) (*Rozier* distinguished).

[13] Buehler v. Whalen, 374 N.E.2d at 467. *See also* Delvecchio v. General Motors Corp., 255 Ill. App. 3d 189 (Ill. App. Ct. 1993); Thomas M. Fleming, J.D., Annotation, *Propriety And Extent of State Court Protective Order Restricting Party's Right to Disclose Discovered Information to Others Engaged In Similar Litigation*, 83 A.L.R.4th 987 (1991). (This annotation collects and analyzes those civil cases in which the courts have considered the propriety or extent of a protective order, issued or sought in a state court action, which expressly or allegedly restricts a party's freedom to disclose or disseminate information obtained through discovery in that action to others who are engaged, or who may in the future be engaged, in similar litigation.)

§ 19.07 ANNOYANCE, EMBARRASSMENT, OPPRESSION

Corporations often seek protective orders on the basis that they will suffer significant *annoyance, embarrassment and oppression* if their documents are not protected from dessimination to other lawyers or the television and print media.[14] The discovery rules require that defense counsel point out with specificity each document or portion thereof which would lead to those results. Due to the obvious risk of illustrating the strength of plaintiff's case in doing so, such arguments are rarely forthcoming. The formal showing of annoyance embarrassment and oppression should be insisted upon for each document so specified. Corporations seldom are specific with supporting reasons, since the greatest number of defense motions for protective orders based in these claims are actually grounded in fear of information sharing. They are also used as the basis for orders alleging that the documentation sought is commercially sensitive, a claim with much more legitimacy.

§ 19.08 TRADE SECRETS AND CONFIDENTIAL COMMERCIAL INFORMATION

In most products liability cases, defendants cannot support trade secret as the basis for a protective order with any degree of credibility. The factors of aggressive advertising and marketing and the obvious physical and public dessimination of the product wouls tend to militate against any legitimate trade secret basis for a protective order. The traditional test for determining whether information qualifies as a trade secret is threefold:

1. Is the matter sought to be protected a trade secret or other confidential research, development or commercial information entitled to protection?

2. Would disclosure cause a cognizable harm sufficient to warrant a protective order?

---

[14] Federal Rule 26 — General Provisions Governing Discovery:

   (c) Protective Orders. Upon motion by a party or by the person from whomdiscovery is sought, accompanied by a certification that the movant has in good faith conferred or attempted to confer with other affected parties in an effort to resolve the dispute without court action, and for good cause shown, the court in which the action is pending or alternatively, on matters relating to a deposition, the court in the district where the deposition is to be taken may make any order which justice requires toprotect a party or person *from annoyance, embarrassment, oppression, or undue burden or expense.*

3. Has the party seeking protection shown good cause for invoking the court's protection?[15]

The question of competitive disadvantage resulting from the disclosure of discovery materials is considered to fall within the annoyance, embarrassment and oppression factors of Rule 26(c). The party seeking the order on this basis has a heavy burden to establish a sufficient basis for its entry.[16]

In the leading case of *Parsons v. General Motors Corp.*, 85 F.R.D. 724 (N.D. Ga.1980), the court gave an extensive discussion of the type of factual pleading that must accompany any claim of protection on the basis of confidential commercial information.

In *Parsons*, plaintiff claimed injury as a result of burns suffered from a ruptured fuel tank on an Oldsmobile automobile. Plaintiff sought discovery of information from General Motors relative to fuel system design and certain crash tests results. General Motors objected to the discovery and moved for a protective order based upon the confidentiality of the information. In denying its motion, the court stated:

> GM admits that this material is not a "trade secret" but argues that it constitutes "confidential research, development or commercial information," within the meaning of the Rule 26(c)(7). Fed. R. Civ. P. 26 (c)(7). GM has asked the Court to enter a protective order which would prohibit plaintiff and her attorneys from reproducing the crash test results or fuel system design information and from disclosing the material to any third party without the Court's permission. . . . Restrictions of discovery are allowed for "good cause" when disclosure of "a trade secret or other confidential research development or commercial information" is involved. Fed.R. Civ. P. 26(c) (7).
>
> The Court interprets "good cause" in the context of Rule 26(c) (7) to mean that the parties seeking the protective order must demonstrate that the material sought to be protected in confidential and that disclosure will create a competitive disadvantage for the party. The Court finds that the two Affidavits filed by GM do not establish that the information in question is confidential.

---

[15] The term "trade secret" itself has a variety of state and federal court defintions, as noted in 26 CHARLES ALAN WRIGHT, ARTHUR R. MILLER & EDWARD H. COOPER, FEDERAL PRACTICE & PROCEDURE § 5644 (WRIGHT & MILLER Treatise) (2005 Pocket Part, Chapter 6, Privileges). (An inspection of judicial definitions of "trade secret" reveals great variety in the understanding of this crucial phrase. . . .These definitions have been criticized on many grounds but perhaps the most telling for purposes of the privilege is the assertion that they are devised ad hoc to meet the needs of a particular case and the criticism that most of them are "open-ended and fact intensive." It is little wonder that Wigmore wrote that he used the phrase "trade secret" to describe the privilege only "for lack of a better term.")

[16] Zenith Radio Corp. v. Matsushita Elec. Co., 529 F. Supp. 866 (E.D. Pa. 1981).

One affidavit states that disclosure of crash test results and design information within GM is limited to the technical and engineering staffs of respective divisions. The affidavit does not reveal how many persons worked on their staffs, or how the secrecy of the reports is maintained. The second affidavit states that "initial distribution" of reports of crash tests is limited to "only a few employees." Circulation to others is permitted although reproduction of the reports of crash tests is controlled. The second affidavit mentions no specific controls on fuel system design information. Some of the information plaintiff seeks is ten years old; GM does not show that the information is still confidential after ten years. Moreover, GM admits that some of the information which plaintiff seeks must be disclosed to the government.

GM has not attempted to show what specific information is already part of the public record and what information remains confidentially held at GM. GM has not made a particularized showing that the information sought is confidential as required by Fed. R. Civ. P. 26(c) (7) for entry of a protective order. Moreover, GM's allegations of competitive harm are vague and conclusory when specific examples are necessary [17]

§ 19.09 FACTUAL COMPONENTS OF THE ARGUMENT IN OPPOSITION

In *United States v. International Business Machines, Inc.*, 67 F.R.D. 40 (S.D.N.Y 1975), Chief Judge Edelstein of the Southern District of New York set forth the key facts that should be considered to determine if commercial information warrants the protection of a protective order on the basis of confidential commercial information:

1. The extent to which such information is known outside the business.

2. The extent to which such information is known to those in the business.

3. Measures taken to guard the secrecy of the information.

---

[17] *Parsons*, 85 F.R.D. at 725-726. On this topic, see also *Federal Court Discovery in the 80's-Making the Rules Work*, 95 F.R.D. 245, 295 (1982); AMERICAN LAW OF PRODUCTS LIABILITY, § 53:67, Particular grounds for issuing protective orders — Trade Secrets (2005); Discovery Proceedings in Federal Court, § 20:13, Protective orders specifically authorized; Preclusion of disclosure discovery — Limitation on disclosure of confidential business information (2004).

4. The value of the information to the business and its competitors.[18] The ultimate test, however, was whether disclosure would work a "clearly defined and very serious injury."[19]

In drafting the memorandum in opposition to the protective order, the argument will thus focus on the general availability of the technical processes that defendant manufacturer seeks to protect. Plaintiff's memorandum should demonstrate the commercial availability of the technology underlying the documents. The manufacturer's chances of success on the basis of *confidential commercial information*, decreases in direct proportion to the time that has passed since the introduction of the technology underlying the documents into the marketplace.

Counsel must educate the court as to the nature of the technology and research underlying defendant's motion. The expert witness affidavit can be used to great advantage here, setting out what is or is not "out there" with respect to the technology, pharmacology, or chemical formulation sought to be protected from disclosure. Here, however, that tutorial is directed to the technology and manufacturing processes themselves, rather than the arguable relevancy of underlying documentation to the legal and factual issues in the litigation.[20]

§ 19.10 MEETING THE ARGUMENTS FOR EACH DOCUMENT

Counsel should insist that defendant establish the basis of protection for each document covered by the motion. The burden is on the corporation to demonstrate both the degree and manner in which each would reveal the processes deemed *commercially sensitive*. Defense arguments directed to general document types are inadequate to warrant protection for the specific processes reflected in any one individual document.

Expert witness affidavits can provide significant support for plaintiff's position that the technology or commercial information reflected in the disputed documents are not *commercially sensitive*. For each area of technology for which protection is sought counsel should consult with his expert to estimate the validity of defendant's claim.

---

[18] 67 F.R.D. 40, 46 (S.D.N.Y. 1975).

[19] *Id.*

[20] *See* TERRENCE F. KIELY, SCIENCE AND LITIGATION: PRODUCTS LIABILITY IN THEORY AND PRACTICE 412 (CRC Press 2002).

§ 19.11 DISCOVERY ENFORCEMENT

The central problem faced by plaintiff counsel in products liability liti-gation is the enforcement of their discovery requests. These matters are generally resolved after a long period of squabbling and one or more motions by plaintiff for sanctions for failure to comply with discovery. It is important to note that a defendant manufacturer is under no obligation to answer poorly drafted, vague or clearly irrelevant interrogatories or requests to produce documents. There is, of course a wide margin of dif-ferences of opinion on just what is or is not *relevant* to the cases. Poorly pre-pared or inexperienced plaintiff counsel often make a variety of "any and all, anywhere, whenever" type of requests that are clearly without the ken of even the most liberal interpretation of wide-ranging discovery. Having said that, it is clear that products defense counsel have there own "irrele-vant, burdensome, oppressive, work product, attorney-client" shotgun response to discovery that is equally improper.

An often encountered defense counsel position regarding discovery com-pliance was recently set forth in a recent article in the *Practical Litigator*:[21]

THE PROBLEM

Every defense attorney who has ever handled a products liability action is all too familiar with the unbelievably broad discovery requests propounded by plaintiffs' attorneys. More often than not, plaintiffs' attorneys serve defense counsel with interrogatories or requests for production of documents which request volumes of information regarding not only the product at issue, but other prod-ucts that have also been manufactured by the defendant. These interrogatories and requests for production of documents often request information regarding the design, manufacture, produc-tion, distribution, and sale of any product the defendant has ever manufactured which is remotely similar (or in some cases not even remotely similar) to the product which the plaintiff claims caused his or her injury. When faced with such expansive discovery requests, defense counsel must take a restrictive, conservative approach to providing information to plaintiff's counsel regarding products other than the product at issue in that particular case.[22]

Plaintiff counsel counter that at the discovery stage, similar product lines that incorporate technology of the very type at issue in the case are

---

[21] Nahrstadt, *Narrowing the Scope of Discovery for Substantially Similar Products*, 15 No. 6 PRAC. LIT. 37, 38 (2004). (This is a brief, well-written summary of the issues from a defense attorney standpoint.)

[22] *Id.* at 38. The author goes on to say that aggressive attempts to limit the amount and type of information supplied about the manufacture of other products or product lines is required because such evidence can confuse the jury and may lead it to wrongly conclude that the prod-uct at issue is defective.

clearly fair game. This position has always found significant support in United States courts. Justice Powell of the United States Supreme Court, writing in 1978 for a unanimous court in *Oppenheimer Fund, Inc. v. Sanders* stated:[23]

> . . . The key phrase in this definition — "relevant to the subject matter involved in the pending action" — has been construed broadly to encompass any matter that bears on, or that reasonably could lead to other matter that could bear on, any issue that is or may be in the case.[24] Consistently with the notice-pleading system established by the Rules, discovery is not limited to issues raised by the pleadings, for discovery itself is designed to help define and clarify the issues. Nor is discovery limited to the merits of a case, for a variety of fact-oriented issues may arise during litigation that are not related to the merits.[25]

Numerous cases have held that a request for discovery should be considered relevant if there is "any possibility" that the information sought may be relevant to the subject matter of the action. The primary focal point to determine the actual scope of discovery relevancy is the plaintiff's complaint. As noted in the leading cases of *Roseberg v. Johns-Manville Corp.*[26]:

> . . . The detail in the complaint specifies the necessary relevance of the interrogatories . . . The burden now falls upon GAF, the party resisting discovery,to clarify and explain its objections and to provide support therefor. . . .[27]

The allegations of each count in the complaint determine the broad subject matters involved in the case. However, relevance is to be measured, not strictly according to the specific fact issues raised by the pleadings, but by reference to the broader logical parameters of those facts.[28]

A routine response of products defendants is to answer or produce materials that could not credibly be objected to and to then refuse to answer interrogatories or produce the bulk of the requested documents. The phrase "defendant refuses to answer plaintiff interrogatories 3-30 [or document request 1-15] on the basis that the information sought is not relevant or not reasonably calculated to lead to the discovery of such information" is a familiar one in state and federal courtrooms across America.[29] This response

---

[23] 437 U.S. 340 (1978).

[24] *See* Hickman v. Taylor, 329 U.S. 495, 501 (1947).

[25] *Id.* at 500-501.

[26] 85 F.R.D. 292, 296-297 (E.D. Pa. 1980)

[27] *Id.* at 297.

[28] Smith v. F.T.C., 403 F. Supp. 1000 (D. Del. 1975).

[29] As noted by Nahrstadt:

Obviously, the defense attorney who is successful in preventing the introduction of "extraneous" issues to the jury will be far ahead of the game in terms of limiting the

sets the stage for each side's opportunity to attempt to draw the relevancy and time frame lines that will govern the remainder of discovery and the broad outlines of the trial itself.

§ 19.12 SAMPLE DISCOVERY ENFORCEMENT MEMORANDUM — STAINLESS STEEL PRESSURIZED BEVERAGE CANISTER LITIGATION[30]

Set out below is a sample memorandum in support of a plaintiff motion to strike the answer of the Defendant Fremantle Tire and Rubber Company for failure to answer plaintiff's interrogatories. This Sample Memorandum illustrates the manner in which the various liability and discovery theories discussed in this book may come together in an aggressive litigation in a hypothetical products liability case. Plaintiff's position was chosen as the most illustrative setting out this memorandum here, continues the effort of this book to supply real life examples of the application of the products liability theories set out in Chapters 2-10.[31]

§ 19.13 THE DENTON v. FREMANTLE DISCOVERY ENFORCEMENT SUPPORT MEMORANDUM

MEMORANDUM IN SUPPORT OF PLAINTIFF'S MOTION
TO STRIKE DEFENDANT'S ANSWER FOR FAILURE TO
ANSWER INTERROGATORIES

I

INTRODUCTION

This is a products liability case brought by Plaintiff John Denton against the manufacturers of a pressurized stainless steel commercial soft-drink beverage canister. The gist of plaintiff's complaint alleges that the defendant

---

scope of the case and concentrating the jury's focus on the salient legal issues. One of the most successful ways of limiting the introduction of "extraneous" issues is to prevent the plaintiff's attorney from finding out about them during the course of discovery.

Nahrstadt, *supra* note 21, at 38.

[30] *John Denton v. The Fremantle Tire & Rubber Company, Polymer Plastic Company, Apex Grinding Company, and the Premier Plastic Corporation* — Complaint set forth and examined in Chapter 14, Drafting the Complaint and Discovery Focus.

[31] The full *Denton v. Fremantle* complaint is set out in Chapter 14, Drafting the Complaint and Discovery Focus §14.03-14.12. The *Denton* Interrogatories are set out in Chapter 16, Interrogatories and Request to Admit Facts, §16.11 Sample Interrogatories — Pressurized Stainless Steel Beverage Canister. The *Denton* Requests for Documents are provided in Chapter 17, Requests to Produce Documents, §17.09 Sample Request for Documents: Pressurized Stainless Steel Beverage Canister.

manufactured this container in a manner that caused it to be in an unreasonably dangerous condition when used by workers, such as Plaintiff, in the commercial soft-drink beverage industry. Specifically, Plaintiff alleges four basic problems with respect to the canister that is the subject of this action:

1. The canister was not reasonably safe in design due to the foreseeable risk that a canister lid or cap constructed of plastic materials would shatter or explode during the course of foreseeable routine handling by workers in the commercial soft-drink vending industry.

2. The canister was not reasonably safe in design due to inadequate pressure relief mechanisms to prevent the shattering or exploding of the plastic lid or cap or other portions of the canister during the course of routine foreseeable handling by workers in the commercial soft-drink vending industry.

3. The canister was not reasonably safe in design due to inadequate mechanisms to prevent the over pressurization of the canister, thereby creating the risk of the shattering or exploding of the plastic lid or cap or other portions of the canister during the course of foreseeable routine handling by workers in the commercial soft-drink vending industry.

4. The canister was not reasonably safe in that defendant failed to provide adequate warnings of the dangers involved in the handling of the canister, including, but not limited to the shattering or exploding of the plastic lid or cap or other portions of said canister during the course of foreseeable routine handling by workers in the commercial soft-drink vending industry.

The complaint contains three counts, sounding in strict liability, negligence and punitive damages. The defendant is the Fremantle Tire and Rubber Company.

In January of 2001, the Plaintiff John Denton was in the process of preparing a pallet of returned canisters for recycling at his place of employment, Joyce Beverages, when the plastic cap on one of the canisters exploded, causing permanent injury to his left eye and face.

Plaintiff has served both a First and Second Set of Interrogatories and Requests for the Production of Documents on defendant. Defendant has filed responses to both sets of discovery requests, which, with minor exceptions, constitute a total refusal to respond to Plaintiff's focused and reasonable requests for information.

The Interrogatories and Requests for the Production of Documents directed to defendant Fremantle Tire and Rubber Company seek information relative to the design, testing, production and marketing of pressurized beverage syrup containers of the type involved in this lawsuit. Plaintiff's

requests are focused on matters that are clearly either relevant to these proceedings or reasonably calculated to lead to the discovery of such relevant
data.

The requests seek information from each defendant for a time frame
ranging from 1975 to the present. The years-long manufacture of the suspect canisters by defendant and the complex nature of the scientific facts
surrounding this case, require extensive interrogatories that might not be
required in a simpler factual setting. The Defendant manufacturer has
either refused to answer Plaintiff's Interrogatories or supplied "answers"
that merely object to each individual question without supporting reasons.
(*See* Section V.)

Plaintiffs must now come before this Court and seek an order compelling
Defendant to fully and adequately supply answers to Plaintiff's legitimate,
relevant and essential requests for information. It should be noted, that
Plaintiff has fully responded to all discovery requests submitted by this
defendant. In some instances Plaintiffs have answered supplemental interrogatories and document requests.

The defendant has based its refusal to answer these interrogatories on the
following reasons:

- The interrogatories are too lengthy;

- They cover too long a period of time;

- It would take considerable man hours to locate the requested
information;

- It would cost too much money to conduct the required search;

- The requested information is not kept in a central file where it
could be readily accessed;

- The questions themselves are:

  (a.) Not relevant or likely to lead to the discovery of relevant
information;

  (b.) Overly broad;

  (c.) Vague;

  (d.) Unreasonably burdensome;

  (e.) Incapable of reasonable response.

These motions in opposition typically go well beyond what might be
expected from a company legitimately attempting to protect its private
papers from outside scrutiny. There has been a conscious decision by the
defendant to totally ignore principles of discovery obvious to the novice
attorney practicing in the Federal courts. For that reason, Plaintiff is
requesting costs and attorneys fees necessitated by the hours of unnecessary
work needed to bring this motion and prepare this memorandum.

Defendant is no stranger to product liability litigation and the discovery rules of the federal courts. They have been through the process of responding to discovery in cases involving their other product lines to a sufficient degree that their expressed perplexity at the nature of the information sought by Plaintiff truly rings hollow. That same experience makes their studied ignoring of familiar case law interpretations of the Federal Rules and the language of the Rules themselves, totally unacceptable.

It should be noted that defendant does not question the propriety of the information *categories* addressed in the interrogatories themselves. It is important in a case of this complexity to address the general issue of just what categories of information are routinely and necessarily subject to discovery in a products liability case grounded in allegations of defective design, failure to warn and punitive damages.

II

DISCOVERABLE TYPES OF INFORMATION

Defendant Fremantle cannot take the position that it is not required to supply *any* information to plaintiffs in this case. All parties agree that certain categories of information are discoverable from this manufacturer over *some* past period of time in their manufacturing and marketing history with respect to the stainless steel pressurized beverage canister at issue in this case.The period of defendant's manufacturing history within which appropriate information is discoverable, is really separate from the question of the appropriate categories of information that are discoverable in the first instance. Accordingly, Plaintiff will address the question of information categories first.

In any products liability design or failure to warn case, the overriding fact question is the extent of the manufacturer's knowledge of the alleged risks associated with the normal use of the product. That central question can only be answered in part by examining the authoritative literature in the relevant fields of engineering.The study of such sources will identify the extent, if any, to which the alleged risks have been identified by knowledgeable scientists and alternative design principles noted. The only other major source of information on the question of feasible alternative designs and a manufacturer defendant's knowledge of the alleged risks is their own internal corporate documents.

Such documents reflect the extent of their experience with the suspect product, through the course of their formulating, testing, producing and marketing of it. The first stage of efficient discovery in products liability cases thus revolves, initially, around the issue of what categories of information contained in the defendant manufacturer's archives are arguably subject to discovery.

Regardless of the type of product being manufactured and whether or not it is a new offering or a subsequent model in a pre-existing line of goods,

there are routine stages or steps that are followed in the manufacturing company to move the product from the idea stage to the inventory shelf.

Each broad stage in this multi-year process is further broken down into more focused sets of activity that consistently generate routine types and forms of documentation such as test reports and test analyses. These materials, in turn, are generally channeled along fairly fixed lines of distribution within the company for purposes of review by management. Accordingly, the principal initial goal in the discovery process in this litigation, is the identification of the categories of documentary information arguably generated by this defendant as a result of the various activities involved in the development, testing, manufacturing and marketing of the subject pressurized stainless steel beverage canister manufactured by them. Equally important is identifying the manner in which that documentation was disseminated throughout the company.

Requiring defendant to respond to structured, detailed and specific interrogatories seeking such information, will go a long way in eliminating costly and time consuming discovery motion practice in this litigation. It clearly meets the stated goals of Federal discovery practice, by facilitating efficient and effective discovery and trial planning.

While courts and litigators may differ in terminology, Plaintiff submits that the major stages along the product development and manufacturing continuum in large corporations, such as the defendant, are basically four in number:

1. Product Design or Drug Formulation

2. Product Testing

3. Product Manufacturing

4. Product Marketing

Defendant certainly would not dispute the fact that some information is accessible by Plaintiffs in this case during each of the above basic manufacturing stages, for some historical period of time. Due to the very nature of corporations, whatever information there may be that Plaintiff is entitled to, will be contained in company documents. These materials will have been generated by company technical and managerial staff as a result of specific activities occurring within the above-noted basic manufacturing stages.

These broad categories can be further sub-divided for discovery planning purposes by a functional breakdown of the activities that have traditionally been a primary focus of corporate energies in the course of product development and manufacture. Such activities would undoubtedly include some form of the following:

DESIGN:

- Overall Product Planning
- Marketing Feasibility Studies
- Technical, Pharmacological or Chemical Feasibility Studies
- Financial Feasibility Studies
- Federal or State Regulatory Reviews
- Detailed Component or Laboratory Studies
- Project Approval Discussions

TESTING:

- Prototype Testing, Animal Testing or Clinical Trials
- Testing Required By Regulatory Agencies
- Alternative Design Testing
- Drafting of Instructions and Warnings

PRODUCTION:

- Finalization of Product Specifications
- Actual Production Runs
- Quality Control Activities

MARKETING:

- Marketing Plans and Arrangements
- Advertising and promotional literature, films or documents
- Customer Complaint Processing

In addition to these basic information categories, plaintiffs in products liability cases are clearly entitled to access a certain amount of information respecting the organizational structure of the defendant company. This information is essential to identify the origination and flow of materials through the various offices, departments, sections and committees within the large scale manufacturing corporation. In this latter regard, Plaintiff submits that some information in the following categories is accessible by them in this case:

CORPORATE ORGANIZATION

- Overall Organization Charts
- Central Staff Organization Charts
- Listings of Groups, Offices, Departments and Sections and Managing

- Personnel

- Committee Structures and Membership

- Functional Employee Groupings

OPERATIONAL DOCUMENTATION

- Standard Operating Procedures

- Record Retention Policies

- Electronic creation, destruction and storage methods and history

- Complaint Processing Procedures

Plaintiff submits that selected information in the above-noted information categories is discoverable in this case, to the degree that such reflects on defendant's knowledge of risks, if any, associated with the design of the stainless steel pressurized beverage canister that is the subject of this case and was manufactured by them. Plaintiffs' Second Set of Interrogatories and Requests for Documents seek to access information in each of these obviously relevant categories, in a well organized, focused and clear manner.

Defendant has repeatedly stressed that the development, testing, production and marketing of a product such as the subject canister, is a very complex process, involving many people, over a substantial period of time. Plaintiff does not quarrel with that assertion. However, that reality results in the generation of a large body of corporate documentation. Often, that information is difficult and costly to locate. Defendant, however, cannot use the complexity inherent in modern industrial manufacture as a basis for refusing to supply any information.

Plaintiff clearly understands that it is not defendant's burden to try and figure out what information Plaintiff is seeking. What is required from Plaintiff is a reasonable, comprehensive, focused, precise and well organized set of information requests. Plaintiff has provided just that in the Interrogatories and Document Requests heretofore filed in this case.

The complexity of defendant Fremantle's business and the extensive corporate and engineering information involved in analyzing the possible risks associated with the use of the type of pressurized beverage canister involved in this case requires extensive discovery.Those same factors require that each question contain several sub-parts in order to provide defendant with the necessary degree of specificity for each information category addressed.The degree of specificity of Plaintiff's Interrogatories and Document Requests are intended to facilitate their record search.

Set out below is a categorization of the Plaintiff's Interrogatories:[32]

INTERROGATORIES 1-3: Corporate organization

---

[32] See full set in Chapter 16, Interrogatories and Request to Admit Facts, §16.11.

INTERROGATORY 4: Engineering literature reviewed

INTERROGATORY 5: Component parts and manufacturers

INTERROGATORY 6: Trade Association activities

INTERROGATORY 7: Sales data

INTERROGATORY 8: Testing activities

INTERROGATORY 9: Comparable product lines

INTERROGATORY 10: Other lawsuits

INTERROGATORY 11: Injury history and complaints

INTERROGATORY 12: Profits information

INTERROGATORY 13: Optional safety equipment

INTERROGATORY 14: Foreign sales data

INTERROGATORY 15: Manufacturing standards

III

TIME FRAME FOR DISCOVERY

Once court and counsel agree on the subject areas to which focused discovery requests may be directed, it must be determined over what historical period of time in the corporation's history any such information may be accessed. Defendant cannot seriously take the position that no period within their company histories is applicable.The Court must resolve this central discovery issue.

Plaintiffs have requested that defendant provide information in the above-noted information categories for a period from 1975 to date. This period is reasonable and was chosen for the following reasons:

1. Defendant has manufactured the type of canister involved in this case for at least that period of time. During that period, the overall design of the canister and its component parts has not changed, thereby allowing a constant factor against which to assess the appropriateness of defendant's response to the engineering literature and their own experience with the product.

2. The engineering literature addressing the relevant technologies stretches over a period of close to twenty-five years.

3. Plaintiff's complaint includes a punitive damage count against this defendant and such counts have traditionally been grounded in a defendant's long term knowledge of a substantial risk to foreseeable users such as John Denton.

The appropriate time frame for discovery will vary with each case. Manufacturers in products liability cases must often search for information over

lengthy periods in order to fully respond to discovery requests. This is especially the case in drug products litigation, where the chemical formulation of the drug has normally not been changed for decades. That reality, however, has never been considered by federal courts to be an adequate reason for not supplying any information.

Plaintiff's have, without objection, fully and seasonably answered the discovery requests submitted by defendant. Plaintiffs in a products liability action simply have much less information to provide in discovery than would a defendant manufacturer.The relevancy of information and the appropriate time over which it must be forthcoming are directly related to the information a party actually has and its relation to the allegations of the complaint. In the instant case, the period within which Plaintiff is seeking focused, specific information, is reasonable and well within the parameters of the scope of discovery in this litigation.

In the leading case of *Roesberg v. Johns-Manville Corp.*, 85 F.R.D. 292 (E.D. Pa. 1980), the court, in rejecting defendant's argument that a fifty-five year time frame specified in plaintiff's interrogatories was burdensome, stated:

> "In Interrogatory Number Three plaintiff seeks to discover asbestos products which GAF manufactured, processed, compounded, converted, sold, supplied or distributed since 1925. GAF's primary objection to this interrogatory is the broad time frame included by plaintiff, whose employment spanned the years 1942 to 1979. However, plaintiff alleges conspiracies antedating plaintiff's employment history and intended to disguise and distort information which would have suggested to plaintiff the unreasonably dangerous and ultrahazardous nature of working with asbestos.

Accordingly, plaintiff's selected time frame is not wholly unreasonable or irrelevant. Such a request for discovery should be considered relevant."

In the instant action, a thirty-year time frame, especially given the inclusion by Plaintiff of a punitive damage count, is reasonable and does not, by its terms, create any undue burden on this defendant.

IV

RELEVANCY IN THE DISCOVERY PROCESS

In the interests of fair trial, eliminating surprise and achieving justice, relevancy, construed liberally, creates a broad vista for discovery. *Oppenheimer Fund, Inc. v. Sanders*, 437 U.S. 340, 351, 98 S. Ct. 2380, 57 L.Ed.2d 253 (1978), *Schlagenhauf v. Holder*, 379 U.S. 104, 121, 85 S. Ct. 234, 13 L.Ed.2d 152 (1964), *Hickman v. Taylor*, 329 U.S. 495, 507, 67 S. Ct. 385, 91 L.Ed. 451 (1947), *United States v. Purdome*, 30 F.R.D. 338, 340 (W.D. Mo. 1962), *Stonybrook Tenants Association, Inc. v. Alpert*, 29 F.R.D. 165, 168 (D. Conn.1961). It makes the trial "less a game of blind man's bluff and more a fair contest with the basic issues and facts disclosed to the fullest practi-

cable extent." *United States v. Proctor & Gamble Co.*, 85 F.R.D. 292, 356 U.S. 677, 682, 78 S.Ct. 983, 2 L.Ed.2d 1077 (1958); *McClain v. Mack Trucks, Inc.*, 85 F.R.D. 53, 57 (E.D. Pa. 1979).

The facts and circumstances of each case determine and limit relevance of interrogatories. *Shang v. Hotel Waldorf Astoria Corp.*, 77 F.R.D. 468, 469 (S.D.N.Y.1978), *Hoffman v. Wilson Line, Inc.*, 7 F.R.D. 73, 74 (E.D. Pa. 1946).The standard to be used to determine the factual information available to the parties in the course of discovery under the Federal discovery rules is as follows:

> . . . Parties may obtain discovery regarding any matter, not privileged, which is relevant to the subject matter involved in the pending action, whether it relates to the claim or defense of any party, including the existence, description, nature, custody, condition and location of any books, documents, or other tangible things and the identity and location of persons having knowledge of any discoverable matter. It is not ground for objection that the information sought will be inadmissible at the trial if the information sought appears reasonably calculated to lead to the discovery of admissible evidence.

F.R.C.P 26(b)(1).

The definition of relevance is provided by Rule 401 of the Federal Rules of Evidence. That provision defines relevant evidence as follows: " 'Relevant evidence' means evidence having any tendency to make the existence of a fact that is of consequence to the determination of the action more probable or less probable than it would be without the evidence." By referencing this broad standard and providing for the free discovery of data that may be reasonably calculated to lead to the discovery of such, the Federal courts have mandated a liberal discovery scheme.

As noted by Justice Powell of the United States Supreme Court, writing for a unanimous court:

> . . . The key phrase in this definition — "relevant to the subject matter involved in the pending action" — has been construed broadly to encompass any matter that bears on, or that reasonably could lead to other matter that could bear on, any issue that is or may be in the case. (citations omitted). . . . Consistently with the notice-pleading system established by the Rules, discovery is not limited to issues raised by the pleadings, for discovery itself is designed to help define and clarify the issues. (citation omitted.) Nor is discovery limited to the merits of a case, for a variety of fact-oriented issues may arise during litigation that are not related to the merits.

Oppenheimer Fund, Inc. v. Sanders, 437 U.S. 340, 351(1978).

A request for discovery should be considered relevant if there is any possibility that information sought may be relevant to the subject matter of the action. Discovery is not limited to formally admissible evidence because its primary purpose is to formulate, define and narrow issues to be tried, increase the chances for settlement, and give each party the opportunity to inform himself of the facts that may come out at trial. *Detweiler Bros., Inc. v. John Graham & Co.*, 412 F. Supp. 416 (D.C. Wash. 1976); *Duplan Corp. v. Deering Milliken Inc.*, 397 F. Supp. 1146 (D.S.C. 1975); *Carlson Companies Inc. v. Sperry & Hutchinson Co.*, 374 F.Supp.1080 (D. Minn. 1974); *Sylgab Steel & Wire Corp. v. Imoco-Gateway Corp.*, 357 F. Supp. 659 (N.D. Ill. 1973).

As stated in the 1984 case of *Chubb Integrated Systems v. National Bank of Washington et al*:

> . . . Whether this information is found to be admissible at trial has little bearing on the issue of discoverability. Rule 26(b) makes a clear distinction between information that is relevant to the subject matter for pretrial discovery and the ultimate admissibility of that information at trial.

Admissibility at trial is not the yardstick of permissible discovery." 103 F.R.D 52 (1984). FED. R. CIV. P. 26 (b)(1), advisory committee note, 1970 Amendment. The relevancy of the information sought bears directly on the issue of whether discovery requests are burdensome. If the requested material is relevant, no matter the volume, it must be produced. The initial focal point to determine the actual scope of this broadly interpreted concept is the plaintiff's complaint. As noted in *Roesberg v. Johns-Manville Corp., supra*:

> . . . The detail in the complaint specifies the necessary relevance of the interrogatories . . . The burden now falls upon GAF, the party resisting discovery, to clarify and explain its objections and to provide support therefor.

The allegations of the complaint serve to determine the broad subject matters involved in the case, and relevance is to be measured, not according to the specific issues raised by the pleadings, but rather, by reference to such subject matters. *Smith v. F.T.C.*, 403 F. Supp. 1000 (D. Del. 1975).

In the instant case, defendant Fremantle does not question the appropriateness of the categories of information sought by Plaintiff. That is because the subject categories for which information is sought are those involved in any product liability case — i.e., the design, testing, production and marketing of the suspect product.

V

SPECIFICITY IN OBJECTION

Defendant raises four recurring and totally unsupported objections as the basis for its refusal to provide anything close to adequate information to Plaintiff:

(1.) The information sought is not relevant nor likely to lead to the discovery of relevant evidence;

(2.) The interrogatories are overbroad;

(3.) The interrogatories are oppressive or burdensome;

(4.) The interrogatories are vague; In no instance does Fremantle specify in what respect any particular inquiry falls into any one or more of the above categories.

The initial failing of Fremantle's argument is that their various allegations are totally unsupported by affidavits that address the substance of the questions. Equally fatal, is the defendant's failure to provide the Court and Plaintiff with detailed objections to each question and sub-part to which objection may be had. Federal case law is clear that such unsupported "shotgun" responses constitute no answer.

The Federal Rules of Civil Procedure provide that if the party receiving interrogatories or document requests objects to any inquiry contained therein, the reasons for such objection shall be stated. FRCP Rule 33(a).The Federal trial courts have been uniform in holding that the objections must point to specific facts supporting the objection, and that a simple reiteration of "irrelevant," "oppressive," "burdensome" or "privilege" constitutes no answer. *Pressley v. Boehlke*, 33 F.R.D. 316 (W.D.N.C. 1963); *Josephs v. Harris Corp.*, 677 F.2d 985 (3d Cir. 1982); *Goodman v. Wagner*, 553 F. Supp. 255 (E.D. Pa. 1982).

In *Chubb Integrated Systems v. National Bank of Washington et al.*, decided in 1984, the court soundly rejected factually unsupported objections to interrogatories:

> An objection must show specifically how an interrogatory is overly broad, burdensome or oppressive, by submitting affidavits or offering evidence which reveals the nature of the burden. Plaintiff's objections do not reveal the nature of its burden. Without more, this Court cannot conclude that Chubb will be unduly burdened by the interrogatories. Accordingly, we reject this argument.

Chubb Integrated Systems Limited v. National Bank of Washington et al., 103 F.R.D 52 (1984). *See generally* 4A J. MOORE & J. LUCAS, MOORE'S FEDERAL PRACTICE § 33.27 (2d ed. 1983).

In the leading case of *Roesberg v. Johns-Manville Corp.*,85 F.R.D.292, 296-297 (E.D. Pa. 1980), the court stated:

> . . . Finally, GAF objects generally to this interrogatory as "overly broad, burdensome, oppressive, and irrelevant," a complaint which GAF echoes with virtually every other interrogatory. To voice a successful objection to an interrogatory, GAF cannot simply intone this familiar litany. Rather, GAF must show specifically how, despite the broad and liberal construction afforded the federal discovery

rules, each interrogatory is not relevant or how each question is overly broad, burdensome, or oppressive, (citations omitted) by submitting affidavits or offering evidence revealing the nature of the burden.(citations omitted). The court is not required to "sift each interrogatory to determine the usefulness of the answer sought." (citations omitted). . . .

See also Trabon Engineering Corp. v. Easton Manufacturing Co., 37 F.R.D. 51, 54 (N.D. Ohio 1964); *Stanley Works v. Haeger Potteries, Inc.*, 35 F.R.D. 551, 555 (N.D. Ill. 1964); *Klausen v. Sidney Printing & Publishing Co.*, 271 F. Supp. 783, 784 (D. Kan. 1967).

In the case of *In re Folding Carton Antitrust Litigation*, 83 F.R.D. 260, 264 (E.D. Ill. 1979), the court, as in *Roesberg, supra*, condemned the practice engaged in by the manufacturing defendant in the instant case, of rubber stamping each legitimate discovery request with an unsupported litany of objections:

. . . Objections to interrogatories must be specific and supported by a detailed explanation why the interrogatories are improper. General objections may result in waiver of the objections. . . . Plaintiff's catch-all objection named every conceivable ground including that the interrogatories are duplicative, not relevant to the subject matter of the litigation, oppressive, and overly vague. Plaintiff's response was so broad as to be meaningless. . . .

Also see United States v. 58.16 Acres of Land, 66 F.R.D. 570, 572 (E.D. Ill. 1975); *Chubb Integrated Systems Limited v. National Bank of Washington et al.*, 103 F.R.D 52 (1984).

Defendant's objections to Plaintiff's legitimate and specific discovery requests in the instant case are a mirror image of the responses found totally lacking in the cases cited above. By responding with unsupported "shotgun" objections to or otherwise simply refusing to answer the Plaintiff's interrogatories and document requests, defendant "intone(s) the litany of stock objections" condemned in *Roesberg, supra*. This is totally inadequate to replace the factually supported objections to each question submitted, as is clearly required by federal case law.

Plaintiff understands that it is much easier for attorneys to dash off one and one-half page "affidavits" without having to bother examining the materials in their client's possession that may contain the requested information. Plaintiff also recognizes that it is much easier to address an entire set of interrogatories or document requests without having the bother of objecting to each request submitted. However, that approach is totally unsupported in repeated federal case law addressing the responsibilities of parties objecting to interrogatories or document requests.

Objections to each interrogatory and document request must be complete, explicit and responsive. If a party cannot furnish details, he must say so under oath, and say why and set forth the efforts used to obtain the

information. *Milner v. National School of Health Technology*, 73 F.R.D. 628 (D.C. Pa. 1977). This basic requirement of federal discovery practice was reiterated in the case of *Chubb Integrated Systems v. National Bank of Washington et al.*, where the court stated:

> "Defendant must show specifically how, despite the broad and liberal construction afforded the federal discovery rules, each interrogatory is not relevant or how each question is overly broad, burdensome or oppressive, by submitting affidavits or offering evidence revealing the nature of the burden." (Emphasis added). 105 F.R.D. 12, 107 (S.D.N.Y. 1984)

VI

OVERBROAD, BURDENSOME AND OPPRESSIVE INTERROGATORIES

The allegedly burdensome and oppressive nature of Plaintiff's interrogatories and document requests are a standard component of the litany of the totally unsupported objections raised by defendant to them. Defendants' unsupported reiteration of the stock objections of "burdensome," "vague" and "oppressive," does not constitute a proper objection. *Sherman Park Community Ass'n v. Wauwatosa Realty Co.*, 486 F. Supp. 838 (D.C. Wis. 1980). *See also Swain v. General Motors Corp.*, 81 F.R.D. 698 (D.C. Pa. 1979) (scope of discovery in products cases).

The clear burden is on this defendant to indicate with specificity exactly in what respect each Interrogatory or document request is overbroad. Having failed to do so to any degree, defendant's allegation that such requests are overbroad fails to rise to the level of a proper answer. (See Authorities cited above.)

Rule 33 of the Federal Rules of Civil Procedure requires a corporation to furnish such information as is available from the corporation itself or from sources under its control after an examination of the requested materials. *Brunswick Corp. v. Suzuki Motor Co.*, 96 F.R.D. 684 (E.D. Wis. 1983).

The number and detailed nature of the interrogatories and document requests at issue here, per se, are simply not a sufficient reason for disallowing them unless they are "egregiously burdensome or oppressive." *Wirtz v. Capital Air Service, Inc.*, 42 F.R.D. 641 (D. Kan. 1967). Nor is the fact that answering them will require these companies to expend considerable time, effort and expense or may even interfere with their company business. *Wirtz, supra. See also In re Folding Carton Antitrust Litigation*, 83 F.R.D. 260 (N.D. Ill. 1979); *Krantz v. United States*, 56 F.R.D. 555 (W.D. Va. 1970). The bare allegation of oppressiveness is patently insufficient to warrant refusal to answer. *Josephs v. Harris Corp.*, 677 F.2d 985 (3d Cir. 1982); *Goodman v. Wagner*, 553 F. Supp. 255 (E.D. Pa. 1982).

Defendant's assertion that certain of Plaintiff's requests do not comport with its record keeping or organizational practices, is likewise, prima facie,

an inadequate response. If corporations do not classify data in the manner requested, the defendant must seek the required answers by whatever reasonable means are available to it, whether by personal observation, recollection or otherwise. *Equal Employment Opportunity Commission v. Hickey-Mitchell Co.*, 372 F. Supp. 1117 (D.C. Mo. 1973).

In the case of *Altech Industries v. Al Tech Specialty Steel,* 528 F. Supp. 521, 523-524 (D. Del. 1981), the defendant's objection was nearly identical to the posture taken here that records are hard to find and that compliance would unduly burden and oppress defendant. In rejecting any such general objection as insufficient, the court applied the uniform requirement of a specific demonstration of burden for each interrogatory submitted:

> . . . A second objection of the defendant is that it would be unduly burdensome for it to respond more fully than it has to interrogatory 4 of the first and third sets. In objecting to augmenting its answer . . . defendant alleges that to do so would be burdensome in that "plaintiff seeks information concerning possible meetings involving hundreds of present and former employees of GATX and the company maintains no separate records as to any such meetings involving such persons." Similarly, defendant's objection to augmenting the answers which it has supplied to interrogatory 4 . . . is that this too would be burdensome since plaintiff "seeks information concerning possible communications or conversations involving hundreds of present and former employees of GATX and the company maintains no separate records as to any such communications or conversations involving such persons." The defendant has provided no evidence to support its objection of burdensomeness. Consequently, no validity can be attributed to it.

Similarly, in the case of *F.D.I.C. v. Mercantile Nat. Bank of Chicago*, 84 F.R.D. 345, 348 (N.D. Ill. 1979), Judge Marovitz, in the face of a similar objection, stated:

> . . . Concerning Mercantile's argument that compliance with plaintiff's interrogatories will be unduly burdensome, the Court begins with the proposition that the fact that a party will be put to some trouble and expense in the process of answering interrogatories is not alone a sufficient ground for objection. . . . An objection to a set of interrogatories on the ground that compliance would be unduly burdensome will only be sustained if the objecting party establishes that the burden upon him outweighs the benefit the information would provide to the party submitting the interrogatories.

Also see Pollock v. Deere and Co., 282 N.W.2d 735 (Iowa 1979); *Roberts v. DeKalb Agr. Ass'n, Inc.*, 259 Iowa 131, 143 N.W.2d 354 (1966).

As with each of their objections, defendant Fremantle has failed to even minimally meet its burden of specifying a factual basis for their refusal to answer.

Defendant suggests that such detailed questions are more appropriate for deposition than written interrogatories. The permissible number and detail of interrogatories are directly related to the complexity of the case in which they are submitted. Plaintiff has asked the defendant to supply a listing of relevant documents or the documents themselves.This practice, in a case involving many more questions and sub-parts than involved here, was recently found fair and adequate under modern, liberal discovery rules.

In the recent case of *Compagnie Francaise D'Assurance Pour Le Commerce Exterieur and Constructions Navales Et Industrielles De La Mediterranee v. Phillips Petroleum Co.*, the court ruled:

> Defendant objects to several interrogatories on the ground that they purportedly ask for evidentiary detail more appropriately elicited at depositions.However, information obtained by interrogatories . . . may effect judicial economy and economic savings to the parties. Plaintiffs will know whom they have to depose; unnecessary depositions may be avoided; information which might not be obtained from the corporate defendants; important conversations, communications and documents will be highlighted; delay may be avoided, and the issues for trial may be narrowed. For these reasons, the Court believes plaintiffs' interrogatories may effect judicial economy. As a result, we find defendant's objection to be without merit.

105 F.R.D. 16, 111 (1984). *Also see In re Shopping Carts Antitrust Litigation*, 95 F.R.D. 299, 1982-1 Trade Cas. p 64, 561, at 73,074 (S.D.N.Y. 1982).

Federal Rule of Civil Procedure 33(c), provides:

> Option to Produce Business Records.Where the answer to an interrogatory may be derived or ascertained from the business records of the party upon whom the interrogatory has been served or from an examination, audit or inspection of such business records, or form a compilation, abstract or summary based thereon, and the burden of deriving or ascertaining the answer is substantially the same for the party serving the interrogatory as for the party served, it is a sufficient answer to such interrogatory to specify the records from which the answer may be derived or ascertained and to afford to the party serving the interrogatory reasonable opportunity to examine, audit or inspect such records and to make copies, compilation, abstracts or summaries.

F.R.C.P. 33(c).

This rule permits a party to answer detailed interrogatories by providing business records where the answers can be found. A specification supplied by the responding party should be in sufficient detail to permit the interrogating party to locate and to identify, as readily as can the party served, the records from which the answer may be ascertained. The idea behind the rule is that when the burden of deriving information from documents is

equal between the parties, the interrogating party should bear the burden of compiling the information. *Sandler v. Musicland Pickwick Int'l, Inc.*, 31 Fed. R. Serv. 2d 760, 761-62 (E.D. Tex. 1980); *Webb v. Westinghouse Elec. Corp.*, 81 F.R.D. 431, 435-36 (E.D. Pa. 1978); *Mid-America Facilities, Inc. v. Argonaut Co.*, 78 F.R.D.497, 498 (E.D. Wis. 1978).One party's familiarity with the documents does not necessarily create a disparity in the ease of discovery that would preclude resort to Rule 33(c). Sandler, 31 Fed. R. Serv. 2d at 761.

However, Rule 33(c) is not an available alternative if an interrogatory can be responded to more readily and conveniently by written answer. *See Daiflon, Inc. v. Allied Chemical Corp.*, 534 F.2d 221, 226 (10th Cir.), *cert. denied*, 429 U.S. 886, 97 S.Ct. 239, 50 L. Ed. 2d 168 (1976); *Atlanta Fixture & Sales Co. v. Bituminous Fire & Marine Ins. Co.*, 51 F.R.D. 311, 312 (N.D. Ga. 1970).

VII

VAGUE INTERROGATORIES

In addition to the above noted, factually unsupported objections to Plaintiffs' First and Second Set of Interrogatories and Requests for Documents, defendant also alleges that they are so vague as to be incapable of a reasonable answer. The court's examination of those interrogatories will demonstrate that each question is precise and clearly drawn. If any interrogatory is unclear, it is defendant's burden to specifically identify the questionable language in each interrogatory and answer the rest. The problem raised by Fremantle does not reside in any lack of specificity or clarity in Plaintiff's Interrogatories. Defendants would simply prefer not to answer them. In any event, the burden is squarely on the defendant to state in detail in what respect each interrogatory is unclear. In the event of uncertainty, the defendant must give each questioned term its common sense meaning. There is no option to simply refuse to answer.

As stated in *Compagnie Francaise D'Assurance Pour Le Commerce Exterieur et Constructions Navales et Industrielles De La Mediterranee v. Phillips Petroleum Company, supra*:

> Defendant argues that the ambiguity of the interrogatories precludes it from responding. The Court directs defendant, in answering the interrogatories, to attribute to any terms which it thinks are ambiguous their common, everyday meaning. . . .

105 F.R.D. 16. *Also see Roesberg*, 85 F.R.D. at 298.

VIII

Conclusion

Roesberg v. Johns-Manville Corp., 85 F.R.D. 292 (E.D. Pa. 1980) is considered the leading case delineating the broad scope of modern discovery.

The Roesberg case was centered in defendant's objections to answering a set of interrogatories in an asbestos products liability case.

Those interrogatories are attached as an appendix to the decision and are supplied here for the Court's examination. As the court will see, they are substantially longer and more complex than the two sets of interrogatories involved in this case.

The *Roesberg* holding was cited in virtually every decision noted in this brief as containing the most lucid discussion of the problem of the scope of modern federal discovery. The *Roesberg* court concluded its lengthy opinion with the following observations, which have compelling relevancy to this motion:

> In light of plaintiff's panoply of allegations his interrogatories have been tailored carefully to establish both the nature and extent of GAF's knowledge of the interrelationship between handling asbestos products and asbestos related diseases and what GAF did in connection therewith. Clearly this information relates to any duty GAF may have had to refrain from manufacturing or distributing unreasonably dangerous or ultrahazardous goods and whether GAF breached that duty. In a nutshell these interrogatories aim at establishing notice and causation. The exactitude of discovery, the lawyer's tool for fact finding, properly lies somewhere between the acuity of the surgeon's scalpel and the carpenter's hammer. Ideally, the lawyer probes for facts with the precision and delicacy of a cardiologist incising the aorta to receive a by-pass vehicle. Realistically, the lawyer's fact finding search shares a closer propinquity with the carpenter's trade and pounds much more bluntly. Balancing the one party's need for discovery against the other party's burden in producing it requires honing the need as narrowly as possible to prevent unreasonable burden. (Citations omitted). In the case at bar plaintiff has attained this desideratum artfully.

Roesberg, 85 F.R.D. at 304.

Based on the above arguments, points and authorities, Plaintiffs' request that this Court order the defendant Fremantle Tire and Rubber Company to fully answer Plaintiff's Interrogatories and Requests for Documents, within a reasonable time as determined by the Court.

§ 19.14 CONCLUSION

Pre-trial motion practice requires a significant amount of counsel's time and energy in products liability litigation. It is the most frustrating aspect of the preparation of these cases. The key to achieving success in product liability litigation is thorough prefiling research. That research provides the basis for aggressive discovery and addressing motions for protective orders and typically contentious discovery enforcement motion practice.

Table of Cases

References are to pages.

C

H

N

INDEX

[References are to page numbers.]

[References are to page numbers.]

[References are to page numbers.]

[References are to page numbers.]

[References are to page numbers.]

[References are to page numbers.]

[References are to page numbers.]

[References are to page numbers.]

INTRODUCTION

The completion of this book (in October 2005) comes at an important time in the continuing development of products liability law. First, 2005 is the 40th anniversary of the American Law Institute's promulgation of § 402A which ushered in the era of strict liability for defective products. It is impossible to overstate the effect this section has had on the development of products liability law, as all but five states have come to use some form of strict liability based on § 402A. However, since 1998 attention has shifted to the lengthier and more complex approach to products liability taken by the Restatement (Third) of Torts: Products Liability. While some courts have rejected the Restatement (Third), many have adopted specific sections of it. Second, the number of products liability suits filed in federal and state courts has risen sharply in the past few years. In addition to the increase in suits filed, there have been a number of high profile products liability cases involving asbestos, the fast-food industry, lead-paint, medical devices, pharmaceuticals, and tobacco. However, as products liability lawsuits have become more complex and many have become class action cases, Congress has reacted by enacting new rules governing class action lawsuits and passing legislation shielding gun manufacturers from liability for the criminal acts of third parties and granting the food industry immunity from liability for weight gain or obesity.

In order to provide an *understanding* of the products liability law that is the basis of litigation and the focus of debate, this book is divided into two parts. First, Part I (Chapters 1-10) consists of an overview of the complex body of products liability case law and statutes that has developed over the past century. The chapters follow a functional approach and begin with the four theories that are the foundation of all products liability case: warranty, misrepresentation, negligence, and strict liability. Separate chapters in Part I then examine the principle types of product defects (design, manufacturing, and failure to warn) and some of the problems involved with proving that the product was defective and that the defect was the cause of the jury. Finally, chapters focus on the various defenses available in a products liability action and the types of damages that a plaintiff may seek.

An *understanding* of products liability law also requires an examination of the issues involved in the prosecution or defense of a products liability case. Part II (Chapters 11-19) addresses a range of those issues, including: researching the case; drafting the complaint; interrogatories and requests to admit facts; requests for the production of documents; discovery and evidence depositions; protective orders; and discovery enforcement. It is hoped that this combination of the theory and the practice of products liability law will make the book useful to not only law students and law professors but those are or may become involved in products liability cases, whether as judges, corporate counsel, plaintiff or defendant counsel, or expert witnesses.

As with any project of this size, this book is the product of the efforts of more than the two authors. First, the authors would like to thank Younghee Jin Ottley for her practical comments and suggestions and for reading the manuscript. In addition, the authors want to thank Professor Rogelio Lasso for his many helpful suggestions and comments. Second, the authors want to acknowledge the excellent support of various DePaul University College of Law students for their research assistance: Marie Abdul-Marek, Maureen Bantz, Tim Bell, Chris Brown, Jennifer Burgess, John Calabrese, Kim Collins, Paul Daugherity, Chris Dely, Andrea Garcia, Eric Garcia, Benjamin Gehrt, Susie Groh, Anne Hopkins, Sarah Kaufmann, Aaron Kaye, Tim Koppang, Audrey Lane, Lindsay LaVine, Caroline Miller, David Morris, Valerie Phillips, Elizabeth Rogers, Brian Shallcross, Kate Van Bokkelen, and Jing Zhang.

TABLE OF CONTENTS